R. G

UGC-NET

Junior Research Fellowship and Assistant Professor Exam

Environmental Sciences

Previous Years' Papers

(Solved)

2019
EDITION

RAMESH PUBLISHING HOUSE, New Delhi

Published by
O.P. Gupta *for* Ramesh Publishing House

Admin. Office
12-H, New Daryaganj Road, Opp. Officers' Mess,
New Delhi-110002 ☎ 23261567, 23275224, 23275124

E-mail: info@rameshpublishinghouse.com
Website: www.rameshpublishinghouse.com

Showroom
● Balaji Market, Nai Sarak, Delhi-6 ☎ 23253720, 23282525
● 4457, Nai Sarak, Delhi-6, ☎ 23918938

Book Code: R-1403

ISBN: 978-93-5012-103-0

HSN Code: 49011010

Price: ₹ 410

Printed at: Deepak Offset, Delhi

CONTENTS

PREVIOUS PAPERS (SOLVED)

COMPULSORY PAPER I (With Explanatory Answers)

Environmental Science, November-2017*

PAPER-II

Note: *This paper contains* **fifty** (*50*) *objective type questions of* **two** (*2*) *marks each.* **All questions are compulsory.**

1. The innermost layer of the earth is made up of:
   A. Silicon and alumina
   B. Silicon and magnesium
   C. Silicon and nickel
   D. Nickel and iron

2. The heat is distributed through a vertical mixing process called:
   A. Advection   B. Diffusion
   C. Convection   D. Turbulance

3. Which of the following statement(s) is/are true for an isothermal process?
   (*a*) There is no change in enthalpy
   (*b*) There is no change in internal energy
   (*c*) There is change in temperature

   Choose the correct code:
   A. (*a*) only   B. (*b*) and (*c*) only
   C. (*a*) and (*b*) only   D. (*a*), (*b*) and (*c*)

4. Match the List-I and List-II. Identify the correct answer from the code given below:

List-I (Aerosol)	List-II (Source)
(*a*) Primary natural aerosol	(*i*) Organic matter from biogenic gases
(*b*) Secondary natural aerosol	(*ii*) Soot from biomass burning
(*c*) Primary anthropogenic aerosol	(*iii*) Sulphate aerosol from powerplant SO_2 emissions
(*d*) Secondary anthropogenic aerosol	(*iv*) Soil dust

   Code:

	(*a*)	(*b*)	(*c*)	(*d*)
A.	(*i*)	(*ii*)	(*iii*)	(*iv*)
B.	(*ii*)	(*iii*)	(*iv*)	(*i*)
C.	(*iii*)	(*iv*)	(*i*)	(*ii*)
D.	(*iv*)	(*i*)	(*ii*)	(*iii*)

5. Which of the following is not a heavy metal?
   A. Lead   B. Mercury
   C. Bismuth   D. Aluminum

6. The dominant dissolved carbon dioxide species in sea water is:
   A. Bicarbonate ion
   B. Carbonate ion
   C. Carbonic acid
   D. Aquated carbon dioxide

7. A solution of chemical 'A' having its 0.14 mol L^{-1} concentration has an absorbance of 0.42. Another solution of 'A' under the same conditions has an absorbance of 0.36. What is the concentration of this solution of 'A'?
   A. 0.108 mol L^{-1} B. 0.35 mol L^{-1}
   C. 0.12 mol L^{-1} D. 0.10 mol L^{-1}

8. Which one of the following is not a soil micronutrient?
   A. Sulphur   B. Boron
   C. Iron   D. Zinc

9. If life of NO_2 be 0.693 day, its residence time is:
   A. 1.44 days   B. 1.0 day
   C. 0.693 day   D. 0.48 day

10. The general molecular formula of PAN type compound is:

A. $C_X H_Y OONO_2$　　B. $C_X H_Y OO_2 NO_2$
C. $C_x H_x OO_2 NO_2$　　D. $C_x H_Y ONO_2$

11. In an ecosystem, which one of the following is a micro-consumer?
　　A. Herbivores　　　　B. Omnivores
　　C. Carnivores　　　　D. Saprotrophs

12. A structure with hundreds of species non-linearly interlinked for their livelyhood is called:
　　A. Guild　　　　　　B. Food chain
　　C. Food web　　　　D. Pyramid

13. The process of examination of change in species diversity between ecosystems is a measure of:
　　A. Alpha diversity　　B. Beta diversity
　　C. Gamma diversity　D. Genetic diversity

14. Red tide is caused by:
　　A. Diatoms　　　　　B. Dianoflagillates
　　C. Navicula　　　　　D. Desmids

15. The unidirectional series of changes from an uninhabited water body to a water body inhabited by a stable aquatic community are called:
　　A. Eutrophication　　B. Succession
　　C. Regeneration　　　D. Reclamation

16. Under the clear Sunny day, the maximum depth of the ocean at which photosynthesis can occur is:
　　A. 10 m　　　　　　B. 250 m
　　C. 80 m　　　　　　D. 600 m

17. The organism likely to be most similar to the first life form that evolved on the earth is:
　　A. Blue - green algae
　　B. Methane producing bacteria
　　C. Protozoan
　　D. Red algae

18. A landform that results from free fall of rocks is called:
　　A. Alluvial fan　　　B. Debris flow
　　C. Talus slope　　　D. Valley fills

19. In India lignite is mined in:
　　A. Neyveli　　　　　B. Jharia
　　C. Singrauli　　　　D. Singareni

20. Tree height can be measured using remote sensing data from:
　　A. Resourcesat　　　B. Landsat
　　C. Cartosat　　　　D. RISAT

21. Ecosystem restoration deals with restoring:
　　A. Ecosystem integrity
　　B. Biodiversity
　　C. Physical environment
　　D. Ecosystem resistance

22. A single solar cell (10 cm × 10 cm) produces a voltage of 0.5 V and a current upto 2.5 A. If the solar insolation is 800 W/m^2, the efficiency of the solar cell is:
　　A. ~ 15.6 %　　　　B. ~ 24.6 %
　　C. ~ 12.3 %　　　　D. ~ 10.2 %

23. Which of the following atoms is not fissile?
　　A. $^{238}_{92}U$　　　　　B. $^{235}_{92}U$
　　C. $^{233}_{92}U$　　　　　D. $^{239}_{94}U$

24. Which of the following fuels has minimum nitrogen content?
　　A. Crude oil　　　　B. CNG
　　C. Producer gas　　D. LPG

25. Maximum sulfur content is found in which grade of coal?
　　A. Bituminous　　　B. Sub - bituminous
　　C. Lignite　　　　　D. Anthracite

26. Which of the following solar cell materials has maximum efficiency?
　　A. Cd Te, thin film
　　B. Si, polycrystalline
　　C. Amorphous Si : Ge : H film
　　D. Ga As, single crystal

27. Noise level of 70 dB corresponds to sound intensity of:
　　A. 10^{-5} Wm^{-2}　　　B. $10^{-7} Wm^{-2}$
　　C. $10^{-4} Wm^{-2}$　　　D. $10^{-3.5} Wm^{-2}$

28. At 25°C and 1 atm. pressure, 1 ppm concentration of SO_2 is equivalent to:
　　A. 1310 µg/m^3　　　B. 1826 µg/m^3
　　C. 2620 µg/m^3　　　D. 5240 µg/m^3

29. Given below are two statements. One labelled as **Assertion (A)** and the other labelled as **Reason (R):**

Assertion (A) : Arsenic (III) is more toxic than arsenic (V).

Reason (R) : Arsenic (V) binds the sulfhydryl group more strongly than arsenic (III).

Choose the **correct** answer:
A. Both (A) and (R) are correct and (R) is the correct explanation of (A).
B. Both (A) and (R) are correct and (R) is not the correct explanation of (A).
C. (A) is true, but (R) is false.
D. (A) is false and (R) is true.

30. The half life period of a radioactive substance is 32 h. How much time it would take for its 75% disintegration?
    A. 16 h   B. 96 h
    C. 128 h   D. 64 h

31. Match the List-I and List-II. Identify the correct answer from the code given below:

List-I (Pesticides)	List-II (Target)
(a) Avicide	(i) Fish
(b) Disinfectant	(ii) Plants
(c) Herbicide	(iii) Birds
(d) Piscicide	(iv) Micro-organisms

    Code:

	(a)	(b)	(c)	(d)
A.	(i)	(ii)	(iii)	(iv)
B.	(ii)	(i)	(iii)	(iv)
C.	(iii)	(iv)	(ii)	(i)
D.	(iv)	(ii)	(i)	(iii)

32. Nitrogen fixation in nature is not accomplished by:
    A. Lightning
    B. Cyanobacteria
    C. Rotifers
    D. Bacteria in root nodules of Leguminous plants

33. Which country has opted out of Paris Agreement on climate change?
    A. USA   B. Canada
    C. Australia   D. Russia

34. Under the EIA notification of 14th September, 2006, preparation of EIA is not required for the projects falling in the:

A. Category 'A' projects
B. Category 'B' projects
C. Category B_1 projects
D. Category B_2 projects

35. Which type of projects usually require an EIA?
    A. Community garden development
    B. Mining and mineral development projects
    C. Outdoor recreation
    D. Development of community wells

36. Match the List-I and List-II. Identify the correct answer from the code given below:

List-I (Series)	List-II (Environmental labelling)
(a) ISO 14021	(i) Principles and procedures
(b) ISO 14022	(ii) Self declaration of environmental claims
(c) ISO 14023	(iii) Symbols
(d) ISO 14024	(iv) Testing and verification methods

    Code:

	(a)	(b)	(c)	(d)
A.	(i)	(ii)	(iii)	(iv)
B.	(ii)	(iii)	(iv)	(i)
C.	(iii)	(iv)	(i)	(ii)
D.	(iv)	(i)	(iii)	(ii)

37. Match the List-I and List-II. Identify the correct answer from the code given below:

List-I (Acts)	List-II (Year)
(a) Environmental Protection Act	(i) 1991
(b) Air (Prevention and Control of Pollution) Act	(ii) 1977
(c) Water (Prevention and Control of Pollution) Act	(iii) 1981
(d) Public Liability Insurance Act	(iv) 1986

    Code:

	(a)	(b)	(c)	(d)
A.	(i)	(ii)	(iii)	(iv)
B.	(ii)	(iii)	(iv)	(i)
C.	(iii)	(iv)	(i)	(ii)
D.	(iv)	(iii)	(ii)	(i)

38. Articles 21, 48-A and 51-A(g), which aim to protect and improve the environment and safe guard forests and wildlife, incorporate which of the following principles of environmental law?
A. Polluter pays principle
B. Precautionary principle
C. Principle of strict liability
D. Moral duty of the state

39. Which is the correct classification of forests under the Indian Forest Act, 1927?
A. Grasslands, tropical forests, wetlands
B. Protected forest, reserved forest, village forest
C. Wildlife sanctuary, national parks, biosphere reserve
D. Private forest, social forest, town forest

40. Hardening of the steel releases the hazardous waste containing:
A. Brine sludge containing mercury
B. Cyanide - nitrate containing sludge
C. Lead bearing residues
D. Tar containing waste

41. Red coloured containers in the hospitals are used to dump:
A. Waste from laboratory cultures
B. House keeping waste
C. Human anatomical waste
D. Waste sharps

42. Mercury pollution is considered hazardous to human health because,
A. Mercury is a pure metal and hard to digest
B. Mercury accumulates and its concentration increases high up in the food chain
C. Mercury is highly soluble in water and easily absorbed by human body
D. Mercury is heavy and is not dispersed by the wind

43. In the context of Gaussian Plume Dispersion model assumptions, consider the following statements:
(*a*) The pollutants have the same density as the air surrounding them.
(*b*) The atmosphere is stable.

Choose the correct code:
A. Both (*a*) and (*b*) are true
B. (*a*) is true, (*b*) is false
C. (*a*) is false, (*b*) is true
D. Both (*a*) and (*b*) are false

44. Graphically depicting a group of numerical data through their Quartile is:
A. Histogram   B. Frequency polygon
C. Box plot   D. Pie chart

45. If, out of 50 fish of a pond, 12 had no ectoparasite and remaining had varying numbers of parasites on them, then how many of fish had at least one parasite?
A. 4   B. 24
C. 38   D. 16

46. In a One-way ANOVA, explained variance was found to be 8.0 and unexplained variance was 3.67. The F-ratio is:
A. 0.46   B. 4.26
C. 2.0   D. 2.18

47. In total global emissions of CO_2, India's contribution is about :
A. ~ 3%   B. ~ 6%
C. ~ 9%   D. ~ 12%

48. According to IPCC, in order to restrict global mean temperature rise to 2°C by the year 2050, global energy related CO_2 emissions (reference year 2005) need to be cut down by the year 2050 by:
A. ~ 50%   B. ~ 90%
C. ~ 40%   D. ~ 30%

49. Global average water consumption (L/person/day) is:
A. ~ 53   B. ~ 20
C. ~ 42   D. ~ 80

50. In a city, half a million cars travel approximately 20 km on a given day. The average HC emission rate is 2.0 g per car km. Assuming that the average molecular weight of all the emitted HCs is equal to that of CH_4, how much volume of HC is released in the city each day?
A. 1.4×10^4 m³/day B. 2.8×10^4 m³/day
C. 6.1×10^4 m³/day D. 11.3×10^4 m³/day

ANSWERS

1	2	3	4	5	6	7	8	9	10
D	C	C	D	D	A	C	A	B	B
11	**12**	**13**	**14**	**15**	**16**	**17**	**18**	**19**	**20**
D	C	B	B	B	B	B	C	A	C
21	**22**	**23**	**24**	**25**	**26**	**27**	**28**	**29**	**30**
A	A	A	D	A	D	A	C	C	D
31	**32**	**33**	**34**	**35**	**36**	**37**	**38**	**39**	**40**
C	C	A	D	B	B	D	B	B	B
41	**42**	**43**	**44**	**45**	**46**	**47**	**48**	**49**	**50**
A	B	B	C	C	D	B	A	A	B

EXPLANATORY ANSWERS

1. The Earth comprises of four separate layers. Most of the geologist believes that as the Earth cooled the heavier, the materials denser sank into the center, and the lighter ones rose towards the top. Due to this, the outermost layer is made of lightest materials such as rocks and granites and the innermost layer consists of nickel and iron.

   Our Earth consists of four different layers namely:

   - Inner core
   - Outer core
   - Mantle
   - Crust

   Inner Core: It is the center and the hottest layer of the Earth. The inner core is solid and made up of iron and nickel with temperature up to 5,500°C. Due to its immense heat energy, the inner core is more like the engine room of the Earth.

2. Vertical mixing, in the atmosphere or oceans, an upward and downward movement of air or water that occurs as a result of the temperature gradients. In the atmosphere vertical mixing is sometimes discernible as a form of atmospheric turbulence.

   When the surface of Earth is substantially warmer than the overlying air, mixing will spontaneously occur in order to redistribute the heat. This process, referred to as free convection or natural convection, occurs when the environmental lapse rate — the rate of change of an atmospheric variable, such as temperature or density, with increasing altitude of temperature — decreases at a rate greater than 1°C per 100 metres.

3. An isothermal process is a thermodynamic process in which the temperature stays constant. In isothermal processes, there is no change in internal energy because internal energy is directly related to temperature.

   For an ideal gas the internal energy (U) depends on temperature. Hence, if temperature is constant (isothermal process), the internal energy remains constant and hence, $\Delta U = 0$.

   Enthalpy change (ΔH) can be directly measured using coffee-cup calorimeter and when we measure heat change (q_P) at constant pressure we actually measure change in enthalpy (ΔH).

   We know that $\Delta H = \Delta U + \Delta n\ RT$ and since for isothermal process ΔT as well ΔU are equal to zero and hence, $\Delta H = 0$.

4. Global sources of major aerosol types

Natural	Primary	Soil dust (mineral aerosol), sea salt, volcanic dust, primary organic aerosols
	Secondary	Sulphates from biogenic gases, sulphates from volcanic SO_2, organic matter from biogenic VOCs, nitrate from NO_x
Anthropogenic	Primary	Industrial dust (except soot), black carbon (includes biomass burning)
	Secondary	Sulphate from SO_2, nitrates from NO_x, organic matter from biogenic VOCs

5. Heavy metals are generally defined as metals with relatively high densities, atomic weights, or atomic numbers. The criteria used, and whether metalloids are included, vary depending on the author and context. In metallurgy, for example, a heavy metal may be defined on the basis of density, whereas in physics the distinguishing criterion might be atomic number, while a chemist would likely be more concerned with chemical behaviour. The definitions encompass up to 96 out of the 118 known chemical elements; only mercury, lead and bismuth meet all of them.

6. When CO_2 from the atmosphere comes into contact with seawater, it can become dissolved into the water where is undergoes chemical reactions to form a series of products, as described in the following:

1. CO_2 (dissolved gas) $+ H_2O \Leftrightarrow$

   H_2CO_3 (carbonic acid)

2. H_2CO_3 (carbonic acid) $\Leftrightarrow H+ + HCO_3^-$ (hydrogen ion + bicarbonate)

3. $HCO_3^- \Leftrightarrow H^+ + CO_3^{-2}$ (hydrogen ion + carbonate)

The amount of CO_2 as dissolved gas is what controls the concentration of CO_2. This concentration depends strongly on the temperature — it is low in cold water and it is high in warm water, which means that the colder parts of the ocean absorb CO_2 from the atmosphere and the warm parts of the ocean release CO_2 into the atmosphere.

All of these reactions mean that in seawater, you can find all of these different forms or species of inorganic carbon co-existing, dissolved in seawater. In reality though, bicarbonate (HCO_3^-) is the dominant form of inorganic carbon; carbonate (CO_3^{2-}) and dissolved CO_2 are important, but secondary.

7. Beer's law governs the amount of radiation absorbed and indicates that absorbance is directly proportional to concentration. Thus, as the concentration of a compound dissolved in a given solvent increases, the absorbance of the solution should also increase proportionally.

Concentration of Solution A

$$= \frac{0.14 \times 0.36}{0.42} = 0.12 \text{ mol/L.}$$

8. Micronutrients are essential for plant growth and play an important role in balanced crop nutrition. They include boron (B), copper (Cu), iron (Fe), manganese (Mn), molybdenum (Mo), zinc (Zn), nickel (Ni) and chloride (Cl). They are as important to plant nutrition as primary and secondary macronutrients, though plants don't require as much of them. A lack of any one of the micronutrients in the soil can limit growth, even when all other nutrients are present in adequate amounts. They constitute in total less than 1% of the dry weight of most plants.

9. Residence times can be determined for a reservoir itself (such as the water in a lake) or for a substance within it (such as a contaminant). The residence time for any reservoir can be determined by taking the ratio of the total amount (mass or volume) of the reservoir to the flux.

The residence time can be calculated as the reciprocal of the sum of all first order rate constants.

Residence time of substance

$$= \frac{\text{amount of substance}}{\text{total of all removal rates}}$$

$$= \frac{1}{\Sigma \text{ removal rate constants}}$$

Half-life: $t_{1/2} = \frac{\ln 2}{k} = \frac{0.693}{k}$

Residence time: $\tau = \frac{1}{k'}$, where k' represents the sum of all first order (or *pseudo*-first order) rate constants

Therefore;

$$\text{Half-life} = 0.693 \times (\text{Residence time})$$

$$\Rightarrow \quad \text{Residence time} = \frac{\text{Half life}}{0.693}$$

$$= \frac{0.693}{0.693} = 1 \text{ day.}$$

10. **Peroxyacyl nitrates** (also known as **Acyl peroxy nitrates**, **APN** or **PAN**s) are powerful respiratory and eye irritants present in photochemical smog. They are nitrates produced in the thermal equilibrium between organic peroxy radicals by the gas-phaseoxidation of a variety of volatile organic compounds (VOCs), or by aldehydes and other oxygenated VOCs oxidizing in the presence of NO_2.

For example, peroxyacetyl nitrate, $CH_3COOONO_2$:

Hydrocarbons + O_2 + NO_2 + light $\rightarrow$

$$CH_3COOONO_2$$

The general equation is:

$$C_xH_yO_3 + NO_2 \rightarrow C_xH_yO_3NO_2$$

They are good markers for the source of VOCs as either biogenic or anthropogenic, which is useful in the study of global and local effects of pollutants.

11. **Microconsumers or Saprotrophs:** The organisms which decompose complex compounds and dead cells and release in organic substances and belong chiefly in the group of bacteria, fungi. Item 1 to 2 - abiotic component u-6 biotic community.

12. A food web is a series of interacting food chains. Food chains show the order in which animals consume food. Food chains and food webs are made up of Producers, Consumers, and Decomposers. It is a structure with hundreds of species non-linearly interlinked for their livelihood.

13. (a) **Alpha diversity** [within-community diversity]: the diversity within a site, or quadrant. Also called as the local diversity.

    (b) **Beta diversity** [between-community diversity] : the change in species composition from site to site. Also called as species turnover. Higher the heterogenecity in the habitats in a region, greater is the beta diversity.

    (c) **Gamma diversity:** the diversity of a landscape, or of all sites combined. Also called as regional diversity.

    (d) **Genetic diversity**
       1. Genetic variation is the cornerstone of all biodiversity.
       2. It enables a population to adapt to its environment and to respond to natural selection. The more individuals there are, the greater the chance of genetic variation. Species with a small population of individuals have limited variability and, therefore, have limited ability to respond to change.
       3. The amount of genetic variation is the basis of speciation.
       4. Genetic diversity within a species often increases with environmental variability.

14. Red tides are caused by an explosive growth and accumulation of certain microscopic

algae, predominantly dinoflagellates, in coastal waters. Some species of dinoflagellates produce toxins that are among the most potent known to man. These harmful algae blooms, or HABs for short, pose a serious and recurring threat to human health, wildlife, marine ecosystems, fisheries, coastal aesthetics and our economy. The most troublesome species in the Gulf of Mexico is *Karenia brevis*. Like other dinoflagellates these tiny, single-celled organisms photosynthesize using chlorophyll like a plant yet they are mobile with the use of two flagella that propel them through the water column.

15. Two important subclasses of lakes are ponds, which typically are small lakes that intergrade with wetlands, and water reservoirs. Over long periods of time, lakes, or bays within them, may gradually become enriched by nutrients and slowly fill in with organic sediments, a process called succession.

   Succession is recognizable only if the colonization of plant communities takes place in artificial small and shallow ponds, lakes, etc. where wave action speeds up the process by allowing the erosion of soil towards edge regions. In this way, the filling process also speeds up quickly and consequently the body of water disappears within few years time.

16. Photosynthesis is the process by which plants and other organisms, also known as photoautotrophs, use energy from sunlight to produce glucose. This process can occur both on land and underwater.

   Photosynthesis can occur underwater as long as enough light is available. In the ocean, significant amounts of photosynthetically active radiation can be detected as deep as 250 m below the surface. Within this euphotic zone (sunlight zone), photosynthesis can occur. This process only requires light, carbon dioxide, and water. As long as a photosynthesizing organism, on land or underwater, has enough of these molecules, it can produce glucose and oxygen.

17. Genetically, the earliest bacteria are thought to have been archaebacteria, a classification that includes methane-producing bacteria, halophiles that survive conditions too hypersaline (salt-rich) for most other organisms, and sulfur bacteria able to tolerate the extreme heat radiating from earth's interior.

18. Rockfall talus slopes result from the accumulation of rockfall debris from discrete rockfall events over long periods of time. The plan morphology of talus slopes depends on the form of the cliffs supplying the debris and the morphology of the surface on which the debris accumulates. Relatively simple cliffs, straight in plan view and of uniform or similar geology, tend to produce sheet (straight) rockfall talus slopes lacking.

19. In 1935, the presence of black particles was discovered and the analysis led to the discovery of lignite reserves beneath the areas in and around Neyveli village. Lignite or brown coal occurs in (i) Neyveli in Tamil Nadu, (ii) Pallu fields in Rajasthan (iii) Masi in Kashmir and (iv) Parts of Assam, Meghalaya and other hilly tracts on the foothills of the Himalayas. By far the largest deposits occur in Neyveli in South Arcot district of Tamil Nadu. The Neyveli Lignite Corporation was formed as a corporate Body in 1956 by the Government of India and the mining of lignite started in 1962. The first thermal power station was commissioned in 1962 with assistance from U.S.S.R.

   India is the fifth largest coal producing country in the world. The coal production was 295.09 million tons and lignite production was 20.01 million tons in 1996-97.

20. The **Cartosat** series of satellites are a type of earth observation satellites indigenously built by India. Up till now 6 Cartosat satellites have been launched by ISRO. The Cartosat series is a part of the Indian Remote Sensing Programme. They were specifically launched

for Earth's resource management and monitoring.

Indian Earth Observation Satellite Cartosat-1 data were evaluated for the estimation of biophysical variables, including as tree height, crown diameter, canopy density and canopy gap, that are crucial for the estimation of stand volume, biomass and generation of site index. Investigations were carried out at a site covering the major dominant forest species grown in India. Cartosat-1 stereo data were analysed in conjunction with differential global positioning system (DGPS) measurements to generate a digital elevation model (DEM) and an orthoimage, which were used to estimate the biophysical variables. Analysis using grey level co occurrence texture measures was performed for separation of forest species, homogeneity of the classes of forest stands, stratification and measurement of crown area, canopy gap and stand density. Field measurements of tree height, diameter at breast height (DBH), stand density, age and crown diameter were conducted for each stand. Empirical models for the estimation of DBH were developed and validated with Cartosat 1 derived height and crown diameter.

21. Ecosystem Restoration is the "process of assisting the recovery of an ecosystem that has been degraded, damaged or destroyed". Ecosystem Restoration should be an important component of conservation and sustainable development programmes so that the livelihoods of people depending on these degraded ecosystems can be sustained.

The time has come to bridge the gap between the discipline of restoration ecology and communities around the world attempting to restore the ecological integrity of their surrounding landscapes.

22. The efficiency of a solar cell is determined as the fraction of incident power which is converted to electricity and is defined as:

$$P_{max} = V_{OC}I_{SC}FF$$

$$\eta = \frac{V_{OC}I_{SC}FF}{P_{in}}$$

Where:

V_{OC} is the open-circuit voltage;

I_{SC} is the short-circuit current;

FF is the fill factor and

η is the efficiency.

$$\eta = \frac{0.5 \times 2.5}{800 \times 0.1 \times 0.1} \times 100$$

$$= 15.6\%.$$

23. In nuclear engineering, **fissile material (nuclide)** is material that is capable of undergoing fission reaction after absorbing thermal (slow or low energy) neutron. These materials are used to fuel thermal nuclear reactors, because they are capable of sustaining a nuclear fission chain reaction.

For heavy nuclides with atomic number of higher than 90, most of fissile isotopes meet the **fissile rule**:

Fissile isotopes have $2 \times Z - N = 43 \pm 2$ (example for ^{235}U: $2 \times 92 - 143 = 41$)

where Z is number of protons and N is number of neutrons.

- **Fissile material** consist of fissionable isotopes that are capable of undergoing nuclear fission **only after capturing a thermal neutron**. ^{238}U is not fissile isotope, because ^{238}U cannot be fissioned by thermal neutron. ^{238}U does not meet also alternative requirement to fissile materials. ^{238}U is not capable of sustaining a nuclear fission chain reaction, because neutrons produced by fission of ^{238}U have lower energies than original neutron (usually below the threshold energy of 1 MeV). Typical fissile materials: ^{235}U, ^{233}U, ^{239}Pu, ^{241}Pu.

- **Fertile material** consist of isotopes that are not fissionable by thermal neutrons, but **can be converted into fissile isotopes** (after neutron absorption and subsequent nuclear decay). Typical fertile materials: ^{238}U, ^{232}Th.

25. Coal is a readily combustible rock containing more than *50 per cent* by weight of carbonaceous material formed from compaction and indurations of variously altered plant remains similar to those in peat.

   - **Lignite** increases in maturity by becoming darker and harder and is then classified as sub-bituminous coal. After a continuous process of burial and alteration, chemical and physical changes occur until the coal is classified as bituminous - dark and hard coal.

   - **Bituminous coal** ignites easily and burns long with a relatively long flame. If improperly fired bituminous coal is characterized with excess smoke and soot.

   - **Anthracite coal** is the last classification, the ultimate maturation. Anthracite coal is very hard and shiny.

   Typical Sulfur Content in Coal
   - Anthracite Coal : *0.6 - 0.77 weight %*
   - Bituminous Coal : *0.7 - 4.0 weight %*
   - Lignite Coal : *0.4 weight %*

26. The primary objective of the worldwide photovoltaic (PV) solar cell research and development is to reduce the cost of PV cells and modules to a level that will be competitive with conventional ways of generating power.

   Photovoltaic conversion efficiencies greater than 20% can be achieved by using single-crystal silicon or single junction GaAs semiconductor materials. Extraordinary progress has been made in recent years in achieving record-level efficiencies of 22% and 24% in single-crystal Si materials grown by the Czochralski (CZ) and 3 Float Zone (FZ) methods, respectively.

28. Concentration ($\mu g/m^3$)

$$= \frac{ppm \times \text{molecular weight (g/mol)} \times 1000\ (\mu g*L/m^3*g)}{24.5\ (L/mol)}$$

$$= \frac{1 \times 64.2 \times 1000}{24.5} = 2620\ \mu g/m^3.$$

29. Arsenic is one of the most toxic metals derived from the natural environment. The major cause of human arsenic toxicity is from contamination of drinking water from natural geological sources rather than from mining, smelting, or agricultural sources.

   Unbound arsenic also exerts its toxicity by generating reactive oxygen intermediates during their redox cycling and metabolic activation processes that cause lipid peroxidation and DNA damage. As III, especially, binds thiol or sulfhydryl groups in tissue proteins of the liver, lungs, kidney, spleen, gastrointestinal mucosa, and keratin-rich tissues (skin, hair, and nails).

31. **Pesticides and Their Targets**

Pesticide Type	Target Organism
Acaricide	Mites
Algicide	Algae
Avicide	Birds
Bactericide	Bacteria
Disinfectant	Microorganisms
Fungicide	Fungi
Herbicide	Plants
Insecticide	Insects
Larvicide	Insect larvae
Molluscicide	Snails, slugs
Nematicide	Nematodes
Piscicide	Fish
Rodenticide	Rodents
Termiticides	Termites

32. The process of converting free nitrogen gas of atmosphere into compounds of nitrogen (which can be used by plants) is called fixation of nitrogen. Nitrogen gas of the atmosphere can be fixed in three ways:

1. Fixation by bacteria
2. Fixation by algae
3. Fixation by lightning

1. **Fixation of nitrogen by bacteria:** The root nodules of certain leguminous plants (like peas, beans, etc.) contain nitrogen fixing bacteria called rhizobium. These nitrogen fixing bacteria convert nitrogen gas to nitrogen compounds, which can then be used by plants. Some non-leguminous plants like alnus and ginkgo also convert atmospheric nitrogen to usable nitrogen compounds for plants.

2. **Fixation of nitrogen by blue green algae:** Algae is the simplest green plant. Blue-green algae is also able to do nitrogen fixation. The nitrogen-fixing blue-green algae is found in paddy fields.

   Thus the two living organisms which can do fixation of nitrogen are rhizobium bacteria and blue-green algae. The fixation of nitrogen by bacteria and algae is called biological fixation of nitrogen. Most of the nitrogen in nature is fixed by this method.

3. **Fixation of nitrogen by lightning:** During lightning in the sky, a high temperature is produced, and the nitrogen gas present in the atmosphere reacts with oxygen, also present in the atmosphere to form nitrogen oxides. These nitrogen oxides dissolve in rain-water to form a very dilute solution of nitric acid which comes down to the Earth. This nitric acid reacts with the alkalies of soil (like limestone) to form nitrates. These nitrates get stored in the soil. In this way, the atmospheric nitrogen gets fixed. The nitrates present in the soil are then absorbed by the plants.

33. The United States withdraw from the Paris climate agreement, "In order to fulfill my solemn duty to protect America and its citizens, the United States will withdraw from the Paris climate accord," Trump said. Withdrawing, he said, "represents a reassertion of America's sovereignty."

   He added that he hoped to "begin negotiations to reenter either the Paris accord or really entirely new transition on terms that are fair to the United States."

34. The objective of EIA Notification 2006 is to address the limitations in the old EIA Notification (1994). Therefore, various modifications have been incorporated in the old Notification, which the ministry claims have been done after taking into account the feedback from the different stakeholders.

   EIA Notification 2006: Projects in Schedule-1 have been divided into two categories, Category A and B.

   Category A project will require clearance from Central Government (MEF). Category B will require clearance from State Government. However, the state government will first classify if the B project falls under B1 or B2 category. B1 projects will require preparation of EIA reports while remaining projects will be termed as B2 projects and will not require EIA report.

   This has the potential of being a good move as decentralization of power may speed up the project clearance process. However, it may be misused and there is an urgent need to build the capacity of the state regulators to deal with their new responsibilities.

36. **ISO 14021:** Environmental labels and declarations. Self-declaration of environmental claims: guidelines, definitions and usage of terms. This document is currently at the ISO DIS voting stage. It is expected to be completed and published by the end of the second quarter of 1998. This standard was combined with ISO 14022 and ISO 14023.

   ISO 14022: Environmental labels and declarations. Self-declaration of environmental claims: symbols. Currently this document is at the ISO committee draft (CD) voting stage. It is expected to be completed and published by the first quarter of 1999. This standard was combined with ISO 14021 and ISO 14023.

ISO 14023: Environmental labels and declarations. Self-declaration of environmental claims: testing and verification methodologies. This document is currently at the ISO CD voting stage. It is expected to be completed and published by the first quarter of 1999. This standard was combined with ISO 14021 and ISO 14023.

ISO 14024: Environmental labels and declarations. Environmental labeling Type I: guiding principles and procedures. This document is currently at the ISO DIS voting stage. It is expected to be completed and published by the end of 1998.

37. 1. **Rules framed under the Air (Prevention and Control of Pollution) Act, 1981:** Under section 54 of the Air (Prevention and Control of Pollution) Act, 1981 confers that every state government shall make their rules of the respective state. Similarly, under section 53 of Air Act, 1981, the central government framed the Air (Prevention and Control of Pollution) Rules 1982.

2. **Rules frame under the Environment (Protection) Act, 1986:** The Environment (Protection) Act, 1986 under sections 6 and 25 empowers that the Government of India formulated the Environment (Protection) Rules, 1986. In exercise of powers conferred by sections 6, 8 and 25 of the Environment (Protection) Act, 1986, the Government of India formulated the following Rules.

   (a) The hazardous wastes (Management and Handling) Rules, 1989

   (b) The manufacture, storage, and import of hazardous chemicals Rules, 1989

   (c) The chemical accidents (Emergency Planning, Preparedness and Response) Rules, 1996

   (d) The biomedical wastes (Management and Handling) Rules, 1998.

3. **The Water (Prevention and Control of Pollution) Cess Act, 1977:** This Act was passed in 1977. This Act deals with the various provisions relating to levy and collection of a cess on water consumed by person carrying on certain industries and by local authorities, with a view to augment the resources of the Central and the State Boards constituted under the Water (Prevention and Control of Pollution) Act, 1974 for the Prevention and Control of Water Pollution.

4. **Rules framed under National Environment Appellate Authority Act, 1997 and Public Liability Insurance Act, 1991:** Under section 22 of the National Environment Appellate Authority Act, 1997 the central government made the National Environment Appellate Authority (Appeal) Rules 1997. Similarly, Under section 22 read with section 13 of the National Environment Appellate Authority Act, 1997 (22 of 1997) the central government of India made the National Environment Appellate Authority (Financial and Administrative powers) Rules, 1998. In exercise of the powers conferred by section 23 of the Public Liability Insurance Act 1997, the central government made the Public Liability Insurance Rules, 1991.

38. Article 21 of the constitution of India provides for the right to life and personal liberty. It states that "no person shall be deprived of his life or personal liberty except according to procedure established by law." In Rural Litigation and Entitlement.

In addition, the Constitution (Forty Second Amendment) Act 1976 explicitly incorporated environmental protection and improvement as a part of state policy. Article 48A, a Directive Principle of State Policy, provides that: The State shall endeavour to protect and improve the environment and safeguard the forests and wildlife of the country'. Moreover, article 51A (g) imposes a similar resonsibility on every citizen to protect and improve the natural environment including forest, lakes, rivers and wildlife, and to have compassion for living creatures ..... 'Therefore, protection of natural environment and compassion for living creatures were made the positive fundamental duty of every citizen. Both the provisions substantially send the same message. Together, they highlight the national consensus on the importance of the protection and improvement of the environment.

39. The Indian Forest Act was enacted to preserve and safeguard the forests generally in India. The Act makes various provisions for such conservation of forests and in the scheme it provides for a State Government to constitute any forest land or waste land, which are property of Government or which the Government has proprietary rights, as a reserved forest.

Although the Indian Forest Act deals specifically with (i) reserved forests; (ii) village forest, viz., reserved forest which have been assigned to any village community; and (iii) protected forests. The preamble and other provisions of the Forest Act are wide enough to cover all categories of forests. This Act is one curtailing proprietary rights of individuals and so the Act and the notifications issued under it must be construed strictly where the rights of individuals are trenched upon.

40. Hardening involves heating of steel, keeping it at an appropriate temperature until all pearlite is transformed into austenite, and then quenching it rapidly in water or oil. The temperature at which austentizing rapidly takes place depends upon the carbon content in the steel used. The heating time should be increased ensuring that the core will also be fully transformed into austenite. The microstructure of a hardened steel part is ferrite, martensite, or cementite.

Hardening of steel releases hazardous waste containing cyanide-, nitrate-, or nitrite-containing sludge and spent hardening salt.

41. Red coloured disinfected containers or bags be used for the disposal of microbial and biological wastes and the soiled wastes. Waste of category 3, 6 and 7 are to be kept together in red container.

The hazardous hospital waste has been divided into various categories, such that each category should contain different type of waste, also requiring different treatment procedures, according to nature of component. The categories 3, 6 and 7 are discussed below.

Category 3: Microbiological and biotechnological wastes, such as waste from laboratory culture, specimens from microorganisms, vaccines, cell cultures, toxins, dishes, devices used to transfer cultures are included under the category 3. Their treatment and disposal options are- local autoclaving or micro waving or incineration.

Category 6: This includes soiled wastes, contaminated with blood and body fluids including cotton, dressing, soiled plasters, linen etc. Their treatment and disposal options are- autoclaving, micro waving or incineration.

Category 7: This category of hospital waste consists of solid wastes such as tubes, catheters, IV sets etc. Their recommended disposal is by means of chemical disinfection, autoclaving, micro waving, mutilation and shredding.

42. Methylmercury is special among organic mercury compounds because large numbers of people are exposed to it and its toxicity is better understood. Methylmercury in food, such as fish, is a particular health hazard because it is easily taken up into the body through the stomach and intestines.

It is a poison for the nervous system. Exposure during pregnancy is of most concern, because it may harm the development of the unborn baby's brain. Some studies suggest that small increases in exposure may affect the heart and circulatory system.

Moreover, there is some evidence at present that methylmercury can cause cancer in humans, but it is far from conclusive: the International Agency for Research on Cancer (IARC) has classified methylmercury as "possibly carcinogenic to humans".

43. Gaussian model: The Gaussian model is perhaps the oldest (circa 1936) and perhaps the most commonly used model type. It assumes that the air pollutant dispersion has a Gaussian distribution, meaning that the pollutant distribution has a normal probability distribution. Gaussian models are most often used for predicting the dispersion of continuous, buoyant air pollution plumes originating from ground-level or elevated sources. Gaussian models may also be used for predicting the dispersion of non-continuous air pollution plumes (called *puff models*). The primary algorithm used in Gaussian modeling is the *Generalized Dispersion Equation For A Continuous Point-Source Plume.*

44. In descriptive statistics, a box plot or boxplot is a convenient way of graphically depicting groups of numerical data through their quartiles. Box plots may also have lines extending vertically from the boxes (whiskers) indicating variablility outside the upper and lower quartiles, hence the terms box-and-whisker plot and box-and-whisker diagram. Outliers may be plotted as individual points.

Advantages of Box and Whisker Plot

1. It helps us to learn how the data is spread in the series.
2. The graph is not sophisticated. It is clear and easy to understand.
3. It uses the range and the median values.
4. It is easy to compare the stratified data using the Box Whisker Plot.

Disadvantages of Box and Whisker Plot

1. Original data is not clearly shown in the Box Plot.
2. Mean and mode cannot be identified using the Box Plot.
3. It can be easy misinterpreted.
4. If large outliers are present, the Box Plot is more likely to give an incorrect representation.

45. Total number of fish in the pond $n(F) = 50$

Number of fishes without ectoparasite $n(A) = 12$

Number of fishes with atleast one parasites

$$= n(F) - n(A)$$
$$= 50 - 12 = 38.$$

46. To use the F-test to determine whether group means are equal, it's just a matter of including the correct variances in the ratio. In one-way ANOVA, the F-statistic is this ratio:

F = variation between sample means / variation within the samples

$$= \frac{8}{3.67} = 2.18.$$

47. India and China are among the world's biggest contributors to fossil fuel emissions with India's carbon dioxide discharge increasing by a whopping 7.7 per cent last year.

Indian CO_2 emissions increased by a whopping 7.7 per cent, with those from coal growing 10.2 per cent, said the report coinciding with the UN climate talks in Warsaw, the Polish capital.

48. Global CO_2 emissions would have to start coming down by about 2015 and by 2050 should be around 50-85% below the year 2000 levels. For a 550 ppm CO_2 equivalent stabilization level (leading to about 3°C warming), global CO_2 emissions should start declining no later than about 2030 and should be 5-30% below 2000 levels by 2050.

49. We use water not just to drink or shower or wash our clothes, we use it through the products we consume too. The average person will need 5 liters of water to drink daily, to survive in a moderate climate with little activity. An average American uses 100 to 175 gallons of water per day. Globally, we consume around 4 trillion cubic meters of fresh water a year!

Agriculture alone can consume 75 to 90% of a region's available freshwater. Global average water consumption (L/person/day) is 53.

PAPER-III

Note: *This paper contains seventy five (75) objective type questions of two (2) marks each. All questions are compulsory.*

1. The sum of the internal energy and product of pressure and volume is known as:
   A. Enthalpy
   B. Gibbs free energy
   C. Entropy
   D. Helmholtz free energy

2. If at latitude $\phi = 30°$, pressure gradient is 15 mb per 1000 km, the geostrophic wind velocity will be:
   A. ~ 20.54 m/s   B. ~ 15.92 m/s
   C. ~ 7.96 m/s   D. ~ 10.27 m/s

3. In a cloud free weather, there is an atmospheric window, which is transparent to terrestrial radiation in the wavelength band:
   A. 1618 nm - 23400 nm
   B. 2168 nm - 4610 nm
   C. 12500 nm - 17000 nm
   D. 7000 nm - 13500 nm

4. If $\Gamma_{env} < \Gamma_d$, where Γ_{env} and Γ_d are environmental and dry adiabatic lapse rates respectively, which of the following types of plume emitted from a stack of a thermal power plant is observed?
   A. Fanning   B. Fumigating
   C. Looping   D. Coning

5. Out of the following two statements, identify the correct one(s):
   (a) An aqueous solution of sodium carbonate is alkaline.
   (b) An aqueous solution of carbon dioxide is acidic.

A. (a) is correct, (b) is incorrect
B. (a) is incorrect, (b) is correct
C. Both (a) and (b) are incorrect
D. Both (a) and (b) are correct

6. The photodissociation of NO_2 yields which oxygen species?
   A. $O(^3P)$ B. $O(^1D)$
   C. O^+ D. O^-

7. The vapour pressure of bromobenzene above its ideal dilute aqueous solution of molality 0.1 mol kg^{-1} is 24.0 kPa. Calculate the Henry's law constant of bromobenzene:
   A. 240 kPa kg mol^{-1}
   B. 220 kPa kg mol^{-1}
   C. 460 kPa kg mol^{-1}
   D. 400 kPa kg mol^{-1}

8. In the Spectrophotometric Study, if a sample has transmittance of 50%, then its absorbance is:
   A. 0.5   B. 0.3
   C. 1.0   D. 0.7

9. Given below are two statements. One labelled as **Assertion (A)** and the other labelled as **Reason (R):**

   Assertion (A): Sandy soil helps promote good drainage and aeration.

   Reason (R): Sandy soil particles have size in the range 0.05 – 2.0 mm.

   Choose the **correct** answer:
   A. Both (A) and (R) are correct and (R) is the correct explanation of (A).
   B. Both (A) and (R) are correct and (R) is not the correct explanation of (A).
   C. (A) is true, but (R) is false.
   D. (A) is false and (R) is true.

10. Night–time tropospheric chemistry is dominated by which of the following radicals?
    A. NO_3
    B. OH
    C. HO_2
    D. O

11. Given below are two statements. One labelled as **Assertion (A)** and the other labelled as **Reason (R)**:

    Assertion (A): Chlorine, which is widely used as an effective and relatively inexpensive disinfectant in water, generates toxic organochlorine compounds in water.

    Reason (R): Hypochlorous acid reacts rapidly with humic acids and hydroxobenzenes.

    Choose the **correct** answer:
    A. Both (A) and (R) are correct and (R) is the correct explanation of (A).
    B. Both (A) and (R) are correct and (R) is not the correct explanation of (A).
    C. (A) is true, but (R) is false.
    D. (A) is false and (R) is true.

12. In the context of argentometric titration of chloride ions in a water sample, identify the **incorrect** statement:
    A. Titrant is silver nitrate solution
    B. Indicator is potassium chromate
    C. Colour of the end - point is lemon - yellow
    D. pH of water sample should be less than 5

13. The reaction of OH radicals with which of the following species generates hydrogen atom?
    A. CH_4
    B. NH_3
    C. CO
    D. NO_2

14. Which of the following statements is true for an ideal dilute solution?
    A. Solute and solvent both obey Raoult's law
    B. Solute obeys Raoult's law and solvent obeys Henry's law
    C. Solute obeys Henry's law and solvent obeys Raoult's law
    D. Solute and solvent both obey Henry's law

15. Given below are two statements. One labelled as **Assertion (A)** and the other labelled as **Reason (R)**:

    Assertion (A): The living components of ecosystems are not immortal.

    Reason (R): Depending on the biological longevity, all living systems become abiotic constituents.

    Choose the **correct** answer:
    A. Both (A) and (R) are correct and (R) is the correct explanation of (A).
    B. Both (A) and (R) are correct and (R) is not the correct explanation of (A).
    C. (A) is true, but (R) is false.
    D. (A) is false and (R) is true.

16. The movement of energy from primary producers to consumers is effected by:
    A. The process of eating
    B. The rate of rainfall
    C. The rate of evaporation
    D. The rate of transpiration

17. The result of removal of primary producers and subsequent reduction in population size leading to change in community attributes is referred to as:
    A. Top - down cascade
    B. Bottom - up cascade
    C. Population decline
    D. Community collapse

18. The amount of accumulated dead organic matter in different forest types:
    A. Decreases from pole to equator.
    B. Increases from tropic of cancer to tropic of Capricorn.
    C. Increases from pole to equator.
    D. Stabilizes at any point between two poles.

19. Which one of the following termite gut microbe contributes to degradation of cellulose?
    A. *Trichonympha* sp.
    B. *Enterococcus* sp.
    C. *Enterobacter* sp.
    D. *Citrobacter* sp.

20. Match the List-I and List-II. Identify the correct answer from the code given below:

List-I (Group of Plankton)	List-II (Example)
(a) Macroplankton	(i) Rotifera
(b) Nanoplankton	(ii) Copepoda
(c) Mesoplankton	(iii) Pyrrophyta
(d) Microplankton	(iv) Amphipoda

Code:

	(a)	(b)	(c)	(d)
A.	(iii)	(iv)	(i)	(ii)
B.	(ii)	(i)	(iv)	(iii)
C.	(i)	(ii)	(iii)	(iv)
D.	(iv)	(iii)	(ii)	(i)

21. The size of the Femtoplankton is in the range:
   A. 0.2 - 2.0 μm   B. < 0.2 μm
   C. > 5.0 μm   D. 0.5 - 1.0 μm

22. As of July 2017, the total number of National Parks existing in India is:
   A. 127   B. 103
   C. 97   D. 100

23. Given below are two statements. One labelled as **Assertion (A)** and the other labelled as **Reason (R):**

   Assertion (A) : Some infectious particles loose their infectious - ability in territories closer to equator, with high average of daily sunshine hours.

   Reason (R): UV incidence can determine the survival of infectious particles.

   Choose the **correct** answer:
   A. Both (A) and (R) are correct and (R) is the correct explanation of (A).
   B. Both (A) and (R) are correct and (R) is not the correct explanation of (A).
   C. (A) is true, but (R) is false.
   D. (A) is false and (R) is true.

24. An organism that represents both primary producer and primary consumer of an aquatic ecosystem is:
   A. Phytoplankton   B. Bacterioplankton
   C. Benthic algae   D. Zooplankton

25. Given below are two statements. One labelled as **Assertion (A)** and the other labelled as **Reason (R):**

   Assertion (A): The $^{18}O/^{16}O$ ratio in a natural system can be used as a thermometer.

   Reason (R): The fractions of $^{18}O/^{16}O$ depend on temperature.

   Choose the **correct** answer:
   A. Both (A) and (R) are correct and (R) is the correct explanation of (A).
   B. Both (A) and (R) are correct and (R) is not the correct explanation of (A).
   C. (A) is true, but (R) is false.
   D. (A) is false and (R) is true.

26. Most suitable spectral region for studying Urban Heat Island (UHI) effect is:
   A. 3 - 5 μm   B. 8 - 10 μm
   C. 10 - 12 μm   D. 1 - 3 μm

27. Which factor(s) may affect species richness on island?
   (a) Area of the island
   (b) Distance from the mainland
   (c) Shape of the island

   Choose the **correct** code:
   A. (a) and (b) only   B. (b) and (c) only
   C. (a) and (c) only   D. (a), (b) and (c)

28. Delineation of water - nonwater boundary in remote sensing is best done using:
   A. 0.5 - 0.6 μm   B. 0.6 - 0.7 μm
   C. 0.7 - 0.9 μm   D. 1 - 3 μm

29. Environmentalists oppose the mining of antarctic mineral resources because:
   A. The demand for minerals is expected to decline as the world's nations become more industrialized.
   B. Environment of Antarctica is extremely vulnerable and fragile to the disturbance that would occur with the development.
   C. Territorial claims to Antarctica are unresolved.
   D. Currenty known reserves of minerals and metals are considered inexhaustible.

30. Which of the following statements is not true for the solubility of CO_2 in seawater?
   A. It increases with increase in partial pressure of CO_2.
   B. It increases with increase in pH.
   C. It increases with increase in temperature.
   D. It decrease with increase in salinity.

31. What was the theme for the International Ozone Day (year 2017)?

A. 'Caring for all life under the Sun'
B. 'Ozone : All there is between you and UV'
C. 'Ozone and Climate : Restored by a World United'
D. '30 years of healing Ozone Together'

32. Given below are two statements. One labelled as **Assertion (A)** and the other labelled as **Reason (R)**:

Assertion (A): OTEC power plants have low efficiences.

Reason (R): Efficiency is governed by 2nd law of thermodynamics.

Choose the **correct** answer:
A. Both (A) and (R) are correct and (R) is the correct explanation of (A).
B. Both (A) and (R) are correct and (R) is not the correct explanation of (A).
C. (A) is true, but (R) is false.
D. (A) is false and (R) is true.

33. Given below are two statements. One labelled as **Assertion (A)** and the other labelled as **Reason (R)**:

Assertion (A): The efficiency of a silicon solar cell decreases with increase in temperature.

Reason (R): The intrinsic resistance of the solar cell increases with rise in temperature.

Choose the **correct** answer:
A. Both (A) and (R) are correct and (R) is the correct explanation of (A).
B. Both (A) and (R) are correct and (R) is not the correct explanation of (A).
C. (A) is true, but (R) is false.
D. (A) is false and (R) is true.

34. Given below are two statements. One labelled as **Assertion (A)** and the other labelled as **Reason (R)**:

Assertion (A): The rotor blades of wind - turbine execute rotational motion when moving air impinges on them.

Reason (R): The momentum of the moving air is transferred to the moving blades.

Choose the **correct** answer:
A. Both (A) and (R) are correct and (R) is the correct explanation of (A).
B. Both (A) and (R) are correct and (R) is not the correct explanation of (A).
C. (A) is true, but (R) is false.
D. (A) is false and (R) is true.

35. A tidal power station has basin area = $10,000$ m^2 and water trapped at height = 2.0 m above low tide. If the density of sea water is 1025 kgm^{-3}, the potential energy available for every tidal period is:
A. ~ 201 MJ   B. ~ 402 MJ
C. ~ 240 MJ   D. ~ 480 MJ

36. A typical fission reaction involving an atom of $^{235}_{92}$U leads to a mass defect = 0.37×10^{-27} kg. How much energy is going to be released by 1.0 g of $^{235}_{92}$U ?
A. 3.33×10^{-11} MJ   B. 2.23×10^{12} MJ
C. 2.56×10^4 MJ   D. 8.53×10^4 MJ

37. Given below are two statements. One labelled as **Assertion (A)** and the other labelled as **Reason (R)**:

Assertion (A) : To exploit renewable energy, quite large structures are required relative to the power produced.

Reason (R): Power flux densities of renewable energy sources are appreciably lower compared to fossil fuels.

Choose the **correct** answer:
A. Both (A) and (R) are correct and (R) is the correct explanation of (A).
B. Both (A) and (R) are correct and (R) is not the correct explanation of (A).
C. (A) is true, but (R) is false.
D. (A) is false and (R) is true.

38. Biodiesel is produced from oils and fats using:
A. Transesterification
B. Anaerobic digestion
C. Pyrolysis
D. Fermentation

39. On take - off, an aeroplane generates noise level of 120 dB. If 5 such aeroplanes take - off simultaneously what will be the noise level?
   A. ~ 126.98 dB
   B. ~ 124.98 dB
   C. ~ 123.86 dB
   D. ~ 122.98 dB

40. CRIEGEE intermediate is formed in which of the following atmospheric reactions?
   A. Olefin and Ozone
   B. Ethane and Ozone
   C. Acedaldehyde and Ozone
   D. NO_2 and Ozone

41. In the purification of drinking water, the purpose of aeration is not to:
   A. Remove dissolved gases such as H_2S
   B. Remove volatile organic compounds
   C. Oxidize soluble Fe^{2+} to Fe^{3+}
   D. Precipitate colloidal particles

42. Which of the following is an organocarbamate insecticide?
   A. Parathion
   B. Chloropyritos
   C. Aldicarb
   D. Malathion

43. A bag containing a mixed feitilizer is labelled 5 - 10 - 5. It indicates:
   A. 5% P ; 10% N ; 5% K
   B. 5% N ; 10% P_2O_5 ; 5% K_2O
   C. 5% N_2O ; 10% PH_3 ; 5% K_2O
   D. 5% N ; 10% PH_3 ; 5% K_2O

44. The bioremediation technique of a contaminated soil does not require the fulfilment of which of the following conditions?
   A. Waste must be present in a physical form that is susceptible to microbes.
   B. Waste must be susceptible to biodegradation.
   C. Environmental conditions such as pH, temperature and oxygen level must be appropriate.
   D. Microbes of any type must be available.

45. Given below are two statements. One labelled as **Assertion (A)** and the other labelled as **Reason (R)**:

Assertion (A): Organophosphate insecticides have lower values of partition coefficient, Kow, than organochlorine pesticides.

Reason (R): Organophosphate insecticide molecules have lower ability to form hydrogen bonds with water than organochlorine pesticides.

Choose the **correct** answer:
A. Both (A) and (R) are correct and (R) is the correct explanation of (A).
B. Both (A) and (R) are correct and (R) is not the correct explanation of (A).
C. (A) is true, but (R) is false.
D. (A) is false and (R) is true.

46. Given below are two statements. One labelled as **Assertion (A)** and the other labelled as **Reason (R)**:

Assertion (A): NOX and volatile organic compounds (VOCs) are primary precursors in photochemical smog formation.

Reason (R): NOX and VOCs form oxidants by thermal reactions.

Choose the **correct** answer:
A. Both (A) and (R) are correct and (R) is the correct explanation of (A).
B. Both (A) and (R) are correct and (R) is not the correct explanation of (A).
C. (A) is true, but (R) is false.
D. (A) is false and (R) is true.

47. The dominant species, which removes hydroxyl radical in troposphere, is:
   A. CH_4
   B. CO
   C. NO
   D. NO_2

48. Match the List-I and List-II. Identify the correct answer from the code given below:

List-I (EIA methods)	List-II (Features)
(a) Overlays	(i) Environmental Evaluation System
(b) Networks	(ii) Adaptive environmental assessment
(c) Battelle Columbus	(iii) Environmental Systems as a complex web
(d) Simulation modelling	(iv) Composite impact by superimposing maps

Code:

	(a)	(b)	(c)	(d)
A.	(i)	(ii)	(iii)	(iv)
B.	(ii)	(iii)	(iv)	(i)
C.	(iii)	(iv)	(i)	(ii)
D.	(iv)	(iii)	(i)	(ii)

49. The baseline studies in EIA pertain to:
    A. Collection of demographic data only
    B. Prediction of significant residual environmental impact
    C. Existing environmental setting of the proposed development area
    D. Selection of the best project option available

50. Which one of the following steps is not included in the scoping process?
    A. Baseline descriptions and potential additional data collection needs
    B. Description of environmental impacts and creation of contingency plan
    C. Defining a set of criteria to assess the project
    D. Setting of experts team that will conduct EIA

51. A company conducted an environmental risk assessment to evaluate the possible impacts of releasing various levels of pollutants from a chemical plant. An environmental risk assessment should focus on:
    A. Beneficial aspects of the products produced by the plant
    B. The legislative requirements related to the human health effects as a result of exposure to the pollutant
    C. The quantification of hazards to the local environment from pollutants released
    D. Detailed outline of the management process to reduce the health effects related to exposure to the pollutants

52. In EIA the multi - attribute utility theory is used to describe:
    A. The identification of the alternatives to be evaluated and structuring of environmental parameters
    B. Existing environmental quality of study area

C. The socio - economic status of the area
D. The risk involved in a development project

53. Under the Air Act, 1981, which body is empowered to set standard for ambient air quality?
    A. MOEFCC
    B. Ministry of Home Affairs
    C. Central Pollution Control Board (CPCB)
    D. State Ministry of Home Affairs

54. What is meant by the doctrine of riparian rights?
    A. Prevention is better than cure.
    B. One who pollutes the water, must pay for it.
    C. Every owner has a right to get unpolluted water without alteration.
    D. All of the above.

55. Which environmental legislation in India makes it compulsory to obtain prior approval of the Central Government for diversion of forest lands for non - forest purposes?
    A. Environment (Protection) Act, 1986
    B. Indian Forest Act, 1927
    C. Forest Conservation Act, 1980
    D. Traditional forest - Dwellers (Forest rights) Act, 2006

56. The Lime stabilization and drying of biosolids ensure:
    (a) Creating unfavourable condition to vector
    (b) High pH of contents in biosolids
    (c) Reduction of all toxic elements

    Choose the **correct** answer:
    A. (a), (b) and (c)   B. (a) and (c) only
    C. (a) and (b) only   D. (b) and (c) only

57. Which one of the following waste may undergo exothermic self - accelerating decomposition?
    A. Organic peroxides
    B. Arsenic bearing sludges
    C. Organo - Chlorines
    D. Vinylchlorides

58. According to Plastic Waste (Management and Handling) Rules 2011, recycling of the plastic should be done according to:

A. IS/ISO 14852 : 1991
B. IS/ISO 17088 : 2008
C. IS 9833 : 1981
D. IS 14534 : 1998

59. Which of the following is not a Millennium Development Goal?
A. Ensuring environmental sustainability
B. Eradicating extreme hunger and poverty
C. Developing global partnership for development
D. Achieving universal energy security

60. The definition of 'air pollutant' as per section 2(a) of Air Act, 1981 includes:
A. Liquid and gaseous substances
B. Solid, liquid and gaseous substances including noise
C. Gaseous substances
D. Solid, liquid and gaseous substances

61. In a population of 210 individuals, 72 are smokers and 138 are non - smokers. If a person is selected with an equal chance to each category, what is the probability of that person being a smoker?
A. 0.25   B. 0.50
C. 0.34   D. 0.75

62. If the mean value ($\bar{X}$) of a normally distributed data is 10 and number of observation (n) = 36 with an standard deviation (sd) of 0.3, then 90% confidence interval is:
A. 10 ± 0.08 B. 10 ± 8.23
C. 10 ± 0.16 D. 10 ± 4.15

63. Consider a tall stack emitting a pollutant at the rate 5.0 gms^{-1} in the atmosphere where wind is blowing in X-direction with an average velocity of 2.0 ms^{-1} at the stack height. What will be the maximum ground level concentration if the effective stack height is 30.0 m and the Gaussian plume is assumed with dispersion parameters σ_y = 50.0 m and σ_z = 30.0 m?
A. ~ 180 µgm^{-3} B. ~ 320 µgm^{-3}
C. ~ 240 µgm^{-3} D. ~ 415 µgm^{-3}

64. Which of the following material(s) are used as land fill liner for the control of gas and leachate movement?

(a) Sand   (b) Bentonite
(c) Fly ash   (d) Butyle rubber
Choose the **correct** code:
A. (a) and (b) only   B. (a) and (c) only
C. (c) and (d) only   D. (b) and (d) only

65. Assume that the population (N) of a species follows the logistic growth represented by following equation:

$$\frac{dN}{dt} = 0.8N - 0.01N^2$$

At what value of N, the population exhibits maximum growth?
A. 40   B. 80
C. 160   D. 800

66. Given below are two statements. One labelled as **Assertion (A)** and the other labelled as **Reason (R):**

Assertion (A) : In regression analysis, smaller the p - values, the more significant is the result of the experiment.

Reason (R) : The magnitude of p - value is an indicator of the association between the changes in the predictor's value and the changes in the response variable.

Choose the **correct** answer:
A. Both (A) and (R) are correct and (R) is the correct explanation of (A).
B. Both (A) and (R) are correct and (R) is not the correct explanation of (A).
C. (A) is true, but (R) is false.
D. (A) is false and (R) is true.

67. The mean and median of a moderately skewed distribution are 21 and 20 respectively. The mode of the distribution is:
A. 24   B. 12
C. 18   D. 26

68. The 90th percentile value for the data : 6, 6, 6.5, 7.0, 7.5, 6.5, 6, 7.5 and 8 is:
A. 7.50   B. 6.50
C. 7.75   D. 7.00

69. Given below are two statements. One labelled as **Assertion (A)** and the other labelled as **Reason (R):**

Assertion (A): Sustainable mountain development should be the global priority.

Reason (R): Mountain people are particularly vulnerable to impacts of climate change and natural disasters.

Choose the **correct** answer:
A. Both (A) and (R) are correct and (R) is the correct explanation of (A).
B. Both (A) and (R) are correct and (R) is not the correct explanation of (A).
C. (A) is true, but (R) is false.
D. (A) is false and (R) is true.

70. In the total global ecological footprint, which country has the maximum share:
A. USA　　　　B. China
C. India　　　D. Brazil

71. Given below are two statements. One labelled as **Assertion (A)** and the other labelled as **Reason (R):**

Assertion (A): Climate change induced monsoon variability may have serious consequences for Indian agriculture.

Reason (R): Two third (2/3rd) of area under cultivation in India is rain dependent.

Choose the **correct** answer:
A. Both (A) and (R) are correct and (R) is the correct explanation of (A).
B. Both (A) and (R) are correct and (R) is not the correct explanation of (A).

C. (A) is true, but (R) is false.
D. (A) is false and (R) is true.

72. Namami Gange (Integrated Ganga Conservation Mission / Programme under National Ganga River Basin Authority) programme was launched in which year?
A. 2014　　　B. 2015
C. 1989　　　D. 2012

73. Which state in India is pioneer in making rain water harvesting as a compulsory measure in towns to avoid ground water depletion?
A. Kerala
B. Arunachal Pradesh
C. Tamil Nadu
D. Maharashtra

74. Environmental education:
(a) Increases public awareness
(b) Provides knowledge of environmental issues
(c) Does not provide disciplinary focus
(d) Sensitizes individuals about the necessity of sustainable development

Choose the **correct** answer:
A. (a), (c) and (d) only
B. (a), (b) and (d) only
C. (b), (c) and (d) only
D. (a), (b), (c) and (d)

75. The greenhouse gas, ozone, absorbs and emits long wave radiation near the wavelength :
A. 9.6 µm　　　B. 11.2 µm
C. 6.9 µm　　　D. 17.3 µm

ANSWERS

1	2	3	4	5	6	7	8	9	10
A	B	D	A	D	A	A	B	A	A
11	12	13	14	15	16	17	18	19	20
A	D	C	C	A	A	B	A	A	D
21	22	23	24	25	26	27	28	29	30
B	B	B	B	A	C	D	C	B	C
31	32	33	34	35	36	37	38	39	40
A	A	A	B	A	D	A	A	A	A

41	42	43	44	45	46	47	48	49	50
D	C	B	D	C	C	B	D	C	B

51	52	53	54	55	56	57	58	59	60
D	A	C	C	C	C	A	D	D	B

61	62	63	64	65	66	67	68	69	70
C	A	B	D	A	C	C	C	B	B

71	72	73	74	75
A	A	C	B	A

EXPLANATORY ANSWERS

1. *The* enthalpy *of a system may be defined as the sum of the internal energy and the product of pressure and volume of the system.*

   The *physical significance of enthapy* may be put as under:

   The **enthlpy** *of a substance is the amount of energy stored within the substance, i.e., available for conversion into heat.*

   Like internal energy, *the heat content or enthalpy of a substance is also a state function, i.e.,* depends only on the state of the system and is independent of the manner by which the state has been attained.

   Enthalpy change: Like internal energy, the absolute value of enthalpy of a substance cannot be determined. However, the change in the enthalpy when a system undergoes a change can be determined experimentally accurately and that serves our purpose.

   A relation between enthalpy change and internal energy change exists as follows:

   $$\Delta H = \Delta E + P\,\Delta V$$

   where $\quad \Delta E = E_2 - E_1$ represents the change in internal energy

   and $\quad \Delta V = V_2 - V_1$ represents the change in volume of the system

   Thus, enthalpy change *of a system may be defined as the sum of internal energy change and the pressure-volume work done.*

   If q_p is the heat absorbed at constant pressure, then $q_p = \Delta H$

   Thus, enthalpy change *is the heat absorbed or evolved at constant pressure.*

2. **Hint:** The speed of the geostrophic wind can be approximated by

   $$V_g \cong \frac{1}{pf}\left|\frac{\Delta p}{\Delta n}\right|$$

   where Δp is the difference in pressure between adjacent isobars (in Pascals, not millibars), and Δn is the horizontal distance between the two adjacent isobars.

4. **Plume Types:** Plume types are important because they help us understand under what conditions there will be higher concentrations of contaminants at ground level.

   Looping Plume
   - High degree of convective turbulence
   - Super adiabatic lapse rate — strong instabilities
   - Associated with clear daytime conditions accompanied by strong solar heating & light winds
   - High probability of high concentrations sporadically at ground level close to stack.
   - Occurs in unstable atmospheric conditions.

   Coning Plume
   - Stable with small-scale turbulence
   - Associated with overcast moderate to strong winds

- Roughly $10°$ cone
- Pollutants travel fairly long distances before reaching ground level in significant amounts
- Occurs in neutral atmospheric conditions

Fanning Plume

- Occurs under large negative lapse rate
- Strong inversion at a considerable distance above the stack
- Extremely stable atmosphere
- Little turbulence
- If plume density is similar to air, travels downwind at approximately same elevation

Fumigation

- Most dangerous plume: contaminants are all coming down to ground level.
- They are created when atmospheric conditions are stable above the plume and unstable below.
- This happens most often after the daylight sun has warmed the atmosphere, which turns a night time fanning plume into fumigation for about a half an hour.

5. (a) **Sodium carbonate** acts as an alkali because when dissolved in **water**, it dissociates into the weak acid: carbonic acid and the strong alkali: **sodium hydroxide**.

$$H_2O \rightarrow 2H^+ + OH^-$$

$$NaCO_3 \rightarrow Na^+ + CO_3(2^-)$$

Net reaction:

$$H_2O + NaCO_3 \rightarrow H_2CO_3 + NaOH$$

(b) Carbon dioxide (CO_2) gas dissolved in water can cause water to become acidic.

The acidity of water from dissolved CO_2 can be reduced by a base such as baking soda (sodium bicarbonate).

6. The photochemical dissociation of NO_2 illustrates the importance of photochemistry, because one of the products is atomic oxygen.

Many photochemical reactions in the atmosphere yield atoms or free radicals and these are much more reactive than molecular species. The oxygen atoms generated in the photodissociation of nitrogen dioxide can subsequently lead to the formation of ozone:

$$O + O_2 + M \rightarrow O_3 + M$$

where M is a third body, *i.e.*, a molecule such as N_2 that carries off excess energy that might disrupt the ozone molecule. Ozone produced by this reaction may photodissociate:

$$O_3 + hv \rightarrow O(^3P)$$

where ^3P describe the spectral state of the atom.

7. The Henry's law constant is defined here as the ratio of the aqueous-phase concentration of a chemical to its equilibrium partial pressure in the gas phase.

Thus, Hengy's law constant

$$= \frac{24}{0.1} = 240 \text{ kPa kg/mol.}$$

8. The amount of monochromatic light absorbed by a sample is determined by comparing the intensities of the incident light (Io) and transmitted light (I). The ratio of the intensity of the transmitted light (I) to the intensity of the incident light (Io) is called *transmittance (T)*.

$$T = I/Io$$

From the transmittance or % transmittance, one can calculate the quantity known as *absorbance (A)*. Absorbance is the amount of light absorbed by a sample. It is calculated from T or %T using the following equations:

$$A = -\log_{10} T \quad \text{or} \quad A = \log_{10}(1/T)$$

$$A = \log_{10}\left(\frac{1}{0.5}\right)$$

$$= \log_{10}(2) = 0.3.$$

9. Sandy soils have a higher percentage of macro pores. Typically, sandy soils never become water logged and allow water to percolate downward more rapidly than clay soils. Typically, moisture content in sandy soils is relatively low when compared to clay soils.

The terms sand, silt, and clay refer to particle size; sand is the largest and clay is the smallest. Gravel particles are larger than 2 millimeters (mm), sand particles are 0.05-2 mm, silt particles are 0.002-0.05 mm, and clay is smaller than 0.002 mm.

10. The night-time oxidant, NO_3 is predominantly formed in the troposphere by the reaction of NO_2 and ozone, and therefore, the regional distribution follows the same pattern as ozone and NO_x.

11. Chlorine (Cl_2) is the most common disinfectant in water treatment because it is easy to use and has effective germicide properties and a low cost. However, chlorine also reacts with dissolved organic material and produces disinfection byproducts, such as trihalomethanes (chloroform) and haloacetic acids. Chlorine, which is widely used as an effective and relatively inexpensive disinfectant in water, generates toxic organochlorine compounds in water because Hypochlorous acid reacts rapidly with humic acids and hydroxobenzenes.

12. Argentometric is a process of determining the content of a substance based on precipitation reaction from component of the test substance, using precipitation of Ag^+.

Titrations with Ag^+ are called argentometric titrations. For argentometric titrations, three classical methods based on colour indicators can be used for end point detection.

Preparation of standard $AgNO_3$ solution:

- Titrate the sample with 0.1 mole Liter^{-1} silver nitrate solution. Although the silver chloride that forms is a white precipitate, the chromate indicator initially gift the cloudy solution faint lemon-yellow colour.

- The endpoint of the titration is identified as the first appearance of a red-brown colour of silver chromate.

13. Carbon monoxide is used to generate hydrogen atom. The reaction is like this:

$$OH + CO \Rightarrow CO_2 + H(atom)$$

Hydroxyl radicals are capable of oxidizing carbon monoxide by hydrogen abstraction.

14. *In an ideally dilute solution, the solvent obeys Raoult's law and the solutes obey Henry's law.*

Henry's law states that the vapour partial pressure of solute i above an ideally dilute solution is proportional to the mole fraction of i in the solution.

Raoult's law states that the vapour pressure of a solution is equal to the sum of the vapour pressures of each volatile component if it were pure multiplied by the mole fraction of that component in the solution. As a result, adding more components to a solution decreases each partial vapour pressure because the mole fraction decreases. Raoult's law can be used to calculate the molecular mass of an unknown solute.

At sufficiently high dilutions, all nonelectrolyte solution become ideally dilute. For less dilute solutions, the solution is no longer ideally dilute and shows deviations from Raoult's and Henry's laws.

15. An ecosystem can be described simply as the collection of all living and non-living components in a particular area. The living components of the environment are known as biotic factors. Biotic factors include plants, animals, and micro-organisms. The non-living components of the environment are known as abiotic factors. Abiotic factors include things such as rocks, water, soil, light, etc.

The living components of ecosystems are not immortal. Because depending on the

26

biological longevity, all living systems become abiotic constituents.

16. In ecology, **energy flow**, also called the **calorific flow**, refers to the flow of energy through a food chain, and is the focus of study in **ecological energetics**. In an ecosystem, ecologists seek to quantify the relative importance of different component species and feeding relationships. The movement of energy from primary producers to consumers is affected by the process of eating.

17. **Trophic cascades** occur when predators in a food web suppress the abundance or alter the behaviour of their prey, thereby releasing the next lower trophic level from predation (or herbivory if the intermediate trophic level is a herbivore).

The trophic cascade is an ecological concept which has stimulated new research in many areas of ecology. For example, it can be important for understanding the knock-on effects of removing top predators from food webs, as humans have done in many places through hunting and fishing.

A **top-down cascade** is a trophic cascade where the food chain or food web is disrupted by the removal of a top predator, or a third or fourth level consumer. On the other hand, a **bottom-up cascade** occurs when a primary producer, or primary consumer is removed, and there is a reduction of population size through the community.

18. In some communities dead organic matter accumulates, but in most forest environments the rate at which litter is added to the soil equals the rate at which it is removed by decomposition. The amount of dead organic matter measured in forests at different latitudes is greatest towards the poles and least at the equator (Table). As the total biomass per unit area in a forest is *greatest* at the equator, this means that almost all of the organic matter in a tropical rainforest is tied up in the living organisms.

Table: The amount of accumulated dead organic matter in different forest types is greatest in forests near the poles and decreases towards the equator.

Forest type	Mass of organic matter in the forest layer
Tropical rainforest	2 tons/ha
Subtropical forest	10 tons/ha
Broad-leaved forest	15-30 tons/ha
Taiga	30-45 tons/ha
Shrub tundra	85 tons/ha

19. Termites depend upon the microbes in their gut or digestive tract to digest the complex sugars in wood into simpler molecules that they can use for food. Cellulose is a major sugar in wood and it is broken down in the hindgut of the termite by microbes into molecules called short-chain fatty acids.

Cellulose degradation: Protists reside in the termite gut ingest wood particles in the form of cellulose and degrade it within their cells. Cellulolytic protists known as Trichonympha and mixotricha produce cellulases and various glycolytic enzymes that can break down cellulose and convert it into an intermediate product, malate. In addition, they carry specific anaerobic energy- generating organelle, hydrogenosome, where transferred malate from the cytoplasm is further fermented to produce CO_2, H_2, and acetate with the help of hydrogenase enzyme. During this fermentation process, ATP is also produced in the way and stored as energy available for both microbes and termite.

20. **Plankton** (singular **plankter**) are the diverse collection of organisms that live in large bodies of water and are unable to swim against a current. They provide a crucial source of food to many large aquatic organisms, such as fish and whales.

Plankton are also often described in terms of size. Usually the following divisions are used:

Group	Size range (ESD)	Examples
Megaplankton	> 20 cm	metazoans; *e.g.* jellyfish; ctenophores; salps and pyrosomes (pelagic Tunicata): Cephalopoda; Amphipoda
Macroplankton	2-20cm	metazoans; *e.g.* Pteropods; Chaetognaths; Euphausiacea (krill); Medusae; ctenophores; salps, doliolids and pyrosomes (pelagic Tunicata); Cephalopoda; Janthinidae (one family of gastropods); Amphipoda
Mesoplankton	0.2-20 mm	metazoans; *e.g.* copepods; Medusae; Cladocera; Ostracoda; Chaetognaths; Pteropods; Tunicata; Heteropoda
Microplankton	20-200 µm	large eukaryote protists; most phytoplankton; Protozoa Foraminifera; tintinnids; other ciliates; Rotifera; juvenile metazoans - Crustacea (copepod nauplii)
Nanoplankton	2-20 µm	small eukaryote protists; Small Diatoms; Small Flagellates; Pyrrophyta; Chrysophyta; Chlorophyta; Xantnopnyta
Picoplankton	0.2-2 µm	small eukaryotic protists; bacteria; Chrysophyta
Femtoplankton	< 0.2 µm	marine viruses

21. **Femtoplankton** is the plankton composed of cells smaller than 0.2 micrometers.

22. An area, whether within a sanctuary or not, can be notified by the state government to be constituted as a National Park, by reason of its ecological, faunal, floral, geomorphological, or zoological association or importance, needed to for the purpose of protecting & propagating or developing wildlife therein or its environment. No human activity is permitted inside the national park except for the ones permitted by the Chief Wildlife Warden of the state under the conditions given in CHAPTER IV, WPA 1972.

There are 103 existing national parks in India covering an area of 40,500.13 km^2, which is 1.23% of the geographical area of the country.

Name of State & Union Territory	State Area km^2	No. of NPs	Area km^2	% of State Area
1. Andhra Pradesh	1,60,205	2	356.02	0.22
2. Arunachal Pradesh	33,743	2	2,290.82	2.74
3. Assam	78,438	5	1,977.79	2.52
4. Bihar	94,163	1	335.65	0.38
5. Chhattisgarh	1,35,191	3	2,899.08	2.14
6. Goa	3,702	1	107.00	2.89
7. Gujarat	1,96,022	4	480.12	0.24
8. Haryana	44,212	2	48.25	—

24. Bacterioplankton are the bacterial component of the plankton. They are comprised of prokaryotes. Some of them serve as primary producers and others as primary consumers in aquatic ecosystems (*e.g.*, marine and freshwater ecosystems). Primary producer bacterioplankton are those that are capable of photosynthesis, *e.g.*, blue-green algae (cyanophyta). It should be noted though that cyanophyta are also referred to as phytoplankton since they are also regarded as one of the photosynthetic algal groups. However, they are the only algal group that is prokaryotic and therefore are also considered as bacteria. Bacterioplankton are ecologically essential since they are involved in the remineralization processes of organic material. They drive global biogeochemical cycling of elements (*e.g.*, carbon fixation, nitrogen fixation, denitrification, nitrification, etc.). Many of them are saprotrophic as they obtain energy from organic material they consume.

25. **Oxygen isotope ratio cycles** are cyclical variations in the ratio of the abundance of oxygen with an atomic mass of 18 to the abundance of oxygen with an atomic mass of 16 present in some substances, such as polar ice or calcite in ocean core samples, measured with the isotope fractionation. The ratio is linked to water temperature of ancient oceans, which in turn reflects ancient climates. The calculated ratio of the masses of each present in the sample is then compared to a standard, which can yield information about the temperature at which the sample was formed.

^{8}O is two neutrons heavier than ^{16}O and causes the water molecule in which it occurs to be heavier by that amount. The addition of more energy is required to vaporize $H_2^{18}O$ than $H_2^{16}O$, and $H_2^{18}O$ liberates more energy when it condenses. In addition, $H_2^{16}O$ tends to diffuse more rapidly.

Because $H_2^{16}O$ requires less energy to vaporize, and is more likely to diffuse to the liquid surface, the first water vapour formed during evaporation of liquid water is enriched in $H_2^{16}O$, and the residual liquid is enriched in $H_2^{18}O$. When water vapour condenses into liquid, $H_2^{18}O$ preferentially enters the liquid, while $H_2^{16}O$ is concentrated in the remaining vapour.

As an air mass moves from a warm region to a cold region, water vapour condenses and is removed as precipitation. The precipitation removes $H_2^{18}O$, leaving progressively more $H_2^{16}O$-rich water vapour. This distillation process causes precipitation to have lower $^{18}O/^{16}O$ as the temperature decreases. Additional factors can affect the efficiency of the distillation, such as the direct precipitation of ice crystals, rather than liquid water, at low temperatures.

Due to the intense precipitation that occurs in hurricanes, the $H_2^{18}O$ is exhausted relative to the $H_2^{16}O$, resulting in relatively low $^{18}O/^{16}O$ ratios. The subsequent uptake of hurricane rainfall in trees, creates a record of the passing of hurricanes that can be used to create a historical record in the absence of human records.

26. Urban development has some negative impacts on the global environmental quality, including air quality, temperature increases and landscape alteration. It also leads to conversion of agricultural land and loss of biodiversity (Santamouris et al., 2001) . Urban heat island (UHI) is a climatic phenomenon where urban areas have higher air temperature than their rural surroundings due to the anthropogenic modifications of land surfaces.

There are two types of urban heat islands, surface and atmospheric UHI. A combination of factors leads to the development of the UHI. UHI is measured by surface temperature, which can vary between the city and rural area by up to 5°C.

The split-window algorithms have been widely used for estimating LST from two thermal bands in the 10.5 - 12.5 μm region with given surface emissivity.

27. Islands have relatively low species richness, but there are some islands such as Galapagos, Hawaii, Madagascar and Mauritius which possess a very high biodiversity. Islands are recognized as hotspots of endemicity and evolutionary marvels. Islands play a vital role as refuges of biodiversity.

The Theory of Island Biogeography is determined by two factors. The first is the effect of distance from the **mainland**. The mainland is where new immigrant species originally inhabited. The second is the effect of island size.

These two factors establish how many species an island can hold at equilibrium. **The equilibrium species number** is the species richness of an island at which immigration balances extinction and which remains roughly constant.

29. Antarctica and its surrounding waters are under pressure from a variety of forces that are already transforming the area, scientists warn.

The most immediate threats are regional warming, ocean acidification and loss of sea ice, all linked to global levels of carbon dioxide. Environmentalists oppose the mining of antarctic mineral resources because Environment of Antarctica is extremely vulnerable and fragile to the disturbance that would occur with the development.

Last year nearly 20,000 tourists visited the Antarctic Peninsula, according to the International Association of Antarctica Tour Operators. There are also more researchers, and there is more exploration for minerals and other resources. An increase in visitors means more disturbances to the fragile ecosystem, more pollution and more opportunities to bring organisms onto the continent from elsewhere in the world.

30. The CO_2 system in the ocean is dependent upon five major parameters: salinity, temperature, pressure, biologic activity and carbonate precipitation (or dissolution). Increased temperature will increase reaction rates of the CO_2 species, but also will decrease the solubility of gaseous CO_2 in sea water. Thus, in an open system (where CO_2 can enter or escape) pH will increase with increasing temperature; in a closed system (such as the deep sea), in which CO_2 cannot readily escape, pH will fall with increasing temperature. The decrease in pH is in response to increases in K_1' and K_2' which cause further dissociations and the release of hydrogen.

The solubilities of CO_2 and H_2CO_3 are inversely related to salinity, while the solubilities of HCO_3^- and $CO_3^=$ are directly related. Pressure increases the solubility of CO_2 and the dissociation constants increase at the following rates:

$$\Delta pK_1' = -0.48 \times 10^{-4}\ \Delta z$$
$$\Delta pK_2' = -0.18 \times 10^{-4}\ \Delta z$$

where z = depth in meters (SVERDRUP and others, (1942).

Biologic activity (photosynthesis and respiration) has perhaps the greatest effect upon the CO_2 system in the oceans:

$$H_2O + CO_2 \underset{\text{respiration}}{\overset{\text{photosynthesis}}{\rightleftharpoons}} HCOH + O_2 \text{ (organic matter)}$$

During photosynthesis, the partial pressure of CO_2 decreases and pH increases. During respiration, CO_2 increases and pH decreases.

31. The theme for the 2017 International Day for the Preservation of the Ozone Layer to be marked on September 16 is: 'Caring for all life under the sun'. This year, to mark the 30th anniversary of the Montreal Protocol celebration, the Ozone Secretariat in cooperation with the Government of Canada hosted the Ozone Awards to be held in Montreal, Canada. That would recognize the achievements of individuals, groups and organizations that have demonstrated extraordinary commitment and contribution in the past 10 years.

32. OTEC power systems operate as cyclic heat engines. They receive thermal energy through heat transfer from surface sea water warmed by the sun, and transform a portion of this energy to electrical power. The Second Law of Thermodynamics precludes the complete conversion of thermal energy in to electricity. A portion of the heat extracted from the warm sea water must be rejected to a colder thermal sink. The thermal sink employed by OTEC systems is sea water drawn from the ocean depths by means of a submerged pipeline. A steady-state control volume energy analysis yields the result that net electrical power produced by the engine must equal the difference between the rates of heat transfer from the warm surface water and to the cold deep water. The limiting (i.e., maximum) theoretical Carnot energy conversion efficiency of a cyclic heat engine scales with the difference between the temperatures at which these heat transfers occur. For OTEC, this difference is determined by T and is very small; hence, OTEC efficiency is low. Although viable OTEC systems are characterized by Carnot efficiencies in the range of 68%, state-of-the-art combustion steam power cycles, which tap much higher temperature energy sources, are theoretically capable of converting more than 60% of the extracted thermal energy into electricity. The low energy conversion efficiency of OTEC means that more than 90% of the thermal energy extracted from the ocean's surface is 'wasted' and must be rejected to the cold, deep sea water. This necessitates large heat

exchangers and seawater Sow rates to produce relatively small amounts of electricity.

33. Solar cell performance decreases with increasing temperature, fundamentally owing to increased internal carrier recombination rates, caused by increased carrier concentrations. The operating temperature plays a key role in the photovoltaic conversion process. Both the electrical efficiency and the power output of a photovoltaic (PV) module depend linearly on the operating temperature. The various correlations proposed in the literature represent simplified working equations which can be apply to PV modules or PV arrays mounted on free-standing frames, PV-Thermal collectors, and building integrated photovoltaic arrays, respectively. The electrical performance is primarily influenced by the material of PV used. Numerous correlations for cell temperature which have appeared in the literature involve basic environmental variables and numerical parameters which are material or system dependent.

34. Wind is essentially a moving gas and like all matter, it is formed of particles. Motion means kinetic energy, so what wind turbines do is capture the kinetic energy in the wind. This energy can then be transferred from one medium into another, namely into electric energy.

There are three essential parts to a wind turbine. The *rotor blades* act as "barriers" to the wind. When the wind forces the blades to move, kinetic energy is transferred from the wind to the blades. Then, the wind-turbine *shaft* is connected to the center of the rotor and acts as a bridge between the rotor and the third component, the *generator*. When the rotor spins, the shaft spins as well, transferring the wind's kinetic energy into the shaft's rotational energy. The shaft then transfers this mechanical, rotational energy from the rotor to the generator.

37. The power densities realized by harnessing these energy flows are appreciably lower than the power densities of fossil fuel-based systems, something that even often uncritical proponents of wind and solar energy—the new renewables, in addition to the two traditional renewable energies, hydro energy and fuelwood—cannot ignore. Thus, to exploit renewable energy, quite large structures are required relative to the power produced.

38. Biodiesel is an alternative fuel similar to conventional or 'fossil' diesel. Biodiesel can be produced from straight vegetable oil, animal oil/fats, tallow and waste cooking oil. The process used to convert these oils to Biodiesel is called transesterification.

Biodiesel can be produced from straight vegetable oil, animal oil/fats, tallow and waste oils. There are three basic routes to biodiesel production from oils and fats:

- Base catalyzed transesterification of the oil.
- Direct acid catalyzed transesterification of the oil.
- Conversion of the oil to its fatty acids and then to biodiesel.

The Transesterification process is the reaction of a triglyceride (fat/oil) with an alcohol to form esters and glycerol. A triglyceride has a glycerine molecule as its base with three long chain fatty acids attached. The characteristics of the fat are determined by the nature of the fatty acids attached to the glycerine. The nature of the fatty acids can in turn affect the characteristics of the biodiesel. During the esterification process, the triglyceride is reacted with alcohol in the presence of a catalyst, usually a strong alkaline like sodium hydroxide. The alcohol reacts with the fatty acids to form the mono-alkyl ester, or biodiesel and crude glycerol. In most production methanol or ethanol is the alcohol used (methanol produces methyl esters, ethanol produces ethyl esters) and is base catalysed by either potassium or sodium hydroxide. Potassium hydroxide has been found to be more suitable for the ethyl ester biodiesel production, either base can be used for the methyl ester. A common product of the transesterification process is Rape Methyl Ester (RME) produced from raw rapeseed oil reacted with methanol.

39. The logarithmic properties of the decibel are best illustrated by a few examples: Two equal noises when sounded simultaneously will produce a noise 3 decibels higher in sound level than either alone; 10 equal noise sources, when sounded simultaneously, will produce a noise 10 decibels higher than one alone; a hundred will produce a noise 20 decibels higher than one alone; a thousand will produce a noise 30 decibels higher than one alone; and 10,000 will produce a noise 40 decibels higher than one alone.

The sound insulation of a wall R, can be defined as

$$R = 10 \log(I_i/I_t)$$

where I_i and I_t are the incident and transmitted sound intensities.

Here, $\dfrac{I_i}{I_t} = 5$

$10 \log(5) = 6.98$

So, $\quad R' = R + 6.98$

$\qquad\qquad = 120 + 6.98 = 126.98$ dB

Hence, five such aeroplane will produces 126.98 dB noise while take-off.

40. The presence of the double bond renders alkenes susceptible to reaction with ozone. Reactions with ozone are, in fact, competitive with the daytime OH radical reactions and the nighttime NO_3 radical reaction as a tropospheric loss process for the alkenes. The ozone-alkene reaction proceeds via initial O_3 addition across the olefinic C=C bond, forming a cyclic 1,2,3-trioxolane intermediate species, referred to as the primary ozonide (denoted POZ). The POZ is formed with a large amount of excess energy, which results in rapid decomposition of the POZ to a stable ketone or aldehyde and a carbonyl oxide reactive intermediate, referred to as a *Criegee intermediate*. In the case of asymmetrically substituted alkenes, two pairs of products are formed:

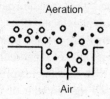

The relative importance of the reaction pathways *a* and *b* are generally assumed to be equal. The Criegee intermediates are represented as biradicals. The simplest Criegee intermediate is CH_2OO, which is formed in the ozonolysis of ethene and 1-alkenes.

41. Aeration water treatment is effective for management of dissolved gases such as radon, carbon dioxide, some taste and odor problems such as methane, and hydrogen sulfide, as well as volatile organic compounds, like MTBE or industrial solvents. It is also effective in precipitating dissolved iron and manganese. Aeration raises the pH of water.

Aeration of water Removal of dissolved gases (*e.g.*, H_2S) and organosulfur compounds

Removal of volatile organic compounds

Oxidation of Fe^{2+} to Fe^{3+} and precipitation as insoluble $Fe(OH)_3$.

Aeration

Air

42. Organocarbamate pesticides are one of several classes of insecticides: including compounds such as carbaryl, aldicarb, and zectran. The organocarbamates are not broad-spectrum insecticides, and some common household insect pests are relatively immune to the effects of these chemicals. Unlike the organophosphate insecticides, most of the organocarbamate insecticides have low dermal toxicities. However, due to the high toxicity of aldicarb by both the oral and dermal routes, it has restricted use in the United States and is recommended only for limited use in greenhouse operations. Aldicarb is released to soil as a systemic insecticide for soil use.

43. Every container (bag, bucket, etc.) of fertilizer on the market must have, by law, a label giving the guaranteed nutrient content of the fertilizer. The information required on the label and the way in which the information is given are specified by the fertilizer law. The information on the label is the guaranteed amount of the primary nutrients given in a series of three numbers, such as 5-10-5, and is referred to as the "fertilizer grade." A fertilizer grade gives the minimum guaranteed primary nutrient content as percentage of total nitrogen (N), percentage of available phosphate (P_2O_5), and percentage of water-soluble potash (K_2O). The fertilizer grade always specifies the nutrient content in this order:

Nitrogen (N) $\rightarrow$ 5-10-5 $\leftarrow$ Soluble Potash (K_2O)
$\uparrow$

Available Phosphate (P_2O_5)

The first number indicates the pounds of nitrogen (N) contained in each 100 pounds of fertilizer. The middle figure refers to the amount of phosphate (P_2O_5), and the last figure shows the pounds of potash (K_2O) in each 100 pounds of a particular fertilizer. By referring to these numbers printed on the bag, you can tell the amount, of each nutrient in the fertilizer. This labeling is the same nationwide.

44. Bioremediation is defined as the acceleration of the natural metabolic process whereby microorganisms alter and break down organic molecules into other substances. In situ bioremediation involves the placement of amendments directly into contaminated media, whereas ex situ bioremediation transfers the contaminated media to a selected site for treatment.

The bioremediation technique of a contaminated soil require the fulfilment of:

Waste must be present in a physical form that is susceptible to microbes.

Waste must be susceptible to biodegradation.

Environmental conditions such as pH, temperature and oxygen level must be appropriate.

Organic contaminants are often classified as biodegradable, persistent or recalcitrant, depending on their behaviour in the environment:

Biodegradable: they undergo a biological transformation.

Persistent: they do not undergo biodegradation in certain environments.

Recalcitrant: they resist biodegradation in a wide variety of environments.

45. Organophosphorus group of pesticides are known to be the best insecticides and acaricides, and also they are equally effective as fungicides, nematicides, herbicides, plant growth regulators, insect chemosterilants and rodenticides. All organophosphorus pesticides are derived from phosphoric acid. Pesticides containing phosphorus include phosphates, phosphoronates, phosphoroamides, pyrophosphates and their sulphur analogues.

Organophosphorus pesticides offer a broad range of toxicity to insect-pests, and are

generally among the most toxic of all pesticides to vertebrate animals. Organochlorine pesticides are, in general, of lower toxicity than organophosphorus pesticides, but are causing environmental problems due to their higher persistence and higher toxicity. The organophosphorus pesticides are easily degradable and consequently less persistent and are often preferred to organochlorines in conventional agricultural applications. Organophosphorus compounds are highly effective and rapid in its action on aphides, spider mites, small caterpillars and many other insects. It is highly toxic to man and other animals. In water solution, it gets easily decomposed by hydrolysis into non-toxic water-soluble products.

46. Nitrogen oxides (the mixture of NO and NO_2 together referred to as NOx) and volatile organic compounds (VOCs) are primary air pollutants, released in the atmosphere by automobiles and industrial processes. Nitrogen dioxide absorbs ultraviolet light and formation of nitric oxide and atomic oxygen takes place. Ozone is generated by the reaction of oxygen gas with this atomic oxygen. Ozone, aldehydes and peroxyacetyl nitrate so formed are thus secondary air pollutants. Photochemical smog is a mixture of primary and secondary air pollutants.

NOX and VOCs form antioxidants by thermal reactions.

47. Carbon monoxide (CO) is the dominant sink of OH in most of the troposphere, and that CH_4 is next in importance. The resulting OH lifetime is of the order of one second. Because of this short lifetime, atmospheric concentrations of OH are highly variable; they respond rapidly to changes in the sources or sinks.

48. Overlay maps are a series of transparencies used to identify, predict, assign relative significance to and communicate impacts, normally at a scale larger than local.

(*i*) The composite impact of the project is found by superimposing the overlay maps and noting the relative intensity of total shading. Unshaded areas would be those where development project would have no impacts. Overlay maps are easy to represent and understand.

(*ii*) Network methods explicitly recognize that environmental systems consist of a complex web of relationships, and try to reproduce that web. Impact identification using networks involves following in effects of development through changes in the environmental parameters in the model.

(*iii*) The use of simulation modelling, adaptive environmental assessment, has been advocated as a means of assessing a wide range of development proposals and environmental management schemes as a means of accommodating the behaviour of ecosystems. It has been used to assess forest pest management, fish stock management, tourist development, regional development, hydroelectric development and a water-resource study.

(*iv*) The Battelle Environmental Evaluation System (EES) is a methodology for conducting environmental impact analysis developed at Battelle Columbus Laboratories by an interdisciplinary research team under contract with the U.S. Bureau of Reclamation. It is based on a hierarchical assessment of environmental quality indicators.

The system is based on a classification consisting of four levels:
- Level I: Categories,
- Level II: Components,
- Level III: Parameters, and
- Level IV: Measurements.

49. Baseline studies are perhaps the most commonly recognized, and yet least understood, element of EIA. The term usually refers to the collection of background information on the environmental and socioeconomic setting for a proposed development project and it is normally one of the first activities undertaken in an EIA. A baseline studies programme may be designed around the results of a scoping exercise. Whether it involves the collation of existing information or requires the acquisition of new data through field sampling, baseline studies frequently account for a large part of the overall cost of an EIA.

Environmental impact assessments are often conducted under severe time restrictions and, since it is relatively easy to collect information and data, there is a tendency to give too much emphasis to baseline studies early in the assessment process. The result is that there is often a great deal of information made available on the environmental setting of a particular project, but it may be irrelevant to the resolution of certain critical questions raised at later stages in the EIA.

50. Scoping is the process of determining which are the most critical issues to study and will involve community participation to some degree. It is at this early stage that EIA can most strongly influence the outline proposal.

Steps included in the scoping process:

(a) Set up the team of experts that will conduct the EIA.

(b) Describe the project area and the area of the project influence.

(c) Outline project alternative for preparation, implementation and closure.

(d) Conduct public meetings and stakeholder consultations; integrate comments and collected feedback into project planning and alternatives.

(e) Create a set of environmental, biological and socioeconomic areas that will be used in the assessment.

(f) Define a set of criteria to assess the project.

(g) Identify a set of data for baseline descriptions and potential additional data collection needs.

(h) Start inserting this information in the appropriate section of the TOR.

51. Risk assessment provides a basis for risk management. However, while risk assessment is a scientific procedure, risk management is more pragmatic, involving decisions and actions that aim at preventing, or reducing to acceptable levels, the occurrence of agents which may pose hazards to the health of workers, surrounding communities and the environment, also accounting for the socio-economic and public health context.

The classical steps in occupational hygiene practice are:

- the recognition of the possible health hazards in the work environment
- the evaluation of hazards, which is the process of assessing exposure and reaching conclusions as to the level of risk to human health
- prevention and control of hazards, which is the process of developing and implementing strategies to eliminate, or reduce to acceptable levels, the occurrence of harmful agents and factors in the workplace, while also accounting for environmental protection.

52. In decision theory, a **multi-attribute utility** function is used to represent the preferences of an agent over bundles of goods either under conditions of certainty about the results of any potential choice, or under conditions of uncertainty. In EIA the multi-attribute utility theory is The identification of the alternatives to be evaluated and structuring of environmental parameters.

53. Ambient air quality refers to the condition or quality of air surrounding us in the outdoors. National Ambient Air Quality Standards are the standards for ambient air quality set by the Central Pollution Control Board (CPCB) that is applicable nationwide. The CPCB has been conferred this power by the Air (Prevention and Control of Pollution) Act, 1981.

Ambient Air Quality Standards in India

The Air (Prevention and Control of Pollution) Act 1981 was enacted by the Central Government with the objective of arresting the deterioration of air quality. The Air (Prevention and Control of Pollution) Act 1981 describes the main functions of the Central Pollution Control Board (CPCB) as follows:

- To advise the Central Government on any matter concerning the improvement of the quality the air and the prevention, control and abatement of air pollution.
- To plan and cause to be executed a nation-wide programme for the prevention, control and abatement of air pollution.
- To provide technical assistance and guidance to the State Pollution Control Board.
- To carry out and sponsor investigations and research related to prevention, control and abatement of air pollution.
- To collect, compile and publish technical and statistical data related to air pollution; and
- To lay down and annul standards for the quality of air.

54. The *Indian Easements Act,* 1882 is one of the earlier statutes dealing with the rights of individuals *inter se* in regard to pollution of waters. The Act has, in fact, codified the common law doctrine of riparian rights to unpolluted waters. The illustrations (f) and (h) of section 7 of the Act in particular, refer to water pollution. Illustration (f) says: "The right of every owner of land, within his own limits, the water which naturally passes or percolates by, over or through his land shall not, before so passing or percolating, be unreasonably polluted by other persons."

Illustration (h) among others, protects the right of every riparian owner to get water of a natural stream, a natural lake or pond into or out of which a natural stream flows from any material alteration in temperature of water. There seems to have been an overlapping in illustrations (f) and (h) in regard to alteration in temperature as this aspect is covered under unreasonable pollution.

55. The Indian Forest Act of 1927 led to the Forest Conservation Act of 1980. This law applied to all the lands, which are notified as forests in the government records and is not restricted to reserved and protected forests. It restricts the power of the state governments by making it mandatory for them, to seek permission from the central government for any non-forest use of forest lands, including de-reservation of forest and diversion of forest land.

The states, where de-reservation was practiced, had regularized encroachments and resettled 'project affected people' from development projects such as dams. The need for a new legislation became urgent. The Act made it possible to retain a greater control over the frightening level of deforestation in the country and specified penalties for offenders.

56. Alkaline or lime stabilization is a very simple process. Its principal advantages over other stabilization processes include low cost and simplicity of operation. However, lime stabilization accomplished at a pH of 10.0–11.0, may allow odors to return during storage owing to pH decay. To eliminate this problem and reduce pathogen levels, addition of sufficient quantities of lime to raise and maintain the biosolids pH to 12.0 for 2 h is required. The lime-stabilized biosolids readily dewaters with mechanical equipment and is generally suitable for application on an agricultural land or disposal in a sanitary landfill.

57. Organic substances which contain the bivalent -0-0- structure and may be considered derivatives of hydrogen peroxide, where one or both of the hydrogen atoms have been replaced by organic radicals. Organic peroxides are thermally unstable substances, which may undergo exothermic self-accelerating decomposition. In addition, they may have one or more of the following properties:

(*i*) be liable to explosive decomposition;

(*ii*) burn rapidly;

(*iii*) be sensitive to impact or friction;

(*iv*) react dangerously with other substances;

(*v*) cause damage to the eyes.

58. The Recycled Plastics Manufacture and Usage Rules, 1999 came to be called the Plastic Waste (Management and Handling) Rules, 2011 from 4 February 2011. Under these rules, the use of carry bags and sachets or containers made of recycled plastic or compostable plastic for storing, carrying dispensing, or packaging food is prohibited. Recycling of plastic is to be undertaken strictly in accordance with the Bureau of Indian Standards specifications IS: 14534:1998 entitled 'The Guidelines for Recycling of Plastics' amended from time to time.

59. The **Millennium Development Goals (MDGs)** were the eight international development goals for the year 2015 that had been established following the Millennium Summit of the United Nations in 2000, following the adoption of the United Nations Millennium Declaration. All 191 United Nations member states at that time, and at least 22 international organizations, committed to help achieve the following Millennium Development Goals by 2015:

1. To eradicate extreme poverty and hunger
2. To achieve universal primary education
3. To promote gender equality and empower women
4. To reduce child mortality
5. To improve maternal health
6. To combat HIV/AIDS, malaria, and other diseases
7. To ensure environmental sustainability
8. To develop a global partnership for development.

60. Act of 1981 'air pollution means the presence in the atmosphere of any air pollutant' (section 2 b). The term 'air pollutant means any solid, liquid or gaseous substance including noise present in the atmosphere in such concentration as may be or tend to be injurious to human beings or other living creatures or plants or property or environment' (section 2a).

61. Total population $n(S) = 210$

Number of somker $n(A) = 72$

Number of non-smoker = 138

Probability of selecting a smoker = $\dfrac{n(A)}{n(S)}$

$$= \frac{72}{210} = 0.34.$$

62. Confidence Interval = $\overline{X} \pm 1.74 \dfrac{\sigma}{\sqrt{n}}$

Here, $\overline{X} = 10$, $\sigma = 0.3$, $n = 36$.

So, Confidence Interval = $10 \pm 1.74 \times \dfrac{(0.3)}{\sqrt{36}}$

$$= 10 \pm 1.74 \frac{(0.3)}{6}$$

$$= 10 \pm 0.08.$$

64.

Classification	Representative types
(i) Compound clay	Bentonides, illites, kaolinites.
(ii) Inorganic chemicals	Sodium carbonates, silicate or pyrophosphate.
(iii) Synthetic chemicals	Polymers, rubber latex.
(iv) Synthetic membrane	PVC, buyl rubber, hypation, poly-thene, nylon reinforced liners.
(v) Asphalt	Modified asphalt, asphalt-covered polypropylene fabric, asphalt concrete.
(vi) Others	Gunite concrete, soil cement, plastic soil cement.

The seal material should be more impermeable than the soil. So sand will not be a suitable material. Flyash and lime themselves produce pollutants which dissolve in water. Therefore these materials cannot be used ads sealants.

65.

$$\frac{dN}{dt} = 0.8\,N - 0.01\,N^2$$

For maximum growth, $\dfrac{d^2N}{dt^2} = 0$

$$\frac{d^2N}{dt^2} = 0.8 - 0.01\,(2N)$$

$$\Rightarrow \qquad \frac{d^2N}{dt^2} = 0.8 - 0.02\,N$$

For maximum growth, $0.8 - 0.02\,N = 0$

$$N = \frac{0.8}{0.02} = 40.$$

66. A p-value is used in hypothesis testing to help you support or reject the null hypothesis. The p-value is the evidence **against** a null hypothesis. The smaller the p-value, the strong the evidence that you should reject the null hypothesis. P-values are expressed as decimals although it may be easier to understand what they are if you convert them to a percentage. For example, á p value of 0.0254 is 2.54%. This means there is a 2.54% chance your results could be random.

On the other hand, a large p-value of 0.9 (90%) means your results have a 90% probability of being completely random and *not* due to anything in your experiment. Therefore, the smaller the p-value, the more important ("significant") your results.

67. In a moderately symmetric distribution, the mean, median and mode are connected by the formula:

$$\text{Mode} = 3\ \text{Median} - 2\ \text{Mean}$$
$$= 3 \times 20 - 2 \times 21$$
$$= 60 - 42 = 18.$$

68. Arranging data in ascending order:
6, 6, 6, 6.5, 6.5, 7, 7.5, 7.5, 8
to get 90th percentile of these,
we have $0.9 \times n$
Here, $\qquad n = 9$
So, $\qquad 0.9 \times 9 = 8.1$
Thus, average of 8th and 9th value will give 90th percentile *i.e.,*

$$\frac{7.5 + 8}{2} = 7.75.$$

70. China's total Ecological Footprint has dramatically increased in the past 15 years and surpassed that of the United States in the early 2000s. China is now the nation with the world's largest total Ecological Footprint. Two factors that drive increasing total Ecological Footprint are increasing per capita Ecological Footprint (a measure of increasing consumption) and population growth.

It is widely known that China has the world's largest population. Over the last 30 years, however, China's population growth rate has stabilized and started to decrease.

71. Climate change refers to a long-term change in the state of climate, that can be identified by changes in the means and/or changes in the variability.

    Climate change also include gradual and/or abrupt changes of the frequencies and intensities of extreme events.

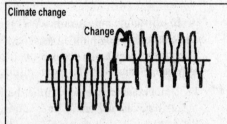

Change of the chatecteristics of climate. Here, a change in the mean state is shown.

Climate Change and Indian Agriculture
- Large country with diverse climate
- Two thirds area rain dependent
- High monsoon dependency
- Diverse seasons, crops and farming systems
- Close link between climate and water resources
- Small holdings, poor coping mechanisms and low penetration of risk management products

72. **'Namami Gange Programme'**, is an Integrated Conservation Mission, approved as 'Flagship Programme' by the Union Government in June 2014 with budget outlay of ₹ 20,000 Crore to accomplish the twin objectives of effective abatement of pollution, conservation and rejuvenation of National River Ganga.

    The key achievements under Namami Gange programme are:

    1. **Creating Sewerage Treatment Capacity:** 63 sewerage management projects under implementation in the States of Uttarakhand, Uttar Pradesh, Bihar, Jharkhand and West Bengal. 12 new sewerage management Projects launched in these states. Work is under construction for creating Sewerage capacity of 1187.33 (MLD). Hybrid Annuity PPP Model based two projects has been initiated for Jagjeetpur, Haridwar and Ramanna, Varanasi.

    2. **Creating River-Front Development:** 28 River-Front Development projects and 33 Entry level Projects for construction, modernization and renovation of 182 Ghats and 118 crematoria has been initiated.

    3. **River Surface Cleaning:** River Surface cleaning for collection of floating solid waste from the surface of the Ghats and River and its disposal are afoot and pushed into service at 11 locations.

    4. **Bio-Diversity Conservation:** Several Bio-Diversity conservation projects are namely: Biodiversity Conservation and Ganga Rejuvenation, Fish and Fishery Conservation in Ganga River, Ganges River Dolphin Conservation Education Programme has been initiated. 5 Bio-Diversity center's at Dehradun, Narora, Allahabad, Varanasi and Barrackpore has been developed for restoration of identified priority species.

    5. **Afforestation:** Forestry interventions for Ganga through Wildlife Institute of India; Central Inland Fisheries Research Institute and Centre for Environment Education has been initiated. Forestry interventions for Ganga has been executed as per the Detailed Project Report prepared by Forest Research Institute, Dehradun for a period of 5 years (2016-2021) at project cost of ₹ 2300 Crores. Work has been

commenced in 7 districts of Uttarakahnd for medicinal plants.

6. **Public Awareness:** A series of activities such as events, workshops, seminars and conferences and numerous IEC activities were organized to make a strong pitch for public outreach and community participation in the programme. Various awareness activities through rallies, campaigns, exhibitions, shram daan, cleanliness drives, competitions, plantation drives and development and distribution of resource materials were organized and for wider publicity the mass mediums such as TV/Radio, print media advertisements, advertorials, featured articles and advertorials were published. Gange Theme song was released widely and played on digital media to enhance the visibility of the programme. NMCG ensured presence at Social Media platforms like Facebook, Twitter, You Tube etc.

7. **Industrial Effluent Monitoring:** Real Time Effluent Monitoring Stations (EMS) has been installed in 572 out of 760 Grossly Polluting Industries (GPIs). Closure notice have been issued to 135 GPIs so far and others have been given deadlines for compliance to stipulated norms and for installations of online EMS.

8. **Ganga Gram:** Ministry of Drinking Water and Sanitation (MoDWS) identified 1674 Gram Panchayats situated on the bank of River Ganga in 5 State (Uttarakhand, Uttar Pradesh, Bihar, Jharkhand, West Bengal). ₹ 578 Crores has been released to Ministry of Drinking Water and Sanitation (MoDWS) for construction of toilets in 1674 Gram Panchayats of 5 Ganga Basin States. Out of the targeted 15, 27,105 units, MoDWS has completed construction of 8,53,397 toilets. Consortium of 7 IITs has been engaged in the preparation of Ganga River basin Plan and 65 villages has been adopted by 13 IITs to develop as model villages. **UNDP** has been engaged as the executing agency for rural sanitation programme and to develop Jharkhand as a model State at an estimated cost of ₹ 127 Crore.

R. Gupta's®
OBJECTIVE QUESTION BANK

	Book Code	Price (₹)		Book Code	Price (₹)
Objective Biotechnology	R-1472	150	Objective Electronics & Telecommunication Engineering	R-110	120
वस्तुनिष्ठ पर्यावरण विज्ञान	R-1261	210	Objective Civil Engineering (Small Size)	R-103	95
Objective Botany	R-1212	140	Objective Electronics & Telecommunication Engineering (enlarged edition)	R-443	180
Objective Zoology	R-1213	210	Objective History	R-681	210
Objective Environmental Sciences	R-1203	210	Objective Public Administration	R-679	130
Objective Agriculture Science	R-1157	195	Objective Geography	R-712	170
वस्तुनिष्ठ कृषि विज्ञान	R-1134	210	Objective Economics	R-720	180
वस्तुनिष्ठ शारीरिक शिक्षा	R-1084	140	वस्तुनिष्ठ गृह विज्ञान	R-899	130
Objective Computer Awareness	R-1031	135	वस्तुनिष्ठ संस्कृत	R-661	140
ऑब्जेक्टिव कम्प्यूटर ज्ञान	R-1032	110	ऑब्जेक्टिव सिविल इंजीनियरिंग	R-99	220
वस्तुनिष्ठ सामाजिक ज्ञान	R-1017	120	ऑब्जेक्टिव इलेक्ट्रीकल इंजीनियरिंग	R-101	180
Objective Social Studies	R-1016	195	वस्तुनिष्ठ इलेक्ट्रॉनिकी तथा दूरसंचार अभियांत्रिकी	R-442	195
वस्तुनिष्ठ विज्ञान	R-1015	110	ऑब्जेक्टिव मैकेनिकल इंजीनियरिंग	R-549	190
Objective Science	R-1014	140	वस्तुनिष्ठ इतिहास	R-532	160
वस्तुनिष्ठ हिन्दी-वृहत् परिचय	R-986	120	वस्तुनिष्ठ भूगोल	R-535	140
वस्तुनिष्ठ सामान्य विज्ञान	R-977	145	वस्तुनिष्ठ अर्थशास्त्र	R-536	150
Objective Psychology	R-966	140	वस्तुनिष्ठ राजनीतिशास्त्र	R-537	160
Objective Home Science	R-898	170	वस्तुनिष्ठ हिन्दी (साहित्य तथा व्याकरण)	R-527	170
Objective Philosophy	R-808	160	वस्तुनिष्ठ इतिहास (बड़ा संस्करण)	R-496	170
Objective Commerce	R-809	230	वस्तुनिष्ठ लोक प्रशासन	R-566	140
Objective Sociology	R-802	170	वस्तुनिष्ठ समाज शास्त्र	R-572	110
Objective Political Science	R-786	160	वस्तुनिष्ठ वाणिज्य	R-748	140
Objective Physics (enlarged edition)	R-755	180	वस्तुनिष्ठ दर्शनशास्त्र	R-713	75
Objective Chemistry	R-658	150	वस्तुनिष्ठ मनोविज्ञान	R-776	120
Objective Biology	R-663	140	वस्तुनिष्ठ जन्तु विज्ञान	R-1377	360
Objective Mathematics	R-662	180	वस्तुनिष्ठ वनस्पति विज्ञान	R-1378	365
Objective Computer Science	R-426	160	वस्तुनिष्ठ भौतिकी	R-1379	260
Objective Physics	R-427	130	वस्तुनिष्ठ रसायन विज्ञान	R-1380	470
Objective General Science	R-265	130	ऑब्जेक्टिव गणित	R-1381	435
Objective Civil Engineering	R-100	210			
Objective Electrical Engineering	R-102	190			
Objective Mechanical Engineering	R-111	240			

Ramesh Publishing House
12-H, New Daryaganj Road, Opp. Officers' Mess, Delhi-110002
For Online Shopping: www.rameshpublishinghouse.com

Previous Paper (Solved)

UGC-NET-Junior Research Fellowship & Assistant Professor Exam

Environmental Science, January-2017*

PAPER-II

Note: *This paper contains **fifty** (**50**) objective type questions of **two** (**2**) marks each. **All** questions are compulsory.*

1. Which of the following methods is generally not adopted for the safe disposal of biomedical waste?
   A. Incineration
   B. Hydroclaving
   C. Landfilling
   D. Shredding after disinfection

2. Which of the following prompted the Govt. of India to enact Environment (Protection) Act, 1986?
   A. River Ganga Water Pollution
   B. Endosulfan tragedy in Kerala
   C. London Smog
   D. Bhopal Gas Tragedy

3. Protection and improvement of environment and safeguarding of forest and wildlife is emphasized in constitution of India under the Article
   A. 48 A   B. 21
   C. 47   D. 46

4. Environmental Relief Fund was established under the provisions of
   A. The Environment (Protection) Act, 1986
   B. The Indian Wild Life (Protection) Act, 1972
   C. The Public Liability Insurance Act, 1991
   D. The Forest (Conservation) Act, 1980

5. A type of lake that forms in the depression of the earth's crust between two parallel faults is known as
   A. Grade lake   B. Surface lake
   C. Graben lake   D. Glacial lake

6. In case of plumes from a tall stack located on flat terrain 'Lofting' type of plume behaviour is observed when in the atmosphere
   A. inversion conditions prevail below the stack height.
   B. strong lapse rate conditions exist.
   C. inversion conditions exist above the stack height.
   D. weak lapse rate conditions exist.

7. Turbulent updrafts and downdrafts flows are an example of
   A. Synoptic scale phenomena
   B. Planetary scale phenomena
   C. Meso-scale phenomena
   D. Micro-scale phenomena

8. A niche of the species where there is no competition from other species is called
   A. hyper volume niche
   B. habitat
   C. fundamental niche
   D. realized niche

9. Dissipative process of energy during photosynthesis in a plant is
   A. Decomposition
   B. Senescence
   C. Respiration
   D. Mineralization of humus

10. Which of the following substances is generally not considered toxic?
    A. Carbonic acid   B. Carbon monoxide
    C. Acetaldehyde   D. Benzene

11. Percentage of tropospheric ozone in relation to total atmospheric ozone is about
    A. 90%   B. 10%
    C. 50%   D. 80%

12. Among the following, which one is the most hazardous chemical in the atmosphere?
    A. Dioxin   B. Carbon monoxide
    C. Halons   D. CFCs

13. The technique, which is fastest for measuring organic carbon is,
    A. COD   B. BOD_5
    C. BOD_7 D. TOC

14. With increase in temperature, the specific conductivity of water
    A. remains unchanged
    B. increases
    C. decreases
    D. makes the water turbid

15. According to ZSI (GOI), which one of the following birds declined by 99%?
    A. Sparrow
    B. Pink-headed Duck
    C. Pond heron
    D. White backed Vulture

16. According to Convention on International Trade in Endangered species (CITES) COP 17, which one of the following is transferred from CITES Appendix II to Appendix I by January 2017.
    A. Gorilla   B. Pangolin
    C. Tapir   D. Mongoose

17. Taxonomic diversity of a region with several ecosystems is:
    A. Alpha diversity   B. Beta diversity
    C. Gamma diversity   D. Sigma diversity

18. Soil water available to roots is
    A. Surface water
    B. Hygroscopic water
    C. Gravitational water
    D. Capillary water

19. C_4 plants are commonly found in
    A. Arid and hot environment
    B. Humid and low temperature environment
    C. Temperature environment
    D. Semi-humid and rainy environment

20. The point at which the light intensity is just enough to produce energy by photosynthesis which equal to the energy used in respiration is called
    A. Equal point
    B. Regulatory point
    C. Compensation point
    D. Complementary point

21. The global pattern of prevailing winds drives the cell-like circulation pattern of ocean currents called
    A. Trade winds   B. Gyres
    C. Jet Streams   D. Shallow drifts

22. As the number of species in a food web increases
    A. Food chain length tends to increase
    B. System tends to be unstable
    C. Energy flow decreases
    D. System tends to collapse completely

23. Each degree of latitude on the earth's surface represents approximately
    A. 91 km   B. 101 km
    C. 111 km   D. 121 km

24. Remote sensing satellites for earth observation are normally located in
    A. Elliptical orbit
    B. Sun-synchronous orbit
    C. Geo-synchronous orbit
    D. Equatorial orbit

25. Asian Ministerial Conference on Disaster Risk Reduction–2016 (AMCDRR–2016) was held in
    A. Bangkok   B. Beijing
    C. New Delhi   D. Colombo

26. Groundwater movement depends on the following characteristics of rock materials.
    (a) Porosity
    (b) Permeability
    (c) Specific yield
    (d) Specific retention capacity
    Choose the correct code:
    A. (a) only
    B. (a) and (b) only
    C. (a), (b) and (c) only
    D. (a), (b), (c) and (d)

27. Magma starts to crystallise when it loses heat during its upward rise to shallower level from a deep source. Which among the following is Bowen's Reaction Series?
  A. Pyroxene, Hornblende, Olivine, Mica, Quartz
  B. Olivine, Pyroxene, Hornblende, Mica, Quartz
  C. Hornblende, Olivine, Mica, Pyroxene, Quartz
  D. Olivine, Pyroxene, Hornblende, Mica, Quartz

28. A 2000 MW dam has maximum head of 200 m. What is the rate of falling water on the turbines? (Neglect losses)
  A. ~ 102.00 m^3/s
  B. ~ 1560.24 m^3/s
  C. ~ 1020.41 m^3/s
  D. ~ 800.00 m^3/s

29. A hydro power plant has a reservoir storage capacity of 2×10^3 m^3 and its maximum head is 500 m. What is its potential energy?
  A. ~ 10 PJ   B. ~ 18.6 PJ
  C. ~ 27.5 PJ   D. ~ 49 PJ

30. The maximum efficiency of hydrogen fuel cell is
  A. 0.96   B. 0.92
  C. 0.83   D. 0.72

31. In a biogas digestor having biomass and animal wastes as feed, for optimum methane production, the value of pH should be such that initially
  A. pH is in the range 6.6 to 7
  B. pH < 6.2
  C. pH is in the range 7 to 7.2
  D. pH is in the range 7.6 to 8

32. Which of the following statements is true in relation to solar flat plate collectors? Glazing (glass or plastic) above the absorber plate?
  A. Reduces convection losses
  B. Reduces conduction losses
  C. Reduces conduction and radiation losses
  D. Enhances the absorption of solar radiation onto the absorber plate.

33. Marine pollution is caused by
  (a) Sewage
  (b) Land runoff
  (c) Oil spills
  (d) Ocean mining
  Choose the correct code:
  A. (a), (c), and (d) only
  B. (c) and (d) only
  C. (a), (b), (c) and (d)
  D. (d), (c), (b) only

34. Which of the following wave properties is *not* taken advantage of in controlling noise?
  A. Absorption
  B. Damping
  C. Interference
  D. Diffraction

35. The reaction $O_2 \rightarrow 2O$, which occurs in the stratosphere, does not occur in the troposphere to produce ozone due to
  A. lower tropospheric temperature
  B. absence of $\lambda < 242$ nm radiation
  C. high air pressure
  D. high gas molecule concentrations

36. The most important global sink process for aerosols is
  A. Interception
  B. Sedimentation
  C. Impaction
  D. Wet deposition

37. Identify the correct sequence with reference to environmental clearance process for new projects :
  A. Appraisal → Screening → Scoping → Public Consultation
  B. Screening → Scoping → Public Consultation → Appraisal
  C. Scoping → Public Consultation → Appraisal → Screening
  D. Public Consultation → Appraisal → Screening → Scoping

38. Which of the following elements has the longest oceanic residence time?
  A. Iron   B. Lead
  C. Calcium   D. Sodium

39. The purpose of offshore islands is focussed for site or landscape restoration to
A. provide linkage between movement and genetic interchange of species.
B. foster populations of endangered species without native or introduced predators.
C. increase the availability of habitats.
D. increase the stabilization of surface cover and protect the animal corridor on land.

40. Match the List-I and List-II. Identify the correct answer from the codes given below:

List–I (Series)	List–II (Life Cycle Analysis)
(a) ISO 14040	1. Interpretation
(b) ISO 14041	2. Impact assessment
(c) ISO 14042	3. Principles and framework
(d) ISO 14043	4. Inventory Analysis

Codes:

	(a)	(b)	(c)	(d)
A.	1	2	3	4
B.	4	3	2	1
C.	1	4	2	3
D.	4	1	3	2

41. Which of the following can be used for valuing environmental amenities?
(a) Hedonic pricing
(b) Travel cost
(c) Contingent valuation
Choose the correct code:
A. (a) only   B. (b) only
C. (a), (b) and (c)   D. (b) and (c) only

42. A graphical representation where frequencies are plotted against class intervals is called
A. Stem and leaf plot B. Pie chart
C. Histogram   D. Box plot

43. Which one of the following is a density–independent factor that limits the size of the natural population?
A. Predation   B. Territoriality
C. Severe drought   D. Sex ratio

44. In a multiple regression analysis, if the variance of the observed variable Y is 1.57 and variance of the residue is 0.52, then R-square value is
A. 0.85   B. 0.67
C. 0.72   D. 0.52

45. The median value of the following data:
1, 2, 3, 5, 8 and 100 ; is
A. 3   B. 5
C. 4   D. 20

46. Exchangeable Sodium Percentage (ESP) > 40, and pH > 9.8 are characteristic of
A. Acidic soil
B. Weak saline soil
C. Strongly saline soil
D. Eroded soil

47. The climate meet COP-22 was held in which country?
A. Morocco
B. South Africa
C. Malaysia
D. Indonesia

48. In an aquatic system, the presence of noxious gases such as H_2S and CH_4 is associated with
A. abundant algal growth
B. oxygen depletion
C. absence of macrophytic vegetation
D. excess of dissolved oxygen

49. Severe drought is declared if
A. Deficit of rainfall is more than 50 per cent of the normal.
B. Deficit of rainfall varies between 25-45 per cent of the normal.
C. Rainfall deficit exceeds 25 per cent of the normal.
D. Rainfall deficit is between 15-25 per cent of the normal.

50. The Global Warming Potential (GWP) of a substance depends on
(a) the spectral band of its absorbing wavelengths.
(b) its residence time in atmosphere.
(c) its number of carbon molecules.
(d) concentration of the substance.

Choose the correct answer:
A. (a), (b) and (c) only
B. (b), (c) and (d) only
C. (a), (c) and (d) only
D. (b), (d) and (a) only

ANSWERS

1	2	3	4	5	6	7	8	9	10
C	D	A	C	C	A	D	C	C	A
11	12	13	14	15	16	17	18	19	20
B	A	D	B	D	B	C	D	A	C
21	22	23	24	25	26	27	28	29	30
B	A	C	B	C	D	*	C	*	C
31	32	33	34	35	36	37	38	39	40
A	A	C	D	B	D	B	D	B	*
41	42	43	44	45	46	47	48	49	50
C	C	C	B	C	C	A	B	A	D

Error in Questions.

EXPLANATORY ANSWERS

1. **Biomedical waste** is any kind of waste containing infectious materials.

   There are mainly five technology options available for the treatment of biomedical waste. They can be grouped as follows:
   - Chemical processes
   - Thermal processes
   - Mechanical processes
   - Irradiation processes
   - Biological processes

   Chemical processes : These processes use chemicals that act as disinfectants. Sodium hypochlorite, dissolved chlorine dioxide, peracetic acid, hydrogen peroxide, dry inorganic chemical and ozone are examples of such chemicals. Most chemical processes are water-intensive and require neutralising agents.

   Thermal processes : These processes utilise heat to disinfect. Depending on the temperature they operate, it is been grouped into two categories, which are Low-heat systems and High-heat systems

   Low-heat systems (operates between 93 -177 °C) use steam, hot water, or electromagnetic radiation to heat and decontaminate the waste. Autoclave & Microwave are low heat systems.

   High-heat systems employ combustion and high temperature plasma to decontaminate and destroy the waste. Incinerator & Hydroclaving are high heat systems.

   Mechanical processes : These processes are used to change the physical form or characteristics of the waste either to facilitate waste handling or to process the waste in conjunction with other treatment steps. The two primary mechanical processes are

   Compaction : Used to reduce the volume of the waste

   Shredding : Used to destroy plastic and paper waste to prevent their reuse. Only the disinfected waste can be used in a shredder.

   Irradiation processes : In these processes, wastes are exposed to ultraviolet or ionizing radiation in an enclosed chamber. These systems require post shredding to render the waste unrecognizable.

   Biological processes : Biological enzymes are used for treating medical waste. It is claimed that biological reactions will not only decontaminate the waste but also cause the destruction of all the organic constituents so that only plastics, glass, and other inert will remain in the residues.

2. In the wake of the Bhopal Tragedy, the Government of India enacted the Environment Protection Act of 1986 under Article 253 of

the Constitution. Passed in March 1986, it came into force on 19 November 1986. It has 26 sections. The purpose of the Act is to implement the decisions of the United Nations Conference on the Human Environments they relate to the protection and improvement of the human environment and the prevention of hazards to human beings, other living creatures, plants and property. The Act is an "umbrella" legislation designed to provide a framework for central government coordination of the activities of various central and state authorities established under previous laws, such as the Water Act and the Air Act.

3. **Environmental values** are also emphasized in the Constitution of India in the following articles:

   Article 51A(g) : The constitution expects citizen of the country to 'protect and improve the natural environment including forests, lakes, rivers and wildlife and to have compassion for all living creatures'.

   Article 48A : The state shall endeavour to protect and improve the environment and to safeguard the forests and wildlife in the country.

   Value education in the context of the environment must teach us the following:

   (i) Environmental values.

   (ii) Values for nature.

   (iii) Values for culture.

   (iv) Values for social justice.

   (v) Values for human heritage.

   (vi) Values for equitable use of resources.

   (vii) Values for sharing common property resources.

   (viii) Values to stop/minimize environmental degradation.

4. Deposit of amount payable for damage to environment
   1. Where any amount of compensation is ordered to be paid under any award by the Tribunal on the ground of any damage to environment, that amount shall be remitted to the authority specified under sub-section (3) of section 7A of the Public Liability Insurance Act, 1991 for being credited to the Environmental Relief Fund established under that section.
   2. The amount of compensation credited to the Environmental Relief Fund under sub-section (1) may be utilised by such person or authority, in such manner and for such purposes of environment as may be prescribed.

5. In geology, a graben is a depressed block of the Earth's crust bordered by parallel faults.

   A graben is a valley with a distinct escarpment on each side caused by the displacement of a block of land downward. Graben often occur side-by-side with horsts. Horst and graben structures indicate tensional forces and crustal stretching.

   Graben are produced from parallel normal faults, where the displacement of the hanging wall is downward, while that of the footwall is upward. The faults typically dip toward the center of the graben from both sides. Horsts are parallel blocks that remain between graben; the bounding faults of a horst typically dip away from the center line of the horst. Single or multiple graben can produce a rift valley.

6. When the reverse condition of the fumigation occurs the plume is said to be lofting (Fig.).

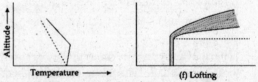

Fig. : *Plume behaviour (Lofting)*

Under this condition the lapse rate above the plume is unstable while below the plume is stable. When the pollutants are emitted from elevated source, they move above the inversion layer and are dispersed well vertically. This is also very suitable condition for dispersion of pollutants. Under these conditions the pollution ground level gets minimum.

7. **Microscale :** The size of microscale is less than 2 km. The time scale is a few seconds to a few minutes. Some examples of microscale are turbulent flow (updrafts and downdrafts).

8. A fundamental niche is the term for what an organism's niche would be in the absence of competition from other species.

Generally, however, there are competitors for the same lifestyle. Rabbits compete with groundhogs for food. Grasses compete with shrubs for soil, and bacteria compete with mold for nutrients among the leaf litter. The niche that a species actually inhabits, taking into account interspecific competition, is its realized niche.

Examples of Fundamental Niches

The male red-winged blackbird's mating call can be heard in the marshes in early spring. At that time, they hold the prime real estate in the marsh. However, as the season progresses, the more aggressive tri-colour blackbirds move in. The tri-colours take over the best territory and force the red-wings to choose the leftovers. The entire marsh represents the red-winged blackbirds' fundamental niche.

9. Dissipative processes are also at work within the biosphere, even under conditions of a steady state of minimum entropy production. These dissipative processes are exemplified by such processes as respiration and senescence that degrade photosynthesized molecules and structures back into smaller molecules such as CO_2, H_2O and less complex mineral compounds and structures. Ordering and dissipative processes in the soil-plant ecosystem can be categorized. Soil and land degradation occur when dissipative processes become excessive; *e.g.,* soil profile destruction by erosion resulting from tillage and poor residue management or overgrazing.

10. **Table :** *Toxic Gases Found in House Fire Smoke*

Substance	Source	Effect
Ammonia	Melamine resins	Inflammation
Aldehydes (acrolein, acetaldehyde, formaldehyde)	Wood, cotton, paper	Inflammation
Benzene	Petroleum products	Irritation and coma
Carbon dioxide	Organic materials	Asphyxiation and coma
Carbon monoxide	Organic materials	Asphyxiation and coma
Hydrogen chloride	Polyvinyl chloride	Inflammation
Hydrogen cyanide	Polyurethanes	Cellular asphyxia
Isocyanate	Polyurethanes	Inflammation and bronchospasm
Organic acids (acetic and formic acid)	Wood, cotton, paper	Inflammation
Oxides of nitrogen and sulphur	Nitrocellulose film	Pulmonary edema
Phosgene	Polyvinyl chloride	Inflammation

11. There are only 10 per cent of atmospheric ozone resides in the troposphere, it plays a critical role in the chemistry of the region. Photolysis of ozone in the presence of water (H_2O) is the primary source of the hydroxyl radical (OH), which for example, partly determines the removal rates of such climatically important trace gases as methane and the chlorofluorocarbons.

12. Doxin is one of the most toxic chemical known.

    Combustion : Dioxins form during poorly controlled combustion in municipal-waste incinerators and other combustion sources– they are products of incomplete combustion. Dioxin particles released into air settle onto vegetation, and are eaten by cattle and other animals. Animals concentrate dioxins in their fat. Humans receive about 90% of their total exposure to dioxins when they eat contaminated fatty meat such as hamburgers and fatty dairy products.

    Chlorine-using processes : A pulp mill using elemental chlorine to bleach pulp releases trace amounts of dioxins into their effluent. Released into a river, most dioxin is not soluble; most attaches to sediment particles. Bottom-feeding creatures ingest dioxins as they eat the tiny organisms living there. From there, dioxins biomagnify in the food web.

13. Total Organic Carbon (TOC) is one of the simplest and fastest to measure. Total organic carbon (TOC) is the amount of carbon found in an organic compound and is often used as a non-specific indicator of water quality or cleanliness of pharmaceutical manufacturing equipment. TOC may also refer to the amount of organic carbon in soil, or in a geological formation, particularly the source rock for a petroleum play; 2% is a rough minimum. For marine surface sediments, average TOC content is 0.5% in the deep ocean, and 2% along the eastern margins .

14. Pure water is not a good conductor of electricity, because electrical current in liquids is conducted by dissolved ions. But, as the concentration of ions in water increases, the conductivity increases. The measurement of conductivity or specific conductance is an excellent indicator of the degree of mineralization of a water.

    The conductance of a water sample will decrease with decreasing temperature, and it can be adjusted to 25 °C (k_{25}) with the equation

    $$k_{25} = \frac{k_m}{1 + 0.0191(T - 25)}$$

    where k_m = measured k at any temperature (T in °C). This equation assumes that the specific conductance measurement has been corrected for the cell constant—the value necessary to adjust for variation in the dimensions of the electrode. Specific conductance increases with increasing temperature.

15. Out of nine species of vultures, the population of three species—White-backed Vulture (*Gyps bengalensis*), Slender-billed Vulture (*Gyps tenuirostris*) and Long-billed Vulture (*Gyps indicus*) has declined by 99%. The Red-headed Vulture (*Sarcogyps calvus*) has also suffered a rapid decline in the recent past. Vultures keep the environment clean, by scavenging on animal carcasses. The decline in vulture populations has associated disease risks, including increased risk of spread of rabies and anthrax, besides adversely impacting the observance of last rites by the Parsis in the Towers of Silence.

    Habitat: Forests, villages etc.

    Distribution: Across India.

    Threats: A major threat to vultures is the painkiller diclofenac used by veterinarians to treat cattle. When vultures consume these carcasses, diclofenac enters their system, but they are unable to metabolize it. Accumulation of diclofenac results in gout-like symptoms such as neck-drooping, ultimately leading to death.

16. The 17th meeting of the Conference of the Parties to CITES (CoP17) took place between 24th September and 4th October 2016 in Johannesburg, South Africa.

The CITES CoP is a meeting of CITES Parties to review the implementation of the Convention. The CoP provides a forum for Parties to:

- Review progress in the conservation of species listed under CITES
- Consider, and where appropriate adopt, proposals to amend the lists of species under CITES
- Recommend measures to improve the effectiveness of the Convention
- Make provisions (including budget matters) necessary to allow the CITES Secretariat to function effectively.

The 17th meeting of the Conference of the Parties to CITES (CoP17) African pangolin species from Appendix II to Appendix I.

17. Biodiversity can be measured by the numbers and types of different species, or the genetic variations within and between species. The Ecologists use different indices to measure biodiversity. Whittaker emphasized on species richness or species evenness as common matrices to measure the species and land diversity. Three indices are commonly used by ecologists to measure biodiversity. These are known as alpha, beta and gamma.

The **Alpha diversity** refers to the diversity within a particular area, and is measured by counting the number of taxa within the ecosystem. It refers to the concept of species richness in a particular habitat or ecosystem.

The **Beta Diversity** is species diversity between ecosystems. For this the numbers of taxa are compared that are unique to each of the ecosystem. If the species composition of a particular community changes from place to place in a particular area, we may say that the beta diversity in that area is high. However, if the whole area is occupied by the species, the beta diversity is said to be low.

The **Gamma Diversity** is a measure of the overall diversity for different ecosystems within a region. In other words, the gamma diversity is defined as the rate of coming up of additional species due to geographical replacements for a given type of habitat in different types of localities.

18. **Capillary water** is that fraction of soil water that is held in the small spaces of the soil against the force of gravity by adhesive forces between water molecules and soil particles; about 75% of this soil water is available to plants. This water is held in the interspaces or thin capillaries between the soil particles after the gravitational water has drained down. It is held against the force of gravity by capillary forces and is called capillary water. The capillary water is readily available to plants for absorptions. Capillary water is important because cohesive forces permit both upward and lateral movement. Often it is the rate, not the distance traversed, that is the critical factor influencing the relative importance of capillary flow.

19. C_4 plants tend to be most abundant in warm, fairly dry environments. The C_4 system is especially often found in grasses in semi-arid environments such as the western and especially the southwestern parts of the North American prairies (no trees have the C_4 metabolism). There is a gradient in C_4 abundance going from cool to warm, and from wet to dry. However, the pattern is not always quite as expected.

A C_4 plant, avoids photorespiration because it shuttles the fixed carbon to have the final sugar-making reaction occur in special cells deep within its leaf that aren't producing any oxygen. And concentrating CO_2 at high levels relative to oxygen also helps suppress photorespiration. Having special "CO_2-gathering" cells that take up CO_2 without producing any CO_2 through photorespiration helps to ensure maximum efficiency in CO_2 uptake (it is like a vacuum cleaner for CO_2), in terms of "stomatal opening time" and water loss. Hence, in a C_4 plant stomata need not be open for as long to take up a unit of carbon, and—for this reason too—water use is more efficient. Thus, the C_4 plant loses less water per unit time per unit of carbon fixed. This should help it to do better in dry environments.

20. Daily and seasonal variations in light intensity affect plant growth; at least 1% intensity of full sunlight is necessary to trigger photosynthesis. Plants are said to have reached a compensation point when the light intensity is enough to produce an equivalent amount of energy by photosynthesis that is being used in respiration. From there, photosynthesis increases linearly, up to between 10 and 20% of full sunlight, when light saturation may be reached. Beyond the saturation point, light intensity may actually impair photosynthesis by causing photooxidation of recently produced photosynthetic products or by increasing the breakdown rate of chlorophyll beyond its renewal rate. Inadequate light intensity limits the radiant energy available for photosynthesis. Only 1–2% of total radiant energy is absorbed and converted into chemical energy through photosynthesis.

21. This global pattern of prevailing winds drives the cell-like circulation pattern of ocean currents called gyres. Most currents are called "drifts" because they lag far behind the average speeds of the surface winds, averaging only about 8 km hr^{-1}. Variations in water temperature, density, and salinity are another major source of oceanic circulation. For example, increases in salinity or decreases in temperature make water denser and cause it to sink. Cold currents of the polar areas sink and flow toward the equator, while warm currents from the equator flow toward the higher Latitudes transporting heat.

22. It appears that the average number of feeding links per species (linkage density) increases as the size of the web (i.e., number of species) increases. This implies that the number of prey that a predator will eat increases in proportion to the total number of species in that community. However, the number of links relative to all possible links (connectance) decreases as the number of groups in a food web increases. Martens suggested that this might reflect an increase in ecosystem stability. However, Christensen and Pauly conclude that any interpretation of connectance is ambiguous due to the binary nature of its scoring.

23. Lines of latitude are always parallel with each other and, therefore, are also known as parallels. Any number of parallels can be designated using degrees, minutes, and seconds. Neglecting Earth's oblate shape, one degree of latitude is anywhere equivalent to approximately 111 km. Important lines of latitude usually shown on maps or globes are the Tropic of Cancer, Tropic of Capricorn, Arctic Circle, Antarctic Circle, and the equator.

Important Parallels of Latitudes

Equator : The equator is the line of 0° latitude and is so named because it divides the Earth into two equal halves.

Tropic of Cancer : It lies at an angle of 23½ °N of the equator.

Tropic of Capricorn : It lies at an angle of 23½ °S of the equator.

Arctic Circle : It lies at an angle of 66½ °N of the equator.

Antarctic Circle : It lies at an angle of 66½ °S of the equator.

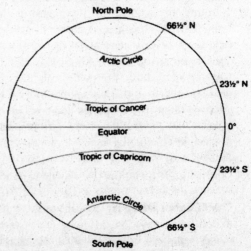

Fig. : *Important Parallels of Latitudes*

- The lines of latitude are horizontal and parallel, running from east to west.
- The equator is the largest line of latitude as it encircles the earth in the middle.
- The lines of latitudes become progressively shorter as they near the poles.
- All the lines of latitudes are circles, except the North and South Poles, which are points.
- If the lines of latitude are 1° apart from each other, there will be 90 parallels in the Northern.

  Hemisphere and 90 parallels in the Southern Hemisphere (total 181 parallels including the equator).
- Each degree of latitude is divided into 60 minutes, and each minute is divided into 60 seconds.

24. Sun-synchronous Orbit

An orbit is said to be sun-synchronous, if the orbit precession of the satellite compensates for the Earth's rotation around the sun. For near-Earth satellite orbits (altitude < 1000 km) sun-synchronous orbits are polar orbits at an orbital inclination and altitude such that a satellite passes over a given site always at the same local time. The orbital nodes maintain a near constant solar time. The satellite always crosses the equatorial plane at the same local time. This means that the sun position (lighting conditions) is always the same (within certain limits) for a repeat observations of any given site. There are advantages and disadvantages to the measurement at constant sun–angle depending on the application. Varying sun angles may be of importance to geologists to reveal subtle structural details not visible at higher sun angles.

25.

India had host the Asian Ministerial Conference for Disaster Risk Reduction (AMCDRR) from 3 November to 5 November 2016.

Prime Minister Narendra Modi inaugurated the conference that was held in New Delhi in collaboration with the United Nations Office for Disaster Risk Reduction (UNISDR). The Conference was focus on partnership with governments and stakeholders to imbibe the practices in the region's development narrative.

Key Highlights of the Conference

- The conference aims at transforming the commitments of governments and stakeholders during the Sendai Conference into national and local action.
- The meet was focus on collaboration, consultation and partnership with governments and stakeholders to mainstream DRR in the region's development narrative.
- The conference adopted the Asian Regional Plan for implementation of the Sendai Framework endorsed by the Asian countries.
- It was also consolidate the political commitment of governments towards preventing and reducing risk as well as strengthening resilience in the form of a political declaration.

26.

Movement of groundwater depends on rock and sediment properties and the groundwater's flow potential. Porosity, permeability, specific yield and specific retention are important properties of groundwater flow. Porosity is the volume of pore space relative to the total volume (rock and/or sediment + pore space). Primary porosity (% pore space) is the initial void space present (intergranular) when the rock formed. Secondary porosity (% added openings) develops later. It is the result of fracturing, faulting, or dissolution. Grain shape and cementation also affect porosity.

Permeability is the capability of a rock to allow the passage of fluids. Permeability is dependent on the size of pore spaces and to what degree the pore spaces are connected. Grain shape, grain packing, and cementation affect permeability.

Specific yield (S_y) is the ratio of the volume of water that drained from a rock (due to gravity) to the total rock volume. Grain size has a definite effect on specific yield. Smaller grains have larger surface areas. Larger surface areas mean more surface tension. Fine-grained sediment will have a lower specific yield than more coarsely-grained sediment. Sorting of material affects groundwater movement. Poorly sorted material is less porous than well-sorted material.

Specific retention (S_r) is the ratio of the volume of water a rock can retain (in spite of gravity) to the total volume of rock.

Specific yield plus specific retention equals porosity.

$$S_r + S_y = \Phi$$

Porosity, permeability, specific yield, and specific retention are all components of hydraulic conductivity.

27. By using Bowen's Reaction Series (Fig.) illustrating the order of crystallization of minerals from a magma, depending on temperature, it becomes apparent how such a varied collection of rocks may be formed from a single source. At the highest temperatures, the rocks formed tend to be free or virtually free of fieldspars, containing olivine and pyroxene, and are called ultrabasic. Basic rocks contain a calcium rich plagioclase feldspar, and a pyroxene; intermediate rocks, a plagioclase in between calcium and sodium rich and an amphibole, with less than 10% quartz; acid rocks, a sodic plagioclase and/or an alkali feldspar, and more than 10% quartz. So, the minerals which crystallize out at any particular temperature combine to form a representative rock type, leaving the chemical composition of the still molten portion of the magma changed. Hence, as the high temperature minerals become crystallized out, elements such as Mg, Fe and Ca, are taken from the melt, along with relatively small amounts of silica combined with these as a silicate radical. Thus, the melt is enriched in

Al, Na and silica, and the lower temperature minerals and hence, rocks are rich in these.

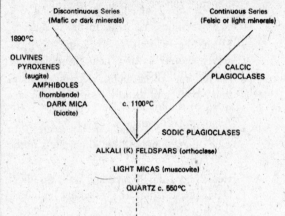

Fig. : *Bowen's Reaction Series showing the order of crystallization of common rock forming minerals from a silicate magma*

28. We know that 1 m^3/sec = 1000 l/sec

Again from formula,

Power (w) = Net head (m) × Flow (l/sec)
$$\times\ 9.8\ (m/sec^2)$$

$$2 \times 10^9 = 200 \times \text{Flow } (l/\text{sec}) \times 9.8$$

$$\text{Flow } (l/\text{sec}) = \frac{10^7}{9.8}$$

$$= 10.2041 \times 10^5$$

Flow (m^3/sec) = 10.2041×10^2

Flow = 1020.41 m^3/sec.

30. The thermal efficiency of fuel cell is given by the ratio of useful electrical energy produced to the enthalpy formation of fuel and is given by Eq. and rewritten as follows.

$$\eta_{FC} = \frac{\Delta G}{\Delta H}$$

where ΔG is change in Gibbs free energy and ΔH is the enthalpy of formation of the reaction. In practice, the actual efficiency of fuel cell is given as follows.

$$\eta = 0.83 \times \left(\frac{V_{CELL}}{V_{IDEAL}}\right)$$

where V_{CELL} = The actual voltage of fuel cell; V_{IDEAL} = The voltage obtained from Gibbs free energy for the ideal case and 0.83 is the theoretical maximum efficiency of fuel cell.

31. Environmental factors such as substrate concentration, temperature, pH and metal ions have great influences on methane production. A high concentration of VFAs has been reported to inhibit methane production from VFAs by mixed anaerobic microorganisms. The optimum pH range for anaerobic digestion producing methane is 6.8–7.2. The growth rate of methanogens can be greatly reduced when the pH value is less than 6.6. An excessively alkaline pH can lead to the disintegration of microbial granules and subsequent failure of the digestion process. Therefore, a buffer is needed in the methane production process in order to provide the resistance to significant and rapid pH changes in the system. Buffer capacity is proportional to the concentration of bicarbonate. $NaHCO_3$ has been widely used to create a buffer system during the anaerobic digestion process. Speece found that an alkalinity to COD concentration ratio (w/w) of 1.2–1.6 was required to sufficiently maintain the pH at approximately 6.6 during the anaerobic digestion of carbohydrate waste to produce methane. It is obviously seen that in order to achieve a maximum methane production, the key environmental factors should be optimized.

32. Flat-plate collector is one of the most important components of a solar water heater. Flat-plate collectors are the simplest and most commonly used collectors for converting the sun's radiation into useful heat. They are designed for applications requiring energy delivery at moderate temperature (less than 100°C) as in water and space heating. They have the advantages of using both beam and diffuse solar radiation, not requiring orientation towards the sun and requiring little maintenance. A conventional flat-plate collector is made up of a flat absorbing plate,

normally metallic upon which solar radiation falls and is absorbed, changing to heat energy. The absorb plate is usually black in colour for optimum collection and its area is the same as the area intercepting the radiation.

To reduce convective and radiative heat losses from the absorber, one or two transparent covers (glazing) are generally placed above the absorber plate.

They usually be made from glass or plastic.

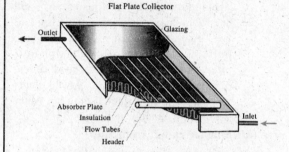

Flat Plate Collector

33. **Marine Pollution :** Oceans are the ultimate sink of all natural and man-made pollutants. Rivers discharge their pollutants into the sea. The sewerage and garbage of coastal cities are also dumped into the sea. The other sources of oceanic pollution are navigational discharge of oil, grease, detergents, sewage, garbage, and radioactive wastes. Capsized oil tankers, offshore oil mining and soil exploration operations and oil-refineries mainly contribute to oil pollution of marine ecosystem. An accidental discharge of petroleum in oceans and estuaries is called oil spills.

The water pollutants are generated by different sources and activities, some of these are briefly described below:

(*i*) **Household detergents and domestic sewage :** Domestic sewage is mainly the liquid wastes from kitchen, toilets and other household domestic activities. In most cases they are discharged into a river or a water body nearby. A mere 0.1% impurities make domestic sewage unfit for human use.

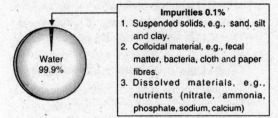

Impurities 0.1%
1. Suspended solids, e.g., sand, silt and clay.
2. Colloidal material, e.g., fecal matter, bacteria, cloth and paper fibres.
3. Dissolved materials, e.g., nutrients (nitrate, ammonia, phosphate, sodium, calcium)

Fig. : *Composition of domestic sewage*

(ii) Industrial waste and effluents : Small and large scale industries like iron and steel industries, chemical plants, soap and detergent manufacturing industries and food processing industries emit inorganic pollutants like chlorides, sulphates, nitrates, acids, alkalis, suspended solids, heavy metals, etc. Electric power plants and nuclear power stations emit hot water which is a notable pollutant.

(iii) Surface runoff from land

1. Runoff from agricultural land—Pesticide residues and inorganic residues of fertilisers.
2. Runoff from urban areas—Contain biodegradables organic pollutants.
3. Runoff from industries—Contain heavy metals, acids and various inorganic compounds.

(iv) Oil spills : An oil spill is the accidental discharge of oil from various sources/activities like by:

(a) Capsized oil tankers : Oil, grease, petroleum products

(b) Offshore oil mining and oil exploration operations and oil refineries : Oil, grease, petroleum products

Fig. : *Oil spill damages the biodiversity, birds smeared with oil lose capability to fly.*

Oil spills cause the death of plankton fish and marine birds as shown in the accompanying figure. They are extremely harmful to coral reefs and drastically damage the marine biodiversity.

34. **Controlling noise :** Methods of controlling noise take advantage of some of its wave properties, including absorption, damping, reflection and interference.

Sound-proofing materials absorb noise over a wide range of frequencies. They are materials like expanded polystyrene, fibreglass or even old egg cartons, that are soft and/or contain air pockets, so absorbing the vibrations. These are used in recording studios to reduce incoming noise, and in noisy developments such as clubs or theatres to prevent excess noise escaping to nearby residential areas. The choice of material will depend upon the frequency range of the noise to be controlled, as certain materials absorb more effectively at certain frequencies. Sound insulation is important in walls and ceilings, particularly between neighbouring properties and in apartment blocks. The sound insulation of a wall, R, can be defined as

$$R = 10 \log\left(\frac{I_i}{I_t}\right)$$

where I_i and I_t are the incident and transmitted sound intensities. This gives the difference in decibel levels at each side of the barrier. It will be reduced in the case of sounds transmitted directly to the wall rather than through the air, for instance where residents in the flat upstars have their hi-fi speakers on the floor. Sound insulation is frequency dependent. To be effective, sound-proofed areas must be solid and without cracks, as sound will be transmitted effectively through quite small holes or cracks reducing any noise insulation significantly.

35. The ozone is produced by the photolysis of oxygen molecules into oxygen atoms, shown in Reaction (1), followed by the reaction of

one oxygen atom with an oxygen molecule:

$$O_2 + UV \text{ light} \rightarrow O + O \quad \lambda < 242 \text{ nm} \quad ...(1)$$
$$O + O_2 + M \rightarrow O_3 + M \quad ...(2)$$
$$\text{Net: } 2\,O_2 + UV \text{ light} \rightarrow O + O_3$$

In Reaction (1), the ultraviolet light required to dissociate the O_2 molecules must have a wavelength less than 242 nm. The oxygen atoms formed in Reaction (1) react with an oxygen molecule to form ozone in Reaction (2). The third molecule, M, is needed to remove the excess energy and can be any other molecule in the atmosphere.

This reaction does not occur in the troposphere to produce ozone due to absence of $\lambda < 242$ nm radiation.

36. For the aerosol in the accumulation mode, the wet deposition is thought to be more of importance. Thus, for sea salt aerosol, dry and wet depositions are the most important sink-processes. The wet deposition process refers to the removal of any species from the atmosphere by precipitation, either by in-cloud or below-cloud scavenging. The in-cloud process is thought to be most important for small sea salt aerosol, which effectively form cloud condensation nuclei, whereas larger aerosol are removed by falling raindrops (below-cloud scavenging). Dry deposition refers to removal mechanisms that do not involve precipitation. For dry deposition of aerosol processes such as gravitational sedimentation, turbulent transfer, Brownian diffusion and impaction are considered.

37. The environmental clearance process comprises of four stages, namely, Stage (1) Screening; Stage (2) Scoping; Stage (3) Public Consultation and Stage (4) Appraisal.

Screening : Screening refers scrutiny of category 'B' projects seeking prior environmental clearance made in Form-1 by the concerned State Level Expert Appraisal Committee for determining whether or not the project requires further environmental studies for preparation of EIA for its appraisal depending upon the nature and location specificity of the project.

Scoping : Scoping refers to the process by which the EAC in the case of Category 'A' projects or activities, and SEAC in the case of Category 'B1' projects or activities determine detailed and comprehensive TORs addressing all the relevant environmental concerns for the preparation of EIA report.

Public Consultation : Public Consultation refers to the process by which the concerns of local affected persons and others who have plausible stake in the environmental impacts of the project or activity are ascertained.

Appraisal : Appraisal means the detailed scrutiny by the Expert Appraisal Committee or State Level Expert Appraisal Committee of the application and other documents submitted by the applicant for grant of environmental clearance.

38. Oceanographers call the time it takes for a substance to be removed from the ocean its *residence time*. Sodium and chloride have the longest residence times of the six major constituents. This explains why table salt is found in the sea in such abundance. Rivers actually add this common salt to oceans very slowly. The other elements have relatively short residence times. For example, potassium lasts seven million years, calcium one million years.

39. The ecological restoration of islands, or island restoration, is the application of the principles of ecological restoration to islands and island groups. Islands, due to their isolation, are home to many of the world's endemic species, as well as important breeding grounds for seabirds and some marine mammals. The purpose of offshore islands is focussed for site or landscape restoration to foster populations of endangered species without native or introduced predators.

41. Estimating Benefits for Nonmarket Goods

Clearly one of the problems with using benefit-cost analysis to help make regulatory decisions is the difficulty involved in estimating the monetary value of nonmarket goods and services, such as improved water quality or the reduced number of sick days. The three techniques that are most commonly used include hedonic pricing (inferring effects of regulations based on changes in the values of market goods such as houses), travel cost and contingent valuation. Each method has its strengths and weaknesses.

42. **Histogram :** It is the most commonly used graphical representation of grouped frequency distribution. Variable characters of the different groups are indicated on the horizontal line (*x*-axis) and frequencies (number of observation) are indicated on the vertical line (*y*-axis). Frequency of each group forms a column or rectangle. Such diagram is called *histogram*. The area of rectangle is proportional to the frequency of the correspondence class interval and the total area of the histogram is proportional to the total frequency of all the class intervals. A histogram may be drawn by using following steps:

● Set of vertical bars the areas of which are proportional to frequencies represented.

● The difference of histogram from bar diagram is that bar diagram is one dimensional and only the length of the bar has its significance while in histogram both length and width matters.

● When class intervals are equal, frequency is taken on *y*-axis, the variables on *x*-axis and adjacent rectangles are constructed.

● When the class intervals are unequal, a correction for unequal class intervals must be made.

The following frequency distribution is represented graphically in the form of histogram.

Age group (years)	No. of males
15-20	15
20-25	20
25-30	40
30-35	60
35-40	50

Here, we will take class boundaries along the horizontal axis and frequencies along with vertical axis. From the data shown above a histogram is drawn, which is presented in fig.

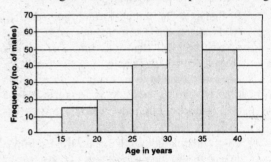

Fig. : *Histogram depicting number of males in different age groups.*

43. Density independent factors influence population size without regard for the population's density. They include events like severe drought or a prolonged cold period, either of which can cause widespread mortality independent of population density. A graph of density-independent effects on populations would show instantaneous, rather than gradual, drops in population size, and these changes would occur at different starting densities.

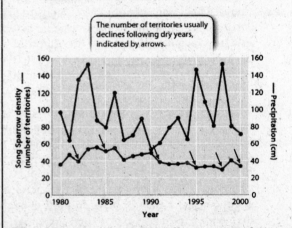

Fig. : *Density-independent effects on population size. Independent of population density, extreme weather (such as drought) lowers the quality of habitat for Song Sparrows, reducing the number of territories occupied.*

44. R-squared $(R^2) = 1 - \left[\dfrac{SS_{Error}}{SS_{Total}} \right]$

$$= 1 - \frac{0.52}{1.57}$$

$$= 1 - 0.33 = 0.67.$$

45. Data in ascending order: 1, 2, 3, 5, 8, 100

Number of term N = 6

So, medium (M)

$= $ Mean of $\dfrac{N}{2}$th term and $\left(\dfrac{N}{2} + 1 \right)$th term

$$= \frac{3+5}{2} = \frac{8}{2} = 4.$$

47. COP-22 was held in Marrakech, in the North-African country of Morocco, on 7-18 November 2016. A focal issue of COP-22 is that of water scarcity, water cleanliness, and water-related sustainability, a major problem in the developing world, including many African states. Prior to the event a special initiative on water was presided by Charafat Afailal, Morocco's Minister in Charge of Water and Aziz Mekouar, COP-22 Ambassador for Multilateral Negotiations. Another focal issue was the need to reduce greenhouse emissions and utilize low-carbon energy sources. Mr. Peter Thompson, President of the UN General Assembly, called for the transformation of the global economy in all sectors to achieve a low emissions global economy.

48. Organic matter in water is broken down by microorganisms, especially bacteria, either aerobically (using oxygen) or, once the oxygen dissolved in water is depleted, anaerobically (without oxygen). The organic matter content of water is described by its biochemical oxygen demand (BOD), a measure of the amount of oxygen needed to break down the organic matter aerobically. Anaerobic decay produces a variety of noxious gases, such as hydrogen sulphide (H_2S) and methane (CH_4), the presence of which in a body of water signals oxygen depletion.

49. Meteorological drought is defined as the deficiency of precipitation from expected or normal levels over an extended period of time (*i.e.,* normal levels accommodate upto 10% deviation from long term average). Meteorological drought usually precedes other kinds of drought and is said to occur when the seasonal rainfall received over an area is less than 25% of its long-term average value. It is classified as moderate drought if the rainfall deficit is 26-50% and severe drought when the deficit exceeds 50% of the normal.

50. **Global warming potential (GWP)** is a relative measure of how much heat a greenhouse gas traps in the atmosphere. It compares the amount of heat trapped by a certain mass of the gas in question to the amount of heat trapped by a similar mass of carbon dioxide. A GWP is calculated over a specific time interval, commonly 20, 100, or 500 years. GWP is expressed as a factor of carbon dioxide.

The substances subject to restrictions under the Kyoto protocol either are rapidly increasing their concentrations in Earth's atmosphere or have a large GWP.

The GWP depends on the following factors:

- The absorption of infrared radiation by a given species
- The spectral location of its absorbing wavelengths
- The atmospheric lifetime of the species

Thus, a high GWP correlates with a large infrared absorption and a long atmospheric lifetime. The dependence of GWP on the wavelength of absorption is more complicated. Even if a gas absorbs radiation efficiently at a certain wavelength, this may not affect its GWP much if the atmosphere already absorbs most radiation at that wavelength. A gas has the most effect if it absorbs in a "window" of wavelengths where the atmosphere is fairly transparent. The dependence of GWP as a function of wavelength has been found empirically and published as a graph.

PAPER-III

Note: *This paper contains **seventy five** (75) objective type questions of **two** (2) marks each. **All** questions are compulsory.*

1. Given below are two statements. One labelled as Assertion (A) and the other labelled as Reason (R):

   Assertion (A): Vertical velocity often equals or exceeds horizontal velocity in mesoscale meteorological systems.

   Reason (R): Rising thermals are susceptible to undergo non-hydrostatic processes such as buoyant acceleration or acceleration through a narrow mountain pass.

   Choose the correct answer:
   A. Both (A) and (R) are correct and (R) is the correct explanation of (A).
   B. Both (A) and (R) are correct and (R) is not the correct explanation of (A).
   C. (A) is true, but (R) is false.
   D. (A) is false and (R) is true.

2. Given below are two statements. One labelled as Assertion (A) and the other labelled as Reason (R):

   Assertion (A): Geostrophic wind velocity is independent of latitude.

   Reason (R): Geostrophic wind velocity is determined by pressure gradient force only.

   Choose the correct answer:
   A. Both (A) and (R) are correct and (R) is the correct explanation of (A).
   B. Both (A) and (R) are correct and (R) is not the correct explanation of (A).
   C. (A) is true, but (R) is false.
   D. (A) is false and (R) is true.

3. Mixing height during night is typically in the range
   A. < few hundred metres
   B. 1 km – 2 km
   C. 2 km – 3 km
   D. 3 km – 4 km

4. At a given urban location, the temperature at an elevation of 25 m above ground is 15 °C. If the inversion conditions prevail and the environmental lapse rate is 1.25 °C per 100 m, the temperature at an elevation of 200 m will be
   A. 12.5 °C   B. 17.5 °C
   C. 12.75 °C   D. 17.25 °C

5. When the temperature of the atmosphere falls at a rate greater than the dry adiabatic lapse rate, the atmosphere is
   A. stable
   B. highly stable
   C. unstable
   D. conditionally unstable

6. Gross Primary Productivity (GPP) of an ecosystem is
   A. net rate of carbon gain by the plant after respiration losses.
   B. total energy used to convert the sugar during growth.
   C. photosynthetic fixation rate of atmospheric carbon dioxide.
   D. rate of release of oxygen through respiration of a plant.

7. The oxygen atom species, which reacts with water to form hydroxyl radical, is produced by the photodissociation of
   A. O_2 B. O_3
   C. NO_2 D. H_2O

8. Match the List–I and List–II given below:

List–I (Element)	List–II (Classification)
(a) Sodium	1. Chalcogen
(b) Calcium	2. Alkali Metal
(c) Chromium	3. Alkaline Earth Element
(d) Sulphur	4. Transition Element

   Choose the correct answer:
   Codes:

	(a)	(b)	(c)	(d)
A.	2	3	4	1
B.	1	2	3	4
C.	3	1	2	4
D.	4	2	1	3

9. Identify the incorrect statement about carbon isotopes:
   A. C-13 is less abundant in vegetation than in oceans.
   B. C-12 is most abundant in nature.
   C. C-14 is absent in fossil fuels.
   D. C-13 is used for carbon-dating.

10. Among the following insecticides, which one is relatively more soluble in water?
    A. Aldicarb   B. Carbaryl
    C. Malathion   D. Aldrin

11. At 25 °C, hydrogen ion concentration in an environmental aqueous solution is found to be 5×10^{-4} mol L^{-1}. This implies that the concentration of hydroxyl ions is
    A. 2×10^{-3} mol L^{-1} B. 1×10^{-7} mol L^{-1}
    C. 2×10^{-11} mol L^{-1} D. 2×10^{-19} mol L^{-1}

12. Identify the incorrect statement about humus.
    A. Humus acts as a reservoir of nitrogen for plants.
    B. By decaying, humus supplies nitrogen to plants.
    C. Its rate of decay and rate of nitrogen release follow plant growth.
    D. Rate of nitrogen release to plants is slow during warm growing season and fast during winter months.

13. Match the List–I and List–II. Identify the correct answer from the codes given below:

List–I (Terms)	List–II (Chromatographic action)
(a) Effluent	1. The eluted solute
(b) Eluate	2. The mobile phase
(c) Eluent	3. The solute-mobile phase mixture which exits the column
(d) Eluite	4. The stream flowing out of the column

    Codes:

	(a)	(b)	(c)	(d)
A.	1	3	2	4
B.	2	4	3	1
C.	3	1	2	4
D.	4	3	2	1

14. A textile industry effluent containing 1×10^{-6} mol L^{-1} of an organic dye has 0.6 absorbance in a cell of 1.0 cm path length. The molar extinction coefficient of the dye is
    A. 6×10^4 L mol^{-1} cm^{-1}
    B. 6×10^7 L mol^{-1} cm^{-1}
    C. 1.66×10^{-5} L mol^{-1} cm^{-1}
    D. 6.0×10^6 L mol^{-1} cm^{-1}

15. Characteristics of successful invasive plant species are:
    (a) Rapid growth and early flowering.
    (b) High phenotypic plasticity
    (c) Production of large number of seeds
    Choose the correct answer:
    A. (a) only   B. (a) and (b) only
    C. (b) and (c) only   D. (a), (b) and (c)

16. Drugs that prevent the formation of bacterial cell wall are
    A. Quinolones   B. Beta-lactams
    C. Tetracyclines   D. Aminoglycocides

17. As a result of El Niño, it has been observed that phytoplankton productivity increases in Eastern Indian Ocean around Indonesia and Gulf of Mexico. This increase is probably due to
    (a) Increased rainfall
    (b) More nutrient inflow
    (c) Turbulence in surface waters
    Codes:
    A. (a) and (b) only   B. (b) and (c) only
    C. (a) and (c) only   D. (a), (b) and (c)

18. Vermi composting process depends on
    (a) Quality of organic resources
    (b) Types of earthworms
    (c) Moisture content of the organic wastes
    Choose the correct answer:
    A. (a) only   B. (a) and (b) only
    C. (b) and (c) only   D. (a), (b) and (c)

19. Photosynthesis in plants is associated with
    (a) decrease in entropy
    (b) increase in entropy
    (c) increase in Gibbs free energy
    Choose the correct answer:
    A. (a) only   B. (b) only
    C. (b) and (c) only   D. (a), (b) and (c)

20. The predominant bioparticulate allergens in the air are
A. Insect debris and house dust mites
B. Pollen grains and fungal spores
C. Animal dander and house dust
D. Wool particles and cockroach calyx

21. The enhancement of the fitness of a recipient individual by acts that reduce the evolutionary fitness of the donor individual is
A. Amensalism   B. Altruism
C. Commonsalism   D. Parasitism

22. The greater proportion of the edges in a national park indicates a
(a) less functional habitat
(b) highly functional habitat
(c) degraded habitat
Choose the correct answer:
A. (a) only   B. (a) and (c) only
C. (b) and (c) only   D. (a), (b) and (c)

23. The change in species composition that is imposed by factors external to the biotic community is known as
A. Autogenic succession
B. Allogenic succession
C. Xerarch
D. Hydrarch

24. Which ecosystem type produces maximum litter mass?
A. Tropical rain forest
B. Tropical seasonal forest
C. Temperate deciduous forest
D. Boreal forest

25. Cyclomorphism is a phenomenon observed in certain planktonic crustaceans and is generally attributed as a response to
(a) changes in environmental variables of water.
(b) ensure adaptive significance.
(c) growth, reproduction and sudden genetic change
Codes:
A. (a) and (c) only   B. (b) and (c) only
C. (a) and (b) only   D. (a), (b) and (c)

26. Microbes in the environment are likely to be
I. living in biofilms on surfaces
II. non-culturable
III. living solitary and planktonic lines
Choose the correct code:
A. I only   B. II and III only
C. I and III only   D. I and II only

27. Which magma type contains the greatest amount of silica?
A. Basaltic   B. Andesitic
C. Rhyolitic   D. Peridotic

28. Match the List–I and List–II and choose the correct answer from the codes given below:

List–I (Stratigraphic Unit)	List–II (Deposits)
(a) Bailadila Group	1. Mn
(b) Nallamalai Group	2. Phosphorite
(c) Udaipur Group	3. Banded Iron Formation
(d) Sansar Group	4. Pb-Zn

Codes:

	(a)	(b)	(c)	(d)
A.	3	4	2	1
B.	4	1	3	2
C.	1	2	4	3
D.	2	3	1	4

29. Which group of following factors determine the discharge of a stream?
A. Width, length and depth
B. Width, length and velocity
C. Width, depth and velocity
D. Length, depth and run-off

30. Which among the following zones has the highest erosion rate in the journey of a river?
A. Head water
B. Potamon
C. Mouth
D. Sediment transforming zone

31. In the decreasing order of hardness on Moh's scale, choose the correct sequence from the following:
A. Quartz, Feldspar, Calcite, Talc
B. Feldspar, Calcite, Talc, Quartz
C. Talc, Quartz, Feldspar, Calcite
D. Quartz, Calcite, Feldspar, Talc

32. Wind transport of materials entails the following processes:
   I. Saltation
   II. Reptation
   III. Suspension
   IV. Creep
   Choose the correct answer:
   A. I, II, III, IV
   B. II, III and IV only
   C. III and IV only
   D. I and II only

33. According to Darcy's law for ground water movement, velocity is proportional to
   A. Hydraulic gradient.
   B. Square of hydraulic gradient.
   C. Square root of hydraulic gradient.
   D. Reciprocal of hydraulic gradient.

34. Which of the following types of coal has maximum ash content (%)?
   A. Anthracite
   B. Sub-Bituminous
   C. Lignite
   D. High volatile Bituminous

35. Given below are two statements. One labelled as Assertion (A) and the other labelled as Reason (R):
   Assertion (A): The amount of energy available in a single fusion event is small compared to a fission event.
   Reason (R) : Isotopes of hydrogen are much lighter than uranium.
   Choose the correct answer:
   A. Both (A) and (R) are correct and (R) is the correct explanation of (A).
   B. Both (A) and (R) are correct and (R) is not the correct explanation of (A).
   C. (A) is true, but (R) is false.
   D. (A) is false and (R) is true.

36. Given below are two statements. One labelled as Assertion (A) and the other labelled as Reason (R):
   Assertion (A): The thermal efficiency of nuclear reactors is lower than that of fossil fuelled steam plants.

Reason (R) : Temperature of water generating stream in a nuclear reactor has relatively lower values compared to fossil fuelled steam plants.
Choose the correct answer:
   A. Both (A) and (R) are correct and (R) is the correct explanation of (A).
   B. Both (A) and (R) are correct and (R) is not the correct explanation of (A).
   C. (A) is true, but (R) is false.
   D. (A) is false and (R) is true.

37. Given below are two statements. One labelled as Assertion (A) and the other labelled as Reason (R):
   Assertion (A): Natural gas contributes less to smog formation than gasoline.
   Reason (R) : Unburnt CH_4 molecules are considerably less reactive with respect to the free radical chemistry for smog than the hydrocarbon molecules with more than one C atom.
   Choose the correct answer:
   A. Both (A) and (R) are correct and (R) is the correct explanation of (A).
   B. Both (A) and (R) are correct and (R) is not the correct explanation of (A).
   C. (A) is true, but (R) is false.
   D. (A) is false and (R) is true.

38. Consider ocean waves of amplitude 2.0 m and wavelength 200 m. Assuming the gravity to be the only active force, the power available per metre perpendicular to the propagation of the wave is
   A. 86.24 kW m^{-1}
   B. 172.48 kW m^{-1}
   C. 344.90 kW m^{-1}
   D. 800.00 kW m^{-1}

39. A wind mill has cross-sectional area 25.0 m^2. The wind speed is 6.0 m/s. What will be the power generated by the wind mill in the Betz limit?
   A. ~ 2.064 kW
   B. ~ 3.483 kW
   C. ~ 11.162 kW
   D. ~ 18.321 kW

40. Given below are two statements. One labelled as Assertion (A) and the other labelled as Reason (R):

Assertion (A): The power output from an OTEC system installed at a tropical site is steady.

Reason (R) : At tropical sites, the temperatures of warm surface water and cold water in the depth of ocean hardly vary from season to season.

Choose the correct answer:

A. Both (A) and (R) are correct and (R) is the correct explanation of (A).

B. Both (A) and (R) are correct and (R) is not the correct explanation of (A).

C. (A) is true, but (R) is false.

D. (A) is false and (R) is true.

41. An electric power plant based on solar energy uses collectors with concentrators which can achieve temperature of about 700 °C to operate a heat engine to generate electricity. If the solar insolation is 1 kW/m², how much total collector area will be required to supply on average 10 MW of electricity? (Take ambient air temperature to be 25 °C)

A. 5.15×10^3 m²   B. 1.44×10^3 m²

C. 3.18×10^3 m²   D. 10.61×10^3 m²

42. The potency factor of $CHCl_3$ is 6.1×10^{-3} kg-day/mg. The concentration in drinking water that would result in 2×10^{-6} risk for a 70-kg man, who drinks 2L/day throughout of his life, is

A. 11.4 μg/L   B. 20.6 μg/L

C. 6 μg/L   D. 25 μg/L

43. Which of the following compounds used for disinfection of water is not stable but is prepared *in situ*?

A. Cl_2 B. $Ca(OCl)_2$

C. NaOCl   D. HOCl

44. Identify the incorrect statement from the following regarding soil pollution by heavy metals:

A. Soils act as a sink for heavy metals.

B. Humic materials have great affinity for heavy metal cations.

C. Humic materials extract heavy metals from soil water by forming complexes.

D. Complexes formed by humic acids are normally water soluble.

45. A point source of noise produces a sound of 60 dB at a distance of 10 m from it. If the sound is measured at a distance of 40 m, what will be its value?

A. 48 dB   B. 54 dB

C. 57 dB   D. 44 dB

46. Identify the incorrect statement with regard to water purification by coagulation.

A. Particles suspended in water are in colloidal form.

B. Suspended particles carry a positive charge.

C. Suspended particles due to similar charge repel each other.

D. When alum is added it works as a coagulant.

47. In relation to drinking water source without conventional treatment but after disinfection, water parameters and their permissible values are given in the lists given below:

Match the List–I and List–II. Identify the correct answer from the codes given below:

List–I (Water parameters)	List–II (Permissible values)
(a) Total coliform organism MPN per 100 ml	1. 6.5 – 8.5
(b) pH	2. < 50 per 100 mL
(c) DO	3. 2 mg/L or less
(d) BOD (5 days, 20 °C)	4. 6 mg/L or more

Codes:

	(a)	(b)	(c)	(d)
A.	2	1	4	3
B.	2	1	3	4
C.	3	4	2	1
D.	4	2	3	1

48. Given below are two statements. One labelled as Assertion (A) and the other labelled as Reason (R):

Assertion (A) : Ozone depletion is much less over arctic stratosphere than over Antarctic stratosphere.

Reason (R) : Antarctic atmosphere is on an average about 10 °C cooler than the arctic stratosphere.

Choose the correct answer:

A. Both (A) and (R) are correct and (R) is the correct explanation of (A).

B. Both (A) and (R) are correct and (R) is not the correct explanation of (A).

C. (A) is true, but (R) is false.

D. (A) is false and (R) is true.

49. Match the List–I and List–II. Identify the correct answer from the codes given below:

List–I (Water type)	List–II (Conductivity ($\mu S\ cm^{-1}$))
(a) Fresh water	1. > 500
(b) Clean tap water	2. < 300
(c) Clean upland river	3. 60 – 100
(d) Organically enriched river	4. 2 – 4

Codes:

	(a)	(b)	(c)	(d)
A.	4	3	2	1
B.	1	4	3	2
C.	2	1	4	3
D.	3	2	1	4

50. Match the List–I and List–II. Identify the correct answer from the codes given below :

List–I (Auditing types)	List–II (Set of terms)
(a) Implementation audit	1. External review of the procedures used
(b) Performance audit	2. Compare actual with predicted impacts
(c) Project impact audit	3. To cover full operation
(d) Procedures audit	4. To cover a start-up

Codes:

	(a)	(b)	(c)	(d)
A.	3	4	1	2
B.	1	3	2	1
C.	1	2	3	4
D.	2	3	4	1

51. Given below are two statements. One labelled as Assertion (A) and the other labelled as Reason (R):

Assertion (A): The ecological restoration is a difficult proposition both in principle and in practice.

Reason (R) : Identity and population sizes of plants and animals once present at a particular site are largely unknown.

Choose the correct answer:

A. Both (A) and (R) are correct and (R) is the correct explanation of (A).

B. Both (A) and (R) are correct and (R) is not the correct explanation of (A).

C. (A) is true, but (R) is false.

D. (A) is false and (R) is true.

52. During the EIA process under the EIA notification of September 14, 2006, no public hearing is required for

(a) all A′ category projects

(b) all 'B$_1$' category projects

(c) all 'B$_2$' category projects

Choose the correct code:

A. (a) only

B. (a) and (b) only

C. (b) and (c) only

D. (c) only

53. Given below are two statements. One labelled as Assertion (A) and the other labelled as Reason (R):

Assertion (A): Evaporation of surface water is reduced due to black carbon in atmosphere.

Reason (R) : Presence of aerosols having black carbon is responsible for dimming effect.

Choose the correct answer:

A. Both (A) and (R) are correct and (R) is the correct explanation of (A).

B. Both (A) and (R) are correct and (R) is not the correct explanation of (A).

C. (A) is true, but (R) is false.

D. (A) is false and (R) is true.

54. Match the List–I and List–II. Identify the correct answer from the codes given below:

List–I (Methods)	List–II (Description)
(a) Network Method	1. Possible impacts by composite environmental parameters.
(b) Overlays Method	2. Structured approaches by involving scaling-weighing techniques.
(c) Checklists Method	3. Environmental systems as a complex web of relation-ships.
(d) Adhoc Method	4. Spatial distribution of environmental impacts using GIS.

Codes:

	(a)	(b)	(c)	(d)
A.	4	3	2	1
B.	1	2	3	4
C.	4	1	3	2
D.	3	4	2	1

55. In environmental Impact Assessment, the baseline studies describe the

A. socio-economic mapping of the area.

B. consequences of the development activity.

C. assessment of the risk involved during project implementation.

D. environmental setting existing in the project area.

56. An ecosystem restoration project should have the outcomes which are

I. Specific
II. Measurable
III. General
IV. Realistic
V. Time bound

Choose the correct code:

A. I, II, III, V   B. I, II, IV, V

C. II, III, IV, V   D. I, II, III, IV

57. When applied to field populations, Lotka-Volterra equations suffer from the following:

I. Competition coefficients are assumed to be constant.

II. Carrying capacity is assumed to be constant.

III. There are no time lags.

IV. Maximal rate of increase is assumed to be constant.

Choose the correct answer:

A. I and II only   B. II and III only

C. II, III and IV only D. I, II, III and IV

58. In a city, the daily per capita inhalation (m^3) values of contaminated air over a period of 5 days are 6.3, 6.3, 6.2, 6.4 and 5.8, respectively. The sample mean with standard deviation of the data is

A. 6.2 ± 0.02 B. 6.2 ± 0.23

C. 6.0 ± 0.15 D. 6.2 ± 0.18

59. The population (N) of fish in a pond follows the logistic equation $\frac{dN}{dt} = 0.1\,N - 0.001\,N^2$. What is the maximum sustainable yield?

A. 100   B. 50

C. 25   D. 200

60. Given below are two statements. One labelled as Assertion (A) and the other labelled as Reason (R):

Assertion (A): For power stations and polluting industries, tall stacks are installed.

Reason (R): The maximum ground level concentration of a pollutant released from a stack is inversely proportion to the height of the stack.

Choose the correct answer:

A. Both (A) and (R) are correct and (R) is the correct explanation of (A).

B. Both (A) and (R) are correct and (R) is not the correct explanation of (A).

C. (A) is true, but (R) is false.

D. (A) is false and (R) is true.

61. Consider a box model for an airshed over a city and assume that the initial concentration of a pollutant is zero and that the air entering the box is clean. If the length of the box is 10 km and the wind speed along the length of the box is 5 m/s, what is the time taken for the pollutant concentration to reach ~ 95% of its final value?
A. 1 h 40 minutes
B. 1 h 7 minutes
C. 33 minutes 20 seconds
D. 2 h 13 minutes 20 seconds

62. For a sample size $n = 16$, the mean $(\bar{X})$ value and standard deviation (S) are found to be 5.667 and 0.934, respectively. If the population mean is $\mu = 5.2$, then t – statistic is
A. 0.5
B. 0.47
C. 1.76
D. 2.0

63. Which of the following are sources of the greenhouse gas methane (CH_4)?
(a) Coal mining areas
(b) Ruminants
(c) Wetlands
(d) Low land paddy
Choose the correct answer:
A. (a), (b) and (c) only
B. (b) and (c) only
C. (b), (c) and (d) only
D. (a), (b), (c) and (d)

64. Which of the following convention/protocols/treaties is legally binding on the signatory countries?
A. Basel Convention
B. Montreal Protocol
C. Kyoto Protocol
D. Paris Agreement

65. For untreated municipal wastewater, BOD/COD ratio is in the range
A. 1.3 – 3
B. 0.3 – 0.8
C. 3.0 – 6.5
D. > 10

66. Organic wetland soils have
I. High porosity
II. Low density
III. High Ion exchange capacity
IV. Low nutrient availability

Choose the right answer:
A. I, II, III, IV
B. II, III, IV only
C. III, IV only
D. I, II only

67. Consider following statements about the ozone hole?
I. Ozone formation and destruction keeps on happening.
II. Ozone destruction rate is higher than its formation rate.
III. Ozone destruction rate is equal to its formation rate.
Choose the correct answer:
A. I only
B. I and II only
C. I and III only
D. III only

68. Consider following statements about an estuary:
I. Estuary is the ecotonal region between fresh water and oceanic water.
II. This area is highly productive.
III. This area is highly unproductive.
Choose the correct answer:
A. I only
B. I and II only
C. III only
D. I and III only

69. The ionic species, O^+, O_2^+ and N_2^+ are found generally in
A. Troposphere
B. Stratosphere
C. Mesosphere
D. Heterosphere

70. As part of recently signed international agreement on phasing out synthetic hydrofluorocarbons (HFCs), India will start phasing them out from the year
A. 2019
B. 2024
C. 2028
D. 2032

71. In the tropospheric ozone formation reaction sequence, which of the following chemical species does not act as a catalyst?
A. OH
B. HO_2
C. NO_2
D. O_2

72. Which of the following are useful indicators of pollution potential of organic effluents?
(a) Total Organic Carbon (TOC)
(b) Biological Oxygen Demand (BOD)
(c) Turbidity
(d) Conductivity

Choose the correct code:
A. (a) and (b) only   B. (a) and (c) only
C. (b) and (d) only   D. (a), (b), (c) and (d)

73. Which of the following power plants releases radioactive materials as well as hazardous metals such as lead and arsenic under normal operating conditions?
A. Nuclear power plant
B. Solar power installations
C. Hydro power
D. Coal based thermal power plants

74. Match the List-I and List-II. Identify the correct answer from the codes given below :

List–I (Convention)	List–II (Purpose)
(a) Paris Convention 1992	1. Transboundary Movement of Waste
(b) Vienna Convention 1985	2. Protection of Marine Environment
(c) Bamako Convention 1998	3. Protection of ozone layer
(d) Basel Convention 1992	4. Ban on import of hazardous waste to Africa

Codes:

	(a)	(b)	(c)	(d)
A.	2	3	4	1
B.	3	4	1	2
C.	4	1	2	3
D.	1	2	3	4

75. Match the List-I and List-II. Identify the correct answer from the codes given below:

List–I (Colour Codes)	List–II (Hospital Wastes)
(a) Yellow Bags	1. Infected metal sharps
(b) Red Bags	2. Outdated Medicine bottles
(c) Blue Bags	3. Used Catheters
(d) Black Carboy	4. Infectious waste placenta

Codes:

	(a)	(b)	(c)	(d)
A.	4	3	2	1
B.	3	2	1	4
C.	2	1	4	3
D.	1	4	3	2

ANSWERS

1	2	3	4	5	6	7	8	9	10
A	*	A	D	C	C	B	A	D	A

11	12	13	14	15	16	17	18	19	20
C	D	D	*	D	B	A	D	A	B

21	22	23	24	25	26	27	28	29	30
B	B	B	D	C	C	C	A	C	A

31	32	33	34	35	36	37	38	39	40
A	A	A	C	B	A	A	B	A	A

41	42	43	44	45	46	47	48	49	50
*	A	D	D	A	B	A	C	A	B

51	52	53	54	55	56	57	58	59	60
B	D	A	D	D	B	D	B	B	C

61	62	63	64	65	66	67	68	69	70
A	D	D	B	B	A	B	B	D	C

71	72	73	74	75
D	A	D	A	A

* Error in Questions.

EXPLANATORY ANSWERS

1. Mesoscale meteorology is the study of weather systems smaller than synoptic scale systems but larger than microscale and storm-scale cumulus systems. Horizontal dimensions generally range from around 5 km to several hundred kilometers. Examples of mesoscale weather systems are sea breezes, squall lines, and mesoscale convective complexes.

   Vertical velocity often equals or exceeds horizontal velocities in mesoscale meteorological systems due to nonhydrostatic processes such as buoyant acceleration of a rising thermal or acceleration through a narrow mountain pass.

2. The geostrophic wind speed is a function of latitude, pressure gradient and air density. Hence, assertion is false.

   The geostrophic wind is a theoretical wind calculated from surface pressure data. A balance is assumed between the flow of air from high to low pressure regions and the effects of the rotation of the Earth as manifested in the "Coriolis Effect". The geostrophic wind flows parallel to the isobars, and a good approximation to the actual wind in the free atmosphere.

   The geostrophic wind is the horizontal equilibrium wind (V_G), blowing parallel to the isobars, which represents the exact balance between the horizontal pressure gradient force:

$$-\left(\frac{1}{\rho}\right)\Delta_H p$$

   and the horizontal component of the Coriolis Force:

$$f V_G$$

   where $\Delta_H p$ is the horizontal pressure gradient, ρ is the air density, and f is the Coriolis parameter.

3. Mixing height (also called mixing depth) is the height above ground level through which relatively vigorous vertical mixing occurs.

Low mixing heights mean that the air is generally stagnant with very little vertical motion; pollutants usually are trapped near the ground surface. High mixing heights allow vertical mixing within a deep layer of the atmosphere and good dispersion of pollutants.

Mixing heights usually are lowest late at night or early morning and highest during mid to late afternoon. This daily pattern often causes smoke to be concentrated in basins and valleys during the morning and dispersed aloft in the afternoon. Average night mixing heights range from 300 m (~980 ft) to over 900 m (~2,900 ft) above ground level. The highest morning mixing heights occur in coastal areas that are influenced by moist marine air and cloudiness that inhibit radiation cooling at night.

4. Lapse rate, $\dfrac{\Delta T}{\Delta Z} = \dfrac{T_2 - T_1}{Z_2 - Z_1}$

$$\frac{1.25}{100} = \frac{T_2 - 15°C}{200 - 25}$$

$$\frac{1.25}{100} = \frac{T_2 - 15}{175}$$

$$T_2 - 15 = \frac{1.25 \times 175}{100}$$

$$T_2 - 15 = 2.1875$$

$$T_2 = 15 + 2.1875$$

$$\Rightarrow \quad T_2 = 17.1875°.$$

5. **Unstable Atmosphere :** If the temperature of the atmosphere falls at a rate greater than Γ, the lapse rate is said to be *superadiabatic,* and the atmosphere is unstable. Using Figure, we can see that this is so. The actual lapse rate is shown by the solid line. If we capture a balloon full of polluted air at elevation A and adiabatically displace it 100 m vertically to elevation B, the temperature of the air inside the balloon will decrease from 21.15° to 20.15°C. At a lapse rate of –1.25°C/100 m, the temperature of the air outside the balloon

will decrease from 21.15° to 19.90°C. The air inside the balloon will be warmer than the air outside; this temperature difference gives the balloon buoyancy. It will behave as a hot gas and continue to rise without any further mechanical effort. Thus, mechanical turbulence is enhanced and the atmosphere is unstable. If we adiabatically displace the balloon downward to elevation C, the temperature inside the balloon would rise at the rate of the dry adiabat. Thus, in moving 100 m, the temperature will increase from 21.15° to 22.15°C. The temperature outside the balloon will increase at the superadiabatic lapse rate to 22.40°C. The air in the balloon will be cooler than the ambient air and the balloon will have a tendency to sink. Again, mechanical turbulence (displacement) is enhanced.

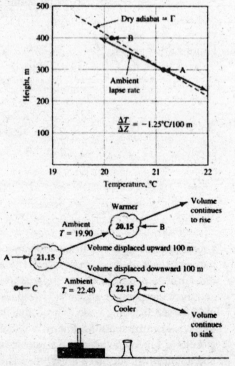

Fig. : *Unstable atmosphere*

6. The photosynthetic fixation rate of atmospheric carbon dioxide is called gross primary productivity (GPP). Net primary productivity (NPP) is the net rate of carbon gain after respiration losses (R). This can be expressed as: NPP = GPP – R. Net production, which accumulates as biological mass in plant organs over time, is referred to as biomass and can be expressed in terms of dry weight (g) or energy content (kcal). The overall photosynthetic efficiency of plants, measured as the amount of solar energy available to them that they actually covert to biomass is typically about 1% or less.

7. The hydroxyl radical (OH) is one of the most important of the trace species in the troposphere, even though its globally averaged concentration is only a few tenths of a pptv ($\sim 10^{12}$ OH m^{-3}; or 3OH per 10^{13} air molecules).

The hydroxyl radical is produced by the high-energy photodissociation of ozone:

$O_3 + h\nu \rightarrow O_2 + O(^1D)$ ($\lambda < 320$ nm)

Here, $O(^1D)$ is an excited state of the oxygen atom. We should know that the stratospheric ozone layer absorbs almost all photons with wavelengths less than ~300 nm, steadily decreasing amounts of radiation up to ~330 nm.

8. By convention, the groups in the periodic tables are assigned certain names:
   - group 1 – "alkali metals"
   - group 2 – "alkaline earth metals"
   - group 3 to 12 – "transition metals"
   - group 13 – "boron group elements"
   - group 14 – "carbon group elements"
   - group 15 – "pnictogens"
   - group 16 – "chalcogens"
   - group 17 – "halogens"
   - group 18 – "noble gases".

9. (i) Carbon-13 isotope, is less common in vegetation or fossil fuels formed from long-dead vegetation and is more abundant in carbon found in the oceans and in volcanic or geothermal emissions.
   (ii) C-12 for the most common carbon isotope and C-14 for the rare isotope.
   (iii) C-14 is absent in fossil fuels.
   (iv) C-13 is not used for carbon-dating.

10. Aldicarb : Technically pure aldicarb is a white crystal, and sparingly miscible in water and most organic solvents. For instance, the solubility of aldicarb in acetone is 34%, in ethanol 25%, and in toluene 10%. Aldicarb is extremely toxic to animals. The acute oral and dermal LD_{50} value for rat is 0.6 to 0.8 mg/kg and 2.5 to 3.0 mg/kg respectively. The female rat is more sensitive than the male rat.

11. Given that, $[H^+] = 5 \times 10^{-4}$ mol/L
and from $\quad K_w = [H^+][OH^-]$
where K_w is the dissociation constant for water
At 25°C, $\quad K_w = 1 \times 10^{-14}$

$$1 \times 10^{-14} = 5 \times 10^{-4} \times [OH^-]$$

$$[OH^-] = \frac{1 \times 10^{-14}}{5 \times 10^{-4}}$$

$$= 2 \times 10^{-11} \text{ mol/L}$$

13. Effluent : The mobile phase that exits the column.

Eluate : The solute-mobile phase mixture which exits the column.

Eluent : Another word for the mobile phase.

Eluite : The eluted solute.

Elute : The use of elution chromatography.

Elution : The passing of mobile phase through the chromatographic bed to transport solutes.

15. Characteristics of Successful Invasive Plant Species : Rapid growth and early flowering. ● Able to cope with a range of nutritional conditions. ● High phenotypic plasticity. ● Different growth forms depending on the ecosystem type. ● Large numbers of seeds produced that are easily dispersed. ● Seed set in a wide range of temperatures and photo-periods. ● Germination "polymorphisms" (i.e., some germinate early, some late).

16.

Antimicrobial action	Examples of antibiotics
Antimetabolites interrupt metabolic pathways causing death, such as blocking nucleic acid synthesis	Sulphonamides
Cell wall agents prevent formation of cross-linking in cell walls so bacteria are killed by lysis (bursting)	Beta-lactams, e.g., penicillins, glycopeptides
Cell membrane agents damage the cell membrane, so metabolites leak out or water moves in, killing the bacteria	Some penicillins, cephalosporins
Protein synthesis inhibitors interrupt or prevent transcription and/or translation of microbial genes, so protein production is affected	Tetracyclines, chloramphenicol
DNA gyrase inhibitors stop bacterial DNA coiling up so it no longer fits within the bacterium	Quinolone

17. El Nino is a climate cycle in the Pacific Ocean with a global impact on weather patterns. The cycle begins when warm water in the western tropical Pacific Ocean shifts eastward along the equator toward the coast of South America. Normally, this warm water pools near Indonesia and the Philippines. As a result of El Nino, it has been observed that phyto-plankton productivity increases in Eastern Indian Ocean around Indonesia and Gulf of Mexico. This increase is probably because of increase in rainfall and more nutrient inflow.

18. Vermicompost is the product of the composting process using various species of worms, usually red wigglers, white worms, and other earthworms, to create a heterogeneous mixture of decomposing vegetable or food waste, bedding materials, and vermicast. This process of producing vermicompost is called vermicomposting. Vermicast (also called worm castings, worm humus or worm manure) is the end-product of the breakdown of organic matter by an earthworm. These castings have been shown to contain reduced levels of contaminants and a higher saturation of nutrients than do organic materials before vermicomposting. Vermicompost contains water-soluble nutrients and is an excellent, nutrient-rich organic fertilizer and soil conditioner. It is used in farming and small scale sustainable, organic farming.

19. Photosynthesis in green plants results in the conversion of simple substances like CO_2 and H_2O into an enormously complex organism. There is a very large decrease in entropy associated with the growth of a plant, but it comes at the expense of an enormous increase in entropy in the Sun to produce the light that is essential for photosynthesis to occur. It is a pessimistic but accurate view that anything we do will always add to the disorder of the universe.

20. Aerobiology is a branch of science which studies these airborne bio-particles with respect to their source, take off, dispersal, deposition and their effect on other organisms. Pollen grains and fungal spores form an important constituent of airspora (airborne spores) all over the world. The atmosphere also contains an incredible diversity of pollen grains and fungal spores and they are very light weight. Pollen grains are amongst the earliest known aeroallergens and are found to be the major cause of bronchial asthma and allergic rhinitis. Seasonal pollen grains and fungal spores are the most predominant allergens in the air.

21. In biology, altruism refers to behaviour by an individual that increases the fitness of another individual while decreasing the fitness of the actor. Altruism in this sense is different from the philosophical concept of altruism, in which an action would only be called "altruistic" if it was done with the conscious intention of helping another. In the behavioural sense, there is no such requirement. As such, it is not evaluated in moral terms—it is the consequences of an action for reproductive fitness that determine whether the action is considered altruistic, not the intentions, if any, with which the action is performed.

22. Edge effects were seen in the majority of species; however, the magnitude of these effects was influenced by the ecotone type. At the assemblage level, more species avoided edges in the ecotone with tree plantations compared with open habitats. The effect of edges on the calculated habitat suitability was either positive or negative, depending on the function that best described the response of the species to edges and whether they avoided edges or penetrated into the less-preferred habitat. In general, forest species penetrated deeper into tree plantations but moved only short distances into open habitats.

23. **Allogenic succession** is definded as the changes in species composition that are imposed by factors external to the biotic community. Physical factors, which produce allogenic succession, such as fire, wind, snow-storm, flood, landslide, or changes induced by climate change. These processes are controlled by forces external to the ecosystem in question and they cause ecosystem disturbance—they alter the rates and patterns of ecosystem change expected from autogenic succession.

24. In the boreal forests, tree stands, mosses and dwarf shrubs produce the majority of the litterfall, which becomes a component of humus as it decomposes.

25. The term cyclomorphosis has been applied to the cyclic morphological changes that supposedly occur with fairly strict seasonality in certain freshwater plankton. Seasonal changes in the morphology within popula- tions involve the alternation of different morphs in time. Forms with external protu- berances e.g., helmets, crests, peaks of the head, humps or spikes of the carapace, spines, elongation of the antennules, usually alternate with forms lacking these exuberances. Cyclomorphosis has been reported for some planktonic algae, rotifers and crustaceans. It ensure adaptive significance and changes in environmental variables of water.

26. A **biofilm** is any group of microorganisms in which cells stick to each other and often these cells adhere to a surface. These adherent cells are frequently embedded within a self-produced matrix of extracellular polymeric substance (EPS). Microbes form a biofilm in response to many factors, which may include cellular recognition of specific or non-specific

attachment sites on a surface, nutritional cues, or in some cases, by exposure of planktonic cells to sub-inhibitory concentrations of antibiotics. When a cell switches to the biofilm mode of growth, it undergoes a phenotypic shift in behaviour in which large suites of genes are differentially regulated.

27. Rhyolitic magma has the greatest silica content, with silica making up about 70 per cent of the magma. Basaltic and andesitic magma have lower silica contents at 50 per cent and 60 per cent, respectively.

Magma with a higher silica content is more viscous, meaning it is thicker and doesn't flow as easily. The more explosive volcanic eruptions are caused by this more viscous magma, which means that rhyolitic magma causes the most explosive eruptions.

Rhyolitic magma contributes to the explosive character of siliceous lava flows and lava domes. The Vulcanian and Plinian types of volcanic eruptions feature rhyolitic magma. Eruptions involving rhyolitic magma produce obsidian and pumice rocks, and rhyolitic volcanoes are typically cinder cone volcanoes.

29. Stream flow or discharge is the volume of water that moves through a specific point in a stream during a given period of time. Discharge is usually measured in units of cubic feet per second (cfs). To determine discharge, a cross-sectional area of the stream or river is measured. Then, the velocity of the stream is measured using a Flow Rate Sensor.

Flow velocity is influenced by the slope of the surrounding terrain, the depth of the stream, the width of the stream, and the roughness of the substrate or stream bottom.

Factors Influencing Flow Velocity:
● Depth of stream channel
● Width of stream channel
● Roughness of stream bottom
● Slope or incline of surrounding terrain

30. Rivers are part of the hydrological cycle. Water generally collects in a river from precipitation through a drainage basin from surface runoff and other sources such as groundwater recharge, springs, and the release of stored water in natural ice and snowpacks

(e.g., from glaciers). Potamology is the scientific study of rivers while limnology is the study of inland waters in general. A river begins at a source (or more often several sources), follows a path called a course, and ends at a mouth or mouths. The water in a river is usually confined to a channel, made up of a stream bed between banks. Head water has the highest erosion rate in the journey of a river.

31. Abrasives are hard substances capable of wearing down soft surfaces by cutting, grinding or polishing action. Some of the commonly used abrasives include diamond, quartz, emery, corundum, carborundum, alundum and boron carbide in the form of powder, paste, sheet, or wheel. The most important property of abrasives is their hardness usually measured in Moh's scale or Vicker's scale. Diamond is rated as the hardest substance with a maximum value of 10 on the Moh's scale. Others in the decreasing order of hardness include corundum. (9) topaz or emery, (8) quartz, (7) feldspar, (6) apatite, (5) fluorite, (4) calcite, (3) gypsum (2) and talc, (1).

32. Wind transport encompasses four processes—saltation, reptation, suspension, and creep (Figure):

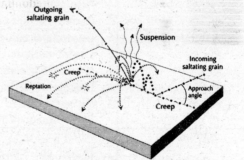

Fig. : *Modes of grain transport by wind.*

1. **Saltation :** Sand grains bound, land, and rebound, imparting, renewed impetus to other sand grains. Such motion is confined to short distances and heights of about 2 m.

2. **Reptation :** On hitting the surface, saltating grains release a small splash-like shower of particles that make small hops from the point of impact. This process is reptation.

3. **Suspension :** Particles of silt and clay lifted into the atmosphere become suspended and may be carried great distances. Sand particles may be lifted into the lower layers of the atmosphere, as in sandstorms, but will fall out near the point of takeoff. Dust particles may be carried around the globe. Dust storms may carry 100 million tonnes of material for thousands of kilometres. A dramatic dust storm, which carried in estimated 2 million tonnes of dust, engulfed Melbourne, Australia, on 8 February 1983.

4. **Creep** and related near-surface activity. Coarse sand and small pebbles inch forward by rolling and sliding with the momentum gained from the impact of jumping sand particles and down the tiny craterslopes produced by an impacting particle.

33. The rates and direction of flow between two points are described by Darcy's law, or

$$Q = -KA \ (dh/dL)$$

where Q is the rate of flow through the media, K is the hydraulic conductivity of the material, A is the total cross-sectional area of the porous medial including both pores and particles, h is the head, and L is the length of the porous media. According to Darcy's law, the rate of ground water movement is proportional to the hydraulic gradient, dh/dL. The proportionality factor, K, is known as the hydraulic conductivity. High values of hydraulic conductivity mean that the material readily transmits water. Among other things, hydraulic conductivity depends on the size, shape, and connectivity of pores and fractures in the aquifer.

34. Characteristics of the Different Ranks of Coals

Rank (from lowest to highest)	Properties
Lignite	1. The lowest rank of coal that has been transformed into a brown-black coal from peat. 2. Contains recognizable plant structures. 3. Excessive moisture (25%–50%). 4. Heating value less than 8300 BTU/lb on a mineral matter free basis. 5. Carbon content between 60% and 70% on a dry ash-free basis.
Sub-bituminous	1. Denser and harder than lignite. 2. Lower moisture content (12%-25%). 3. With higher carbon content (71%-77%) on dry ash-free basis. 4. Heating value much higher than lignite or sub-bituminous coal. 5. On the basis of hating value, it is subdivided into sub-bituminous A. Sub-bituminous B. and sub-bituminous C ranks.
Bituminous	1. Alternate bright and dull bandings. 2. Harder and denser than sub-bituminous coal. 3. Carbon content between 77% and 87% on dry ash-free basis. 4. Heating value much higher than lignite or sub-bituminous coal. 5. On the basis of volatile content, bituminous, coals are subdivided into low volatile bituminous, medium volatile bituminous, and high volatile bituminous.
Anthracite	1. Anthracite is the highest rank of coal. 2. Carbon content over 87% on dry ash-free basis. 3. Anthracite coal generally has the highest heating value per ton on a mineral matter free basis. 4. It is often subdivided into semi-anthracite, anthracite, and meta-anthracite on the basis of carbon content.

37. Natural gas is formed in the earth's crust as a result of transformation of organic matter due to heat and pressure of overlying rock. Natural gas mainly consists of saturated aliphatic hydrocarbons like methane. Components such as carbon dioxide, hydrogen sulphide, nitrogen and helium constitute an insignificant proportion of natural gas composition. Natural gas is the cleanest of all fossil fuels and the main products of combustion of natural gas are carbon dioxide and water vapour. The combustion of natural gas releases very small amounts of nitrogen oxides (NOx), sulphur dioxide (SO_2), carbon dioxide (CO_2), carbon monoxide (CO), other reactive hydrocarbons and virtually no particulate matter.

Natural gas contributes less to smog formation than gasoline. Unburnt CH_4 molecules are considerably less reactive with respect to the free radical chemistry for smog than the hydrocarbon molecules with more than one C atom.

Natural gas can be used in many ways to help reduce the emissions of pollutants into the atmosphere as it emits fewer harmful pollutants and an increased reliance on natural gas can potentially reduce the emission of many of these harmful pollutants.

39. Power generated by the wind in the Betz limit

$$= A \times (V)^3 \times 38\%$$

$$= 25 \times (6)^3 \times \frac{38}{100} \approx 2.064 \text{ kW}.$$

40. Ocean thermal energy conversion (OTEC) uses the temperature difference between cooler deep and warmer shallow or surface seawaters to run a heat engine and produce useful work, usually in the form of electricity. OTEC is a base load electricity generation system.

Among ocean energy sources, OTEC is one of the continuously available renewable energy resources that could contribute to base-load power supply. At tropical sites, the temperatures of warm surface water and cold water in the depth of ocean hardly vary from season to season, and the power output from an OTEC system installed at a tropical site is steady.

43. Disinfection of water:

$$Cl_2 + H_2O \rightleftharpoons HCl + HOCl$$

$$HOCl \rightleftharpoons H^+ + OCl^-$$

The hypochlorous acid (HOCl) and hypochlorite ions (OCl^-) are responsible for the disinfection of water. The action of chlorine is directly proportional to the pH value of water. At high pH value, say above 8.50, chlorine is not a suitable bacterial removal. Disinfection is rapid when pH of water is below 7.0. Chlorine is applied for disinfection as free chlorine, chloramines and bleaching powder.

The term free chlorine is used to indicate the sum of hypochlorous acid, hypochlorite ions and molecular chlorine existing in a sample of water. Free chlorine is available in gaseous or liquid forms. Chlorine is not stable in water, but when it is mixed in water with ammonia, stable compounds known as chloramines are formed. These compounds have adequate and good disinfecting properties and especially used for disinfecting swimming pools. They also remove odour from water to some extent.

46. The process of chemically neutralizing the negative charge on colloidal matter in waste waters to form small floc particles is called "coagulation." Most colloidal suspended matter in water carries a negative charge by nature. It can consist of emulsified oil particles, solid particles, dirt, metal fines, or biological particles. These particles will not settle until this charge is neutralized. Water treatment polymers that carry a positive charge and low molecular weight (coagulants) can be added to the water to neutralize the colloidal charges.

47. Surface water quality classes used in India

Class   Criteria

A   1. Total coliform organisms MPN/100 ml shall be 50 or less.

       2. pH between 6.5 and 8.5

       3. Dissolved oxygen 6 mg/L or more.

       4. BOD 5 days 20°C 2 mg/L or less.

B   1. Total coliform organisms MPN/100 ml 500 or less.

2. pH between 6.5 and 8.5.

3. Dissolved oxygen 5 mg/L or more.

4. BOD 5 days 20°C 3 mg/L or less.

C   1. Total coliform organisms MPN/100 mL 5000 or less.

2. pH between 6 and 9.

3. Dissolved oxygen 4 mg/L or more.

4. BOD 5 days 20°c 3 mg/L or less

D   1. pH between 6.5 and 8.5.

2. Dissolved oxygen 4 mg/L or more.

3. Free ammonia (as N) 1.2 mg/L or less.

E   1. pH between 6.0 and 8.5.

2. Electrical conductivity at 25°C µmhos/cm Max. 2250.

3. Sodium absorption ratio max. 26

4. Boron max. 2 mg/L.

Below-E : Not meeting A, B, C, D & E criteria.

Note : Class A is suitable for drinking water without conventional treatment but after disinfection.

Class B suitable for outdoor bathing (organized).

Class C suitable for drinking water after conventional treatment and disinfection.

Class D suitable for propagation of wild life and fisheries.

Class E suitable for irrigation, industrial cooling controlled waste disposal.

48. Ozone depletion occurs in the Arctic stratosphere, but much less than over Antarctica. The Arctic winter stratosphere has fewer and shorter-lived stratospheric clouds than the Antarctic stratosphere. Thus, assertion is true. The winter Antarctic stratosphere is on the average more than 10 K colder than the Arctic stratosphere, the Antarctic polar vortex lasts longer, and the winter build-up of ozone is weaker. Hence, reason is false.

50. Auditing is a term frequently used to describe a systematic process of examining, documenting, and verifying that EIA procedures and outcomes correspond to its objectives and recommendations. This process can be undertaken during and/or after project construction and draws upon surveillance reports and monitoring data. The main types of audits related to post-decision activities are as follows:

- **Implementation audit :** It essentially "polices" projects to ensure that recommended mitigation measures are in place and operated correctly.

- **Performance audit :** It is regarded as a management activity that examines the response of personnel concerned with the project operation to potential environmental problems and determines whether the actions required to deal with a major environmental incident are satisfactory.

- **Project impact audits :** It is designed to identify environmental changes that have occurred as a consequence of a development.

- **Predictive techniques audit :** It is to assess the accuracy and utility of predictive techniques by a comparison of actual consequences with the predicted environmental impacts of a project.

- **EIA procedure audit :** It includes any or all of the previously mentioned audits with the intention of improving procedures in general rather than individual EIAs.

- **Compliance audit :** It is undertaken to verify that the project complies with environmental standards and regulatory requirements.

52. Environmental Impact Assessment (EIA) is an important tool for integrating the objectives of environmental management into the decision making process to ensure environmentally sound and sustainable development. Earlier, any developmental project/activity were reviewed keeping in view the technical feasibility and financial viability of the project only. However, with the introduction of concept of EIA the environmental considerations have also been included as one of the factors to be considered

while deciding about the feasibility and sustainability of any developmental/industrial project/activity. In fact, the main purpose of EIA is to mitigate adverse environmental impacts of any project/activity and bringing them to an acceptable level and to project the community likely to be affected by the proposed project.

The EIA notification has undergone several amendments incorporating provisions for "Public Hearing" and bringing in several important projects/activities into the purview of EIA, requiring "Environmental Clearance" by Ministry of Environment and Forest (MoEF), Govt of India. To further improve the EIA procedure in India, EIA notification was revised on September 14th, 2006. According to the notification, different projects/developmental activities have been divided into 8 major heads requiring "Environmental Clearance" (EC) either from Central Government, *i.e.,* MoEF (Category 'A') or at State Level from State Environmental Impact Assessment Authority (SEIAA) (Category 'B'). The category 'B' has been further divided into category 'B1' (project requires to submit EIA report) and 'B2' project activities which don't require EIA report). All categories 'A' and 'B1' projects necessarily have to carry out EIA studies along with the "public hearing" as per the procedure stipulated in the notification.

53. Evaporation of surface water is reduced due to black carbon in atmosphere.

Black carbon aerosols absorb incoming solar radiation, which both reduces radiation reaching the surface and cools the surface, but they also warm the troposphere by absorbing solar radiation with peak heating at 2–6 km in the atmosphere. The effect of cooling the surface and warming above is to make the atmosphere more stable, which tends to reduce precipitation as well. These aerosol effects taken together can lead to a weaker hydrological cycle, a weaker monsoon circulation, less freshwater availability, and drought. In addition, black carbon aerosols

nucleate more cloud droplets, making the clouds more reflective and less efficient in producing precipitation. These effects have been noted in southern Asia, where there is a persistent brown haze due to aerosols from biomass burning and fossil fuel consumption. Hence, reason is correctly explain the assertion.

54. **Ad Hoc methods :** This is the most common approach to impact assessment. Basically ad hoc methods indicate broad areas of likely impact by listing composite environmental parameters (for example, flora and fauna) likely to be affected by development activities.

Checklist Methods : Checklists annotate the environmental features or factors that need to be addressed when identifying the impacts of projects and activities. They can vary in complexity and purpose, from a simple checklist to a structured methodology or system that also assigns significance by scaling and weighting the impacts.
Checklists provide a systematized means of identifying impacts. They also have been developed for application to particular types of projects and categories of impacts (such as dams or road building)

Networks Methods : Networks illustrate the cause-effect relationship of project activities and environmental characteristics. They are, therefore, particularly useful in identifying and depicting secondary impacts (indirect, cumulative, etc). Simplified networks, used in conjunction with other methods, help to ensure that important second-order impacts are not omitted from the investigation.

Overlays Methods : Overlays and geographic information systems Overlays can be used to map impacts spatially and display them pictorially.
A modern version of the overlay method is the computer-based geographical information system (GIS). In simple terms, a GIS stores, retrieves, manipulates and displays environmental data in a spatial format. A set of maps or overlays of a given area provide different types of information and scales of

resolution. The use of GIS for EIA purposes is not as widespread as commonly imagined. The main drawbacks are the lack of appropriate data and the expense of creating a usable system.

55. Baseline studies will characterize and document the existing environmental conditions prior to development. Those environmental elements that have a likelihood of being affected by the proposed project will be the focus of data collection. Knowledge of baseline environmental conditions is important for two reasons: first, to form a basis for the assessment and second, to provide a record of initial conditions, which will be essential both during operations, and when project decommissioning takes place.

In the baseline Studies, the environmental assessment will include a description of the project location on a national, regional and local basis with increasingly more detailed maps. The regional and local geology and geography lead into a description of the local terrestrial habitat. Descriptions of climate, surface water hydrology, hydrogeology, soil, water and air quality, and natural radiological conditions are required in the baseline document. Any rare or endangered animal or plant species in the area of the project must be identified. A description of resource use including land use, agriculture, livestock, wildlife harvesting, fishing, tourism, etc. is also an integral part of the document. Finally, a description of the socio-economic environment indicating the inhabitants of the areas potentially impacted areas and the nature of their livelihood and culture will round out the description of baseline conditions.

56. The goals and objectives of a river restoration are to identify, usually in a short but clear sentence, the desired outcome or results of any action to restore the river. This is a critical step in the overall planning process in order to avoid failed or poorly performing restoration as well as to evaluate the restoration project after the completion of the project. General and broad scopes and expressions of the objectives can make the project team lose focus and how well to perform for the restoration. Narrowing the objectives reduces any ambiguity for the project team. The objectives of river restoration should be:
● Specific ● Realistic ● Achievable ● Measurable

57. The Lotka–Volterra equations can also be written in a more general form for a community composed of n different species:

$$\frac{dN_i}{dt} = r_i N_i \left(\frac{\{K_i - N_i - \Sigma \alpha_{ij} N_j\}}{K_i} \right)$$

where the i and j subscripts denote species and range from 1 to n and the summation is from 1 to n over all other species.

Implicit in the Lokta-Volterra competition equations are a number of assumptions; some can be relaxed, although the Mathematics rapidly become unmanageable. Maximal rates of increase, competition coefficients, and carrying capacities are all assumed to be constant and immutable; they do not vary with population densities, community composition, or anything else. As a result, all inhibitory relationships within and between populations are strictly linear, and every N_1 individual is identical as is every N_2 individual.

Also there is no time lag in this equation.

59. For maximum sustainable yield

$$\frac{dy}{dN} = 0$$

Here,

$$y = \frac{dN}{dt} = 0.1 \, N - 0.001 \, N^2$$

$$\frac{dy}{dN} = 0.1 - 0.001 \, (2N)$$

So, $0.1 - 0.002N = 0 \Rightarrow N = \dfrac{0.1}{0.002} = 50.$

60. Some countries set minimum heights for industrial stacks (chimneys) on the assumption that the taller the stack the greater the dispersion of pollutants away from the point of origin. Wind speeds normally increase with height, so tall stacks emit pollutants into stronger winds, which encourage dispersion and dilution. Tall stacks are needed for industrial plants located in valleys and basins because these locations are prone to low-level temperature inversions. The tall stacks enable

emitted plumes to penetrate an inversion. Thus assertion is true.

For continuous source the following type of Gaussian Distribution is assumed normally.

$$C(x, y, z) = \frac{Q}{\pi \sigma_y \sigma_z \bar{u}} \exp - \left\{ \left(\frac{h^2}{2\sigma_z^2} \right) + \left(\frac{y^2}{2\sigma_y^2} \right) \right\}$$

Where,

- C = Concentration (g/m^3)
- Q = Pollutant release rate (g/s)
- σ_y, σ_z = Crosswind and vertical plume standard deviations (m)
- $\bar{u}$ = Mean wind speed (m/s) at h_s, the height of the stack
- h = Effective stack height (m)
- x, y = Downwind and crosswind distances.

From the above equation it is seen that C, the ground level (Z = 0) concentration of a pollutant at a point (x, y) downwind from a source is proportional to the rate of emission (Q). Further, it is inversely proportional to the wind speed ($\bar{u}$), and to the parameters σ_y and σ_z. Also, it can be shown that the maximum ground level concentration of a gaseous pollutant is inversely proportional to the square of the effective stack height.

Hence, reason is false.

62. Given datas: Mean $(\bar{X})$ = 5.667

Standard deviation (S) = 0.934

Population mean (μ) = 5.2

Sample size (n) = 16

Test statistic = ?

From formula

Test statistic (z)

$$= \frac{\bar{X} - \mu}{\dfrac{S}{\sqrt{n}}} = \frac{5.667 - 5.2}{\dfrac{0.934}{\sqrt{16}}} = \frac{0.467}{\dfrac{0.934}{4}}$$

$$= \frac{0.467}{0.2335} = 2.$$

63. Methane (CH_4) is one of the most widespread greenhouse gases (GHGs) emitted from paddy fields and other sources such as wetlands, ruminants, coal mines as well as anthropogenic activities such as leakage from natural gas systems and the raising of livestocks.

The concentration of CH_4 in the atmosphere is increasing due to discrepancy in CH_4 emanation and its removal. The lifetime of CH_4 in the atmosphere in 8–12 years, but it is more efficient in trapping radiation and 23–30 times more potential than CO_2 Global surface temperature has increased by 0.8 °C in the last 100 years and CH_4 also contributed to this phenomenon as a potent GHG.

64. All over the world, efforts are on to save the ozone layer. The United Nations formed a committee which drafted an agreement that calls for a stepwise reduction of CFCs. This agreement, called the Montreal Protocol, came into effect in 1987. Under this legally binding agreement, the consumption and production of CFCs and halons is to be stopped within a stipulated time. The committee keeps a regular check on the amount of ozone depleting substances in the world. It also provides technical and financial assistance to developing countries to reduce CFC consumption. Under the Montreal Protocol, all the signatory countries have to assess their consumption and production of ODS every year.

65. Typical values for the ratio of BOD/COD for untreated municipal wastewater are in the range from 0.3 to 0.8. If the BOD/COD ratio for untreated wastewater is 0.5 or greater, the waste is considered to be easily treatable by biological means. If the ratio is below about 0.3, either the waste may have some toxic components or acclimated microorganisms may be required in its stabilization. The corresponding BOD/TOC ratio for untreated wastewater varies from 1.2 to 2.0. In using these ratios it important to remember that they will change significantly with the degree of treatment the waste has undergone, as reported in Table.

Type of wastewater	BOD/COD	BOD/TOC
Untreated	0.3–0.8	1.2–2.0
After primary settling	0.4–0.6	0.8–1.2
Final effluent	0.1–0.3A[a]	0.2–0.5[b]

a : CBOD/COD

b : CBOD/TOC

66. Organic soils, or histosols, develop under conditions of almost continuous saturation where drainage is poor, anaerobic conditions prevail, and litter production exceeds decomposition. If soils become deficient in oxygen because they are waterlogged, oxidation of organic matter is limited and rate of decomposition slows because anaerobic decomposition processes are much less efficient than aerobic ones.

Organic soils typically have lower bulk density (dry weight per volume less than 1 g/cm^3) and a higher porosity (volume of water held per volume of soil) and higher water holding capacity than mineral soils. Consequently, flooded organic soils can often hold more water than flooded mineral soils. In spite of higher porosity, organic soils may have low to high hydraulic conductivities, indicating that they may impede horizontal or vertical groundwater flows. Thus, organic soils can act as an aquitard to seal a wetland and increase hydroperiod. Organic soils typically have a lower stock of available plant nutrients than mineral soils and are less capable of storing some cations and anions in wastewater effluents.

67. Ozone is constantly being produced and destroyed in a natural cycle in the environment.
Large increases in stratospheric chlorine and bromine, however, have upset that balance. In effect, they have added a siphon downstream, removing ozone faster than natural ozone creation reactions can keep up. Therefore, ozone levels fall.
Research has shown that ozone depletion occurs over the latitudes that include North America, Europe, Asia and much of Africa, Australia and South America. Over the U.S., ozone levels have fallen 5–10%, depending on the season. Thus, ozone depletion is a global issue and not just a problem at the South Pole. Reductions in ozone levels will lead to higher levels of UVB reaching the Earth's surface. The sun's output of UVB does not change; rather, less ozone means less protec-tion, and hence more UVB reaches the Earth. Studies have shown that in the Antarctic, the amount of UVB measured at the surface can double during the annual ozone hole.

68. **Estuarine ecology :** River mouths, coastal bays, tidal marshes and any other semi-enclosed coastal body of water which is influenced by tidal action and in which sea water is constantly in interaction with fresh-water are called estuaries. Hence they are 'transitional ecotones' between freshwater and marine habitats. Drowned river valleys, ford-type estuaries, bar-built estuaries, estuaries created by tectonic processes and river delta estuaries are some of the types of estuaries. Various estuaries have various amounts of salinity value, some being homogenous, whole others not. Estuaries are highly productive because of their 'being trapped' in between the sea and the freshwater ecosystem.

69. **Composition of the heterosphere**
Above the turbopause (about 100 km), the Earth's atmosphere begins to have a composition that varies with altitude. This is essentially because, in the absence of mixing, the density of a gas falls off exponentially with increasing altitude, at a rate that depends on the molecular mass of the gas. Higher mass constituents, such as oxygen and nitrogen, fall off more quickly than lighter constituents such as helium, molecular hydrogen, and atomic hydrogen. Thus, as the altitude increases in the heterosphere, the atmosphere is dominated successively by helium, molecular hydrogen, and atomic hydrogen. The precise altitude of the heterosphere and the layers it contains varies significantly with temperature.

70. The Kigali deal on HFCs is in fact fiendishly complicated and has taken years to negotiate in various technical and political forums. The final agreement, announced on Saturday morning caps and reduces the use of HFCs in a gradual process beginning in 2019.
Worldwide use of HFCs has soared in the past decade as rapidly growing countries such as

China and India adopted air-conditioning in homes, offices and cars. But HFC gases are thousands of times more destructive to the climate than carbon dioxide, and scientists say their growing use threatens to undermine the Paris accord, agreed last year by 195 countries.

Rich countries, including the US, Japan and Europe, will start phasing out synthetic HFCs in 2019, China in 2024, and India and less ambitious countries in 2028.

71. Hydroxyl radicals are present in the atmosphere at very low concentrations. Since the hydroxyl radical is reformed in the atmospheric photooxidation of hydrocarbons, it effectively acts as a catalyst for the oxidation of hydrocarbons. Figure illustrates the role of the hydroxyl radical in initiating a chain of reactions that oxidize hydrocarbons, forming peroxy radicals that can oxidize NO to NO_2 and re-form hydroxyl radicals. The NO_2 can photolyze, leading to the formation of ozone.

$$NO_2 + OH + M \rightarrow HNO_3 + M$$

NO_2 may also photolyze and produce a ground state O atom, which will go on to produce ozone:

$$NO_2 + hv \rightarrow NO + O \ (\lambda < 410 \text{ nm})$$
$$O_2 + O + M \rightarrow O_3 + M$$

72. The key measurands relate to the composite loading of organic compounds in the water (the sources of which are familiar to us all and need not be detailed) and provide general indicators of pollution level, rather than specific chemical contaminant levels. These are biological oxygen demand (BOD), chemical oxygen demand (COD), total organic carbon (TOC) and dissolved oxygen (DO). Water returned to natural courses with low oxygen levels or with contaminants which consume oxygen significantly will have a damaging effect on the plant and animal life in the water.

BOD is a measure of the biodegradable substances in a sample, COD the oxygen required to oxidise the organic and inorganic substances present. TOC indicates the total carbon compounds present but does not differentiate between degradable and nondegradable compounds. DO in a sample is lowered if BOD or COD are high. Typically, BOD is used to indicate final pollutant load in effluent. Either COD, TOC or DO act as control parameters for the blending and treatment processes. The parameters are related and not usually all measured on the same site.

73. Coal Based Thermal power plants which generated electricity by burning coal releases radioactive materials during it's normal operation. Radioactive leakage may occur from a Nuclear plant, but only due to a fault or damages. Hydroelectric or solar power plants can't produce radioactive materials or toxic bi-products.

74. **Paris Convention 1992:**

Regional Sea Agreements Relevant to Pollution

Two regional agreements focusing on regional sea management may serve as avenues for controlling land-based pollution: Paris Convention for the Protection of the Marine Environment of the North-East Atlantic, 1992 and the Convention on the Protection of the Marine Environment of the Baltic Sea Area, 1992 and this often referred to as the Helsinki Convention, 1992.

The Vienna Convention for the Protection of the Ozone Layer, 1985

The conference of the plenipotentiaries for a Convention for the Protection of the Ozone Layer took place in Vienna on 18-22 March 1985. Thirty-four countries attended the meeting, including ten developing countries. Attending, as observers, were China, industrial organizations – including two from Europe – and the International Chamber of Commerce. The United Nations Industrial Development Organization (UNIDO), WMO, the European Economic Community and OECD were also present. No environmental NGO was present.

Basel Convention 1992

The Basel Convention on the Control of Transboundary Movements of Hazardous Wastes and their Disposal (the Basel Convention) entered into force on 5 May 1992. The Convention regulates the transboundary import and export of hazardous wastes and obliges Parties to ensure that such wastes are managed and disposed of in an environmentally sound manner.

Bamako Convention 1998

Many African states considered the Basel Convention insufficient, and in 1998, the Organization for African Unity adopted the Bamako Convention on the Ban of Import into Africa and the Control of Transboundary Movement and Management of Hazardous Wastes within Africa to address specific regional concerns regarding hazardous waste.

The provisions of the Bamako Convention generally correspond to those of the Basel Convention, with a few important distinctions. First, the Bamako Convention defines waste in a much broader context, including radioactive wastes that are subject to any international control system. Parties must also strive to apply the precautionary approach in their activities. Most importantly, Parties to the Bamako Convention commit to prohibit and criminalize the importation of all hazardous wastes, for any reason, into Africa from non-contracting parties. Additionally, it bans the dumping of hazardous wastes at sea by contracting parties or in internal waters by non-contracting parties, and it requires Parties to impose strict, unlimited liability, along with joint and several liability, on those parties that generate hazardous waste.

75. Table : *Colour-coding system for waste, recommended by the DH*

Colour receptacle	Waste type and management
Yellow	Infectious waste that has an additional characteristic that means that it must be incinerated in a suitably licensed or permitted facility. Examples: anatomical waste, chemically contaminated samples and diagnostic kits, medicinally contaminated infectious waste; and Category A (as specified in the Carriage Regulations) pathogens (often when in culture form) as these are capable of causing permanent disability, life-threatening or fatal disease.
Orange	Infectious waste, for example, incontinence pads, stoma bags and soiled wound dressings where the patient has an infection and the causative agent is likely to be in the waste. For example, the stoma bag of a patient with a gastrointestinal infection. A used wound drain would always go into this waste steam. This waste steam must not contain non-infectious waste or infectious waste with additional characteristics (chemicals, medicines, anatomical waste), which mean it must be incinerated.
Purple	Waste consisting of, or contaminated with cytotoxic and/or cytostatic products.
Yellow with black stripe	Offensive/hygiene waste, such as stoma bags, incontinence pads, catheter bags and soiled wound dressings, when they are not considered infectious. In the community, a patient who is self-managing can put small amounts of these items into their domestic waste stream.
Red	Anatomical waste, which includes recognisable body parts and placenta.
Black (or clear)	Domestic waste which is similar to waste generated at home. Domestic waste should not contain any infectious materials, sharps or medicinal products. Examples: Non-recyclable packaging, such as crisp packets, polystyrene cups, flowers.
Blue	Medicinal waste.

Environmental Science, July-2016*

PAPER-II

Note: *This paper contains **fifty (50)** objective type questions of **two (2)** marks each. **All questions are compulsory.***

1. Photoionization of gas molecules maintain the temperature profile of which atmospheric layer?
   A. Troposphere   B. Stratosphere
   C. Mesosphere   D. Thermosphere

2. Around the mid latitude, the surface winds are generally
   A. Gradient   B. Geostrophic
   C. Subgeostrophic   D. Cyclonic

3. How many biogeographic regions are reported to exist in India?
   A. Five   B. Seven
   C. Ten   D. Three

4. Energy transfer and nutrient flow through various trophic levels can be described as
   A. Linear
   B. Cyclic
   C. Linear and cyclic respectively
   D. Cyclic and linear respectively

5. The highest rate at which individuals can be harvested without reducing the population size is called maximum sustainable yield of a
   A. Population   B. Community
   C. Ecosystem   D. Landscape

6. Leslie matrix population model is generally used to determine
   (a) the growth of population.
   (b) the age distribution within population over time.
   (c) the prey-predator interactions.

Choose the correct answer:
A. (a) only   B. (a) and (c) only
C. (b) and (c) only   D. (a) and (b) only

7. If ΔN_n is equal to production of new individual in the population, Δt and N represent time and initial number of individuals of a population, then natality rate per unit of population is

   A. $\dfrac{\Delta N_n}{\Delta t}$ B. $\dfrac{\Delta N_n}{N\Delta t}$

   C. $\Delta N_n - N\Delta t$ D. $\dfrac{N\Delta t}{\Delta N_n}$

8. In a health survey, 38 of 120 men and 24 of 80 women are found to be affected by nicotine by smoking. What is the probability of a randomly selected male being a smoker?
   A. 0.32   B. 0.19
   C. 0.38   D. 0.12

9. If for a sample size (N) of 64, the mean $(\bar{X})$ and standard deviation (SD) are found to be 82 and 6. Then standard error (SE) for the mean is
   A. 0.75   B. 0.14
   C. 10.4   D. 2.2

10. 'Public hearing' is not mandatory for project like
    A. building construction project
    B. mining project
    C. oil refinery project
    D. river valley project

11. The preparedness for prevention of chemical accidents and emergency in industry should be made according to the statutory framework of
    (*a*) The National Environmental Tribunal Act, 1975
    (*b*) The Public Liability Insurance Act, 1991
    (*c*) The Factories Act, 1948
    (*d*) The Water (Prevention and Control of Pollution) Act, 1974
    Choose the correct answer:
    A. (*a*), (*b*) and (*c*) only
    B. (*b*), (*c*) and (*d*) only
    C. (*b*) and (*c*) only
    D. (*a*), (*b*), (*c*) and (*d*)

12. The term (life) of a patent from the date of filing is
    A. 5 years   B. 100 years
    C. 20 years   D. 50 years

13. According to the Hazardous Waste (Management and Handling) Rules, 1989, the limit for Polyaromatic Hydrocarbons (PAH) in waste oil suitable for recycling should be less than
    A. 8%   B. 10%
    C. 6%   D. 15%

14. The main objectives of the Wildlife (Protection) Act, 1972 are
    (*a*) Restricting hunting, killing or overexploitation of species.
    (*b*) Protection of wildlife, preservation of natural habitats and environment.
    (*c*) Recognizing the right of people to a healthy environment.
    Choose the correct answer:
    A. (*a*) and (*b*) only   B. (*b*) and (*c*) only
    C. (*a*) and (*c*) only   D. (*a*), (*b*) and (*c*)

15. The signing ceremony of Paris agreement on climate change was held on April 22, 2016 at UN headquarters. The agreement will be open for signatures by the countries till
    A. December 22, 2016
    B. April 21, 2017
    C. December 21, 2017
    D. March 21, 2018

16. The committee, which reviews the EIA and EMP reports of developmental projects in Ministry of Environment, Forest and Climate Change, is called
    A. Project Assessment Committee
    B. Environment Appraisal Committee
    C. Project Evaluation Committee
    D. Environmental Clearance Committee

17. In EIA, after official notification, time given to hold public hearing is
    A. 10 days   B. 15 days
    C. 30 days   D. 50 days

18. The corporate social responsibility has been made mandatory since
    A. 2010   B. 2014
    C. 2015   D. 2013

19. The guiding principles for the National Land Utilization Policy are as follows:
    (*a*) Inclusive growth, poverty eradication and gender equality – equal opportunities.
    (*b*) Balanced development and intergenerational justice.
    (*c*) Efficient utilization of resources and mitigation of impacts.
    (*d*) Integrated and comprehensive development planning.
    Choose the correct answer:
    A. (*a*) and (*b*) only
    B. (*a*), (*b*) and (*c*) only
    C. (*b*), (*c*) and (*d*) only
    D. (*a*), (*b*), (*c*) and (*d*)

20. Degradation of different categories of pesticides by soil microorganism is called
    A. Biotransformation
    B. Biomineralization
    C. Bioaugmentation
    D. Biomagnification

21. Given below are two statements. One labelled as Assertion (A) and the other labelled as Reason (R):
    Assertion (A) : CO can contribute to the photochemical smog problem in cities.
    Reason (R) : It aids in formation of surface ozone.

Choose the correct answer:

A. Both (A) and (R) are correct and (R) is the correct explanation of (A).

B. Both (A) and (R) are correct and (R) is not the correct explanation of (A).

C. (A) is true but (R) is false.

D. (A) is false but (R) is true.

22. For spherical aerosol particles smaller than about 30 μm and with density much greater than air, their settling velocity varies with their size (d) as

A. $\propto d$

B. $\propto d^{-1}$

C. $\propto d^{-2}$

D. $\propto d^2$

23. Given below are two statements. One labelled as Assertion (A) and the other labelled as Reason (R):

Assertion (A) : Sound barriers alongside motorways in urban areas are very effective in controlling noise.

Reason (R) : They act as reflectors of sound back into motorways and upwards.

Choose the correct answer:

A. Both (A) and (R) are correct and (R) is the correct explanation of (A).

B. Both (A) and (R) are correct and (R) is not the correct explanation of (A).

C. (A) is true but (R) is false.

D. (A) is false but (R) is true.

24. The effect of sulphate aerosol in the Earth's atmosphere is to

A. decrease precipitation

B. destroy ozone

C. cool global climate

D. warm global climate

25. Solar radiation of average energy ~ 1.25 eV and intensity 500 W/m^2 are incident on the surface of a solar flat plate collector. What is the approximate photon flux density impinging on the surface of the collector?

A. ~ 5×10^{22} photons $m^{-2} s^{-1}$

B. ~ 2×10^{22} photons $m^{-2} s^{-1}$

C. ~ 2.5×10^{20} photons $m^{-2} s^{-1}$

D. ~ 2.5×10^{21} photons $m^{-2} s^{-1}$

26. A solar pond based electricity generation plant has an efficiency of 5% and power output of 500 mW. If the solar insolation is 1000 W/m^2, what is the area of solar pond?

A. 5 km^2

B. 10 km^2

C. 1.0 km^2

D. 20 km^2

27. Intended nationally determined contribution of India envisages reduction in carbon intensity by 2030 below 2005 level by what percentage?

A. 22–25 %

B. 33–35 %

C. 35–40 %

D. 40–50 %

28. By the year 2022, India's target of producing power from wind energy is

A. 50 GW

B. 60 GW

C. 75 GW

D. 120 GW

29. Which among the following surfaces has maximum albedo?

A. Leafy crops

B. Dry sand

C. Calm sea water

D. Dark asphalt

30. A wetland ecosystem has a very high Biological Oxygen Demand (BOD). Which of the following statement about such a wetland is correct?

A. It has high level of microbial pollution.

B. It has very low level of microbial pollution.

C. There is no microbial pollution.

D. It is highly turbid.

31. Desertification is the process of

A. increase in desert area

B. sand dune movement

C. land degradation

D. arid zone management

32. Ecological restoration is the process of rebuilding a degraded ecosystem till

A. it becomes pollution free and provides solace to the people.

B. it becomes free of disturbance.

C. its structure and functions are restored.

D. it starts providing some ecosystem services.

33. Consider the following four statements about wetland ecosystems:

(a) They are the transitional zones between terrestrial and aquatic ecosystems.

(b) They are highly productive.

(c) They are the source of greenhouse gases.

(d) They normally occur in the floodplain of rivers.

Choose the correct answer:

A. (a) and (b) only

B. (a), (b) and (c) only

C. (b), (c) and (d) only

D. (a), (b), (c) and (d)

34. In soil conservation programme, the tillage where residues of previous crops are left in the soil is called

A. Reduced tillage

B. No tillage

C. Conservation tillage

D. Contour plowing

35. Which of the following will provide the most valuable information for determining risk of mass wasting of an area?

A. Seismometer

B. Analysis of stereo satellite data

C. Measurement of acceleration due to gravity

D. Geological map of the region

36. The rapid downslope movement of ice or snow is called as

A. Mudflow   B. Solifluction

C. Lahars   D. Avalanches

37. The landform created by subglacial meltwater is known as

A. Moraine   B. Eskers

C. Cirques   D. Kames

38. Among the following gases, which is not emitted by volcano?

A. NO_x B. SO_x

C. CO_2 D. H_2S

39. In remote sensing, ground truth data is generally required for

(a) calibration of sensor

(b) analysis of remotely sensed data

(c) accuracy assessment

Choose the correct answer:

A. (a) only   B. (b) and (c) only

C. (a), (b) and (c) D. (a) and (b) only

40. A species the population of which is low enough for it to be at risk of becoming extinct, but not low enough that it is in imminent danger of extinction is called

A. Endangered species B. Threatened species

C. Vulnerable species D. Rare species

41. Landscape mosaic comprises

A. matrices and patches

B. patches and corridors

C. matrices, patches and corridors

D. matrices and corridors

42. Which of the following country is not a megadiversity centre of biodiversity?

A. Columbia   B. India

C. Brazil   D. Argentina

43. Sclerophyllous leaves are the characteristic features of

A. Chaparral Vegetation

B. Grassland Vegetation

C. Tropical Vegetation

D. Alpine Vegetation

44. Among the plants listed below, which is not producing allergenic pollen grain?

A. Mango   B. Neem

C. Fan Palm   D. Pine

45. A species having a dominating influence on the structure and function of a community or ecosystem is known as

A. Fundamental species

B. Functional species

C. Keystone species

D. Indicator species

46. Which of the following trace atmospheric gases is not an acid rain precursor?

A. Dimethyl sulphide B. Hydrogen sulphide

C. Nitrous oxide   D. Nitric oxide

47. According to WHO report 2015, out of 20 most polluted cities of the world, India has

A. 12   B. 18

C. 10   D. 13

48. With respect to sea, increase in CO_2 abundance is not responsible for which of the following?

A. Increase in pH of sea water.

B. Increase in concentration of bicarbonate ions.
C. Coral bleaching.
D. Enhanced dissolution of calcareous materials.

49. Elements that cycle in the environment and that also have a gaseous phase at some point in their cycle include which of the following?
(a) Phosphorus

(b) Sulphur
(c) Carbon
Choose the correct answer:
A. (a) only   B. (b) only
C. (b) and (c) only   D. (a) and (c) only

50. Poor aeration and high water holding capacity are characteristic features of
A. Sandy soil   B. Loam soil
C. Clay soil   D. Sandy Loam soil

ANSWERS

1	2	3	4	5	6	7	8	9	10
D	B	C	C	C	D	B	B	A	A
11	12	13	14	15	16	17	18	19	20
A	C	C	D	B	B	C	B	D	A
21	22	23	24	25	26	27	28	29	30
A	D	C	C	D	B	B	B	B	A
31	32	33	34	35	36	37	38	39	40
C	C	D	C	C	D	B	A	C	B
41	42	43	44	45	46	47	48	49	50
C	D	A	A	C	C	D	A	C	C

EXPLANATORY ANSWERS

1. The **thermosphere** is the layer of the Earth's atmosphere directly above the mesosphere and directly below the exosphere. Within this layer of the atmosphere, ultraviolet radiation causes photoionization/photo-dissociation of molecules, creating ions in the ionosphere.

2. The **geostrophic wind** is the theoretical wind that would result from an exact balance between the Coriolis effect and the pressure gradient force. This condition is called geostrophic balance.

The geostrophic wind neglects frictional effects, which is usually a good approximation for the synoptic scale instantaneous flow in the midlatitude mid-troposphere. Although ageostrophic terms are relatively small, they are essential for the time evolution of the flow and in particular are necessary for the growth and decay of storms.

3. Biogeographic classification of India is the division of India according to biogeographic characteristics. Biogeography is the study of the distribution of species (biology), organisms, and ecosystems in geographic space and through geological time. There are ten biogeographic zones in India.
   1. Trans Himalayan zone,
   2. Himalayan zone,
   3. Desert zone,
   4. Semiarid zone,
   5. Western ghat zone,
   6. Deccan plateau zone,
   7. Gangetic plain zone,
   8. North east zone,
   9. Coastal zone, and
   10. Islands present near the shore line.

5. In population ecology and economics, maximum sustainable yield or MSY is

theoretically, the largest yield (or catch) that can be taken from a species' stock over an indefinite period. Fundamental to the notion of sustainable harvest, the concept of MSY aims to maintain the population size at the point of maximum growth rate by harvesting the individuals that would normally be added to the population, allowing the population to continue to be productive indefinitely. Under the assumption of logistic growth, resource limitation does not constrain individuals' reproductive rates when populations are small, but because there are few individuals, the overall yield is small. MSY is extensively used for fisheries management.

6. In applied mathematics, the Leslie matrix is a discrete, age-structured model of population growth that is very popular in population ecology. The Leslie matrix (also called the Leslie model) is one of the most well known ways to describe the growth of populations (and their projected age distribution), in which a population is closed to migration, growing in an unlimited environment, and where only one sex, usually the female, is considered.

The Leslie matrix is used in ecology to model the changes in a population of organisms over a period of time. In a Leslie model, the population is divided into groups based on age classes.

9. **Standard Error Formula:**

$$SE_{\bar{x}} = \frac{s}{\sqrt{n}}$$

where,

$SE_{\bar{x}}$ = Standard Error of the Mean

s = Standard Deviation of the Mean

n = Number of Observations of the Sample

From question,

$s = 6, n = 64$

$$SE_{\bar{x}} = \frac{6}{\sqrt{64}} = \frac{6}{8} = 0.75$$

10. The concept of Public Hearing was introduced for the first time in the Environment Impact Assessment *vide* Notification S.O. 60 (E) dated 27.01.1994 and subsequently formalized *vide* Notification S.O. 318 (E) dated 10.04.1997 making amendment in the Environment Impact Assessment Notification, 1994. Whereas, the Industrial Estates were added in the Schedule to the EIA Notification mandating the requirement of environmental clearance *vide* notification S.O. 801 (E) dated 7.07.2004. In between, the above two notifications, another notification No. S.O. 737 (E) dated 1st August, 2001 introducing the concept of exemption from public hearing for certain category of projects and activities in the process of environmental clearance was published. The said notification reads as "However, Public Hearing is not required in respect of (*i*) small scale industrial undertakings located in (*a*) notified/designated industrial areas/industrial estates or (*b*) areas earmarked for industries under the jurisdiction of industrial development authorities; (*ii*) widening and strengthening of Highways; (*iii*) mining projects (major minerals) with lease area up to twenty-five hectares (*iv*) units located in Export Processing Zones, Special Economic Zones and (*v*) Modernization of existing irrigation projects."

12. The term of a patent is the maximum period during which it can be maintained in force. It is usually expressed in a number of years either starting from the filing date of the patent application or from the date of grant of the patent.

"The term of protection available (for patents) shall not end before the expiration of a period of twenty years counted from the filing date."

Consequently, in most patent laws nowadays, the term of patent is 20 years from the filing date of the application. This however does not forbid the states party to the WTO from providing, in their national law, other type of patent-like rights with shorter terms. Utility models are an example of such rights. Their term is usually 6 or 10 years.

14. Wildlife Protection Act of 1972 is a comprehensive legislation that was enacted by the Government of India in 1972. The first comprehensive legislation relating to protection of wild life was passed by the Parliament and it was assented by the President on 9th September, 1972 and came to be known as The Wild Life (Protection) Act, 1972.

Objective of Wildlife Protection Act of 1972

The main objective behind the enactment of Wildlife Protection Act of 1972 was to control poaching and illegal trading of wildlife in the country. The act also aims at providing a powerful legal framework for conserving the wildlife by introduction of regulations such as prohibition of hunting, protection and management of wildlife habitats, establishment of protected areas, regulation and control of trade in parts and products derived from wildlife and management of zoos. The protected areas under the Act are categorized as National Parks, Wildlife Sanctuaries, Tiger Reserves, Conservation Reserves and Community Reserves.

15. The Paris Agreement calls for the Agreement to be open for signature from 22 April, 2016 to 21 April, 2017. To mark the first day that the Agreement will be open for signing (which coincides with Earth Day), United Nations Secretary-General Ban Ki-moon invited leaders from all countries to attend a high-level signing ceremony to accelerate climate action and to drive the political momentum towards ratification and early entry into force of the Paris Agreement.

17. Public Consultation - All Category A and Category B1 projects or activities have to undertake public consultation except for 6 activities for which public consultation has been exempted. Some of the projects exempted include expansion of roads and highways, modernization of irrigation projects, etc. Some of these may have potential, social and environmental impact. The responsibility for conducting the public hearing still lies with the state PCBs. Member-Secretary of the concerned State Pollution Control Board or Union Territory Pollution Control Committee has to finalise the date, time and exact venue for the conduct of public hearing within 30 days of the date of receipt of the draft Environmental Impact Assessment report, and advertise the same in one major National Daily and one Regional vernacular Daily. A minimum notice period of 30 days will be given to the public for furnishing their responses.

The public consultation will essentially consist of two components - a public hearing to ascertain the views of local people and obtaining written responses of interested parties.

18. India became the first country in the world to write CSR into legislation in April 2014, forcing companies to invest in sustainability programs. This should spell great news for development in India but business leaders are split over the effectiveness of such a law.

19. Guiding Principles for the National Land Utilization Policy

1st Principle: *Human beings are at the centre*—Human beings are at the centre of concerns for sustainable development. They are entitled to a healthy and productive life in harmony with nature.

2nd Principle: *Inclusive growth, poverty eradication and gender equality-equal opportunities*—Inclusive growth, poverty eradication and gender equality are indispensable requirements for sustainable development of India, and must be addressed in all policies, plans and programmes.

3rd Principle: *Balanced development and intergenerational justice*—Developmental sectors and activities must be planned in a balanced manner to meet economic, social and environmental needs of present and future generations, and should aim to minimize any large-scale displacement of population.

4th Principle: *Efficient utilisation of resources and mitigation of impacts*—Long-term planning for optimum utilisation of land

and saving scarce land resource is essential and as far as possible, projects should be set up on recycled lands, wastelands, degraded lands or un-irrigated lands provided these are not performing any other important function like biodiversity, water resources etc.

5th Principle: *Integrated and comprehensive development planning*—Development planning must be comprehensive, sustainable, and integrated vertically (national, state, regional and local levels) taking into consideration the interest of all other sectors and stakeholders.

6th Principle: *The States are custodian of land*—States are custodian of land and state governments must eliminate unsustainable patterns of land utilisation/land management and provide necessary legal and institutional support to facilitate capacity building and participatory, transparent and comprehensive land use planning.

7th Principle: *Harmonization with existing policy, legislative and regulatory framework*—The existing constitutional provisions and rights, the existing laws, rules, standards, procedures, guidelines and stipulations brought out by various ministries, departments and institutions of the Government of India, as applicable to land utilisation policy shall continue to be in force for taking decisions on land matters and land use changes.

23. A noise barrier (also called a soundwall, sound berm, sound barrier, or acoustical barrier) is an exterior structure designed to protect inhabitants of sensitive land use areas from noise pollution. Noise barriers are the most effective method of mitigating roadway, railway, and industrial noise sources - other than cessation of the source activity or use of source controls.

24. Aerosols are minute particles suspended in the atmosphere. When these particles are sufficiently large, we notice their presence as they scatter and absorb sunlight. Their scattering of sunlight can reduce visibility (haze) and redden sunrises and sunsets. As a direct effect, the aerosols scatter sunlight directly back into space. As an indirect effect, aerosols in the lower atmosphere can modify the size of cloud particles, changing how the clouds reflect and absorb sunlight, thereby affecting the Earth's energy budget.

27. On the domestic front, India continued to take ambitious targets in its actions against climate change. As a part of its contributions to the global climate change mitigation efforts, India announced its intended nationally determined contribution (INDC) which set ambitious targets for domestic efforts against limate change. Including other efforts, the country has set itself an ambitious target of reducing its emissions intensity of its gross domestic product (GDP) by 33-35 per cent by 2030, compared to 2005 levels, and of achieving 40 per cent cumulative electric power installed capacity from non-fossil fuel-based energy resources by 2030.

28. India has committed to generating 60 GW (60,000 MW) of wind power by 2030, while the Prime Minister has given a much tighter deadline of 2022. Where are we in relation to this goal in terms of actual generation, installed capacity and capacity being installed.

"We have a target for renewable energy generation of 175 gigawatts by 2022. We have got off to a good start with nearly 12 GW likely to be installed by 2016, more than three times the current capacity," Prime Minister Narendra Modi said during the inauguration of India's pavilion at the ongoing Paris climate change conference.

Of the target capacity, 100 GW would be from solar power, 60 GW from wind, 10 GW from biomass and 5 GW from small hydro power, according to the Union ministry of new and renewable energy.

29. Sand surface had a higher albedo (0.266) than BSCs (0.226) when the surfaces were very dry. However, sand surface albedo became

increasingly lower than that of BSCs when the surfaces were in wet conditions and when the soil moisture exceeded a critical value. The changes in soil surface albedo from sand dune to BSCs after revegetation in shallow soil profiles associated with the variation of the surface soil moisture can be seen as an indicator of the degree of sand dune stabilization when compared with the original shifting sand dune soil.

31. Desertification can be considered to be a subset of land degradation, occurring in more arid areas; though land degradation is usually defined as being caused by human actions. The main direct actions are over-clearing, over-grazing and over-cultivation. There is a host of more complex direct and underlying causes including the introduction and spread of exotic plants, animals, pests and diseases, fire, economic pressures, people's attitudes, perceptions and knowledge, actions or inactions by government agencies, and inappropriate government policies.

32. Interestingly, ecosystem restoration can give to the science of ecology as well as take from it because it represents and experimental application of our knowledge of ecosystem function and structure. As Bradshaw put it, "Ecologists working in the field of ecosystem restoration are in the construction business and, like their engineering colleagues, can soon discover if their theory is correct by whether the airplane falls out of the sky, the bridge collapses, or the ecosystem fails to flourish."

36. Avalanche is a rapid, downslope movement of snow, ice, water, rock, soil, vegetation, etc., mixed in various proportions. The term avalanche is used most often when snow or ice is the major component.

Avalanches require a combination of steep slopes and a heavy snowfall. A common trigger is the deposition of wet snow over ice or a hard crust, with failure occurring at the base of the snow. Alternatively, high winds can produce a cornice, which may break off, causing an avalanche on the slope below.

37. Eskers are the chief landform created by subglacial meltwater. Minor forms include sediment-filled Nye channels and moulin kames, which are somewhat fleeting piles of debris at the bottom of a moulin (a pothole in a glacier that may extend from the surface to the glacier bed). Esker is an Irish word and is now applied to long and winding ridges formed mostly of sand and gravel and laid down in a meltwater tunnel underneath a glacier.

38. The major volcanic gases emitted from basaltic magma are H_2O, CO_2, SO_2, H_2, CO, H_2S, HCl and HF. The most abundant gas is water vapour (H_2O), followed by carbon dioxide (CO_2) and sulphur dioxide (SO_2).

41. To understand landscape ecology, we have to focus on some of its important principles: landscape composition, structure, function and change.

   – Structure involves the variety of habitat patches or ecosystems and thier patterns- the size and arrangement of patches, stands, or ecosystems—including the sequence of pools in a stream, vertical layering of vegetation.

43. Mediterranean Shrublands or Chaparral biome is found along the coasts of the Mediterranean Sea, California, Central Chile, south-western part of South Africa and south-western parts of Australia.

   The dominant shrubs that occupy these regions are stunted and tough in their ability to with-stand hot-summer drought and due to this, the chaparral vegetation is also known as sclerophyllous. It averages as metre or two in height and has deep, well developed roots, leathery and uneven low branches.

45. A keystone species is a species that has a disproportionately large effect on its environment relative to its abundance. Such species are described as playing a critical role in maintaining the structure of an

ecological community, affecting many other organisms in an ecosystem and helping to determine the types and numbers of various other species in the community.

47. World Health Organization (WHO) has revealed a report with the most polluted cities across the world according to WHO's guidelines. The most shameful thing about this list is that, out of 20 most polluted cities of the world, 13th are Indian cities.

50. In suspension, particles of largest dimensions will settle first and those of smaller dimensions will settle afterwards. Individual soil separates are identified on the basis of their respective diameter ranges. Soil separates (sand, silt and clay) differ not only in their sizes but also in their bearing on some of the important factors affecting plant growth, such as, soil aeration, workability, movement and availability of water and nutrients.

PAPER-III

Note: *This paper contains seventy five (75) objective type questions of two (2) marks each. All questions are compulsory.*

1. In India audit on conservation and protection of tigers in all 28 Tiger reserves was conducted in
   A. 2001   B. 2004
   C. 2006   D. 2007

2. In the screening stage of EIA, the impact level of a development project is not discernible, then what step should be adopted?
   A. Scoping stage ought to be initiated
   B. Detailed EIA study ought to be conducted
   C. A rapid EIA study ought to be conducted
   D. The project may not be given environmental clearance

3. Biodiversity hotspots are regions of high
   A. stationary population of common species
   B. richness of endemic species
   C. migratory population
   D. richness of dominant species

4. Given below are two statements. One labelled as Assertion (A) and the other labelled as Reason (R):
   Assertion (A) : Ocean Thermal Energy Conversion (OTEC) plants have very low efficiencies.
   Reason (R) : The temperature difference between warm surface water and cold deeper ocean water is not all that great.

Choose the correct answer:
   A. Both (A) and (R) are correct and (R) is the correct explanation of (A).
   B. Both (A) and (R) are correct and (R) is not the correct explanation of (A).
   C. (A) is true, but (R) is false.
   D. (A) is false, but (R) is true.

5. In respect of geothermal power production, identify the correct sequence of the countries:
   A. Iceland > Russia > Japan > USA
   B. Japan > Iceland > USA > Russia
   C. USA > Iceland > Japan > Russia
   D. USA > Japan > Iceland > Russia

6. Among the forest types of India, which category of forest covers maximum geographical area:
   A. Tropical grassland
   B. Mangrove forest
   C. Tropical deciduous forest
   D. Temperate evergreen forest

7. The overall diversity of a landscape comprising several ecosystems is known as
   A. Alpha diversity   B. Beta diversity
   C. Gamma diversity   D. Delta diversity

8. The ratio between the amount of radiation emitted by earth upto the wavelength at which maximum radiation is emitted and total amount of radiation emitted by earth is approximately
   A. ~ 25%   B. ~ 50%
   C. ~ 40%   D. ~ 66%

9. Milankovitch cycles refer to
   A. Shifts in the temperature of surface water in the middle latitudes of the Pacific Ocean.
   B. The timing of the northern lights in the thermosphere.
   C. The changes in the Earth's rotation and orbit around the sun that may trigger climate variation.
   D. Upwelling and down-welling in the ocean.

10. El Niño and La Niña phenomena
    A. decrease water temperatures in the eastern Pacific Ocean
    B. increase water temperatures in the Gulf of Mexico
    C. occur in a definite pattern every ten years
    D. cause changes in global temperature and precipitation pattern

11. Given below are two statements. One labelled as Assertion (A) and the other labelled as Reason (R):
    Assertion (A) : At a constant temperature, the solubility of ammonia in water increases with decrease in pH.
    Reason (R) : The solubility of all gases increase with decrease in pH.
    Choose the correct answer:
    A. Both (A) and (R) are correct and (R) is the correct explanation of (A).
    B. Both (A) and (R) are correct and (R) is not the correct explanation of (A).
    C. (A) is true, but (R) is false.
    D. (A) is false, but (R) is true.

12. Given below are two statements. One labelled as Assertion (A) and the other labelled as Reason (R):
    Assertion (A) : Temperature of sea water generally decreases with increasing latitude.
    Reason (R) : Surface layers of sea water tend to contract and sink in cold waters.
    Choose the correct answer:
    A. Both (A) and (R) are correct and (R) is the correct explanation of (A).

B. Both (A) and (R) are correct and (R) is not the correct explanation of (A).
C. (A) is true, but (R) is false.
D. (A) is false, but (R) is true.

13. A normal sand dune is characterized by
    A. Gentle windward and steeper leeward sides.
    B. Both gentle sides.
    C. Steeper windward and gentle leeward sides.
    D. Both steeper sides.

14. Given below are two statements. One labelled as Assertion (A) and the other labelled as Reason (R):
    Assertion (A) : The distribution of animals over the world is much more complex and irregular compared to plants.
    Reason (R) : The animals are mobile and therefore capable of more rapid dispersal.
    Choose the correct answer:
    A. Both (A) and (R) are correct and (R) is the correct explanation of (A).
    B. Both (A) and (R) are correct and (R) is not the correct explanation of (A).
    C. (A) is true, but (R) is false.
    D. (A) is false, but (R) is true.

15. Consider the following statements in case of Gaussian Plume Model.
    (a) The wind speed is constant both in time and with elevation.
    (b) The emission rate from the source is constant.
    (c) The pollutant is conservative.
    Choose the answer:
    A. (a) only   B. (b) only
    C. (a) and (b) only   D. (a), (b) and (c)

16. A stream flowing at 5.0 m^3/s converges with another stream with the same flow rate. The concentration of the phosphate upstream to the junction is 10.0 mg/L and that in the other stream is 5.0 mg/L. The downstream concentration of phosphate is
    A. 2.5 mg/L   B. 5.0 mg/L
    C. 7.5 mg/L   D. 10 mg/L

17. Lotka-Volterra model for an ecosystem can be used to study
(a) oscillations in prey-predator population.
(b) effect of predator on prey population.
(c) effect of prey on predator population.
Choose the correct answer:
A. (a) and (b) only
B. (b) and (c) only
C. (a) and (c) only
D. (a), (b) and (c)

18. In an ecosystem following logistic growth model initial population was 900 with growth rate constant of 0.1. If the carrying capacity of the ecosystem is 1000, what is the instantaneous rate of change of population?
A. 10   B. 25
C. 1.1   D. 9

19. Choose an appropriate hypothesis testing method for the condition where the variance is an unknown parameter of a population of independent observations:
A. Z-test   B. χ^2-test
C. t-test   D. F-test

20. For sampling error of 1.96σ; where σ is the standard deviation, and at critical value of 1.96, the significance level is
A. 5.0 %   B. 1.0 %
C. 2.7 %   D. 4.5 %

21. Qualitatively a sampling error in a survey based environmental experiment is the sum of
A. Frame error + Response error + Chance error
B. Frame error + Non-sampling error
C. Chance error + Frame error + Systematic error
D. Non-sampling error + Chance error + Systematic error

22. Ecosensitive zones are declared by the Ministry of Environment, Forest and climate change, Govt. of India under the provisions of
A. Forest Act, 1927
B. Forest (Conservation) Act, 1980
C. Environment (Protection) Act, 1986
D. Biological Diversity Act, 2002

23. Basel convention on trans-boundary movement of hazardous waste and disposal was adopted in the year
A. 1969   B. 1979
C. 1999   D. 1989

24. Which method reduces the volume of waste but could release toxic air emissions into the atmosphere?
A. Biological treatment
B. Sanitary landfill
C. Incineration
D. Chemical treatment

25. As per CRZ (Coastal Regulation Zone) 2011 Notification, which of the following activities is permitted?
A. Dumping of untreated sewage, effluents or solid waste.
B. Traditional fishing and allied activities.
C. Construction of Housing Complexes.
D. Infrastructural projects.

26. Match the List-I and List-II. Identify the correct answer from the codes given below:

List-I (Biomedical Waste)	List-II (Treatment/Disposal)
(a) Human tissues	(i) Incineration
(b) Scalpels	(ii) Autoclaving
(c) Solid plaster casts	(iii) Microwave mutilation
(d) Catheters	(iv) Deep burial

Codes:

	(a)	(b)	(c)	(d)
A.	(iv)	(ii)	(i)	(iii)
B.	(iii)	(i)	(iv)	(ii)
C.	(ii)	(iv)	(iii)	(i)
D.	(i)	(iii)	(ii)	(iv)

27. An organisation implementing an EMS under ISO 14001 should set environmental targets in order to achieve environmental objectives within a specified time-frame. The target should be
A. implemented on a trial basis
B. generic in nature
C. related to financial aspects
D. measurable and specific

28. ISO 14001 requires an organisation to
A. set improvement targets for every department.
B. define a quality policy within the defined scope of its EMS.
C. define the scope of its EMS.
D. define the scope of its audit.

29. Cost-benefit analysis is performed during
A. Design phase
B. Feasibility study phase
C. Implementation
D. Maintenance phase

30. Given below are two statements. One labelled as Assertion (A) and the other labelled as Reason (R):
Assertion (A) : The ecosystem surrounding a river gets damaged due to the construction of a dam on it.
Reason (R) : The area in upper catchment of the river gets inundated.
Choose the correct answer:
A. Both (A) and (R) are correct and (R) is the correct explanation of (A).
B. Both (A) and (R) are correct and (R) is not the correct explanation of (A).
C. (A) is true but (R) is false.
D. (A) is false but (R) is true.

31. Match the List-I and List-II. Identify the correct answer from the codes given below:

List-I (Auditing)	List-II (Actions)
(a) Implementation audit	(i) External review
(b) Predictive techniques audit	(ii) Initial activities
(c) Performance audit	(iii) Validation of impacts
(d) Procedures audit	(iv) Comprehensive operational activities

Codes:

	(a)	(b)	(c)	(d)
A.	(ii)	(iii)	(iv)	(i)
B.	(iii)	(iv)	(i)	(ii)
C.	(iv)	(i)	(ii)	(iii)
D.	(i)	(ii)	(iii)	(iv)

32. The interaction matrix developed by Leopold consists of how many parameters?
A. 30 B. 60
C. 70 D. 90

33. Given below are two statements. One labelled as Assertion (A) and the other labelled as Reason (R):
Assertion (A) : The goal of the National Land Utilisation Policy is to achieve improvement of livelihood, food and water security under the umbrella of sustainable development in India.
Reason (R) : The National Land Utilisation Policy envisages a guiding framework for state specific needs, potentials, priorities and legal provisions.
Choose the correct answer:
A. Both (A) and (R) are correct and (R) is the correct explanation of (A).
B. Both (A) and (R) are correct and (R) is not the correct explanation of (A).
C. (A) is true but (R) is false.
D. (A) is false but (R) is true.

34. Which of the following is a major photochemical oxidant?
A. PAN
B. Ozone
C. Aldehydes
D. Peroxybenzoyl nitrates (PBzN)

35. In terms of toxicity, identify the correct sequence:
A. Arsenic > Cadmium > Methylene chloride
B. Cadmium > Arsenic > Methylene chloride
C. Methylene chloride > Cadmium > Arsenic
D. Methylene chloride > Arsenic > Cadmium

36. Upwelling of oceanic waters is important for
A. enrichment of nutrients in pelagic waters.
B. balancing water circulation pattern in oceans and seas.
C. making the pelagic waters nutrient deficient.
D. helping survival of benthic organisms.

37. Arrange the following in terms of increasing productivity:

(a) Antarctica sea   (b) Arctic sea
(c) Dead sea   (d) Arabian sea

Choose the correct answer:
A. $(c) < (a) < (d) < (b)$
B. $(c) < (a) < (b) < (d)$
C. $(d) < (b) < (c) < (a)$
D. $(a) < (c) < (d) < (b)$

38. Match the List-I and List-II. Identify the correct answer from the codes given below:

List-I (Process/Event)	List-II (Consequences/Links)
(a) Assimilative capacity	(i) DO, BOD, Coliform
(b) Critical water parameter	(ii) Cadmium
(c) Itai-Itai disease	(iii) Blue baby syndrome
(d) Excess nitrate in water	(iv) Waste discharge

Codes:

	(a)	(b)	(c)	(d)
A.	(i)	(ii)	(iii)	(iv)
B.	(iv)	(i)	(ii)	(iii)
C.	(ii)	(i)	(iii)	(iv)
D.	(ii)	(iii)	(i)	(iv)

39. Which type of plume behaviour one would expect from a tall stack located on a flat terrain if adiabatic lapse rate (Γ) and environmental lapse rate (Γ_{env}) are as shown in the diagram below:

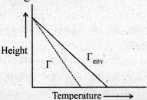

A. looping   B. fanning
C. coning   D. trapping

40. A road carrying heavy traffic has an average noise level of 90 dB when measured at a distance of 10 metres. What would be the noise level at 20 metres distance?

A. 87 dB   B. 84 dB
C. 60 dB   D. 45 dB

41. When biomass is converted to CO and H_2O, the energy made available is ~450 kJ per mol of carbon per unit of reduction level. What would be the heat of combustion per gram of methane?

A. 28.125 kJ/g   B. 56.25 kJ/g
C. 67.5 kJ/g   D. 135 kJ/g

42. Given below are two statements. One labelled as Assertion (A) and the other labelled as Reason (R):

Assertion (A) : Hydrogen, as a fuel, when burned, does produce some amount of pollution.

Reason (R) : Heat produced during combustion of hydrogen chemically combines N_2 and O_2 in atmosphere to produce NO_x.

Choose the correct answer:
A. Both (A) and (R) are correct and (R) is the correct explanation of (A).
B. Both (A) and (R) are correct and (R) is not the correct explanation of (A).
C. (A) is true but (R) is false.
D. (A) is false but (R) is true.

43. Given standard enthalpies for methane, carbon dioxide and water vapour as ~75 kJ/mol, 394 kJ/mol and 240 kJ/mol, respectively. What is the net heat of combustion of methane?

A. – 799 kJ/mol   B. – 802 kJ/mol
C. + 1598 kJ/mol   D. + 799 kJ/mol

44. In an ideal magnetohydrodynamic power plant, the speed of flow of the hot ionized gas is u m/s. The maximum power output from the plant varies as

A. $\propto u$ B. $\propto u^{3/2}$
C. $\propto u^2$ D. $\propto u^3$

45. An ideal wind turbine located on a hill top produces electrical power. If wind speed changes by 5%, by what percentage the electrical power will change?

A. 12.5 %   B. 25 %
C. 30 %   D. 15 %

46. A person working in a nuclear reactor is exposed to a beam of thermal neutrons and receives a dose of 20 millirads per hour for an exposure of 12 minutes. What is the equivalent dose in millirems, the person is exposed to?

   A. 4   B. 8
   C. 12   D. 16

47. What is the approximate increase in radiative forcing if the CO_2 concentration increases from 400 ppm to 800 ppm?

   A. ~ 4.37 W/m^2 B. ~ 3.81 W/m^2
   C. ~ 2.72 W/m^2 D. ~ 1.62 W/m^2

48. Given below are two statements. One labelled as Assertion (A) and the other labelled as Reason (R):

Assertion (A) : Large parts of India have already become water stressed.

Reason (R) : Climate change may be the main reason.

Choose the correct answer:

   A. Both (A) and (R) are correct and (R) is the correct explanation of (A).
   B. Both (A) and (R) are correct and (R) is not the correct explanation of (A).
   C. (A) is true, but (R) is false.
   D. (A) is false, but (R) is true.

49. Ecosystem degradation refers to

   (a) loss or decrease in biodiversity.
   (b) modification in structure of abiotic components.
   (c) impairment of ecosystem processes such as nutrient cycling.

Choose the correct answer:

   A. (a) only   B. (a) and (b) only
   C. (b) and (c) only   D. (a), (b) and (c)

50. In addition to their role in ozone depletion, CFCs play a role in global warming by

   A. reducing the albedo of the earth's surface
   B. absorbing solar radiation
   C. blocking UV-B radiation on earth
   D. absorbing terrestrial radiation

51. Given below are two statements. One labelled as Assertion (A) and the other labelled as Reason (R):

Assertion (A) : As per equilibrium theory of island biogeography, distance of the islands from the mainland determines the dispersal rate of new species.

Reason (R) : Size of an island is important in determining number of species.

Choose the correct answer:

   A. Both (A) and (R) are correct and (R) is the correct explanation of (A).
   B. Both (A) and (R) are correct and (R) is not the correct explanation of (A).
   C. (A) is true, but (R) is false.
   D. (A) is false, but (R) is true.

52. Given below are two statements. One labelled as Assertion (A) and the other labelled as Reason (R):

Assertion (A) : All cloud processes have implications for climate change.

Reason (R) : Clouds strongly affect the flux of both shortwave and infra-red light through atmosphere.

Choose the correct answer:

   A. Both (A) and (R) are correct and (R) is the correct explanation of (A).
   B. Both (A) and (R) are correct and (R) is not the correct explanation of (A).
   C. (A) is true, but (R) is false.
   D. (A) is false, but (R) is true.

53. Using remote sensing for height measurement of trees, which microwave band is most suitable?

   A. X   B. C
   C. S   D. L

54. For public use, Survey of India publishes topographical maps on 1 : 50,000 scale. These maps use

   A. UTM projection and WGS 84 datum
   B. Polyconic projection and WGS84 datum
   C. UTM projection and Modified Mount Everest datum
   D. Polyconic projection and Modified Mount Everest datum

55. Sub-geostrophic winds in the earth-atmospheric system are caused by the balance involving
   A. pressure gradient force, Coriolis force and frictional force
   B. pressure gradient force and Coriolis force
   C. pressure gradient force and frictional force
   D. Coriolis force and frictional force

56. Which one of the following is not a set of polymorphous minerals?
   A. Calcite, aragonite, vaterite
   B. Quartz, coesite, tridymite
   C. Graphite, anthracite, diamond
   D. Kyanite, alusite and sillimanite

57. Match the List-I and List-II. Identify the correct answer from the codes given below:

List-I (Geological events)	List-II (Processes)
(a) Exfoliation dome	(i) Landform change
(b) Rift valleys	(ii) Ultisols
(c) Palaeomagnetism	(iii) Mechanical weathering
(d) Pedogenesis	(iv) Seafloor spreading

   Codes:

	(a)	(b)	(c)	(d)
A.	(i)	(ii)	(iii)	(iv)
B.	(ii)	(i)	(iv)	(iii)
C.	(iii)	(i)	(iv)	(ii)
D.	(iv)	(ii)	(i)	(iii)

58. Given below are two statements. One labelled as Assertion (A) and the other labelled as Reason (R):

   Assertion (A) : Soil development begins with physical, chemical and biological weathering of rocks.

   Reason (R) : Anthropogenic factors play a major role in soil formation.

   Choose the correct answer:
   A. Both (A) and (R) are correct and (R) is the correct explanation of (A).
   B. Both (A) and (R) are correct and (R) is not the correct explanation of (A).
   C. (A) is true but (R) is false.
   D. (A) is false but (R) is true.

59. The most common ferromagnesian rock forming minerals are as follows:
   A. Amphibole and Biotite Mica
   B. Muscovita mica and Quartz
   C. Galena and Pyrite
   D. Calcite and Dolomite

60. Underground coal mine fires can best be monitored by remote sensing technique in the spectral region
   A. 3–5 μm   B. 10–12 μm
   C. 1–3 μm   D. 1–10 mm

61. Our inability to address the conflict between short term individual well-being and long term societal welfare is responsible for the
   A. Tragedy of the population
   B. Tragedy of the community
   C. Tragedy of the environment
   D. Tragedy of the commons

62. Proportion of representation of each species allows ecologists to compare different communities through graphical representation. Such a graph is called
   A. Rank abundance curve
   B. Species accumulation curve
   C. Survivorship curve
   D. Sigmoid curve

63. Lincoln index is a mark-recapture method used in animals to estimate the
   A. total population density
   B. total number
   C. total frequency
   D. total dominance

64. K-selected population during ecological succession tends to dominate in
   A. mature stages   B. early stages
   C. pioneer stages   D. seral stages

65. Evolution can be viewed as
   (a) genetic change over time
   (b) a process of descent with modification
   (c) a sudden change in organism
   (d) a man-made change in oraganism

   Choose the correct code:
   A. (a) and (b) only   B. (b) and (c) only
   C. (c) and (d) only   D. (a) and (d) only

66. Given below are two statements. One labelled as Assertion (A) and the other labelled as Reason (R):

Assertion (A) : C_4 photosynthesis lowers photorespiratory energy loss.

Reason (R) : The greater supply of CO_2 lowers the rate of O_2 uptake by rubisco substantially reducing photorespiration.

Choose the correct answer:

A. Both (A) and (R) are correct and (R) is the correct explanation of (A).
B. Both (A) and (R) are correct and (R) is not the correct explanation of (A).
C. (A) is true, but (R) is false.
D. (A) is false, but (R) is true.

67. Symbiotic blue-green algal biofertilizer is obtained from

A. *Nostoc* species
B. *Rhizobium* species
C. *Azolla* mass culture
D. *Azospirillum* mass culture

68. With reference to smog consider the following statements:

(*a*) Los Angeles smog is oxidizing.
(*b*) London smog is reducing.

Choose the correct answer:

A. Both (*a*) and (*b*) are false.
B. Both (*a*) and (*b*) are true.
C. (*a*) is false, but (*b*) is true.
D. (*a*) is true, but (*b*) is false.

69. Match the List-I and List-II. Identify the correct answer from the codes given below:

List-I (Chemical Species)	List-II (Measurement Techniques)
(*a*) DO	(*i*) West-Gaeke Method
(*b*) SO_2	(*ii*) Non-dispersive infrared analyser
(*c*) CO	(*iii*) Chemiluminescence
(*d*) NO	(*iv*) Winkler's Method

Codes:

	(*a*)	(*b*)	(*c*)	(*d*)
A.	(*iv*)	(*i*)	(*ii*)	(*iii*)
B.	(*iii*)	(*ii*)	(*i*)	(*iv*)
C.	(*ii*)	(*iii*)	(*iv*)	(*i*)
D.	(*i*)	(*iv*)	(*iii*)	(*ii*)

70. Disintegration of $_{226}^{88}Ra$ yields $_{222}^{86}Rn$ owing to the emission of

A. two β-particles
B. one α-particle
C. γ-radiation
D. one β-particle followed by an α-particle

71. Given below are two statements. One labelled as Assertion (A) and the other labelled as Reason (R):

Assertion (A) : Temperature in stratosphere increases with increase in altitude.

Reason (R) : Photodissociation of O_2 in stratosphere makes the lapse rate positive.

Choose the correct answer:

A. Both (A) and (R) are correct and (R) is the correct explanation of (A).
B. Both (A) and (R) are correct and (R) is not the correct explanation of (A).
C. (A) is true, but (R) is false.
D. (A) is false, but (R) is true.

72. At 15 °C, a manufacturer dissolves CO_2 at 2.4 atm in water in a bottle. If Henry's law constant of CO_2 in water be 0.045 mol L^{-1} atm^{-1} at 15 °C, calculate the concentration of CO_2 dissolved in water.

A. 5.6 mol L^{-1} B. 0.019 mol L^{-1}
C. 0.098 mol L^{-1} D. 0.108 mol L^{-1}

73. Match the List-I and List-II. Identify the correct answer from the codes given below:

List-I (Pesticides)	List-II (Purpose)
(*a*) Malathion	(*i*) Molluscicide
(*b*) Metaldehyde	(*ii*) Fungicide
(*c*) Diethyl Tolumide (DEET)	(*iii*) Insecticide
(*d*) Chloroneb	(*iv*) Insect repellant

Codes:

	(*a*)	(*b*)	(*c*)	(*d*)
A.	(*iv*)	(*ii*)	(*i*)	(*iii*)
B.	(*i*)	(*iii*)	(*ii*)	(*iv*)
C.	(*ii*)	(*iv*)	(*iii*)	(*i*)
D.	(*iii*)	(*i*)	(*iv*)	(*ii*)

74. Which of the following is not an Advanced Oxidation Process for the treatment of waste water?
- A. PhotoFenton Process
- B. Photocatalytic TiO_2 Process
- C. UV/H_2O_2 Process
- D. Acidified Potassium Dichromate Oxidation Process

75. If a material containing humic substances is extracted with a strong base, and the resulting solution is acidified, products are

(*a*) humin   (*b*) humic acid

(*c*) fulvic acid

Choose the correct answer:
- A. (*a*) only
- B. (*a*) and (*b*) only
- C. (*a*), (*b*) and (*c*)
- D. (*b*) and (*c*) only

ANSWERS

1	2	3	4	5	6	7	8	9	10
C	C	B	A	C	C	C	A	C	D

11	12	13	14	15	16	17	18	19	20
C	B	A	A	D	C	D	D	B	A

21	22	23	24	25	26	27	28	29	30
A	C	D	C	B	A	D	C	B	B

31	32	33	34	35	36	37	38	39	40
A	D	A	B	A	A	B	B	A	A

41	42	43	44	45	46	47	48	49	50
B	A	A	C	D	B	A	C	D	D

51	52	53	54	55	56	57	58	59	60
B	A	D	A	A	C	C	C	A	B

61	62	63	64	65	66	67	68	69	70
D	A	A	A	A	A	C	B	A	B

71	72	73	74	75
C	D	D	D	C

EXPLANATORY ANSWERS

1. The IX Plan proposal for the continuation of the Centrally Sponsored Scheme (CSS) "Project Tiger" was approved by the Government in June 1999 with the direction that for monitoring purposes, a master plan for development of each of the reserves should be prepared.

Achievement of physical targets was to be compared with the master plan. PTD stated in March 2006 that the Management Plans (MPs) of the Tiger Reserves were the master plans.

3. Nowadays there is serious concern about the effectiveness of existing strategies for biodiversity protection. A central issue in conservation is to identify biodiversity-rich areas to which conservation resources should be directed. Based on the observation that some parts of the world have far more species than others, the area-based approaches are widely advocated for species conservation planning. Areas with high concentrations of endemic species (species that are found nowhere else on Earth) and with high habitat loss are often referred to as "hotspots". The hotspot approach can be applied at any geographical scale and both in terrestrial and marine environments.

4. Ocean Thermal Energy Conversion (OTEC) plants have very low efficiencies. OTEC works best when the temperature difference between the warmer, top layer of the ocean and the colder, deep ocean water is about 36°F (20°C). These conditions exist in tropical coastal areas, roughly between the Tropic of Capricorn and the Tropic of Cancer. To bring the cold water to the surface, ocean thermal energy conversion plants require an expensive, large-diameter intake pipe, which is submerged a mile or more into the ocean's depths.

5. **Geothermal power** is power generated by geothermal energy. Technologies in use include dry steam power stations, flash steam power stations and binary cycle power stations.

Installed geothermal electric capacity

Country	Capacity (MW) 2007	Capacity (MW) 2010	Capacity (MW) 2013	Capacity (MW) 2015	Share of national generation (%)
USA	2687	3086	3389	3450	0.3
Iceland	421.2	575	664	665	30.0
Japan	535.2	536	537	519	0.1
Russia	79	82	97	82	

6. Temperate Deciduous Forests are those, which consist of predominantly broad-leafed trees. Deciduous forests are of two types: Temperate and Tropical. Temperate deciduous forests occur in areas of moderate temperature and rainfall with chilly winters. It covers maximum geographical area. Species belonging to these forests drop leaves in autumn. The deciduous forests in tropical areas shed leaves only by December (in the Northern Hemisphere) when water becomes scarce. The tropical monsoon deciduous forests are found in areas receiving an annual rainfall of 100 to 200 cms in India, with a distinct dry and rainy season and minimum temperature. The deciduous forest can further be divided into Moist and Dry.

7. Diversity is a combination of two factors; the number of species present, species richness, and the distribution of individuals among the species are referred to as evenness or equitability. Whittaker distinguishes three types of diversity:

1. *Alpha*-diversity – diversity within a particular area or ecosystem.

2. *Beta*-diversity – the change in diversity between ecosystems, and

3. *Gamma*-diversity – the overall diversity of a landscape comprising of several ecosystem.

The two most widely used species diversity indices are Shannon and Simpson indices. They are adopted by ecologists to describe the average degree of uncertainty in predicting the species of an individual picked at random from a given community.

9. **Milankovitch cycles** describes the collective effects of changes in the Earth's movements upon its climate, named after Serbian geophysicist and astronomer Milutin Milankovic, who in the 1920s had theorized that variations in eccentricity, axial tilt, and precession of the Earth's orbit determined climatic patterns on Earth through orbital forcing.

10. The ENSO cycle, both El Niño and La Niña, causes global changes of both temperatures and rainfall.

13. Sand dunes form when the wind carries small particles of sand that are deposited against an obstacle, such as a shrub, rock, tree or any other kind of obstruction. As small particles of sand are deposited around the obstacle,

the dune grows in size, forming rows that grow perpendicular to the wind's direction. The wind will continue to erode the sand particles that were deposited on the windward side of the dune and deposit them on the leeward side of the dune. Sand dunes migrate when erosion by the wind forces the sand particles to move by saltation on the upwind slope. These particles are then deposited on the slip face, creating repose angles of 30-34°.

14. Zoogeographic Regions

1. Distribution of animals over the world is more complex and irregular than plants because they are mobile.
2. Broad distribution of animals is reflective of the distribution of energy and food diversity: (a) richest faunal assemblages are in the permissive environment of the humid tropics (b) sparsest representations of both species and individuals are in the dry lands and cold lands.

15. Point Source Gaussian Plume Model

Model Structure and Assumptions

- pollutants released from a "virtual point source".
- advective transport by wind.
- dispersive transport (spreading) follows normal (Gaussian) distribution away from trajectory.
- constant emission rate.
- wind speed constant with time and elevation.
- pollutant is conservative (no reaction).
- terrain is flat and unobstructed.
- uniform atmospheric stability.

17. The **Lotka-Volterra equations,** also known as the **predator-prey equations,** are a pair of first-order, non-linear, differential equations frequently used to describe the dynamics of biological systems in which two species interact, one as a predator and the other as prey.

The Lotka-Volterra model makes a number of assumptions about the environment and evolution of the predator and prey populations:

1. The prey population finds ample food at all times.
2. The food supply of the predator population depends entirely on the size of the prey population.
3. The rate of change of population is proportional to its size.
4. During the process, the environment does not change in favour of one species and genetic adaptation is inconsequential.
5. Predators have limitless appetite.

22. The Environment (Protection) Act (EPA), 1986, under the jurisdiction of the Indian Ministry of Environment and Forests (MoEF) is officially considered to be the umbrella legislation to regulate environment degradation and pollution. It also attempts to provide a critical framework to enable the coordination of bodies such as Pollution Control Boards set up through air and water related legislations that precede the EPA.

23. The Basel Convention on the Control of Transboundary Movements of Hazardous Wastes and their Disposal was adopted on 22 March 1989 by the Conference of Plenipotentiaries in Basel, Switzerland, in response to a public outcry following the discovery, in the 1980s, in Africa and other parts of the developing world of deposits of toxic wastes imported from abroad.

24. Incineration is a waste treatment process that involves the combustion of organic substances contained in waste materials. Incineration of waste materials converts the waste into ash, flue gas, and heat. The ash is mostly formed by the inorganic constituents of the waste, and may take the form of solid lumps or particulates carried by the flue gas. The flue gases must be cleaned of gaseous and particulate pollutants before they are dispersed into the atmosphere. In some cases, the heat generated by incineration can be used to generate electric power.

Incineration reduces the volume of waste but could release toxic air emissions into the Atmosphere.

25. The dwelling units of the traditional coastal communities including fisherfolk, tribals as were permissible under the provisions of the CRZ notification, 1991, but which have not obtained formal approval from concerned authorities under the aforesaid notification shall be considered by the respective Union territory CZMAs and the dwelling units shall be regularized subject to the following condition, namely–
    (*i*) These are not used for any commercial activity.
    (*ii*) These are not sold or transferred to non-traditional coastal community.

28. The ISO 14000 family includes most notably the ISO 14001 standard, which represents the core set of standards used by organizations for designing and implementing an effective Environmental Management System (EMS). ISO 14001 sets out the criteria for an Environmental Management System (EMS). It does not state requirements for environmental performance, but maps out a framework that a company or organization can follow to set up an effective EMS. It can be used by any organization that wants to improve resource efficiency, reduce waste, and drive down costs. Using ISO 14001 can provide assurance to company management and employees as well as external stakeholders that environmental impact is being measured and improved. ISO 14001 can also be integrated with other management functions and assists companies in meeting their environmental and economic goals..

29. A unique problem-set of the smaller-size software project is that technically qualified personnel for performing feasibility studies and cost-benefit analysis are often not available. Therefore, linking the feasibility study to risk analysis and cost-benefit analysis techniques may result in no feasibility study being performed. Since in most system development projects it is important that some form of feasibility study be executed, to the highest degree of rigor that circumstances permit, then it is preferable to consider risk analysis and cost-benefit analysis as alternative phases.

32. Simple 'interaction matrices' as developed by Leopold *et al.* display project actions or activities along one axis with appropriate environmental factors listed along the other (Canter 1996). Leopold *et al.* (1971) constructed a generic interaction matrix based on about 100 categories of action and 90 categories of 'environmental item'. To use the 'Leopold' matrix, each action and its potential for creating an impact must be considered for each environmental item or receptor. Where an impact is anticipated, the matrix is marked with a diagonal line in the appropriate cell. It is also possible to indicate the possibility of beneficial or detrimental impacts using + or − signs, respectively.

34. Photochemical oxidants are the products of reactions between NO_x and a wide variety of volatile organic compounds (VOCs). The most well known 'oxidants' are ozone (O_3), peroxyacetyle nitrate (PAN) and hydrogen peroxide (H_2O_2). The main impact on the natural environment is mostly due to elevated O_3. Excessive concentrations of tropospheric (ground level) O_3 have toxic effects on both plants and human health.

49. Environmental degradation is the deterioration of the environment through depletion of resources such as air, water and soil; the destruction of ecosystems and the extinction of wildlife. It refers to loss or decrease in biodiversity, modification in structure of abiotic components and impairment of ecosystem processes such as nutrient cycling.

50. CFCs were phased out via the Montreal Protocol due to their part in ozone depletion. This anthropogenic compound is also a greenhouse gas, with a much higher potential to enhance the greenhouse effect than CO_2.

52. All cloud processes have the potential to change as the climate state changes. Cloud feedbacks are of intense interest in the context of climate change. Any change in a cloud process that is caused by climate change - and in turn influences climate - represents a cloud-climate feedback. Because clouds interact so strongly with both sunlight and infrared light, small changes in cloudiness can have a potent effect on the climate system. Many possible types of cloud-climate feedbacks have been suggested, involving changes in cloud amount, cloudtop height and/or cloud reflectivity. The literature shows consistently that high clouds amplify global warming as they interact with infrared light emitted by the atmosphere and surface. There is more uncertainty, however, about the feedbacks associated with low-altitude clouds, and about cloud feedbacks associated with amount and reflectivity in general.

53. Interaction of SAR microwaves with canopies, trees and soil is of interest. The longer wavelengths (*e.g.*, L-band 15-20 cm) penetrate the canopy, and its backscatter data contains information that relates to leaves, branches, stems and soil conditions; the longer the wavelength the greater the penetration. It has been proven that radar is sensitive to the structure of the canopy. The received backscatter intensity represented in the image is a composition of interactions with the crown, the trunk and the ground surface. Using fully polarimetric SAR it is possible to derive a relationship between backscatter, texture and crop status.

54. **Open Series Maps (OSM)** – These are prepared on 1:250,000; 1:50,000 and 1:25,000 scales for the use of general public/civilians for supporting development activities in the country. Technically maps of this series are based on WGS-84 Datum and UTM Projection. They do not contain grid and classified information; therefore, they are kept under unrestricted category. They can be obtained from all map sale centre and other authorized agents deputed all over the country. Few sheets are also printed in Hindi and other regional languages.

55. An air parcel initially at rest will move from high pressure to low pressure because of the pressure gradient force (PGF). However, as that air parcel begins to move, it is deflected by the Coriolis force to the right in the northern hemisphere (to the left on the southern hemisphere). As the wind gains speed, the deflection increases until the Coriolis force equals the pressure gradient force. At this point, the wind will be blowing parallel to the isobars. When this happens, the wind is referred to as geostrophic.

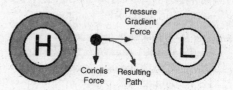

57. Exfoliation refers to the *spalling,* or breaking off, of curved rock shells roughly parallel or concentric to the surface. Exfoliation is especially common in granite and was once thought to be caused by temperature changes. However, this process may actually be related to both chemical and physical weathering processes. Exfoliation that produces thin sheets or spalls a few millimeters or so thick is associated with hydration, a chemical weathering process.

A rift valley is a lowland region that forms where Earth's tectonic plates move apart, or rift. Rift valleys are found both on land and at the bottom of the ocean, where they are created by the process of seafloor spreading. Rift valleys differ from river valleys and glacial valleys in that they are created by tectonic activity and not the process of erosion.

Paleomagnetists led the revival of the continental drift hypothesis and its transformation into plate tectonics. Apparent polar wander paths provided the first clear geophysical evidence for continental drift, while marine magnetic anomalies did the same for seafloor spreading. Paleomagnetism continues to extend the history of plate tectonics back in time and are applied to the movement of continental fragments, or terranes.

Pedogenesis is the process of soil formation as regulated by the effects of place, environment, and history. Pedogenesis is studied as a branch of pedology, the study of soil in its natural environment. Other branches of pedology are the study of soil morphology, and soil classification. The study of pedogenesis is important to understanding soil distribution patterns in current (soil geography) and past (paleopedology) geologic periods.

59. Ferromagnesian silicates contain iron and magnesium. Since these two metal ions are nearly identical in size, they easily substitute for one another in the crystal structure. Ferromagnesian silicates are usually dark in colour. Olivine, pyroxene, amphibole and biotite mica are ferromagnesian silicates.

61. Our inability to address the conflict between short term individual well-being and long term societal welfare is responsible for the tragedy of the commons.

62. A rank abundance curve or Whittaker plot is a chart used by ecologists to display relative species abundance, a component of biodiversity. It can also be used to visualize species richness and species evenness. It overcomes the shortcomings of biodiversity indices that cannot display the relative role different variables played in their calculation.

The rank abundance curve visually depicts both species richness and species evenness. Species richness can be viewed as the number of different species on the chart i.e., how many species were ranked. Species evenness is reflected in the slope of the line that fits the graph (assuming a linear, i.e., logarithmic series, relationship). A steep gradient indicates low evenness as the high-ranking species have much higher abundances than the low-ranking species. A shallow gradient indicates high evenness as the abundances of different species are similar.

63. **Mark and recapture** is a method commonly used in ecology to estimate an animal population's size. A portion of the population is captured, marked, and released. Later, another portion is captured and the number of marked individuals within the sample is counted. Other names for this method is the Lincoln method.

The Lincoln-Petersen method (also known as the Petersen-Lincoln index or Lincoln index) can be used to estimate population size if only two visits are made to the study area. This method assumes that the study population is "closed".

64. K-selected species possess relatively stable populations and tend to produce relatively low numbers of offspring; however, individual offspring tend to be quite large in comparison with r-selected species. K-selected species are characterized by long gestation periods lasting several months, slow maturation (and thus extended parental care), and long life spans. In addition, they tend to inhabit relatively stable biological communities, such as late-successional or climax forests.

65. "Evolution" commonly is used more narrowly to refer to the specific theory that all organisms have descended from common ancestors, also known as the "theory of descent with modification," or to refer to one explanation for the process by which change occurs, the "theory of modification through natural selection". The term also is used with reference to a comprehensive theory that includes both the non-causal pattern of descent with modification and the causal mechanism of natural selection.

Evolution can be viewed as genetic change over time or as a process of descent with modification. Biological evolution is change in organisms over time.

68. The London smog has been called reducing or sulphurous smog. This type is identified by high concentrations of sulphur dioxide (SO_2) and particulate matter. London smog is therefore composed of air pollutants that are emitted directly by combustion processes and are called "Primary pollutants".

The Los Angeles smog is an oxidizing smog formed from the photochemical reactions of nitrogen oxides and volatile organic hydrocarbons, which are primary pollutants released from the combustion of fossil fuels in automobiles, power plants, etc.

70. When one α-particle emitted from a radioactive substance, its atomic number is decreases by two and its mass number is decreases by 4.

$$^{226}_{88}Ra \xrightarrow[\alpha-particle]{} {}^{222}_{86}Rn .$$

71. The air at the surface up to around 10 kilometers is called the troposphere. The reason it is warmer at the surface is simple. The air is warmed by heat given off by the Earth! The farther away from the surface the air moves, the less heat there is to absorb.

The stratosphere lies roughly 12 to 50 km above the surface and is marked by a temperature profile that increases with height. This is due to the absorbtion by ozone of the sun's UV radiation and is in sharp contrast to the lower atmosphere. There it generally gets colder as you go higher due to the expansion of gases as the pressure decreases. Technically, the stratosphere has a negative 'lapse rate' (temperature increases with height), while the lower atmosphere's lapse rate is positive.

72. When a gas is dissolved in a liquid, the concentrations will eventually reach equilibrium between the source of the gas and the solution. Henry's Law shows the concentration of a solute gas in a solution is directly proportional to the partial pressure of the gas over the solution.

$$P = K_H C; \text{ where}$$

P is the partial pressure of the gas above the solution

K_H is the Henry's Law constant for the solution

C is the concentration of the dissolved gas in solution.

$$P = 2.4 \times 0.045$$
$$= 0.108 \text{ mol/L}^{-1}$$

75. The most important class of complexing agents that occur naturally is the humic substances. These are degradation-resistant materials formed during the decomposition of vegetation that occur as deposits in soil, marsh sediments, peat, coal, lignite, or in almost any location where large quantities of vegetation have decayed. They are commonly classified on the basis of solubility. If a material containing humic substances is extracted with a strong base, and the resulting solution is acidified, the products are (1) a nonextractable plant residue called humin; (2) a material that precipitates from the acidified extract, called humic acid; and (3) an organic material that remains in the acidified solution, called fulvic acid. Because of their acid-base, sorptive, and complexing properties, both the soluble and insoluble humic substances have a strong effect upon the properties of water. In general, fulvic acid dissolves in water and exerts its effects as the soluble species. Humin and humic acid remain insoluble and affect water quality through exchange of species, such as cations or organic materials, with water.

UGC–NET Environmental Science

Junior Research Fellowship and Assistant Professor Exam

December–2015

PAPER-II

Note : *This paper contains* ***fifty (50)*** *objective type questions of* ***two (2)*** *marks each.* ***All questions are compulsory.***

1. Which one of the following elements contributes maximum to the earth crust by weight?
   A. Iron   B. Silicon
   C. Oxygen   D. Carbon

2. The lowest temperature is observed in which layer of the atmosphere?
   A. Troposphere   B. Stratosphere
   C. Mesosphere   D. Thermosphere

3. Which of the following gases has the lowest residence time?
   A. CO_2 B. N_2O
   C. CFCs   D. CH_4

4. Which of the following statement is **incorrect**?
   A. Chromium (VI) is highly toxic
   B. Methyl mercury is most toxic mercury species
   C. Arsenic (III) is more toxic than arsenic (V)
   D. Cadmium is a criteria pollutant

5. The most abundant functional group present in fulvic acid, commonly found in soils, is:
   A. Peptide group
   B. Carboxylate group
   C. Phenolic group
   D. Amino group

6. The source of Stratospheric NO_x is:
   A. Atmospheric N_2
   B. Tropospheric N_2O
   C. Tropospheric NO
   D. Tropospheric NO_2

7. In troposphere, which of the following processes does **not** generate hydroxyl radical?
   A. $O(^1D) + H_2O$ B. $O(^3P) + H_2O$
   C. $HCHO + hv$ D. $HNO_2 + hv$

8. The most common form of lead present in pesticide is:
   A. Lead acetate   B. Lead arsenate
   C. Lead azide   D. Lead telluride

9. Consider the following four statements about benzo[a]pyrene:
   (*a*) It is a group I carcinogen
   (*b*) It is a polycyclic aromatic hydrocarbon
   (*c*) Its molecular formula is $C_{20}H_{12}$
   (*d*) It has four benzene rings
   Choose the **correct** code:
   A. (*a*) and (*b*) only
   B. (*a*), (*b*) and (*c*) only
   C. (*b*), (*c*) and (*d*) only
   D. (*a*), (*b*), (*c*) and (*d*)

10. Given below are two statements. One labelled as **Assertion (A)** and the other labelled as **Reason (R)**.
    Assertion (A): Radon is an inert gas and it is radioactive.
    Reason (R): All inert gases are radioactive.
    Choose the **correct** answer:
    A. Both (A) and (R) are correct and (R) is the correct explanation of (A).
    B. Both (A) and (R) are correct and (R) is not the correct explanation of (A).
    C. (A) is true, but (R) is false.
    D. (A) is false, but (R) is true.

11. Most of Epiphytes are examples of type of biotic interactions called:

A. Mutualism   B. Coevolution

C. Commensalism   D. Parasitism

12. Inhalation of airborne mold spore leads to disease in man such as:

A. Bronchitis

B. Allergy

C. Cardiac congestion

D. Eye irritation

13. Biological diversity is mainly a function of:

(a) Latitude

(b) Longitude

(c) Distance from sea

Choose the **correct** answer:

A. (a) only   B. (a) and (b) only

C. (b) and (c) only   D. (a), (b) and (c)

14. The ability of a living system to be restored through secondary succession after a more severe disturbance is known as:

A. Rehabilitation   B. Resistance

C. Resilience   D. Restoration

15. The characteristic feature of the background extinction is disappearance of a species at a:

A. low rate   B. fast rate

C. lapse rate   D. intrinsic rate

16. Speciation means:

A. Natural process of extinction of different species

B. Artificial process of extinction of different species

C. One species splits into two or more different species naturally

D. Characterisation of different species

17. Topological modelling is a well organized cluster of functions in GIS to process:

(a) Spatial data

(b) Attribute data

(c) Physico-chemical data

(d) Species richness data

Choose the **correct** code:

A. (a) and (b) only

B. (b) and (c) only

C. (a), (b) and (c) only

D. (a), (b), (c) and (a)

18. A rock body or formation which may be porous enough to hold enough quantity of water but which by virtue of its other properties does not allow an easy and quick flow through it, is called:

A. Aquitard   B. Aquifuge

C. Aquiclude   D. Aquifer

19. For many decades, geologists noted the high number of earthquakes and active volcanoes occurring around the rim of the Pacific Ocean basin. This is called:

A. Volcanic ring   B. Ring of fire

C. Earthquake zone   D. Volcanic hot spot

20. Inversion that occurs near Earth's Surface is called:

A. Radiation inversion

B. Advectional inversion

C. Subsidence inversion

D. Cold-air-drainage inversion

21. The radiation flux emitted per unit solid angle in a specified direction by a unit area of source is called:

A. irradiance   B. radiance

C. exitance   D. radiant flux

22. Mean residence time of soil organic matter in an ecosystem is maximum in:

A. Tropical rain forest

B. Boreal forest

C. Temperate coniferous forest

D. Dry deciduous forest

23. Worst affected area by Indian Ocean Tsunami of December 2004 in India was:

A. Andaman and Nicobar Islands

B. Tamil Nadu

C. Andhra Pradesh

D. Odisha

24. Consider solar insolation of 400 W/m^2 incident on a single solar cell of area 100 cm^2. If only 15% of the photons cause electron - hole pairs and the average energy of incident photons is ~1 eV, the short circuit current of the cell is:

A. 1.2 A   B. 1.5 A

C. 1.6 A   D. 1.8 A

25. For which of the following renewable resources of energy, sun is not directly responsible?
A. Wind
B. Biomass
C. OTEC
D. Tidal

26. In terms of the calorific value, identify the **correct** sequence:
A. Methane > hydrogen > ethanol > methanol
B. Hydrogen > methane > ethanol > methanol
C. Methane > hydrogen > methanol > ethanol
D. Hydrogen > ethanol > methane > methanol

27. At a given location the wind speeds are predominantly in the range 6 to 6.4 m/s. This location's wind power class will be termed as:
A. Fair
B. Good
C. Excellent
D. Outstanding

28. Which of the following nuclides does **not** undergo fission with low energy (slow) neutrons?
A. 235 U
B. 238 U
C. 239 Pu
D. 233 U

29. According to CPCB standards, the annual average concentration of $PM_{2.5}$ should not exceed:
A. $60 \ \mu g \ m^{-3}$
B. $40 \ \mu g \ m^{-3}$
C. $80 \ \mu g \ m^{-3}$
D. $100 \ \mu g \ m^{-3}$

30. Which of the following is a secondary aerosol?
A. Pollens
B. Virus
C. Sodium Chloride
D. Ammonium Sulphate

31. In the colorimetric determination of ambient SO_2 by WEST-GAEKE method, the absorbance of the coloured complex should be measured at which of the following wavelengths?
A. 550 nm
B. 650 nm
C. 450 nm
D. 350 nm

32. A healthy human ear, before experiencing pain, can detect sound pressure levels as high as:
A. 50 Pa
B. 100 Pa
C. 200 Pa
D. 1000 Pa

33. The resultant of two noise levels of 80 dB and 50 dB will be about:
A. ~80 dB
B. ~82 dB
C. ~60 dB
D. ~130 dB

34. The half life of radioactive iodine −131 is:
A. 30 years
B. 15 years
C. 5 years
D. 8 days

35. Which of the following best describes the function of the environmental management plan as a part of the environmental statement?
A. It describes the environmental impacts of the proposal.
B. It describes the baseline environmental data.
C. It describes the project proposal in detail.
D. It describes the actions and auditing procedures needed.

36. India submitted its INDCs related to climate change to the UN recently. What does INDCs stand for?
A. Intended Nationally Devoted Contributions
B. Intended Nationally Determined Contributions
C. Intended Notified Decisive Contributions
D. India's Nationally Determined Contributions

37. Formal EIA became an integral part of Environmental Management in India by a Notification for the first time in:
A. 1988
B. 1990
C. 1992
D. 1994

38. EIA is necessary because:
(a) Development is not good for environment
(b) Environmental impacts of development are in public interest
(c) There is growing interest in sustainability

Choose the **correct** answer:
A. (a) only
B. (b) only
C. (b) and (c) only
D. (a), (b) and (c)

39. A moist air parcel at 24°C has a mixing ratio of 10 g per kg. Its virtual temperature is:
A. ~25.81°C
B. ~20.68°C
C. ~ 31.25°C
D. ~28.12°C

40. The Vienna Convention is basically related to:
A. International trade in endangered species
B. Protection of O_3 layer
C. Biodiversity conservation
D. Preservation of cultural environment

41. According to Wildlife Protection Act in India, who is the authority to issue permission to hunt rogue animals?
A. Chief Minister of the State
B. Chief Wildlife Warden
C. Conservator of Forest
D. Deputy Commissioner

42. According to MOEF (now MOEFCC) notification of 1992, for labelling cosmetics as environment friendly product, the presence of fluoride (F) in tooth paste/powder should not exceed:
A. 20 ppm   B. 50 ppm
C. 100 ppm   D. 10 ppm

43. Which one of the following methods converts decomposed liquid or solid hazardous organic waste effectively?
A. Open incineration
B. Plasma incineration
C. Sanitory landfill
D. Bioremidiation

44. For a bi-variate sample, the correlation coefficient is 0.25 and it is found to be significantly different from zero at 5% level of significance. Given $t_{0.05}$ = 1.645, what is the minimum size of the sample?
A. 43   B. 50
C. 55   D. 63

45. Which one of the following is non-probability sampling?
A. Convenience probability
B. Stratified
C. Cluster
D. Systemic

46. A parametric test generally used to compare sample variance to a theoretical population variance, is:
A. F - test   B. Z - test
C. t - test   D. χ^2 - text

47. From a random sample of 36 fish caught in a sample, the mean length ($\bar{X}$) and sample standard deviation (sd) were found to be 30 cm and 6 cm respectively. If at 95% confidence level z is 1.96, then the mean length of fish in this population is in the range:
A. 27 < X < 33   B. 27.5 < X < 32.5
C. 24 < X < 36   D. 28.04 < X < 32

48. One of the natural causes of occurrence of inland soil alkalinity is the presence of:
A. Sodium hypochlorite
B. Potassium nitrate
C. Sodium chloride
D. Sodium carbonate

49. The Supreme Court of India directed the government to implement environmental education in all educational institutions as compulsory subject in:
A. 1976   B. 2003
C. 1988   D. 2014

50. Organic wetland soils have:
A. high cation capacity
B. high bulk density
C. low porosity
D. high nutrient availability

ANSWERS

1	2	3	4	5	6	7	8	9	10
C	C	D	D	B	B	B	B	B	C
11	**12**	**13**	**14**	**15**	**16**	**17**	**18**	**19**	**20**
C	B	A	C	A	C	A	C	B	A

21	22	23	24	25	26	27	28	29	30
B	B	A	A	D	B	C	B	B	D
31	32	33	34	35	36	37	38	39	40
A	C	A	D	D	B	D	C	A	B
41	42	43	44	45	46	47	48	49	50
B	D	B	A	A	D	D	D	B	A

EXPLANATORY ANSWERS

1. This table includes the average weight percentage each element contributes to the composition of the earth's crust.

Table: *Weight percentages of the earth's crust*

Oxygen	46.7
Silicon	27.7
Aluminum	8.15
Iron	5.00
Calcium	3.65
Sodium	2.85
Potassium	2.60
Magnesium	2.10
Hydrogen	.15
Phosphorus	.15
Total	**99.05**

2. The mesopause is the temperature minimum at the boundary between the mesosphere and the thermosphere atmospheric regions. Due to the lack of solar heating and very strong radiative cooling from carbon dioxide, the mesosphere is the coldest region on Earth with temperatures as low as $-100°C$ ($-148°F$ or 173 K). The altitude of the mesopause for many years was assumed to be at around 85 km (52 mi.), but observations to higher altitudes and modelling studies in the last 10 years have shown that in fact the mesopause consists of two minima - one at about 85 km and a stronger minimum at about 100 km.

5. **Fulvic acids:** The fraction of humic substances that is soluble in water under all pH conditions. They remain in solution after removal of humic acid by acidification. Fulvic acids are light yellow to yellow-brown in colour.

Fulvic acids contain more functional groups of an acidic nature, particulary COOH. The total acidities of fulvic acids (900 - 1400 meq/100 g) are considerably higher than for humic acids (400 - 870 meq/100 g).

6. **Nitrogen substances:** Nitrous oxide (N_2O). The dominant sources of N_2O are natural, but anthropogenic contributions are becoming increasingly important. Nitrous oxide is the primary source of stratospheric NO_x, which play a vital role in controlling the abundance of stratospheric ozone.

Nitrogen oxides (NO_x). Ground-level sources of NO_x play a major direct role only in tropospheric photochemical processes and an indirect role in stratosphere photochemistry, whereas injection of NO_x close to the tropopause may lead directly to a change in upper tropospheric and stratospheric ozone.

8. Most common form of lead present in pesticide is Lead arsenate. Lead arsenate is a pentavalent form of inorganic arsenic. It normally exists as white crystals with no discernible odour. Lead arsenate contains 22% arsenic and is very slightly soluble in cold water. The melting point of lead arsenate is $1042°C$, the density is 7.80 and the molecular weight is 347.12.

9. **Benzo[a]pyrene** is a polycyclic aromatic hydrocarbon found in coaltar with the formula $C_{20}H_{12}$. Its metabolites are mutagenic and highly carcinogenic, and it is listed as a Group

I carcinogen by the IARC. The compound is one of the benzopyrenes, formed by abenzene ring fused to pyrene, and is the result of incomplete combustion at temperatures between 300°C (572°F) and 600°C.

11. Commensalism is an interaction that benefits one species but has little, if any, effect on the other species. One example is some kinds of silverfish insects that move along with columns of army ants to share the food left over during their raids. The army ants receive no apparent harm or benefit from the silverfish.

Birds can benefit from trees by making their nests in them. But generally this does not affect the trees in any way. Another example is plants called *epiphytes* such as some types of orchids and bromeliads, which attach themselves to the trunks or branches of large trees in tropical and subtropical forests.

12. The molds that produce airborne toxins that can cause serious symptoms, such as breathing difficulties, memory and hearing loss, dizziness, flu-like symptoms, and acid reflux. Common ailments from toxigenic mold— including allergies (hypersensitivity after initial toxicity), and excessive bruising— usually can be treated and reduced after people leave their contaminated environment.

13. The word "biodiversity" is a contracted version of "biological diversity". The Convention on Biological Diversity defines biodiversity as: "the variability among living organisms from all sources including, *inter alia*, terrestrial, marine and other aquatic ecosystems and the ecological complexes of which they are a part; this includes diversity within species, between species, and of ecosystems."

14. **Resilience:** The ability of a living system to be restored through secondary succession after a more severe disturbance.

16. Under certain circumstances, natural selection can lead to an entirely new species. In this process, called speciation, one species splits into two or more different species. For sexually reproducing organisms, a new species forms when one population of a species has evolved to the point where its members can no longer breed and produce fertile offspring with members of another population that did not change or that evolved differently.

17. A geographic information system or geographical information system (GIS) or geospatial information system is a system designed to capture, store, manipulate, analyze, manage, and present all types of spatial or geographical data. The acronym GIS is sometimes used for geographic information science (GIScience) to refer to the academic discipline that studies geographic information systems and is a large domain within the broader academic discipline of geoinformatics.

18. **Aquiclude:** A rocky body or formation which may be porous enough to hold enough quantity of water but which by virtue of its other properties does not allow an easy and quick flow through it. It is to be treated as a practically impermeable rock mass. Compacted clay formations are the best examples of aquicludes.

19. The greater depths of the oceans are found in trenches at the margins of the oceans. Excepting the Indonesia, Antilles, and Scotia deeps, the major trenches are found in the Pacific Ocean floor. However, as pointed out by Uyeda, in a broad sense, even these three exceptions may be regarded as part of the Pacific margin because they comprise the belts of active volcanoes, sometimes called the Ring of Fire around the Pacific. These are also belts of high seismic activity and margins with trenches are Pacific-type or active margins.

20. *Ground surface inversion* also called as *radiation inversion* occurs near the earth's

7

surface due to radiation mechanism. This is also called as non-advectional inversion because it occurs in static atmospheric condition characterized by no movement of air whether horizontal or vertical (it may be noted that air is never static). Such inversion normally occurs during the long cold winter nights in the snow-covered regions of the middle and high latitudes. In fact, surface inversion is caused due to excessive nocturnal cooling of the ground surface due to rapid rate of loss of heat from the ground through outgoing longwave terrestrial radiation. Thus, the air coming in contact with the cool ground surface also becomes cold while the air layer lying above is relatively warm. Consequently, temperature inversion develops because of cold air layer below and warm air layer above.

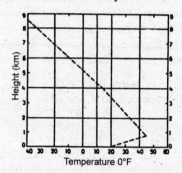

Fig.: *Ground surface inversion of temperature*

21. **Radiance:** An element of surface with an area dS emits a flux $d\mathbf{F}$ in a direction specified by an angle ψ with respect to the normal. When the element is projected at right angles to the direction of the flux, its projected area is $dS \cos \psi$ which is the apparent or effective area of the surface viewed from an angle ψ. The radiance of the element in this direction is the flux emitted in the direction per unit solid angle, or $d\mathbf{F}/\omega$, divided by the projected area $dS \cos \psi$. In other words, radiance is equivalent to the intensity of radiant flux observed in a particular direction divided by the apparent area of the source in the same direction. This quantity may be expressed in W m^{-2} sr^{-1}.

22. The boreal forest is the world's largest land-based biome. Spreading over continents and covering many countries, the boreal plays a significant role in the planet's biodiversity and even its climate. In Boreal forest mean residence time of soil organic matter in an ecosystem is maximum.

23. **The Asian Tsunami, 26 December 2004:** The Asian Tsunami, which occurred on 26 December 2004, was generated by a great underwater earthquake—the Indian Ocean earthquake, also known as the Sumatra-Andaman earthquake.

Affected areas: The Asian Tsunami has been one of the deadliest disasters in modern times. It killed large numbers of people and inundated coastal areas across south and south-east Asia, including parts of Indonesia, Sri Lanka, Thailand and India. Coastal areas of other south Asian countries like Malaysia, Myanmar, Bangladesh and Maldives, and east African countries like Somalia, Kenya, Tanzania and Madagascar also suffered serious damage. In India, the coastal areas of Andhra Pradesh, Tamil Nadu, Kerala, Pondicherry and Andaman and Nicobar Islands were the worst affected. The Indira Point in the Nicobar Islands, which was the southernmost point of India, was completely submerged, as were a few other islands.

25. Renewable energy is not always connected to the Sun. We can use energy that is created from the earth's heat to heat and cool our homes and other buildings. This source is geothermal energy. Geothermal energy is also a reliable source for the production of electricity.

Our earth is made up of seven continents, which are surrounded by oceans, which provide two important sources of energy. Tides and wind create waves. Tidal energy is renewable, and wave energy is consistently renewable with wind, water, and tides. That is not all there is! The difference in temperature of ocean water from the icy cold depths to the shallower, warmer water that has been heated by the Sun is also a source of energy.

26. The Calorific Value:

Fuel	Higher Calorific Value (Gross Calorific Value-GCV)		Lower Calorific Value (Net Calorific Value - NCV)
	kJ/kg	Btu/lb	kJ/kg
Ethanol	29700	12800	
Hydrogen	141790	61000	121000
Kerosene	46200		43000
Lignite	16300	7000	
Methane	55530		50000
Methanol	23000		

28. Uranium-238 (238U) is fissionable, but because it cannot sustain a neutron chain reaction, it is not fissile. Neutrons produced by fission of 238U have lower energies than the original neutron (they behave as in an inelastic scattering), usually below 1 MeV (*i.e.*, a speed of about 14,000 km/s), the fission threshold to cause subsequent fission of 238U, so fission of 238U does not sustain a nuclear chain reaction.

Fast fission of 238U in the secondary stage of a nuclear weapon contributes greatly to yield and to fallout. The fast fission of 238U also makes a significant contribution to the power output of some fast-neutron reactors.

30. Atmospheric particulate matter - also known as particulate matter (PM) or particulates - are microscopic solid or liquid matter suspended in the Earth's atmosphere. The term aerosol commonly refers to the particulate/air mixture, as opposed to the particulate matter alone.

In the presence of ammonia, secondary aerosols often take the form of ammonium salts; *i.e.* ammonium sulphate and ammonium nitrate (both can be dry or in aqueous solution); in the absence of ammonia, secondary compounds take an acidic form as sulphuric acid (liquid aerosol droplets) and nitric acid (atmospheric gas), all of which may contribute to the health effects of particulates.

31. SO_2 forms a complex salt with sodium tetra chloromercurate. Formaldehyde and pararosalinine dye are added to obtain a red purple colour (under controlled pH) the intensity of which can be measured at 550 nm wave length colorimetrically. (West-Gaeke method).

32. **Human Acoustics:** The human ear is a remarkable organ, which is capable of hearing sound pressures as low as 2×10^{-5}Pa (Pascals) to as high as 200 Pa before experiencing pain. The audible frequency response for a good ear ranges between 16 to 20,000 Hz. Sounds below 16 Hz are called infrasound, while those above 20,000 Hz are called ultrasound. The audio sense of human ear is most sharp in the frequency range of 2,000 to 5,500 Hz.

34. Iodine-131 (^{131}I), is an important radioisotope of iodine discovered by Glenn Seaborg and John Livingood in 1938 at the University of California, Berkeley. It has a radioactive decay half-life of about eight days. It is associated with nuclear energy, medical diagnostic and treatment procedures, and natural gas production. It also plays a major role as a radioactive isotope present in nuclear fission products, and was a significant contributor to the health hazards from open-air atomic bomb testing in the 1950s, and from the Chernobyl disaster, as well as being a large fraction of the contamination hazard in the first weeks in the Fukushima nuclear crisis. This is because I-131 is a major uranium, plutonium fission product, comprising nearly 3% of the total products of fission (by weight).

36. India has submitted its Intended Nationally Determined Contributions (INDCs) at midnight on 1st October to The United Nations Framework Convention on Climate Change (UNFCCC), making it one of the last countries to submit its climate action plan in run up to the climate change conference— Conference of Parties (COP21)—that will be held in Paris this December. A total of 146 countries, representing 87 per cent of global greenhouse gas emissions have submitted their INDCs to UNFCCC before the deadline.

37. Environmental Impact Assessment (EIA) is the formal process used to predict the environmental consequences (positive or negative) of a plan, policy, program, or project prior to the decision to move forward with the proposed action.

In India, EIAs of development projects were first started in 1977-78 when the Department of Science and Technology took up environmental appraisal of river valley projects. Subsequently, various other projects were brought under the purview of EIA. It was, however, in 1994 when EIA was made mandatory in India under the Environmental Protection Act of 1986.

40. The Vienna Convention for the Protection of the Ozone Layer is a Multilateral Environmental Agreement. It was agreed upon at the Vienna Conference of 1985 and entered into force in 1988. In terms of universality, it is one of the most successful treaties of all time, having been ratified by 197 states as well as the European Union.

41. The Chief Wildlife Warden may, on an application, grant to any person a permit to enter or reside in a sanctuary for the following purposes;

(a) Investigation or study of wildlife and any purpose ancillary or incidental thereto;

(b) Photography

(c) Scientific research

(d) Tourism

(e) Transaction of lawful business with any person in the sanctuary

42. Tooth Paste/Tooth Powder: For the purpose of formulation of these products, the ingredients listed in IS : 6356 (1979) and ISL: 5383 (1978) shall only be used. Moreover, tooth paste shall not be fluoridated and presence of fluoride (F) as impurity shall not exceed the limit of 10 ppm.

43. Incineration is a disposal method in which solid organic wastes are subjected to combustion so as to convert them into residue and gaseous products. This method is useful for disposal of residue of both solid waste management and solid residue from waste water management. This process reduces the volumes of solid waste to 20 to 30 per cent of the original volume. Incineration and other high temperature waste treatment systems are sometimes described as "thermal treatment". Incinerators convert waste materials into heat, gas, steam, and ash.

Incineration is carried out both on a small scale by individuals and on a large scale by industry. It is used to dispose of solid, liquid and gaseous waste. It is recognized as a practical method of disposing of certain hazardous waste materials (such as biological medical waste). Incineration is a controversial method of waste disposal, due to issues such as emission of gaseous pollutants.

45. In non-probability sampling designs, the elements in the population do not have any probabilities attached to their being chosen as sample subjects. This means that the findings from the study of the sample cannot be confidently generalized to the population. However, the researchers may at times be less concerned about generalisability than obtaining some preliminary information in a quick and inexpensive way. Sometimes non-probability could be thee only way to collect the data.

Examples of non-probability sampling include:

● **Convenience, haphazard or accidental sampling:** Members of the population are chosen based on their relative ease of access. To sample friends, co-workers, or shoppers at a single mall, are all examples of convenience sampling. Such samples are biased because researchers may unconsciously approach some kinds of respondents and avoid others and respondents who volunteer for a study may differ in unknown but important ways from others.

- **Snowball sampling:** The first respondent refers an acquaintance. The friend also refers a friend, and so on. Such samples are biased because they give people with more social connections an unknown but higher chance of selection but lead to higher response rates.

- **Judgmental sampling or purposive sampling:** The researcher chooses the sample based on who they think would be appropriate for the study. This is used primarily when there is a limited number of people that have expertise in the area being researched, or when the interest of the research is on a specific field or a small group. Different types of purposive sampling include:

- **Deviant case:** The researcher obtains cases that substantially differ from the dominant pattern (a special type of purposive sample). The case is selected in order to obtain information on unusual cases that can be specially problematic or specially good.

- **Case study:** The research is limited to one group, often with a similar characteristic or of small size.

- **Ad hoc quotas:** A quota is established (*e.g.* 65% women) and researchers are free to choose any respondent they wish as long as the quota is met.

46. The chi-square value is often used to judge the significance of population variance *i.e.*, we can use the test to judge if a random sample has been drawn from a normal population with mean (μ) and with a specified variance (σ_P^2). The test is based on χ^2-distribution. Such a distribution we encounter when we deal with collections of values that involve adding up squares. Variances of samples require us to add a collection of squared quantities and, thus, have distributions that are related to χ^2-distribution. If we take each one of a collection of sample variances, divide them by the known population variance and multiply these

quotients by $(n - 1)$, where n means the number of items in the sample, we shall obtain a χ^2-distribution. Thus,

$$\frac{\sigma_S^2}{\sigma_P^2} \, (n - 1) = (d.f.)$$ would have the same

distribution as χ^2-distribution with $(n - 1)$ degree of freedom.

48. Alkali, or alkaline, soils are clay soils with high pH (> 8.5), a poor soil structure and a low infiltration capacity. Often they have a hard calcareous layer at 0.5 to 1 metre depth. Alkali soils owe their unfavourable physico-chemical properties mainly to the dominating presence of sodium carbonate, which causes the soil to swell and difficult to clarify/settle.

49. In 2003, the Supreme Court (SC) of India mandated compulsory Environmental Education (EE) at all stages of education throughout the country. It directed the National Council of Education Research and Training (NCERT) to prepare a model syllabus for this purpose. In 2004, NCERT published the first edition of the syllabus, which the Supreme Court approved and directed all the boards and councils for school education in the country to adopt, to suitably modify their existing syllabi and textbooks, or to develop them a new.

50. **Table: Comparison of Mineral and Organic Soils in Wetlands**

	Mineral Soil	Organic Soil
Organic content, per cent	Less than 20-35	Greater than 20-35
Organic carbon, per cent	Less than 12-20	Greater than 12-20
pH	Usually circumneutral	Acid
Bulk density	High	Low
Porosity	Low (45-55%)	High (80%)
Hydraulic conductivity	High (except for clays)	Low to high
Water holding capacity	Low	High
Nutrient availability	Generally high	Often low
Cation exchange capacity	Low, dominated by major cations	High, dominated by hydrogen ion
Typical wetland	Riparian forest, some marshes	Northern peatland, southern swamps, and marshes

PAPER-III

Note : *This paper contains seventy five (75) objective type questions of two (2) marks each. All questions are compulsory.*

1. Which one of the following statements is not true in the case of point source Gaussian Plume Model?
   A. Wind speeds are constant in time
   B. Pollutants are conservative
   C. Rate of emission of pollutants from the stack is constant
   D. The ground level concentration is inversely proportional to effective stack height

2. Consider the simple regression equation $Y = a + bX$ between the variables Y and X. If the standard deviation S_X and S_Y are 3 and 2 respectively and correlation coefficient $r = 0.75$, the estimate of b is:
   A. 0.25
   B. 0.5
   C. 1.125
   D. 1.5

3. Consider two normal populations with variances of 10 and 20, respectively. If two independent random samples drawn from the two populations are of the sizes 30 and 24 and their variances 10 and 15 respectively, the value of static $F_{(29,23)}$ is:
   A. 1.33
   B. 2.50
   C. 1.56
   D. 3.0

4. A normal population has $\sigma^2 = 6$. The sum of squares of deviations of 15 sample values from their mean being 120, what is the χ^2 (chi-square) value?
   A. 9
   B. 48
   C. 20
   D. 1.33

5. Choose the correct sequence of phases associated with a population growth that exhibits logistic model represented by
   $$\frac{dN}{dt} = rN\left(1 - \frac{N}{k}\right).$$

   A. Stationary phase → Exponential phase → Lag phase
   B. Lag phase → Stationary phase → Exponential phase
   C. Lag phase → Exponential phase → Stationary phase
   D. Exponential phase → Stationary phase → Lag phase

6. The toxic substances of special concern emitted during incineration process from waste to energy plants are:
   (a) Carbon monoxide (b) Carbon dioxide
   (c) Dioxins   (d) Furans
   Choose the **correct** answer:
   A. (a) and (b) only   B. (b) and (c) only
   C. (a) and (d) only   D. (c) and (d) only

7. Sanitary land fills have following properties. They:
   (a) reduce trash volume in a short time
   (b) release CH_4 and CO_2
   (c) eventually produce leachate which contaminate ground water
   Choose the **correct** answer:
   A. (a) and (b) only   B. (b) only
   C. (a) and (c) only   D. (a), (b) and (c)

8. For providing information related to environment to decision makers, policy makers, scientists and environmental engineers all over the country, ENVIS was established in the year belonging to:
   A. Sixties   B. Seventies
   C. Eighties   D. Nineties

9. The total radiative forcing of all major and minor green-house gases in the year 2014 is estimated to be:
   A. ~ 2.51 W/m²   B. ~ 2.93 W/m²
   C. ~ 1.87 W/m²   D. ~ 2.7 W/m²

10. For the range of temperatures observed in the earth's atmosphere, the saturation mixing ratio (W_s) and the total pressure are related as:

A. $W_s \propto \dfrac{1}{p}$ B. $W_s \propto p$

C. $W_s \propto p^{3/2}$ D. $W_s \propto p^{-3/2}$

11. A thermal power plant based on coal produces 100 MW of electrical power with conversion efficiency of 30%. If the ash content of coal is 5% and net heating value is 30 MJ per kg, how much ash is produced daily?
A. 48 metric tons   B. 24 metric tons
C. 90 metric tons   D. 60 metric tons

12. Under which section of Wildlife (Protection) Act 1972, the state government can declare an area closed to hunting for a specified period?
A. Section 35   B. Section 27
C. Section 38-A   D. Section 37

13. Which one of the following criteria should **not** contribute to the process of establishing significance of the impact of a developmental project on environment?
A. Sensitivity of surrounding environment
B. Probability of the impact occurring
C. Views and values of the developer
D. Views and suggestions of the public

14. The following benefits may accrue as a result of environmental audit:
(a) Material audit leads to improvement in the production efficiency and cost
(b) Pollution monitoring leads to environmental quality improvement
(c) Approach towards zero discharge and zero emission leads to clean development
(d) Incentive for pollution abatement in the form of reduction in import tax leads to cleaner environment

Choose the **correct** answer:
A. (a) only
B. (b) and (c) only
C. (b) and (d) only
D. (a), (b), (c) and (d)

15. Environmental Impact Assessment (EIA) was incorporated under which one of the following legislations?

A. Air (Prevention and Control of Pollution) Act 1981
B. Wildlife (Protection) Act, 1981
C. Indian Forest Act, 1927
D. Environmental (Protection) Act 1986

16. A company operating a vehicle Manufacturing plant has developed Environmental Management System (EMS) to enhance its performance and to improve quality of its products. The key aspects of this EMS would include:
A. Audit of manufacturing plant safety procedure
B. Maximizing returns to stakeholders of the company
C. The development of an overall framework for environmental affairs of the company
D. The aspects of costs involved in developing an environmental policy.

17. Best practice in scoping requires:
(a) A site visit
(b) Relevant experience of other similar developmental projects
(c) Employing formal scoping techniques

Choose the **correct** answer:
A. (a) only   B. (a) and (b) only
C. (b) and (c) only   D. (a), (b) and (c)

18. Match the **List-I** and **List-II**. Identify the **correct** answer from the codes given below:

List-I (Stages in EIA)	List-II (Actions in EIA)
(a) Screening	(i) Reduce or avoid the impacts
(b) Scoping	(ii) Establish present and future stages of environment
(c) Baseline description	(iii) Early indication of crucial impacts
(d) Mitigation measures	(iv) Narrowing the application of EIA

Codes:

	(a)	(b)	(c)	(d)
A.	(iv)	(iii)	(ii)	(i)
B.	(i)	(iv)	(iii)	(ii)
C.	(ii)	(i)	(iv)	(iii)
D.	(iii)	(ii)	(i)	(iv)

19. The decision making process in EIA generally **does not** include:
    A. Cost-benefit analysis
    B. Procedural information
    C. Socio-economic aspects
    D. Operational management

20. Which of the following actions may be recommended for acidified lakes?
    A. Ammoniation   B. Liming
    C. Ozonation   D. Chlorination

21. Given below are two statements. One labelled as **Assertion (A)** and the other labelled as **Reason (R)**.

    Assertion (A): All types of aerosols contribute to radiative forcing.

    Reason (R): Aerosol effectively absorb electromagnetic radiations.

    Choose the **correct** answer:
    A. Both (A) and (R) are correct and (R) is the correct explanation of (A).
    B. Both (A) and (R) are correct and (R) is not the correct explanation of (A).
    C. (A) is true, but (R) is false.
    D. (A) is false, but (R) is true.

22. Given below are two statements. One labelled as **Assertion (A)** and the other labelled as **Reason (R)**.

    Assertion (A): The efficiency of fuel cells is not limited by the second law of thermodynamics.

    Reason (R): There is no intermediate heat to work conversion in a fuel cell.

    Choose the **correct** answer:
    A. Both (A) and (R) are correct and (R) is the correct explanation of (A).
    B. Both (A) and (R) are correct and (R) is not the correct explanation of (A).
    C. (A) is true, but (R) is false.
    D. (A) is false, but (R) is true.

23. Given below are two statements. One labelled as **Assertion (A)** and the other labelled as **Reason (R).**

    Assertion (A): A wind rose with approximately equal length spokes (or petals) represents great variation of wind direction over a given duration.

    Reason (R): The length of the spokes is a measure of wind speeds in a given duration.

    Choose the **correct** answer:
    A. Both (A) and (R) are correct and (R) is the correct explanation of (A).
    B. Both (A) and (R) are correct and (R) is not the correct explanation of (A).
    C. (A) is true, but (R) is false.
    D. (A) is false, but (R) is true.

24. Given below are two statements. One labelled as **Assertion (A)** and the other labelled as **Reason (R).**

    Assertion (A): Large scale OTEC development may exacerbate the green-house effect.

    Reason (R): Methane is a green-house gas.

    Choose the **correct** answer:
    A. Both (A) and (R) are correct and (R) is the correct explanation of (A).
    B. Both (A) and (R) are correct and (R) is not the correct explanation of (A).
    C. (A) is true, but (R) is false.
    D. (A) is false, but (R) is true.

25. In a spectrophotometric cell of 2.0 cm path length, the solution of a substance shows the absorbance value of 1.0. If the molar absorptivity of the compound is 2×10^4 L $mol^{-1} cm^{-1}$, calculate the concentration of the substance in solution. What is the concentration of the substance in that solution?
    A. 2.5×10^{-5} mol L^{-1}
    B. 4.0×10^{-4} mol L^{-1}
    C. 1.0×10^4 mol L^{-1}
    D. 5.0×10^{-4} mol L^{-1}

26. In order to obtain useful fusion energy from a thermonuclear fusion reactor, if the confinement time of the D + T Plasma ions is 1 μ sec, the ion density (per m^3) must be:

A. $\geq 10^{26}$ m^{-3} B. $\geq 10^{23}$ m^{-3}
C. $\geq 10^{20}$ m^{-3} D. $\geq 10^{14}$ m^{-3}

27. Which of the following is **not** a detrivore?
A. Vultures B. Earthworms
C. Insects D. *Hydrilla*

28. Secondary succession begins at:
A. base rock
B. newly cooled lava
C. burnt forest
D. newly created shallow pond

29. Given below are two statements. One labelled as **Assertion (A)** and the other labelled as **Reason (R).**

Assertion (A): It is generally agreed that life on earth began between 3.5 and 4.5 billion years ago.

Reason (R): The first form of life was the anaerobic bacteria as environment was devoid of oxygen.

Choose the **correct** answer:
A. Both (A) and (R) are correct and (R) is the correct explanation of (A).
B. Both (A) and (R) are correct and (R) is not the correct explanation of (A).
C. (A) is true, but (R) is false.
D. (A) is false, but (R) is true.

30. The total number of Sustainable Development Goals (SDGs) announced by UN in 2015 are:
A. 15 B. 17
C. 19 D. 21

31. The total area of productive ecosystem required to support the population sustainably is known as:
A. Ecological footprint
B. Ecological handprint
C. Carrying capacity
D. Ecological services

32. Carrying capacity of a population determines that a particular habitat for a given species can sustain:
A. Minimum Population
B. Maximum Population
C. Average Population
D. A Fraction of Migrating Population

33. Which one of the following is the most productive ecosystem?
A. Lakes and Streams
B. Estuaries
C. Continental shelf
D. Open ocean

34. A measure that combines the number of species and their relative abundances compared with one another is termed:
A. Species richness
B. Species evenness
C. Species diversity
D. Species relationships

35. The figures of humanity's global footprint (million hectares) for different countries estimated by WWF and Global Footprint Network in 2008 fall in the sequence:
A. US > China > European Union > Japan > India
B. China > US > Japan > India > European Union
C. European Union > US > China > Japan > India
D. US > European Union > China > India > Japan

36. A common features of the synoptic and mesoscale motions in the atmosphere is that their:
A. Vertical motion component is more in magnitude than the horizontal wind component.
B. Vertical motion component is roughly comparable to horizontal wind component.
C. Vertical motion component is an order of magnitude smaller than the horizontal wind component.
D. Properties can be studied by conventional synoptic networks.

37. The shape of a plume from a tall stack located on a flat terrain is found to be of "fanning" type. It implies that the atmosphere is under the condition of:

A. Strong lapse rate
B. Weak lapse rate
C. Inversion
D. Weak lapse rate below inversion

38. Given below are two statements. One labelled as **Assertion (A)** and the other labelled as **Reason (R).**

Assertion (A): Thunderstorm is a violent convective event accompanied by thunder and lightening.

Reason (R): Thunderstorm is not associated with vertical air movement, humidity and instability.

Choose the **correct** answer:
A. Both (A) and (R) are correct and (R) is the correct explanation of (A).
B. Both (A) and (R) are correct and (R) is not the correct explanation of (A).
C. (A) is true, but (R) is false.
D. (A) is false, but (R) is true.

39. According to National Ambient Air Quality Standards in India, the permissible 24 hour average concentration of lead in ambient air of an industrial area is:
A. $1.0 \ \mu g/m^3$
B. $2.0 \ \mu g/m^3$
C. $3.03 \ \mu g/m^3$
D. $4.0 \ \mu g/m^3$

40. Peat soils, which have undergone prolonged drought in the forests are prone for:
(a) ground forest fire
(b) underground forest fire
(c) tree crown fire

Choose the **correct** code:
A. (a) only
B. (b) only
C. (a) and (b) only
D. (a), (b) and (c)

41. Insect pests can be controlled by the use of:
(a) Insecticide
(b) Pheromones
(c) Juvenile Hormones
(d) Nitrophosphate

Choose the **correct** answer:
A. (a) only
B. (a) and (b) only
C. (a), (b) and (c) only
D. (a), (b), (c) and (d)

42. Dioxins and Furans are two toxic gaseous pollutants which can be measured by:
A. GC - MS
B. TLC
C. ICP - AES
D. AAS

43. Based on the pE value for four water samples given below, the concentration of dissolved oxygen shall be highest in:
A. pE = –4.1
B. pE = 13.9
C. pE = 1.0
D. pE = 7.0

44. A total of 10 instantaneous sound pressure level measurements at 10 sec intervals for a traffic site are given in the table below:

S. No.	1	2	3	4	5	6	7	8	9	10
SPL (dB)	71	75	70	78	80	84	76	74	75	74

The estimated L_{90} from these measurement is:
A. ~71 dB
B. ~70 dB
C. ~74 dB
D. ~75 dB

45. The composition of rhizospheric micro organisms are dependent on the soil:
(a) Texture
(b) Organic matter
(c) pH
(d) Elasticity

Choose the **correct** answer:
A. (a) only
B. (a) and (b) only
C. (a), (b) and (c) only
D. (a), (b), (c) and (d)

46. Given below are two statements. One labelled as **Assertion (A)** and the other labelled as **Reason (R).**

Assertion (A): The fundamental goal of a dose - response assessment is to obtain a mathematical relationship between the amount of a toxicant that a human is exposed to and the risk that there will be.

Reason (R): To apply dose - response data obtained from animal bioassay to humans, a scalling factor must be introduced.

Choose the **correct** answer:
A. Both (A) and (R) are correct and (R) is the correct explanation of (A).
B. Both (A) and (R) are correct and (R) is not the correct explanation of (A).
C. (A) is true, but (R) is false.
D. (A) is false, but (R) is true.

47. Tropical grasslands with scattered trees are also known as:
    A. Taigas
    B. Steppe
    C. Savannas
    D. Meadows

48. On 18th April 2015, Global Alliance to Eliminate Lead Paint (GAELP) announced the goal of eliminating lead paint around the world by:
    A. 2020
    B. 2025
    C. 2028
    D. 2022

49. The form of coal/fuel in the ascending order of heating value can be best represented as:
    A. Lignite < Peat < Bituminous < Anthracite
    B. Bituminous < Lignite < Peat < Anthracite
    C. Peat < Lignite < Bituminous < Anthracite
    D. Peat < Lignite < Anthracite < Bituminous

50. In India wetland conservation is presently done by the Ministry of Environment, Forest and Climate Change under:
    A. National Wetland Conservation Programme
    B. National Plan for Conservation of Aquatic Ecosystems
    C. National Lake Conservation Programme
    D. Coastal Regulation Zone

51. Soil salination is **not** caused by:
    A. Agricultural area with high ground water irrigation
    B. Coastal swampy area
    C. Flood prone area
    D. Upland lateritic area with waste water irrigation

52. Ground water occurs under:
    (a) Unconfined condition in shallow aquifers
    (b) Semi-confined aquifers
    (c) Confined aquifers
    Choose the **correct** answer:
    A. (a) only
    B. (a) and (b) only
    C. (b) and (c) only
    D. (a), (b) and (c)

53. DEM (Digital Elevation Model) is best represented using:
    A. Vector Data Models
    B. Raster Data Models
    C. Coverage Data Structure
    D. Non-topological Data Structure

54. Delta are classified into six basic types taking cognissance and importance of:
    (a) Rivers
    (b) Waves
    (c) Tides
    Choose the **correct** answer:
    A. (a) only
    B. (a) and (b) only
    C. (a) and (c) only
    D. (a), (b) and (c)

55. Large elongated depression with steep walls formed by the downward displacement of a block of the earth surface between nearly parallel faults or fault system:
    A. Thrust faults
    B. Horst
    C. Grabben
    D. Rift Valley

56. Which form of scattering in visible region in the atmosphere is not dependent on wavelength?
    (a) Rayleigh
    (b) Mie
    (c) Non-selective
    Choose the **correct** answer:
    A. (a) only
    B. (a) and (b) only
    C. (c) only
    D. (b) and (c) only

57. Best spatial configuration for designing a core natural area is:
    A. Circular
    B. Rectangular
    C. Square
    D. Triangle

58. Ecosystem resilience is the capacity of an ecosystem to sustain its:
    (a) Fundamental function
    (b) Structure
    (c) Feedbacks in the face of a spectrum of shock and perturbations
    Choose the **correct** answer:
    A. (a) and (b) only
    B. (b) and (c) only
    C. (a) and (c) only
    D. (a), (b) and (c)

59. With regard to ozone depletion over Antarctica, select the false statement:
    A. Circumpolar vortex acts as a reaction chamber
    B. Polar Stratospheric Clouds (PSCs) are formed within the vortex

C. There is very low temperature inside the vortex

D. The heterogenous reaction

$$ClONO_2(s) + HCl(g) \rightarrow Cl_2(g) + HNO_3(s) \text{ takes over PSCs}$$

60. Match the **List-I** and **List-II**. Choose the **correct** answer from the codes given below:

List-I (Horizon)	List-II (Type/Characteristics)
(a) A - horizon	(i) Subsoil
(b) O - horizon	(ii) Leaf litter
(c) C - horizon	(iii) Parent material
(d) B - horizon	(iv) Top soil

Codes:

	(a)	(b)	(c)	(d)
A.	(iv)	(ii)	(iii)	(i)
B.	(i)	(iii)	(iv)	(ii)
C.	(ii)	(iv)	(i)	(iii)
D.	(iii)	(i)	(ii)	(iv)

61. A laboratory analysis of a waste water sample indicated BOD of 750 mg L^{-1} with rate constant (K) 0.20 day^{-1} at 20°C. The 5-day BOD at 20°C is:

A. 675 mg L^{-1} B. 650 mg L^{-1}

C. 400 mg L^{-1} D. 600 mg L^{-1}

62. A stream with a flow of 0.2 m^3/sec and a chloride concentration of 50 mg/L receives a discharge of mine drainage water with a flow of 0.05 m^3/sec and chloride concentration of 1500 mg/L. The downstream concentration of chloride is:

A. 150 mg/L   B. 200 mg/L

C. 340 mg/L   D. 380 mg/L

63. Four students (**List-A**) working independently in a chromatographic analysis (**List-B**) reported the Retention Factor (R_f) values:

List-A (Students)		List-B (R_f Values)
(a) R	→	(i) 0
(b) S	→	(ii) 0.5
(c) T	→	(iii) 1.3
(d) U	→	(iv) 1.0

The result of which student(s) is (are) definitely **incorrect**:

A. R and U   B. S and T

C. S, T and U   D. T

64. The mechanism of the formation of gaseous N_2O_5 from NO_2 and O_2 gases in the gas phase within clouds is:

$$NO_2(g) + O_3(g) \rightarrow NO_3(g) + O_2(g) \quad (i)$$
$$NO_3(g) + NO_2(g) \rightarrow N_2O_5(g) \quad (ii)$$

The experimentally determined rate law is

$$-d\,[NO_2(g)]\,/dt = K\,[NO_2(g)]\,[O_3(g)]$$

Based on the information provided which of the following statement is **incorrect**?

A. Overall reaction is : $2NO(g) + O_3(g) \rightarrow N_2O_5(g) + O_2(g)$

B. The reaction intermediate is NO_3

C. The rate determining step is reaction (i)

D. The rate reaction (ii) is slower than the rate of reaction (i)

65. In a rain water sample of pH = 8.45, the dominant species of dissolved sulphur dioxide shall be:

A. $SO_2 \cdot H_2O$ B. HSO_3^-

C. SO_3^{2-} D. $S_2O_5^{2-}$

66. An aquifer of sand has a saturated column of cross-sectional area 0.2 m × 5 m and a depth of 3 m. If the specific yield of sand is 25%, how much water can be extracted from the aquifer?

A. 0.5 m^3 B. 0.75 m^3

C. 1.2 m^3 D. 1.5 m^3

67. Atmospheric life times of CFCs is typically in the range:

A. 50 - 102 years   B. 140 - 200 years

C. 200 - 400 years   D. 152 - 210 years

68. With respect to CO_2, Global Warming Potential (GWP) for N_2O over a time horizon of 100 years is estimated to be:

A. 156   B. 210

C. 296   D. 240

69. The green-house gas N_2O strongly absorbs infra-red radiations of wavelength(s):
A. ~4.5 μm
B. ~7.8 μm and 8.6 μm
C. ~9.6 μm
D. ~10.6 μm

70. By the year 2022, Indian government has set a new target of Solar Power generation of:
A. 4 GW   B. 60 GW
C. 75 GW   D. 100 GW

71. Match the **List-I** and **List-II**. Identify the **correct** answer from the codes given below the lists.

List-I (Causes)	List-II (Effects)
(a) Soil organisms	(i) Algal bloom
(b) Phosphorous assimilation	(ii) Chronic obstructive pulmonary diseases
(c) Water pollution	(iii) Decomposition
(d) Air pollution	(iv) Complexing agent

Codes:

	(a)	(b)	(c)	(d)
A.	(i)	(ii)	(iii)	(iv)
B.	(iii)	(iv)	(i)	(ii)
C.	(ii)	(iii)	(iv)	(i)
D.	(iv)	(ii)	(i)	(iii)

72. The Wavelengths that are most important in the context of stratospheric ozone depletion are:
A. 280 - 320 nm   B. 400 - 700 nm
C. 700 - 900 nm   D. > 900 nm

73. Remote sensing satellites such as RESOURCESAT are usually placed in polar:
(a) Low Earth Polar orbit
(b) Sunsynchronous orbit
(c) Geosynchronous orbit
Codes:
A. (b) and (c) only   B. (a) and (b) only
C. (a) and (c) only   D. (a), (b) and (c)

74. Gills of marine fishes perform the functions of the following:
A. Water loss and salt excretion
B. Water gain and salt excretion
C. Water uptake and solute uptake
D. Water loss and solute uptake

75. The instrument used for determination of soil water loss by percolation, evapotranspiration and run off is called:
A. Lysimeter
B. Rain Gauze
C. Soil moisture meter
D. Soil porosity meter

ANSWERS

1	2	3	4	5	6	7	8	9	10
D	B	A	C	C	D	B	C	B	A

11	12	13	14	15	16	17	18	19	20
A	D	C	D	D	C	D	A	D	B

21	22	23	24	25	26	27	28	29	30
C	A	C	B	A	A	D	C	B	B

31	32	33	34	35	36	37	38	39	40
A	B	B	C	D	C	C	C	A	C

41	42	43	44	45	46	47	48	49	50
C	A	B	A	C	B	C	A	C	B

51	52	53	54	55	56	57	58	59	60
C	D	B	D	D	C	A	D	D	A

61	62	63	64	65	66	67	68	69	70
A	C	D	D	C	B	A	C	B	D

71	72	73	74	75
B	A	B	A	A

EXPLANATORY ANSWERS

1. Assumptions in Gaussian plume model:

(*i*) Steady-state conditions, which imply that the rate of emission from the point source is constant.

(*ii*) Homogeneous flow, which implies that the wind speed is constant both in time and with height (wind direction shear is not considered).

(*iii*) Pollutant is conservative and no gravity fallout.

(*iv*) Perfect reflection of the plume at the underlying surface, *i.e.* no ground absorption.

(*v*) The turbulent diffusion in the *x*-direction is neglected relative to advection in the transport direction (*x*), which implies that the model should be applied for average wind speeds of more than 1 m/s ($\bar{u} >$ 1 m/s).

(*vi*) The coordinate system is directed with its *x*-axis into the direction of the flow, and the *v* (lateral) and *w* (vertical) components of the time averaged wind vector are set to zero.

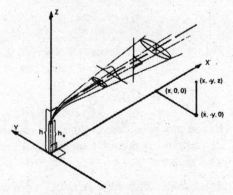

Fig.: *Cross section of a Gaussian plume profile in the horizontal and vertical directions.*

(*vii*) The terrain underlying the plume is flat.

(*viii*) All variables are ensemble averaged, which implies long-term averaging with stationary conditions.

2. For simple linear regression,

$$b = r\frac{s_y}{s_x}, \qquad b_0 = \bar{y} - b_1\bar{x}$$

Given that $r = 0.75$,
$s_x = 3, \quad s_y = 2$

$$b = 0.75 \times \frac{2}{3} = 0.5.$$

5. Four characteristic phases of the growth cycle are recognized.

1. **Lag Phase:** Immediately after inoculation of the cells into fresh medium, the population remains temporarily unchanged. Although there is no apparent cell division occurring, the cells may be growing in volume or mass, synthesizing enzymes, proteins, RNA, etc., and increasing in metabolic activity.

2. **Exponential (log) Phase:** The exponential phase of growth is a pattern of balanced growth wherein all the cells are dividing regularly by binary fission, and are growing by geometric progression. The cells divide at a constant rate depending upon the composition of the growth medium and the conditions of incubation.

3. **Stationary Phase:** Exponential growth cannot be continued forever in a **batch culture** (*e.g.* a closed system such as a test tube or flask). Population growth is limited by one of three factors: 1. exhaustion of available nutrients; 2. accumulation of inhibitory metabolites or end products; 3. exhaustion of space, in this case called a lack of "biological space".

4. **Death Phase:** If incubation continues after the population reaches stationary phase, a death phase follows, in which the viable cell population declines. During the death phase, the number of viable cells decreases geometrically (exponentially), essentially

the reverse of growth during the log phase.

6. Dioxins and furans are chemicals that are created by burning chlorine in the presence of hydrocarbons and oxygen. Hydrocarbons (the bulk of the TDF itself, as well as coal, wood or gas it's co-fired with) and oxygen (from the air) are readily available when TDF is incinerated. Dioxins and furans are produced by tire incineration because tires contain chlorine. The manufacture of synthetic rubber for tires uses up to 25% aromatic extender oils, a toxic waste product of oil refining which can contain chlorine.

7. Landfills produce both gaseous and aqueous emissions. Biomass in landfills quickly depletes oxygen by aerobic biodegradation of microorganisms in the landfill,

$$\{CH_2O\} \text{ (biomass)} + O_2 \rightarrow CO_2 + H_2O$$

emitting carbon dioxide. Over a period of many decades the buried biodegradable materials undergo anaerobic biodegradation

$$2\{CH_2O\} \rightarrow CO_2 + CH_4$$

releasing methane as well as carbon dioxide. Although often impractical and too expensive, it is desirable to reclaim the methane as fuel, and some large sanitary landfills are major sources of methane. Released methane is a greenhouse gas and can pose significant explosion hazards to structures built on landfills.

8. Realising the importance of Environmental Information, the Government of India, in December, 1982, established an Environmental Information System (ENVIS) as a plan programme. The focus of ENVIS since inception has been on providing environmental information to decision makers, policy planners, scientists and engineers, research workers, etc. all over the country. Since environment is a broad-ranging, multi-disciplinary subject, a comprehensive information system on environment would necessarily involve effective participation of concerned institutions/organisations in the country that are actively engaged in work relating to different subject areas of environment. ENVIS has, therefore, developed itself with a network of such participating institutions/organisations for the programme to be meaningful.

10. **Saturation mixing ratios**

The *saturation mixing ratio* w_s, with respect to water is defined as the ratio of the mass m_{vs} of water vapour in a given volume of air that is saturated with respect to a plane surface of pure water to the mass m_d of the dry air. That is

$$w_s = \frac{m_{vs}}{m_d}$$

Because water vapour and dry air both obey the ideal gas equation

$$w_s = \frac{p'_{vs}}{p'_d} = \frac{e_s}{(R_yT)} \bigg/ \frac{(p-e_s)}{(R_dT)}$$

where p'_{vs} is the partial density of water vapour required to saturate air with respect to water at temperature T, p'_d is the partial density of the dry air and p is the total pressure. Combining the equations, we obtain

$$w_s = 0.622 \frac{e_s}{p-e_s}$$

For the range of temperatures observed in the Earth's atmosphere, $p \gg e_y$; therefore

$$w_s = 0.622 \frac{e_s}{p}$$

Hence, at a given temperature, the saturation mixing ratio is inversely proportional to the total pressure.

12. The Wildlife Protection Act, 1972, provides for protection to listed species of flora and fauna and establishes a network of ecologically-important protected areas. The Act consists of 60 Sections and VI Schedules-divided into Eight Chapters. The Wildlife Protection Act, 1972 empowers the central

and state governments to declare any area a wildlife sanctuary, national park or closed area. There is a blanket ban on carrying out any industrial activity inside these protected areas. It provides for authorities to administer and implement the Act; regulate the hunting of wild animals; protect specified plants, sanctuaries, national parks and closed areas; restrict trade or commerce in wild animals or animal articles; and miscellaneous matters. The Act prohibits hunting of animals except with permission of authorized officer when an animal has become dangerous to human life or property or as disabled or diseased as to be beyond recovery.

Section-37: Declaration of closed area: (1) The State Government may, by notification, declare any area closed to hunting for such period as may be specified in the notification. (2) No hunting of any wild animal shall be permitted in a closed area during the period specified in the notification referred to in sub-section (1).

15. Under the Environment (Protection) Act, 1986 EIA for projects was made mandatory in India in 1994 with the objective to predict environment impact of projects, find ways and means to reduce adverse impacts, and if these impacts were too high, to disallow such projects.

16. The key to effective environmental management is the use of a systematic approach to planning, controlling, measuring and improving an organization's environmental efforts. Potentially significant environmental improvements (and cost savings) can be achieved by reviewing and improving your organization's management processes. Not all environmental problems need to be solved by installing expensive pollution control equipment.

18. **Screening:** Screening helps to focus resources on those projects most likely to have significant impacts, those where the impacts are uncertain and those where environmental management input is likely to be required.

Scoping: Scoping is a crucial part of the impact assessment process and involves the identification and 'narrowing-down' of potential environmental impacts to ensure that the assessment focuses on the key issues for decision-making. It also offers a crucial opportunity to involve local people in determining the scope and focus of the impact assessment.

The description of the environmental baseline includes the establishment of both the present and future state of the environment, in the absence of the project, taking into account changes resulting from natural events and from other human activities.

Mitigation involves the introduction of measures to avoid, reduce, remedy or compensate for any significant adverse impacts.

20. **Liming:** The only sure way to prevent acidification of freshwater bodies is to reduce the emissions of acid pollutants in the first place . At present, the main way of reversing acidification in freshwaters is liming the water body or its surrounding catchment. The main liming method is to add the lime directly to the water body.

Acidified lakes in Sweden have been restored in the short-term by liming. Liming provides only a temporary solution, hence it is far better to attack the source of the problem by reducing emissions of acidifying pollutants.

22. **Fuel cells:** A fuel cell converts chemical energy of a fuel into electricity directly, with no intermediate combustion cycle. Since there is no intermediate 'heat to work' conversion, the efficiency of fuel cells is not limited by the second law of thermodynamics, unlike conventional 'fuel $\rightarrow$ heat $\rightarrow$ work $\rightarrow$ electricity' systems. The efficiency of conversion from chemical energy to electricity by a fuel cell may theoretically be 100%.

27. **Detritivore:** Organisms that eat dead things, also known as decomposers.

    Decomposer: Organisms that break down dead organisms by consuming them.

    Decomposers are like nature's garbage collectors. Common detritivores include vultures, many types of insects, fungi, and bacteria but hydrilla is not a detrivore.

28. Secondary succession is one of the two types of ecological succession of plant life. As opposed to the first, primary succession, secondary succession is a process started by an event (*e.g.*, forest fire, harvesting, hurricane) that reduces an already established ecosystem (*e.g.*, a forest or a wheat field) to a smaller population of species, and as such secondary succession occurs on pre-existing soil whereas primary succession usually occurs in a place lacking soil.

30. On September 25th 2015, countries adopted a set of goals to end poverty, protect the planet and ensure prosperity for all as part of a new sustainable development agenda. Each goal has specific targets to be achieved over the next 15 years.

    The total number of sustainable development Goals (SDGs) announced by UN in 2015 are 17.

    1. No Poverty, 2. Zero Hunger, 3. Good Health and Well-Being, 4. Quality Education, 5. Gender Equality, 6. Clean Water and Sanitation, 7. Affordable and Clean Energy, 8. Decent Work and Economic Growth, 9. Industry, Innovation and Infrastructure, 10. Reduced Inequalities, 11. Sustainable Cities and Communities, 12. Responsible Consumption and Production, 13. Climate Action, 14. Life Below Water, 15. Life on Land, 16. Peace, Justice and Strong Institutions, 17. Partnerships for the Goals.

31. **Total Ecological Impact and Ecological Footprint:** The concept of an ecological footprint is concerned with determining how much productive land and water area in various ecosystems is required to support a region's human population indefinitely at current consumption levels. This approach essentially inverts traditional carrying-capacity measures that are concerned with the maximum size of population that a given ecological region can sustain indefinitely.

    Related to the ecological footprint concept is the notion of total ecological impact—the total human impact on ecosystems of the resource degradation and pollution caused by human production and consumption activities.

32. **Carrying capacity (K):** The maximum population of a given species that a particular habitat can sustain indefinitely without degrading the habitat. The growth rate of a population decreases as its size nears the carrying capacity of its environment because resources such as food and water begin to dwindle.

33. An estuary is a partially enclosed body of water along the coast where freshwater from rivers and streams meets and mixes with salt water from the ocean. Estuaries and the lands surrounding them are places of transition from land to sea and freshwater to salt water. Although influenced by the tides, they are protected from the full force of ocean waves, winds, and storms by barrier islands or peninsulas. Estuaries are among the most productive ecosystems in the world. Many species of animals rely on the sheltered waters of estuaries for food, secure places to breed and migration stopovers.

34. Biodiversity is one of the primary interests of ecologists, but quantifying the species diversity of ecological communities is complicated. In addition to issues of statistical sampling, the rather arbitrary nature of delineating an ecological community, and the difficulty of positively identifying all of the species present, species diversity itself has two separate components: (1) The number of

species present (species richness). (2) Their relative abundances (termed dominance or evenness).

Total Ecological Footprint (million hectares) and Share of Global Biological Capacity (%)

- United States 2,810 (25%)
- European Union 2,160 (19%)
- China 2,050 (18%)
- India 780 (7%)
- Japan 540 (5%)

36. A common features of the synoptic and mesoscale motions in the atmosphere is that their Vertical motion component is an order of magnitude smaller than the horizontal wind component.

The vertical component of atmospheric motions, typically on the order of 1 – 10 cm/sec., is generally much weaker than its horizontal counterpart, often by 2 orders of magnitude when examined at the synoptic scale. In spite of their relatively small magnitude, vertical motions are necessary in maintaining the global energy cycle and shaping the temperature structure of the atmosphere.

37. Plume Behaviour: One way to quickly determine the stability of the lower atmosphere is to view the shape of a smoke trail, or *plume,* from a tall stack located on flat terrain. Visible plumes usually consist of pollutants emitted from a smoke stack into the atmosphere. The formation and fate of the plume itself depend on a number of related factors: (1) the nature of the pollutants, (2) meteorological factors (combination of vertical air movement and horizontal air flow), (3) source obstructions, and (4) local topography, especially downwind. Overall, maximum ground-level concentrations will occur in a range from the vicinity of the smokestack to some distance downwind.

When the atmosphere is slightly stable or neutral, a typical plume *cones.* This is likely to occur on cloudy days or sunny days between the breakup of a radiation inversion

35. The per capita ecological footprint is an estimate of how much of the earth's renewable resources an individual consumes.

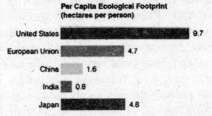

Per Capita Ecological Footprint (hectares per person)

- United States 9.7
- European Union 4.7
- China 1.6
- India 0.8
- Japan 4.8

and the development of unstable daytime conditions. When the atmosphere is highly unstable, a *looping plume* forms. In the looping plume, the stream of emitted pollutants undergoes rapid mixing, and the wind causes large eddies, which may carry the entire plume down to the ground, causing high concentrations close to the stack before dispersion is complete. In an extremely stable atmosphere, usually in the early morning during a radiation inversion, a *fanning plume* spreads horizontally, with little mixing. When an inversion layer occurs a short distance above the plume source, the plume is said to be *fumigating.* Ground-level pollutant concentrations can be very high when fumigation occurs. Sufficiently tall stacks can prevent fumigation in most cases. When inversion conditions exist below the plume source, the plume is said to be *lofting.* When conditions are neutral, the plume issuing from a smoke stack tends to rise directly into the atmosphere. When an inversion layer prevails both above and below the plume source, the plume issuing from a smokestack tends to be *trapped.*

39. The environmental quality is based on three physical parameters *viz.* Air quality, Water quality and Noise level.

Lead (Pb): No systematic date is available to compare the status of lead (Pb) in the district. But the present data show that average concentration of Pb (0.45) lies within the limit of National Ambient Air Quality Standard (NAAQS) for residential area (1.0 $\mu g/m^3$).

41. Insect pheromones: Pheromones serve as a means of communication between animals like light and sound. They transfer informations from one animal to another by smell or taste. Pheromones evoke specific behavioural, developmental or reproductive responses in the recipients, and these responses may be of great importance for the survival of the species. A class of pheromones called sex pheromones are mainly used in the behavioural control of insect pests. A trap containing female sex pheromones is placed in the pest infested region. The males aggregate at the trap and are destroyed. Natural pheromone of gypsy moth, *Prothetria dispar,* a pest of forest can be used for its control. A synthetic compound gypture, similar to the hormone of gypsy moth, has become important in insect control. If the air is filled with synthetic pheromones, the males would fail to locate the females for insemination. This method is called 'male inhibition technique'.

In another method, early death of the insect pests can be brought about by the introduction of juvenile hormone at the late stage of larval development. The larva develops into giant larva (immature adult) which die quickly without attaining maturity. Insecticide can also be used to insect pests.

42. Gas chromatography (GC) is a dynamic method of separation and detection of volatile organic compounds. GC separates the gaseous components of a mixture by partitioning them between the inert gas mobile phase and a stationary phase.

Mass Spectrometry: Mass spectrometry (MS) is a technique that is used to measure the mass of atoms or molecules. To obtain a mass spectrum, gaseous sample atoms are introduced into the source of the MS where they are ionized. Dioxins and Furans are two toxic gaseous pollutants that are created by burning chlorine in the presence of hydrocarbon and oxygen and measured by GC-MS method.

45. The plant root zone hosts not only an increase in the numbers of micro-organisms, but also a rich variety of microbial species. The actual composition of the rhizosphere microbial community is dependent on host plant species, plant age, and soil type as well as other selection pressures including the presence of xenobiotic compounds Rhizosphere communities typically consist of (1) bacteria which are very abundant and reproduce rapidly under favourable conditions, and (2) fungi which form mycelia on plant roots and extend into the surrounding soil to seek nutrients. Aerobic bacteria, particularly Pseudomonads, are generally abundant in the root zone and play an important role in organic contaminant degradation. The composition of rhizospheric micro organisms are also depends on the soil pH and its texture.

47. Grasslands are large areas of grass with scattered trees. They can be divided into two types—tropical grasslands or savannas and temperate grasslands. They are often given local names like veldts in South Africa, pampas in Argentina, outback or scrub in Australia, steppe on Central Asia and prairies in North America.

Tropical Grasslands

Location: Tropical grasslands, also known as savannas, are found between 20° north and south of the Equator. They cover large parts of Africa, Australia, South America and India.

48. At the April 18 Global Citizen 2015 Earth Day, the Global Alliance to Eliminate Lead Paint (Lead Paint Alliance), co-led by the United Nations Environment Programme (UNEP) and the World Health Organization (WHO), announced the goal of eliminating lead paint around the world by 2020. The event in Washington, DC, was organized by the Global Poverty Project and Earth Day Network to commemorate the 45th anniversary of the first Earth day.

49. Coal is the principal energy source, particularly in India because of its large deposits and availability. According to geological order of formation, coal may be of the following types: (1) Peat, (2) Lignite, (3) Subbituminous, (4) Bituminous, (5) Subanthracite, and (6) Anthracite, with increasing percentages of carbon. After anthracite, graphite is formed. Anthracite contains more than 86% fixed carbon (in amorphous form) and less volatile matter. Volatile matter helps in the ignition of coal. So, it is often difficult to burn anthracite. Bituminous coal is the largest group containing 46-86% of fixed carbon and 20-40% of volatile matter. It can be low-volatile, medium-volatile and high-volatile. The lower the volatility, the higher the heating value. Lignite is the lowest grade of coal containing moisture as high as 30% and high volatile matter. According to ASTM (American Society of Testing and Materials), peat is not regarded as a rank of coal. Peat contains up to 90% moisture and is not attractive as a utility fuel. Rank carries the meaning of degree of maturation (carbonisation) and is a measure of carbon content in coal. Lignite is considered to be low rank and anthracite to be high rank.

50. National Plan for Conservation of Aquatic Eco-systems (NPCA) will help promote better synergy and avoid overlap of administrative functions. It will be governed by a uniform policy and clear guidelines, and will operate through the implementation of sustainable conservation plans. The principal objectives of NPCA will be holistic conservation and restoration of lakes and wetlands through an integrated and multidisciplinary approach with a common regulatory framework.

This will enable enhancement of water quality, as well as enrichment of biodiversity and the ecosystem. The scheme will also contribute to reduction of pollution loads and improvement in goods and services provided by these water bodies to stakeholders, say ministry officials.

The new scheme includes within its scope the conservation and management of lakes and wetlands, the maintenance of an inventory and information system on these water bodies, a national-level directive on criteria for lakes and wetlands, a regulatory framework, the inclusion of capacity building at state government and local body levels, and evaluation.

51. Soil salinity is the salt content in the soil; the process of increasing the salt content is known as salinization. Salts occur naturally within soils and water. Salination can be caused by natural processes such as mineral weathering or by the gradual withdrawal of an ocean. It can also come about through artificial processes such as water irrigation in agriculture area and Upland lateritic area. Salinity from irrigation can occur over time wherever irrigation occurs, since almost all water (even natural rainfall) contains some dissolved salts. Water in excess of plant needs is called the leaching fraction. Salination from irrigation water is also greatly increased by poor drainage and use of saline water for irrigating agricultural crops.

53. A digital elevation model (DEM) is a digital model or 3D representation of a terrain's surface — commonly for a planet, moon, or asteroid — created from terrain elevation data.

A DEM can be represented as a raster (a grid of squares, also known as a heightmap when representing elevation) or as a vector-based triangular irregular network (TIN). The TIN DEM dataset is also referred to as a primary (measured) DEM, whereas the Raster DEM is referred to as a secondary (computed) DEM.

54. Deltas are discrete shoreline protuberances formed where a river enters a standing body of water and supplies sediments more rapidly than they can be redistributed by basinal processes, such as tides and waves. In that

sense, all deltas are river-dominated and deltas are fundamentally regressive in nature. The morphology and facies architecture of a delta is controlled by the proportion of wave, tide, and river processes; the salinity contrast between inflowing water and the standing body of water, the sediment discharge and sediment caliber, and the water depth into which the river flows. The geometry of the receiving basin (and proximity to a shelf edge) may also have an influence. The simple classification into river-, wave-, and tide-dominated end members must be used with caution because the number of parameters that control deltas is more numerous.

55. **Rift valley:** It is a Elongated depression, trough, or graben in the earth's crust, bounded on both sides by normal faults and occurring on the continents or under the oceans. The central flat block forming the trough slips downward relative to the crustal blocks on either side. The appearance is that of a fallen keystone in a broken arch. Rift valleys form by tensional forces, typically those associated with the initiation of plate separation. The development of a rift valley in a continent is believed to be a precursor to the breakup of the continent and the development of a new ocean basin by seafloor spreading. Rift valleys, such as the Red Sea and the African rift valleys, are commonly the sites of volcanism and the locus of much earthquake activity.

56. Scattering is a condition whereby suspended particles and molecules in the atmosphere redirect solar radiation in every direction. The Solar radiation reaches the Earth's surface by a direct transmission as well as an indirect transmission from scattering by particulates. A portion of the scattered energy is redirected back toward space, and a portion is re-scattered by other particulates. If we did not have scattering, we would not be able to see light when standing in shadows, because there

would be no redirected light that our eyes could detect. There are 3 defined types of scattering: Rayleigh, MIE, and Non-selective scattering; Rayleigh scattering happens at the upper atmosphere and occurs when atmospheric particles have a diameter smaller than the incident wavelength. Since Blue and UV light is more readily scattered than red light, we generally see the sky as blue. MIE scattering is caused by particulates that exist in the Earth's lower atmosphere, and when particulates are roughly equal to the incident wavelength. Dust, smoke, and water droplets in the lower atmosphere cause Mie scattering to create a dark or grey appearance in the sky. Non-selective scattering is caused by particles much larger than the incident wavelength and occurs in the very lowest portion of the atmosphere to the Earth's surface. Non-selective scattering by aerosols is the primary cause of haze. Non-selective scattering in visible region in the atmosphere is not dependent on wavelength.

57. The best spatial configuration for a core natural area is circular.

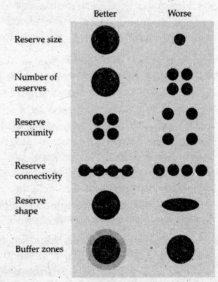

Fig.: *The Best Spatial Configurations for a Core Natural Area*

58. Ecosystem resilience is the capacity of an ecosystem to sustain its fundamental function, structure, and feedbacks in the face of a spectrum of shocks and perturbations Ecosystems are particularly resilient to those fluctuations to which organisms are well-adapted, including day-night or seasonal cycles of light and temperature.

60. A Horizon or Surface Soil:

- It is the part of top soil.
- In this layer, organic matter is mixed with mineral matter.
- It is the layer of mineral soil with the most organic matter accumulation and soil life.
- This layer is depleted of (eluviated of) iron, clay, aluminum, organic compounds, and other soluble constituents.
- When depletion is pronounced, a lighter coloured "E" subsurface soil horizon is apparent at the base of the "A" horizon.

O Horizon:

- Layers dominated by organic material.
- Some O layers consist of undecomposed or partially decomposed litter (such as leaves, needles, twigs, moss, and lichens).
- They may be on top of either mineral or organic soils.

C Horizon or Parent Rock:

- Weathered parent material accumulates in this layer, *i.e.* the parent material in sedimentary deposits.
- It is a layer of large unbroken rocks.
- This layer may accumulate the more soluble compounds (inorganic material).

B Horizon or Subsoil

- It is subsurface layer reflecting chemical or physical alteration of parent material.
- This layer accumulates all the leached minerals from A and E horizon.
- Thus iron, clay, aluminum and organic compounds accumulate in this horizon [illuviation (opposite of eluviation)].

62. Using mass balance equation

$0.2 \times 50 + 0.05 \times 1500$

$= (0.2 + 0.05) \times$ downstream concentration

i.e., downstream concentration = 340 mg/L.

63. In chromatography, a retardation factor (R_f) describes the ratio of time spent in the stationary phase relative to time spent in the mobile phase basically is the distance travelled by the compound divided by the distance travelled by the solvent can be determined using Equation.

$$R_f = \frac{\text{Migration Distance of Substance}}{\text{Migration Distance of Solvent Front}}$$

An R_f value will always be in the range 0 to 1: if the substance moves at all, it moves along the direction the solvent ("mobile phase") does less, but cannot move further than the solvent does. R_f values are only useful if they are between these two extremes. So, student T with R_f values 1.3 is definitely incorrect.

67. Molina and Rowland estimated in 1974 the average lifetime of a molecule of CFC-11 in the atmosphere at 40 to 80 years, and at 75 to 150 years for CFC-12. These predictions have been confirmed by measurements over the last 23 years which have shown their actual atmospheric lifetimes to be about 50 years for CFC-11 and 100 years for CFC-12.

68. The global warming potential (GWP) of a GHG is a relative measure of its ability to act as a GHG with respect to carbon dioxide. For example, nitrous oxide has a 100-year GWP of 296. This means that 1 tonne of nitrous oxide gas emitted into the atmosphere is the same as the emission of 296 tonnes of carbon dioxide.

69. The green-house gas N_2O strongly absorbs infra-red radiations of wavelength(s) ~7.8 μm and 8.6 μm.

70. The Government has up-scaled the target of renewable energy capacity to 175 GW by the year 2022 which includes 100 GW from solar, 60 GW from wind, 10 GW from bio-power and 5 GW from small hydro-power. Stepping up capacity target under the Jawaharlal Nehru National Solar Mission (JNNSM) by five times now India is aiming to generate reaching 1,00,000 MW solar power by 2022. The target will principally comprise of 40 GW Rooftop and 60 GW through Large and Medium Scale Grid Connected Solar Power Projects. With this ambitious target, India will become one of the largest Green Energy producers in the world, surpassing several developed countries. The total investment in setting up 100 GW will be around ₹ 6,00,000 crore.

72. High levels of UV-B radiation (280 to 320 nm wavelength) are responsible for many biologically harmful effects in both plants and animals. Some effects include DNA damage, eye cataracts, skin cancer, and immune system suppression in animals, as well as lower growth rates and depressed rates of leaf photosynthesis in plants. Results of calculations of the transmission of UV-B through the atmosphere indicate that a 1% decrease in ozone results in a 1.3% to 2% increase in the UV-B levels at the surface of the earth.

73. Indian earth observation system began with the launch of *remote sensing satellites* from 1988 onwards: with the largest constellation of IRS satellites in operation today. They fall into two broad categories: satellites in *medium-earth* orbits at 10,000 km above the earth (in a sun-synchronous polar orbit) carrying payload up to 1500 kg; and satellites in *low-earth* polar orbit with payloads 1000-1200 kg or less. The Polar Satellite Launch Vehicle (PSLV) is now India's workhorse launcher, which has launched its ninth IRS satellite CARTOSAT-1 (2005) for cartographic applications and a small satellite HAMSAT, as piggyback, for amateur radio (HAM) operators.

IRS-P6, called RESOURCESAT-1 (2003), was a multi-institutional endeavour at 620 km high, with academic and private participation from IIT Chennai, M/S Godrej, Bharat Aluminium Company (BALCO), Hindustan Aeronautics (HAL) and Bharat Electronics (BEL) for making data products available to end-users. It is placed in low earth polar sunsynchronous orbit.

74. Freshwater fishes adapted very successfully to their aquatic habitats. Thus, when some freshwater fishes returned to the sea about 200 mya, their blood and body fluids were less salty than (hypotonic to) their surroundings. They tended to lose water osmotically and to take in salt. To compensate for fluid loss, many marine bony fishes drink seawater. They retain the water and excrete salt by the action of specialized cells in their gills. Very little urine is excreted by the kidneys; the kidneys have only small (or no) glomeruli.

75. A lysimeter is a measuring device which can be used to measure the amount of actual evapotranspiration which is released by plants, usually crops or trees. By recording the amount of precipitation that an area receives and the amount lost through the soil, the amount of water lost to evapotranspiration can be calculated.

A lysimeter is most accurate when vegetation is grown in a large soil tank which allows the rainfall input and water lost through the soil to be easily calculated. The amount of water lost by evapotranspiration can be worked out by calculating the difference between the weight before and after the precipitation input.

UGC–NET Environmental Science, June–2015*

Note : *This paper contains fifty (50) objective type questions of two (2) marks each. All questions are compulsory.*

1. An endotherm's basal metabolic rate stays constant throughout a range of environmental temperatures known as the:
   I. Lower critical temperature zone
   II. Thermoneutral zone
   III. Higher critical temperature zone
   Choose the correct answer:
   A. I only   B. II only
   C. I and II only   D. II and III only

2. Which state has the largest coastline in India?
   A. West Bengal   B. Karnataka
   C. Gujarat   D. Odisha

3. Indicators for sustainable development are:
   I. environmental pressures
   II. environmental quality
   III. society's response
   Choose the correct answer:
   A. I and II only   B. II and III only
   C. I and III only   D. I, II and III

4. Stoichiometric calculations are based on:
   A. Moles   B. Atomic weight
   C. Atomic number   D. Loss of mass

5. BOD of the effluents discharged on land for irrigation should not exceed:
   A. 30 mg/L   B. 100 mg/L
   C. 300 mg/L   D. 60 mg/L

6. Which of the following adds to the carbon dioxide concentration in atmosphere?
   I. Volcanic action
   II. Respiration
   III. Photosynthesis
   IV. Decay of organic matter
   Choose the correct answer:
   A. I and III only
   B. II only
   C. I, II and IV only
   D. I, II, III and IV

7. Corrosion normally occurs when an electrochemical cell is set up on a metal surface. The corroded area is:
   A. cathode
   B. anode
   C. electrolyte
   D. entire metal surface

8. Acid sulphate soils are characteristic of marine coastal plains in areas rich in:
   I. Organic matter
   II. Brackish water
   III. Mangrove swamps
   Choose the correct answer:
   A. I only   B. I and II only
   C. II only   D. I, II and III

9. The amount of energy at one trophic level divided by the amount of energy at the trophic level immediately below it is termed as:
   A. Trophic efficiency
   B. Consumption efficiency
   C. Assimilation efficiency
   D. Production efficiency

10. Blue whale is placed under the category of:
    A. Endangered species
    B. Critically endangered species
    C. Vulnerable species
    D. Extinct species

11. Maximum density of detritivorus micro organisms in pond ecosystem are present in:
    A. Limnetic zone   B. Photic zone
    C. Littoral zone   D. Benthic zone

12. Species diversity show a marked pattern as one moves from equator to the poles. Species diversity:
    A. increases as one moves towards the poles from the equator
    B. decreases as one moves from equator to poles
    C. remains constant as one moves from equator to poles
    D. is highest in the arctic and antartic regions

13. Coral reefs are mainly distributed globally in:
    A. Temperate waters
    B. Tropical waters
    C. Antartic waters
    D. Arctic waters

14. Most common soil borne bacterial pathogen that manipulates plant by injecting its DNA segment into plant cell is:
    A. *Acidaminococcus fermentans*
    B. *Clostridium thermoacetium*
    C. *Rhizobium leguminosarum*
    D. *Agrobacterium tumefaciens*

15. Which among the following are the best tools/ techniques to study landscape fragmentation?
    I. Remote sensing
    II. Geodesy
    III. Cartography
    IV. Geographical Information System
    Choose the correct answer:
    A. I and II only
    B. I, III and IV only
    C. II, III and IV only
    D. I, II, III and IV

16. An earthquake's epicentre is:
    A. usually in the lower part of the mantle
    B. determined by analysing S-wave arrival time at seismic stations
    C. determined by analysing P-wave arrival time at seismic stations
    D. a point on the surface directly above the focus

17. Water entrapped at the time of formation of the sedimentary rocks is called:
    A. Meteoric water   B. Connate water
    C. Juvenile water   D. Ground water

18. Which of the following pairs of igneous rocks have the same mineral composition?
    A. Granite – basalt
    B. Andesite – rhyolite
    C. Basalt – gabbro
    D. Pumic – basalt

19. Traps for petroleum and natural gas formed by deformation such as folding and fracturing of rocks are known as:
    A. Lithification traps
    B. Reservoir traps
    C. Structural traps
    D. Stratigraphic traps

20. In which one of the following areas does radiant drainage fully develop?
    A. On a point bar
    B. Around an ox-bow lake
    C. Near a delta
    D. Around a volcano

21. Which of the following countries produce highest amount of hydropower?
    A. Australia   B. Canada
    C. Italy   D. India

22. A solar cell of area 10 cm × 10 cm produces a voltage of 0.6 V and a current upto 2A. If solar insolation is 1000 Wm^{-2}, the efficiency of the solar cell is:
    A. 15%   B. 12%
    C. 25%   D. 24%

23. An ocean wave has a height of 3 m and has time period of 10 sec. The power available for extraction from this wave in the units of kW per meter of the wavefront is approximately:
    A. 30   B. 45
    C. 90   D. 300

24. In the case of Silicon solar cell (Eg = 1.12 eV), the maximum wavelength of solar radiations for production of electron-hole pairs is:
   A. ~ 560 nm   B. ~ 480 nm
   C. ~ 720 nm   D. ~ 1100 nm

25. The share of India in the total annual GHG emissions of the world is approximately:
   A. 5 - 7%   B. 10 - 12%
   C. 17 - 20%   D. 20 - 25%

26. In biogas, the percentage (%) of methane is in the range of:
   A. 50 - 70%   B. 30 - 40%
   C. 70 - 90%   D. 40 - 50%

27. Indira Gandhi canal passes through the following state:
   I. Punjab   II. Haryana
   III. Uttar Pradesh   IV. Rajasthan
   Choose the correct answer:
   A. I, II only   B. I, II, III only
   C. I, II, IV only   D. I, II, III, IV

28. Trichloromonofluoromethane is:
   I. Freon-II
   II. A spray can propellent
   III. A chlorofluorocarbon
   Choose the correct answer:
   A. I only   B. II and III only
   C. I and III only   D. I, II and III

29. Which of the following air pollutants are released by thermal power plants?
   I. Oxides of nitrogen
   II. Oxides of sulphur
   III. Ammonia
   IV. Carbon monoxide
   Choose the correct answer:
   A. I, III and IV only B. II and III only
   C. I, II and IV only   D. I, II, III and IV

30. The Noise Index L_{eq} for a specific duration is a measure of:
   A. acoustic energy content
   B. average noise amplitude
   C. sum of instantaneous sound pressure levels
   D. fluctuations in noise levels

31. When DDT enters the human body, it is:
   A. water soluble and easily excreted in urine
   B. stored in the bones
   C. fat soluble and stored in fat tissues
   D. processed by enzymes and becomes a different compound which is toxic

32. In which EIA guidelines notification, developmental projects were categorized as 'A' and 'B' in India?
   A. EIA guidelines notification, 1994
   B. EIA guidelines notification, 1986
   C. EIA guidelines notification, 2006
   D. EIA guidelines notification, 2000

33. Three important rivers of Indian sub-continent have their source near the Mansarovar lake in Tibet. These rivers are:
   A. Indus, Jhelum, Ganga
   B. Indus, Sutlej, Yamuna
   C. Indus, Sutlej, Brahmaputra
   D. Yamuna, Brahmaputra, Gandak

34. Which state in India has the highest area of wastelands under barren/stony/rock category?
   A. Jammu and Kashmir
   B. Himachal Pradesh
   C. Arunachal Pradesh
   D. Uttarakhand

35. During clearance of any developmental project, the minimum distance required for site selection from eco-sensitive zone is:
   A. 5 km   B. 10 km
   C. 15 km   D. 20 km

36. Which of the following are true regarding 'Jhum' cultivation in India?
   I. It is largely practiced in N-E India
   II. Fertility is exhausted in a few years
   III. It is referred as 'Slash and Burn' technique
   Choose the correct answer:
   A. I, II, and III   B. I and II only
   C. II and III only   D. I and III only

37. Compensatory afforestation provisions are covered under the Environment Act names as:
   A. Indian Forest Act (Revised), 1982
   B. Environment Protection Act, 1986

C. Forest Conservation Act, 1980
D. Public Liability Insurance Act, 1981

38. When a disaster has occurred, the early action in a Disaster Management Plan could be:
A. Response and Rescue
B. Warning and preparedness
C. Relief and Rehabilitation
D. Shelter and Food supply

39. An environmental problem associated with landfill waste disposal site is:
  I. Methane production
  II. Ground water pollution
  III. Incomplete decomposition
Choose the correct answer:
A. I and II only   B. I, II and III
C. I and III only   D. II and III only

40. Eco-labelling of commercial products is regulated by:
A. ISO 14020   B. ISO 14010
C. ISO 14030   D. ISO 14040

41. Which one of the following is not a part of 'Waste Reduction' strategy?
A. Reduced use of raw material
B. Material Reuse
C. Recycling of waste
D. Decreased toxicity

42. The expanded form of ISWM is:
A. International Standards of Waste Management
B. Indian Standards for Waste Material
C. Integrated Solid Waste Management
D. International Solid Waste Management

43. Municipal Solid Waste (Handling and Management) rule and Biomedical Waste (Handling and Management) rule were implemented in the years respectively:
A. 2000 and 1998   B. 1998 and 2002
C. 1996 and 1998   D. 1990 and 1985

44. If a phosphorous limited lake having surface area equal to 80×10^6 m^2 is fed by stream with flow rate 20 m^3/s that has phosphorous concentration of 0.01 mg/L, then the phosphorous loading from the incoming stream is:

A. 4.0 g/s   B. 0.2 g/s
C. 0.4 g/s   D. 0.6 g/s

45. If K is the carrying capacity of a population N in an ecosystem following the logistic growth, its growth rate becomes zero when:
A. N/K = 0
B. Mortality > Natality
C. N/K = 1
D. N = Half of the carrying capacity of the habitat

46. A good sample design should result in:
A. A truely representative sample
B. Highly varied sampling error
C. Low level of confidence
D. Unsystemic bias

47. The mean of a Poisson's distribution is 8. Its standard deviation is:
A. 2   B. $2\sqrt{2}$
C. 4   D. $\dfrac{8}{5}$

48. Destructive powers of Tsunami result mainly from its:
A. Incredible Height
B. Unpredictability
C. Momentum and long wavelength
D. Cold water

49. Which one of the following is **not** correct for drip irrigation?
A. Drip consists of a network of perforated plastic tubing below the ground surface
B. Drip irrigation increases fertilizer use and water pollution from fertilizer run-off
C. Small holes in the tubing drops off water at a slow rate close to plant roots
D. This technique was developed in Israel in the 1960's

50. The non-formal Environmental Education in India provides support to:
  I. Eco-clubs
  II. GLOBE
  III. Environmental appreciation courses
Choose the correct answer:
A. I and II only   B. II and III only
C. I and III only   D. I, II and III

5

ANSWERS

1	2	3	4	5	6	7	8	9	10
B	C	D	A	B	C	B	D	A	A

11	12	13	14	15	16	17	18	19	20
D	B	B	D	B	D	B	C	C	D

21	22	23	24	25	26	27	28	29	30
B	B	C	D	A	A	C	B	C	A

31	32	33	34	35	36	37	38	39	40
C	C	C	A	B	A	C	A	B	A

41	42	43	44	45	46	47	48	49	50
D	C	A	B	C	A	B	C	B	A

SOME SELECTED EXPLANATORY ANSWERS

2. Gujarat—longest coast line 1600 km, dotted with 41 ports; 1 major, 11 intermediate and 29 minor ports. Andhra Pradesh is the second longest coast line 972 km (604 mi).

3. Environmental and sustainable development indicators proliferated in the wake of the Rio Earth Summit's call for indicators of sustainable development.

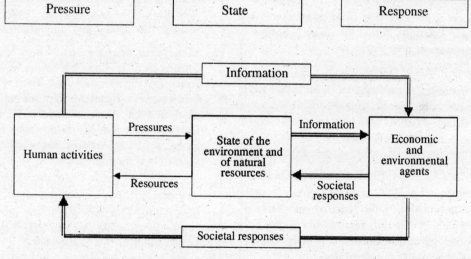

7. Corrosion normally occurs when an electrochemical cell is set up on a metal surface. The area corroded is the anode, where the following oxidation reaction occurs, illustrated for the formation of a divalent metal ion from a metal, M:

$$M \rightarrow M^{2+} + 2e^-$$

9. Trophic levels are the feeding position in a food chain such as primary producers, herbivore, primary carnivore, etc. Green plants form the first trophic level, the producers. Herbivores form the second trophic level, while carnivores form the third and even the fourth trophic levels.

Trophic efficiency is the transfer of energy through tropic levels, the trophic level is the

same as the food chain.
Trophic efficiency

$$= \frac{\text{Amount of energy at } n^{th} \text{ trophic level}}{\text{Amount of energy at } (n+1)^{th} \text{ trophic level}}$$

10. Blue whales are the largest mammals that ever lived, but they are also an endangered species. Due to aggressive hunting and environmental changes, these ocean-dwellers could become extinct.

13. Coral reefs are found in all three of the Earth's oceans that have portions in the tropics—the Atlantic, Pacific and Indian.

   However, coral reefs are **not randomly scattered** throughout each of these great ocean basins.

   Because the global distribution of coral reefs is largely determined by the ecological requirements of the reef-building corals themselves.

   The coral animals that build tropical reefs require **sunlight** found in **clear, shallow ocean waters**.

14. The soil-borne pathogen *Agrobacterium tumefaciens* carries flagellin variants that are non-detectable by the Arabidopsis FLS2, yet it triggers a typical innate immune response through the EF-Tu protein.

   Agrobacterium tumefaciens is the causal agent of crown galls. It infects plants by integrating a segment of its DNA (transfer DNA) into the host chromosomal DNA. *efr1* mutants fail to recognize EF-Tu and, presumably owing to reduced defence responses, are more easily transformed by Agrobacterium.

16. The epicentre, epicentre or epicentrum is the point on the Earth's surface that is directly above the hypocentre or focus, the point where an earthquake or underground explosion originates.

17. **Sources of Ground water:** There are three sources of ground water:

- **Connate Water:** Water entrapped in the interstices of a sedimentary rock at the time the rock was deposited.
- **Meteoric Water:** Meteoric water originates in the atmosphere, falls as precipitation and becomes groundwater by infiltration. Meteoric water constitutes the bulk of groundwater and this is evident in the fluctuation of water level in wells during the rainy season when the level goes up, and in summer season when the level goes down.
- **Juvenile Water:** Juvenile water is that water which is considered to have been generated in the interior of the Earth and have reached the upper levels of the Earth's surface for the first time. It is also called magmatic water.

18. **Basalt-Gabbro:** *Basalt* and *Gabbro* are the aphanitic and phaneritic rocks that crystallize from mafic magma (45-52% silica). Thus, both have the same composition—mostly calcium-rich plagioclase and pyroxene, with smaller amounts of olivine and amphibole.

19. **Structural traps** result when rocks are deformed by folding, fracturing, or both. In sedimentary rocks that have been deformed into a series of folds, hydrocarbons migrate to the high parts of these structures. Displacement of rocks along faults fractures along which movement has occurred also yields traps for hydrocarbons.

21. Canada is the world's second largest producer of hydroelectricity after China which is more than double Canada's level, and one of few countries to generate the majority of its electricity from hydroelectricity.
- Hydropower produced 63 per cent of Canada's electricity production in 2010.
- Canada is the world's second largest hydropower producer, generating 363 TWh/year.
- Every province with the exception of Prince Edward Island produces hydropower to varying degrees.
- There is 163, 173 megawatts of undeveloped hydro potential in Canada.

22. Efficiency of the Solar Cell

$$= \frac{\dfrac{Voltage \times Current}{Area(in\ m^2)} \times 100}{Solar\ insolation}$$

$$= \frac{\dfrac{0.6 \times 2}{10 \times 10} \times 100}{100 \times 100} \times 1000 = 12\%.$$

26. Biogas is a mixture of different gases produced by the breakdown of organic matter and is used as a renewable energy source that exerts a very small carbon footprint. The composition of biogas is typically 40-60 per cent methane, 40-50 per cent carbon dioxide, and the remainder being water, hydrogen sulfide, and other impurities. The composition of a specific biogas depends on the type of waste it is being obtained from, what it's being purified for, as well as the purpose for which the biogas is being used.

27. Indira Gandhi Canal is the largest canal in India. The canal is 650 km long and starts from the Harike Barrage, a few kilometers below the confluence of the Sutlej and Beas rivers in Punjab. It flows through Punjab, Haryana, and Rajasthan, with the major length of the canal flowing through Rajasthan. The canal terminates near Jaisalmer in Rajasthan.

30. The most common general noise indice is: The equivalent sound pressure level $L_{eq,T}$, defined in ISO 1996-1, expresses the level of a continuous noise that would have the same total acoustic energy as a fluctuating noise measured for the same specific period

$$T : L_{eq,T} = 10 \log_{10} \left(\frac{1}{T} \int_0^T \frac{p^2(t)}{p_0^2} dt \right) [dB].$$

31. DDT is fat soluble and is disseminated by air and water to terrestrial and aquatic ecosystems. When DDT enters a water environment, it is taken up by aquatic animals and becomes part of the food chain, accumulating and concentrating in the fat of predatory species. DDT also remains residual in upper soil layers and accumulates in many terrestrial animal species.

33. The Indus River originates in the northern slopes of the Kailash range near Lake Manasarovar in Tibet. While the Sutlej river originates from the Rakas Lake (Rakshas Tal), which is connected to the Manasarovar lake by a stream, in Tibet and the Brahmaputra river also originated from Manasarovar lake in tibet.

35. Restrictions have been imposed for any project operations in wildlife, sanctuaries, national parks, near the national monuments, areas of cultural heritage, ecological fragile areas rich in biological diversity, gene pool etc. Prior environmental clearance is required in respect of any project to be located within 10 km of the boundary of reserve forests or a designated ecologically sensitive area or within 25 km of the boundary of national park or sanctuary.

40. **Eco-labels** and **Green stickers** are labelling systems for food and consumer products. Eco-labels are voluntary, but green stickers are mandated by law. This International Standard establishes guiding principles for the development and use of environmental labels and declarations. It is intended that other applicable standards in the ISO 14020 series be used in conjunction with this International Standard.

41. Waste minimisation can be defined as "systematically reducing waste at source". It means:
   - Prevention and/or reduction of waste generated
   - Efficient use of raw materials and packaging
   - Efficient use of fuel, electricity and water
   - Improving the quality of waste generated to facilitate recycling and/or reduce hazard
   - Encouraging re-use, recycling and recovery.

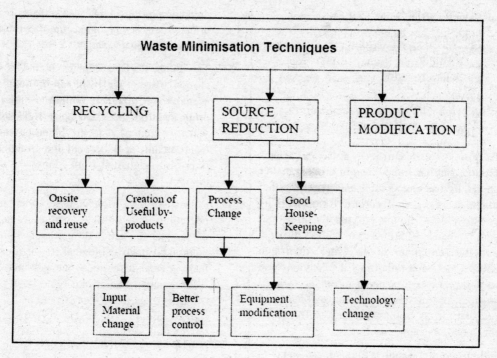

42. ISWM stand for Integrated Solid Waste Management. There is a clear need for strategies to redesign conventional waste generation systems in such a way that they can effectively and efficiently handle growing amounts of waste with diversified waste streams. To respond to this need, the work plan for the focal area on integrated solid waste management (ISWM) proposes to promote an integrated approach to solid waste management, which will enable local/national authorities to reduce the overall amount of waste generated and to recover valuable materials for recycling and for the generation of energy.

44. Phosphorous loading from the incoming stream is

$$OC_{in} = 20 \text{ m}^3/\text{sec} \times 0.01 \text{ mg/l} \times 1\frac{g/l}{mg/l}$$

$$= 0.2 \text{ g/sec.}$$

45. Logistic population growth model follows an S-shaped or sigmoid growth form. In this the population increases slowly at first, then more rapidly, before slowing to an equilibrium level where the population may fluctuate around a maximum. This equilibrium density is termed the carrying capacity and is represented by K in the following model (logistic growth equation):

$$\frac{dN}{dt} = \frac{rN(K-N)}{K}$$

where r is the intrinsic rate of growth and N is the population size. Note that, as N increases, N/K approaches one and the population growth rate keeps falling. When $N = K$, the pupulation growth rate (dN/dt) becomes zero.

46. Characteristics of a good sample design as under:
- Sample design must result in a truly representative sample.
- Sample design must be such which results in a small sampling error.
- Sample design must be viable in the context of funds available for the research study.

- Sample design must be such so that systematic bias can be controlled in a better way.
- Sample should be such that the results of the sample study can be applied, in general, for the universe with a reasonable level of confidence.

47. Properties of Poisson Distribution
1. Mean and Variance of Poisson distribution are same, each equal to λ.
2. Poisson distribution is always a skewed distribution.

∴ Standard deviation

$$S.D. = \sqrt{8} = 2\sqrt{2}.$$

48. Tsunamis (seismic sea waves) are triggered by earthquakes or volcanic eruptions beneath the ocean floor. These waves have wavelengths of approximately 160 kilometers and a speed of 600 to 700 kilometers per hour. Their high speed gives them great momentum and large destructive power.

PAPER-III

Note : *This paper contains **seventy five (75)** objective type questions of **two (2)** marks each.* ***All** questions are compulsory.*

1. Biological zonation in the ocean is determined by:
   I. Ocean depth
   II. Light availability
   III. Bottom substrate
   Choose the correct answer :
   A. I only
   B. I and II only
   C. I, II and III
   D. II and III only

2. Given below are two statements. One labelled as Assertion (A) and the other labelled as Reason (R):
   Assertion (A): Methanogenic archae (methanogens) grow in swamps and sewage.
   Reason (R): Methanogens are obligate anaerobes.
   Choose the correct answer :
   A. Both (A) and (R) are correct and (R) is the correct explanation of (A).
   B. Both (A) and (R) are correct and (R) is not the correct explanation of (A).
   C. (A) is true, but (R) is false.
   D. (A) is false, but (R) is true.

3. Filamentous Cyanobacteria differentiate 5 to 10% of their vegetative cells into heterocysts. Heterocysts are characterized by :

   I. Thick cell wall
   II. Only PSI activity
   III. Nitrogenase activity

   Choose the correct answer :
   A. I only
   B. I and II only
   C. II and III only
   D. I, II and III

4. A critically endangered species :
   A. Do not exist in wild habitat
   B. Face extremely high risk of extinction in immediate future
   C. Face high risk of extinction in the medium term future
   D. Will not face any risk of extinction in future 1000 years

5. Which of the following characteristics of desert animals are physiological adaptation to conserve water ?
   I. Thick outer covering
   II. Release dry faeces
   III. Avoid exposure to direct sunlight

   Choose the correct answer :
   A. I and III only
   B. II and III only
   C. I and II only
   D. I, II and III

6. The balance between photosynthesis and photorespiration is related to :
   I. The ratio of O_2 and CO_2 in the atmosphere

II. Temperature

III. Kranz anatomy

IV. The ratio of CO_2 and H_2O

Choose the correct answer :
A. I and II only
B. II, III and IV only
C. I, II and III only
D. I, II, III and IV

7. Individual organism respond to environmental change through short-term adjustment(s) by :
A. Physiological changes
B. Cytological changes
C. Genetic changes
D. Phytochemical and genetic alterations

8. The hurricanes have spatial scale of :
A. 100 Km - 1000 Km
B. 10 Km - 100 Km
C. 100 m - 100 Km
D. 100 m - 10 Km

9. In SDS - PAGE :
A. Polymeric proteins are not only converted into monomers, but monomers are also denatured by SDS.
B. Polymeric proteins converted into monomeric units, but monomers are not denatured.
C. Polymeric proteins are retained as single unit.
D. SDS donot have any negative impact on native structure of monomers.

10. Which of the following is the major source of mercury pollution in India ?
A. Coal based thermal power plants
B. Pesticides manufacturing
C. Dental amalgam fillings
D. Electrical and electronic gadgets

11. A non-metal 'X' occurs in nature in free state. It combines with hydrogen to form a gas, which is colourless and highly toxic. Apart from this, 'X' is oxidized to 'XO_2' which is a colourless, pungent and irritating gas. 'X' represents :
A. Sulphur   B. Carbon
C. Phosphorus   D. Nitrogen

12. Elemental carbon influences the regional climate because :
A. It influences the radiative flux in the atmosphere due to its absorbing properties.
B. It reacts with other pollutants.
C. It coagulates with other atmospheric pollutants.
D. Its concentration is usually more in the atmosphere.

13. Bioremediation of xenobiotics (like melathion) through hydrolysis involves their detoxification by :
A. Removal of water
B. Addition of water
C. Both removal and addition of water
D. Removal of phosphate

14. To determine the cation-exchange capacity, it is necessary to calculate the total positive charge associated with ions like :
A. Ca^{2+}, Mg^{2+}, K^+, Na^+
B. Ca^{2+}, Mn^{2+}, Fe^{3+}, Cr^{3+}
C. Mg^{2+}, Fe^{3+}, Ni^{2+}, Cd^{2+}
D. K^+, BO^{2+}, Pb^{2+}, Hg^{2+}

15. Given below are two statements. One labelled as Assertion (A) and the other labelled as Reason (R) :

Assertion (A): Organometals/organometalloids such as trimethylarsine and dimethylmercury are more toxic to living systems (including humans) compared to their inorganic forms.

Reason (R): Organometals/organometalloids are more hydrophilic than their inorganic forms and hence can move easily across lipid bilayer.

Choose the correct answer :
A. Both (A) and (R) are correct and (R) is the correct explanation of (A).
B. Both (A) and (R) are correct and (R) is not the correct explanation of (A).
C. (A) is true, but (R) is false.
D. (A) is false, but (R) is true.

16. Project elephant was launched in the year :
A. 1973
B. 1985
C. 1992
D. 1998

17. Biological communities in a stream vary based on :
I. Water velocity
II. Allochthonous material
III. Size of the particle on the stream bed
IV. Depth of the stream

Choose the correct answer :
A. I and II only
B. I, II and III only
C. II, III and IV only
D. I, II, III and IV

18. Champion and Seth (1968) classify Indian forests based on :
I. Floristic Composition
II. Precipitation
III. Distance from Sea

Choose the correct answer :
A. I Only
B. I and II only
C. II only
D. I, II and III

19. Which one of the following statements is **not** correct ?
A. The solubility of gases varies considerably with pressure.
B. Hydrocarbons chiefly occur in coal, natural gas and petroleum.
C. Polynuclear aromatic hydrocarbons are present in coal tar and fossil fuels.
D. All hydrocarbons are hydrophilic in nature.

20. Gauss exclusion principle states that :
A. Complete competitors co-exist
B. Complete competitors cannot co-exist
C. Complete competitors tend to co-operate
D. Symbionts evolve into complete competitors

21. Parasites in a population/community can :
I. Influence host population cycles
II. Change ecological communities
III. Change community structure

Choose the correct answer :
A. I, II and III
B. II and III only
C. III only
D. I only

22. Long-term patterns of evolution are shaped by large scale process(s) such as :
I. Speciation
II. Mass extinction
III. Adaptive radiation

Choose the correct answer:
A. I only
B. II and III only
C. I and III only
D. I, II and III

23. Match the List-I with List-II. Identify the correct answer from the codes given below the lists :

List–I (Organism)	List–II (Interaction)
(a) *Albugo* and Indian mustard	(i) Symbiosis
(b) *Penicillium* and *Staphyllococcus*	(ii) Ammensalism
(c) Lichens	(iii) Commensalism
(d) Barnacles and whales	(iv) Parasitism

Codes:

	(a)	(b)	(c)	(d)
A.	(i)	(ii)	(iii)	(iv)
B.	(ii)	(i)	(iv)	(iii)
C.	(iv)	(ii)	(i)	(iii)
D.	(iv)	(iii)	(ii)	(i)

24. Extreme of seasonal variation (as much as 80°C swing) from summer to winter is represented by :
A. Boreal forest
B. Tropical forest
C. Deciduous forest
D. Evergreen forest

25. Aeromycoflora can be trapped and quantified by :
A. Rotorod air sampler
B. Anderson air sampler
C. Gregory air sampler
D. Respirable dust sampler

26. Which among the following frequencies in microwave region of electromagnetic spectrum is better suited for determination of tree height ?
   A. C - band (4 - 8 GHz)
   B. X - band (8 - 12.5 GHz)
   C. P - band (0.3 - 1.0 GHz)
   D. K - band (18 - 26.5 GHz)

27. Which of the common mineral is not a silicate?
   A. Quartz   B. Calcite
   C. Pyroxene   D. Feldspar

28. Which among the following is the best model in GIS spatial relationships?
   A. Spaghetti model
   B. Topological model
   C. Relational database model
   D. Parent-child model

29. One of the warning signs of an impending volcanic eruption is volcanic tremor, which is :
   A. A change in ground levels
   B. Inflation of a volcano as magma rises
   C. Ground shaking lasting for minutes or hours
   D. Emission of large quantities of gases

30. Time slot for measuring thermal inertia (TI) differences between land and water is :
   A. 1000 hrs.   B. 1100 hrs.
   C. 1200 hrs.   D. 1400 hrs.

31. Slump is a complex slide which consists of :
   A. Curved shear surface
   B. Curved and planar shear surfaces
   C. Planar shear surface
   D. No definite shear surface

32. In rainwater harvesting, the purpose of percolation tank is :
   A. Recharge ground water only
   B. Surface water supply for irrigation
   C. Both surface water supply and ground water recharge
   D. Drinking water supply

33. Which of the following minerals causes fluoride pollution in the groundwater ?
   A. Fluorite and Apatite
   B. Olivine and Haematite
   C. Calcite and Magnetite
   D. Quartz and Orthoclase

34. Indian monsoon is greatly influenced by :
   I. Sea surface temperature in pre-monsoon season
   II. El Nino
   III. La Nina
   IV. Depression over Tibet

   Choose the correct answer :
   A. I and II only
   B. II and III only
   C. III and IV only
   D. IV only

35. The important continental silicate mineral weathering process of lowering carbon dioxide levels is :
   A. Hydrolysis   B. Oxidation
   C. Carbonation   D. Reduction

36. The set of processes by which soil and rock are loosened and move downhill are called :
   A. Erosion   B. Saltation
   C. Weathering   D. Abrasion

37. Wind mills are most suited for :
   I. Deserts
   II. Offshore
   III. High altitude
   IV. Roof tops

   Choose the correct answer :
   A. I and II only
   B. II and III only
   C. I and III only
   D. II, III and IV only

38. Main source of energy for a tropical cyclone formation comes from :
   I. Heat of condensation of water vapours in the atmosphere
   II. Torrential rains
   III. Large ocean waves

13

Choose the correct answer :
A. I only
B. II only
C. III and II only
D. I and III only

39. In the following nuclear fusion reaction $^2_1D + {}^2_1D = {}^3_2He + {}^1_0n + E$ the value of the energy E is :
A. 17.6 MeV   B. 18.3 MeV
C. 4.03 MeV   D. 3.27 MeV

40. Fast neutrons produced in nuclear fission reactions involving ^{235}U have average energy of the order of :
A. 2 MeV   B. 5 MeV
C. 100 MeV   D. 200 MeV

41. As the population growth rate increases the doubling time :
A. Increase   B. Double
C. Remain constant   D. Decrease

42. A tidal estuary of tidal range 2 m has trapped water area 5000 m^2. If g = 9.8 m/s^2, the maximum energy available per tidal cycle is:
A. 2.45 kW   B. 9.8 kW
C. 98 kW   D. 19.6 kW

43. The power (P) from an ocean wave varies with time period (T) of the wave as :
A. $P \propto T$ B. $P \propto T^2$
C. $P \propto \dfrac{1}{T}$ D. $P \propto \dfrac{1}{T^2}$

44. With reference to pre-industrial times, the present day average global surface temperature is higher approximately by :
A. ~ 0.56 °C   B. ~ 0.85 °C
C. ~1.3 °C   D. ~1.5 °C

45. Burning of 1 mol of CH_4 liberates 890 kJ of energy and 1 mol of CO_2. Since 1 mol of CO_2 has 12 g of carbon, the higher heating value (HHV) of methane is :
A. 13.5 gC/MJ   B. 18.5 gC/MJ
C. 12.0 gC/MJ   D. 10.0 gC/MJ

46. pH of 1 mM HCl is :
A. 1   B. 2
C. 3   D. 11

47. Priority air pollutants included in the air quality index for urban areas in India are :
A. CO, NO_x, PM_{10} and $PM_{2.5}$, SO_x, O_3, ammonia and Pb
B. CO, NO_x, SO_x and Pb
C. NO_x, SO_x, O_3, and Pb
D. PM_{10} and $PM_{2.5}$, NO_x, SO_x, O_3, and Pb

48. Present day advanced anaerobic digestors can generate power in the range :
A. 2 - 10 MW
B. 20 - 100 MW
C. 100 - 200 MW
D. 200 - 500 MW

49. Cement dust is characterized by very fine particulates. Which of the following air pollution control devices is appropriate for removing them from hot exhaust gases emanating from cement kiln?
A. Baghouse
B. Cyclones
C. Venturi scrubber
D. Electrostatic precipitator

50. The sources of aliphatic hydrocarbons in indoor environment are :
A. Paints, adhesives and gasoline
B. Aerosol sprays and solvents
C. Spirits and cleansers
D. Solvents and vinyl flooring

51. Given the following data of sound pressure levels measured at equal intervals: 60 dB, 62 dB, 63 dB, 59 dB, 60 dB, 80 dB, 58 dB, 59 dB, 65 dB, 57 dB, 62 dB. The value of the background noise level (L_{90}) is :
A. 62.5 dB   B. 57 dB
C. 61 dB   D. 58 dB

52. The air-to-fuel ratio (A/F) for complete combustion in an internal combustion engine is about :
A. 14.6   B. 11.2
C. 12.1   D. 15.5

53. Phytovolatilization of mercuric pollutants involves volatalization of mercury in :
A. Elemental state
B. Ionic state
C. Organic state
D. Both ionic and organic state

54. Match the List - I with List - II. Identify the correct answer from the codes given below the lists :

List–I	List–II
(a) Texture	(i) Vertical zonation
(b) Profile	(ii) Land degradation
(c) Erosion	(iii) Planting tree
(d) Conservation	(iv) Mineral particle size

Codes :

	(a)	(b)	(c)	(d)
A.	(iv)	(i)	(ii)	(iii)
B.	(i)	(ii)	(iii)	(iv)
C.	(ii)	(iii)	(iv)	(i)
D.	(iii)	(iv)	(i)	(ii)

55. Environmental Management Plan is associated with :
A. EIS
B. Environmental audit
C. ISO 14000
D. LCA

56. ISO 14000 is connected with :
A. Adoption of environmental safety guideline
B. Energy audit in industries
C. Adoption of clean development
D. Adoption of environmental management system in industry/organisation

57. CAPART in India stands for :
A. Committee for Advancement and Promotion of Rural Technology
B. Council for Advancement of Rural Technology
C. Council for Advancement of People's Action and Rural Technology
D. Committee for Advancement and Privatization of Rural Technology

58. EIA of Port and Harbour projects involve impact assessment on :
  I. Biological environment
  II. Air environment
  III. Soil environment
  IV. Social environment

Choose the correct answer :
A. I only
B. II only
C. III only
D. I, II and IV only

59. Which act provided provisions for enforcing levy and collection of a tax on water consumed by industries ?
A. Water (prevention and control of pollution) Act 1974
B. Water (prevention and control of pollution) Cess Act 1977
C. Environment (protection) Act 1986
D. Public Liability Insurance Act 1991

60. Disaster risk reduction in degraded wilderness areas is better achieved using :
A. People's participation
B. Ecosystem based management
C. Strengthening of people's economic conditions
D. Afforestation

61. The major conventions of Rio Earth Summit are :
A. CBD and climate change
B. Kyoto protocol and Montreal protocol
C. CDM and Nagoya protocol
D. Basel convention and Bameco convention

62. If $\lceil s < \lceil e < \lceil d$ where $\lceil s$, $\lceil e$ and $\lceil d$ are saturated adiabatic lapse rate, environmental lapse rate and dry adiabatic lapse rate, the atmosphere is :
A. Stable
B. Conditionally unstable
C. Unstable
D. Neutral

63. Match the List–I with List–II. Identify the correct answer from the codes given below the lists:

List–I (Tests)	List–II (Application)
(a) Z-test	(i) Judging the significance of differences between means of two small samples
(b) t-test	(ii) Judging the significance of mean, median, mode
(c) Chi-square (χ^2) test	(iii) Compare the variance of two - independent samples
(d) F-test	(iv) Compare sample variance to a theoretical population variance

Codes:

	(a)	(b)	(c)	(d)
A.	(ii)	(i)	(iv)	(iii)
B.	(iii)	(ii)	(i)	(iv)
C.	(iv)	(iii)	(ii)	(i)
D.	(i)	(iv)	(iii)	(ii)

64. Chocolates of 250 g produced in a factory were observed to have standard deviation of 2 g. A random sample of 20 chocolates showed a standard deviation of 1.5 g. What is the χ^2 value for the sample ?
A. 7.2
B. 6.0
C. 12.0
D. 33.3

65. Which one of the following would indicate that a dataset is NOT distributed in a bell - shape?
A. The range is equal to 5 standard deviation
B. The range is larger than the inter quartile range
C. The mean is much smaller than the median
D. There are no outliers

66. In a random sample of $x = 16$, the mean ($\overline{X}$) is 40, and the standard deviation (sd) is 4.0. The 95% confidence interval (Z = 1.96) for the mean is :
A. ±4.0
B. ±1.96
C. ±0.25
D. ±0.30

67. The title of the Brundtland report is :
A. Caring for Earth
B. Caring of Biosphere
C. Our Common Future
D. The Silent Spring

68. According to Gaussian Plume Model, the maximum ground level concentration (C) varies with height (H) of chimney:
A. $C \propto \dfrac{1}{H}$
B. $C \propto H^{-2}$
C. $C \propto H^{-\frac{1}{2}}$
D. $C \propto H^{-\frac{3}{2}}$

69. Given below are two statements. One labelled as Assertion (A) and the other labelled as Reason (R) :

Assertion (A): A wetland of international importance is brought under the 'Montreux Record'.

Reason (R): The country in which the wetland is located should enact a law to prohibit any human activity within five kilometers from the edge of the wetland.

Choose the correct answer :
A. Both (A) and (R) are correct and (R) is the correct explanation of (A).
B. Both (A) and (R) are correct and (R) is not the correct explanation of (A).
C. (A) is true, but (R) is false.
D. (A) is false, but (R) is true.

70. Which of the following methods related to fly ash utilization has future ecofriendly and economic benefits?
  I. Direct application to cropland
  II. Converting to Bricks
  III. Using as a road-sub-base material

Codes:
A. I and II only
B. II and III only
C. I and III only
D. I, II and III

71. Which of the following is NOT one of the twelve principles of green chemistry?
A. Minimize or eliminate the need for waste cleanup by emphasizing waste prevention
B. Minimize energy consumption

C. Maximize use of products from green plants

D. Avoid the use and generation of hazardous substances that may harm humans or the environment

72. Match the List-I with List-II. Identify the correct answer from the codes given below the lists :

List–I (Halocarbons)	List–II (Atmospheric residence time)
(a) CF_4	(i) ~ 50 years
(b) CF_2Cl_2	(ii) ~ 50,000 years
(c) $CFCl_3$	(iii) ~ 65 years
(d) CF_3Br	(iv) ~ 102 years

Codes :

	(a)	(b)	(c)	(d)
A.	(ii)	(iv)	(i)	(iii)
B.	(iii)	(i)	(ii)	(iv)
C.	(iv)	(ii)	(iii)	(i)
D.	(i)	(iii)	(iv)	(ii)

73. Climate change has become a buzz word throughout the world. In case of the Himalayas the best way to infer whether there is a climate change or not is to :
   I. Monitor tree line
   II. Monitor migration of glaciers
   III. Study alteration in species composition
   Choose the correct answer :
   A. I only   B. I and II only
   C. II only   D. I, II and III

74. Landslide hazards in the Himalayan region are the consequence of :
   I. Road cutting
   II. Seismic activity
   III. Deforestation
   IV. Urbanization

   Choose the correct answer :
   A. I only
   B. I and II only
   C. I, II and III only
   D. I, II, III and IV

75. Consider the following International agreements.
   I. The International Treaty on Plant Genetic Resources for Food and Agriculture
   II. The United Nations Convention to Combat Desertification
   III. The World Heritage Convention

   Which of the above has/have a bearing on the biodiversity ? Choose the correct answer:
   A. I and II only   B. III only
   C. I and III only   D. I, II and III

ANSWERS

1	2	3	4	5	6	7	8	9	10
C	A	D	B	C	C	A	A	A	A
11	12	13	14	15	16	17	18	19	20
A	A	B	A	C	C	D	B	D	B
21	22	23	24	25	26	27	28	29	30
A	D	C	A	B	C	B	B	C	D
31	32	33	34	35	36	37	38	39	40
B	A	A	A	A	A	A	A	D	D
41	42	43	44	45	46	47	48	49	50
D	C	A	B	A	C	A	A	D	A
51	52	53	54	55	56	57	58	59	60
D	A	A	A	B	D	C	D	B	B
61	62	63	64	65	66	67	68	69	70
A	B	A	A	C	B	C	B	C	B
71	72	73	74	75					
C	A	D	D	D					

SOME SELECTED EXPLANATORY ANSWERS

1. Marine biological zones are determined by ocean depth, light availability, and the stability of the bottom substrate.

   Marine Biological Zones

   - Nearshore zones reflect the influence of tides and substrate stability

   - Shallow ocean zones are diverse and productive

   - Open ocean and deep benthic zones are determined by light availability and proximity to the bottom

   - Marine biological zones have been impacted by human activities

2. **Methanogens (methane generators)** live in reducing environments, and represent about one-half of all known species of archaeans. All known methanogens, for example *Methanococcus* and *Methanobacterium* species, belong to the Euryarchaeota. Methanogens are obligate anaerobes, meaning they are killed by oxygen. They are found in the anoxic (oxygen-lacking) sediments of, for instance, swamps and marshes, as well as in more moderate environments, such as the rumen of cattle and sheep; the large intestine of dogs and humans; and the hindguts of insects such as termites and cockroaches. Methanogens generate energy by converting at least ten different substrates such as carbon dioxide and hydrogen gas, methanol, or acetate into methane gas (CH_4), which is released into the atmosphere.

4. Critically Endangered species face an extremely high risk of extinction in the wild in the immediate future, whilst Endangered species face a high risk of extinction in the wild in the near future. Those categorised as Vulnerable face a high risk of extinction in the medium term.

7. Aquatic crustaceans respond to environmental change in a number of ways. In order to avoid the most immediate effects, individuals move away from the problem and show a range of unusual behaviours, such as the aggregation of both predators and prey to avoid bouts of hypoxia. Physiological responses further enhance the ability of individuals to survive relatively short-term changes in either O_2, temperature, or pH levels in the surrounding water. Compensatory responses are observed in a range of crustacean species and are focused on adjustments in respiratory physiology, including acid-base homeostasis and ion regulation. Survival depends on the ability to maintain the most appropriate conditions for protein function. The physiological responses and consequent survival of aquatic crustaceans to simultaneous changes in environmental pH and either temperature or O_2 over the longer term remain to be studied.

8. A hurricane is a type of tropical cyclone or severe tropical storm that forms in the southern Atlantic Ocean, Caribbean Sea, Gulf of Mexico, and in the eastern Pacific Ocean.

9. **SDS** (sodium dodecyl sulphate) is a detergent (soap) that can dissolve hydrophobic molecules but also has a negative charge (sulphate) attached to it. Therefore, if a cell is incubated with SDS, the membranes will be dissolved, all the proteins will be solubilized by the detergent, plus all the proteins will be covered with many negative charges. The end result has two important features: (1) all proteins retain only their primary structure and (2) all proteins have a large negative charge which means they will all migrate towards the positive pole when placed in an electric field. All proteins converted into monomers and monomers are also denatured by SDS.

10. The major sources of mercury pollution in India are chloralkali industries, industrial processes in thermal power plants, steel and cement industries, coal fired power and heat production, mercury-containing products such as thermometers, blood pressure equipment, pesticides, dental amalgam, and waste incineration processes.

16. Elephant (*Elephas maximus*) is the largest terrestrial mammal of India. Project Elephant (PE) was launched by the Government of India in the year 1992 as a Centrally Sponsored Scheme with following objectives:

 1. To protect elephants, their habitat & corridors

 2. To address issues of man-animal conflict

 3. Welfare of captive elephants

18. Champion and Seth classified forest into five major groups based on climatic factors, precipitation and floristic composition. These major groups have been further divided into 16 type groups based on temperature and moisture content. A few of these type groups have been further divided into several subgroups. Ultimately the type groups have been classified into 221 forest types and subtypes based on location specific climate factors and vegetation formation. Structure, physiognomy, floristics, temperature, edaphic factors, and moisture are all used as characters to define the types. Previous classification systems and profile diagrams were also used as input data for classification. The system is valid even now, to prepare working plans and for silvicultural practises.

20. In ecology, the **competitive exclusion principle**, sometimes referred to as **Gauss's law of competitive exclusion** or just **Gauss's law**, is a proposition that states that two species competing for the same resource cannot coexist at constant population values, if other ecological factors remain constant. When one species has even the slightest advantage or edge over another then the one with the advantage will dominate in the long term. One of the two competitors will always overcome the other, leading to either the extinction of this competitor or an evolutionary or behavioural shift toward a different ecological niche. The principle has been paraphrased into the maxim **"complete competitors cannot coexist"**.

21. Parasite-modified changes in predator-prey dynamics can have ramifications throughout the community, affecting community structure and productivity.

24. The **Boreal forest** is the world's largest land-based biome. Spreading over continents and covering many countries, the Boreal plays a significant role in the planet's biodiversity and even its climate. The seasonal variation from summer to winter is represented by boreal forest.

27. Calcite is a carbonate mineral and the most stable polymorph of calcium carbonate. The other polymorphs are the minerals aragonite and vaterite. Aragonite will change to calcite at 380-470 °C, and vaterite is even less stable.

28. A GIS topology is a set of rules and behaviours that model how points, lines, and polygons share coincident geometry. For example:
 - Adjacent features, such as two counties, will have a common boundary between them. They share this edge.
 - The set of county polygons within each state must completely cover the state polygon and share edges with the state boundary.

Topology has long been a key GIS requirement for data management and integrity. In general, a topological data model manages spatial relationships by representing spatial objects (point, line, and area features) as an underlying graph of topological primitives—nodes, faces, and edges. These primitives, together with their relationships to one another and to the features whose boundaries they represent, are defined by representing the feature geometries in a planar graph of topological elements.

30. **Thermal Inertia** is the degree of slowness with which the temperature of a body approaches that of its surroundings and which is dependent upon its absorptivity, its specific heat, its thermalconductivity, its dimensions, and other factors.

Thermal inertia is an important parameter in geological and agricultural applications. Time slot for measuring thermal inertia (TI) differences between land and water is 1400 hrs.

31. A **slump** is a form of mass wasting that occurs when a coherent mass of loosely consolidated materials or rock layers moves a short distance down a slope. Movement is characterized by sliding along a concave-upward or planar surface. Causes of slumping include earthquake shocks, thorough wetting, freezing and thawing, undercutting, and loading of a slope.

32. In scientific terms, water harvesting broadly refers to collection and storage of rain water and also other activities such as harvesting surface water, extracting ground water, prevention of losses through evaporation and seepage. In general, water harvesting is the activity of direct collection of rain water, collected rain water can be stored for direct use or can be recharged into ground water.

RWH helps conserve and augment the storage of ground water aquifers, thereby improving the ground water table. In coastal areas over extraction of ground water leads to saline water intrusion. Therefore recharging the ground water aquifer helps arrest the saline water intrusion. Continuous recharge of ground water using rain water helps improve the ground water quality considerably.

36. **Erosion:** The set of all processes by which soil and rock are loosened and moved downhill or downwind.

41. A useful way to demonstrate growth rate is to present it as *doubling time,* or the number of years for a human population to double its size. The doubling time can be calculated according to the following relationship:

doubling time = 0.70/growth rate

This relationship is derived from the formula for calculating compound interest at the bank and is an approximation. It is useful to remember that a growth rate in any population compounds itself since the individuals entering the population will ultimately reproduce and add more people to that population. As the growth rate increases, the doubling time decreases.

45. Balanced chemical oxidation reaction of methane:

$$CH_4 + 2O_2 = CO_2 + 2H_2O$$

Burning 1 mol of CH_4 liberates 890 kJ of energy while producing 1 mol of CO_2. Since 1 mol of CO_2 has 12g of carbon, the HHV carbon intensity of methane is

$$HHV \text{ carbon intensity} = \frac{12g}{890kJ}$$
$$= 0.0135 \text{ gC/kJ} = 13.5 \text{ gC/MJ.}$$

46. mM HCl = 10^{-3} M HCl

HCl dissociates completely, so

$$[H^+] = M \text{ HCl}$$
$$[H^+] = 10^{-3}$$
$$pH = -\log[H^+]$$
$$= -\log 10^{-3}$$
$$pH = 3.$$

50. The sources of aliphatic hydrocarbons (octane, decane, undecane) in indoor environment are paints, adhesives, gasoline, combustion sources, etc.

52. Internal combustion engines burn a mixture of fuel and air; the air is the source of oxygen needed to engage in the chemical reaction with the fuel known as combustion, or burning. In standard engines, the ratio of air to fuel is set at or very near that which ensures that there is sufficient oxygen in the mixture to burn all of the fuel, yet not an excess amount of air.

A stoichiometric air/fuel ratio (A/F) of approximately 14.6, when gasoline is the fuel, which yields lower fuel economy for complete combustion in an internal combustion engine.

53. Phytovolatilization is a process, in which plants take up contaminants from soil and release them as volatile form into the atmosphere through transpiration. The process occurs as growing plants absorb water and organic contaminants. As water travels from the roots to the leaves along the vascular system of the plant, it is changed and modified along the way. Then, some of the contaminants move through the plants to the leaves and evaporate or volatilize into the atmosphere. Phytovolatilization has been primarily used to remove mercury; the mercuric ion is converted into less toxic elemental mercury.

56. The ISO 14000 family of standards provides practical tools for companies and organizations of all kinds looking to manage their environmental responsibilities.

57. **Council for Advancement of People's Action and Rural Technology** (CAPART) is a nodal organization for rural development. The main purpose of this organization is to promote and organize the joint venture emerging between the Government of India and the voluntary organizations pertaining to the development of the rural sector. The voluntary organizations are responsible for motivating and promoting the rural sector towards change.

59. An Act to provide for the levy and collection of a cess on water consumed by persons carrying on certain industries and by local authorities, with a view to augment the resources of the Central Board and the State Boards for the prevention and control of water pollution constituted under the Water (Prevention and Control of Pollution) Act, 1974.

Levy and Collection of Cess

1. There shall be levied and collected a cess for the purpose of the Water (Prevention and Control of Pollution) Act, 1974 (6 of 1974) and utilisation thereunder.

2. The cess under sub-section (1) shall be payable by—

   (a) every person carrying on any specified industry; and

   (b) every local authority

60. Disasters can have adverse consequences on the environment and on ecosystems in particular, which could have immediate to long-term effects on the populations whose life, health, livelihoods and well-being depend on a given environment or ecosystem.

Environmental degradation also contributes to risk by increasing socio-economic vulnerability to hazard impacts, as the capacity of damaged ecosystems to meet people's needs for food and other products is reduced. Appropriate management of ecosystems can therefore play a critical role in reducing vulnerability and enhancing resilience of local communities, as healthy socioecological systems are better able to prevent, absorb and recover from disasters.

61. The three major Rio Conventions—on Biodiversity, Climate Change and Desertifi-

cation—derive directly from the 1992 Earth Summit. The three conventions are intrinsically linked, operating in the same ecosystems and addressing interdependent issues.

Convention on Biological Diversity

The objectives of the CBD are the conservation of biological diversity, the sustainable use of its components, and the fair and equitable sharing of the benefits arising from commercial and other utilization of genetic resources. The agreement covers all ecosystems, species, and genetic resources.

63. The important parametric tests are: the z-test, the t-test, the Chi-square (χ^2) test and the F-test.

    (a) **The z-test:** This test is widely used for testing the significance of statistics such as mean, median, mode, coefficient of correlation and others. This test is used even when binomial distribution or 't' distribution is applicable on the presumption that such a distribution tends to approximate normal distribution as the sample size (n) becomes larger. The elevant test statistic, 'z', is calculated and compared with its probable value at a specified level of significance for judging the significance of the measure concerned.

    (b) **The t-test:** This test is suitable for testing the significance of a sample mean or for judging the significance of difference between the means of two samples, when the samples are less than 30 in number and when the population variance is not known. When two samples are related, the paired t-test is used. The t-test can also be used for testing the significance of the coefficients of simple and partial correlations. The relevant test statistic, 't', is calculated from the sample data,

and it is compared with its corresponding critical value in the t-distribution table for rejecting or accepting a null hypothesis.

    (c) **The Chi-square (χ^2) test:** The chi-squared calculation is between observed and expected values. This approach applies whether we are looking at comparing a theoretical with an empirical distribution, testing a sample variance against the population variance (expected), or using a contingency table.

    Use the basic chi-squared formula to calculate a value

$$\chi^2 = \sum_i \frac{(\text{observed}_i - \text{expected}_i)^2}{\text{expected}_i}$$

    (d) **The F-test:** This test is based on F-distribution which is a distribution skewed to the right, and tends to be more symmetrical, as the number of degrees of freedom in the numerator and denominator increase. The F-test is used to compare the variances of two independent samples. It is also used in the analysis of variance (ANOVA) for testing the significance of more than two sample means at a time. It is also used for judging the significance of multiple correlation coefficients.

66. The module on confidence intervals provided methods for estimating confidence intervals for various parameters. Confidence intervals for every parameter take the following general form:

    Point Estimate ± Margin of Error

In the module on confidence intervals we derived the formula for the confidence interval for μ as

$$\bar{X} \pm Z \frac{\sigma}{\sqrt{n}}$$

For this question, Z is the value from the table of probabilities of the standard normal distribution for the desired confidence level (*e.g.*, Z = 1.96 for 95% confidence), mean = ± 1.96.

67. **Our Common Future**, also known as the **Brundtland Report**, from the United Nations World Commission on Environment and Development (WCED) was published in 1987.

Its targets were multilateralism and interdependence of nations in the search for a sustainable development path. The report sought to recapture the spirit of the United Nations Conference on the Human Environment—the Stockholm Conference—which had introduced environmental concerns to the formal political development sphere. *Our Common Future* placed environmental issues firmly on the political agenda; it aimed to discuss the environment and development as one single issue.

68. In the Gaussian equation, it is assumed that the plume spread has a Gaussian distribution in both the horizontal and vertical planes. The standard deviation of the plume concentration distribution in the horizontal (crosswind) is denoted by sigma $y(\sigma_y)$ and the corresponding concentration distribution in the vertical is denoted by sigma $z(\sigma_z)$. These are frequently referred to as dispersion or diffusion coefficients. The values for these diffusion coefficients vary depending on the height above the surface, the surface roughness, sampling time, wind speed and distance downwind from the source.

$$\text{Concentration (c)} \propto \frac{1}{\{height(H)\}^2}$$

72. A halocarbon is an organic chemical molecule composed of at least one carbon atom bound covalently with one or more halogen atoms. The residence time (or atmospheric lifetime) of a halocarbon is defined by its rate of removal or sink. The average atmospheric lifetime not only controls the build-up of the halocarbon in the atmosphere, but also impacts on the global distribution of halocarbons and the role in evaluating the impact of individual species on the stratospheric and tropospheric ozone depletion, climate change, regional pollution and on future scenarios, and finally determines the timescale for the atmosphere to recover after emissions cease.

	Lifetime (years)	Radiative forcing (Wm^{-2}/ppb)
CF_4	50000	0.08
CCl_3F	50	0.25
CCl_2F_2	10	0.32
$CBrF_3$	65	0.32

74. The sudden movement of rock, debris or earth along the slope is called landslide.

The various causes of landslides are-

(*a*) **Natural causes:**
   1. Landslides are generally associated with natural calamities like earthquake, volcanic eruptions, floods, cloudburst, etc
   2. Long spell of rainfall
   3. Loose soil cover and sloping terrain

(*b*) **Anthropogenic causes:**
   1. Rapid urbanization and changes in land use patterns
   2. Rampant deforestation and mining activities like blasting and quarrying, etc
   3. Increased industrialisation leading to climate change and weather disturbances
   4. Change in river flow due to construction of dams, barriers, etc.

R.Gupta's®
USEFUL BOOKS FOR UGC EXAM

R. Gupta's®
OBJECTIVE QUESTION BANK

	Book Code	Price (₹)		Book Code	Price (₹)
Objective Biotechnology	R-1472	140	Objective Electronics & Telecommunication Engineering	R-110	120
वस्तुनिष्ठ पर्यावरण विज्ञान	R-1261	195	Objective Civil Engineering (Small Size)	R-103	95
Objective Botany	R-1212	120	Objective Electronics & Telecommunication Engineering (enlarged edition)	R-443	180
Objective Zoology	R-1213	195			
Objective Environmental Sciences	R-1203	210	Objective History	R-681	195
Objective Agriculture Science	R-1157	180	Objective Public Administration	R-679	130
वस्तुनिष्ठ कृषि विज्ञान	R-1134	140	Objective Geography	R-712	150
वस्तुनिष्ठ शारीरिक शिक्षा	R-1084	110	Objective Economics	R-720	150
Objective Computer Awareness	R-1031	135	वस्तुनिष्ठ गृह विज्ञान	R-899	110
ऑब्जेक्टिव कम्प्यूटर ज्ञान	R-1032	95	वस्तुनिष्ठ संस्कृत	R-661	95
वस्तुनिष्ठ सामाजिक ज्ञान	R-1017	85	ऑब्जेक्टिव सिविल इंजीनियरिंग	R-99	210
Objective Social Studies	R-1016	125	ऑब्जेक्टिव इलेक्ट्रीकल इंजीनियरिंग	R-101	180
वस्तुनिष्ठ विज्ञान	R-1015	75	वस्तुनिष्ठ इलेक्ट्रॉनिकी तथा दूरसंचार अभियांत्रिकी	R-442	195
Objective Science	R-1014	140	ऑब्जेक्टिव मैकेनिकल इंजीनियरिंग	R-549	190
वस्तुनिष्ठ हिन्दी-वृहत् परिचय	R-986	90	वस्तुनिष्ठ इतिहास	R-532	130
वस्तुनिष्ठ सामान्य विज्ञान	R-977	145	वस्तुनिष्ठ भूगोल	R-535	130
Objective Psychology	R-966	140	वस्तुनिष्ठ अर्थशास्त्र	R-536	120
Objective Home Science	R-898	140	वस्तुनिष्ठ राजनीतिशास्त्र	R-537	120
Objective Philosophy	R-808	140	वस्तुनिष्ठ हिन्दी (साहित्य तथा व्याकरण)	R-527	150
Objective Commerce	R-809	195	वस्तुनिष्ठ इतिहास (बड़ा संस्करण)	R-496	140
Objective Sociology	R-802	150	वस्तुनिष्ठ लोक प्रशासन	R-566	95
Objective Political Science	R-786	150	वस्तुनिष्ठ समाज शास्त्र	R-572	110
Objective Physics (enlarged edition)	R-755	150	वस्तुनिष्ठ वाणिज्य	R-748	130
Objective Chemistry	R-658	130	वस्तुनिष्ठ दर्शनशास्त्र	R-713	75
Objective Biology	R-663	140	वस्तुनिष्ठ मनोविज्ञान	R-776	120
Objective Mathematics	R-662	160	वस्तुनिष्ठ जन्तु विज्ञान	R-1377	320
Objective Computer Science	R-426	150	वस्तुनिष्ठ वनस्पति विज्ञान	R-1378	345
Objective Physics	R-427	95	वस्तुनिष्ठ भौतिकी	R-1379	245
Objective General Science	R-265	130	वस्तुनिष्ठ रसायन विज्ञान	R-1380	430
Objective Civil Engineering	R-100	185	ऑब्जेक्टिव गणित	R-1381	395
Objective Electrical Engineering	R-102	180			
Objective Mechanical Engineering	R-111	240			

For Cash on Delivery (COD), E-mail your order to: order@rameshpublishinghouse.com

Ramesh Publishing House
12-H, New Daryaganj Road, Opp. Traffic Kotwali, Delhi-110002
For Online Shopping: www.rameshpublishinghouse.com

1509

UGC–NET Environmental Sciences, December–2014

PAPER-II

Note : *This paper contains **fifty (50)** objective type questions of **two (2)** marks each. All questions are compulsory.*

1. Thermal stratification of aquatic ecosystems takes place in
   A. tropical lakes
   B. temperate lakes
   C. glacier lakes
   D. meandering rivers

2. The scale length of pressure variations in atmosphere in vertical direction is about
   A. 3 km
   B. 4.8 km
   C. 7 km
   D. 12 km

3. Which radioactive element is considered as an indoor pollutant?
   A. Oxygen – 18
   B. Nitrogen – 15
   C. Carbon – 13
   D. Radon

4. In a closed thermodynamic system, across its boundaries
   A. no transfer of heat is possible.
   B. no transfer of work is possible.
   C. transfer of heat is possible but not of work.
   D. transfer of heat and work is possible.

5. In an urban area, moist air at 27 °C has a mixing ratio of 50 gm per kg. Its virtual temperature is
   A. 33.69 °C
   B. 38.15 °C
   C. 36.15 °C
   D. 32.30 °C

6. Under aerobic biodegradation of DDT, which of the following compound is formed?
   A. DDD
   B. DDE
   C. DDN
   D. DDS

7. Among the following heavy metals, which has highest concentration in earth's crust?
   A. Chromium
   B. Copper
   C. Nickel
   D. Zinc

8. Composition-wise halons are related to
   A. CFCs
   B. Halides
   C. Hydrocarbons
   D. Peptides

9. Which of the following gases has highest absorption co-efficient for solubility in water?
   A. Hydrogen
   B. Nitrogen
   C. Oxygen
   D. Carbon dioxide

10. Quantity of glucose (MW 180) required to prepare 1000 ml of 5% solution is
    A. 5 g
    B. 50 g
    C. 900 g
    D. 9000 g

11. Endemic species are
    A. Uniformly distributed across the landscape
    B. Widely distributed
    C. Restricted to a particular area
    D. Continuously distributed globally

12. Which of the following is the *in-situ* biodiversity conservation site?
    A. Arboretum
    B. Botanical garden
    C. Biosphere reserve
    D. Orchidarium

13. The largest unit of climax communities representing well defined climatic zone is referred to as
    A. Biosphere
    B. Biome
    C. Biota
    D. Landscape

14. An active, adaptive control process which is able to maintain the overall balance is known as
    A. Bohr's Hypothesis
    B. Miller Hypothesis
    C. Gaia Hypothesis
    D. Kepler's Law

15. Niche of an organism is
    A. Address
    B. Profession
    C. Location
    D. Range

16. Out of the total fresh water volume of the frozen form constitutes
   A. 60%
   B. 70%
   C. 80%
   D. 50%

17. If Q = stream flow, P = precipitation, E = evapotranspiration, ΔS = net change in storage and ΔT = net underground transfers, then the basic water balance equation is
   A. $Q = (P + E) - (\Delta S + \Delta T)$
   B. $Q = (P - E) - (\Delta S + \Delta T)$
   C. $Q = (P - E) + (\Delta S + \Delta T)$
   D. $Q = (P - E) - (\Delta S - \Delta T)$

18. Particles with a diameter smaller than 0.002 mm are classed as
   A. Cobble
   B. Pebble
   C. Silt
   D. Colloids

19. Water storage capacity of which soil is maximum?
   A. Sandy loam
   B. Loam
   C. Clay loam
   D. Heavy clay

20. Which among the following is not a hot desert?
   A. Sahara
   B. Kalahari
   C. Thar
   D. Gobi

21. In an ideal MHD power generator, the maximum power P output varies with the velocity (u) of conducting fuel as
   A. $P_{max} \propto u$
   B. $P_{max} \propto u^2$
   C. $P_{max} \propto u^3$
   D. $P_{max} \propto u^{3/2}$

22. Which is the most efficient energy source for producing electricity?
   A. Nuclear power
   B. Hydro power
   C. Wind power
   D. Solar power

23. Which of the following types of coal has highest water content?
   A. Anthracite
   B. Bituminous coal
   C. Lignite
   D. Subbituminous coal

24. Energy intensity is the amount of energy
   A. produced per unit gross domestic product
   B. consumed per unit gross domestic product
   C. produced per year per unit area of the country
   D. consumed per year per unit area of the country

25. Which is the cleanest fuel for power generation?
   A. Coal
   B. Uranium
   C. Hydrogen
   D. Water

26. The mountain that rises a kilometre or more above the surrounding sea floor is called
   A. Oceanic island
   B. Atoll
   C. Seamount
   D. Island arc

27. Which form of As is most toxic?
   A. As^{+3}
   B. As^{+2}
   C. As^{+6}
   D. As^{+4}

28. Noise climate is represented by
   A. $L_{10} - L_{90}$
   B. L_{eq}
   C. L_{50}
   D. $(L_{10} - L_{90})^2 / 60$

29. The classical smog is mainly composed of
   A. NO_x and smoke particulates
   B. O_3 and SO_2
   C. SO_2 and NO_x
   D. SO_2 and smoke particulates

30. According to National Ambient Air Quality Standards the annual average concentration of SPM in a residential area should not exceed
   A. 80 $\mu g/m^3$
   B. 100 $\mu g/m^3$
   C. 140 $\mu g/m^3$
   D. 200 $\mu g/m^3$

31. "Blue baby syndrome" is caused due to intake of water high in
   A. Ammonia
   B. Nitrates
   C. Sulphates
   D. Sulphides

32. EIA of mining activities involve impact assessment on
   I. Geological Environment
   II. Biological Environment
   III. Aerial Environment
   Codes :
   A. I only
   B. II and III only
   C. I and III only
   D. I, II and III

33. Accreditation of Environmental Consultant Organizations in India is done by
   A. Ministry of Environment, Forest and Climate Change
   B. Central Pollution Control Board
   C. Ministry of Earth Sciences
   D. Quality Council of India

34. Life Cycle Assessment (LCA) does not include
   A. Life Cycle Inventory of the product
   B. Quantitative improvement in the process of the product
   C. Life Cycle Impact Analysis
   D. Emergency Preparedness Plan

35. A developmental project requires both environmental clearance as well as approval under
   A. Water Act, 1974
   B. Forest (Conservation) Act, 1980
   C. National Environmental Tribunal Act, 1995
   D. Air Act, 1981

36. The best practice of disposal of construction and demolition (C & D) debris is
   A. Incineration   B. Recycling
   C. Land fills   D. Solidification

37. Pyrolysis of Solid Waste refers to
   A. High temperature aerobic incineration
   B. High temperature anaerobic distillation of waste for energy generation
   C. Ambient aerobic distillation
   D. Ambient anaerobic distillation

38. Kyoto Protocol of 1997 introduced the concept of carbon trading in the year of
   A. 2000   B. 2004
   C. 2001   D. 2002

39. Citizen's Charter on Environment in the Constitution of India is embodied in
   A. Article 48   B. Article 48A
   C. Article 49A   D. Article 51A

40. United Nation's Conference on Environment and Development was held in
   A. December, 1993   B. June, 1992
   C. December, 1995   D. November, 1996

41. The geometric mean of the numbers 4, 6 and 9 is
   A. 6   B. 8
   C. 5   D. 7

42. A complete enumerate of all items in the population is
   A. Unrestricted sampling
   B. Non-probability sampling
   C. Census
   D. Sample survey

43. The term 'parameter' is an attribute associated with the data pertaining to
   A. sample
   B. population
   C. descriptive statistics
   D. sampling technique

44. A solar cell of surface area $= 5$ cm^2 delivers a current of 0.1 A at 0.6 V. If the intensity of solar radiation impinging on the solar cell is 1.0 kW/m^2, the efficiency of the solar cell is
   A. 6%   B. 3%
   C. 30%   D. 12%

45. **Assertion (A)** : Living systems exposed to drought salinity and freezing show enhanced levels of osmolytes.
   Reason (R) : Drought, salinity and freezing stress induce water deficit.
   In the context of the two statements, which one of the following is correct?
   A. Both (A) and (R) are true and (R) is the correct explanation of (A).
   B. Both (A) and (R) are true, but (R) is not the correct explanation of (A).
   C. (A) is true, but (R) is false.
   D. (A) is false, but (R) is true.

46. UN Decade of Education for Sustainable Development is
   A. 2000 – 2009   B. 2005 – 2014
   C. 2010 – 2019   D. 2020 – 2031

47. Two kinds of the values distinguished in environmental ethics are
   A. Instrumental value and intrinsic value
   B. Direct use values and social values

C. Social values and existence value
D. Indirect use value and aesthetic value

48. The natural sources of methyl bromide in the atmosphere is
A. Ocean   B. Volcanoes
C. Landslide   D. Vegetation

49. The part of an actual resource which can be developed profitably in the future is

A. Non-renewable resources
B. Potential resources
C. Reserved resources
D. Stock resources

50. Trophic state index of aquatic ecosystem is determined by the concentration of
A. Chlorophyll-a   B. NO_3^-
C. PO_4^{-3} D. NO_2^-

ANSWERS

1	2	3	4	5	6	7	8	9	10
B	C	D	D	C	B	B	A	D	B

11	12	13	14	15	16	17	18	19	20
C	C	B	C	B	B	C	D	D	D

21	22	23	24	25	26	27	28	29	30
B	A	C	B	C	C	A	A	D	C

31	32	33	34	35	36	37	38	39	40
B	D	D	D	B	C	B	D	D	B

41	42	43	44	45	46	47	48	49	50
A	C	B	D	A	B	A	A	C	A

SOME SELECTED EXPLANATORY ANSWERS

1. An important feature of most lakes is that the water is divided into layers (strata) which tend not to mix. Many temperate lakes exhibit thermal stratification. In the summer the top few metres of the lake may reach a temperature of 20°C, a pleasant temperature for swimming. However, at a depth of 20 m, the summer temperature may be only 5°C. Most humans would die from hypothermia within an hour of being in water this cold. In winter the reverse happens; the surface of the lake is *colder* than lower down. Stratification can be understood if one remembers that water is densest at 4°C. Consequently, water that is either cooler or warmer than this will rise.

2. The atmosphere is considerably thinner in its vertical extent (scale height 7 km) than in its horizontal extent. The largest scales of motion are in the horizontal direction and form the basis for the general circulation of the atmosphere.

3. Radon is a dangerous indoor air pollutant that comes from the ground through rocky soil. Radon is a radioactive gas, whose decay particles cling to dust and can mutate lung tissue. The concentration of radon varies widely, both regionally and within regions. Energy conservation work probably has little effect on radon concentrations. However, all housing specialists should be aware of radon's danger, radon testing procedures, and radon mitigation strategies.

4. A **thermodynamic system** is the content of a macroscopic volume in space, along with its walls and surroundings; it undergoes thermodynamic processes according to the principles of thermodynamics. The walls of a closed system allow transfer of energy as heat

and as work, but not of matter, between it and its surroundings. The walls of an *open system* allow transfer both of matter and of energy.

5. $T_v = T (1 + 0.61 \ W)$

$$= (273 + 27)\left(1 + 0.61 \times \frac{50}{1000}\right)$$

$$= 300 \ (1 + 0.61 \times 0.05)$$

$$= 300 \ (1 + 0.0305)$$

$$= 300 \ (1.0305)$$

$$= 309.15 \ K = 36.15°C.$$

6. During biodegradation of DDT, both DDE and DDD are formed in soils. Both metabolites may undergo further transformation but the extent and rate are dependent on soil conditions and, possibly, microbial populations present in soil. DDT under both aerobic and anaerobic conditions, forming 4-chlorobenzoic acid and DDE, respectively. Biodegradation of DDT and its metabolites involves cometabolism, a process in which the microbes derive nutrients for growth and energy from sources other than the compound of concern. DDE, the dominant DDT metabolic found, is often resistant to biodegradation under aerobic and anaerobic conditions. In laboratory experiments with marine sediments, DDT has been shown to degrade to DDE and DDD under anaerobic and anaerobic conditions, respectively.

7. Copper is a reddish metal that occurs naturally in rock, soil, water, sediment, and at low levels air. Its average concentration in the earth's crust is about 50 parts copper per million parts soil (ppm) or, stated another way, 50 grams of copper per 1,000,000 grams of soil (1.8 ounces or 0.11 pounds of copper per 2,200 pounds of soil). Copper also occurs naturally in all plants and animals. It is an essential element for all known living organisms including humans and other animals at low levels of intake.

8. Chlorofluorocarbons (CFCs) and halons are man-made chemicals that exist as gases or liquids. Chlorofluorocarbons contain chlorine, fluorine and carbon. Halons are similar but contain bromine or iodine. They are neither toxic nor flammable.

9. Solubility of gases in a liquid is generally expressed in terms of volume rather than weight. It is generally expressed in terms of *absorption coefficient (α) which is defined as the volume of gas, reduced to 0°C and 1 atm pressure (STP), dissolved in unit volume of the solvent at the experimental temperature under a partial pressure of 1 atm of the gas.* Higher the absorption coefficient higher is the solubility of the gas. Absorption coefficient of some common gases in water at 20°C are given in the table.

Table : *Absorption Coefficient of some gases at 20°C*

He	N_2	H_2	O_2	CO_2	H_2S	HQ	NH_3
0.009	0.015	0.017	0.028	0.88	2.62	442	710

11. **Endemism** is the ecological state of a species being unique to a defined geographic location, such as an island, nation, country or other defined zone, or habitat type; organisms that are indigenous to a place are not endemic to it if they are also found elsewhere. The extreme opposite of endemism is cosmopolitan distribution. Another term for a species that is endemic is precinctive, which applies to species (and subspecific categories) that are restricted to a defined geographical area. A native species, such as a native plant, is one that is considered to have been endemic for a relatively long period of time.

12. In-situ conservation is on site conservation or the conservation of genetic resources in natural populations of plant or animal species, such as forest genetic resources in natural populations of tree species. It is the process of protecting an endangered plant or animal species in its natural habitat, either by protecting or cleaning up the habitat itself, or by defending the species from predators.

In India following types of natural habitats are being maintained:

1. National parks
2. Wildlife sanctuaries
3. Biosphere reserves

Biosphere Reserves: It is a special category of protected areas where human population also forms a part of the system. They are large protected area of usually more than 5000 sq.km.

14. An active, adaptive control process, able to maintain the Earth in over-all balance, is known as the Gaia hypothesis.

    The updated Gaia hypothesis proposes that Earth's atmosphere, oceans, and land masses are held in equilibrium by the living inhabitants of the planet, which includes millions of species besides humans. The Gaia concept suggests that this living world keeps itself in worldwide environmental balance.

    One example of this balancing act takes place in the oceans. Salts are constantly added to the oceans by physical and chemical processes, raising salinity. Eventually, affected seas (like the Dead Sea) reach an uninhabitable salinity level. According to the Gaia hypothesis, the sea's salinity is controlled biologically through the mutual action of ocean organisms. In fact, living sea creatures, primarily algae and protozoa, have processed and removed salt throughout geological time, balancing salinity levels that allow life to thrive.

15. The concept of the ecological niche is an important one; it helps us to understand how organisms in an ecosystem interact with each other. The ecological niche of an organism depends not only on where it lives but also on what it does. By analogy, it may be said that the habitat is the organism's "address", and the niche is its "profession", biologically speaking.

16. Over 70% of our Earth's surface is covered by water. Although water is seemingly abundant, the real issue is the amount of fresh water available.

    - 97.5% of all water on Earth is salt water, leaving only 2.5% as fresh water
    - Nearly 70% of that fresh water is frozen in the icecaps of Antarctica and Greenland; most of the remainder is present as soil moisture, or lies in deep underground aquifers as groundwater not accessible to human use.
    - Only ~1% of the world's fresh water is accessible for direct human uses. This is the water found in lakes, rivers, reservoirs and those underground sources that are shallow enough to be tapped at an affordable cost. Only this amount is regularly renewed by rain and snowfall, and is therefore available on a sustainable basis.

18. Clay particles range downward in diameter from 0.002 mm or 2 microns to smaller than 0.001 micron. Clay particles finer than about 0.01 micron are classed as *colloids*. A property of mineral colloids is their ability to remain in suspension indefinitely in water, once the particles have become dispersed (separated one from another). A colloidal suspension appears clouded or murky.

19. The plant-available water-holding capacity of soil varies from around 50 to 400 mm per metre of soil depth. The maximum volume of water available to a plantation therefore depends on the depth of its root zone and on the water storage properties of the soil. In general, Water storage capacity of heavy clay soil is maximum.

20. Gobi is a cold desert, and it is not uncommon to see frost and occasionally snow on its dunes. Besides being quite far north, also is situated on a plateau about 910-1,520 meters above sea level, further contributing to its low temperature. Generally temperate desert climate is typical continental, with extremely low winter temperatures (–40° C) and very

hot summers (temperatures can rise up to 40 Celsius). The extreme temperature difference between winter and summer, and that between day and night can be explained by lack of water. Thus, the difference in temperature within 24 hours can reach 32° C.

22. Nearly a third of the world's energy demands are met through nuclear power plants. The waste and potential environmental hazards posed are minimal, however, when compared with other major energy sources, such as fossil fuels. The electricity produced by nuclear energy, if produced using coal, would release nearly 147 million metric tons of carbon dioxide into the atmosphere. With nuclear energy, waste production is smaller and contained. The total volume of nuclear waste produced since the nuclear power industry began is only enough to fill a football field to a depth of about 15 yards. This is easily managed and held on site or in underground repositories, safely out of environmental or public contact.

23. **Lignite coal**—The softest of the four types of coal. It is a brownish black in color, very crumbly and primarily used for the generation of electricity. Because of its color, it is often referred to as "brown coal." Lignite is the result of millions of tons of plants and trees that decayed in a swampy atmosphere about 50-70 million years ago. The material on top of the lignite deposits in North Dakota and Montana - called *overburden* - was deposited by runoff from the west as the Rocky Mountains formed. The heating content of lignite is approximately 4,000-8,000 Btu's per pound. The carbon content of lignite is 25%-35% and it has a very high water content - about 35 percent.

24. **Energy intensity** is a *measure* of the *energy efficiency* of a nation's *economy*. It is calculated as units of *energy* per unit of *GDP*.
   • High energy intensities indicate a high price or cost of converting energy into GDP.
   • Low energy intensity indicates a lower price or cost of converting energy into GDP. Energy Intensity as defined here is not to be confused with Energy Use Intensity (EUI), a measure of building energy use per unit area.

25. In many ways, hydrogen is the perfect fuel. It is the cleanest burning and the most efficient. Hydrogen can produce electricity and electricity can produce hydrogen, creating an energy loop that is renewable and harmless to the environment. Hydrogen combines chemically with most elements, so it has been utilized as an industrial chemical in a wide range of applications for many years. In vehicles, hydrogen can be used as a fuel in two ways: to produce electricity in a fuel cell for the cleanest option; or in an internal combustion engine where emissions are still significantly reduced compared with other fuels.

26. A **seamount** is a mountain rising from the ocean seafloor that does not reach to the water's surface (sea level), and thus is not an island. Seamounts are typically formed from extinct volcanoes that rise abruptly and are usually found rising from the seafloor to 1,000-4,000 metres in height. They are defined by oceanographers as independent features that rise to at least 1,000 metres above the seafloor. The peaks are often found hundreds to thousands of meters below the surface, and are therefore considered to be within the deep sea.

28. **Noise Climate (NC)**

Noise Climate = $L_{10} - L_{90}$

where L_{90} = the level exceeded for 90% of the time of record

L_{10} = level exceeded for 10% of the time of record.

29. Smoke-fog like condition is known as smog. Classical smogs occur in cold humid climate and are result of buildup of sulphur dioxide

and particulate matter from fuel combustion. Classical smog is chemically reducing smog with high concentration of SO_2.

31. There are two health concerns when drinking water with high levels of nitrates or nitrites. The first health concern is with infants being at risk for **"blue baby syndrome"**, also called **methemoglobinemia:**
    - Poisoning can occur when infants drink formula made with nitrate or nitrite contaminated tap water.
    - The infant's blood is less able to carry oxygen due to the poisoning.
    - Affected infants develop a blue-grey color and need emergency medical help immediately.
    - Infants under six months of age are more susceptible.

    The second health concern with nitrates and nitrites is the formation of chemicals called **nitrosamines** in the digestive tract. Nitrosamines are being studied for long term links to cancer. No standards have been set for this yet.

33. Quality Council of India (QCI) was set up jointly by the Government of India and the Indian Industry represented by the three premier industry associations i.e. Associated Chambers of Commerce and Industry of India (ASSOCHAM), Confederation of Indian Industry (CII) and Federation of Indian Chambers of Commerce and Industry (FICCI), to establish and operate national accreditation structure and promote quality through National Quality Campaign. It is among the world's leading national apex quality facilitation, accreditation and surveillance organisations, to continuously improve the climate, systems, processes and skills for total quality.

35. The environmental clearance process is required for 39 types of projects and covers aspects like screening, scoping and evaluation of the upcoming project. The main purpose is to assess impact of the planned project on the environment and people and to try to abate/ minimise the same.

    Issues of clearance or rejection letter: When a project requires both environmental clearance as well as approval under the Forest (Conservation) Act, 1980. Proposals for both are required to be given simultaneously to the concerned divisions of the ministry. The processing is done simultaneously for clearance/rejection, although separate letters may be issued. If the project does not involve diversion of forest land, the case is processed only for environmental clearance.

37. **Pyrolysis** is a thermochemical decomposition of organic material at elevated temperatures in the absence of oxygen (or any halogen). It involves the simultaneous change of chemical composition and physical phase, and is irreversible. The word is coined from the Greek-derived elements *pyro* "fire" and *lysis* "separating".

    Pyrolysis of Solid Waste refers to High temperature anaerobic distillation of waste for energy generation.

38. In response to the threat of climate change, UN passed the Kyoto Protocol in 1997, which was gradually ratified by 156 countries, and later infamously rejected by the world's biggest polluters - the US and Australia. The protocol sets the target of reducing emissions by an average of 5.2 percent below 1990 greenhouse gas levels by the year 2012. Russia and Canada ratify the Kyoto Protocol to the UNFCCC bringing the carbon treaty into effect on 16 February 2005.

39. The chapter on fundamental duties of the Indian Constitution clearly imposes duty on every citizen to protect environment. Article 51-A (g), says that "It shall be duty of every citizen of India to protect and improve the natural environment including forests, lakes, rivers and wild life and to have compassion for living creatures."

40. The **United Nations Conference on Environment and Development (UNCED),** also known as the Rio Summit, Rio Conference, and Earth Summit was a major United Nations' conference held in Rio de Janeiro from 3 to 14 June 1992.

41. Geometric mean (G.M.) = $\{4.6.9\}^{\frac{1}{3}}$

$$= \sqrt[3]{216} = 6.$$

42. Surveys are used as a tool to collect information from some or all units of a population and compile the information into a useful form. There are two different types of surveys that can be used to collect information in different circumstances to satisfy differing needs. These are *sample surveys* and *censuses.*

Sample Surveys: In a sample survey, only part of the total population is approached for information for the topic under study. These data are then 'expanded' or 'weighted' to make inferences about the whole population. We define the sample as the set of observations taken from the population for the purpose of obtaining information about the population.

Censuses: A census is a collection of information from all units in the population or a 'complete enumeration' of the population. We use a census when we want accurate information for many subdivisions of the population. Such a survey usually requires a very large sample size and often a census offers the best solution.

46. The United Nations Decade of Education for Sustainable Development (2005-2014), for which UNESCO is the lead agency, seeks to integrate the principles, values, and practices of sustainable development into all aspects of education and learning, in order to address the social, economic, cultural and environmental problems we face in the 21st century.

47. Values are an assessment of measure of the worth of something. Two broad types of values can be distinguished in environmental ethics:

1. *Instrumental* is the value that something has as a means to an end. So money might be good only because it leads to other good things (purchase of goods). Putting monetary value on environmental goods, or considering nature in terms of natural resources and ecosystem services, are typical expressions of instrumental value in relation to nature.

2. *Instrinsic* is the value that a thing has in itself, or for its own sake, or in its own right. Money for example is not intrinsically good (unless you are a collector of historic or different currencies) whereas most other goods might arguably be considered as having some intrinsic value. Environmentalism as a soical movement in the mid-twentieth century grew from an appreciation of the intrinsic value for nature.

A third type of value can be associated with the valuer as against the valued. Here, value is linked with obligations and the boundaries of the *moral community*--who or what is worthy of respect (past, present, future generations? other animals? all living organisms? ecosystems? biosphere? universe? multiverse?).

3. Personal (or individual) is the internally held value of the valuer usually attached to character traits such as having integrity. Behind any value is a valuer with particular perspectives on the world guided by personal values. Two perspectives on the environment based on personal values can be distinguished– anthropocentric and ecocentric.

49. **Natural resources** occur naturally within environments that exist relatively undisturbed by humanity, in a natural form. A natural resource is often characterized by amounts of biodiversity and geodiversity existent in various ecosystems.

Considering their stage of development, natural resources may be referred to in the following ways:

- *Potential resources*–Potential resources are those that exist in a region and may be used in future. For example *petroleum* occurs with sedimentary rocks in various regions, but until the time it is actually drilled out and put into use, it remains a potential resource.

- *Actual resources*–Actual resources are those that have been surveyed, their quantity and quality determined and are being used in present times. The development of an actual resource, such as *wood processing* depends upon the technology available and the cost involved.

- *Reserve resources*–The part of an actual resource which can be developed profitably in the future is called a reserve resource.

- *Stock resources*–Stock resources are those that have been surveyed but cannot be used by organisms due to lack of technology. For example: *hydrogen.*

50. Quantitive evaluation of trophic state conditions has been aided by use of simple trophic state indices. The most widely used TSIs are those developed by Carlson (1977), based on Secchi disk transparency and on concentrations of total phosphate and chlorophyll *a*. These strongly intercorrelated parameters are, respectively, the best quantified physical, chemical and biological measures of trophic conditions, and Carlson developed a simple index based on each parameter.

PAPER-III

Note : *This paper contains **seventy five (75)** objective type questions of **two (2)** marks each. **All** questions are compulsory.*

1. Which of the following ranges of scale lengths represents meso-scale motions in atmosphere?
   A. 30 km – 400 km
   B. 500 m – 10 km
   C. 1 km – 2 km
   D. 100 m – 1 km

2. Rayleigh scattering in the atmosphere is caused by
   A. molecules larger than the wavelength
   B. molecules equal to the size of wavelength
   C. molecules whose size is much smaller than the wavelength
   D. molecules and particles of all sizes

3. Wind rose is a
   A. graphical representation of wind velocity vector over a period of time in a polar diagram.
   B. graphical representation of wind velocity vector in a spherical coordinate system over a period of time.
   C. graphical representation of horizontal and vertical wind speeds over a period of time in polar diagram.
   D. graphical representation of instantaneous wind velocity at a particular time.

4. The key groups of organic molecules that help in chelation of metal ions are
   I. –COOH
   II. –SH
   III. $-CH_3$
   IV. –CHO
   Choose the correct answer from the codes given below:
   A. I only
   B. I and II only
   C. II, III and IV only
   D. I, II and IV only

5. Geostrophic winds are the result of the balance between
   A. coriolis force and pressure gradient force
   B. coriolis force and centrifugal force
   C. pressure gradient force and frictional force
   D. pressure gradient force and centrifugal force

6. A possible mechanism for photochemical smog inhibition is to add compounds like diethylhydroxylamine (DEHA) as it reacts with
   A. hydrocarbon
   B. nitrogen dioxide
   C. PAN
   D. hydroxyl radicals

7. In the determination of sulphur dioxide by p-rosaniline method, the end product is
   A. p-rosaniline sulfonic acid
   B. methyl p-rosaniline
   C. p-rosaniline methyl sulfonic acid
   D. sulfo methyl p-rosaniline

8. Number of molecules present in 10 ml of proline is
   A. 6.023×10^{23} B. 6.023×10^{20}
   C. 6.023×10^{18} D. 6.023×10^{17}

9. Nitrogenous biochemical oxygen demand refers to the quantity of O_2 needed to convert
   A. N_2 to NO_3^-
   B. N_2 to NH_4^+
   C. NH_4^+ to NO_3^-
   D. Protein to $CO_2 + H_2O + NO_2$

10. Beer-Lambert's law defines
    A. The degree of absorption of monochromatic light by a homogeneous medium
    B. Atomic absorption spectrophotometry
    C. Atomic emission spectrophotometry
    D. Gas chromatography

11. Chemically phytochelatins are
    A. Proteins   B. Polysaccharides
    C. Lipids   D. Polypeptides

12. Mixture of organic pollutants X and Y were separated using paper chromatography and the R_f values obtained for X and Y were 0.75 and 0.25, respectively. Which relationship holds good for the solubility of these pollutants in mobile phase?
    A. X > Y   B. X < Y
    C. X = Y   D. X + Y = 1

13. Overall reaction of Winkler's method is
    $$4S_2O_3^{2-} + 4H^+ + O_2 \rightarrow 2S_4O_6^{2-} + 2H_2O$$
    This equation indicates:
    A. One mole of O_2 is equivalent to one mole of thiosulphate.
    B. One mole of O_2 is equivalent to two moles of thiosulphate.
    C. One mole of O_2 is equivalent to three moles of thiosulphate.
    D. One mole of O_2 is equivalent to four moles of thiosulphate.

14. Return of an ecosystem to a condition prior to disturbance refers to as
    A. Rehabilitation   B. Restoration
    C. Rejuvenation   D. Reclaimation

15. **Assertion (A)** : Shade loving species show better natural regeneration under highly disturbed condition.
    Reason (R) : Heliophilic species needs more exposure to light for better natural regeneration.
    In the context of the two statements, which one of the following is correct?
    A. Both (A) and (R) are true and (R) is the correct explanation of (A).
    B. Both (A) and (R) are true, but (R) is not the correct explanation of (A).
    C. (A) is true, but (R) is false.
    D. (A) is false, but (R) is true.

16. Which one of the following enzymes work under strict anaerobic conditions to fix atmospheric nitrogen?
    A. Nitrate reductase
    B. Nitrite reductase
    C. Transaminase
    D. Nitrogenase

17. Predatory strategy followed by an alligator for hunting is
   A. Chase
   B. Stalk
   C. Ambush
   D. Camouflage

18. In a tropical peat forest, the carbon storage (tonnes/ha) is typically in the range
   A. 3000 – 6000
   B. 13000 – 16000
   C. 300 – 600
   D. 300 – 1600

19. Which one of the following bacterial species convert NO_2^- to NO_3^- ?
   A. *Nitrosomonas*
   B. *Nitrobacter*
   C. *Rhizobium*
   D. *Azospirillum*

20. **Assertion (A) :** Living system adapted to low temperatures invariably show higher unsaturated to saturated fatty acid in membrane lipids.
   Reason (R) : Fluidity of membranes is directly proportional to unsaturated to saturated fatty acids in membrane lipids.
   In the context of the two statements, which one of the following is correct?
   A. Both (A) and (R) are true and (R) is the correct explanation of (A).
   B. Both (A) and (R) are true, but (R) is not the correct explanation of (A).
   C. (A) is true, but (R) is false.
   D. (A) is false, but (R) is true.

21. Which of the following is/are produced during fermentation?
   I. Ethanol
   II. Citrate
   III. Lactate
   IV. Succinate
   Choose the correct answer from the codes given below:
   A. I only
   B. I and II only
   C. I and III only
   D. II and IV only

22. Salinity of the ocean varies from 2.0% to 4.2% in
   A. Red Sea and Gulf of Kachchh
   B. Black Sea and Omura Bay
   C. Baltic Sea and Persian Gulf
   D. Mediterranean Sea and Bay of Fundy

23. Uranium in Indian agricultural soils is mainly contributed by
   A. Weathering of Uranium rich minerals
   B. Excess addition of NPK fertilizers
   C. Excess addition of pesticides
   D. Excess addition of fungicides

24. Loamy sand contains
   A. > 80% silt and > 80% clay
   B. 10% silt and 5% clay
   C. 15 to 30% silt and 10 to 15% clay
   D. > 80% silt and < 20% clay

25. Spectral reflectance of leaf is highest for which band?
   A. Blue
   B. Green
   C. Near infrared
   D. Middle infrared

26. Match the List–I with List–II and choose the correct answer from the given codes:

List–I (Elements)	List–II (Concentration in Earth's Crust by weight %)
(a) Oxygen	(i) 8.13
(b) Aluminium	(ii) 46.60
(c) Iron	(iii) 27.72
(d) Silicon	(iv) 5.00

   Identify the correct code:
   Codes :

	(a)	(b)	(c)	(d)
A.	(i)	(iv)	(iii)	(ii)
B.	(iii)	(ii)	(i)	(iv)
C.	(ii)	(i)	(iv)	(iii)
D.	(iv)	(iii)	(ii)	(i)

27. Indian Microwave Remote Sensing Satellite is
   A. RISAT
   B. Resourcesat
   C. IRS
   D. Bhaskara

28. Mount Etna in Sicily and Mauna Loa in Hawaiian Islands are the most noteworthy examples of
   A. shield volcanoes
   B. plug dome
   C. strato volcanoes
   D. pyroclastic cones

29. Match the List–I with List–II and choose the correct answer from the given codes:

List–I (Mineral Deposit)	List–II (Top producer)
(a) Bauxite	(i) Peru
(b) Copper	(ii) India
(c) Mica	(iii) USA
(d) Guano	(iv) Australia

Identify the correct code :
Codes :

	(a)	(b)	(c)	(d)
A.	(i)	(ii)	(iii)	(iv)
B.	(iv)	(iii)	(ii)	(i)
C.	(iii)	(i)	(iv)	(ii)
D.	(ii)	(iv)	(i)	(iii)

30. Which of the following fuels has the highest HHV carbon intensity?
A. Natural gas   B. Oil
C. Bituminous coal D. Nuclear fuel

31. If fission of 1 atom of U^{235} produces 200 MeV energy, how much energy will be produced by 1 metric ton of U^{235}?
A. 4.1×10^7 MJ   B. 8.2×10^7 MJ
C. 1.23×10^8 MJ   D. 2×10^5 MJ

32. The Green Climate Fund recently set up to help poor countries adapt to climate impacts envisages financial support to the extent of (in $ per year)
A. 100 bn   B. 30 bn
C. 10 bn   D. 3 bn

33. Which of the following biomass conversion processes produces biogas from crop residues?
A. Anaerobic digestion
B. Fermentation
C. Pyrolysis
D. Aerobic digestion

34. Which among the following is superior carbon fixer per unit area for bioenergy generation?
A. Trees   B. Shrubs
C. Blue-green algae   D. Crops

35. Energy flow in ecosystem is governed by
A. First law of thermodynamics
B. Second law of thermodynamics
C. Planck's law
D. Kirchoff's law

36. Average number of carbon in diesel ranges between
A. $C_{18} - C_{24}$ B. $C_{10} - C_{16}$
C. $C_4 - C_6$ D. $C_{25} - C_{30}$

37. Knocking effect in the gasoline cannot be reached by one of the following additives:
A. $(C_2H_5)_4Pb$ B. BTX
C. Kerosene   D. n-Butane

38. Radioactive mineral available in the Indian coastal region is
A. Rutile   B. Monazite
C. Apatite   D. Magnetite

39. Thermal pollution in the coastal region is caused by
(i) Atomic power plants
(ii) Thermal power plants
(iii) Industrial plants
(iv) Tourism industry
Choose the correct answer from the codes given below:
Codes :
A. (i), (ii) and (iii) only B. (i) and (ii) only
C. (iii) and (iv) only D. (ii) and (iii) only

40. **Assertion (A) :** Metallic contaminants are toxic to the microorganism.
Reason (R) : Heavy metal tends to precipitate in the form of phosphatic compounds and decrease soil fertility.
In the context of the two statements, which one of the following is correct?
A. Both (A) and (R) are true and (R) is the correct explanation of (A).
B. Both (A) and (R) are true, but (R) is not the correct explanation of (A).
C. (A) is true, but (R) is false.
D. (A) is false, but (R) is true.

41. A point source of sound produces a noise of 70 dB at a distance of 20 m from it. What will be the noise level at 80 m from it?
A. 35 dB   B. 64 dB
C. 58 dB   D. 52 dB

42. Stratospheric ozone absorbs UV radiations principally in the wavelength of range
A. 320 – 400 nm
B. 230 – 320 nm
C. < 290 nm
D. 180 – 240 nm

43. If Γ_d, Γ_s and Γ represent dry adiabatic, saturated adiabatic lapse rate and environ-mental lapse rate, respectively, the condition for unstable atmosphere is

A. $\Gamma > \Gamma_d$ B. $\Gamma < \Gamma_d$
C. $\Gamma < \Gamma_s$ D. $\Gamma < \Gamma_s < \Gamma_d$

44. At initial time (t_0) number of *E. coli* per ml was 10. If generation time is 30 minutes, what would be number of cells per ml after a duration of 4 hours?
A. 256   B. 2560
C. 240   D. 300

45. Emission inventories involved in urban air quality assessment include parameters on
(i) SO_2, NO_x, particulate matter pollutants
(ii) Industry, traffic, domestic sources
(iii) Fuel type, gasoline, wood as energy carrier
Choose the correct answer from codes given below:
Codes:
A. (i) and (ii) only
B. (ii) and (iii) only
C. (i) and (iii) only
D. (i), (ii) and (iii)

46. **Assertion (A) :** Leopold matrix can be expanded or contracted.
Reason (R) : Leopold matrix is a checklist designed to show possible interactions between developmental activities and set of environmental characteristics.
In the context of the two statements, which one of the following is correct?
A. Both (A) and (R) are true and (R) is the correct explanation of (A).
B. Both (A) and (R) are true, but (R) is not the correct explanation of (A).
C. (A) is true, but (R) is false.
D. (A) is false, but (R) is true.

47. In Battele environment evaluation system the total parameter importance units is lowest for
A. Ecology
B. Environmental Pollution
C. Aesthetics
D. Human interest

48. ISO 14040 is
A. Environmental Management : Life cycle assessment principle and framework.
B. Environmental Management – environmental assessment of sites and organization.
C. Guidelines for environmental audit – general principle.
D. Environmental Management – vocabulary.

49. Given below are stages within each tier of risk assessment:
(i) identification of consequences
(ii) hazard identification
(iii) probability assessment
(iv) assessment of consequences as well as significance of risk
(v) magnitude assessment for consequences
Which one of the following code represent correct sequences?
A. (ii), (i), (v), (iii), (iv)
B. (i), (ii), (iii), (iv), (v)
C. (iii), (ii), (iv), (v), (i)
D. (iv), (ii), (i), (iii), (v)

50. Ecolabels are indicators of
(i) Acceptable level of environmental impact of a product.
(ii) Environmental performance of a product.
(iii) Claims of environmental friendliness of a product.
Choose the correct answer from the codes given below:
A. (i), (ii), (iii)   B. (i) and (ii) only
C. (i) only   D. (ii) only

51. Ecosystem diversity can be best studied using the
A. Topographical maps
B. Geoinformatics
C. Geodesy
D. Geology

52. Biennial assessment of forest cover in India is done by
    A. Indian Institute of Remote Sensing, Dehradun
    B. Forest Research Institute, Dehradun
    C. Indian Institute of Forest Management, Bhopal
    D. Forest Survey of India, Dehradun

53. Soil moisture using remote sensing techniques is determined best in
    A. Optical region
    B. Thermal region
    C. Microwave region
    D. Infrared region

54. Which one of the following statements is not connected to ISO 14000 series of Environmental Management?
    A. Promotes eco-labelling of the product
    B. It is based on the recommendation of TC-207 committee
    C. Make the environmental audit mandatory
    D. Promotes human rights and women empowerment

55. As per colour coding of plastic bags for biomedical wastes, match the List–I with List–II and choose the correct answer from the codes given below:

List–I (Colour Code)	List–II (Option for disposal)
(a) Yellow plastic bags	(i) Disposal in secured land fills
(b) Black plastic bags	(ii) Incineration and deep burials
(c) Blue/White plastic bags	(iii) Autoclaving and chemical treatment
(d) Red plastic bags	(iv) Microwave treatments and destruction

Codes :

	(a)	(b)	(c)	(d)
A.	(iv)	(iii)	(ii)	(i)
B.	(i)	(iv)	(iii)	(ii)
C.	(ii)	(i)	(iv)	(iii)
D.	(iii)	(ii)	(i)	(iv)

56. Given below is a list of natural disasters:
    (i) Hudhud cyclone
    (ii) Chernobyl nuclear plant disaster
    (iii) Tsunami in Indian Ocean
    (iv) Bhopal gas tragedy
    Which is the correct chronological sequence for the above events in the codes given below?
    Codes:
    A. (iii), (i), (ii), (iv)   B. (ii), (iii), (i), (iv)
    C. (iv), (ii), (iii), (i)   D. (i), (ii), (iii), (iv)

57. Benchmarking in environmental management refers to
    A. Potential risk assessment.
    B. Reporting of environmental performance.
    C. Assessment of organization's business processes against the best-in-class operations to improve the performance.
    D. Setting of environmental standards to be followed by environmental managers.

58. Basel convention is related to
    A. Control of ozone depletion.
    B. Control of water pollution.
    C. Transboundary movement of hazardous wastes and their disposal.
    D. Environmental auditing.

59. Concept of intergenerational equity on natural resources refers to
    A. Legal obligations of present generation to future generations.
    B. Moral obligation of the present generation to future generation.
    C. Equitable responsibility of pollution generating industries.
    D. Prudent use of resources inherited from previous generation.

60. Which among the following is not correct in regard to the sources of nitrate in the soils?
    (i) Microbial breakdown of soil organic matter, organic manure and plant residues.
    (ii) Fertilizers which add nitrate and that formed by microbial oxidation of NH_4^+ from ammonium fertilizers or urea.
    (iii) Addition from the atmosphere.

(iv) Pesticides containing nitrogen atoms.
Choose the correct answer from the following codes:

Codes:

A. (i)   B. (ii)
C. (iii)   D. (iv)

61. Which one of the following protozoan is related to water borne disease?
A. *Spumella* sp.
B. *Entamoeba histolytica*
C. *Paramoecium*
D. *Plasmodium vivax*

62. Match the List–I with List–II, choose the correct answer from the given codes:

List–I (Group of Analysis)	List–II (Test)
(a) Unidimensional analysis	(i) Testing of hypothesis
(b) Multivariate analysis	(ii) Measure of central tendency
(c) Interferential analysis	(iii) Two-way ANOVA
(d) Bivariate analysis	(iv) Canonical analysis

Codes :

	(a)	(b)	(c)	(d)
A.	(i)	(iii)	(iv)	(ii)
B.	(ii)	(iv)	(i)	(iii)
C.	(iii)	(i)	(ii)	(iv)
D.	(iv)	(ii)	(iii)	(i)

63. The differences between crude birth rate and crude death rate in a population is called
A. Population momentum
B. Demographic transition rate
C. Net migration rate
D. Rate of natural increase

64. Which set of stoichiometric coefficient correctly balance the equation?
(a) H_2O_2 + (b) $KMnO_4$ + (c) H_2SO_4 → (d) K_2SO_4 + (e) $MnSO_4$ + (f) H_2O + (g) O_2
Select the correct answer from the codes given below :

Codes :

	(a)	(b)	(c)	(d)	(e)	(f)	(g)
A.	1	1	1	1	1	1	1
B.	1	2	3	1	2	4	3
C.	2	5	3	2	1	8	5
D.	5	2	3	1	2	8	5

65. **Assertion (A) :** The hypothesis testing can proceed on the basis of null hypothesis.
Reason (R) : If null hypothesis is true probabilities to different possible sample result can be assigned to it.
In the context of the two statements, which one of the following is correct?
A. Both (A) and (R) are true and (R) is the correct explanation of (A).
B. Both (A) and (R) are true, but (R) is not the correct explanation of (A).
C. (A) is true, but (R) is false.
D. (A) is false, but (R) is true.

66. The advantage of Leslie matrices are
I. Stable age distribution is not required for valid population projections.
II. Can derive finite rate of population change.
III. Requires large amount of data on population structure.
Choose the correct answer from the codes given below:

Codes :

A. I and III only   B. I only
C. I and II only   D. II and III only

67. Important characteristics of χ^2 test are
I. As a non-parametric test, it is based on frequencies.
II. It is not useful for estimation and to test hypothesis.
III. Can be applied to a complex contingency table.
Choose the correct answer from the codes given below:

Codes :

A. I and II only   B. I and III only
C. II and III only   D. I, II and III

68. The quantity of 0.2% solution needed to prepare 1000 mL of 10 ppm solution is
A. 5 mL   B. 10 mL
C. 20 mL   D. 200 mL

69. Which one of the following international events was not related to climate change?
    A. UN framework convention on climate change, 1992.
    B. Montreal Protocol, 1987
    C. Stockholm conference on "Human and Environment", 1972
    D. Kyoto Protocol, 1997

70. Which of the following has the lowest Ozone depletion potential?
    A. HCFC – 22   B. HCFC – 123
    C. Halon – 1211   D. CFC – 12

71. **Assertion (A) :** Rain water harvesting, primarily aims at artificial recharge of ground water to uplift the ground water table.
    Reason (R) : Under rain water harvesting, the primary aim is to let the rain water infiltrate into the underground aquifer.
    In the context of the two statements, which one of the following is correct?
    A. Both (A) and (R) are true and (R) is the correct explanation of (A).
    B. Both (A) and (R) are true, but (R) is not the correct explanation of (A).

C. (A) is true, but (R) is false.
D. (A) is false, but (R) is true.

72. For environmental mass awareness, *Paryavaran Vahini* Scheme was launched in the year
    A. 1988   B. 2003
    C. 1992   D. 1998

73. Disaster Management Act in India came into existence in the year
    A. 2003   B. 2005
    C. 1998   D. 2006

74. Which one of the following is most reactive oxygen species?
    A. $^1O_2$ B. $O_2^{\cdot-}$
    C. H_2O_2 D. $\overset{\cdot}{O}H$

75. If we move through the group I elements from top to bottom we first encounter Lithium, Sodium and Potassium. If we move further which elements we will encounter in sequence?
    A. Caesium, Calcium, Rubidium
    B. Rubidium, Caesium, Francium
    C. Rubidium, Caesium, Rhodium
    D. Magnesium, Rubidium, Francium

ANSWERS

1	2	3	4	5	6	7	8	9	10
A	C	A	D	A	D	C	C	C	A
11	12	13	14	15	16	17	18	19	20
D	A	D	B	D	D	C	A	A	A
21	22	23	24	25	26	27	28	29	30
C	C	B	C	C	C	A	A	B	C
31	32	33	34	35	36	37	38	39	40
B	A	A	C	A	B	C	B	B	A
41	42	43	44	45	46	47	48	49	50
C	B	A	B	D	A	C	A	A	B
51	52	53	54	55	56	57	58	59	60
B	D	C	D	C	C	C	C	B	D
61	62	63	64	65	66	67	68	69	70
B	B	D	B	A	C	D	A	C	B
71	72	73	74	75					
B	C	B	D	B					

SOME SELECTED EXPLANATORY ANSWERS

1. Mesoscale meteorology is the study of weather systems smaller than synoptic scale systems but larger than microscale and storm-scale cumulus systems. Horizontal dimensions generally range from around 5 kilometers to several hundred kilometers. Examples of mesoscale weather systems are sea breezes, squall lines, and mesoscale convective complexes.

   Mesocyclone: A horizontal atmospheric rotation on a scale between 4 and 400 km. It is a rotation within a thunderstorm typically surrounding a small area of low pressure. Typically within thunderstorms the rotation is 4-12 km across and 4-10 km in height.

   Mesoscale: On a scale of 4 km to 400 km.

2. **Rayleigh Scattering:** It is largely due to gas molecules and other very small particles, many times smaller than the wavelength of radiation under consideration, such as visible light (0.4–0.7 μm) by pure gas molecules of size 10^{-4} μm, in a clean atmosphere. Rayleigh scattering is inversely proportional to the fourth power of the wavelength. The scattering is accomplished through absorption and re-emission of radiation by atoms and molecules. For a wavelength ratio of 1:2 between 0.4 μm (blue) and 0.8 μm (beyond red), the ratio of scattered light is 16:1. This is the reason for bluish appearance of clear sky.

3. A **wind rose** is a graphic tool used by meteorologists to give a succinct view of how wind speed and direction are typically distributed at a particular location. Using a polar coordinate system of gridding, the frequency of winds over a long time period is plotted by wind direction, with color bands showing wind ranges. The directions of the rose with the longest spoke show the wind direction with the greatest frequency.

5. The **geostrophic wind** is the theoretical wind that would result from an exact balance between the Coriolis effect and the pressure gradient force. This condition is called geostrophic balance. The geostrophic wind is directed parallel to isobars (lines of constant pressure at a given height). This balance seldom holds exactly in nature. The true wind almost always differs from the geostrophic wind due to other forces such as friction from the ground. Thus, the actual wind would equal the geostrophic wind only if there were no friction and the isobars were perfectly straight.

6. A possible mechanism for photochemical smog inhibition is to add compounds like diethylhydroxylamine (DEHA) as it reacts with hydroxyl radicals. Diethylhydroxylamine (DEHA) reacts with gas-phase hydroxyl radicals on every third collision, whereas the corresponding reaction in aqueous solution is considerably slower. The high gas-phase reactivity explains the predicted inhibitory effect of DEHA in atmospheric smog processes.

9. **Biochemical oxygen demand (BOD)** is the amount of dissolved oxygen needed by aerobic biological organisms in a body of water to break down organic material present in a given water sample at certain temperature over a specific time period. It is the amount of oxygen required for microbial metabolism of organic compounds in water. This demand occurs over some variable period of time depending on temperature, nutrient concentrations, and the enzymes available to indigenous microbial populations.

   The first step in the process, conversion of ammonia to nitrite and then to nitrate, is called nitrification. The process is summarized in the following equations:

$$NH_4 + 3/2\ O_2 \rightarrow NO_2^- + 2H^+ + H_2O$$
$$NO_2^- + 1/2O \rightarrow NO_3^-$$

Nitrification Process

It is important to note that this process requires and consumes oxygen. This contributes to the BOD or biochemical oxygen demand of the sewage. The process is mediated by the bacteria *Nitrosomhas* and *Nitrobacter* which require an aerobic (presence of oxygen) environment for growth and metabolism of nitrogen. Thus, **the nitrification process must proceed under aerobic conditions.**

10. **Beer's law:** The physical law stating that the quantity of light absorbed by a substance dissolved in a nonabsorbing solvent is directly proportional to the concentration of the substance and the path length of the light through the solution; the law is sometimes also referred to as the Beer-Lambert law or the Bouguer-Beer law. Beer's law is commonly written in the form $A = \varepsilon cl$, where A is the absorbance, c is the concentration in moles per liter, l is the path length incentimeters, and ε is a constant of proportionality known as the molar extinction coefficient. The law is accurate only for dilute solutions; deviations from the law occur in concentrated solutions because of interactions between molecules of the solute, the substance dissolved in the solvent.

11. Phytochelatins are small, cysteine-rich peptides capable of binding heavy metal ions via thiolate coordination. They primarily form a M_r 3600 complex with cadmium. Phytochelatins are assumed to be involved in the accumulation, detoxification, and metabolism of metal ions such as cadmium, zinc, copper, lead and mercury in plant cells.

13. **Winkler Method for Determining Dissolved Oxygen (DO):** An accurate method of measuring the amount of DO in water is the Winkler method. Oxygen dissolved in water is able to oxidize manganese (II) ions in alkaline solution to manganese (IV) ions. The alkali is necessary to convert the manganese (II) sulphate to manganese hydroxide, which is readily oxidized.

The titration end point can be easily detected visually from blue to colorless, the overall reaction of the Winkler method is:

$$2S_2O_3^{2-} + 2H^+ + \tfrac{1}{2}O_2 \rightarrow S_4O_6^{2-} + H_2O$$

The above reaction indicates that 1 mol of O_2 is equivalent to 4 mol of thiosulphate $(S_2O_3^{2-})$ in the final titration. The DO can be calculated by the following equation:

$$DO\ (mg/L) = \frac{N \times V \times 8000}{V_S}$$

where N and V are the normality and volume (mL) of $Na_2S_2O_3$, respectively, Vs is the sample volume (typically 200 mL is withdrawn from 300 mL sample).

14. Restoration is ... the return of an ecosystem to a close approximation of its condition prior to disturbance. In restoration, ecological damage to the resource is repaired. Both the structure and the functions of the ecosystem are recreated ... The goal is to emulate a natural, functioning, self-regulating system that is integrated with the ecological landscape in which it occurs.

17. **Ambush predators** or **sit-and-wait predators** are carnivorous animals or other organisms, such as some nematophagous fungi and carnivorous plants, that capture or trap prey by stealth or by strategy (typically not conscious strategy), rather than by speed or by strength.

Alligator gars (*Atractosteus spatula*) are relatively passive, seemingly sluggish solitary fish, but voracious ambush predators. They are opportunistic night predators and are primarily piscivores, but they will also ambush and eat water fowl and small mammals that may be floating on the surface. Their method of ambush is to float a few feet below the surface, and wait for unsuspecting prey to swim within reach. They lunge forward, and with a sweeping motion grab their prey, impaling it on their double rows of sharp teeth.

19. Ammonia is very soluble. It moves in the soil rapidly and is acted upon by microorganisms of the category of chemosynthetic autotrophs. The nitrifying bacteria which convert ammonia into nitrite is *Nitrosomonas* and which converts nitrite into nitrate is *Nitrobacter.*

$$NH_4 + 2O_2 \xrightarrow{\text{Nitrosomonas}} 2H_2O + NO_2$$

$$NO_2^- + 1/2O_2 \xrightarrow{\text{Nitrobacter}} NO_3^-.$$

22. Although the average salinity of the oceans is 3.5 per cent, it varies geographically. High rainfall near the equator dilutes salinity to 3.45 per cent. Conversely, in dry subtropical regions, where evaporation is high and low precipitation, salinity can be as high as 3.6 per cent. Salinity varies more dramatically along coastlines. The Baltic Sea is a shallow ocean basin fed by many large, fresh water rivers and diluted further by rain and snow. As a result, its salinity is as low 2.0 per cent. In contrast, the Persian Gulf has low rainfall; high evaporation; and few large, inflowing rivers; its salinity exceeds 4.2 per cent.

24. **Loamy Sand:** This category contains 70 to 85 percent sand, 0 to 30 percent silt, and 10 to 15 percent clay. Because loamy sand contains more clay than does sand, it is slightly cohesive and can be molded into a ball that will maintain its form under gentle pressure. Soil squeezed between the thumb and forefinger, will not form a ribbon.

25. When solar radiation hits a target surface, it may be **transmitted, absorbed** or **reflected**. Different materials reflect and absorb differently at different wavelengths. The reflectance spectrum of a material is a plot of the fraction of radiation reflected as a function of the incident wavelength and serves as a unique signature for the material. In principle, a material can be identified from its spectral reflectance signature if the sensing system has sufficient **spectral resolution** to distinguish its spectrum from those of other materials. This premise provides the basis for multispectral remote sensing.

27. **Radar Imaging Satellite 1,** or **RISAT-1,** is an Indian remote sensing satellite which was built and is operated by the Indian Space Research Organisation (ISRO). The second RISAT satellite to be launched, it uses C-band 5.35 GHz Synthetic Aperture Radar for earth observation irrespective of the light and weather conditions of the area being imaged.

28. **Shield volcanoes** are huge, gently sloping volcanoes built of very thin lava spreading out in all directions from a central vent. They have wide bases several miles in diameter with steeper middle slopes and a flatter summit. The gentle convex slopes give them an outline like a medieval knight's shield. Eruptions are not generally explosive, more like liquid overflowing around the edges of a container. Mount Etna in Sicily and Mauna Loa in Hawaiin Islands are the most noteworthy examples of shield volcanoes. The world's largest volcano, Mauna Loa in Hawaii, is a shield volcano. Mauna Loa is about 55,770 feet (17,000 meters) from its base beneath the ocean to the summit, which is 13,681 feet (4,170 meters) above sea level. It is also one of the Earth's most active volcanoes and is carefully monitored. The most recent eruption was in 1984.

30. The calorific value of a fuel is the **quantity of heat produced by its combustion**—at constant pressure and under "normal" ("standard") conditions.
Higher Calorific Value (or Gross Calorific Value–GCV, or Higher Heating Value–HHV)– the water of combustion is entirely condensed and that the heat contained in the water vapor is recovered.

Table : *Carbon Intensity of Fossil Fuels Based on High-Heating Values (HHV)*[*]

	Energy Density (kJ/kg)	Carbon Content (%)	Carbon Intensity (kgC/GJ)
Anthracite coal	34,900	92	26.4
Bituminous coal	27,330	75	27.4
Crude oil	42,100	80	19.0
Natural gas	55,240	77	13.9

* HHV includes latent heat in exhaust water vapour.

32. The Green Climate Fund (GCF) is a cornerstone of the emerging architecture of the global climate regime. The volume of funds must be sufficient to inspire developing countries confidence in the commitment of developed countries to support climate action and inspire developing countries to put sufficient effort into creating projects and programs to make good use of this funding. ECO wonders how serious developed countries are about the GCF, really. As soon as the GCF is fully operational, and the institutional arrangements are in place for direct access by developing countries, ECO suggests that regular contributions to the GCF increase rapidly, surpassing USD$10 billion annually. This must also scale up further to account for a substantial part of the $100 billion committed by developed countries by 2020.

33. Anaerobic digestion is the natural biological process which stabilizes organic waste in the absence of air and transforms it into biofertilizer and biogas. Anaerobic digestion is a reliable technology for the treatment of wet, organic waste. Organic waste from various sources is biochemically degraded in highly controlled, oxygen-free conditions circumstances resulting in the production of biogas which can be used to produce both electricity and heat.
An anaerobic digestion plant produces two outputs, biogas and digestate, both can be further processed or utilized to produce secondary outputs. Biogas can be used for producing electricity and heat, as a natural gas substitute and also a transportation fuel. A combined heat and power plant system (CHP) not only generates power but also produces heat for in-house requirements to maintain desired temperature level in the digester during cold season.

35. The first laws of thermodynamics deals with the conservation of matter and energy and states that energy cannot be created or destroyed but can only change from one form to another. For example, the energy of visible light is absorbed by green plants through photosynthesis; it is changed into chemical energy stored in the glucose molecules. Almost all living organisms including plants consume glucose in respiration and use the stored chemical energy for their metabolic activity. Some of the energy is dissipated as heat, another form of energy.

37. **Knocking** in spark-ignition internal combustion engines occurs when combustion of the air/fuel mixture in the cylinder does not start off correctly in response to ignition by the spark plug, but one or more pockets of air/fuel mixture explode outside the envelope of the normal combustion front. *Knocking effect in the gasoline cannot be reached by additive like kerosene.*

38. **Monazite** is a reddish-brown phosphate mineral containing rare earth metals. It occurs usually in small isolated crystals. Monazite is an important ore for thorium, lanthanum, and cerium. It is often found in placer deposits. India, Madagascar, and South Africa have large deposits of monazite sands. The deposits in India are particularly rich in monazite. It has a hardness of 5.0 to 5.5 and is relatively dense, about 4.6 to 5.7 g/cm^3.

42. The UV (ultraviolet) region of solar radiation covers the wavelength range 100-400 nm and is divided into three bands:

- UV-A (315-400 nm)
- UV-B (280-315 nm)
- UV-C (100-280 nm)

Stratospheric ozone levels are near their lowest point since measurements began, so current UV-B radiation levels are thought to be close to their maximum. Total stratospheric content of ozone-depleting substances is expected to reach a maximum before the year 2000. All other things being equal, the current ozone losses and related UV-B increases should be close to their maximum.

47. The Battelle Environmental Evaluation System (EES) is a methodology for conducting environmental impact analysis developed at Battelle Columbus Laboratories by an interdisciplinary research team under contract with the U.S. Bureau of Reclamation. It is based on a hierarchical assessment of environmental quality indicators. In Battele environment evaluation system the total parameter importance units is lowest for aesthetics.

48. ISO 14040:2006 describes the principles and framework for life cycle assessment (LCA) including: definition of the goal and scope of the LCA, the life cycle inventory analysis (LCI) phase, the life cycle impact assessment (LCIA) phase, the life cycle interpretation phase, reporting and critical review of the LCA, limitations of the LCA, the relationship between the LCA phases, and conditions for use of value choices and optional elements.

49. With regards to the risk assessment undertaken at each tier of the framework, it is important that the following are taken into account:
- Have the hazards been identified?
- Have the consequences been identified?
- Have the magnitudes of consequences been determined?
- Have the probabilities of the consequences been determined?
- Has the significance of the risk been determined?

51. **Geoinformatics** is the science and the technology which develops and uses information science infrastructure to address the problems of geography, geosciences and related branches of engineering.
Geoinformatics has been described as "the science and technology dealing with the structure and character of spatial information, its capture, its classification and qualification, its storage, processing, portrayal and dissemination, including the infrastructure necessary to secure optimal use of this information" or "the art, science or technology dealing with the acquisition, storage, processing production, presentation and dissemination of Geoinformation".

52. **Forest Survey of India** (FSI) is a government organization in India under the union Ministry of Environment and Forests for conducting forest surveys and studies. The organization came into being in June, 1981. It is head-quartered at Dehradun of Uttarakhand in India.

53. Satellite sensors can observe large areas but the spatial resolution of these is dependent on microwave frequency, antenna dimensions, and height above the earth's surface. The higher the sensor, the lower the spatial resolution and at low elevations the spacecraft would use more fuel. Higher spatial resolution requires larger diameter antennas that in turn require more fuel to maintain in space.

56. (a) The **Bhopal disaster,** also referred to as the **Bhopal gas tragedy,** was a *gas leak* incident in India, considered *the world's worst industrial disaster.*
It occurred on the night of 2-3 December 1984 at the *Union Carbide India Limited* (UCIL) pesticide plant in Bhopal, Madhya Pradesh. Over 500,000 people were exposed to *methyl isocyanate (MIC)* gas and other chemicals. The toxic substance made its way into and around the *shanty towns* located near the plant.

(b) The **Chernobyl disaster** was a catastrophic nuclear accident that occurred on 26 April 1986 at the Chernobyl Nuclear Power Plant in Ukraine (then officially the Ukrainian SSR), which was under the direct jurisdiction of the central authorities of the Soviet Union. An explosion and fire released large quantities of radioactive particles into the atmosphere, which spread over much of the western USSR and Europe.

(c) **The 2004 Indian Ocean earthquake** occurred at 00:58:53 UTC on 26 December with an epicentre off the west coast of Sumatra, Indonesia. The event is known by the scientific community as the **Sumatra-Andaman earthquake.** The resulting tsunami was given various names, including the **2004 Indian Ocean tsunami, South Asian tsunami, Indonesian tsunami,** the **Christmas tsunami** and the **Boxing Day tsunami.**

(d) Very Severe Cyclonic Storm Hudhud was a strong tropical cyclone that caused extensive damage and loss of life in eastern India and Nepal during October 2014.

Hudhud originated from a low pressure system that formed under the influence of an upper-air cyclonic circulation in the Andaman Sea on October 6. Hudhud intensified into a cyclonic storm on October 8 and as a Severe Cyclonic Storm on October 9.

57. Benchmarking, a management approach for implementing best practices at best cost, is a recent concept in the healthcare system. Benchmarking is often thought to consist simply of comparing indicators and is not perceived in its entirety, that is, as a tool based on voluntary and active collaboration among several organizations to create a spirit of competition and to apply best practices. The key feature of benchmarking is its integration within a comprehensive and participatory policy of continuous quality improvement (CQI). Conditions for successful benchmarking focus essentially on careful preparation of the process, monitoring of the relevant indicators, staff involvement and inter-organizational visits.

58. The Basel Convention is to protect human health and the environment against the adverse effects of hazardous wastes. Its scope of application covers a wide range of wastes defined as "hazardous wastes" based on their origin and/or composition and their characteristics, as well as two types of wastes defined as "other wastes" - household waste and incinerator ash.

The provisions of the Convention center around the following principal aims:

- the reduction of hazardous waste generation and the promotion of environmentally sound management of hazardous wastes, wherever the place of disposal;
- the restriction of transboundary movements of hazardous wastes except where it is perceived to be in accordance with the principles of environmentally sound management; and
- a regulatory system applying to cases where transboundary movements are permissible.

59. Intergenerational equity is a concept that says that humans 'hold the natural and cultural environment of the Earth in common both with other members of the present generation and with other generations, past and future'. It means that we inherit the Earth from previous generations and have an obligation to pass it on in reasonable condition to future generations.

63. In demographics, the **rate of natural increase (NIR)** is the crude birth rate minus the crude death rate of a population. When looking at countries, it gives an idea of what position in the Demographic Transition Model, but to find out how much a country is growing, the

population growth rate should be observed. The formula for the rate of natural increase is: (Crude birth rate – Crude death rate) / 10, where birth and death rates are in per mile. The result is the rate of natural increase in percentage form.

72. Paryavaran Vahini, was launched in 1992-93 to create environmental awareness and to ensure active public participation by involving the local people in activities related to environmental protection. Paryavaran Vahinis are proposed to be constituted in 194 selected districts all over the country which have a high incidence of pollution and density of tribal and forest population. The Vahinis also play a watch-dog role by reporting instance of environmental pollution, deforestation, poaching, etc.

73. The Disaster Management Act, 2005 came into the statute book on 26 December 2005 by a Gazette notification, exactly on the first anniversary of the devastating tsunami of 2004, which killed nearly 13,000 people in India alone and affected 18 million people. The Act provides a legal and institutional framework for "the effective management of disasters and for matters connected there with or incidental thereto." It provides for establishment of *National Disaster Management Authority (NDMA),* State Disaster Management Authority (SDMA) and *District Disaster Management Authorities (DDMA)* at the National, State and District levels with adequate financial and administrative powers and creation of the National Institute of Disaster Management (NIDM) with the mandate of undertaking training and capacity building, Develop Training Modules on various aspects of Disaster management, Undertake Research and Documentation, Formulate and implement comprehensive *HRD Plan* covering all aspects of DM, Provide assistance in national level policy formulation and Provide assistance to state governments and State Training Institutions.

Previous Paper (Solved)

UGC-NET Environmental Science, June 2014

PAPER-II

Note : *This paper contains fifty (50) objective type questions of two (2) marks each. All questions are compulsory.*

1. For a clear night and with windspeeds < 3 m/s, the atmosphere is
   A. stable
   B. slightly unstable
   C. neutral
   D. slightly stable

2. **Assertion (A) :** Chemosynthesis plays an important role in 'S' cycle.
   Reason (R) : In chemosynthesis, some sulphur compounds act as source of energy.
   Codes:
   A. Both (A) and (R) are true and (R) is the correct explanation.
   B. Both (A) and (R) are true and (R) is not the correct explanation.
   C. (A) is true, but (R) is false.
   D. (A) is false, but (R) is true.

3. Which of the following is **NOT** a correct statement?
   A. Tropics are the warmest and wettest regions.
   B. Subtropical high pressure zones create dry zones at about 30° N and S.
   C. Temperature and precipitation are lowest at the poles.
   D. Temperature is lowest and precipitation is highest at the poles.

4. Protecting nature and the wilderness for its own sake is referred as
   A. Deep ecology
   B. Shallow ecology
   C. Self ecology
   D. Selfless ecology

5. For the analysis of oxides of Nitrogen, which of the following set of reagents are used?
   A. Sulphanilic acid, NEDA, H_2O_2, HNO_3
   B. Sulphamic acid, NEDA, H_2O_2, HNO_3
   C. Sulphamic acid, Nicotine, H_2O, HNO_3
   D. Sulphomolybdic acid, NEDA, H_2O_2, H_2SO_4

6. Number of ions of cadmium present in $3n$ moles of cadmium nitrate is
   A. 18.069×10^{23}
   B. 18.069×10^{20}
   C. 18.069×10^{17}
   D. 18.069×10^{14}

7. Which one of the following organisms is a free living nitrogen fixer?
   A. *Rhizobium*
   B. *Azotobacter*
   C. *Frankia*
   D. *Dorylimes*

8. Which one of the following has highest bioconcentration factor (BCF)?
   A. DDT
   B. DDE
   C. Chlordane
   D. Heptachlor

9. Consider an Ocean Thermal Energy Conversion (OTEC) process operating between 30°C and 5°C. What would be the maximum possible efficiency for an electricity generator station operating with these temperatures?
   A. 8%
   B. 15%
   C. 25%
   D. 40%

10. The process of 'Nebulisation' in Atomic Absorption Spectrophotometry is to
    A. convert the liquid sample to gaseous form.
    B. convert the liquid sample into small droplets.
    C. sublimate the sample.
    D. solubilization of the solute.

11. Individuals of a plant species occurring in a particular area constitute
    A. fauna
    B. flora
    C. flora and fauna
    D. population

1

12. A local population genetically, structurally and functionally adapted to its local environment is called
    A. ecotype   B. ecophene
    C. ecad   D. ecocline

13. Mycorrhizae is an example of
    A. Ammensalism   B. Commensalism
    C. Parasitism   D. Symbiosis

14. The entire series of communities of biotic succession from pioneer to climax community is known as
    A. Troph   B. Sere
    C. Population   D. Biome

15. In which of the following ecosystems the pyramid of biomass is inverted?
    A. Forest   B. Grassland
    C. Pond   D. Desert

16. The first National Park established in India is
    A. Kaziranga National Park
    B. The Jim Corbett National Park
    C. Hazaribagh National Park
    D. Gir National Park

17. The animals that rest or swim on the surface of the lakes are called
    A. Nektons   B. Neustons
    C. Benthos   D. Peritons

18. Which of the following is an example of *in situ* conservation of biodiversity?
    A. Captive breeding
    B. Seed bank
    C. National park
    D. Pollen bank

19. A biome contains
    A. many ecosystems
    B. many communities
    C. many populations
    D. a single ecosystem

20. In Bhopal gas tragedy, the quantity of Methyl Isocyanate leaked into the atmosphere was around
    A. ~ 180 tonnes   B. ~ 60 tonnes
    C. ~ 112 tonnes   D. ~ 40 tonnes

21. What is the sequence of arrival of seismic waves at a recording station?
    A. P-wave, S-wave, L-wave, R-wave.
    B. S-wave, P-wave, R-wave, L-wave.
    C. R-wave, L-wave, P-wave, S-wave.
    D. S-wave, L-wave, R-wave, P-wave.

22. The presence of ammonia in groundwater may indicate a nearby
    A. coal mine
    B. municipal solid waste dumping site
    C. thermal power plant
    D. granite quarry

23. Given below are statements in the context of a truly vertical aerial photograph:
    (i) The principal point, nadir point and isocentre coincide.
    (ii) Isocentre is the centre from where the radial displacements of images take place.
    (iii) Tilt is a character of vertical aerial photograph
    Identify the correct answer from the codes given below:
    A. (i) only
    B. (i) and (ii) only
    C. (i) and (iii) only
    D. (ii) and (iii) only

24. Kaolinite is a type of clay Mineral with layers of silicon and aluminium in the ratio of
    A. 1 : 1   B. 1 : 2
    C. 2 : 1   D. 3 : 1

25. In an ideal Magneto Hydro Dynamic Power Generator, the separation between the plates = 0.5 m, magnetic flux density = 2 Wb/m^2 and average fuel velocity = 500 m/sec. The voltage developed across the plates will be
    A. 500 V   B. 1000 V
    C. 2000 V   D. 5000 V

26. If the wind speed in a certain area increases by a factor of 2 from 4 m/s to 8 m/s, the power output from an ideal wind mill will increase by a factor of
    A. 4   B. 8
    C. 16   D. 2

27. Under Jawaharlal Nehru Solar Mission of Government of India, a total of 20,000 MW of utility Grid Power (including roof to solar power) is sought to be installed by the year.
    A. 2020
    B. 2022
    C. 2025
    D. 2030

28. In which country dry steam deposits have been used as such for electricity generation?
    A. Italy
    B. Iceland
    C. Austria
    D. New Zealand

29. The resources which are unlimited and where quality is not degraded are termed as
    A. renewable
    B. reusable
    C. immutable
    D. exhaustible

30. The most toxic form of mercury in water is
    A. $2 Hg^+$
    B. $Hg2^+$
    C. $CH_3^- Hg^+$
    D. $Hg°$

31. Hardness of water is due to the presence of
    A. Calcium and Magnesium ions
    B. Strontium and Nitrate ions
    C. Sodium and Chloride ions
    D. Potassium and Nitrite ions

32. Principal constitutents of atmospheric brown clouds are
    I. Soot
    II. Soil dust
    III. Fly ash
    IV. Sulphates and nitrates
    Identify the correct code:
    A. I and II only
    B. I and IV only
    C. II, III and IV only
    D. I, II, III and IV

33. The famous 'London Smog' was observed in the year
    A. 1750
    B. 1952
    C. 1972
    D. 2000

34. The permissible limit of day time industrial noise as recommended by WHO is
    A. 80 dB
    B. 75 dB
    C. 90 dB
    D. 76 dB

35. Surface litter layer on ground soil is also known as
    A. 'O' horizon
    B. 'A' horizon
    C. 'B' horizon
    D. 'C' horizon

36. Which one of the following represents the correct Uranium decay series?
    A. Uranium → Radium → Radon → Polonium
    B. Uranium → Radon → Radium → Polonium
    C. Uranium → Radium → Polonium → Radon
    D. Uranium → Radon → Polonium→ Radium

37. Hydropower projects with large reservoirs affect the environment by release of
    A. CO
    B. CO_2
    C. CH_4
    D. NO_2

38. Terms of reference is fixed at which stage of EIA process?
    A. Screening stage
    B. Scoping stage
    C. Detailed EIA stage
    D. Project Appraisal stage

39. Arrange the functions associated with EIA in a sequential manner
    (i) Identification
    (ii) Prediction
    (iii) Defining the scope
    (iv) Impact evaluation and analysis
    Codes :
    A. (i)   (iii)   (iv)   (ii)
    B. (ii)   (iv)   (i)   (iii)
    C. (iii)   (i)   (ii)   (iv)
    D. (iv)   (ii)   (iii)   (i)

40. The role of State Pollution Control Board in EIA is
    (i) Public hearing/consultation
    (ii) Issue of NOC
    (iii) Collecting environmental data
    (iv) Survey of fauna and flora
    Codes :
    A. (i) and (iii) only
    B. (i) and (ii) only
    C. (iii) and (iv) only
    D. (ii) and (iii) only

41. Percentage of carbon in a typical municipal solid waste ranges from
    A. 50 – 60%
    B. 40 – 50%
    C. 30 – 40%
    D. 20 – 30%

42. Which one of the following has maximum destruction and removable efficiency?
A. Incineration
B. Biological Treatment
C. Chemical Treatment
D. Landfill

43. Wastes are known to be corrosive if the pH is
A. ≤ 2 B. ≤ 3
C. ≤ 4 D. ≤ 5

44. Hazardous Waste Management and Handling Rule was enacted in the year
A. 1989   B. 1979
C. 1969   D. 1999

45. For a given set of data 5, 8, 12, 15 and 20, the comparison of geometric ($\bar{G}$), harmonic ($\bar{H}$) and arithmetic mean ($\bar{X}$) will be
A. $\bar{H} > \bar{G} > \bar{X}$ B. $\bar{H} > \bar{G} < \bar{X}$
C. $\bar{H} < \bar{G} < \bar{X}$ D. $\bar{H} < \bar{G} > \bar{X}$

46. Algal bloom follows a population growth pattern, which is
A. J-shaped
B. S-shaped
C. Exponential
D. Linear

47. t-distribution is approximately normal for sample size η
A. ≥ 30 B. ≥ 10
C. ≥ 15 D. ≥ 20

48. Two sets of data consisting of 10 and 20 observations have same mean 8 with standard deviations of 1 and 2, respectively. If the two data sets are combined, then the variance is
A. 3
B. 2
C. 5
D. 1.5

49. Match the List-I with List-II and choose the correct answer from the given codes:

List–I (Event)	List–II (Date)
(a) Earth Day	(i) 5th June
(b) World Environment Day	(ii) 3rd October
(c) Ozone Day	(iii) 22nd April
(d) World Nature Day	(iv) 16th September

Codes :

	(a)	(b)	(c)	(d)
A.	(i)	(ii)	(iv)	(iii)
B.	(iii)	(i)	(iv)	(ii)
C.	(ii)	(i)	(iii)	(iv)
D.	(iv)	(iii)	(ii)	(i)

50. CBD stands for
A. Convention on Biological Diversity
B. Conservation Biodiversity Development
C. Conservation Association for Biodiversity and Management
D. Cumulative Plan for Biological Diversity

ANSWERS

1	2	3	4	5	6	7	8	9	10
A	A	D	A	A	D	B	A	A	B
11	12	13	14	15	16	17	18	19	20
D	A	D	B	C	B	B	C	A	D
21	22	23	24	25	26	27	28	29	30
A	B	A	A	A	B	B	A	C	C
31	32	33	34	35	36	37	38	39	40
A	D	B	B	A	A	C	B	C	B
41	42	43	44	45	46	47	48	49	50
A	A	A	A	C	A	A	A	B	A

Some Selected Explanatory Answers

1. Relation between the Monin-Obukhov Length, L and Other Meteorological Stability Conditions

Description	Time and weather	Wind speed u	Monin-Obukhov Length, L	Pasquill-Gifford stability class
Very stable	Clear night	< 3 m/s	10 m	F
Stable	↓	2–4 m/s	50 m	E
Neutral	Cloudy or windy	Any	> |100 m|	D
Unstable	↓	2-6 m/s	–50 m	B or C
Very unstable	Sunny	< 3 m/s	– 10 m	A

3. On a global scale the effects of **latitude** are of greatest importance. The highest temperatures are recorded in low latitudes in the tropics between 0° and 23½° north and south of the Equator. Lowest temperatures are recorded in polar latitudes north and south of 66½°. There is a gradual decrease in temperature between the Equator and the Poles because of reduced **insolation**. The lowest precipitation **amounts** at **high latitudes** are on the plateau of Antarctica and in the central area of Greenland.

4. In the 1970s, a new thinking on environmental concerns began to emerge, protecting nature and the wilderness for its own sake, which is now referred to as 'Deep Ecology'. It recognizes the intrinsic value of all living beings and looks upon mankind as a small segment of a great living community of life-forms. It teaches that the well-being and flourishing of human and non-human life on Earth have value in themselves and that these values are independent of the usefulness of the non-human world for human purposes. Deep Ecologists on the other hand stress that wilderness preservation is a means to achieve the conservation and protection of biological diversity. Thus, it is not enough to protect the fragments that are that left of the wilderness, but we must also attempt to restore degraded areas to their former natural ecological state.

7. Azotobacter are free living bacteria which grow well on a nitrogen free medium. These bacteria utilize atmospheric nitrogen gas for their cell protein synthesis. This cell protein is then mineralised in soil after the death of Azoto-bacter cells thereby contributing towards the nitrogen availability of the crop plants. Azotobacter naturally fixes atmospheric nitrogen in the rhizosphere. Azotobacter uses carbon for its metabolism from simple or compound substances of carbonaceous in nature. Besides carbon, Azotobacter also requires calcium for nitrogen fixation.

8. Some compounds with very high bioconcentration factors, 10^3 to 10^4, show lower than expected EM values, (See Table). Since the accumulation values for DDT, PCB, hexachlorobenzene (HCB), and di-2-ethylhexyl phthalate (DEHP) in the real aquatic environment are high, the laboratory data should also rank these compounds among the highest in accumulative potential.

Table : *Predicting the more accumulative compounds*

Compounds	Bioconcentration Factors	Ecological Magnification	
	Trout Muscle	Terrestrial and Aquatic	Aquatic
PCB	12,400 ± 2290	11,900	17,840

Compounds	Bioconcentration Factors	Ecological Magnification	
	Trout Muscle	Terrestrial and Aquatic	Aquatic
HCB	7,880 ± 350	287	343
DDT	1,390 (191)	84,545	16,950
DEHP	800 (143)	130	3

10. **Nebulization is where the sample is converted to a fine mist of finely divided droplets but using a jet of compressed gas.**

    Pneumatic nebulization is the technique used in most atomic spectroscopy determinations. The sample solution is introduced through an orifice into a high-velocity gas jet, usually the oxidant. The sample stream may intersect the gas stream in either a parallel or perpendicular manner. Liquid is drawn through the sample capillary by the pressure differential generated by the high velocity gas stream passing over the sample orifice. The liquid stream begins to oscillate, producing filaments. Finally, these filaments collapse to form a cloud of droplets in the aerosol modifier or spray chamber. In the spray chamber the larger droplets are removed from the sample stream by mixer paddles or broken up into smaller droplets by impact beads or wall surfaces.

11. A population is the set of individuals of a species that live in a particular area at the same time and that can interbreed with each other. **Population genetics** deals with the abundance of different alleles within a population and the manner in which the abundance of a particular allele increases, decreases, or remains the same with time.

12. **Ecotypes (Ecological or Physiological races).** These are genetically adapted local populations that evolve from a species having a wide range of distribution.

14. The first commodity, which inhabit a bare area is called pioneer community. It has very little diversity and takes longest time to change the environment for invasion of the next community. The last and stable community in the area is called climax community. It is in perfect harmony with the physical environment. It is also termed as **climatic climax community**. It has maximum diversity and niche specialization. The intermediate communities between pioneer and climax communities are called **seral** or **transitional communities**. The entire series of communities of biotic succession from pioneer to climax community is known as **sere**.

15. **Pyramid of biomass:** It is based upon the total biomass (dry matter) at each trophic level in a food chain. The pyramid of biomass can also be *upright* or *inverted*. Fig. (*a, b*) show pyramids of biomass in a forest and an aquatic ecosystem. The pyramid of biomass in a forest is upright in contrast to its pyramid of numbers. This is because the producers (trees) accumulate a huge biomass while the consumers' total biomass feeding on them declines at higher trophic levels, resulting in broad base and narrowing top.

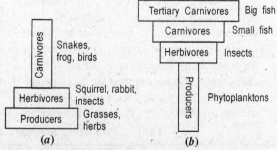

Fig.: Pyramid of biomass (*a*) Grassland (*b*) Pond

The pond ecosystem shows an inverted pyramid of biomass (Fig. *b*). The total biomass of producers (phytoplanktons) is much less as compared to herbivores (zooplanktons, insects), Carnivores (Small fish) and tertiary carnivores (big fish). Thus the pyramid takes an inverted shape with narrow base and broad apex.

16. **Jim Corbett National Park:** Jim Corbett National Park was India's first national park, located near Nainital in the state of Uttaranchal. It was established as a national park in 1936 under the United Provinces National Parks Act of India. It is known for its varied wildlife, and as the site for the launching of Project Tiger. The park is named after Jim Corbett, a legendary hunter-turned-conservator, best known for despatching a number of man-eating tigers and leopards in this region in the first half of the 20th century.

18. Conserving wild plants and animals in their original habitats or natural surroundings is referred to as *in situ* conservation. Conserving wild plants and animals in forests, national parks or sanctuaries are examples of *in situ* conservation.

24. **Kaolinite and Halloysite, 1:1 Minerals:** 1:1 clay minerals are composed, for their silicate part, by a two layer structure where one layer is occupied exclusively by silicon cations and the other in large majority by aluminium ions. The aluminium is in octahedral coordination with oxygen atoms, shared with Si cations, and hydroxyl cations. This mineral is highly hydrated (hydrogen content) and therefore less thermally stable than the 2:1 minerals. The ratio of Si to Al is very near one. The kaolinite structure is not subject to cation substitutions for the most part and its composition is thus near Al, Si, O and H.

28. *Dry steam,* that is, steam accompanied by very little water, is the simplest system and is produced by some reservoirs. The steam can be used directly to power turbines for the generation of electric power. It has been used in Italy for electricity generation.

29. **Classification of Natural Resources:** Resources may be classified on the basis of the following:

1. **Availability**
   (*i*) **Inexhaustible:** These resources are unlimited in quantity and quality. With the passage of time quality may be degraded but not the quantity.
   (*ii*) **Exhaustible:** Quantity and quality of these resources may be exhausted soon.

2. **Renewed Capability**
   (*i*) **Renewable:** Resources which can be renewed along with their exploitation. For example, forest, solar energy.
   (*ii*) **Non-renewable:** These cannot be regene-rated if exploited on a large scale. For example, mineral, water and so on.

3. **Quality**
   (*i*) **Immutable:** Quality of these resources are not degraded by human activity. For example, tidal power, wind, atomic power.
   (*ii*) **Mutable:** Quality may be degraded by man's activity. For example, water, hydropower.

4. **Method used**
   (*i*) **Maintainable:** The method used for consumption by human being.
   (*ii*) **Non-maintainable:** Total quantity static when consumption occurs.

5. **Origin**
   (*i*) **Biotic:** (Organic) Biotic resources are obtained from biosphere. For example, crops, birds, animals and so on.
   (*ii*) **Abiotic:** (Inorganic) Resources composed of non-living matter. For example, land, water, minerals.

31. Hardness of water is of two types: *Temporary hardness and Permanent hardness.*
   Temporary hardness: When hardness of water is due to the presence of soluble bicarbonates of calcium and magnesium, it is called temporary hardness. Temporary hardness of water can be removed by boiling. Temporary hardness is also called **carbonate hardness.**

Permanent hardness: It is due to the presence of sulphates and chlorides of magnesium and calcium, *i.e.,* $CaCl_2$, $CaSO_4$, $MgCl_2$ and $MgSO_4$. This type of hardness is called permanent hardness because it can not be removed simply by boiling. Permanent hardness is also called **non-carbonate hardness.**

33. When a thick fog engulfed London from December 5 to December 9, 1952, it mixed with black smoke emitted from homes and factories to create a deadly smog. This smog killed approximately 12,000 people and shocked the world into starting the environmental movement.

34.   **Table : Allowable noise limits (India)**

Area zone	Day-time limits dB(A)	Night-time limits dB(A)
Industrial Area	75	70
Commercial Area	65	55
Residential Area	55	45
Silence zone	50	40

36. The *uranium decay series* consist of a group of nuclides that, when their mass number is divided by 4, have a remainder of 2 (the $4n + 2$ series). The parent of this series is ^{238}U with a natural abundance of 99.3%; it undergoes α-decay with a half-life of 4.46×10^9 y. The stable end product of the uranium series is ^{206}Pb, which is reached after 8 α- and 6 β-decay steps.

The specific activity of ^{238}U is 12.44 MBq/kg ^{238}U. However, because *natural uranium* consists of 3 isotopes, ^{238}U, ^{235}U and ^{234}U, whose isotopic abundances are 99.2745%, 0.7200% and 0.0055%, respectively, the specific activity of natural uranium is 25.4 MBq/kg.

The uranium decay series provides the most important isotopes of elements radium, radon and polonium, which can be isolated in the processing of uranium minerals.

38. Scoping was also introduced as a term which included the generation of Terms of Reference, on the basis of which the EIA report had to be made by Project Proponents. These terms of reference had to be devised by the Expert Appraisal Committee at center and State expert Appraisal Committee at the state level. This enhanced the role and burden on the expert committees.

42. Incineration has maximum destruction and removal efficiency.

43. **Corrosivity:** An aqueous waste is corrosive if it is strongly acidic with a pH of 2 or less, or strongly alkaline with pH of 12.5 or more. Also considered corrosive is a liquid waste capable of corroding steel at a rate of 6.35 mm per year as determined by the National Association of Corrosive Engineers. Examples of corrosive substances are highly alkaline compounds such as caustic soda or strong acids such as sulphuric and nitric acids.

44. **Hazardous Waste Management in India:** In India the need to manage hazardous wastes on scientific lines was felt only after the occurrence of Bhopal accident in the mid eighties (2, December, 1984). The Government then started thinking about the hazardous waste substances and their effect on human health and on the environment. In order to cover the environment as a whole entity, the Ministry of Environment and Forests (MOEF) enacted the law, Environment (Protection) Act 1986. Subsequent to this Act, in order to prevent indiscriminate disposal of hazardous waste, the MOEF initiated the Hazardous Wastes (Handling and Manage-ment) Rules in 1989. Though the Hazardous Waste Handling Rules were enacted in 1989 only, the response towards their implementation was very poor. It may be because of liberalized policy and the pace of industrialization has been accelerated, which was resulted in the increasing amounts of hazardous waste generated and released into the environment every year.

45. Arithmetic mean ($\bar{X}$)

$$= \frac{5+8+12+15+20}{5} = 12$$

Harmonic mean ($\bar{H}$)

$$= \frac{1}{\dfrac{\left(\dfrac{1}{5}+\dfrac{1}{8}+\dfrac{1}{12}+\dfrac{1}{15}+\dfrac{1}{20}\right)}{5}} = 2.625$$

Geometric mean ($\bar{G}$)

$$= \sqrt{\text{A.M.} \times \text{H.M.}}$$

$$= \sqrt{12 \times 2.625}$$

$$= 5.6125$$

Hence, $\bar{H} < \bar{G} < \bar{X}$

47. The t, or Student's t, distribution is an unbounded distribution having a mean of zero and a variance that depends on the scale parameter v, which is sometimes termed the "degrees of freedom". As v increases toward infinity, the t distribution approaches the standard normal density function. In general, the standard normal distribution can be used instead of the t distribution for sample sizes greater than 30.

PAPER-III

*Note : This paper contains **seventy five** (75) objective type questions of **two** (2) marks each. **All** questions are compulsory.*

1. Chemosynthesis involves CO_2 fixation using energy derived from
   A. Sunlight
   B. Infrared radiation
   C. UV-radiation
   D. Inorganic and Organic compounds

2. Wind in the mountain-valley regions are of
   A. Microscale   B. Mesoscale
   C. Macroscale   D. Synoptic scale

3. In tropical region an aircraft is flying at an altitude of 10 km. At that altitude the tempera-ture is $-40\,°C$. What is the ambient temperature on the ground?
   A. 24°C   B. 40°C
   C. 30°C   D. 20°C

4. **Assertion (A) :** Upper atmosphere shields life on earth.
   Reason (R) : Ultraviolet radiations are absorbed in the upper atmosphere.
   Choose the correct answer:
   Codes:
   A. Both (A) and (R) are true and (R) is the correct explanation of (A).
   B. Both (A) and (R) are true, but (R) is not the correct explanation of (A).
   C. (A) is true and (R) is false.
   D. (A) is false and (R) is true.

5. The molar extinction coefficient of proline ninhydrin complex at 520 nm is $0.34\ \mu M^{-1}$ cm^{-1}. A solution of the proline ninhydrin complex has an absorbance of 0.68 in a one centimeter cuvette. The concentration (μM) of proline is
   A. 0.5   B. 0.2312
   C. 2.312   D. 2

6. The principal components of photochemical smog in urban areas are
   A. SO_2 and NO_2
   B. SPM and CO
   C. SPM and NO_2
   D. Oxides of Nitrogen, Hydrocarbons and Ozone.

7. The amount of a particular gas dissolved in water depends on
   (i) its solubility in water.
   (ii) its partial pressure at the air/water interface or sediment/water interface.
   (iii) the water temperature.
   (iv) the levels of salts in the water.
   Identify the correct answer:
   A. (i) and (ii) only
   B. (ii), (iii) and (iv) only
   C. (i), (ii) and (iii) only
   D. (i), (ii), (iii) and (iv)

10

8. A 50 ml solution of pH = 1 is mixed with a 50 ml solution of pH = 2. The pH of the mixture will be nearly
   A. 0.76
   B. 1.26
   C. 1.76
   D. 2.26

9. The solubility product of the following type of reaction:

   $Al(OH)_3 \longrightarrow Al^{3+} + 3\overset{\ominus}{O}H$ is

   A. $Ksp = (Al)(OH)$
   B. $Ksp = (Al^{3+})(3\overset{\ominus}{O}H)$
   C. $Ksp = (Al^{3+})(\overset{\ominus}{O}H)^3$
   D. $Ksp = (Al^{3+})(\overset{\ominus}{O}H)$

10. Cells grown in medium containing isotope sulphur 35 will show radio labelling in
    A. membrane lipids
    B. membrane proteins
    C. glycogen
    D. nucleic acid

11. A stream flowing at 10.0 m³/s has a tributary feeding it with a flow of 5.0 m³/s. The stream concentration of chloride upstream at the junction is 20.0 mg/L and the tributary chloride concentration is 40 mg/L. Treating chloride as a conservative substance and assuming complete mixing of the two streams, find the down stream concentration.
    A. 26.7 mg/L
    B. 30.2 mg/L
    C. 22.6 mg/L
    D. 35.2 mg/L

12. Assume that dilution factor p for an unseeded mixture of waste and water is 0.03. The DO of the mixture is initially 9.0 mg/L and after 5 days, it has dropped to 3.0 mg/L. The reaction rate constant 'K' has been found to be 0.22 / day. Five day BOD of the water will be
    A. 200 mg/L
    B. 150 mg/L
    C. 100 mg/L
    D. 75 mg/L

13. Nudation is generally caused by
    A. migration of species
    B. climate change
    C. invasion of foreign species
    D. modification of habitat

14. Which one of the following is the best tool to study the interacting residues in protein-ligand interaction?
    A. X-ray crystallography
    B. Circular dichroism spectroscopy
    C. UV–V is spectroscopy
    D. Fluorescence spectroscopy

15. During centrifugation, if the centrifugal force is F_c, buoyant force is F_b, and frictional force is F_f, which of the following equations expresses the sedimentation of the molecule?
    A. $F_C = F_b - F_f$
    B. $F_C = F_b + F_f$
    C. $F_C = \dfrac{F_b - F_f}{2}$
    D. $F_C = \dfrac{F_b + F_f}{2}$

16. Match the List-I with List-II and choose the correct answer from the given codes:

List-I (Lakes)	List-II (Characteristics)
(a) Oligotrophic lakes	(i) More nutrient concentration
(b) Dystrophic lakes	(ii) Magmatic water
(c) Eutrophic lakes	(iii) Low nutrient concentration
(d) Volcanic lakes	(iv) Low pH and high humic acid conditions

   Codes :

	(a)	(b)	(c)	(d)
A.	(i)	(ii)	(iii)	(iv)
B.	(ii)	(i)	(iv)	(iii)
C.	(iii)	(iv)	(i)	(ii)
D.	(iv)	(iii)	(ii)	(i)

17. The earthworm used for composting is
    (a) Crassiclitellata excavata
    (b) Octochaetona serrata
    (c) Lumbricus terrestris
    (d) Eisenia foetida
    Choose the correct answer:
    A. (a) and (b) only
    B. (b) and (d) only
    C. (b) and (c) only
    D. (a) and (d) only

18. The amount of the living material present in different trophic levels at a given time is called
    (a) standing crop   (c) standing state

(b) biomass   (d) biosphe
Choose the correct answer:
A. (a) and (c) are correct
B. (d) is correct
C. (b) is correct
D. (c) and (b) are correct

19. Many orchids use trees as a surface to grow. This is an example of
A. Commensalism   B. Mutualism
C. Parasitism   D. Predation

20. The r-strategist is a
A. small organism that has a short life, produces many offsprings and does not reach carrying capacity.
B. small organism that has a longer life, produces offsprings and does not reach carrying capacity.
C. small organism that has a short life, produces numerous offsprings and reach carrying capacity.
D. medium organism that has a short life, produces numerous offsprings and reach carrying capacity.

21. Under the Rhino relocation project, during 1987, Rhinoes were introduced in
A. Assam   B. Meghalaya
C. West Bengal   D. Madhya Pradesh

22. Which of the following is an endangered bird species?
A. Kashmir stag
B. Great Indian Bustard
C. Hangul
D. Black buck

23. In India, Crocodile breeding project started for the first time in
A. Tamil Nadu   B. West Bengal
C. Odisha   D. Goa

24. Identify the correct sequence of materials in terms of their porosity.
A. Sand > clay > gravel
B. Clay > sand > gravel
C. Gravel > sand > clay
D. Gravel > clay > sand

25. For an aquifer of gravel having cross sectional area of 4 m^2 and a depth of 2.5 m, how much water could potentially be extracted? (The porosity and specific yield of gravel are 25% and 20% respectively.)
A. 0.5 m^3 B. 0.25 m^3
C. 0.125 m^3 D. 1 m^3

26. The layers formed by thermal stratification in lakes are
A. Epilimnion, Midlimnion, Hypolimnion
B. Epilimnion, Oligolimnion, Hypolimnion
C. Epilimnion, Dystrolimnion, Hypolimnion
D. Epilimnion, Thermocline, Hypolimnion

27. On an aerial photograph, the focal length (f) of the camera lens is 6 inches and flying height (H) over the datum line is 15,000 ft. What is scale of the aerial photograph?
A. 1 : 30,000   B. 1 : 10,000
C. 1 : 5,000   D. 1 : 25,000

28. Which of the following substrate will have highest reflectance value?
A. Silt loam with 20% moisture.
B. Clay with 36% moisture.
C. Silt loam with 0.8% moisture.
D. Clay with 2% moisture.

29. **Assertion (A) :** For sustainable development of a region, proper land use planning is required.
Reason (R) : Land use planning involves inputs of soil types, rock types, seismicity, weather pattern and socio-economic conditions of a region.
Codes:
A. Both (A) and (R) are true and (R) is the correct explanation of (A).
B. Both (A) and (R) are true, but (R) is not the correct explanation of (A).
C. (A) is true and (R) is false.
D. (A) is false and (R) is true.

30. Tundra is biome characterized by
A. stunted trees and permanently frozen sub-surface soil.
B. coniferous trees and permanently frozen sub-surface soil.

C. lack of trees and permanently frozen sub-surface soil.

D. evergreen trees and permanently frozen sub-surface soil.

31. Acid mine drainage occurs when
A. the combined action of O_2, H_2O and certain bacteria cause sulphur in coal to form H_2SO_4.
B. the combined action of H_2O and certain bacteria cause sulphur in coal to form H_2SO_4.
C. the combined action of O_2 and certain bacteria cause sulphur in coal to form H_2SO_4.
D. the combined action of SO_2 and certain bacteria with coal to form H_2SO_4.

32. In accordance with Saffir-Simpson hurricane scale, a cyclonic storm of category 5 should have wind speeds
A. > 69 ms^{-1} B. $50 - 58$ ms^{-1}
C. $59 - 69$ ms^{-1} D. $33 - 42$ ms^{-1}

33. **Assertion (A):** Large scale OTEC development may not be good for environment.
Reason (R): Release of CO_2 from ocean depths into the atmosphere could exacerbate GHG effect.
Codes:
A. Both (A) and (R) are true and (R) is the correct explanation of (A).
B. Both (A) and (R) are true, but (R) is not the correct explanation of (A).
C. (A) is true, but (R) is false.
D. Both (A) and (R) are false.

34. In a methane fuel cell, what will be the voltage of the cell and its efficiency?
(Given: $\Delta G° = 8 \times 10^5$ Joules/gm-mole $\Delta H° = 8.8 \times 10^5$ Joules/gm-mole and Faraday's constant = 96500 coulomb/gm-mole)
A. ~ 1.23 Volts, $\sim 90.9\%$
B. ~ 1.04 Volts, $\sim 90.9\%$
C. ~ 1.15 Volts, $\sim 11\%$
D. ~ 2.13 Volts, $\sim 92\%$

35. The coefficient of performance for an ideal wind mill is
A. 3/8   B. 5/16
C. 2/5   D. 16/27

36. Assume that the energy released during the combustion of methane is 900 kJ/mol. Its carbon intensity is
A. 13.3 gc/MJ   B. 15.3 gc/MJ
C. 19.7 gc/MJ   D. 24.2 gc/MJ

37. In a nuclear fusion reactor it is envisaged to use a liquid blanket of Li to absorb fast neutrons from D + T reaction. How many neutrons are produced as a result of $^{7}_{3}Li + ^{1}_{0}n$?
A. 1   B. 2
C. 3   D. 4

38. In an ideal MHD power plant, the electrical efficiency corresponding to maximum power production is
A. 50%   B. 75%
C. 25%   D. 100%

39. Energy intensity is a measure of
A. effectiveness of energy utilisation
B. energy produced per unit area
C. energy produced per unit volume
D. energy produced per unit area per unit time

40. One of the criteria for characterizing a region as ABC hotspot is that the annual mean anthropogenic Aerosol Optical Depth (AOD) is greater than
A. 0.3   B. 0.5
C. 0.8   D. 0.1

41. The resultant of two noise levels of 50 dB and 55 dB is
A. 58 dB   B. 55.41 dB
C. 52.5 dB   D. 56.19 dB

42. Which of the following is used as a coagulant for removal of phosphates in water?
A. Aluminium sulphate
B. Iron sulphate
C. Copper sulphate
D. Potassium chromate

43. Which of the following radionuclides has the longest half-life?
   A. C^{14}
   B. Sr^{90}
   C. I^{131}
   D. Cs^{137}

44. Under anaerobic conditions nitrogenase catalises
   A. breakdown of atmospheric nitrogen
   B. oxidation of atmospheric nitrogen
   C. reduction of atmospheric nitrogen
   D. hydrolysis of nitrogenous compounds

45. Size range of atmospheric aerosols is
   A. 5 nm – 100 μm
   B. 100 μm – 150 μm
   C. 150 μm – 200 μm
   D. 0.01 nm – 5 nm

46. Which one of the following is used as microbial indicator of water contamination?
   A. Coliform bacteria
   B. Giardia
   C. Cryptosporidium
   D. Tobacco mosaic virus

47. Elevated salt and Na^+ concentrations in soils are highly toxic to many plants, but relatively high tolerance level (to this toxicity) is seen in
   A. Sugarbeet
   B. Sugarcane
   C. Onion
   D. Lettuce

48. Which of the following hydrocarbons is emitted by vegetation?
   A. Ocimene
   B. Xylene
   C. Acrolein
   D. 1, 3-Pentadions

49. For particles of size > 5 μm, the efficiency of cyclones can be as high as
   A. 50%
   B. 60%
   C. 80%
   D. 90%

50. Given the following parameters of a primary settling chamber:
   Diameter = 50 m, Depth = 2.5 m, average detention time = 2 hours.
   How much quantity of waste water is being treated?
   A. ~ 58928 m^3/day
   B. ~ 48321 m^3/day
   C. ~ 45321 m^3/day
   D. ~ 25321 m^3/day

51. A flat surface type electrostatic precipitator (ESP) has the following parameters: collector plate area A = 4600 m^2, volumetric flow rate Q = 200 m^3/s and effective drift velocity of flue gas = 0.15 m/s
   What is the efficiency of the ESP?
   A. ~ 0.968
   B. ~ 0.981
   C. ~ 0.975
   D. ~ 0.922

52. **Assertion (A) :** Cost-benefit analysis for assess-ment of natural systems is not merely concerned with the effects on environmental quality but seeks the conditions for sustainable use of the natural resources of a region.
   Reason (R) : Cost-benefit analysis is not useful for small scale development projects, but is better suited for the analysis and evaluation of a regional development plan.
   Identify the correct answer:
   Codes:
   A. Both (A) and (R) are true and (R) is the correct explanation.
   B. Both (A) and (R) are true, but (R) is not the correct explanation.
   C. (A) is true and (R) is wrong.
   D. Both (A) and (R) are wrong.

53. Battelle-Columbus weighting – scaling checklist methodology for water-resources projects obtains base line data on how many environmental parameters?
   A. 40
   B. 78
   C. 68
   D. 50

54. Match List-I with List-II and choose the correct answer from the codes given below:

List-I	List-II
(a) Checklists methods	(i) Involve preparation of a set of trans-parent maps, which represent the spatial distribution of an environmental characteristics
(b) Overlays methods	(ii) Highly structured approaches involving importance weightings for factors and

application of scaling
techniques

(c) Adhoc   (iii) Identification and
    methods   evaluation of inter-
                   actions between
                   various activities and
                   environmental
                   parameters

(d) Matrices   (iv) Indicate broad areas
    methods   of possible impacts by
                   listing composite envir-
                   onmental parameters.

Codes :

	(a)	(b)	(c)	(d)
A.	(i)	(ii)	(iii)	(iv)
B.	(iv)	(ii)	(i)	(iii)
C.	(ii)	(i)	(iv)	(iii)
D.	(iii)	(iv)	(ii)	(i)

55. Match List-I with List-II and choose the correct answer from the codes given below:

List-I (Criteria of EIA Methodology)	List-II (Component)
(a) Impact identification	(i) Magnitude
(b) Impact measurement	(ii) Specificity
(c) Impact communication	(iii) Depth of analysis
(d) Impact interpretation	(iv) Comprehensive over-all perspective

Codes :

	(a)	(b)	(c)	(d)
A.	(i)	(iv)	(iii)	(ii)
B.	(ii)	(i)	(iv)	(iii)
C.	(iii)	(iv)	(i)	(ii)
D.	(iv)	(iii)	(ii)	(i)

56. Significant hazard/accident factor to be considered under risk assessment of distillaries are
A. toxic gas release and human accident
B. pressure wave and heat radiation
C. toxic gas release and radiation
D. pressure wave and toxic gas release

57. If 'I' is the impact of the population on the environment, 'P' is the size of the population, 'A' is the per capita affluence or consumption and 'T' is the damage caused by technologies, then which of the following equation is correct?
A. $I = (P \times A)/T$ B. $I = P \times A \times T$
C. $I = T/(P \times A)$ D. $I = P/(A \times T)$

58. According to Environment (Protection) Act, 1986 permissible limits of oil and grease in the effluents to be discharged into public sewers is
A. 10 mg/l B. 20 mg/l
C. 25 mg/l D. 30 mg/l

59. 'Reed swamp stage' is also referred to as
A. submerged stage
B. woodland stage
C. rooted floated stage
D. amphibious stage

60. Match List-I with List-II and choose the correct answer from the given codes:

List-I (Ecosystem types)	List-II (Characteristics)
(a) Coral reefs	(i) Still water
(b) Deltas	(ii) Saline water
(c) Wetlands	(iii) Brackish water
(d) Rivers	(iv) Fresh water

Codes :

	(a)	(b)	(c)	(d)
A.	(i)	(ii)	(iii)	(iv)
B.	(ii)	(iii)	(i)	(iv)
C.	(ii)	(i)	(iv)	(iii)
D.	(iii)	(iv)	(i)	(ii)

61. Maximum energy content (KJ/kg) in a typical municipal solid waste is found in
A. Plastic   B. Leather
C. Wood   D. Textile

62. Public Liability Insurance Act was enacted in the year
A. 1991   B. 1993
C. 1995   D. 1997

63. A sample size of 17 observations is selected from a normal population with mean = 50. The sample mean and variance are 48 and 8 respectively. The value of t–statistic is
A. 0.25   B. –2.82
C. –2.2   D. 0.71

64. A class has equal number of boys and girls. The mean and standard deviation of their weights are $\bar{X}_g = 40$ kg, $S_g = 2$ kg for girls and $\bar{X}_b = 50$ kg, $S_b = 2$ kg for boys. What is the combined variance of the weights of the whole class?
A. 29   B. 16
C. 8   D. 19

65. For a simple regression analysis involving the dependent variable Y and explanatory variable X, the following data is given : No. of observations N = 40, $\Sigma X^2 = 2000$, $\Sigma Y^2 = 2000$, $\bar{X} = 20$, $\bar{Y} = 5$, standard error of estimate of Y on X, $S_{YX} = 4$. The explained variance is
A. 360   B. 860
C. 500   D. 580

66. A ψ^2 distribution with 10 degrees of freedom has variance
A. 10   B. 20
C. 5   D. 40

67. The rank of the matrix
$$\begin{bmatrix} 1 & 1 & 1 \\ 1 & -1 & -1 \\ 3 & 1 & 1 \end{bmatrix}$$ is
A. 2
B. 3
C. 1
D. Not possible to determine

68. Which of the following is not an eigenvector of the matrix $\begin{bmatrix} 2 & 0 \\ 0 & 5 \end{bmatrix}$?

A. $\begin{bmatrix} 1 \\ 0 \end{bmatrix}$ B. $\begin{bmatrix} 0 \\ 1 \end{bmatrix}$

C. $\begin{bmatrix} 0 \\ 2 \end{bmatrix}$ D. $\begin{bmatrix} 1 \\ 1 \end{bmatrix}$

69. **Assertion (A) :** Ground level concentration of pollutants decreases when taller stacks are used.
Reason (R) : The ground level concentration varies inversely proportional to the height of the stacks.
Codes:
A. Both (A) and (R) are true and (R) is the correct explanation of (A).
B. Both (A) and (R) are correct, but (R) is not the correct explanation of (A).
C. (A) is true and (R) is false.
D. Both (A) and (R) are false.

70. Assume that 5.3 billion people live in less developed countries, where average birth rate is 23 and infant mortality rate is 53. Then the total death due to infant mortality are
A. 6.5×10^6/year   B. 5.3×10^6/year
C. 7.3×10^6/year   D. 8.5×10^6/year

71. Which of the following act as 'natural sink for carbon'?
I. Trees   II. Oceans
III. Soils
Choose the correct code:
A. I only   B. I and II only
C. I, II and III   D. II and III only

72. Match List-I with List-II and choose the correct answer from the codes given below:

List-I (GHGs)	List-II (Atmospheric Lifetime) (Years)
(a) CFC-12	(i) 12
(b) Methane	(ii) 50-200
(c) CO_2	(iii) 114
(d) N_2O	(iv) 100

Codes :

	(a)	(b)	(c)	(d)
A.	(iii)	(iv)	(i)	(ii)
B.	(ii)	(iii)	(iv)	(i)
C.	(iv)	(i)	(ii)	(iii)
D.	(i)	(ii)	(iii)	(iv)

73. REDD$^+$ initiatives include
I. Forest carbon partnership facility
II. Forest investment programme
III. Sanitation for all
IV. Food security for all
Choose the correct code:
A. I and IV only   B. I and II only
C. I, II and III only D. III and IV only

74. Match List-I with List-II and choose the correct answer from the codes given below:

List-I (Environment Related Treaties)	List-II (Year)
(a) CITES	(i) 1989
(b) Basel	(ii) 1973
(c) UNFCCC	(iii) 1997
(d) Kyoto Protocol	(iv) 1992

Codes :

	(a)	(b)	(c)	(d)
A.	(iii)	(ii)	(i)	(iv)
B.	(iv)	(iii)	(ii)	(i)
C.	(i)	(iv)	(iii)	(ii)
D.	(ii)	(i)	(iv)	(iii)

75. Identify the correct sequence with reference to sensitization about environmental problems.

A. Knowledge → Awareness → Attitude → Skill → Evaluation ability → Participation

B. Knowledge → Awareness → Skill → Attitude → Participation → Evaluation ability

C. Awareness → Knowledge → Attitude → Skill → Evaluation ability → Participation

D. Awareness → Knowledge → Participation → Attitude → Skill → Evaluation ability

ANSWERS

1	2	3	4	5	6	7	8	9	10
D	B	A	B	D	D	D	B	C	B
11	12	13	14	15	16	17	18	19	20
A	A	B	A	B	C	B	A	A	A
21	22	23	24	25	26	27	28	29	30
A	B	C	B	A	D	A	C	A	C
31	32	33	34	35	36	37	38	39	40
A	A	A	B	D	A	B	A	A	A
41	42	43	44	45	46	47	48	49	50
D	A	D	C	A	A	A	A	D	A
51	52	53	54	55	56	57	58	59	60
A	A	B	C	B	B	B	A	D	B
61	62	63	64	65	66	67	68	69	70
A	A	B	A	A	B	A	D	C	A
71	72	73	74	75					
C	C	B	D	C					

Some Selected Explanatory Answers

1. The principal exception to the creation of organic matter through photosynthesis is *chemosynthesis*. In chemosynthesis, chemical reactions rather than light provide the energy to "fix" CO_2. Regardless of the energy source, however, fixation of CO_2 involves the Benson-Calvin Cycle and RUBISCO. Chemosynthesis typically results in carbon isotope fractionations similar to those of photosynthesis. Thus large carbon isotope fractionations are the signature of both photosynthesis and chemosynthesis.

6. Smog is a type of *air pollution*. Smog is a mixture of smoke and fog, hence the name (SMoke + fOG = SMOG). Victorian-era London was famous for its thick smogs, which resulted from the city's frequent, naturally occurring, heavy fogs that combined with smoke from coal fires which were used to heat homes. The main components of photochemical smog are *nitrogen oxides, Volatile Organic Compounds (VOCs), tropospheric ozone*, and PAN *(peroxyacytyl nitrate)*. All of these substances are very chemically reactive and are irritating to humans and other living things.

8. $[H_3O^+]$ in solution with pH = 1 = 10^{-1} M
$[H_3O^+]$ in solution with pH = 2 = 10^{-2} M
$M_1V_1 + M_2V_2 = M_3V_3$
$10^{-1} \times 50 + 10^{-2} \times 50 = M_3 \times 100$

$M_3 = \dfrac{1}{2}[10^{-1} + 10^{-2}] = 5.5 \times 10^{-2}$

$[H_3O^+]$ after mixing = 5.5×10^{-2}
pH = $-\log 5.5 \times 10^{-2}$ = 1.26
Hence, the choice B is correct.

10. *Sulphur-35* is used to label proteins and nucleic acids. *Cysteine* is an *amino acid* containing a *thiol* group which can be labelled by S-35. For *nucleotides* that do not contain a *sulphur* group, the oxygen on one of the phosphate groups can be substituted with a sulphur. This *thiophosphate* acts the same as a normal phosphate group, although there is a slight bias against it by most *polymerases*. The maximum theoretical specific activity is 1,494 Ci/mmol (55.28 PBq/mol).

11.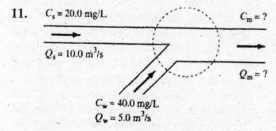

Fig.: *Flow rate and chloride concentrations for example stream and tributary.*

In problems of this sort, it is much easier simply to leave the mixed units in the expression, even though they may look awkward at first, and let them work themselves out in the calculation. The downstream concentration of chlorides is thus

$$C_m = \frac{(20.0 \times 10.0 + 40.0 \times 5.0) \text{mg}/\text{L} \cdot \text{m}^3/\text{s}}{(10.0 + 5.0) \text{ m}^3/\text{s}}$$

= 26.67 mg/L

14. X-ray crystallography is essentially a form of very high resolution microscopy. It enables us to visualize protein structures at the atomic level and enhances our understanding of protein function. Specifically we can study how proteins interact with other molecules, how they undergo conformational changes, and how they perform catalysis in the case of enzymes. Armed with this information we can design novel drugs that target a particular protein, or rationally engineer an enzyme for a specific industrial process.

16. Types of Lakes: Some important types of lakes are:

(*a*) **Oligotrophic** lakes which have low nutrient concentrations.

(*b*) **Eutrophic** lakes which are overnourished by nutrients like nitrogen and phosphorus, usually as a result of agricultural run-off or municipal sewage discharge. They are covered with "algal blooms", *e.g.* Dal lakes.

(*c*) **Dystrophic** lakes that have low pH, high humic acid content and brown waters, *e.g.* Bog lakes.

(*d*) **Endemic** lakes that are very ancient, deep and have endemic fauna which are restricted only to that lake, *e.g.* the Lake Baikal in Russia: the deepest lake, which is now suffering a threat due to industrial pollution.

(*e*) **Desert salt** lakes that occur in arid regions and have developed high salt concentrations as a result of high evaporation, e.g. great salt lake, Utah; Sambhar lake in Rajasthan.

(f) **Volcanic** lakes that receive water from magma after volcanic eruptions, e.g. many lakes in Japan. They have highly restricted biota.

(g) **Meromictic** lakes that are rich in salts and are permanently stratified, e.g. lake Nevada.

(h) **Artificial lakes or impounds** that are created due to construction of dams, e.g. Govindsagar lake at Bhakra-Nangal.

19. Commensalism occurs when one population is benefited but the other is unaffected (+, 0). Small epiphytes such as bromeliads and orchids, which grow on the surfaces of large trees without obvious detriment to the tree, might be an example.

20. R-strategies principally operates to maximize reproductive rates in harsh, unstable environment or during habitat disturbance, while there are only a little competition exist. This R-strategies favour a "gambling" strategies.

22. Endangered Species – Endangered species are those species whose number has been reduced to a critical level. This reduction is specifically attributed to loss of natural habitat of animals. Endangered species are near extinction and may become extinct if causal factors continue operating. Among the important endangered animals are charismatic species such as the tiger, the elephant, the rhino etc. Some others include Indian wild ass, the hangul or Kashmiri stag, the Golden langoor, the Pygmy hog and a host of others. There are also endangered bird species, like the Siberian crane, the Great Indian bustard, the Florican and several birds of prey.

26. Thermal stratification can occur in lakes as well as the ocean. Lakes can be classified according to their mixing regimes. The warm, oxygenated and less dense layer above the thermocline (or metalimnion) is called the epilimnion (Fig-b.).

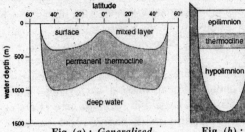

Fig. (a) : *Generalised thermal Stratification of the oceans.*

Fig. (b) : *Corresponding nomenclature for lakes*

The lower layer is termed the hypolimnion and contains colder denser water, which may become depleted in oxygen. Circulation within each layer is independent; it is likely to be more sluggish in the hypo-limnion because it is not affected by wind action.

30. Tundra is the coldest of all the biomes. Tundra comes from the Finnish word **tunturia**, meaning treeless plain. It is noted for its frost-molded landscapes, extremely low temperatures, little precipitation, poor nutrients, and short growing seasons. Dead organic material functions as a nutrient pool. The two major nutrients are nitrogen and phosphorus. Nitrogen is created by biological fixation, and phosphorus is created by precipitation.

35. Power of a wind turbine
= (A coefficient) (Power in the wind)
This coefficient must, obviously, be smaller than 1. It is called **power coefficient.**
Wind turbine power
= ½(Power coefficient) (Density) (Cross-sectional area)(Speed)^3
The power coefficient depends on how good a turbine is in design and how well it can grasp the wind energy. Thus, its value can be small or large. Nevertheless, there is a maximum value that no turbine in its best performance can exceed. It can be theoretically determined and is called the **Betz limit**.
The value for *Betz limit* is 16/27 = 0.59.

39. **Energy intensity** is a *measure* of the *energy efficiency* of a nation's *economy*. It is calculated as units of *energy* per unit of *GDP*.

- High energy intensities indicate a high price or cost of converting energy into GDP.

- Low energy intensity indicates a lower price or cost of converting energy into GDP. Energy intensity as defined here is not to be confused with **Energy Use Intensity** (EUI), a measure of building energy use per unit area.

42. Aluminium sulphate is used in water purification for removal of phosphate and of colloidal matter, for the coagulation of which the high charge on the cation is very effective. Aluminium in food, however, is suspected of causing Alzheimer's disease.

44. $N_2 + 6H^+ + 6e^- \rightarrow 2HN_3$

$12ATP \rightleftharpoons 12(ADP + Pi)$

Nitrogenase catalyzes proton reduction in the absence of nitrogen gas.

46. Coliform bacteria are the natural part of the microbial flora of the intestinal tract of warm-blooded mammals, including man. Coliform bacteria can also be found in soil, vegetation and other animals. The coliform group is relatively easy to culture in the lab and therefore, has been selected as primary indicator bacteria for the presence of disease causing organism. Coliform bacteria are normally non-pathogenic organisms and are only mildly infectious. For this reason these bacteria are relatively safe to work with in the laboratory. If large number of coliform is found in water, there is a high probability of presence of other pathogenic viruses, bacteria, protozoa and helminthes.

48. Ocimene hydrocarbons is emitted by vegetation.

57. I = PAT is the lettering of a formula put forward to describe the impact of human activity on the environment.

$I = P \times A \times T$

In words:

Human Impact (I) on the environment equals the product of P = Population, A = Affluence, T – Technology. This describes how our growing population, affluence, and technology contribute toward our environmental impact.

59. **Reed-swamp stage.** This stage is also known as **amphibious** stage as the plants of community are rooted but most parts of their shoots (assimilatory organs) remain exposed to air. Species of *Scirpus, Typha, Sagittaria* and *Phragmites* etc. are the chief plants of this stage. They have well-developed rhizomes and form a very dense vegetation. The water level is by now very much reduced and finally becomes unsuitable for the growth of these amphibious species.

62. **The Public Liability Insurance Act, 1991**– This law has been enacted to provide for public liability insurance for the purpose of providing immediate relief to the persons affected by accident occurring while handling any hazardous substance and the matters connected therewith or incidental there to. The act came into force with effect from the 1 April 1991. The main rules under this act were notified on the 1 May 1991, and other notifications under various provisions of the Act have also been issued.

63. $t\text{-statistic} = \dfrac{\overline{X} - \mu}{\sigma / \sqrt{n}}$

$= \dfrac{48 - 50}{\sqrt{8}/\sqrt{17}} = \dfrac{-2\sqrt{17}}{2\sqrt{2}} \cong -2.82$

64.

	Boys	Girls
Number :	n	n
Mean Wts :	50 kg	40 kg
Standard deviation :	2 kg	2 kg
Variance :	4 kg	4 kg

Combined variance

$$\sigma_{12}^2 = \frac{N_1\sigma_1^2 + N_1 d_1^2 + N_2\sigma_2^2 + N_2 d_2^2}{N_1 + N_2}$$

Here, $N_1 = N_2 = n$, $\sigma_1 = \sigma_b = 4$, $\sigma_2 = \sigma_g = 4$

To find the value of d_1 and d_2 we will calculate combined mean of the boys and girls

$$a_{12} = \frac{N_1 d_1 + N_2 d_2}{N_1 + N_2} = \frac{(50+40)n}{2n} = 45 \text{ kg}$$

$d_1 = 50 - 45 = 5 \text{ kg}$
$d_2 = 40 - 45 = -5 \text{ kg}$

Substituting the values in the above formula we get:

$$\sigma_{12}^2 = \frac{4n + 25n + 4n + 25n}{2n}$$

$$= \frac{58}{2} = 29 .$$

67. $\begin{bmatrix} 1 & 1 & 1 \\ 1 & -1 & -1 \\ 3 & 1 & 1 \end{bmatrix} = \frac{1}{2} \begin{bmatrix} 2 & 2 & 2 \\ 1 & -1 & -1 \\ 3 & 1 & 1 \end{bmatrix} \{R_1 \to 2R_1\}$

$= \begin{bmatrix} 3 & 1 & 1 \\ 1 & -1 & -1 \\ 3 & 1 & 1 \end{bmatrix} \{R_1 \to R_1 + R_2\}$

68. Given matrix $= \begin{bmatrix} 2 & 0 \\ 0 & 5 \end{bmatrix}$

Eigen values $= \begin{bmatrix} 2-\lambda & 0 \\ 0 & 5-\lambda \end{bmatrix} = 0$

$= (2-\lambda)(5-\lambda) = 0$

$\therefore \qquad \lambda = 2, 5$

Eigen vector for $\lambda = 2$

$= \begin{bmatrix} 2-2 & 0 \\ 0 & 5-2 \end{bmatrix} \begin{bmatrix} x_1 \\ x_2 \end{bmatrix} = \begin{bmatrix} 0 \\ 0 \end{bmatrix}$

$= \begin{bmatrix} 0 & 0 \\ 0 & 3 \end{bmatrix} \begin{bmatrix} x_1 \\ x_2 \end{bmatrix} = \begin{bmatrix} 0 \\ 0 \end{bmatrix}$

so, eigen vector would be $\begin{bmatrix} 0 \\ 1 \end{bmatrix}$ or $\begin{bmatrix} 0 \\ 2 \end{bmatrix}$

again, eigen vector for $\lambda = 5$

$= \begin{bmatrix} 2-5 & 0 \\ 0 & 5-5 \end{bmatrix} \begin{bmatrix} x_1 \\ x_2 \end{bmatrix} = \begin{bmatrix} 0 \\ 0 \end{bmatrix}$

$= \begin{bmatrix} -3 & 0 \\ 0 & 0 \end{bmatrix} \begin{bmatrix} x_1 \\ x_2 \end{bmatrix} = \begin{bmatrix} 0 \\ 0 \end{bmatrix}$

$\therefore$ eigen vector would be $\begin{bmatrix} 1 \\ 0 \end{bmatrix}$

$= \frac{1}{2} \begin{bmatrix} 0 & 0 & 0 \\ 1 & -1 & -1 \\ 3 & 1 & 1 \end{bmatrix} \{R_1 \to R_1 - R_3\}$

Hence, Rank of the given matrix is 2.

70. Population of the developed countries = 5.3 billion
Average birth rate = 23%
and Infant mortality rate = 53%
So, total death due to infant mortality

$= 5.3 \times 10^7 \times \dfrac{23}{100} \times \dfrac{53}{100}$

$= 6.46 \times 10^6 \cong 6.5 \times 10^6 /\text{year}.$

74.	Agreement type and name	Date adopted	Secretariat
	Atmosphere Conventions:		
	United Nations Framework Convention on Climate Change (UNFCCC)	1992	UN
	Kyoto Protocol to the United Nations Framework Convention on Climate Change	1997	UN
	Convention on International Trade in Endangered Species (CITES)	1973	UNEP
	Basel Convention on the Control of Transboundary Movements of Hazardous Wastes and their Disposal	1989	UNEP

UGC-NET Environmental Science December 2013

PAPER-II

Note : *This paper contains **fifty (50)** objective type questions, each question carrying **two (2)** marks. All questions are compulsory.*

1. Mesoscale Meteorological Phenomena occur over areas of horizontal distance in the range (km)
   A. 100 – 200 km
   B. 1 – 100 km
   C. 10 – 50 km
   D. 1 – 10 km

2. The Indian monsoon period is from
   A. October to November
   B. December to February
   C. June to September
   D. March to May

3. Which of the following is not a reactive oxygen species?
   A. Hydrogen peroxide
   B. Hydroxyl ion
   C. Singlet oxygen
   D. Superoxide anion

4. If air quality standard for carbon monoxide is 9.0 ppmV, the percentage as in mg/m^3 at 1 atm. at 25°C is
   A. 10.3 mg/m^3
   B. 15.2 mg/m^3
   C. 20.0 mg/m^3
   D. 5.6 mg/m^3

5. Azaridine, Ethylene dibromide, Bis (chloromethyl) ether are
   A. Alkylating agents
   B. Hydrocarbons
   C. Hydrazines
   D. Aromatic amines

6. Normality of 0.25 M phosphoric acid is
   A. 0.25
   B. 0.50
   C. 0.75
   D. 2.50

7. Match List–I with List–II and choose the correct answer from the codes given below :

List–I (Air Pollutants)	List–II (Sources / Activities)
(a) Carbon monoxide	1. Coal burning
(b) Nitrogen oxide	2. Cigarette Smoking
(c) Sulphur dioxide	3. Chemical reaction with VOCs
(d) Ozone	4. Power and Industrial Plant

   Codes :

	(a)	(b)	(c)	(d)
A.	2	4	1	3
B.	1	2	3	4
C.	3	1	4	2
D.	4	3	2	1

8. The gaseous material which is used for the synthesis of Methyl isocyanate is
   A. Chloranil
   B. Sevin
   C. Phosgene
   D. Chlorine

9. During the determination of COD, sulphanilic acid is added, because
   A. it maintains the acidic nature
   B. it precipitates the mercury ions
   C. it oxidises nitrites to nitrates
   D. it reacts with ferrous ammonium sulphate

10. Which year was declared as International Year of Biodiversity?
    A. 2002
    B. 2010
    C. 2020
    D. 1972

11. The forest biome characterised by 3-4 tree species/km^2 is
    A. Tropical
    B. Temperate
    C. Boreal
    D. Taiga

1

12. Which of the following is a type of biodiversity extinction caused primarily due to anthropogenic activities?
   A. Carboniferous rain forest collapse
   B. Permian — Triassic extinction
   C. Cretaceous paleogene extinction
   D. Holocene extinction

13. The chemical used in a fermenter with molasses as a substrate is
   A. Diammonium sulphate
   B. Diammonium phosphate
   C. Diammonium nitrate
   D. Diammonium chloride

14. Which of the following is an example of lotic ecosystem?
   A. Stream ecosystem
   B. Pond ecosystem
   C. Bog ecosystem
   D. Wetland ecosystem

15. Which pyramid is always straight?
   A. Pyramid of biomass
   B. Pyramid of number
   C. Pyramid of energy
   D. Pyramid of number and biomass

16. Which of the following type of materials present in a landslide suggest that the movement was rotational?
   A. Rockflow, Debris flow, Earthflow
   B. Rock slump, Debris slump, Earth slump
   C. Rockfall, Debris fall, Earth fall
   D. Rock topple, Debris topple, Earth topple

17. Which of the following parameters is not a good indicator of contamination in ground water?
   A. BOD
   B. Nitrates
   C. Silica
   D. Chlorides

18. On an aerial photograph, the distance between the principal point and the conjugate principal point is called
   A. Relief
   B. Tilt
   C. Photo-base
   D. Focal length

19. An equatorial west to east remote sensing satellite orbiting the earth at an altitude of 36,000 km is called
   A. Sun-synchronous satellite
   B. Geostationary satellite
   C. Space shuttle
   D. Stereo imager

20. Which state of Cr (Chromium) is most toxic?
   A. Cr^{4+} B. Cr^{3+}
   C. Cr^{5+} D. Cr^{6+}

21. Assertion (A) : Groundwater may get seriously contaminated in coastal areas.
   Reason (R) : Groundwater overdrafts near coastal areas can contaminate groundwater supplies by allowing salt water to intrude into freshwater aquifers.
   Codes :
   A. Both (A) and (R) are true and (R) is the correct explanation of (A).
   B. Both (A) and (R) are true, but (R) is not the correct explanation of (A).
   C. (A) is true and (R) is false.
   D. (A) is false and (R) is true.

22. Assertion (A) : Tropical and subtropical seas are most suitable for OTEC.
   Reason (R) : There is a certain minimum vertical gradient (> 25°C/km) required for OTEC to become feasible.
   Codes :
   A. Both (A) and (R) are true and (R) is the correct explanation of (A).
   B. Both (A) and (R) are true, but (R) is not the correct explanation of (A).
   C. (A) is true, but (R) is false.
   D. (A) is false, but (R) is true.

23. On burning a certain amount of fuel a total of 500 million tonnes of CO_2 is released to the atmosphere. If the entire amount of CO_2 remains in the atmosphere, what will be the rise in the concentration of CO_2 in ppm?
   A. ~ 0.236 ppm   B. ~ 0.128 ppm
   C. ~ 2.312 ppm   D. ~ 1.216 ppm

24. A thermal power station has a heat rate of 12 mJ/kWh. Its thermal efficiency is
   A. 30%   B. 36%
   C. 40%   D. 25%

25. Assume that world coal production is 6.1 billion tons per year and estimated total recoverable resources of coal is 1.1 trillion tons. How long it would take to use up those reserves at current rate of production?
    A. ~ 180 years   B. ~ 150 years
    C. ~ 120 years   D. ~ 90 years

26. In a salt gradient solar pond, the salinity generally varies from top to bottom of the pond as
    A. < 5% to ~ 20%
    B. ~ 10% to ~ 30%
    C. ~ 20% to ~ 35%
    D. ~ 20% to ~ 40%

27. Which region among the following is not Atmospheric Brown Cloud (ABC) hotspot?
    A. East-Asia
    B. South Africa
    C. Amazon Basin in South America
    D. Australia

28. Prolonged exposure to high levels of noise causes
    (i) Hearing loss
    (ii) Constriction of blood vessels
    (iii) Gastric ulcers
    (iv) Toxicity
    Identify the correct answer :
    A. (i), (ii) and (iv) only
    B. (i), (iii) and (iv) only
    C. (i), (ii) and (iii) only
    D. (i), (ii), (iii) and (iv)

29. *Azolla pinnata* is a
    A. Blue green algae B. Green algae
    C. Red algae   D. Fern

30. **Assertion (A) :** Eruption of the volcano Mt. Pinatobu in 1991 spewed sulphur clouds into the upper reaches of the atmosphere. The following three years were cooler.
    Reason (R) : Sulphate aerosols reflect sunlight away from the Earth.
    Codes :
    A. Both (A) and (R) are correct and (R) is the correct explanation of (A).
    B. Both (A) and (R) are correct and (R) is not the correct explanation of (A).

C. (A) is correct (R) is incorrect.
D. Both (A) and (R) are incorrect.

31. Photolysis of NO_2 occurs due to radiations of wavelength
    A. < 600 nm
    B. < 550 nm
    C. < 480 nm
    D. < 390 nm

32. The efficiency of removing SO_2 from the flue gas by limestone in wet scrubbers can be as high as
    A. 30%
    B. 50%
    C. 70%
    D. 90%

33. The depth of the oxidation ponds is typically
    A. 1–2 m   B. 2–5 m
    C. 5–10 m   D. 10–20 m

34. In EIA the baseline data describes
    A. The environmental consequences by mapping
    B. Existing environmental status of the identified study area
    C. Assessment of risk on the basis of proposal
    D. Demographic and socioeconomic data

35. Which one of the following does not belong to EIA methods used for assessing the impacts of developmental activities on the environment?
    A. Checklist   B. Adhoc
    C. Network   D. Flexible

36. The EIA report of a hydropower project would be valid upto how many years after the environmental clearance of the project?
    A. 5 years   B. 6 years
    C. 30 years   D. 10 years

37. If in the screening stage of EIA, the impact level of a developmental project is not discernible, then what step should be adopted?
    A. Scoping stage is to be followed.
    B. A rapid EIA study is to be conducted.
    C. Detail EIA study is to be conducted.
    D. The project should be given Environmental Clearance.

38. The Committee which reviews the Environmental Impact Assessment and Environmental Management plan reports of a developmental project in Ministry of Environment and Forest is called
   A. Project Assessment Committee
   B. Project Appraisal Committee
   C. Project Evaluation Committee
   D. Project Estimate Committee

39. In a typical municipal solid waste, least percentage of Ash is found in
   A. Textiles
   B. Plastic
   C. Leather
   D. Rubber

40. Highly inflammable liquid/chemicals have flash point
   A. lower than 23°C
   B. between 23 and 26°C
   C. between 27 and 31°C
   D. between 32 and 40°C

41. Which one of the following does not contribute to climate change?
   A. NO
   B. O_3
   C. SF_6
   D. HFCs

42. A population (X) in an ecosystem follows logistic growth curve. If the carrying capacity of the system is K, the growth realisation factor is
   A. $\dfrac{K-X}{X}$
   B. $\dfrac{K-X}{K}$
   C. $\dfrac{K-X}{K^2}$
   D. $(K-X)$

43. Which one of the following conditions would indicate that the dataset is **not** bell shaped?
   A. The mean is much smaller than median
   B. The range is equal to five times the standard deviation.
   C. The range is larger than interquartile range.
   D. The range is twice the standard deviation.

44. For degrees of freedom (df) > 1, the mean (μ) of the t-distribution is
   A. Zero
   B. 1
   C. depends on df
   D. 2

45. Which of the following is an eigen value of the matrix $\begin{bmatrix} 3 & -1 \\ 4 & -2 \end{bmatrix}$?
   A. 2
   B. 0
   C. 1
   D. 3

46. Suppose a 70 kg person drinks 2L of water everyday for 70 years with a chloroform concentration of 0.10 mg/L (the drinking water standard), upper bound cancer risk for these individual will be
   A. 17 in 1 million
   B. 25 in 1 million
   C. 37 in 1 million
   D. 5 in 1 million

47. What is Ecomark?
   A. Label given to recycled products
   B. Label given to an environment friendly products
   C. Land mark indicating the boundaries of bioparks
   D. Label given to non-recyclable products

48. An important source of Arsenic in Municipal Solid Water (MSW) is
   A. Pigments in plastics
   B. Rubber products
   C. Batteries
   D. Household pesticides

49. Which of the following is **not** a nonformal Environment Education and Awareness Programme?
   A. Global Learning and Observations to Benefit the Environment (GLOBE)
   B. National Environment Awareness Campaign (NEAC)
   C. Eco-clubs
   D. Environmental Education in School System

50. REDD stands for
   A. Recurring Emission from Deforestation and Forest Degradation
   B. Reducing Environmental Degradation and Forest Degradation
   C. Reducing Emissions from Deforestation and Forest Degradation
   D. Reducing Emissions from Degradable Deposits of Wastes

ANSWERS

1	2	3	4	5	6	7	8	9	10
B	C	B	A	A	C	A	C	C	B

11	12	13	14	15	16	17	18	19	20
B	D	B	A	C	B	C	C	B	D

21	22	23	24	25	26	27	28	29	30
A	A	A	A	A	A	D	C	D	A

31	32	33	34	35	36	37	38	39	40
D	D	A	B	D	D	B	B	A	A

41	42	43	44	45	46	47	48	49	50
A	B	A	A	A	A	B	D	D	C

SOME SELECTED EXPLANATORY ANSWERS

1. Mesoscale metrology is the study of weather system smaller than synoptic scale systems but larger than microscale and strom scale cumulus systems. Horizontal dimension generally range from around 1–100 km. Example of mesoscale weather systems are seabreezes, squallines and mesoscale convective complexes.

2. The Indian monsoon period is from June to September. Monsoon is traditionally defined as a seasonal reversing wind accompanied by corresponding changes in precipitation, but is now used to describe seasonal changes in atmosphere circulation and precipitation associated with the asymmetric heating of land and sea.

3. Reactive oxygen species (ROS) are chemically reactive moleculus containing oxygen, Examples include oxygen ions and peroxides. ROS are formed as a natural by product of the normal metabolism of oxygen and have important roles in cell signaling and homeostasis. However, during times of environment stress (e.g., UV or heat exposure), ROS levels can increase dramatically. This may result in significant demage to cell structures. Cumulatively, this is known as oxidative stress. ROS are also generated by exogenous sources such as ionizing, radiation.

Damaging Effects : Normally, cells defend themselves against ROS damage with enzymes such as alpha-1 microglobulin, superoxide dismutases, catalases, lactoperoxidases, glutathioxins. Small molecule antioxidants such as ascorbic acid (Vitamin C), tocopherol (Vitamin E), uric acid glutathione also play important roles as cellular antioxidants. In a similar manner, polyphenol antioxidants assist in preventing ROS damage by scavenging free radicals. In contrast, the antioxidant ability of the extra cellular space is less, e.g., the most important plasma antioxidant in humans is uric acid.

Effects of ROS on cell metabolism are well documented in a variety of species. These include not only roles in apoptosis (programmed cell death) but also positive effects such as the induction of host defence genes and mobilisation of ion transport systems. This implicates them in control of cellular function. In particular, platelets involved in wound repair and blood homeostasis release ROS to recruit additional platelets to sites of injury. These also provide a link to the adaptive immune system via the recruitment of leukocytes.

Reactive oxygen species are implicated in cellular activity to a variety of inflammatory responses including cardiovascular disease. They may also be involved in hearing impairment via cochlear damage induced by elevated sound levels in ototoxicity of drugs such as cisplatin and in congenital deafness in both animals and humans. ROS are also implicated in meditation of apoptosis or programmed cell death and ischaemic injury. Specific examples include stroke and heart attack.

In general, harmful effects of reactive oxygen species on the cell are most often.

1. Damage of DNA
2. Oxidations of polyunstaurated fatty acids in lipids.
3. Oxidations of amino acids in proteins.
4. Oxidatively inactivate specific enzymes by oxidation of co-factors.

10. The UN-declared 2010 as international year of Biodiversity.

Biodiversity plays a vital role in human sciences, culture and its diversity, education and communication, contributes in a multidisciplinary way to taking the root causes of biodiversity erosion and loss due to unsustainable development. During the year, UNESCO has lead several activities which aimed to educate and to raise public awareness on the reasons for conserning biodiversity and to catalyte further international action for its sustainable use.

11. **Temperate Forest :** Temperate forest occurs in eastern North America, north-eastern Asia, and Western and Central Europe well defined seasons with a distinct winter characterize this forest biome. Moderate climate and a growing season of 140-200 days during 4-6 forst-trees months distinguish temperate forests.

- Temperature varies from –30°C to 30°C.
- Precipitation (75-150 cm) is distributed evenly throughout the year.
- Soil is fertile, enriched with decaying litter.
- Canopy is moderately dense and allows light to penetrate, resulting in well-developed and richly diversified understory vegetation and stratification of animals.
- Flora is characterized by 3-4 tree species per square kilometre (3-4 tree species/km^2) Trees are distinguished by broad leaves that are lost annually and include such species as oak, hickory, beech, hemlock, maple, basswood, cottonwood, elm, willow, and spring-flowering herbs.
- Fauna is represented by squirrels, rabbits, skunks, birds, deer, mountain black lion, bobeat, timber wolf, fox and bear.

Further sub-divisions of this groups are determined by seasonal distribution of rainfall.

- Moist conifer and evergreen broad-leave forests : Wet winters and dry summers (rainfall is concentrated in the winter months and winters are relatively mild).
- Dry conifer forests : Dominate higher elevation zones; low precipitation.
- Mediterraneam forests : Precipitation is concentrated in winter, less than 100 cm per year.
- Temperate coniferous : Mild winters high annual precipitation (greater than 200 cm).
- Temperate broad-leaved rainforests : Mild, frost-free winters, high precipitation (more than 150 cm) evenly distributed throughout the year.

Only scattered remnants of original temperate forests remain.

12. **Holocene extiction :** The Holocene extinction, sometimes called the sixth Extinction, is name proposed to describe the extinction event of species that has occurred during the present Holocene epoch (since around 10,000 BC). The large number of extinctions span numerous families of plants and animals including mammals, birds, amphibians, reptiles and arthropods. Although 875 extinctions occurring between 1500 and 2009 have been documented by International union for conservation of Nature and Natural Resources, the vast majority are undocumented. According to the species-area theory and based on upper-bound estimating, the present

rate of extinction may be up to 140,000 species per year.

The Holocene extinction includes the disappearance of large mammals known as megafauna, starting between 9,000 and 13,000 years ago, the end of the last Ice Age. This may have been due to the extinction of the mammoth that had maintained grasslands that became brich forests without the mammoths. The new forest and the resulting forest fires may have induced climate change. Such disappearances might be the result of the proliferation of modern humans which led to climate change. These extinctions, occurring near the Pleistocene-Holocene boundry are sometimes referred to as the quaternary extinction event. The Holocene extinction continuous into the 21st century.

There is no general agreement on whether to consider this as merely part of the quaternary extinction event, or just a result of human caused changes. Only during these most recent parts of the extinction can be characterized by humanity's presence.

13. Diammonium Phosphate (DAP) (chemical formula $(NH_4)_2HPO_4$, IUPAC name diammonium hydrogen phosphate) is a series of water-soluble ammonium phosphate salts that can be produced when ammonia reacts with phosphoric acid. Solid diammonium phosphate shows a dissociation pressure of ammonia as given by the following expression and equation,

$(NH_4)_2 HPO_4(s) NH_3(g) + NH_4H_2 PO_4(s)$

log P mmHg = 3063/T + 175 log

T + 3.3

Where, P = the resultant dissociation pressure of ammonia

T = absolute temperature (K)

At 100°C, the dissociation pressure of diammonium phosphate is approximately 5 mmHg.

Uses : DAP is used as a fertilizer. When applied as plant food, it temporally increases the soil pH, but over a long term the treated ground becomes more acidic than before upon nitrification of the ammonium. It is incomplete with alkaline chemical because its ammonium ion is more likely to convert to ammonia in a high pH environment. The average pH in solution in 7.5–8. The typical formulation is 18–46–0 (18% N, 46% P_2O_5, 0% K_2O).

DAP can be used as a fire retardant. It lowers the combustion temperature of the national, decreases maximum weight loss rates and causes an increase in the production of residue or char. These are important effects in fighting wildfiers as lowering the pyrolysis temperature and increasing the amount of char formed reduces that amount of available fuel and can lead to the formation of a firebreak. It is the largest component of some popular commercial firefighting products.

DAP is also used as a yeast nutrient in wine making and brecuing mead; as an addtive in some brands of cigarettes purportedly as a nicotine enhancer; to prevent afterglow in matches, in purifying sugar; as a flux for soldering tin, copper, zinc and brass; and to control precipitation of alkali-soluble and acid-insoluble colloidal dyes on wool.

15. "Pyramid of Energy is a graphic representation of the amount of energy trapped per unit time and area in different trophic level of a food chain with producers forming the base and the top carnivors at the tip."

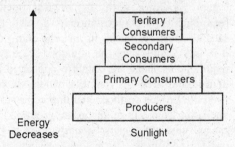

Representation of Pyramid of Energy

Pyramid of energy is always upright. It is so because at each transfer about 80-90% of the energy available at lower trophic level is used upto overcome its entrophy and to perform metabolic activities. Only 10% of the energy is available to next tropic level (as per lindermann's ten per cent rule).

19. A Geostationary satellite is a satellite in geosynchronous orbit, with an orbital period

the same as the Earth's rotation period. Such a Satellite returns to the same position in the sky after each sidereal day and over the course of a day traces out a path in the sky that is typically some form of analemma. A special case of geosynchronous satellite is the geo stationary satellite, which has a geostationary orbit a circular geosynchronous orbit directly above the Earth's equator. Another type of geosynchronous orbit used by satellites is the Tundra elliptical orbit.

Geosynchronous satellites have the advantage of remaining permanently in the same area of the sky, as viewed from a particular location on Earth, and so permanently within view of a given ground station. Geostationary satellites have the special property of remaining permanently fixed in exactly the same position in the sky, meaning that ground based anternnas do not need to track them but can remain fixed in one direction. Such satellite are often used for communication purposes; a geosynchronous network is a communication network based on communication with or through geosynchronous satellites.

Definition : The term "geosynchronous" refers to the satellite's orbital period being exactly one sidereal day which enables it to be synchronized with the rotation of the Earth ('geo-'). Along with the orbital period requirements, to be geostationary as well, the satellite must be placed in an orbit that puts it in the vicinity over the equator. These two requirements make the satellite appear in an unchanging area of visibility when viewed from the Earth's surface, enabling continuous operation from one point on the ground. The special case of a geostationary orbit is the most common type of orbit for communications satellites. If a geosynchronous satellite's orbit is not exactly aligned with the Earth's equator, the orbit is known as an inclined orbit. It will appear (when viewed by someone on the ground). As the angle between the orbit and the equator decreases, the magnitude of this oscillation becomes smaller; when the orbit lies entirely over the equator in circular orbit, the satellite remains stationary relative to the Earth's surface. it is said be geostationary.

20. Chromium is a hard steel-gray metal that is highly resistant to oxidation, even at high temperatures. It is the sixth most abundant element in the earth's crust, where it is combined with iron and oxygen in the form of chromite ore.

Chromium is used in three basic industries:
- Metallurgical,
- Chemical, and
- Refractory (heat-resistant applications)

Chromium exists in series of oxidation states from -2 to $+6$ valence. The most important stable states are O (elemental metal), $+3$ (trivalent), and $+6$ (hexavalent). Chromium in chromite ore is in the trivalent state; industrial processes also produce the elemental metal and hexavalent chromium.

Cr^{6+} is generally considered 1,000 times more toxic than Cr^{3+}.

Cr^{3+} is an essential dietary mineral in low doses. Cr^{6+} compounds are carcinogenic.

Therefore Cr^{6+} state of Cr (chromium) is most toxic.

21. Ground water is get seriously contaminated in coastal areas. It overdrafts near the coastal areas can contaminated ground water supplies by allowing salt water to introduce into freshwater aquifers. Hence, both (A) and (R) are true and R is correct explanations of A.

22. Ocean thermal energy conversion (OTEC) uses the temperature difference between cooler and warmer shallow or surface ocean waterstorum a heat engine and produced a useful work. In ocean, the temperature difference between surface and deep water is greatest in the tropics, although still a modest 20 to 25°C. In OTEC, the tropical and subtropical seas are most suitable and there is minimum vertical gradient >25°C/km required for OTEC to become feasible.

27. Atmospheric Brown Cloud (ABC) hotspot observe as widespread layers of browish haze, regional scale plumes of air pollutants, consisting of many aerosol particles, such as black carbon (BC), and precursor gases which

produce aerosols and ozone. ABCs and their interaction with buildup of greenhouse gases significantly effect, the regional climate, hydrological cycle, glacial melting, agriculture and human health.

Atmospheric Brown Cloud (ABC) hotspot regions are :

● East Asia (Eastern China, Thiland, Vietnam, Comboida), ● Indonesian region, ● South Africa extending southerwords from Sub-Saharan Africa into Angola, Zambia and Zimbabwe, the American basin in South America.

29. Azolla pinnata is a species of fern known by several common names including feathered mosquitofern and water velvet. It is native to much of Africa, Asia from China to Japan, India and the Phillipines, and parts of Australia. It is an aquatic plant, its frond floating upon the surface of the water. It grows in quiet and slow-moving water bodies, because swift currents and waves break up the plant. This is a with a triangular frond measuring up to 2.5 centimeters in length which floats on the water. The frond is made up of many rounded or angular ovelapping leaves each 1 or 2 millimeters long. They are green, blue-green or dark red in colour and coated in tiny hairs, giving them a velvety appearance. The hairs make the top surface of the leaf water-repellent, keeping the plant afloat even after being pushed under. A water body may be coated in a dense layer of the plants, which form a velvety mat that crowds out other plants. The hairlike roots extend out into the water. The leaves contain the cyanobacterium Anabaena azolle, which is a symbiont that fixes nitrogen from the atmosphere that the fern can use.

This gives the fern the ability to grow in habitats that are low in nitrogon. The plant reproduces vegetatively when branches break off the main axis, or sexually when sporocarps on the leaves release spores.

It is present in New Zealand as an introduced species and an invasive weed that has crowded out a native relative, Azolla rubra. Therefore Azolla pinnata is a fern.

30. In 1991, the erruption of the Vocano Mt. Pinatobu spewed sulphur(s) clouds into the upper atmospheres. The sulphate aerosols reflect light of the sun away from the surface of the earth. Therefore, both the statements are true and farmer is correct explanation of later.

45. $\begin{vmatrix} 3 & -1 \\ 4 & -2 \end{vmatrix}$

We know that the eigenvalue are the roots of equation, then characterstic equations

$\begin{vmatrix} 3-\lambda & -1 \\ 4 & -2-\lambda \end{vmatrix}$

Solving this, we get the result $\lambda = 2$.

47. Ecomark or Eco mark is a certification mark issued by the Bureau of Indian Standards (The National Standards Organisation of India) to products conforming to a set of Standards aimed at the least impact on ecosystem. The marking scheme was started in 1991. One of the purposes of the mark inereasing awareness among the consumers towards reducing environment impact. The mark is issued to various product categories and the development of standards for more products is in progress.

Eco-mark Pre-Inked Stamps : Produced using the most environmently friendly manufacturing methods, eco-mark offers the quality you expect at a price that fits your budget. Eco-mark is a pre-inked stamp with a self-inker 'look' without the messy ink pads or noise of a conventional self-inker. The new wrap around lens cover gives you ideal space to advertise your company information. Several private label options are available. Therefore, Label given to an invironmental friendly products.

50. **REDD** involves some kind of incentive for changing are used. As such, it offers a new way of curbing CO_2 emission through paying for actions that prevent forest loss or degradation. These transfer mechanisms can include carbon trading, or paying for forest management. It stands for reducing emissions from Deforestation and forest Degration.

PAPER-III

*Note : This paper contains **seventy five (75)** objective type questions of **two (2)** marks each. **All** questions are compulsory.*

1. For an overcast day or night, the atmosphere is
   A. stable
   B. neutral
   C. slightly stable
   D. unstable

2. **Assertion (A) :** The energy flow in an ecosystem follows the law of thermodynamics.
   Reason (R) : The energy flow in an ecosystem is unidirectional and during the transformation of energy from one trophic level to the other, 80–90% of energy is lost.
   Codes :
   A. Both (A) and (R) are true and (R) is the correct explanation of (A).
   B. Both (A) and (R) are true, but (R) is not the correct explanation of (A).
   C. (A) is true, but (R) is false.
   D. (A) is false, but (R) is true.

3. Match the List–I with List–II and identify the correct answer from the given codes :

List–I (Thermodynamic Variables) (Symbols have their usual meanings.)		List–II (Expression)
(a) ΔG	1.	$\Delta E + P\Delta V$
(b) $\Delta G°$	2.	$-n\,FE°$
(c) ΔS	3.	$RT \ln \dfrac{V_1}{V_2}$
(d) ΔH	4.	$nR \ln \dfrac{V_2}{V_1}$

   Codes :

	(a)	(b)	(c)	(d)
A.	2	4	1	3
B.	3	2	4	1
C.	3	1	4	2
D.	2	3	4	1

4. The environmental lapse rate during day time is governed by
   (i) Wind speed
   (ii) Sunlight
   (iii) Topographical features
   (iv) Cloud cover
   The correct answer is
   A. (i) and (ii) only
   B. (ii) and (iii) only
   C. (i), (ii) and (iii) only
   D. (i) and (iv) only

5. The wavelength range of UV–C radiations is
   A. 200–280 nm
   B. 180–240 nm
   C. 320–400 nm
   D. 240–300 nm

6. In a gas chromatography experiment, the retention factor (R_f) values for pollutant 'A' and pollutant 'B' in a mixture of pollutants were 0.5 and 0.125, respectively. If the distance travelled by solvent front is 12 cms, the distance (in cms) travelled by pollutant 'A' and pollutant 'B' will be
   A. 6 and 1.5
   B. 3 and 1.5
   C. 0.5 and 0.125
   D. 1.5 and 3

7. Using the following equations, which can be determined correctly?

   $$Ca(HCO_3)_2 \xrightarrow{\Delta} CaCO_3 + H_2O + CO_2$$
   (by heating)
   or
   $$Ca(HCO_3)_2 + Ca(OH)_2 \longrightarrow 2CaCO_3 + 2H_2O$$
   (by addition of lime)

   A. Carbon dioxide
   B. Carbonates
   C. Bicarbonates
   D. Carbonates and Bicarbonates

8. Assume that a river having dissolved oxygen 0.5 g/m^3, BOD 0.3 g/m^3 flowing at 80 m^3/sec. converge with another river having Dissolved Oxygen 0.7 g/m^3. BOD 0.6 g/m^3 flowing at a rate of 60 m^3/sec. If after the confluence the Dissolved Oxygen is 0.59 g/m^3, then the BOD is
   A. 0.83 g/m^3
   B. 0.43 g/m^3
   C. 0.73 g/m^3
   D. 0.92 g/m^3

9. Cells grown in a medium containing phosphorous –32 will show radio labelling in
   A. Starch   B. Glycogen
   C. Proteins   D. Nucleic acids

10. C^{14} has a half-life of 5700 years. The fraction of the C^{14} atoms that decays per year is
    A. 1.216×10^{-4} B. 0.52×10^{-3}
    C. 0.78×10^{-4} D. 2.81×10^{-4}

11. **Assertion (A)** : Marine biodiversity tends to be highest in mid-latitudes in all oceans and along coasts in the Western Pacific.
    Reason (R) : Sea surface temperature along coasts in the Western Pacific is highest.
    Codes :
    A. Both (A) and (R) are true and (R) is the correct explanation of (A).
    B. Both (A) and (R) are true, but (R) is not the correct explanation of (A).
    C. (A) is true, but (R) is false.
    D. (A) is false, but (R) is true.

12. "Double digging" is a method of
    A. Bio-intensive agriculture
    B. Deforestation
    C. Aforestation
    D. Water conservation

13. The rate of replacement of species along a gradient of habitats pertains to
    A. Alpha diversity   B. Beta diversity
    C. Gamma diversity   D. Species diversity

14. Match the List–I and List–II. Choose the correct answer from the given codes :

List–I (Vegetation development)	List–II (Nomenclature of succession)
(a) On a rock	1. Psammosere
(b) On sand	2. Lithosere
(c) In aquatic habitat	3. Xerosere
(d) In dry habitat	4. Hydrosere

    Codes :

	(a)	(b)	(c)	(d)
A.	2	1	4	3
B.	1	2	3	4
C.	3	4	2	1
D.	4	3	1	2

15. If individuals of a species remain alive only in captivity or other human controlled conditions, the species is said to be
    A. Ecologically extinct
    B. Mass extinct
    C. Wild extinct
    D. Anthropogenic extinct

16. Which of the following symbolises correct sequence in hydrosere?
    A. Diatoms → Wolffia → Hydrilla → Cyperus → Populus
    B. Hydrilla → Wolffia → Cyperus → Populus → Diatoms
    C. Cyperus → Diatoms → Hydrilla → Wolffia → Populus
    D. Diatoms → Hydrilla → Wolffia → Cyperus → Populus

17. Which of the following is not a class of aquatic ecosystems based on salinity levels?
    A. Stagnant water ecosystem
    B. Freshwater ecosystem
    C. Brackish ecosystem
    D. Marine ecosystem

18. The K-strategists are
    (a) large organisms which have relatively longer life
    (b) provide care for their offsprings
    (c) organisms that stabilise their population at carrying capacity for the area
    Choose the correct answer :
    A. (a) and (b) only   B. (a) and (c) only
    C. (b) and (c) only   D. (a), (b) and (c)

19. Limnetic zone in freshwater ecosystem is characterised by
    A. Presence of rooted vegetation
    B. Absence of rooted vegetation
    C. Presence of large proportion of lime
    D. Absence of phytoplankton

20. Match the List–I with List–II, choose the correct answer from the given codes :

List–I (Plants)	List–II (Family)
(a) *Camellia caduca*	1. Orchidaceae
(b) *Picea brachytyla*	2. Theaceae
(c) *Colchicum luteum*	3. Pinaceae
(d) *Arachnantha clarkei*	4. Liliaceae

Codes :

	(a)	(b)	(c)	(d)
A.	4	2	3	1
B.	1	2	3	4
C.	2	1	4	3
D.	2	3	4	1

21. Vegetation cover shows maximum reflectance in which of the following regions of the electromagnetic radiation spectrum?
A. Ultraviolet   B. Near infrared
C. Middle infrared D. Visible

22. During remote sensing of the vegetation cover, the spectral reflection of vegetation over electromagnetic radiation spectrum depends upon
A. Pigmentation in the leaf
B. Structure of the leaf
C. Moisture content of the leaf
D. All the above characters

23. Given below are statements in the context of biogeochemical cycles :
(i) Ecosystems are black boxes for many of the processes that take place within them.
(ii) Ecosystem boundaries are permeable to some degree or other.
(iii) The energy and nutrients can be transferred to and from one ecosystem to another via imports and exports.

Identify the correct answer from the codes given below:
A. (i) and (ii) only B. (ii) and (iii) only
C. (i) and (iii) only D. (i), (ii) and (iii)

24. The volume of ejecta and the column height for a volcano are $10^{8.5}$ m^3 and 24 km, respectively. What is its volcanic explosivity index value?
A. 2   B. 8
C. 7   D. 4

25. In the context of material balance in hydrological cycle, which of the following equations is correct for oceans?
A. Input + change in storage = output
B. Precipitation + inflow = evaporation
C. Input – change in storage = output
D. Precipitation – inflow = evaporation

26. In disaster management which steps are followed in post-disaster recovery phase?
A. Relief, rehabilitation, reconstruction, learning–review
B. Risk Assessment, mitigation, preparedness, emergency plans.
C. Relief, mitigation, emergency plans.
D. Learning–review, emergency plans, preparedness.

27. Permafrost represents
A. permanently frozen subsurface soil
B. frozen leaves of Oak trees
C. frozen needles of pine trees
D. temporarily frozen subsurface soil

28. Assertion (A) : Estuaries are productive ecosystems.
Reason (R) : Large amounts of nutrients are introduced into the basin from the rivers that run into them.
Choose the correct answer :
A. Both (A) and (R) are true, and (R) is the correct explanation of (A).
B. Both (A) and (R) are true, but (R) is not the correct explanation of (A).
C. (A) is true and (R) is false.
D. (A) is false and (R) is true.

29. A confined aquifer of thickness 25 m has two wells 200 m apart along the direction of flow of water. The difference in their hydraulic heads is 1 m. If hydraulic conductivity is 50 m/day, the rate of flow of water per day per metre of distance perpendicular to the flow of water is
A. 25 m^3/day per metre
B. 50 m^3/day per metre
C. 5 m^3/day per metre
D. 1 m^3/day per metre

30. Which of the following material has the highest hydraulic conductivity?
A. Clay   B. Sandstone
C. Limestone   D. Quartzite

31. Which of the following energy sources is not renewable on human time scale?
A. Solar   B. Hydrothermal
C. Geothermal   D. Biomass

32. For a solar flat plate collector the following data is given : Useful heat gain = 28 watts/m^2 per hour, solar radiation intensity = 350 watts/m^2 per hour and the factor to convert beam radiation to that on the plane of the collector = 1.2. The collector efficiency is
   A. ~ 6.6%   B. ~ 4.8%
   C. ~ 12.2%   D. ~ 15.2%

33. For the reaction in a hydrogenoxygen fuel cell,

$$H_2 + \frac{1}{2}O_2 = H_2O(l)$$

Given $\Delta G° = 240$ kJ/gm – mole of H_2 and Faraday's constant = 96,500 Coulomb/gm mole.
The developed voltage in the fuel cell will be
   A. ~ 1.13 Volts
   B. ~ 2.13 Volts
   C. ~ 1.51 Volts
   D. ~ 1.24 Volts

34. Identify the correct sequence of the fuels in order of their increasing carbon intensity :
   A. Natural gas < Oil < Bituminous coal < Nuclear
   B. Oil < Coal < Natural gas < Nuclear
   C. Nuclear < Coal < Natural gas < Oil
   D. Nuclear < Natural gas < Oil < Bituminous coal

35. In nuclear thermal reactors, which of the following is not used as moderator?
   A. Normal water   B. Heavy water
   C. Graphite   D. Liquid Helium

36. The minimum temperature gradient (°C/km) required for OTEC is about
   A. 20   B. 10
   C. 40   D. 60

37. A solar pond has electricity generating capacity of 600 MWe. If the efficiency of solar energy to electric generation process was 2% and solar energy supply rate was 300 W/m^2, what is the area of solar pond?
   A. 100 km^2 B. 90 km^2
   C. 60 km^2 D. 180 km^2

38. Which of the following causes warming of atmosphere but cooling of the earth's surface?
   A. Ozone
   B. Black carbon aerosols
   C. All Greenhouse gases
   D. Sulphates and nitrates

39. **Assertion (A) :** For noise level surveys in urban areas, weighting A is used for measurements.
   Reason (R) : Weighting A filters out unwanted signals.
   Codes :
   A. Both (A) and (R) are true and (R) is the correct explanation of (A).
   B. Both (A) and (R) are true, but (R) is not the correct explanation of (A).
   C. (A) is true, but (R) is false.
   D. Both (A) and (R) are false.

40. Noise levels of 80 dB refers to a sound pressure level of
   A. 0.2 Pa   B. 0.02 Pa
   C. 20 Pa   D. 200 Pa

41. Asphyxiation is caused by
   A. HCN, $COCl_2$ B. NO_x
   C. $CHCl_3$ D. AsH_3

42. Sequence of a typical sewage treatment plant operation process will be
   A. Aeration → Flocculation → Sedimentation → Recarbonation → Filtration → Disinfection
   B. Aeration → Sedimentation → Flocculation → Filtration → Recarbonation → Disinfection
   C. Flocculation → Aeration → Recarbonation → Sedimentation → Filtration → Disinfection
   D. Sedimentation → Flocculation → Aeration → Filtration → Recarbonation → Disinfection

43. Which one of the following isotopes has maximum half-life period?
   A. Rn^{222}
   B. Pb^{210}
   C. Ti^{210}
   D. Bi^{210}

44. Match the List–I with List–II and identify the correct answer from given codes :

	List–I (Aerosols)	List–II (Constituents)
(a)	Dust	1. Small gas borne particles resulting from combustion
(b)	Mist	2. Black carbon
(c)	Smoke	3. Suspended small liquid droplets
(d)	Atmospheric Brown Cloud	4. Solid suspended particles

Codes :

	(a)	(b)	(c)	(d)
A.	4	3	2	1
B.	3	4	1	2
C.	2	1	3	4
D.	1	2	3	4

45. **Assertion (A)** : Chloroflurocarbons deplete ozone.
   Reason (R) : These compounds contain chlorine, bromine and fluorine.
   Codes :
   A. Both (A) and (R) are true and (R) is the correct explanation of (A).
   B. Both (A) and (R) are true, but (R) is not the correct explanation of (A).
   C. (A) is true, but (R) is false.
   D. (A) is false, but (R) is true.

46. Which of the following organic compounds is not of biogenic origin?
   A. Isoprene   B. α-pinene
   C. Myrcene   D. Acrolein

47. Which of the following is used as plant indicator for detection of presence of SO_2 and HF in air?
   A. Lichen   B. Orchid
   C. Apricot   D. Tobacco

48. Integrated Gasification Combined Cycle (IGCC) technology is best at removing
   A. NO_2 and CO
   B. CO and SO_2
   C. Particulates and sulphur
   D. NO_2 and SO_2

49. A wastewater treatment plant in a city treats 50,000 m^3 wastewater generated per day. For an average flow rate of 25 m^3 per day per sq. metre, what should be the diameter of the circular primary settling tank?
   A. 50.4 m   B. 30.6 m
   C. 20 m   D. 25.8 m

50. An Electrostatic Precipitator (ESP) with collector plate area = 5000 m^2 treats a flue gas with drift velocity = 0.12 m/s with 98% efficiency. The volumetric flow rate (m^3/s) of the flue gas is
   A. ~ 175.2   B. ~ 213.5
   C. ~ 153.4   D. ~ 198.9

51. **Assertion (A)** : Urban heat islands contribute to build up of pollutants in cities.
   Reason (R) : Urban heat islands produce a somewhat stable air mass in the city's atmosphere.
   Codes :
   A. Both (A) and (R) are correct and (R) is the correct explanation of (A).
   B. Both (A) and (R) are correct, but (R) is not the correct explanation of (A).
   C. (A) is true, but (R) is false.
   D. Both (A) and (R) are false.

52. Match List–I with List–II and choose the correct answer from the codes given below :

	List–I (Analytical functions)	List–II (Activity under the function)
(a)	Defining scope of EIA	1. Critical Assessment of impacts
(b)	Identification of impacts	2. Estimation of the probability that a particular impact will occur
(c)	Prediction of Impacts	3. Description of the existing environment system
(d)	Impact Evaluation and Analysis	4. Deciding important issues and concerns

Codes :

	(a)	(b)	(c)	(d)
A.	3	4	1	2
B.	4	3	2	1
C.	2	1	3	4
D.	1	2	4	3

53. A drawback of checklists is
    A. Preliminary analysis is available in scaling checklist
    B. Checklists are too general or incomplete
    C. Checklists summarises information to make it available to experts
    D. Ecosystem functions can be clearly understood from weighting methods

54. If EIU_j = environmental impact units for jth alternative, EQ_{ij} = environmental – quality – scale value for i^{th} factor and j^{th} alternative, PIU_i = parameter importance units for i^{th} factor, then what is the correct formulation for the index expressed in environmental impact units (EIU_i)?

    A. $EIU_i = \sum_{i=1}^{n} \left(\dfrac{E}{Q_{ij}} \right) PIU_i$

    B. $EIU_i = \sum_{i=1}^{n} \left(\dfrac{Q_{ij}}{E} \right) PIU_i$

    C. $EIU_i = \sum_{i=1}^{n} EQ_{ij}\, PIU_i$

    D. $EIU_i = \sum_{i=1}^{n} \dfrac{PIU_i}{EQ_{ij}}$

55. Match List–I with List–II and choose the correct answer from the codes given below :

List–I (Scales used in EIA methods)	List–II (Example)
(a) Nominal	1. Temperature (degrees)
(b) Ordinal	2. Species classification
(c) Interval	3. Map scale
(d) Ratio	4. Worst to best

Codes :

	(a)	(b)	(c)	(d)
A.	1	2	3	4
B.	4	3	2	1
C.	3	1	4	2
D.	2	4	1	3

56. Risk assessment in EIA does not involve
    A. Maximum credible analysis
    B. Hazard and operability studies
    C. Preparation of disaster management plan
    D. Assessment of economic benefit arising out of a project

57. In a gravity flow autoclave, medical waste is subjected to a temperature
    A. $> 120°C$
    B. $< 100°C$
    C. $> 300°C$
    D. $> 800°C$

58. Hierarchy of priorities in hazardous waste management is
    A. Eliminate generation → Reduce generation → Recycle/Reuse → Treatment → Disposal
    B. Reduce generation → Eliminate generation → Recycle/Reuse → Treatment → Disposal
    C. Eliminate generation → Reduce generation → Treatment → Recycle/Reuse → Disposal
    D. Reduce generation → Eliminate generation → Treatment → Recycle/Reuse → Disposal

59. Public Liability Insurance Act was enacted in the year
    A. 1991
    B. 1993
    C. 1995
    D. 1997

60. Match List–I with List–II and choose the correct answer from the codes given below :

List–I (Convention)	List–II (Year)
(a) Convention for the protection of the ozone layer	1. 1979
(b) Conservation of migratory species of wild animals	2. 1985
(c) Kyoto protocol	3. 1982
(d) UN Convention on the law of the sea	4. 1997

Codes :

	(a)	(b)	(c)	(d)
A.	2	1	4	3
B.	2	4	3	1
C.	3	1	2	4
D.	1	2	3	4

61. Match List–I with List–II and choose the correct answer from the codes given below :

List–I (Acts)	List–II (Year when enacted)
(a) Wildlife Protection Act	1. 1980
(b) Forest Conservation Act	2. 1972
(c) Air (Prevention and Control of Pollution) Act	3. 1974
(d) Water (Prevention and Control of Pollution) Act	4. 1981

Codes :

	(a)	(b)	(c)	(d)
A.	2	1	4	3
B.	1	2	3	4
C.	3	2	1	4
D.	4	3	2	1

62. **Assertion (A)** : χ^2 distribution is a non-parametric distribution.
Reason (R) : χ^2 is a sample statistic having no corresponding population parameter.
Codes :
A. Both (A) and (R) are correct and (R) is the correct explanation of (A).
B. Both (A) and (R) are correct, but (R) is not the correct explanation of (A).
C. (A) is true, but (R) is false.
D. Both (A) and (R) are false.

63. In a simple regression analysis of y on x, the standard error of estimate of y on x, $S_{yx} = 5$, number of observations N is 30, and $\Sigma y^2 = 2000$. The unexplained variance is
A. 1500   B. 750
C. 500   D. 250

64. Two normal populations have variances $\sigma_1^2 = 10$ and $\sigma_1^2 = 20$. Two random samples of sizes 25 and 20, independently selected from these populations have variances of $S_1^2 = 8$ and $S_2^2 = 15$, respectively. What is the $F_{(24, 19)}$ statistic?
A. 1
B. 2
C. 2.81
D. 3.6

65. **Assertion (A)** : A matrix is non-singular if and only if none of its eigen values is zero.
Reason (R) : The product of the eigen values equals the determinant of a matrix.
Codes :
A. Both (A) and (R) are correct and (R) is the correct explanation of (A).
B. Both (A) and (R) are correct, but (R) is not the correct explanation of (A).
C. (A) is correct, but (R) is false.
D. Both (A) and (R) are false.

66. In Gaussian Plume Model assume $\sigma_z = cx$, where c is a constant and ratio of σ_y to σ_z to be a constant. If H is the effective height of the stack, the maximum concentration at a distance (x) from the stack is proportional to
A. H^{-1} B. H^{-2}
C. $\exp(-H^2)$ D. $H^{-3/2}$

67. The Pearson Linear correlation coefficient (r) for the following paired data (x, y) : (2, 1.4) (4, 1.8), (8, 2.1), (8, 2.3), (9, 2.6) is
A. 0.623   B. −0.572
C. 0.957   D. 0.823

68. In a rough terrain the wind speed at a height of 10 m is 2.5 m/s. The wind speed at an elevation of 300 m will be
A. 4.9 m/s   B. 1.2 m/s
C. 3.6 m/s   D. 7.9 m/s

69. In the context of REDD⁺ initiatives the land clearing in forest areas is primarily concerned with
A. Physical resources of the area
B. Ecology of the area
C. Carbon budget of the area
D. Water resources of the area

70. What was the objective of Basel Convention (1989) under UNEP?
I. Minimize generation of hazardous wastes in terms of quantity and hazardousness
II. Disposal of hazardous wastes as close to the source of generation as possible.
III. Reduce the movement of hazardous wastes.
Choose the correct code :
A. I and II only   B. II and III only
C. I, II and III   D. I only

71. Global Warming Potential (GWP) of a greenhouse gas (GHG) is a comparison of global warming impact between
   A. 1 kg of GHG and 1 kg of methane
   B. 1 kg of GHG and 1 kg of CO_2
   C. 1 kg of GHG and 1 kg of N_2O
   D. 1 kg of GHG and 1 kg of CFC-11

72. Which of the following mixture of gases is called biogas?
   A. CO_2, CH_4, NH_3, H_2S, H_2O (vapour)
   B. CO, CH_4, NH_3, H_2S, H_2O (vapour)
   C. CO_2, CH_4, N_2O, NH_3, H_2O (vapour)
   D. CO_2, NO_x, H_2O, CH_4

73. Environmental ethics deal with moral relationship of human beings to
   A. the value and moral status of the environment and its non-human contents
   B. the values that are important to development and economic growth
   C. the conservation values of selected species
   D. the development of genetically modified organisms

74. The major source of BaP (Benzo-a-pyrene) in atmospheric environment is
   A. residential wood burning
   B. gasoline
   C. coal tar
   D. cooked meat

75. Match the List–I with List–II and choose the correct answer from the codes given below :

List–I (Materials)	List–I (Applications)
(a) Trichloroethylene	1. Gasoline
(b) Toluene	2. Wood treatment
(c) Zinc	3. Dry cleaning
(d) Phenol	4. Mining

Codes :

	(a)	(b)	(c)	(d)
A.	3	1	4	2
B.	2	3	1	4
C.	1	4	2	3
D.	4	2	3	1

ANSWERS

1	2	3	4	5	6	7	8	9	10
B	A	B	C	A	A	D	B	D	A
11	12	13	14	15	16	17	18	19	20
A	A	B	A	C	D	A	D	B	D
21	22	23	24	25	26	27	28	29	30
B	D	D	D	B	A	A	A	C	B
31	32	33	34	35	36	37	38	39	40
C	A	D	D	D	A	A	B	C	A
41	42	43	44	45	46	47	48	49	50
A	A	B	A	C	D	A	C	A	C
51	52	53	54	55	56	57	58	59	60
A	B	B	C	D	D	A	A	A	A
61	62	63	64	65	66	67	68	69	70
A	A	B	A	A	B	C	A	C	C
71	72	73	74	75					
B	A	A	A	A					

SOME SELECTED EXPLANATORY ANSWERS

1. **Atmospheric Stability and Instability**
Atmospheric stability : The resistance of the atmosphere to vertical motion.

Temperature distribution and lapse rates, where that temperatures normally increases as we get closer to the earth's surface. This is due in part to the greater molecular activity of denser, more compressed air at lower attitudes. These conditions change throughout a 24-hour period, as the daytime solar heating and nighttime heat loss to and through the atmosphere distributions.

Temperature Distribution of vertically moving air

The term 'adiabatic process' which simply means warning by compression, or cooling by expansion, without a transfer of heat or mass into a system. As air moves up or down within the atmosphere, it is affected by this process. This temperature difference will be 5-1/2 degree decreases per 1000 feet increase in attitude. This is also terned the dry adiabatic lapse rate. The atmosphere may or may not have a temperature distribution that fits the dry adiabatic lapse rate.

The actual lapse rate may be greater of less the dry adiabatic lapse rate and may change by levels in the atmosphere. This variation from the dry adiabatic lapse rate is what determines whether the air is stable or unstable. If the air is unstable. The vertical movement of air is encouraged and this tend to increase fire activity. If the air is stable, vertical movement of air is discouraged, and this usually. The importance of the atmosphere property will became evident by the time we have completed this unit.

Dry Lapse Rates : The actual temperature lapse rate in a given portion of the atmosphere could range from a plus 15 per 1000 feet to a minus 15 per 1000 feet. These would represent the extremes of very stable air to very unstable air. Rather than be concerned with all of these degrees of stability or instability, we usually describe the atmosphere as falling into one of five conditions.

The vertical air temperature distribution in the atmosphere is highly variable. For dry air it ranges as follows:

1. **Very stable :** Temperature increases with increase in altitude. This is a 'plus' temperature lapse rate, or an inversion.

2. **Stable :** Temperature lapse rate is less than the dry adiabatic rate, but temperature decreases with altitude increase.

3. **Neutral :** Temperature lapse rate is the same as the dry adiabatic rate of 5.5 degrees Fahrenheit per 1000 feet increase.

4. **Unstable :** Temperature lapse rate is greater than the dry adiabatic rate. It may be 6 degrees Fahrenheit or more.

5. **Very Stable :** Temperature lapse rate is much greater than the dry adiabatic rate and it called super-adiabatic.

Therefore (B) Neutral : the temperature lapse rate is the same as the dry adiabatic rate of 5.5 degree Fahrenheit per 1000 feet increase.

2. In the ecosystem, the flow energy follows the law of thermodynamics, it is because the flow of energy in the ecosystemic is unidirectional. The energy is lost from one trophic level to other is 80-90% during the transfarmation of energy. Hence, both the statements are true and reason (R) is the correct explanation of assertion (A).

3. (a) $\Delta G = RT \ln \dfrac{V_1}{V_2}$

   (b) $\Delta G° = -n \, FE°$

   (c) $\Delta S = nR \ln \dfrac{V_2}{V_1}$

   (d) $\Delta H = \Delta E + P\Delta V$

5. **Electro-magnetic Spectrum :** The electro-megnetic spectrum is a way of visualizing the frequency and wavelength proportions of different forms of energy. Electromagnetic radiation has properties of both waves and particles. We divide the electromagnetic spectrum in the UV range for medical purposes.

- UVA is found in the region between 320 and 400 nm (nm = Nanometer = 1 billionth of a meter) and is the least powerful wavelength band of UV radiation.

- UVB is found in the region between 280 and 320 nm. It comprises the wavelengths primarily associated with erythema (sunburn), is also necessary for the production of vitamin D in the skin and is primarily responsible for stimulating increased milamine production.

UV–B wavelength (at 305 nm) have 1,000 times more erythemal power than UVA wavelengths.

UV–C is found in the region between approximately 200-280 nm and is called germicidal UV because of its proven effectiveness in killing single cell organisms. Solar radiations in the UVC range is absorbed almost entirely by the atmosphere and that is fortunate considering that even a short overexposure to UVC is very harmful to eyes and causes severe erythema (sunburn). UVC is emitted by High Intensity Discharge (HID) lamps, therefore these lamps require special filter glass, its contain the output of the UVC spectrum.

Therefore the wavelength range of UV-C radiations is 200-280 nm.

9. The cells grown in a medium containing phospherous (P-32) will show radio labelling in nucleic acids.

11. In the Western Pacific Ocean, the marine biodiveristy tends to be highest in mid-latitudes in all oceans along coasts. It is because the temperature of surface of sea/ocean along the coasts in the western pacific is the highest.

Hence, both (A) and (R) are true and (R) is the correct explanation of (A).

14. (a) Lithosene   – rock
    (b) Psammosere – sand
    (c) Hydroser   – aquatic (life) aquatic
    (d) Xerosere   – dry habitate.

16. The symbolises correct sequence in hydrosere is

Diatoms → hydrilla → wolffia cyperus → populus.

17. The eco-systems in the hydrosphere are callled aquatic eco-system. For example, include ponds, lakes, rivers, open ocean, coral reefs, estuaries months of rivers or oceans inlets (where salt water and fresh mix and coastal and island wettends) such as swamps marshes and pairie pothdes that are covered with water all or part of the lime. The major differences between these eco-systems are the result of differences in the amount of various nutrients in the depth of sunlight presentation and differences in average water temperature. Therefore, all the class of aquatic eco-systems based on the salinity levels are freshwater eco-systems, brackish eco-system and the marine eco-system. Hence (A) is not a clause of aquatic ecosystem based on the salinity level.

18. **K- Strategists :** These are large organisms that have relatively longer life and provide care for their offsprings.

The organism which stablise their population at the carrying capacity for the area. Hence, all the statements (A), (B) and (C) are correct.

20. Theaceae   → *Camellia caduca*
    Pinaceae   → *Picea brachytyla*
    Liliaceae   → *Colchicum luteum*
    Orchidaceae   → *Arachnantha clarkei*
    Hence option (D) is correct.

23. **Biogeochemical Cycles :** The eco-systems are black boxes for many of the processes that

takes place within them. The boundries of the eco-systems are the permeable to some degree, from one eco-systems to another eco-system via imparts and exports, the energy and the nutrients are transformed. Hence, all the statements are correct. Therefore, (D) is the correct option.

31. Geothermal energy is thermal energy generated and stored in the earth. Thermal energy is the energy that determines the temperature of matter. The geothermal energy of the Earth's crust originates from the original formation of the planet (20%) and form radioactive decay of minerals (80%). The geothermal gradient, which is the difference in temperature between the core of the planet and its surface, drives a continuous conduction of thermal energy in the form of heat from the core to the surface. Geothermal energy is cost effective reliable, sustainable and environmentally friendly, but has historically been limited to areas near tectonic plate boundaries. Recent technological advances have dramatically expanded the range and size of viable resources, especially for applications such as home heating, opening a potential for widespread exploitation. Geothermal wells release greenhouse gases trapped deep within the earth, but these emissions are much lower per energy unit than those of fossil fuels. As a result, geothermal power has the potential to help mitigate global warming if widely deployed in place of fossil fuels.

The Earth geothermal resources are theoretically more than adequate to supply humanity's energy needs, but only a very small fraction may be profitably exploited. Drilling and exploration for deep resources is very expensive. Forecasts for the future of geothermal power depend on assumptions about technology, energy prices, subsidies, and interest rates. Pilot programs like EWEB's customer opt in Green Power Program show that customers would to pay a little more for a renewable energy source like geothermal. But as a result of government assisted research and industry experience, cost of generating geothermal power has decreased by 25% over the past two decades. In 2001, geothermal energy cost between two and ten US cents per kWh.

35. **Liquid Helium :** The chemical element helium exists in a liquid form only at the extremely low temperature of –269 degrees celsius (about 4 kelvin or –452.2 degrees Fahrenheit). Its boiling point and critical point depend on which isotope of helium is present : the common isotope helium 4 or the rare isotope helium-3. These are the only two stable isotopes of helium. The density of liquid helium-4 at its boiling point and a pressure of one atmosphere (101.3 kilo pascals) is about 125 grams per liter.

38. **Black Carbon Aerosols :** The sun provides the energy that drives Earth's climate, but not all of the energy that reaches the top of the atmosphere finds its way to the surface. That is because aerosols and clouds seeded by them reflect about a quarter of the sun's energy back to space. Aerosols play an important role in Earth's climate. Most aerosols are brighter than land or ocean, and cool the earth by reflecting sunlight back to space. Different aerosols scatter or absorb sunlight to varying degrees, depending on their physical properties. Climatologists describe these scattering and absorbing properties as the 'direct effect' of aerosole on Earth's radiation field. However, since aerosols comprise such a broad collection of particles with different properties, the overall effect is anything but simple.

Although most aerosols reflect sunlight, some also absorb it. An aerosols effect on light depends primarily on the composition and colour of the particles. Broadly speaking, bright coloured or translucent particles tend to reflect radiation in all directions and back towards space. Darker aerosols can absorb significant amounts of light.

Pure sulfates and nitrates reflect nearly all radiation they encounter cooking the atmosphere. Black carbon in contrast, absorbs radiation readily, warming the atmosphere but also shading the surface organic carbon, sometimes called brown carbon or organic matter, has a warming influence on the atmosphere depending on the brightness of the underlying ground. Dust impacts radiation to varying degrees, depending on the composition of the minerals that comprise the dust grains, and whether they are coated with black or brown carbon. Salt particles tend to reflect all the sunlight they encounter. Black carbon aerosols, similar to the 500 in a chimney, absorb sunlight rather than reflecting it. This warms the layer of the atmosphere carrying the black carbon, but also shades and cools the surface below.

Aerosols can have a major impact on climate when they scatter light. In 1991 the eruption of Mount Pinatubo in the Phillippines ejected more than 20 million tons of sulfer dioxide– a gas that reacts with other substances to produce sulfate aerosol as high as 60 kilometers (37 miles) above the surface, creating particles in the stratosphere. Those bright particles remained above the clouds and didn't get washed from the sky by rain; they settled only after several years climatologists predicted global temperatures would drop as a result of that global sulfate infusion. They were right: Following the eruption, global temperatures abruptly dipped by about a half-dgree (0.6°C) for about two years. And Pinatubo isn't a unique event large, temperature–altering eruptions occur about once per decade. Large volcanic eruptions may lift sulfate aerosols into the stratosphere, which usually cools the global, climate for the following year or two.

In addition to scattering or absorbing radiation, aerosols can albebo, of the planet. Bright surfaces reflect radiation and cool the climate, whereas darker surfaces absorb radiation and produce a warming effect. White sheets of sea ice, for example, reflect a great deal of radiation, whereas darker surfaces, such as the ocean, tend to absorb solar radiation and have a net warming effect.

Aerosols particularly black carbon, can alter reflectively by depositing a layer of dark residue on ice and other bright surfaces. In the Arctic especially, aerosols from wildfires and industrial pollution are likely hastening the meling of ice.

Dark aerosols dramatically change the reflectivity of the Earth's surface when they land on snow. Black ash covered the summit of New Zealand's Mount Ruapehu after an eruption in 2007, but was soon covered by fresh snow, long-term accumulation of black carbon aerosols in the Arctic and Himalaya is leading to increased melting of snow.

Scientists believe the cooling from sulfates and other reflective aerosols. Overwhelms the warming effect of black carbon and other absorbing aerosols over the planet.

Despite considerable advances in recent decades, estimating the direct climate impacts of aerosols remains an immature science of the 25 climate models considered by the Fourth. Intergovernmental Panel on climate (IPCC), only a handful considered the direct effects of aerosols types other than sufates.

Therefore Black carbon aerosols causes warming of atmosphere but cooling of the earth's surface.

41. Asphyxia or asphyxiation is a condition of severaly deficient supply of oxygen to the body that arises from abnormal breathing. An example of asphyxia is choking. Asphyxia causes generalized hypoxia, which primarily

affects the tissues and organs. There are many circumstances that can induce asphyxia, all of which are characterized by an inability of an individual to acquire sufficient oxygen through breathing for an extended period of time. These circumstances can include but are not limited to the constriction or obstruction of airways, such as from asthma, laryngospasm, or simple blockage from the pressure of foreign materials; from being in environments where oxygen is not readily accessible, such as underwater, in a low oxygen atmosphere, or in a vaccum; environments where sufficiently oxygenated air is present, but cannot be adequately breathed because of air contamination such as excessive smoke. Asphyxia can cause come or death.

48. An Integrated Gastrification combined cycle (IGCC) is a technology that uses a gas fier to turn coal and other carbon based fuels into gas, i.e., synthesis gas. It then removes the impurities from the synthesis gas before it is combusted some of these pollutants, such as particulates and sulphur can be turn into reusable by-products. This results in the lower emission of sulphur dioxides parculates and mercury (Hg) with additional process equipments. The carbon in the synthesis gas can be shifted to hydrogen (H_2) via the water gas shift reaction, resulting is nearly carbon free fuel. This resulting CO_2 from the shift reaction can be compressed and stored. Excess heat from the primary combstion and synthesis gas fixed generation is then passed to a steam cycle similar to the combined cycle. This results in improved efficiency composed to conventional pulverized coal.

61. (a) **Wildlife Protection Act :** In India, the Wildlife Protection Act of 1972 was amended thrice (in 1983, 1986 and 1991). The wildlife crime control Bureau has been constituted through amendment of the Wildlife (Protection) Act, 1972 in

2008. The powers and function of the bureau have been defined u/s 38Z of the act. Wildlife Protection Act, 1972 aimed at rational and modern wildlife management.

(b) **Forest Conservation Act, 1980 :** The Forest Conservation Act, 1980, amended in 1988.

(c) **Air (Prevention and Control of Pollution) Act, 1981 :** The Central Enactment came into force from 16-05-1981. This act was intended to achive effective contral over air pollution caused by various regions. The Act contemplates establishment of the central and state Boards rested with wide powers to enable them to devise means to improve the quality of air and to prevent, control or abate pollution in the country.

The Act is visualized as a measure to implemented some of the decisions taken at the UN conference on Human Environment held at Stockholm in June 1972 to take appropriates steps for the prevention of the natural resources of the earth and central the pollution.

(d) **The Water (Prevention and Control of Pollution) Act, 1974 :** This comprehensive piece of legistation was passed under Article 252 of the constitution mainly with the object of prevention and control of water pollution. The act contemplates establishment of the Central Board of Prevention and Control of Water Pollution and similar Boards at the state level. The penalties against the pollution vary from regrous imprisonment for 6 months to 6 years.

62. χ^2 distribution is a non-parametric distribution, because it is a sample statistic having no corresponding population parameter. Then, both (A) and (R) are true and former is correct explanation of latter.

72. CO_2, CH_4, NH_3, H_2S, H_2O (vapour)

Biogas typically refers to a mixture of gases produced by the breakdown of organic matter in the absence of oxygen. Biogas can be produced from regionally available raw materials such as recycled waste. It is a renewable energy source and it many cases exerts a very small carbon footprint.

Biogas is produced by anaerobic digestion with anaerobic bacteria or fermentation of biodegrable materials such as manure, sewage, municipal waste, green waste, plant material and crops. It is primarily methane (CH_4) and carbon dioxide (CO_2) and may have small amounts of hydrogen sulphide (H_2S), moisture and siloxanes.

The gases methance, hydrogen and carbon monoxide (CO) can be combusted or oxidized with oxygen. This energy release allows biogas to be used as a fuel; it can be used for any heating purpose, such as cooking. It can also be used in gas engine to convert the energy in the gas into electricity and heat.

Biogas can be compressed, the same way natural gas is compressed to CNG and used to power motor vehicles. In the UK, for example, biogas is estimated to have the potential to replace around 17% of vehicle fuel. It qualifies for renewable energy subsidies in some parts of the world. Biogas can be cleaned and upgraded to natural gas thousands when it becomes bio methane.

UGC-NET ENVIRONMENTAL SCIENCE, JUNE 2013

PAPER-II

Note : *This paper contains fifty (50) objective type questions, each question carrying two (2) marks. Attempt all the questions.*

1. **Assertion (A) :** Every country should integrate the principles of sustainable development into its policies and programmes.
   Reason (R) : Environmental resources are a Nation's wealth.
   Choose the correct code from the following:
   A. Both (A) and (R) are true and (R) is the correct explanation of (A).
   B. Both (A) and (R) are true, but (R) is not the correct explanation of (A).
   C. (A) is true, but (R) is false.
   D. (A) is false, but (R) is true.

2. Wind rose represents statistical distribution of
   A. Wind velocity in vector form
   B. Wind speeds in scalar form
   C. Wind speeds in π diagram
   D. Wind speeds in the form of histograms

3. In the redox reaction given below, which one of the substrates in forward reaction is oxidized?
   $$2Fe^{3+} + H_2 \rightarrow 2Fe^{2+} + 2H^+$$
   A. Fe^{3+} B. H_2
   C. H^+ D. Fe^{2+}

4. If soil in a given area is wetted and allowed to drain till percolation is stopped, the amount of water thus retained is called
   A. Storage capacity
   B. Capillary capacity
   C. Hygroscopic capacity
   D. Field capacity

5. Quantity of 5M HCl required for preparing 1000 ml of 0.1 M HCl is,
   A. 20 ml   B. 2 ml
   C. 200 ml   D. 100 ml

6. The method which can be used for the softening of water having high calcium, high magnesium-carbonate hardness and some non-carbonate hardness
   A. single-stage lime process.
   B. excess lime process.
   C. single stage lime-soda ash process.
   D. excess lime-soda ash process.

7. Spotted deer, Asiatic wild ass, Black buck are,
   A. Endangered species B. Vulnerable species
   C. Threatened species D. Key species

8. Specific mortality of members of a population is expressed by
   A. Life table
   B. Survivorship curve
   C. Rate of mortality
   D. Rate of fecundity

9. Which group of vertebrate comprises maximum number of endangered species?
   A. Fish   B. Amphibia
   C. Reptiles   D. Birds

10. Under anaerobic condition denitrifying *Pseudomonas* changes,
    A. Nitrate to molecular nitrogen
    B. Nitrate to ammonia
    C. Nitrate to Nitrite
    D. Nitrite to Nitrate

11. The Phenomenon of having higher number of species in ecotone is called
    A. Dominance effect   B. Edge effect
    C. Abundance   D. Frequency

12. Which specific common feature is not found in zooplankton and rabbit ?
    A. Both are animals
    B. Both are primary consumers
    C. Both are carnivores
    D. Both are herbivores

13. The following exogenous and endogenous factors are the cause of extinction of animal species :
   I. Ecological niche
   II. Decrease in reproductive potency.
   III. Lesser adaptability to fluctuating environment.
   Choose the correct answer from the codes given below:
   Codes :
   A. I only   B. II only
   C. I and II   D. I, II and III

14. Positive mass balance of glaciers has been recently reported from
   A. Eastern Himalayas   B. Nepal Himalayas
   C. Western Himalayas   D. Karakoram

15. Which of the following will lead to reduction in greenhouse gases in atmosphere?
   A. Increased chemical weathering of rocks.
   B. Volcanic eruption
   C. Lowering of mean sea level
   D. An increase in melting of glacial ice

16. The unconsolidated material with highest permeability is
   A. Landslide with clayey component
   B. Altered volcanic ash
   C. Well sorted alluvial sand
   D. Buried mud flows

17. Which of the following component of cryosphere has the longest life ?
   A. Sea ice   B. Icebergs
   C. Valley glaciers   D. Ice sheets

18. Aerobic bacteria is most active in
   A. Moist and saturated soil
   B. Moist and non-saturated soil
   C. Alluvial soil
   D. Permafrost

19. Andisols are formed by
   A. Biological activity B. Erosion by wind
   C. Erosion by waves   D. Volcanoes

20. In case of photovoltaic cell, the maximum theoretical efficiency of conversion is
   A. ~ 45%   B. ~ 30%
   C. ~ 25%   D. ~ 50%

21. Consider an ideal wind power generator, if the wind speed increases 3 times, the power output would increase by how many times?
   A. 3   B. 9
   C. 27   D. 81

22. Identify the correct sequence in increasing order of total CO_2 emissions from various countries at present.
   A. Britain < India < China < USA
   B. India < Britain < China < USA
   C. Britain < USA < India < China
   D. Britain < India < USA < China

23. Arsenic compounds cause
   A. Dwarfism   B. Dermatitis
   C. Thyrotoxicosis   D. Wilson's disease

24. What is the pE value in an acid mine water sample having
   $[Fe^{2+}] = 7.03 \times 10^{-3}$ M and
   $[Fe^{3+}] = 3.71 \times 10^{-4}$ M
   A. 10.5   B. 12.5
   C. 14.5   D. 18.5

25. **Assertion (A) :** Chronic exposure to ozone is a possible contributor to forest decline.
   Reason (R) : Surface ozone is a greenhouse gas.
   Identify the correct code:
   A. Both (A) and (R) are true and (R) is the correct explanation of (A).
   B. Both (A) and (R) are true, but (R) is not the correct explanation of (A).
   C. (A) is true, but (R) is false.
   D. (A) is false, but (R) is true.

26. Identify the most dominant pollutant in terms of its concentration levels in urban atmosphere.
   A. Oxides of nitrogen   B. Oxides of sulphur
   C. Particulate matter   D. Carbon monoxide

27. The main constituents of photochemical smog are
   A. Oxides of sulphur and CO
   B. Oxides of sulphur and hydrocarbons
   C. Oxides of nitrogen and CO
   D. Oxides of nitrogen, hydrocarbons and ozone

28. The air borne fraction of carbon is
   A. ~ 0.72   B. ~ 0.62
   C. ~ 0.46   D. ~ 0.38

29. The noise index L_{eq} is used for noise standards in ambient environment of urban areas. The prescribed duration of the integration associated with L_{eq} is
   A. 12 hours
   B. 8 hours
   C. 1 hour
   D. 30 minutes

30. In alkaline soils, which of the following is not present in soluble state?
   A. Phosphorous
   B. Calcium
   C. Nitrates
   D. Potassium

31. Which one of the following is not a post audit activity under environmental audit process?
   A. Review of draft report by Law department.
   B. Issue of final report to functional specialist.
   C. Develop action plan to establish responsibility.
   D. Report audit findings.

32. Which one of the following pairs is correctly matched?
   A. Specification for   ISO 14001
       environmental management system
   B. Environmental performance   ISO 14040
       evaluation
   C. Guidelines for environmental   ISO 14000
       auditing
   D. Environmental labels   ISO 14004
       and declaration

33. In accordance with the Indian EIA notification 2006, within how many days if Environmental Appraisal Committee do not specify the Terms of Reference, the proponent can go ahead with its own Terms of Reference.
   A. 15 days   B. 45 days
   C. 60 days   D. 90 days

34. Which is the correct sequence for impact assessment process in EIA ?
   A. Description of Environment → Identification of impacts → Prediction of impacts → Evaluation of impacts → Identification of mitigation needs.
   B. Identification of impacts → Prediction of impacts → Evaluation of impacts → Identification of mitigation needs.
   C. Identification of impacts → Description of Environment → Prediction of impacts → Evaluation of impacts → Identification of mitigation needs.
   D. Prediction of impacts → Identification of impacts → Description of environment → Evaluation of impacts → Identification of mitigation needs.

35. Quantifying the energy and raw material requirement as a part of life cycle assessment, is termed as
   A. Life Cycle improvement analysis.
   B. Life Cycle impact analysis.
   C. Life Cycle inventory.
   D. Life Cycle pre-requisites.

36. Which of the following pertains to "high-waste approach" in dealing with the solid and hazardous wastes?
   A. Burying and burning
   B. Recycling
   C. Composting
   D. Reusing

37. **Assertion (A) :** Dumping of sewage to river water may decrease oxygen even below 4 mg/l.
   Reason (R) : Dumping of sewage pollutes river water heavily.
   Identify the correct answer:
   A. Both (A) and (R) are true with (R) being the correct explanation.
   B. Both (A) and (R) are true, but (R) is not the correct explanation.
   C. (A) is true, but (R) is wrong.
   D. Both (A) and (R) are wrong.

38. In most of the studies, a large sample size is anticipated to
   A. get a low level of precision.
   B. maximize the sampling error.
   C. get a high level of precision.
   D. maximize the standard deviation.

39. The geometric mean of 4, 8 and 16 is
   A. 9.3   B. 8.0
   C. 4.8   D. 10.2

40. The covariance between two data of N observations each represented by variables X and Y is given by (A)

A. $\dfrac{\Sigma(X-\overline{X})(Y-\overline{Y})}{N^2}$

B. $\dfrac{\Sigma(X-\overline{X})^2(Y-\overline{Y})^2}{N}$

C. $\dfrac{\Sigma(X-\overline{X})^2(Y-\overline{Y})^2}{N^2}$

D. $\dfrac{\Sigma(X-\overline{X})(Y-\overline{Y})}{N}$

41. The mean and standard deviation of a Binomial distribution are 9 and 1, respectively. The first moment of the distribution is
A. 9
B. 3
C. 1
D. 0

42. Which one of the following is used in manufacturing flexible plastic bags and sheets?
A. Polystyrene (PS)
B. Polyethylene terephthalate (PET)
C. Low density polyethylene (LDPE)
D. TEFLON

43. Which one of the following is a non-formal environment education and awareness programme?
A. Environmental appreciation courses.
B. National Environment Awareness Campaign.
C. Environmental Education in school system.
D. Environmental Management Business Studies.

44. Bioparks are conceived, developed and managed with a goal of conservation of biodiversity through
(i) development of educational and scientific activities.
(ii) promoting silviculture and monoculture.
(iii) promoting local community welfare without harming the natural habitat.

Choose the correct answer from the codes:
Codes :
A. (i) and (ii)
B. (ii) and (iii)
C. (i) and (iii)
D. (i), (ii) and (iii)

45. In about a 7 metre deep pond the series of vegetation development will be
A. Submerged → Floating → Reed → Herb
B. Floating → Submerged → Reed → Herb
C. Floating → Reed → Submerged → Herb
D. Submerged → Reed → Floating → Herb

46. In terrestrial ecosystems, roughly how much NPP ends up being broken down by decomposers?
A. 90%
B. 70%
C. 50%
D. 10%

47. Which of the following BOD level waste water is permitted to be released inlands by industries under water (Prevention and Control of Pollution) Act, 1974 ?
A. 30 mg/l
B. 80 mg/l
C. 100 mg/l
D. 150 mg/l

48. Hydraulic conductivity is a function of
A. medium alone
B. fluid alone
C. either fluid or medium
D. both fluid and medium

49. Dachigan sanctuary is associated with
A. Hangul
B. Rhinoceros
C. Barking deer
D. Leopard

50. Rio + 20 summit was held in
A. Durban
B. Johannesburg
C. Rio de Janeiro
D. Cancun

ANSWERS

1	2	3	4	5	6	7	8	9	10
B	A	B	D	A	D	B	B	D	A

11	12	13	14	15	16	17	18	19	20
B	C	D	D	A	C	D	B	D	A

21	22	23	24	25	26	27	28	29	30
C	D	B	C	B	D	D	C	B	A

31	32	33	34	35	36	37	38	39	40
D	A	C	A	C	A	A	C	B	A

41	42	43	44	45	46	47	48	49	50
D	C	B	C	A	A	A	D	A	C

SOME SELECTED EXPLANATORY ANSWERS

2. The movement of air from higher pressure to lower pressure is an attempt to balance out the pressure differences. As the wind travels it is diverted to its right in the northern hemisphere and to its left in the southern hemisphere *i.e.*, The velocity of wind is represented in the vector form.

Wind rose is a diagram indicating the frequency and strengths of winds in a definite locality for a given period of years.

3. **Redox reaction :** A chemical reaction in which change in valency of elements takes place is called redox reaction. In these reactions, both oxidation and reduction processes take place simultaneously. One substance is oxidised and other is reduced in these reactions.

In the reaction,

$2Fe^{3+} + H_2 \rightarrow 2Fe^{2+} + 2H^+$

H_2 is one of the substrates in forward reaction that is oxidised.

4. When a soil holds all the water it can, but no gravitational water, it is said to be its field capacity. This is generally defined as the water content of an undistributed soil after it is saturated by rainfall and drainage of gravitational water has completely stopped. In practice for determining field capacity, soil is thus sampled about 48 hrs after rain. This value for a soil may be taken as constant. Thus, field capacity of soil may be taken as the total amount of capillary, hygroscopic and combined water plus water vapours.

5. 0.1 M HCl is required 1000 ml

∴ 1 M HCl is required = 1000 × 0.1

∴ 5 M HCl is required = $\dfrac{1000 \times 0.1}{5}$ = 20 Ml.

6. The hardness of water is due to presence of the bicarbonates of calcium and magnesium. Excess of lime-soda ash method can be used for the softening of water having high calcium, high magnesium carbonate hardness and some non-carbonate hardness.

7. Vulnerable species are likely to move into this endangered category in the near future if the causal factors continue to operate. These are species, whose populations have been seriously depleted and also those whose populations are still abundant throughout their range. Spotted deer, asiatic wild ass, black buck etc. are the examples of vulnerable species.

8. Mortality may be expressed as the number of individuals dying in a given period (death per time) or as the specific rate terms of units of the total population.

A birth-death ratio $\left(100 \times \dfrac{\text{births}}{\text{deaths}}\right)$ is called vital index. For a population, the important thing is not which members die but which members survive. Thus, survival rates are of much interest than the death rates.

Survival rates are generally expressed by survivorship curves.

Survivorship curves : The pattern of mortality with age is best illustrated by survivorship curves which plot the number surviving to a particular age. There are three general types of survivorship curves which represent different nature of survivors in different types of population

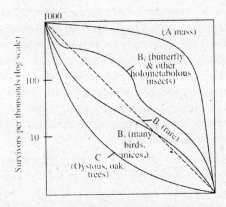

9. Birds group of vertebrate comprises maximum number of endangered species.

10. Ammonia is changed to nitrite by nitrite bacteria (e.g., nitrosomonas, nitrococcus) which is then oxidised to nitrate by nitrate bacteria. There are some bacteria which reduce nitrates and change them into free nitrogen. They are called denitrifying bacteria (e.g., Thiobacillus, denitrificans, pseudomonas denitrificans).

11. Ecotone is a translational area of vegetation between two different plant communities, such as forest and grassland. It has some of the characteristics of each bordering biological community and often contains species not found in the overlapping communities. An ecotone may exist along a broad belt or in a small pocket, such as forest clearing, where two local communities blend together. The influence of the two bordering communities on each other is known as the edge effect. An ecotonal area often has a higher density of organisms of one species and a greater number of species then are found in either flanking community.

12. Zooplankton and rabbit are the small animals, they depend on plants only. They are called herbivores. Carnivores are the animals they depend upon the flesh of animals. That's why their specific common feature is not found in zooplankton and rabbit.

13. An ecological niche is a description of all the physical, chemical and biological factors that a species needs to live, grow and reproduce in an ecosystem, decrease in reproductivity, potency and lesser adaptability to fluctuating environmental factors are the cause of extinction of animal species.

14. **Mass balance glaciers :** Crucial to the survival of a glacier is its mass balance, the difference between accumulation and ablation (sublimation and melting). Climate change may cause variations in both temperature and snowfall, causing changes in mass balance. Changes in mass balance control a glacier's long-term behaviour and are the most sensitive climate indicators on a glacier. From 1980-2008 the mean cumulative mass loss of glaciers reporting mass balance to the World Glacier Monitoring Service is −12m. This includes 19 consecutive years of negative mass balances.

A glacier with a sustained negative balance is out of equilibrium and will retreat, while one with a sustained positive balance is out of equilibrium and will advance. Glacier retreat results in the loss of the low elevation region of the glacier. Since higher elevations are cooler than lower ones, the disappearance of the lowest portion of the glacier reduces overall ablation, thereby increasing mass balance and potentially reestablishing equilibrium. However, if the mass balance of a significant portion of the accumulation zone of the glacier is negative, it is in disequilibrium with the local climate. Such a glacier will melt away with a continuation of this local climate. The key symptom of a glacier in disequilibrium is thinning along the entire length of the glacier. For example, Easton Glacier will likely shrink to half its size, but at a slowing rate of reduction, and stabilize at that size, despite the warmer temperature, over a few decades. However, the Grinnell Glacier will shrink at an increasing rate until it disappears. The difference is that the upper section of Easton Glacier remains healthy and snow-covered, while even the upper section of the Grinnell Glacier is bare, melting and has thinned. Small glaciers with shallow slopes such as Grinnell Glacier are most likely to fall into disequilibrium, if there is a change in the local climate.

In the case of positive mass balance, the glacier will continue to advance expanding its low elevation area, resulting in more melting. If this still does not create an equilibrium balance the glacier will continue to advance. If a glacier is near a large body of water, especially an ocean, the glacier may advance until iceberg calving losses bring about equilibrium. Positive mass balance of glaciers has been recently reported from Karakoram.

15. **Greenhouse gases :** The best known greenhouse gas is carbon dioxide CO_2. It is breathed out or otherwise given off by living organisms as they undergo aerobic respiration, and is taken in by green plants during photo-synthesis. A small amount of CO_2 in atmosphere is an absolute necessity for life on the earth, without it the planet would be too cold to support living organisms and plants would lack an essential raw ingradient. But excess of CO_2 will cause the earth's surface to heating abnormally.

17. The cryosphere is those portions of earth's surface where water is in solid form, including sea ice, lake ice, river ice, snow cover glaciers, ice caps and ice sheets and frozen ground. Thus, there is a wide overlap with the hydrosphere. The cryosphere is an integral part of the global climate-system with important linkages and feedbacks generated through its influence on the surface energy and moisture fluxes, clouds, hydrology atmospheric and oceanic circulation.

18. **Moist and non-saturated soil :** When soil temperatures are below 50°F, these bacterias are fairly inactive. Also, the bacteria require aerobic conditions (unsaturated soil water conditions) to nitrify ammonium.

Thus, the amount of nitrification that occurs in the soil is largely dependent on the soil temperature and the time elapsed from application until the soil becomes saturated with water.

19. Andisols are soils formed in volcanic ash and defined as soils containing high proportions of glass and amorphous colloidal materials, including allophane, imogolite and ferrihydrite. Because they are generally quite young, andisols typically are very fertile except in case where phosphorus is easily fixed. Fossil andisols are found from areas far from present day volcanic activity.

20. Photovoltaics (PV) is a method of generating electrical power by converting solar radiation into direct current electricity using semiconductors that exhibit the photovoltaic effect. Photovoltaic power generation employs solar panels composed of a number of solar cells containing a photovoltaic material. Materials presently used for photovoltaics include monocrystalline silicon, polycrystalline silicon, amorphous silicon, cadmium telluride, and copper indium gallium selenide/sulphide. Due to the increased demand for renewable energy sources, the manufacturing of solar cells and photovoltaic arrays has advanced considerably in recent years.

The maximum theoretical efficiency of conversion is about 45%. In August, the university of New South Wales set a record with a solar cell that could convert 43% of light that struck it into electricity.

22. The emission of carbon due to burning of fossil fuels are produced disproportionately by the people of the industriallized countries. Indeed, the wealthiest nations of the world's population burn nearly 70% of the fossil fuels. China is the biggest single contributor, after USA of the world's CO_2 emission. The correct sequence in increasing order of total CO_2 emissions from various countries at present is :

Britain < India < USA < China.

25. Both A and R are true, but R is not the correct explanation of A.

26. Carbon monoxide is a colourless, odourless inflammable, toxic gas present in large quantities in the waste water from burned gases, especially in exhaust fumes from motor vehicles. This is the pollutant which is mostly produced by mankind, who generates more than 70% of its total volume. The toxic effect of carbon monoxide arises from the fact that it combines with the RBCs pigment haemoglogbin so as impedes the combination that normally occurs in the lungs of oxygen with haemoglobin. It thus arrests the transport of oxygen through the blood and leads to symptoms similar to those occur in suffocation. Carbon monoxide (CO) has a 500 times greater affinity to bind with haemoglobin than oxygen. No person should be exposed to CO at a concentration greater than 35 ppm.

27. **Photochemical Smog :** Smog formed from atmospheric pollutants that are generated under the influence of solar radiations. It manifests itself in the form of a more or less dense haze covering the town which restricts visibility by the blurring, it contrasts due to dissipation of light. The dissipation of light caused by aerosols generated by chemical reactions occasioned by smog. Initial products of reactions are sulphur dioxide, nitrogen oxide various hydrocarbons. Many important reactions include formation of Ozone.

28. The air borne fraction is a scalling factor defined as the ratio of the annual increase in atmospheric CO_2 to the CO. It represents the proportion of human emitted CO_2 that remains in the atmosphere. The fraction average about 46% meaning that approx. half the human emitted CO_2 is absorbed by ocean and land surface.

29. Alkali or Alkaline soils are clay soils with high pH > 8.5, a poor soil structure and a low infiltration capacity. Also they have a hard calcareous layer at 0.5 to 1 m depth. Alkali soils owe their unfavourable physico-chemical properties mainly to the dominating presence of sodium carbonate, phosphorous is not present in soluble state.

31. Report audit findings is not a post audit activity under environmental audit process.

32. Specification for environmental management system – ISO 14001.

33. The draft notification further to amend the Environment Impact Assessment Notification, 2006 published in the Gazette of India, Extraordinary, Part II, Section 3, Subsection (ii) vide number S. 1533 (E) dated the 14th September, 2006, which the Central Government proposes to make, in exercise of the powers conferred by sub-section (1) and clause (v) of sub-section (2) of section 3 of the Environment (Protection) Act, 1986 (29 of 1986), is hereby published for the information of the public likely to be affected thereby and notice is hereby given that the said notification will be taken into consideration after the expiry of sixty days (60 days) from the date on which copies of the Official Gazette containing this notification is made available to the public.

34. Description of environment → Identification of impacts → Prediction of impacts → Evalution of impacts → Identification of mitigation needs.

35. Life Cycle Inventory (LCI) database helps in Life Cycle Assesment (LCA). Practioners answer questions about the environmental impact.

36. Fossil fuels, non renewable natural resources that originate in the earth's crust are being extracted from the earth at breakneck speed

simply for human consumption. The chronology ratio of mineral formation to mineral extraction is remarkably high.

There are two ways to manage municipal solid waste (MSW). The high waste approach involves leaving it somewhere burning it or burying it.

Landfills the symbol of the high waste approach, have the proven reputation of preventing MSW from degrading, not to mention attracting a lot of traffic noise, and dust to the surrounding areas.

37. Both (A) and (R) are correct and Reason (R) is not the correct explanation of A.

39. Here terms, $n = 3$

$\therefore$ GM $= \sqrt[3]{4 \times 8 \times 16}$

$= \sqrt[3]{512} = 8$.

40. The covariance between two data of N observations is given by $\dfrac{\Sigma(X - \overline{X})(Y - \overline{Y})}{N^2}$.

42. Low density polyethylene (LDPE) is a thermoplastic made from the monomer ethylene. It was the first grade of polyethylene, produced by using high pressure process via free radical polymerisation. The EPA estimates 5.7% of LDPE is recycled. LDPE is defined by a density range of 0.910–0.940 g cm^{-3}. It is not reactive at room temperatures except by strong oxydising agents and some solvents come swelling. It can withstand temperatures at 80°C continuously and 95°C for a short time. Made in tranlucent or opaque variations, it is quite flexible and tough but breakable.

43. National Environment Awareness compaign is a non-formal environment education and awareness programme. It is designed for any group, participitating in social, economic and cultural development of the community. They form groups or clubs and arrange exhibition, public lectures, meetings, environment compaigns, etc.

46. NPP (Net Primary Productivity) is the primary measure of biomass accumulation within an ecosystem. Net primary productivity can be calculated by simple formula where the total amount of productivity is adjusted for total productivity losses through maintenance of biological processes.

NPP = GPP – R$_{producer}$

In the terrestrial ecosystem roughly 90% NPP ends up being broken down by decomposers.

47. Regulating marine pollution is the Water (Prevention and Control of Pollution) Act, 1974 (amended up to 1988), which is operative up to 5 km from the shoreline in all coastal States and Union Territories. The enforcement of this Act rests with Central and State Pollution Control Boards. In the case of marine areas, sea water is categorized into five zones, with minimum standards evolved by the Indian Standards Institution (ISI) for the permissible quantities and concentrations of pollutants in each zone.

The prevention and control of marine pollution is one of the responsibilities of the Coast Guard, under the Coast Guard Act, 1978. The prevention and control of marine pollution by oil from ships and liabilities for oil pollution damage are addressed in amendments to the Merchant Shipping Act, 1958, which address provisions of the International Convention for the Prevention of Pollution from Ships (MARPOL) in accordance with the amendments to the 1954 Oil Pollution Convention.

Implementation and enforcement of pollution-related legislation rests with the Central and State Pollution Control Boards and the State Departments of Environment. BOD level waste water is permitted to be released in lands by industries under (PCPA) act 1974 is 30 mg/l.

48. Hydraulic conductivity, symbolically represented as K, is a property of vascular plants, soil or rock, that describes the ease with which a fluid (usually water) can move through pore spaces or fractures. It depends on the *intrinsic permeability* of the material and on the degree of saturation, and on the density and viscosity of the fluid. Saturated hydraulic conductivity,

K_{sat}, describes water movement through saturated media. It is a function of both fluid and medium.

49. Dachigan Sanctuary is associated with Hangul.

50. The UN General Assembly in December 1989 responding to the report of the Brundtland commission decided to hold an international conference on issues concerning environment and development in Rio de Janeiro in June 1992, with the object of a new evolving a new global partnership for saving the earth planet and for sustainable development for the future.

It was decided that the UNCED would beat the level of Heads of State and Government. This made it the first ever earth summit. The Reo Earth marked the 20th anniversary of the Stockholm conference and the founding of the UNTEP, the head for the scintific understanding phenomenon like climatic change acid, rain, global warming, ozone depletion.

The Heads of State and Government assembled at Rio to have the last chance to draw up an action plan, based on global partnership to 'save' the earth planet for future generation.

PAPER-III

*Note : This paper contains **seventy five (75)** objective type questions, of **two (2)** marks each. **All** questions are compulsory.*

1. Most of the day to day weather changes are associated with which scale in meteorology?
   A. Micro scale
   B. Meso scale
   C. Synoptic scale
   D. Planetary scale

2. Match the List-I with List-II and choose the correct answer from the codes given below:

List-I (Date)	List-II (Event)
(a) 5th June	1. National Pollution Prevention Day
(b) 2nd December	2. World Environment Day
(c) 22nd May	3. World Forest Day
(d) 21st March	4. Bio-diversity Day

   Codes :

	(a)	(b)	(c)	(d)
A.	2	1	4	3
B.	3	2	4	1
C.	4	3	2	1
D.	1	4	3	2

3. 'Fanning' smoke stack plumes are observed when
   A. there is an inversion above the ground surface.
   B. there is unstable atmosphere.
   C. there is neutrally stable atmosphere.
   D. the stack height is below an inversion layer.

4. The cyclonic winds are generated by the approximate balance between
   A. Pressure gradient force and coriolis force
   B. Centrifugal force and coriolis force
   C. Centrifugal force, coriolis force and frictional drag force.
   D. Centrifugal force and pressure gradient force.

5. Mixing height is determined by
   A. adiabatic lapse rate and environmental lapse rate.
   B. vertical profile of wind speeds and adiabatic lapse rate.
   C. vertical profiles of wind speeds and ambient temperature.
   D. wind speeds and solar insolation.

6. United Nations has declared "UN Decade of Education for sustainable Development' and the decade identified for this education is
   A. 2006–2015
   B. 2005–2014
   C. 2011–2020
   D. 2012–2021

7. Halon–1301 is a
   A. Fire extinguisher
   B. Solvent
   C. Refrigerant
   D. Aerosol propellant

8. Which of the following is a primary pollutant in atmospheric air?
   A. Cl_2
   B. SO_3
   C. Nitrates
   D. Sulphates

9. Hardness is expressed on the Mohs scale, which ranges from
   A. 1 to 10
   B. 1 to 14
   C. –14 to 14
   D. 1 to 100

10. The halon H-1211 has the following chemical composition :
    A. $CF_2 Cl Br$
    B. $CCl_2 FBr$
    C. $CCl_2 F_2$
    D. $CBr_2 Cl F$

11. The most toxic among the chlorinated hydrocarbons is
    A. Aldrin
    B. DDT
    C. Endrin
    D. Heptachlor

12. Agent orange is a
    A. Weedicide
    B. Fungicide
    C. Nematicide
    D. Rodenticide

13. Major source of SO_2 is
    A. Cement Industry
    B. Forest fires
    C. Thermal Power Stations
    D. Volcanic activity

14. Match each water contaminant in Column-I with its preferred method of removal in Column-II.

Column–I	Column–II
(a) Mn^{2+}	1. Activated Carbon
(b) Ca^{2+} and HCO_3^-	2. Raise pH by addition of Na_2CO_3
(c) Trihalomethane	3. Addition of lime
(d) Mg^{2+}	4. Oxidation

    Codes :

	(a)	(b)	(c)	(d)
A.	4	3	1	2
B.	3	2	4	1
C.	2	4	3	1
D.	1	2	4	3

15. Reverse Osmosis (RO) operated at 200–1200 psig removes particles ranging from
    A. 0.0001 to 0.001 μm
    B. 0.01 to 10 μm
    C. 0.1 to 1.0 μm
    D. 0.1 to 2.0 μm

16. Coagulation is a chemical process, in which charged particles or colloids undergo
    A. Stabilization
    B. Destabilization
    C. Attraction
    D. Precipitation

17. Water has the following chemical composition:
    $[Ca^{2+}]$ = 15 mg/L;
    $[Mg^{2+}]$ = 10 mg/L;
    $[SO_4^{2-}]$ = 30 mg/L;
    The total hardness of water will be
    A. 80 mg/L as $CaCO_3$
    B. 55 mg/L as $CaCO_3$
    C. 160 mg/L as $CaCO_3$
    D. 40 mg/L as $CaCO_3$

18. Two water samples were collected.
    Sample # 1 : pH = 9, but no carbonate or other dissolved proton donors or acceptors.
    Sample # 2 : pH = 8.3, but it contains dissolved $NaHCO_3$ at a concentration of 0.01/mg/L
    Which of the following is true based on the above observations.
    A. Sample # 1 will have more alkalinity.
    B. Sample # 2 will have more alkalinity.
    C. Sample # 1 and sample # 2 will have exactly same alkalinity.
    D. Alkalinity cannot be estimated.

19. Two soil samples, A and B, at different soil moisture levels are placed in contact with each other. Water will more likely move from soil A to soil B if their water potential, expressed in kPa, are :
    A. A = –5; B = +5
    B. A = –5; B = –5
    C. A = –20; B = –10
    D. A = –30; B = –40

20. Blue baby syndrome is caused by
    A. Carbon monoxide
    B. Nitrate
    C. Fluoride
    D. Mercury

21. **Assertion (A) :** For solar cell fabrication, those semiconducting materials which have band-gap energies in the range 1-1.8 eV are most suitable.
    Reason (R) : The maximum solar irradiance is around a wavelength corresponding to 1.5 eV. Identify the correct Code:
    A. Both (A) and (R) are correct and (R) is the correct explanation of (A).
    B. Both (A) and (R) are correct and (R) is not the correct explanation of (A).
    C. (A) is true, but (R) is false.
    D. (A) is false, but (R) is true.

22. **Assertion (A) :** State factors (external factors) control the overall structure of an ecosystem and the way things work within it.

Reason (R) : The state factors are not themselves influenced by the ecosystem.
Identify the correct code:
A. (A) is correct (R) is incorrect.
B. Both (A) and (R) are correct, but (R) is not correct explanation of (A).
C. Both (A) and (R) are correct and (R) is correct explanation of (A).
D. Both (A) and (R) are incorrect.

23. **Assertion (A) :** When energy is transferred between trophic levels, the successive level in the pathway have lesser available energy compared to the preceding level.
Reason (R) : Whenever energy is transformed, there is loss of energy through the release of heat.
A. Both (A) and (R) are true and (R) is the correct explanation.
B. Both (A) and (R) are true and (R) is not the correct explanation.
C. (A) is true and (R) is false.
D. (A) is false and (R) is true.

24. **Assertion (A) :** The ecosystem surrounding a river gets damaged due to construction of a dam.
Reason (R) : The area gets inundated with large volume of water.
Identify the correct answer:
A. Both (A) and (R) are true, with (R) being the correct explanation.
B. Both (A) and (R) are true, but (R) is not correct explanation.
C. (A) is true, but (R) is wrong.
D. Both (A) and (R) are wrong.

25. **Assertion (A) :** Soils rich in clay minerals have high levels of organic matter.
Reason (R) : Clay soils tend to have low decomposition rates.
Identify the correct answer:
A. Both statements are correct and (R) is correct explanation of (A).
B. Both statements are correct, but (R) is not correct explanation of (A).
C. Statement (A) is correct, but (R) is incorrect.
D. Statement (A) is incorrect, but (R) is correct.

26. **Assertion (A) :** Nitrogen cycle is an endogenic biogeochemical cycle.
Reason (R) : Atmospheric N_2 can be fixed by certain prokaryotes in the soil.
Choose correct answer:
A. Both (A) and (R) are true and (R) is the correct explanation of (A).
B. Both (A) and (R) are true, but (R) is not the correct explanation of (A).
C. (A) is true, but (R) is false.
D. (A) is false, but (R) is true.

27. Match the following :

Column–I	Column–II
(a) Nekton	1. Associated with surface film water
(b) Neuston	2. Found at the bottom of an aquatic ecosystem.
(c) Benthos	3. Active swimmer, against water current.
(d) Plankton	4. Incapable of independent movement.

Choose the correct answer from the Codes:
Codes :

	(a)	(b)	(c)	(d)
A.	1	3	4	2
B.	2	4	1	3
C.	3	1	2	4
D.	4	2	3	1

28. Which of the following is not a major biome of India?
A. Tropical rain forest biomes
B. Tropical deciduous forest biomes
C. Temperate needle leaf forest biomes
D. Mountains and glaciers

29. To survive and avoid competition for the same resources, a species usually occupies only part of its fundamental niche in a particular community or ecosystem. This is called
A. Geographic isolation
B. Mutualism
C. Realized Niche
D. Broad Niche

30. Which of the following is *not* a characteristic feature of community?
A. Populations of different species occupying a particular place.

B. Complex interacting network of plants, animals and microbes.

C. Different species interacting with one another and with their environment of matter and energy.

D. Groups of interacting individuals of different species.

31. Which of the following food chain is correct?
A. Krill → Adelie Penguins → Emperor Penguins → Leopard Seal
B. Krill → Crabeater Seal → Leopard Seal → Killer Whale
C. Krill → Leopard Seal → Emperor Penguins → Killer Whale
D. Krill → Crabeater Seal → Killer Whale → Leopard Seal

32. The observation that individuals of a population are uniformly distributed suggests that
A. Density of population is low.
B. Resources are distributed unevenly.
C. The members of the population are neither attracted to nor repelled by one another.
D. The members of the population are competing for access to a resource.

33. Which of the following biomes is correctly paired with the description of its climate?
A. Tropical forests — nearly constant day length and temperature
B. Tundra — long summers, mild winters
C. Savanna — cool temperature year-round, uniform precipitation during the year
D. Temperate grasslands — relatively short growing season, mild winters.

34. Cellulose and hemicellulose are not resistant to decay but are broken down more slowly. They are considered
A. Labile
B. Moderately labile
C. Recalcitrant
D. Nonlabile

35. The parasitic gall formation is related to
A. Host-specific antibodies
B. Parasite specific cysts
C. Parasite specific enzymes
D. Host specific hormones

36. What is the estimate of volume of water yield for saturated pond aquifer of 1 metre width and 2 metre depth and length of 4 metre. Consider the porosity of sand to be 35% and specific yield to be 25%?
A. 2.8 m³
B. 28 m³
C. 0.28 m³
D. 280 m³

37. Arrange the following climate proxies in ascending order of time scales:
(i) Lithological records
(ii) Pollens
(iii) Tree rings
(iv) Historical records
A. (iv), (iii), (i), (ii)
B. (iv), (iii), (ii), (i)
C. (iv), (ii), (i), (iii)
D. (iv), (i), (iii), (ii)

38. Acid drainage is more in mining of
A. Granite
B. Bauxite
C. Lime stone
D. Base metal sulphide

39. Geothermal gradient in Earth is
A. Uniform throughout.
B. Higher in continental lithosphere.
C. Higher in subduction zones.
D. Lower at mid oceanic ridges.

40. Coal mining areas are affected by
(i) Land subsidence
(ii) Fire hazard
(iii) Radioactive waste
(iv) Air pollution
A. (i) and (ii)
B. (i), (ii) and (iii)
C. (i), (ii) and (iv)
D. (i), (ii), (iii) and (iv)

41. Radioactive elements are concentrated in
A. Earth's core
B. Earth's mantle
C. Mid-Oceanic ridges
D. Earth's crust

42. What led to maximum number of fatalities during Indonesian 2004 Earthquake?
A. Death on account of openings on surface
B. Fires generated due to earthquake
C. Epidemic diseases
D. Tsunami

43. Maximum carbon in the world is found in
    A. Oceans
    B. Coal mines
    C. Antarctica
    D. Forests

44. The highest seismic domain in India is
    A. The Himalayas
    B. The Western ghats
    C. The Indogangetic plains
    D. The Dharwar craton

45. Earth's core is mainly composed of
    A. Iron
    B. Nitrogen
    C. Carbon
    D. Magnesium

46. Gasification is
    A. the high temperature (~ 750 – 850 °C) conversion of solid, carbonaceous fuel into flammable gas mixtures.
    B. the high temperature (~ 750 – 850 °C) conversion of solid, carbonaceous fuel into liquid.
    C. the low temperature (~ 250 – 350 °C) conversion of solid, carbonaceous fuel into flammable gas mixture.
    D. the low temperature (~ 250 – 350 °C) conversion of solid, carbonaceous fuel into liquid.

47. In case of magneto hydrodynamic power generation, for maximum power output, the efficiency is
    A. 0.25
    B. 0.5
    C. 0.75
    D. 0.4

48. Which combination of radiative fluxes plays the all important role in climate change?
    A. Visible and infrared
    B. Visible and UV
    C. Visible, UV and infrared
    D. UV, microwaves and infrared

49. The climate sensitivity parameter is defined as the rate of change of
    A. surface temperature with albedo of earth
    B. surface temperature with CO_2 concentration in atmosphere
    C. precipitation with earth's temperature
    D. surface temperature with radiative forcing.

50. Which of the following fuels has highest carbon intensity?
    A. Natural gas
    B. Oil
    C. Bituminous coal
    D. Biomass

51. Solid waste treatment by pyrolysis involves
    A. Autoclaving
    B. Heating in presence of air
    C. Heating in presence of acetic acid
    D. Heating in absence of air

52. In which year Wildlife Protection Act was enacted ?
    A. 1962
    B. 1972
    C. 1982
    D. 1992

53. According to National Ambient Air Quality Standards, the annual average concentration of Sulphur dioxide in residential areas in India is
    A. 20 $\mu g/m^3$
    B. 40 $\mu g/m^3$
    C. 60 $\mu g/m^3$
    D. 80 $\mu g/m^3$

54. Which of the following statements is correct in the context of Environmental Impact Assessment?
    A. The process considers broad range of potential alternatives.
    B. It provides early warning of cumulative effects.
    C. Focusses on sustainability agenda.
    D. Focusses on standard agenda.

55. Match the List-I with List-II and choose the correct answer from the codes given below:

List–I (Components)	List–II (Dimensions)
(a) Equitable utilization of natural resources	1. Social dimensions
(b) Benefit to disadvantaged group	2. Economic dimensions
(c) Creation of additional value	3. Environmental dimensions
(d) Elimination of toxic substances	4. Political dimensions

Codes :

	(a)	(b)	(c)	(d)
A.	4	1	2	3
B.	4	1	3	2
C.	3	2	1	4
D.	2	4	1	3

56. Among the following, which one does not belong to EIA process?
   A. Establishment of base line environmental condition.
   B. Identification, Prediction and assessment of impact.
   C. Suggesting the mitigation measures.
   D. Developing EMS auditing procedures.

57. According to Gaussian Plume Model, the ground level concentration (C) of a pollutant varies with effective height (H) as (σ is the vertical dispersion coefficient):

   A. $C \propto \dfrac{1}{H}$

   B. $C \propto e^{-\frac{H^2}{\sigma^2}}$

   C. $C \propto e^{-\frac{H}{\sigma}}$

   D. $C \propto H^{-2}$

58. In a multiple regression analysis, an examination of variances revealed that explained sum of squares per degree of freedom and residual sum of squares per degree of freedom were 250 and 100, respectively. What is the F-ratio?
   A. 6.25
   B. 5.25
   C. 0.4
   D. 2.5

59. A source of air pollution is emitting a pollutant at the rate S(mg/hours) inside a room of volume V(m³). The air of the room is being changed n times per hour. If k is pollutant decay rate constant, the concentration C(t) of the pollutant at any given instant of time under well mixed conditions is given by

   A. $C(t) = \left(\dfrac{S}{nV}\right)(1-e^{-nt})$

   B. $C(t) = \left(\dfrac{S/V}{n+k}\right)(1-e^{-nt})$

   C. $C(t) = (S/nV)(n+k)$

   D. $C(t) = \left(\dfrac{nV}{S}\right)(1-e^{-nk})$

60. Which one of the following is *not* an eigenvalue of the matrix?

$$\begin{bmatrix} -1 & 2 & 2 \\ 2 & 2 & 2 \\ -3 & -6 & -6 \end{bmatrix}$$

   A. 0
   B. -2
   C. -3
   D. 3

61. A sample of 17 measurements of the diameter of a spherical particle gave a mean = 5 µm and a standard deviation = 0.5 µm. Assuming t-statistic for 16 degrees of freedom $t_{0.05} \approx 2$, the 95% confidence limits of actual diameter are
   A. 4.75 and 5.25 µm.   B. 4.00 and 6.00 µm.
   C. 4.9 and 5.1 µm.   D. 4.5 and 5.5 µm.

62. "Hot spots" are areas,
   (i) extremely rich in species
   (ii) with high endemism
   (iii) extremely scarce in species
   (iv) under constant threat
   Choose the correct answer from the codes:
   Codes :
   A. (i) and (ii)
   B. (ii) and (iii)
   C. (ii), (iii) and (iv)
   D. (i), (ii) and (iv)

63. A paddy field is an example of
   A. Fresh water ecosystem
   B. Terrestrial ecosystem
   C. Auto ecosystem
   D. Engineered ecosystem

64. Which pyramid cannot be inverted in a stable ecosystem?
   A. Pyramid of energy
   B. Pyramid of biomass
   C. Pyramid of number
   D. Pyramid of dry weight

65. Which one of the following environmental factors is responsible for cyclomorphism in animals?
   A. Moisture
   B. Temperature
   C. Photoperiod
   D. Wind

66. Sr^{90} can enter and accumulate in the body through
   A. Drinking water
   B. Inhaling contaminated air
   C. Food chain
   D. Skin

67. Which one of the following is a neurotoxic?
   A. Organophosphate   B. Nitric oxide
   C. 2, 4-D   D. Cuprous oxide

68. If 0.05 M proline-ninhydine complex has an absorbance of 0.15 at 520 nm in a 1 cm curvette, its molar extinction coefficient will be
   A. 50 m M^{-1} cm^{-1} B. 0.1 M^{-1} cm^{-1}
   C. 1 M^{-1} cm^{-1} D. 3 M^{-1} cm^{-1}

69. Which bacterium found in soil is anaerobic?
   A. *Clostridium* Sp   B. *Azatobacter* Sp
   C. *Bacillus* Sp   D. *Thiobacillus* Sp

70. Particles of sizes < 1 μm are most efficiently removed by
   A. Cyclones
   B. Scrubbers
   C. Bag filter
   D. Electrostatic Precipitator

71. The attenuation of sound by reactive type silencers is based on
   A. absorption of sound waves
   B. scattering of sound waves
   C. impedance discontinuity
   D. interference of sound waves

72. "Farmer's lung" is a classic example for
   A. Psittacosis
   B. Extrinsic allergic alveolitis
   C. Legionnaire's disease
   D. Aspergillosis

73. The lichen and moss stages occur in
   A. Lithosere   B. Psamosere
   C. Hydrosere   D. Hydrarch

74. The mean of a data following Poisson distribution is 4. The second moment of the distribution is:
   A. 4   B. 2
   C. 1   D. 0

75. Which of the following rivers has maximum melt water component in its discharge?
   A. Indus   B. Ganges
   C. Brahmaputra   D. Narmada

ANSWERS

1	2	3	4	5	6	7	8	9	10
C	A	A	D	A	B	A	A	A	A

11	12	13	14	15	16	17	18	19	20
C	A	D	A	A	B	A	B	D	B

21	22	23	24	25	26	27	28	29	30
A	B	B	B	A	D	C	D	C	C

31	32	33	34	35	36	37	38	39	40
B	D	A	B	C	A	B	C	B	C

41	42	43	44	45	46	47	48	49	50
D	D	A	A	A	A	B	A	D	C

51	52	53	54	55	56	57	58	59	60
D	B	C	D	A	D	B	D	A	D

61	62	63	64	65	66	67	68	69	70
A	D	D	A	B	C	A	D	A	D

71	72	73	74	75
C	B	A	A	A

SOME SELECTED EXPLANATORY ANSWERS

1. Scale in meteorology is the interdisciplinary scientific study of the atmosphere that focuses on weather processes and short term forecasting (in contrast with climatology). Studies in the filled stretch back millennia, though significant progress in meteorology did not occur until the 18th century, saw breakthrough occur after observing networks developed across several countries. Breakthrough in weather forecasting were achieved in the latter half of the twentieth century, after development of computer. Most of the day weather changes are associated with planetary scale.

2. 5th June : World Environment Day
2nd December : National Pollution Prevention Day
22nd May : Biodiversity Day
21st March : World Forest Day.

3. Tall smoke stacks emit the pollution from the inversion aloft. This fume does not pollute the nearby area. Otherwise, the smoke stack forms a fumigating plume that can cause health problems to those in the nearby area. There are also their plumes sometimes created by the smoke stack. It depends on how the power plant releases the exhaust into the air and how outside forces impact the exhaust, the smoke stack can develop a coning plume, a looping plume, a lofting plume or a fumigation.

4. **Cyclonic winds :** The cyclones are irregular wind movements involving closed air circulation around a low pressure centre. This closed air circulation is caused by atmospheric disturbances over and above the surface of the earth, coupled with the earth's rotation which imparts to these disturbances a whirling motion. Cyclones are associated with destructive and violent disturbances, such a heavy squalls and torrential rainfall. The cyclonic winds are generated by the balance between centrifugal force and pressure gradient force.

6. **UN Decade of Education for Sustainable Development:** Education for Sustainable Development allows every human being to acquire the knowledge, skills, attitudes and values necessary to shape a sustainable future. Education for Sustainable Development means including key sustainable development issues into teaching and learning for example, climate change, disaster risk reduction, biodiversity, poverty reduction, and sustainable consumption. It also requires participatory teaching and learning methods that motivate and empower learners to change their behaviour and take action for sustainable development. Education for Sustainable Development consequently promotes competencies like critical thinking, imagining future scenarios and making decisions in a collaborative way. Education for Sustainable Development requires far-reaching changes in the way education is often practised today. UNESCO is the lead agency for the UN Decade of Education for Sustainable Development (2005-2014).

7. **Halon–1301 :** Halon-1301 was introduced as an effective gaseous fire suppression agent in the 1960s, and was used around valuable materials, such as aircraft, mainframe computers, and telecommunication switching centers, usually in total flooding systems. It was also widely used in the maritime industry to add a third level of protection, should the main and emergency fire pumps become inoperable or ineffective. It is a fire extinguisher.

It is considered good practice to avoid all unnecessary exposure to Halon 1301, and to limit exposures to concentrations of 7 per cent and below to 15 minutes. Exposure to Halon 1301 in the 5 to 7 per cent range produces little, if any, noticeable effect. At levels between 7 and 10 per cent, mild central nervous system effects such as dizziness and tingling in the extremities have been reported. In practice, the operators of many Halon 1301 total flooding systems evacuate the space on impending agent discharge.

8. Primary Pollutant in atmospheric Air : Global satellite data showed that stratospheric ozone levels were decreasing over most of the southern polar latitudes. This pattern, widely referred to as the 'ozone hole' (more accurately, ozone thinning), proved to be caused by high chlorine radical concentrations, as well as by bromine radicals (Br), which also trigger catalytic cycles with chlorine to consume ozone.

The source of the high chlorine radicals was found to be a fast reaction of the chlorine reservoirs HCl and $ClNO_3$ at the surface of icy particles formed at the very cold temperatures of the Antarctic wintertime stratosphere and called polar stratospheric clouds (PSCs). HCl and $ClNO_3$ react on PSC surfaces to produce molecular chlorine (Cl_2) and nitric acid. Cl_2 then rapidly photolyzes in spring to release chlorine atoms and trigger ozone loss.

Ozone depletion has worsened since 1985. Today springtime ozone levels over Antarctica are less than half of levels recorded in the 1960s, and the 2006 Antarctic Ozone hole covered 29 million square kilometers, tying the largest value previously recorded in 2000. In the 1990s, ozone loss by the same mechanism was discovered in the Arctic springtime stratosphere, although Arctic ozone depletion is not as extensive as in Antarctica because temperatures are not as consistently cold. Cl_2 is a primary pollutant in atmospheric air.

9. Mohs Scale: The Mohs scale of mineral hardness characterizes the scratch resistance of various minerals through the ability of a harder material to scratch a softer material. It was created in 1812 by the German geologist and mineralogist Friedrich Mohs and is one of the several definitions of hardness in materials science.

The Mohs scale of mineral hardness is based on the ability of one natural sample of matter to scratch another mineral. The sample of matter used by Mohs are all different minerals.

Minerals are pure substances found in nature. Rocks are made up of one or more minerals. As the hardest known naturally occurring substance, when the scale was designed, diamonds are at the top of the scale. The hardness of material is measured against the scale by finding the hardest material that the given material can scratch and the softest material that can scratch the given material. For example, if some material is scratched by apatite but not by fluorite, its hardness on the Mohs scale, which ranges from 1 to 10.

10. Halon H-1211 : Halon-1211 and Halon-1301 are low toxicity, chemically stable compounds that as long as contained in cylinders, are easily recyclable. Halon-1211 is a CFC, production of new Halon has ceased. There is no cost effective means of safety effectively of the halon-1211. Hence, recycling and reusing the existing supply intelligently and responsibly to protect lives and property is the wisest solution. The halon H-1211 has the chemical composition of CF_2ClBr.

11. Chlorinated Hydrocarbons are a group of chemicals composed of carbon, chlorine and hydrogen. As pesticides, they are also referred to by several other names, including chlorinated organics, chlorinated insecticides and chlorinated synthetics. Although the first chlorinated hydrocarbon was synthesized in 1874, its insecticidal properties were not discovered until 1939 by the Swiss chemist, Paul Müller. It was introduced as DDT in 1942 during World War II and its subsequent use is responsible for saving millions of lives from vectored diseases such as typhus and malaria. The advantages of these synthetic chemicals over previously used botanical or natural insecticides were improved efficacy, lower use rates, lower costs and greater persistence. As with most of the chlorinated hydrocarbons, DDT has been banned for use in the United States, but is still used in some developing countries for combating insect vectors of disease. Other members of this chemical group no longer in use in the United States include aldrin, dieldrin, heptachlor, mirex, chlordecone, and chlordane. Others remaining registered are active ingredients of various home and garden products and some agricultural, structural, and environmental pest control products. One particular subgroup of these chemicals, known as cyclodienes, were especially persistent, which made them useful for controlling structural pests such as termites. Their persistence is attributed to their long soil-life and stability in the presence of the untraviolet radiation from sunlight. Many structures treated with one of these compounds are still protected today. One cyclodiene still registered for use, endosulfan, is less persistent. The Environmental Protection Agency determined that the potential for environmental contamination from the persistent members of this group of chemicals was sufficient to issue a ban on their use. The most toxic among the chlorinated hydrocarbons is Endrin.

12. Agent Orange or Herbicide Orange (HO) is one of the herbicides and defoliants used by the U.S. military as part of its herbicidal warfare program, Operation Ranch Hand, during the Vietnam War from 1961 to 1971. A 50:50 mixture of 2,4,5-T and 2,4-D, it was manufactured for the U.S. Department of Defense primarily by Monsanto Corporation and Dow Chemical. The 2,4,5-T used to produce Agent Orange was contaminated with 2,3,7,8-tetrachlorodibenzodioxin (TCDD), an extremely toxic dioxin compound. It was given its name from the colour of the orange-striped 55 US gallon (208) barrels in which it was shipped and was by far the most widely used of the so-called "Rainbow Herbicides".

During the Vietnam War, between 1962 and 1971, the United States military sprayed nearly 2,00,00,000 US gallons (7,60,00,000) of material containing chemical herbicides and defoliants mixed with jet fuel in Vietnam, eastern Laos and parts of Cambodia, as part of Operation Ranch Hand. The program's goal was to defoliate forested and rural land, depriving guerrillas of cover, another goal was to induce forced draft urbanization, destroying the ability of peasants to support themselves in the countryside, and forcing them to flee to the U.S. dominated cities, thus depriving the guerrillas of their rural support and food supply.

The US began to target food crops in October 1962, primarily using Agent Blue. In 1965, 42 per cent of all herbicide spraying was dedicated to food crops. Rural-to-urban migration rates dramatically increased in South Vietnam, as peasants escaped the war and famine in the countryside by fleeing to the U.S.-dominated cities. The urban population in South Vietnam nearly tripled: from 2.8 million people in 1958, to 8 million by 1971. The rapid flow of people led to a fast-paced and uncontrolled urbanization; an estimated 1.5 million people were living in Saigon slums.

United States Air Force records show that at least 6,542 spraying missions took place over the course of Operation Ranch Hand. By 1971, 12 per cent of the total area of South Vietnam had been sprayed with defoliating chemicals, at an average concentration of 13 times the recommended USDA application rate for domestic use. In South Vietnam alone, an estimated 10 million hectares (25 million acres, 39,000 square miles) of agricultural land was ultimately destroyed. In some areas, TCDD concentrations in soil and water were hundreds of times greater than the levels considered safe by the U.S. Environmental Protection Agency. Overall, more than 20% of South Vietnam's forests were sprayed at least once over a nine-year period. Hence, Agent Orange is weedicide.

13. SO_2 : Sulphur dioxide belongs to the family of gases called sulphur oxides. SO_2 forms when substances containting sulphur are burned usually coal, diesel, or oil and during some industrial processes. SO_2 affects respiratory systems and aggravates cardiovascular disease. It can harm vegetation, including agricultural crops. Mixed with moisture in the atmosphere, SO_2 can create acid rain, which can harm humans, animals and vegetation as well as erode buildings. The major source of SO_2 is volcanic activity.

14. Mn^{2+} → oxidation

$Ca^{2+}HCO_3$ → addition of lime

Trihalomethane → activated carbon

Mg^{2+} → raise pH by addition of Na_2CO_3.

15. **Reverse Osmosis (RO) :** The process of movement of solvent through a semipermeable membrane from the solution to the pure solvent by applying excess pressure on solution side is known as reverse osmosis. This process is used for distillation of sea water obtaining drinking water. It operates at 200–1200 psig, removes particles, ranging from 0.001 to 0.001 μm.

16. The use of nitrate-contaminated drinking water to prepare infant formula is a well-known risk factor for infant methemoglobinemia. Affected infants develop a peculiar blue-gray skin colour and may become irritable or lethargic, depending on the severity of their condition. The condition can progress rapidly to cause coma and death if it is not recognized and treated appropriately. Two cases of blue baby syndrome were recently investigated. Both cases involved infants who became ill after being fed formula that was reconstituted with water from private wells. Water samples collected from these wells during the infants, illnesses contained nitrate-nitrogen concentrations of 22.9 and 27.4 mg/L.

21. Both (A) and (R) are correct and (R) is correct explanation of (A).

22. Both (A) and (R) are correct and (R) is not the correct explanation of (A).

23. Both (A) and (R) are correct and (R) is not the correct explanation of (A).

24. Both (A) and (R) are true, but (R) is not the correct explanation of (A).

34. Using the organic phosphorus fractionation system suggested by Bowman and Cole, this paper studied the dynamics of labile, moderately labile, moderately resistant, and highly resistant organic phosphorus in rhizosphere and non-rhizosphere soil at different development stages of larch, and their relationships with soil available phosphorus and tree growth yield. The results showed that the main components of soil organic phosphorus in larch plantation were moderately labile and moderately resistant organic phosphorus, amounted to 77.07%-86.68% of the total organic phosphorus. The labile and moderately labile organic phosphorus in rhizosphere soil were the main sources of soil available phosphorus at different development stages of larch. The contents of total organic phosphorus, labile organic phosphorus, moderately resistant organic phosphorus and highly resistant organic phosphorus in rhizosphere soil decreased with stand ages from young stand to near mature stand, but increased from near mature stand to mature stand. No apparent change the moderately labile organic phosphorus content was found over stand ages in rhizosphere soil. The contents of various organic phosphorus forms presented a fluctuating increasing tendency in non-rhizosphere soil as stand ages increased. There was a close relationship between the increments of periodic average diameter at breast height and periodic average height and the contents of soil labile organic phosphorus and available phosphorus. Cellulose and hemicelluse are not resistance to decay but are broken down more slowly. They are considered as moderatory labile.

35. In fact, most galls contain both the parasitic larvae of a gall wasp, and the parasitic larvae of a wasp which feeds on the parasitic larvae of the gall wasp. (It's like an Escher drawing! But with parasitic wasps.)

Another interesting fact is that many gall wasps practice parthenogenesis, which is where the female reproduces without any interaction with a male. Some species practice blended methods (sometimes reproducing sexually, and other times using parthenogenesis) and other species alternate generations (with one generation reproducing sexually, and the next generation reproducing through parthenogenesis). Hence, the parasitic gall information is related to parasite specific enzymes.

37. Historical records → Tree rings → Pollens → Lithological records.

38. **Acid drainage :** When rock surfaces are exposed to air and rain, a reaction can occur with the elements in the rock which results in a change in the characteristics of the water that drains off. If the rock contains sulphides, a natural oxidation process can acidify the water. This is known as acid drainage (also acid rock drainage (ARD) or acid mine drainage (AMD)). As the water becomes more acidic, its capacity to leach out other elements from the rock, such as metals, increases. The resulting drainage can become very acidic and contain a number of harmful constituents. In some cases, elements from the rock can leach out into contact water without acidification and result in water contamination—this is known as metal leaching (ML). In either case, polluted water drains away from the exposed rock and can have significant impacts on surrounding water bodies (rivers, lakes, coastal areas, groundwater) and the wildlife or people who come in contact with these sources. Acid drainage is more in mining of lime stone.

Although this is natural process, mining activities can trigger this phenomenon by exposing large surface areas of rock to water and oxygen. Rock is exposed on the walls of open pits and underground structures–but the most significant newly exposed rock surfaces are in the fragmented pieces of waste rock that are removed from the ground and placed in dumps.

39. The geothermal gradient of 25°C/km is thought to be restricted to the upper part of the earth's crust. If it continued at this rate uniformly from the surface, the internal temperature of the earth would be greater than 2,000°C within the lithosphere—a temperature that far exceeds the melting temperatures for all rocks at the depth. Since the crust and upper mantle are solid and brittle, this gradient cannot extend to these depths, where it is more likely about 1°C/km. Recent laboratory studies have suggested the temperature is about 4,800°C at the base of the lower mantle and about 7,000°C in the inner core. The heat flow is the amount of heat from the earth's interior that is lost at the surface. The heat is probably generated by a still–cooling core or by the radioactive decay of elements such as uranium and thorium. Areas of higher heat flow are generally related to magmatic activity or tectonic forces that bring wedges of hot mantle rock (mangle plumes) into thin or faulted crustal areas.

40. Coal mining areas are affected by Land subsidence, fire hazard and air pollution.

41. Uranium, thorium and potassium are the main elements contributing to natural terrestrial radioactivity. The isotopes ^{228}U, ^{235}U, ^{232}Th and ^{40}K decay with half-lives so long that significant amounts remain in the earth, providing a continuing source of heat. The slow decay of these isotopes also provides the basis for radiometric age dating and isotopic modelling of the evolution of the earth and its crust. There is a complex interplay between their heat production and the processes involved in crust formation. The phenomena such as volcanism, earthquakes, and large-scale hydrothermal activity associated with ore deposition reflect the dissipation of heat energy from the earth much of which derived from natural radioactivity.

42. On the morning of December 26, 2004 a magnitude 9.3 earthquake struck off the Northwest coast of the Indonesian island of Sumatra. The earthquake resulted from complex slip on the fault where the oceanic portion of the Indian Plate slides under Sumatra, part of the Eurasian Plate. The earthquake deformed the ocean floor, pushing the overlying water up into a tsunami wave. The tsunami wave devastated nearby areas where the wave may have been as high as 25 metres (80 feet) tall and killed nearly 3,00,000 people from nations in the region and tourists from around the world. The tsunami wave itself also travelled the globe, and was measured in the Pacific and

many other places by tide gauges. Measurements in California exceeded 40 cm in height, while New Jersey saw water level fluctuations as great as 34 cm. Eyewitness accounts, photos, and videos provided unprecedented documentation of the event.

44. Northeast India is seismically, one of the six most active regions of the world, the other five being Mexico, Taiwan, California, Japan and Turkey. It is placed in zone 5, the highest zone, of the seismic zonation map of India. It lies at the junction of Himalayan arc to the north and Burmese arc to the east. The region has experienced 18 large earthquakes ($M \geq 7$) during the last hundred years including the great earthquakes of Shillong (1897, $M = 8.7$) and Assam-Tibet border (1950, $M = 8.7$). Besides, several hundred small and micro earthquakes have also been recorded in the region. The high seismicity in the region is attributed to the collision tectonics between the Indian and the Eurasian plate in the north and subduction tectonics along the Indo-Myanmar range (IMR) in the east.

45. Earth's core is structured in a solid inner core, mainly composed of iron, and a liquid outer core. The temperature at the inner core boundary is expected to be close to the melting point of iron at 330 gigapascal (GPa). Despite intensive experimental and theoretical efforts, there is little consensus on the melting behaviour of iron at these extreme pressures and temperatures. We present static laser-heated diamond anvil cell experiments up to 200 GPa using synchrotron-based fast X-ray diffraction as a primary melting diagnostic. When extrapolating to higher pressures, we conclude that the melting temperature of iron at the inner core boundary is 6230 ± 500 kelvin. This estimation favours a high heat flux at the core-mantle boundary with a possible partial melting of the mantle.

46. Gasification is a processs that converts organic or fossil based carbonaceous materials into carbon monoxide, hydrogen and carbon dioxide. This is achieved by reacting the material at high temperatures ~750°C-850°C, without combustion, with a controlled amount of oxygen and/or steam. The resulting gas mixture is called syngas (from synthesis gas or synthetic gas) or producer gas and is itself a fuel. The power derived from gasification and combustion of the resultant gas is considered to be a source of renewable energy, if the gasified compounds were obtained from biomass.

The advantage of gasification is that using the syngas is potentially more efficient than direct combustion of the original fuel because it can be combusted at higher temperatures or even in fuel cells, so that the themodynamic upper limit to the efficiency defined by Carnot's rule is higher or not applicable. Syngas may be burned directly in gas engines, used to produce methanol and hydrogen, or converted via the Fischer–Tropsch process into synthetic fuel. Gasification can also begin with material which would otherwise have been disposed of such as biodegradable waste. In addition, the high-temperature process refines out corrosive ash elements such as chloride and potassium, allowing clean gas production from otherwise problematic fuels. Gasification of fossil fuels is currently widely used on industrial scales to generate electricity.

51. Pyrolysis is a thermochemical decomposition of organic material at elevated temperatures in the absence of oxygen (or any halogen). It involves the simultaneous change of chemical composition and physical phase, and is irreversible.

Pyrolysis is a type of thermolysis, and is most commonly observed in organic materials exposed to high temperatures. It is one of the processes involved in charring wood, starting at 200-300°C (390-570°F). It also occurs in fires where solid fuels are burning or when vegetation comes into contact with lava in volcanic eruptions. In general, pyrolysis of organic substances produces gas and liquid products and leaves a solid residue richer in carbon content, char. Extreme pyrolysis, which leaves mostly, carbon as the residue, is called carbonization.

The process is used heavily in the chemical industry, for example, to produce charcoal, activated carbon, methanol and other chemicals from wood, to convert ethylene dichloride into vinyl chloride to make PVC, to produce coke from coal, to convert biomass into syngas and biochar, to turn waste into safely disposable substances, and for transforming medium-weight hydrocarbons from oil into lighter ones like gasoline. These specialized uses of pyrolysis may be called various names, such as dry distillation, destructive distillation, or cracking.

Pyrolysis also plays an important role in several cooking procedures, such as baking, frying, grilling and caramelizing. In addition, it is a tool of chemical analysis, for example, in mass spectrometry and in carbon-14 dating. Indeed, many important chemical substances, such as phosphorus and sulfuric acid, were first obtained by this process. Pyrolysis has been assumed to take place during catagenesis, the conversion of buried organic matter to fossil fuels. It is also the basis of pyrography. In their embalming process, the ancient Egyptians used a mixture of substances, including methanol, which they obtained from the pyrolysis of wood.

52. In 1972, new wildlife protection act was passed under this act, possession, trapping, shooting of wild animals alive or dead, serving their meat in eating houses, their transport and export are all controlled and watched by special staff. This acts prohibits hunting of females and young ones. Under this act, threatened species are absolutely protected and the rest afford graded protection according to their state of population size.

53. Literature comparing national ambient air quality standards (AAQSs) globally is scattered and sparse. Twenty-four hour AAQSs for particulate matter <10 μm in aerodynamic diameter (PM_{10}) and sulphur dioxide (SO_2) in 96 countries were identified through literature review, an international survey, and querying an international legal database. Eighty three per cent of the 96 countries with information on the presence or absence of AAQSs, have 24-h AAQSs for either PM_{10} or SO_2. The annual average concentration of SO_2 in residential areas in India by National Ambient Air Quality Standards is 60 μg/m^3.

56. **Environmental management System (EMS):** It EMS is that aspect of the total management structure of the organisation which addresses the immediate as well as long term impact of its products, services and processes on the enviornment. EMS is a tool, which is used by organisations world over to facilitate the implementation of environmental policy of the respective governments.

57. **The Gaussian plume model** is a (relatively) simple mathematical model that is typically applied to point source emitters, such as coal-burning electricity-producing plants. Occassionally, this model will be applied to non-point source emitters, such as exhaust from automobiles in an urban area.

One of the key assumptions of this model is that over short periods of time (such as a few hours) steady state conditions exists with regard to air pollutant emissions and meteorological changes. Air pollution is represented by an idealized plume coming from the top of a stack of some height and diameter. One of the primary calculations is the effective stack height. As the gases are heated in the plant (from the burning of coal or other materials), the hot plume will be thrust upward some distance above the top of the stack—the effective stack height. We need to be able to calculate this vertical displacement, which depends on the stack gas exit velocity and temperature, and the temperature of the surrounding air. According to Gaussian plume model, the grand level concentration (c), $C \propto e^{-H/\sigma}$.

58. In oceanic biogeochemistry, the f-ratio is the fraction of total primary production fuelled by nitrate (as opposed to that fuelled by other nitrogen compounds such as ammonium). This fraction is significant because it is assumed to be directly related to the sinking (export) flux of organic marine snow from the surface ocean by the biological pump. The ratio was originally defined by Richard Eppley and Bruce Peterson in one of the first papers estimating global oceanic production.

$$\text{F-ratio} = \frac{\text{Sum of squares per degree of freedom}}{\text{Residual sum of squares per degree of freedom}}$$

$$= \frac{250}{100} = 2.5.$$

60. We have, $A - \lambda I = \begin{bmatrix} -1 & 2 & 2 \\ 2 & 2 & 2 \\ -3 & -6 & -6 \end{bmatrix} - \begin{bmatrix} \lambda & 0 & 0 \\ 0 & \lambda & 0 \\ 0 & 0 & \lambda \end{bmatrix}$

$$= \begin{bmatrix} -1-\lambda & 2 & 2 \\ 2 & 2-\lambda & 2 \\ -3 & -6 & -6-\lambda \end{bmatrix}$$

$\Rightarrow$ $-(1 + \lambda) \{(\lambda - 2) (6 + \lambda) + 12\} + 2 \{-6 + 12 + 2\lambda\} + 2 \{-12 + 3(2 - \lambda)\} = 0$

$\Rightarrow$ $-(1 + \lambda) \{\lambda^2 + 4\lambda - 12 + 12\} + 2 (2\lambda + 6) + 2 \{-6 - 3\lambda\} = 0$

$\Rightarrow$ $-(1 + \lambda)^2 \{\lambda^2 + 4\lambda\} + 12 + 4\lambda - 12 - 6\lambda = 0$

$\Rightarrow$ $-\lambda (1 + \lambda)^2 \{\lambda + 4\} -2\lambda = 0$

$\Rightarrow$ $-\lambda \{\lambda^2 + 5\lambda + 4 + 2\} = 0$

$\Rightarrow$ $-\lambda (\lambda + 2) (\lambda + 3) = 0$

$\therefore$ $\lambda = 0, -2, -3$

Hence, 3 is not eigenvalue. Therefore option (C) is correct.

62. Hot spot are areas that are extremely rich in species, have high endemism and are under constant threat. Among the 25 hot spots of the world, two are found in India extending into neighbouring countries—the western Ghats/Sri Lanka and the Indo-Myanmar region (covering the eastern Himalayas.) These areas are particularly rich in floral wealth and endemism, not only in flowring plants but also in repetiles, amphibians, swallow-tailed butterflies and some mammals.

63. An ecosystem that is fully designed and controlled by man is called Engineered eco-systems. A paddy field or a fish pond can be quoted as an example for engineered type of eco-system.

64. Pyramid of energy : The energy pyramids give the best picture of overall nature of the ecosystem. Here, number and weight of organisms at any level depends not on the amount of fixed energy present at any one time in the level just below but rather on the rate at which food is being produced. In contrast with the pyramids of numbers and biomass which are pictures of the standing situations, the pyramid of energy is a picture of the rates of passage of food mass through the food chain. Pyramid energy cannot be invested in a stable ecosystem.

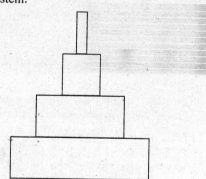

Pyramid of energy

65. The temperature is an environment factor and is responsible for cyclomorphism in animals.

66. Everyone is exposed to small amounts of strontium-90, since it is widely dispersed in the environment and the food chain. Dietary intake of Sr-90, however, has steadily fallen over the last 30 years with the suspension of nuclear weapons testing. People who live near or work in nuclear facilities may have increased exposure to Sr-90. The greatest concern would be the exposures from an accident at a nuclear reactor, or an accident involving high-level wastes. Sr^{90} can enter and accumulates in the body through drinking water.

67. Neurotoxicity occurs when the exposure to natural or artificial toxic substances, which are called neurotoxins, alters the normal activity of the nervous system in such a way as to cause damage to nervous tissue. This can eventually disrupt or even kill neurons, key cells that transmit and process signals in the brain and other parts of the nervous system. Neurotoxicity can result from exposure to substances used in chemotherapy, radiation treatment, drug therapies, certain drug abuse and organ transplants, as well as exposure to heavy metals, certain foods and food additives, pesticides, industrial and/or cleaning solvents, cosmetics, and some naturally occurring substances. Symptoms may appear immediately after exposure or be delayed. They may include limb weakness or numbness, loss of memory, vision, and/or intellect, uncontrollable obsessive and/or compulsive behaviours, delusions, headache, cognitive and behavioural problems and sexual dysfunction. Individuals with certain disorders may be especially vulnerable to neurotoxins.

The name implies the role of a neurotoxin, although the term neurotoxic may be used more loosely to describe states that are known to cause physical brain damage but where no obvious neurotoxin has been identified. Organophosphate is an example of neurotoxic.

69. Clostridium sporogenes is the name given to strains of Clostridium botulinum that do not produce botulinum neurotoxins. Like other strains of C. botulinum, it is an anaerobic Gram-positive, rod-shaped bacterium that produces oval, subterminal endospores and is commonly found in soil. It is being investigated as a way to deliver cancer-treating drugs to tumours in patients.

Clostridium sporogenes is often used as a surrogate for C. botulinum when testing the efficacy of commercial sterilisation.

70. An electrostatic precipitator (ESP), or electrostatic air cleaner is a particulate collection device that removes particles from a flowing gas (such as air) using the force of an induced electrostatic charge. Electrostatic precipitators are highly efficient filtration devices that minimally impede the flow of gases through the device, and can easily remove fine particulate matter such as dust and smoke from the air stream. The particles sizes < 1 μm are most efficiently removed by ESP.

In contrast to wet scrubbers which apply energy directly to the flowing fluid medium, an ESP applies energy only to the particulate matter being collected and therefore is very efficient in its consumption of energy (in the form of electricity).

71. The sound generated by the unsteady motion of a vortex filament moving over a flat boundary with a sharp flow impedance discontinuity is studied theoretically. Theoretical results show that the vortex filament undergoes significant accelerating or decelerating motions and radiates sound at the instant when it moves across the plane of impedance discontinuity. The accelerations and decelerations of the vortex filament are shown to be the major mechanisms of sound generation. The sound so produced has a large low-frequency content such that the change in the flow impedance affects only the sound generation process but not the subsequent sound propagation to the far field. The attenuation of sound by reactive type silencers is based on impedence discontinuity.

72. Farmer's lung is a hypersensitivity pneumonitis induced by the inhalation of biologic dusts coming from hay dust or mold spores or other agricultural products. It results in a type III hypersensitivity, inflammatory response and can progress to become a chronic condition which is considered potentially dangerous. While

inhaled allergens often provoke the creation of IgE antibodies that circulate in the bloodstream, these types of immune response are most often initiated by exposure to thermophilic actinomycetes (most commonly Saccharopolyspora rectivirgula), which generates IgG-type antibodies. Following a subsequent exposure, IgG antibodies combine with the inhaled allergens to form immune complexes in the walls of the alveoli in the lungs. This causes fluid, protein and cells to accumulate in the alveolar wall which slows blood-gas interchange and compromises the function of the lung.

73. **Lithosere** is a type of Xerosere originating on bare rock surfaces. The original substratum is deficient in water and lacks any organic matter having only minerals in disintegrated unweathered state. The pioneers to colonise this primitive substratum are crustose type of lichens and moss stages.

74. **Poisson distribution** is the distribution of a discrete random variable whose probability of occurrence is very small but the mean and variance of the distribution are equal and finite. Thus, the Poisson distribution is the distribution of a rare event with a finite mean and variance. The equality of mean and variance is important property of Poisson distribution.

75. The large area of the Indus river flow in the Himalayas. The Tibetan Plateau contains the world's third-largest store of ice. Qin Dahe, the former head of the China Meteorological Administration, said the recent fast pace of melting and warmer temperatures will be good for agriculture and tourism in the short term, but issued a strong warning:

"Temperatures are rising four times faster than elsewhere in China, and the Tibetan glaciers are retreating at a higher speed than in any other part of the world. In the short term, this will cause lakes to expand and bring floods and mudflows. In the long run, the glaciers are vital lifelines of the Indus River. Once they vanish, water supplies in Pakistan will be in peril."

Hence, Indus river has maximum melt water component in its discharge.

UGC-NET ENVIRONMENTAL SCIENCE, DECEMBER 2012

PAPER-II

Note : *This paper contains fifty (50) objective type questions, each question carrying two (2) marks. Attempt **all** the questions.*

1. **Assertion (A):** Biosphere constitutes an excellent life-support system which is sustainable and can fulfil all human needs.

   Reason (R): The size and productivity of the Biosphere is limited by availability of water, nutrients and environmental conditions. Identify the correct code :

   Codes :
   A. Both (A) and (R) are true and (R) is the correct explanation of (A).
   B. Both (A) and (R) are true, but (R) is not the correct explanation of (A).
   C. (A) is true but (R) is false.
   D. (A) is false but (R) is true.

2. Geostrophic wind occurs when pressure gradient force balances
   A. Coriolis force
   B. Frictional force
   C. Centripetal force
   D. Coriolis and frictional force together

3. Scales of Meteorology are in the following order starting from the least
   A. Macro –, Micro –, Meso –
   B. Macro–, Meso–, Micro–
   C. Meso–, Macro–, Micro–
   D. Micro–, Meso–, Macro–

4. When the full potential of physical, chemical and biological factors, a species can use if there is no competition, it is called
   A. Fundamental niche
   B. Ecological niche
   C. Realized niche
   D. Competitive exclusion

5. The uppermost zone of atmosphere of earth, where shortwave ultraviolet radiations are absorbed, is
   A. Troposphere
   B. Stratosphere
   C. Mesosphere
   D. Thermosphere

6. Which of the following oxides of nitrogen is the major air pollutant released from automobile exhausts?
   A. NO
   B. N_2O
   C. NO_2
   D. N_2O_3

7. Match List-I with List-II which contains pollutant gases and their threshold (safe limit) values as per WHO standards :

List-I (Pollutant gas)	List-II (Thresholds)
(a) CO	(i) 2 ppm
(b) SO_2	(ii) 50 ppm
(c) NO	(iii) 0.08 ppm
(d) PAN	(iv) 25 ppm

   Identity the correct code :
   Codes :

	(a)	(b)	(c)	(d)
A.	(ii)	(iii)	(i)	(iv)
B.	(iv)	(ii)	(i)	(iii)
C.	(ii)	(i)	(iv)	(iii)
D.	(iii)	(iv)	(ii)	(i)

8. The band labelled as UV-C which is lethal to micro-organisms is
   A. 0.29 – V 0.32 μm
   B. 0.2 – V 0.29 μm
   C. 0.17 – V 0.2 μm
   D. 0.07 – V 0.21 μm

9. Which of the following species in the atmosphere is called atmospheric detergent?
   A. Chlorine radical
   B. Hydroxyl radical
   C. Methyl radical
   D. Ozone radical

10. The pOH of a 0.001 M solution of HCl is
    A. 12
    B. 10
    C. 11
    D. 13

11. Identify the pair (element-health effect) which is correctly matched :
    A. Lead — Methaemoglobinemia
    B. Arsenic — Kidney damage
    C. Mercury — Nervous disorder
    D. PAN — Hypoxemia

12. Which of the following organisms can act as primary consumer, secondary consumer, tertiary consumer or scavenger in different types of food chains?
    A. Raven   B. Tiger
    C. Snake   D. Phytoplanktones

13. The tendency of biological systems to resist change and to remain in a state of equilibrium is called
    A. Homeostatis
    B. Feedback mechanism
    C. Ecological efficiency
    D. Carrying capacity

14. If different categories of threatened species are written in a sequence, what is the correct order?
    A. Extinct → Vulnerable → Rare → Endangered
    B. Vulnerable → Rare → Endangered → Extinct
    C. Vulnerable → Rare → Extinct → Endangered
    D. Rare → Vulnerable → Endangered → Extinct

15. Which of the following is not a type of *ex situ* conservation method?
    A. Botanical garden
    B. Zoological park
    C. Wildlife sanctuaries
    D. Gene banks

16. As a consequence of succession the P/B ratio (Gross production/Standing crop biomass) is changed. It is
    A. high during developmental stages and low at mature stage.
    B. low during developmental stages and high at mature stage.
    C. > 1 or < 1 at developmental stages and approximately 1 at mature stage.
    D. remaining unchanged at all stages.

17. Preparation of hazard-zoning map in case of landslide prone regions involves comprehensive investigation of
    A. details of structural and lithological settings.
    B. geomorphic features relating to instability of slopes.
    C. seismicity pattern of the region.
    D. All of the above

18. If ap = specified value of peak acceleration, N = mean rate of occurrence of earthquake per year, t_{ep} = time interval of consideration (exposure period) and F_{ap} = probability that an observed acceleration is less than or equal to ap, then the cumulative probability distribution of peak acceleration for epoch — dependent seismic hazard map is given by which formula?
    A. $F_{max} \, t_{ep} = \exp \{-Nt(1 - Fap)\}$
    B. $F_{max} = \exp \{-Nt(1 - F_{ap})\} \cdot t_{ep}$
    C. $F_{max} \, tep = \exp \{-t(1 - F_{ap})N\}$
    D. All of the above

19. **Assertion (A):** In oceans, Na has the longest residence time, within an order of magnitude of the age of the oceans.

    Reason (R): The long residence time of Na reflects a lack of reactivity of sodium in the marine environment by not being readily incorporated in the common sedimentary minerals, nor being removed by biological reactions.

    Identify the correct code :
    Codes:
    A. Both (A) and (R) are true and (R) is the correct explanation of (A).
    B. Both (A) and (R) are true, but (R) is not the correct explanation of (A).
    C. (A) is true, but (R) is false.
    D. (A) is false, but (R) is true.

20. According to Goldieh the decreasing order of stability of following minerals of igneous rocks towards weathering is
    A. Muscovite > Quartz > Potash feldspar > Biotite
    B. Biotite > Potash feldspar > Muscovite > Quartz
    C. Quartz > Muscovite > Potash feldspar > Biotite
    D. Potash feldspar > Quartz > Muscovite > Biotite

21. In universal polar stereographic coordinate system the eastings and northings are computed using which projection method?
   A. Polar aspect stereographic projection
   B. Non-polar aspect stereographic projection
   C. Polar aspect mercator projection
   D. Non-polar aspect mercator projection

22. Pitchblende is an ore of
   A. Nickel   B. Chromium
   C. Molybdenum   D. Uranium

23. Copper (Cu) is classified according to its geochemical affinity as
   A. Siderophile element
   B. Chalcophile element
   C. Lithophile element
   D. Atmophile element

24. If 'a' is the fractional wind speed decrease at the wind turbine, the maximum extraction of power from the wind occurs when 'a' is equal to
   A. 1/2   B. 1/3
   C. 1   D. 3/5

25. In the following fusion energy reaction
   $D + T = {}_0n^1 + X$
   identify X
   A. Li   B. H_2
   C. He^3 D. He_4

26. **Assertion (A):** Natural gas is a very attractive ecofriendly fuel.

   Reason (R): It produces few pollutants and less carbon dioxide per unit energy than any other fossil fuel on combustion.

   Identify the correct answer :
   Codes:
   A. Both (A) and (R) are true and (R) is the correct explanation of (A).
   B. Both (A) and (R) are true and (R) is not the correct explanation of (A).
   C. (A) is true but (R) is false.
   D. (A) is false but (R) is true.

27. **Assertion (A):** Solar photovoltaic cells are expensive.

   Reason (R): Solar photovoltaic cells are fabricated from crystalline silicon and operate only at 10-12% efficiency.

   Identify the correct answer :
   Codes:
   A. Both (A) and (R) are true and (R) is the correct explanation of (A).
   B. Both (A) and (R) are true and (R) is not the correct explanation of (A).
   C. (A) is true but (R) is false.
   D. (A) is false but (R) is true.

28. Human activities add 7-9 gigatons of CO_2 per annum into the atmosphere. Major contributor to this CO_2 is
   A. Burning of fossil fuels
   B. Clearing of forests for agriculture
   C. Fermentation industries
   D. Cement industries

29. According to WHO, maximum permissible level of chlorides in drinking water is
   A. 100 mg/L   B. 200 mg/L
   C. 600 mg/L   D. 800 mg/L

30. Wilting coefficient of a loam represents
   A. the minimum water content of the soil at which plants can no longer obtain water
   B. water holding capacity
   C. capillary water
   D. field capacity

31. Which one of the following techniques can be used for determining the level of cadmium in soil?
   A. UV – Visible spectrophotometer
   B. Atomic Absorption Spectrophotometer
   C. XRD
   D. IR spectrometer

32. For noise control in automobiles, the exhaust muffler attenuates sound by
   A. Absorption
   B. Destructive interference
   C. Reducing velocity of hot gases
   D. Absorption and destructive interference

33. Five particles (< 2-3 μm) can be effectively collected from industrial stacks by
   A. Fabric filters
   B. Cyclone separators
   C. Venturi scrubbers
   D. Settling chambers

34. Soil fulvic acids are strong chelators of
    A. Iron (II)
    B. Iron (III)
    C. Both A and B
    D. Fe(OH)$_3$

35. Natural source of polycyclic aromatic hydrocarbons (PAHs) is
    A. Root exudates
    B. Anaerobic bacteria
    C. Aerobic bacteria
    D. Grass fires

36. Match the 'phase' with the 'activity' in Environmental Audit. Identify the correct answer from the codes given below. the lists :

List-I (Phase)	List-II (Activity)
(a) Pre-Audit	(i) Human input-output analysis in relation to economy
(b) On-site Audit	(ii) Reviewing audit-check lists
(c) Post-Audit	(iii) Records/Documents Review

    Codes:

	(a)	(b)	(c)
A.	(ii)	(iii)	(i)
B.	(i)	(iii)	(ii)
C.	(i)	(ii)	(iii)
D.	(iii)	(ii)	(i)

37. Match the Impact Assessment Methodologies (List-II) with the corresponding environments (List-I). Identify the correct answer from the codes given below the lists.

List-I	List-II
(a) Air	(i) Ecosystem models
(b) Biological	(ii) Gaussian models
(c) Water	(iii) Mass balance approach
(d) Land	(iv) G.I.S.

    Codes :

	(a)	(b)	(c)	(d)
A.	(ii)	(i)	(iii)	(iv)
B.	(i)	(ii)	(iv)	(iii)
C.	(iii)	(iv)	(ii)	(i)
D.	(iv)	(iii)	(i)	(ii)

38. Public hearing is conducted
    A. Prior to site selection
    B. Prior to approval of Terms of Reference
    C. After preparation of EIA
    D. After environmental clearance

39. IAIA stands for
    A. International Association of Impact Assessment
    B. Indian Association of Impact Assessment
    C. International Assembly of Impact Assessment
    D. Indian Assembly of Impact Assessment

40. Municipal Solid Wastes (MSWs) have the heating value typically in the range
    A. 9,300 to 12,800 kJ/kg
    B. 1000 to 2500 kJ/kg
    C. 1780 to 2830 kJ/kg
    D. 530 to 780 kJ/kg

41. The Motor Vehicles Act, 1938 was amended in which year?
    A. 1972   B. 1980
    C. 1988   D. 1986

42. The following statistical test is used to ascertain whether there is significant difference between the variances of two sets of observations:
    A. t-test   B. F-test
    C. Chi square test   D. Regression

43. The population (N) of an ecosystem obeys the growth equation

    $$\frac{dN}{dt} = \alpha N - \beta N^2$$

    where α and β are constants. The maximum sustainable yield of this ecosystem will be
    A. $\alpha - \beta N$ B. α/β
    C. $\alpha/2\beta$ D. α^2/β

44. The geometric mean of the following data:

    4, 10, 25, 10

    is
    A. 10   B. 5

    C. 12.25   D. $\frac{100}{49}$

45. If the mean and variance of a Poisson distribution are μ and σ, then the following relation is correct.

A. $\sigma = \mu^2$ B. $\sigma = \sqrt{\mu}$

C. $\sigma^2 = \mu$ D. $\sigma = 2\mu$

46. In the Gaussian Plume Model, the plume rise varies with Buoyancy Flux Parameter F as

A. F B. $F^{\frac{1}{2}}$

C. $F^{\frac{1}{3}}$ D. $F^{\frac{1}{4}}$

47. United Nations Conference on Environment, also termed as Earth Summit, was held in 1992 in which city?

A. Rio de Janeiro   B. Kyoto

C. Stockholm   D. Copenhagen

48. In which part of India, the tropical Western Ghats are situated?

A. Punjab   B. Rajasthan

C. Gujarat   D. Kerala

49. Variety of different species, genetic variability among individuals within each species and variety of ecosystems constitute the so called

A. Species diversity

B. Genetic diversity

C. Biological diversity

D. Ecological diversity

50. Baba Amte was the leader of

A. Appiko Movement

B. Chipko Movement

C. Narmada Bachao Andolan

D. Tehri Dam Movement

ANSWERS

1	2	3	4	5	6	7	8	9	10
D	A	D	A	D	A	C	B	B	C
11	**12**	**13**	**14**	**15**	**16**	**17**	**18**	**19**	**20**
D	A	A	B	C	A	D	A	A	C
21	**22**	**23**	**24**	**25**	**26**	**27**	**28**	**29**	**30**
A	D	B	B	D	A	A	A	C	A
31	**32**	**33**	**34**	**35**	**36**	**37**	**38**	**39**	**40**
B	C	C	C	D	A	A	C	A	A
41	**42**	**43**	**44**	**45**	**46**	**47**	**48**	**49**	**50**
C	B	C	A	A	C	A	D	C	C

SOME SELECTED EXPLANATORY ANSWERS

2. An air parcel initially at rest will move from high pressure to low pressure because of the pressure gradient force (PGF). However, as that air parcel begins to move, it is deflected by the Coriolis force to the right in the northern hemisphere (to the left on the southern hemisphere). As the wind gains speed, the deflection increases until the Coriolis force equals the pressure gradient force. At this point, the wind will be blowing parallel to the isobars. When this happens, the wind is referred to as geostrophic wind.

3. Microclimatology—Microclimatological studies often measure small-scale contrasts, such as between hilltop and valley or between city and surrounding country. They may be of an extremely small scale, such as one side of a hedge contrasted with the other, a plowed furrow versus level soil, or opposite leaf surfaces. Climate in the micro scale may be effectively modified by relatively simple human efforts.

Meso Climatology—Meso climatology embraces a rather indistinct middle ground between macro climatology and microclimatology. The areas are smaller than those of macro climatology are and larger than those of microclimatology, and they may or may not be climatically representative of a general region.

Macroclimatology—Macro climatology is the study of the large-scale climate of a large area or country. Climate of this type is not easily modified by human efforts. However, continued pollution of the Earth, its streams, rivers, and atmosphere, can eventually make these modifications

4. **Fundamental niche:** The full range of environmental conditions and resources an organism can possibly occupy and use, especially when limiting factors are absent in its habitat.

   The fundamental niche describes the potential area and resources an organism is capable of using. But the presence of limiting factors such as direct competition with other organisms, the organism tends to occupy a niche narrower than this.

5. The thermosphere is the layer of the Earth's atmosphere directly above the mesosphere and directly below the exosphere. Within this layer, ultraviolet radiation (UV) causes ionization.

   At these high altitudes, the residual atmospheric gases sort into strata according to molecular mass (see turbosphere). Thermospheric temperatures increase with altitude due to absorption of highly energetic solar radiation.

6. Petrol on combustion produces carbon monoxide, hydrocarbons, nitrogen oxides, aldehydes, sulphur compounds, organic acids and ammonia and carbon particles. Incomplete combustion of petrol produces a hydrocarbon, 3, 4 benzpyrene. There is more pollution during acceleration and deceleration than during constant speed. Nitrous oxides, produced as a result of combusting fuel at excessive

temperatures, contribute significantly to car pollution. Nitrogen oxide is a major cause of acid rain. Over the years, better techniques have reduced the amount of nitrous oxide released from cars but these gases are still responsible for around 8% of global warming.

9. Hydroxyl radicals are often called the "detergent" of the atmosphere because they control the atmosphere's capacity to cleanse itself of pollutants. Here, we show that the reaction of electronically excited nitrogen dioxide with water can be an important source of tropospheric hydroxyl radicals. Using measured rate data, along with available solar flux and atmospheric mixing ratios, we demonstrate that the tropospheric hydroxyl contribution from this source can be a substantial fraction (50%) of that from the traditional $O(^1D) + H_2O$ reaction in the boundary-layer region for high solar zenith angles. Inclusion of this chemistry is expected to affect modeling of urban air quality, where the interactions of sunlight with emitted NO_x species, volatile organic compounds, and hydroxyl radicals are central in determining the rate of ozone formation.

10. $pH = -\log [H^+]$

   $pOH = -\log [OH^-]$

Since the HCl is strong acid and dissociates completely hence

[H^+] from HCl is 0.001M.
   The pH = $-\log [0.001]$
   $= -(-3)$
   $= 3$
   $pOH = 14 - pH = 14 - 3 = 11$ **Answer**

13. **Homeostatis:** The ability or tendency of an organism or cell to maintain internal equilibrium by adjusting its physiological processes.

Any self-regulating process by which a biological or mechanical system maintains stability while adjusting to changing conditions. Systems in dynamic equilibrium reach a balance in which internal change continuously compensates for external change in a feedback control process to keep conditions relatively uniform. An example is temperature regulation mechanically in a room by a thermostat or biologically in the body by a complex system controlled by the hypothalamus, which adjusts breathing and metabolic rates, blood-vessel dilation, and blood-sugar level in response to changes caused by factors including ambient temperature, hormones, and disease.

14. The World Conservation Union (IUCN) is the foremost authority on threatened species, and treats threatened species not as a single category, but as a group of four categories, depending on the degree to which they are threatened:

They are written in a sequence as:

Vulnerable $\rightarrow$ Rare $\rightarrow$ Endangered $\rightarrow$ Extinct.

15. Ex-situ conservation means literally, "off-site conservation". It is the process of protecting an endangered species of plant or animal outside its natural habitat; for example, by removing part of the population from a threatened habitat and placing it in a new location, which may be a wild area or within the care of humans. While ex-situ conservation comprises some of the oldest and best known conservation methods, it also involves newer, sometimes controversial laboratory methods.

They are meant to protect and conserve particular species of wildlife. They are not bound by state legislation. Killing, hunting or capturing of any animal species is prohibited. Forestry and other activities such as grazing of domestic animals are permitted as long as these activities do not adversely affect the wild life.

22. Lindgren defines an ore mineral as "a mineral which may be used for the extraction of one or more metals." A uranium ore mineral is therefore a mineral possessing such physical and chemical properties and occurring in a deposit in such concentrations that it may be used for the profitable extraction of uranium, either alone or together with one or more other metals. Pitchblende is Amorphous, dense, black, pitchy form of the crystalline uranium oxide mineral uraninite; it is one of the primary mineral ores of uranium. Pitchblende is found in granular masses and has a greasy lustre. Three chemical elements were first discovered in pitchblende: uranium, polonium, and radium.

23. Copper is a chalcophile element forming several minerals, including chalcopyrite $CuFeS_2$, covellite CuS, and malachite $Cu_2CO_3(OH)_2$, but is more widely dispersed at trace levels in mica (biotite), pyroxene and amphibole, thus showing a greater affinity for mafic than for felsic igneous rocks. Copper can occur in its metallic form in nature (i.e., native copper), and is one of the seven metals known in antiquity. Copper may be redistributed during low-grade metamorphism and metasomatism (Senior and Leake 1978), but its mobility is more restricted at higher metamorphic grades (Nicollet and Andriambololona 1980). In common with other chalcophile elements, Cu is strongly concentrated into sulphide minerals during hydrothermal mineralisation.

28. Burning wood or allowing trees to rot does not increase the amount of carbon dioxide in the atmosphere, as long as old trees are replaced by new ones which absorb as much carbon as the old ones had done. This is essentially part of the natural cycle, in which carbon is continually added to and removed from the atmosphere. But deforestation does increase the amount of carbon dioxide in the atmosphere, because new trees are not allowed to replace those removed.

The most important way in which we add to the amount of carbon dioxide in the atmosphere is by burning fossil fuels. The burning of fossil fuels is a primary source of increased atmospheric carbon dioxide. Motor vehicle exhaust and the burning of fuel oil in ships and factories or power plants puts lots of CO_2 into the air. We also burn a lot of coal worldwide, and this also ups CO_2 output by people. Additionally, the burning of wild lands (either by accident or on purpose) is increasing the amount of combustion byproducts (including CO_2) in the air.

29. Environmental impact of chlorides are not usually harmful to human health; however, the sodium part of the table salt has been linked to heart and kidney diseases. Sodium chloride may impact a salty taste at 250 mg/l; however, calcium or magnesium chloride is usually detected by taste until levels of 1000 mg/l are reached. Public drinking water standards require chloride level not to exceed 250 mg/l. Chlorides may get into surface water from several sources including: rocks contain chlorides, agricultural run-off, waste water from industries, oil well wastes, and effluent waste water from waste water treatment plants. Chlorides can corrode metals and affect the taste of food products. Chlorides can contaminate fresh water streams and lakes. Fish and aquatic communities cannot survive in high level of chlorides. Therefore, water that is used in industry or proceeds for any use has a recommended maximum chloride level.

30. If the roots of a plant are well established in a mass of soil, the plant gradually reduces the water content until permanent wilting occurs. The water remaining in the soil under this condition has been termed non-available by previous writers. We have found, however, that plants can reduce the soil moisture content somewhat below the point corresponding to the permanent wilting of the leaves, so that the water content at the wilting point is not strictly non-available. In fact, this loss of water from the soil to the air goes on through the plant tissues even after the death of the plant, and appears to be limited only by the establishment of a state of equilibrium between the soil and the air. The plant during the drying stage acts simply as a medium for the transference of water, and while the rate of loss is reduced, the final result is the same as if the air and soil were in direct contact. By means of the wax seal method, which effectually prevents all direct loss of water from the soil, we have been able to demonstrate conclusively that there is

a continued loss of water from the soil through the plant long after wilting occurs.

31. Quantitative determination of cadmium can be performed using a variety of methods and techniques, including:
   - Atomic absorption spectroscopy (AAS) with either a graphite furnace (GFAA, EPA Method 213.2) or flame (FAA, EPA Method 231.1)
   - Inductively coupled plasma techniques (ICP) using optical emission spectroscopy (ICP-OES) or atomic emission spectroscopy (ICP-AES, EPA method 200.7)
   - Mass spectrometry (ICP-MS, EPA method 200.8)
   - Electrochemical techniques such as adsorptive cathodic stripping voltametry (ACSV) [8, 9], potentiometric stripping analysis (PSA) [10], and liquid chromatography [10] are also used to analyze and separate cadmium (Cd (II)).

32. The most common element used to silence generator exhausts are reactive mufflers. Reactive mufflers are available in a wide range of cost and performance. The noise is reduced by forcing the exhaust air to pass through a series of tubes and chambers.

Each element in the muffler has sound reduction properties that vary greatly with acoustic frequency, and it is the mixing and matching of these elements that constitutes muffler design.

35. Sources of PAHs can be both natural and anthropogenic.

Natural sources include:
   - forest and grass fires
   - oil seeps
   - volcanoes
   - chlorophyllous plants, fungi, and bacteria

39. IAIA is the leading global network on best practice in the use of impact assessment for informed decision making regarding policies, programs, plans and projects.

The name of the South African Affiliate of the International Association for Impact

Assessment (IAIA) will be the "International Association for Impact Assessment - South African Affiliate (IAIAsa)" herein after referred to as the "Affiliate".

41. After the coming into force of the Motor Vehicles Act, 1988, Government received a number of representations and suggestions from the state govt. transport operators and members of public regarding the inconvenience faced by them because of the operation of some of the provisions of the 1988 Act. A Review Committee was, therefore, constituted by the Government in March, 1990 to examine and review the 1988 Act.

43. Let population of ecosystem at time t is P then $P = \alpha N - \beta N^2$

For maximum sustainable yield

$$\frac{dP}{dN} = 0$$

$$\frac{dP}{dN}(\alpha N - \beta N^2) = 0$$

$$\alpha - 2\beta N = 0$$

$$N = \frac{\alpha}{2\beta}$$

44. Geometric mean of the series
a, b, c, d

$$G.M. = \sqrt[4]{abcd}$$
$$= \sqrt[4]{4 \times 10 \times 25 \times 10}$$
$$= \sqrt[4]{10 \times 10 \times 10 \times 10}$$
$$= 10.$$

45. The *mean* of a data set is simply the arithmetic average of the values in the set, obtained by summing the values and dividing by the number of values. Recall that when we summarize a data set in a frequency distribution, we are approximating the data set by "rounding" each value in a given class to the class mark. With this in mind, it is natural to define the mean of a frequency distribution by

$$\mu = \frac{1}{n}\sum_{i=1}^{n} f_i x_i = \sum_{i=1}^{n} p_i x_i$$

The *variance* of a data set is the arithmetic average of the squared differences between the values and the mean. Again, when we summarize a data set in a frequency distribution, we are approximating the data set by "rounding" each value in a given class to the class mark. Thus, the variance of a frequency distribution is given by

$$\sigma^2 = \frac{1}{n}\sum_{i=1}^{n} f_i (x_i - \mu)^2 = \sum_{i=1}^{n} p_i (x_i - \mu)^2$$

The *standard deviation* is the square root of the variance:

$$\sigma = \mu^2$$

47. The United Nations Conference on Environment and Development (UNCED), also known as the Rio Summit, Rio Conference, and Earth Summit was a major United Nations conference held in Rio de Janeiro from 3 June to 14 June 1992.

48. Western ghats are the continuous range of mountains, rising up from the India's Malabar Coast. The average elevation of the western ghats is approximately 1200 meters. Starting at south of Tapti river (near the border of Gujarat and Maharashtra), Western Ghats cover 1600 Km, and pass through states like Maharashtra, Goa, Kerala, Karnataka and Tamil Nadu. The mountain range of Western Ghats end at Kanyakumari, which is the southern end of India.

50. Baba Amte, (1914-2008), was one of India's most respected social and moral leaders. Most of his life he devoted to the care and rehabilitation of leprosy patients. His community of a few thousand patients at Anandwan has done much to dispel prejudice against the victims of leprosy. In 1990 he left Anandwan with the words: "I am leaving to live along the Narmada... Narmada will linger on the lips of the nation as a symbol of all struggles against social injustice."

PAPER-III

*Note : This paper contains **seventy five** (75) objective type questions, each question carrying **two** (2) marks. **All** questions are compulsory.*

1. In a multiple regression model, the f-ratio is used to test the
   A. Variance of the data
   B. Standard error of mean
   C. R^2 value
   D. Overall goodness of fit of the model.

2. If the mean of a sample is 20, the standard error of mean is 1 and the t-statistic for 95% level of confidence is 2.5, the population mean will be in the range
   A. 17.5 to 22.5   B. 15 to 25
   C. 20 to 25   D. 15 to 20

3. The third moment about the mean of a distribution of a set of observations is a measure of
   A. Mode   B. Skewness
   C. Kurtosis   D. Variance

4. Consider an air shed over a city in the form of a rectangular box. The wind velocity is 5 m/sec normal to left face of the box. The length of the box along the direction of wind is 10 km and mixing height is 1 km. Assuming rapid mixing of the pollutants which are conservative in nature, the concentration of the pollutants in the city would reach 63% of its final value in
   A. 2,000 sec   B. 5,000 sec
   C. 10,000 sec   D. 1,000 sec

5. Which one of the following states of mercury is volatile?
   A. Organic   B. Ionic
   C. Atomic   D. All of the above

6. Molar extinction coefficient of H_2O_2 at 240 nm is 0.04 M^{-1} cm^{-1}. The concentration of H_2O_2 in a solution which has absorbance of 0.6 in a 3 cm curette will be
   A. 5 M   B. 10 M
   C. 15 M   D. 20 M

7. A reference solution is to be prepared with 5 PPM parabenzopyrene (molecular weight = 252). The quantity of parabenzopyrene required for preparing one litre 5 PPM solution is
   A. 252 mg   B. 25.2 mg
   C. 5 mg   D. 252 μg

8. Which one of the following is a peroxyl radical?
   A. OH°   B. R°
   C. RO°   D. ROO°

9. Depending upon the amount of net primary productivity the various ecosystems can be arranged in a decreasing sequence of yield.
   A. Tropical seasonal forest – Tropical rain forest – Temperate Grassland – Woodland and Shrubland.
   B. Tropical seasonal forest – Tropical rain forest – Woodland and Shrubland – Temperate Grassland
   C. Tropical rain forest – Temperate Grassland – Woodland and Shrubland – Tropical seasonal forest.
   D. Tropical rain forest – Tropical seasonal forest – Woodland and Shrubland – Temperate Grassland.

10. Which of the following is a correct sequence of secondary seral vegetation development on any habitat?
    A. Ecesis – Invasion – Aggregation – Stabilization
    B. Ecesis – Aggregation – Invasion – Stabilization
    C. Aggregation – Invasion – Ecesis – Stabilization
    D. Invasion – Ecesis – Aggregation – Stabilization

11. What is common feature among the following?
    Abies delavayi
    Aconitum diennorrhzum
    Adinandra griffthii
    Aglaia perviridis
    A. All have been extinct.
    B. All are gymnosperms.

C. All are identified as endangered species.

D. All are angiosperms.

12. Raunkiaer's normal biological spectrum for phanerogamic flora of the world exhibits one of the following sequence of occurrence (%) of different life forms.

A. Phanerophytes, Hemicryptophytes, Therophytes, Cryptophytes, Chaemophytes.

B. Phanerophytes, Hemicryptophytes, Therophytes, Chaemophytes, Cryptophytes.

C. Phanerophytes, Hemicryptophytes, Cryptophytes, Chaemophytes, Therophytes.

D. Phanerophytes, Chaemophytes, Hemicryptophytes, Cryptophytes, Therophytes.

13. One of the following categories of earthworms is most suitable for wasteland reclamation.

A. Epigeic   B. Anecic

C. Endogeic   D. None of the above

14. How many mega-bio-diverse countries have been identified in the world?

A. 2   B. 12

C. 17   D. 35

15. Which one of the following is an *Ex-situ* method of biodiversity conservation?

A. Seed storage   B. DNA Bank

C. Tissue culture   D. All of the above

16. Which one of the following is a methyl isocyanate (MIC) based pesticide?

A. Sevin (Carbaryl)

B. Temix (Aldicarb)

C. Furadon (Carbofuran)

D. All of the above

17. The sequence of fossil fuels in the order of higher to lower heating value is as follows :

A. Coal, Petroleum, Natural Gas, Hydrogen.

B. Hydrogen, Natural Gas, Petroleum, Coal.

C. Hydrogen, Coal, Natural Gas, Petroleum.

D. Natural Gas, Petroleum, Coal, Hydrogen.

18. Natural ore of radioactive materials does not contain which one of the following isotope?

A. U^{235} B. Pu^{239}

C. U^{238} D. Th^{232}

19. The process of splitting bigger hydrocarbon into smaller hydrocarbon molecules is called

A. Pyrolysis

B. Thermal decomposition

C. Cracking

D. Combustion

20. Which one of the following is a complex inorganic fertilizer?

A. Urea   B. Super phosphate

C. Potash   D. NPK

21. The sequence of ease of decomposition of organic compounds in soil is

A. Lignin – Hemicellulose – Starch – Crude protein – Fat

B. Crude protein – Starch – Fat – Lignin – Hemicellulose

C. Starch – Crude protein – Hemicellulose – Fat – Lignin

D. Fat – Starch – Lignin – Hemicellulose – Crude protein

22. Which one of the following radionuclides has the lowest half life period?

A. C^{14} B. Sr^{90}

C. I^{131} D. Cs^{137}

23. Match the rules mentioned in Column-I with year of enforcement mentioned in Column-II.

Column-I	Column-II
(a) Hazardous Wastes (Management and Handling) Rules	1. 2000
(b) Biomedical Solid Wastes (Management and Handling) Rules.	2. 1978
(c) Municipal Solid Wastes (Management and Handling) Rules	3. 1989
(d) The Water (Prevention and Control of Pollution) Cess Rules	4. 1998

Choose the correct code:

Codes:

	(a)	(b)	(c)	(d)
A.	3	4	1	2
B.	4	1	2	3
C.	2	4	3	1
D.	1	3	4	2

24. Average composition of biodegradable waste in Municipal Solid Waste (MSW) of India is
    A. 30-35%   B. 40-45%
    C. 55-65%   D. 60-70%

25. The treatment method recommended for the human anatomical waste generated from hospitals is
    A. Chemical disinfection
    B. Autoclaving
    C. Incineration
    D. All of the above

26. Match the waste class mentioned in Column-I with Colour Code of the Collection Container mentioned in Column-II.

Column-I		Column-II
(a) Human Anatomical Waste	1.	Blue
(b) Waste Scrap	2.	Green
(c) Discarded glass ware	3.	Red
(d) Disposable plastics	4.	White

    Choose the correct code:

    Codes:

	(a)	(b)	(c)	(d)
A.	2	3	1	4
B.	4	2	3	1
C.	1	2	3	4
D.	3	1	4	2

27. Which of the following is true when frequency of occurrence of risk is remote but possible?
    A. Risk is acceptable.
    B. Risk reduction measures should be implemented.
    C. Risk is unacceptable.
    D. Both A and B are true.

28. Given below are two statements, one labelled as Assertion (A) and the other labelled as Reason (R).

    Assertion (A): Indirect impacts are more difficult to measure, but can ultimately be more important.

    Reason (R): In areas where wildlife is plentiful, such as Africa, new roads often lead to the rapid depletion of animals.

    Choose the correct answer.

    Codes:
    A. Both (A) and (R) are true and (R) is the correct explanation.
    B. Both (A) and (R) are true, but (R) is not the correct explanation.
    C. (A) is true, but (R) is false.
    D. (A) is false, but (R) is true.

29. An earthquake measuring over 8 on Richter Scale is rated as
    A. Destructive   B. Major
    C. Great   D. Damaging

30. Given below are two statements, one labelled as Assertion (A) and the other labelled as Reason (R).

    Assertion (A): It is difficult to judge how changes in localized gas samples represent more general conditions in the Volcano.

    Reason (R): The composition of the juvenile gases emitted from volcanic vents often show considerable variation over short periods and distances.

    Choose the correct answer.

    Codes:
    A. Both (A) and (R) are true and (R) is the correct explanation of (A).
    B. Both (A) and (R) are true, but (R) is not the correct explanation of (A).
    C. (A) is true, but (R) is false.
    D. (A) is false, but (R) is true.

31. In a false - colour set, human visual perception is limited to how many independent coordinates?
    A. Three   B. Four
    C. One   D. Five

32. If D = Detector Dimension, F = Focal Length, H = Flying Height, then Ground Resolution Element (GRE) is equal to
    A. $(D/F) \times H$ B. D/F
    C. H/F D. D/H

33. Darkest level of the associated colour (RGB) would have brightness value equal to
    A. 0   B. 256
    C. 255   D. 2047

34. The efficiency of a MHD power generator for applied electric field $\vec{E}$, magnetic field $\vec{B}$ and velocity of hot ionized gas $\vec{U}$ is

A. $\dfrac{|\vec{E}|}{|\vec{U} \parallel \vec{B}|}$ 　　　　 B. $\dfrac{|\vec{U} \parallel \vec{B}|}{|\vec{E}|}$

C. $\dfrac{|\vec{E}|^2}{|\vec{U} \parallel \vec{B}|^2}$ 　　　　 D. $\dfrac{|\vec{E}|^2}{|\vec{U} \parallel \vec{B}|^2}$

35. Match the List-I with List-II and choose the correct answer from the codes given below :

List-I (Constituents of Particulate matter)	List-II (Sources)
(a) Si	1. Natural Resources
(b) PAH	2. Incomplete combustion of fossil fuels
(c) SO_4^{2-}	3. Elements largely introduced by Human Activities
(d) Pb	4. Reactions of a gas in atmosphere

Choose the correct code :
Codes:

	(a)	(b)	(c)	(d)
A.	1	2	4	3
B.	2	3	4	1
C.	2	4	1	3
D.	3	4	2	1

36. For aerosol particles having sizes > 1 μm, the terminal settling velocity (V_T) of an aerosol particle varies with its diameter (D) as
A. $VT \propto D$ 　　　 B. $V_T \propto D^2$
C. $V_T \propto D^3$ 　　　 D. $V_T \propto D^{3/2}$

37. Scale lengths associated with synoptic scale phenomenon in atmosphere are typically in the range
A. 10 　— 100 km
B. 200 　— 40,000 km
C. 10,000 　— 100,000 km
D. 1 　— 10 km

38. Assume that the atmosphere is isothermal at 25°C and the estimated maximum daily surface temperature is 35°C, the mixing height is (take adiabatic lapse rate to be 1°C per 100 m)
A. 3.5 km 　　　　 B. 2.5 km
C. 1.5 km 　　　　 D. 1 km

39. The wavelengths of UV-A radiations are in the range
A. 200 - 240 nm 　　　 B. 240 - 280 nm
C. 280 - 320 nm 　　　 D. 320 - 400 nm

40. Two sounds of 80 dB and 85 dB superimpose at a location. What is the resultant sound at that location?
A. ~ 82 dB 　　　　 B. ~ 87 dB
C. ~ 91 dB 　　　　 D. ~ 165 dB

41. The coefficient of performance of a wind turbine for maximum power output is
A. 13/18 　　　　 B. 5/8
C. 16/27 　　　　 D. 11/17

42. Which of the following does not have a direct role in climate change?
A. Sulphate and nitrate aerosols
B. Black carbon aerosols
C. Surface ozone
D. Nitric oxide

43. Which method is used to separate molecules on the basis of their sizes?
A. Ion exchange chromatography
B. Molecular exclusion chromatography
C. Adsorption chromatography
D. Thin layer chromatography

44. Which type of support media is used in different types of electrophoresis?
A. Agarose gel
B. Polyacrylamide gel
C. Sodium dedecyl sulphate polyacrylamide gel
D. All of the above

45. Which of the following categories of plants get benefitted more due to elevation of CO_2 level?
A. C_3 plants 　　　 B. C_4 plants
C. CAM plants 　　　 D. All of the above

46. Aquifers that extend continuously from the land surface through material of high permeability are
A. Aquitards 　　　 B. Auicludes
C. Confined aquifers 　 D. Unconfined aquifers

47. Which one of the following is used to determine ambient concentration of suspended particulate matter?
A. Cascade impactor   B. Kjeldahl's Flask
C. Sacchi Disk   D. Folin-Wu method

48. Which of the following laws states that the solubility of a gas in a liquid is proportional to the partial pressure of that gas in contact with liquid?
A. Hick's law
B. Henry's law
C. Hardy-Weinburg law of equilibrium
D. 2nd Law of Newton

49. Maximum CaO is found in
A. Bauxite   B. Limonite
C. Limestone   D. Siderite

50. The sequence of chemical constituents in order of their abundance in a majority of sedimentary rocks is
A. $SiO_2 > TiO_2 > Al_2O_3 > Fe_2O_3$
B. $SiO_2 > Al_2O_3 > Fe_2O_3 > TiO_2$
C. $SiO_2 > Fe_2O_3 > Al_2O_3 > TiO_2$
D. $SiO_2 > Fe_2O_3 > TiO_2 > Al_2O_3$

51. The primary producers in the marine ecosystem are
A. Eubacteria and Algae
B. Cyanobacteria and Algae
C. Algae and Protozoans
D. All of the above

52. Mycorrhizae can be used as biofertilizers because they
A. fix nitrogen
B. fix CO_2
C. solubilise phosphate
D. kill pathogens

53. Given below are two statements, one labelled as Assertion (A) and the other labelled as Reason (R).

Assertion (A): Some plants with mycorrhizal fungi are able to occupy habitats that otherwise could not inhabit.

Reason (R): The importance of mycorrhizal plant interaction is attested by the fact that 95% of all plants have mycorrhizae.

Choose the correct answer :

Codes:
A. Both (A) and (R) are true and (R) is the correct explanation of (A).
B. Both (A) and (R) are true but (R) is not the correct explanation of (A).
C. (A) is true, but (R) is false.
D. (A) is false, but (R) is true.

54. An interactive association between two populations in which one population benefits from the association, while the other is not affected, is
A. Mutualism   B. Neutralism
C. Commensalism   D. Symbiosis

55. The method for downstreaming of ethanol from fermentation broth is
A. Filtration   B. Flow cytometry
C. Distillation   D. Flame Photometry

56. The country which uses maximum nuclear power is
A. U.S.A.   B. Japan
C. France   D. Germany

57. Which bacteria removes copper from low grade copper ore?
A. *Thiobacillus sp*
B. *Bacillus thuringiensis*
C. *Rhizobium sp*
D. All of the above

58. Which of the following is *not* a part of Geographic Information System (GIS)?
A. Projection
B. Overlay
C. Reclassification
D. Measuring distance and connectivity

59. Ultrafiltration can remove
A. Suspended solids   B. Bacteria
C. Protozoa   D. All of the above

60. A good automobile fuel, in addition to having high calorific value, should have
A. High ignition temperature
B. High viscosity
C. Low ignition temperature
D. Moderate ignition temperature

61. Reserve food material in algae is
A. Starch   B. Cellulose
C. Protein   D. None of the above

62. The biodegradability of xenobiotics can be characterized by
    A. Rate of CO_2 formation
    B. Rate of O_2 consumption
    C. Ratio of BOD to COD
    D. All of the above

63. The soil borne plant pathogens could be controlled by
    A. Lowering pH
    B. Increasing pH
    C. Adding lime
    D. All of the above

64. A selective Lignin degrading fungus belongs to
    A. Soft – rot
    B. Brown – rot
    C. White – rot
    D. Red – rot

65. The drastic reduction in the number of intestinal pathogens during activated sludge process is the overall result of
    A. Competition
    B. Competition and adsorption
    C. Predation, competition and adsorption
    D. Competition, adsorption, predation and settling

66. Which of the following disinfection method does not result in synthesis of organochlorine?
    A. Chlorination
    B. Chloroamination
    C. Ozonation
    D. None of the above

67. An organism's niche is
    A. the way the organism uses the range of physical and biological conditions in which it lives.
    B. all the biological and physical factors in the organism's environment.
    C. the function role played by the organism where it lives.
    D. the range of temperature that the organism needs to live.

68. The pyramid of biomass is invented in
    A. Forest ecosystem
    B. Greenland ecosystem
    C. Aquatic ecosystem
    D. All of the above

69. Which of the following chemicals of anthropogenic origin mimics the effect of estrogen in animals?
    A. Alkyl phenol
    B. Polychlorinated biphenyl
    C. O, p' - DDT
    D. All of the above

70. "Black Foot" disease in human beings caused due to use of water contaminated with
    A. Mercury
    B. Cadmium
    C. Silver
    D. Arsenic

71. Largest amount of fresh water is present in
    A. Lakes
    B. Rivers
    C. Glaciers
    D. Polar Ice

72. A threatened species is
    A. only endangered species
    B. only vulnerable species
    C. only rare species
    D. All of the above

73. Given below are two statements, one labelled as Assertion (A) and the other labelled as Reason (R).

    Assertion (A): Animals adopt various strategies to survive in hostile environment.

    Reason (R): Praying mantis is green in colour which emerges with plant foliage.

    Choose the correct code:

    Codes:
    A. Both (A) and (R) are true, with (R) being the correct explanation of (A).
    B. Both (A) and (R) are true but (R) is not the correct explanation of (A).
    C. (A) is true, but (R) is false.
    D. Both (A) and (R) are false.

74. Given below are two statements, one labelled as Assertion (A) and the other labelled as Reason (R).

    Assertion (A): Increasing temperature in the environment influences gonadal growth in fish.

    Reason (R): Increase in day length causes increase in environmental temperature in summer.

    Choose the correct code:

    Codes:
    A. Both (A) and (R) are true, and (R) is the correct explanation of (A).

B. Both (A) and (R) are true, but (R) is not the correct explanation of (A).

C. (A) is true, and (R) is false.

D. (A) and (R) are false.

75. Match Column-I with Column-II:

Column-I	Column-II
(a) The Rio Summit	1. 1997
(b) Johannesburg Earth Summit	2. 1972
(c) Kyoto Protocol	3. 1992
(d) The Stockholm Conference	4. 2002

Codes:

	(a)	(b)	(c)	(d)
A.	3	4	1	2
B.	1	2	3	4
C.	4	3	2	1
D.	2	1	4	3

ANSWERS

1	2	3	4	5	6	7	8	9	10
D	A	B	A	C	A	C	D	D	B
11	**12**	**13**	**14**	**15**	**16**	**17**	**18**	**19**	**20**
C	B	C	C	D	D	B	B	C	D
21	**22**	**23**	**24**	**25**	**26**	**27**	**28**	**29**	**30**
C	C	A	B	C	D	A	B	C	A
31	**32**	**33**	**34**	**35**	**36**	**37**	**38**	**39**	**40**
A	A	A	A	A	B	B	D	D	A
41	**42**	**43**	**44**	**45**	**46**	**47**	**48**	**49**	**50**
C	D	B	D	A	D	A	B	C	B
51	**52**	**53**	**54**	**55**	**56**	**57**	**58**	**59**	**60**
B	C	A	C	C	C	A	A	D	D
61	**62**	**63**	**64**	**65**	**66**	**67**	**68**	**69**	**70**
A	D	A	C	D	C	C	C	D	D
71	**72**	**73**	**74**	**75**					
D	D	C	A	A					

SOME SELECTED EXPLANATORY ANSWERS

1. Significance Testing and Goodness of Fit

In linear regression, we tested for a significant relationship by looking at the t or F-ratios. In multiple regression, the two ratios test two different hypotheses. As before, the t test is used to determine if a slope equals zero. Thus, in this case, we have two tests to perform:

Expenditures	SAT Scores
$H_0 : \beta_2 = 0$	$H_0 : \beta_2 = 0$
$H_A : \beta_1 \neq 0$	$H_A : \beta_2 \neq 0$

The t ratio and significance level in each row of the table of coefficients tell us whether to reject each of the null hypotheses. In this instance, at the .05 level of significance, we reject in both cases, due to the very low P-values. That is to say, both independent variables have statistically significant relationships to tuition.

The F-ratio in a multiple regression is used to test the null hypothesis that all of the slopes are equal to zero:

$$H_0 : \beta_1 = \beta_2 = 0 \text{ vs. } H_A : H_0 \text{ is not true.}$$

Note that the alternative hypothesis is different from saying that all of the slopes are nonzero. If one slope were zero and the other were not, we would reject the null in the F test. In the two *t* tests, we would reject the null in one, but fail to reject it in the other.

Finally, let's return to r^2, the coefficient of multiple determination. In the prior sessions, we noted that the output reports both r^2 and "adjusted" r^2. It turns out that adding any x variable to a regression model will tend to inflate r^2. To compensate for that inflation, we adjust r^2 to account for both the number of x variables in the model, and for the sample size. When working with multiple regression analysis, we generally want to consult the adjusted figure.

3. Skewness is asymmetry in a statistical distribution, in which the curve appears distorted or skewed either to the left or to the right. Skewness can be quantified to define the extent to which a distribution differs from a normal distribution.

In a normal distribution, the graph appears as a classical, symmetrical "bell-shaped curve." The **mean**, or average, and the **mode**, or maximum point on the curve, are equal.

- In a perfect normal distribution (green solid curve in the illustration below), the tails on either side of the curve are exact mirror images of each other.

- When a distribution is skewed to the left (red dashed curve), the tail on the curve's left-hand side is longer than the tail on the right-hand side, and the mean is less than the mode. This situation is also called negative skewness.

- When a distribution is skewed to the right (blue dotted curve), the tail on the curve's right-hand side is longer than the tail on the left-hand side, and the mean is greater than the mode. This situation is also called positive skewness.

8. The analog of the perhydroxyl radical in which the H atom is replaced by an organic group is called a peroxyl radical (ROO •). Peroxyl radicals do not dissociate to O_2^- because of the stability of the carbon-oxygen bond. The principal pathway of peroxyl radical formation in biological systems is autoxidation.

13. By their activity in the soil, earthworms offer many benefits: increased nutrient availability, better drainage, and a more stable soil structure, all of which help improve farm productivity.

14. The **megadiverse countries** are a group of countries that harbor the majority of the Earth's species and are therefore considered extremely *biodiverse. Conservation International* identified 17 megadiverse countries in 1998. All are located in, or partially in, the *tropics*.

India is one of the 17 Megabiodiverse countries in the world and accounts for 7-8 % of the recorded species. The State of Assam is a constituent unit of the Eastern Himalayan Biodiversity Region; one of the two biodiversity "Hot Spots" in the country. The climatic condition and wide variety in physical features witnessed in Assam have resulted in a diversity of ecological habitats such as forests, grasslands, wetlands, which harbour and sustain wide ranging floral and faunal species placing.

15. **Ex-situ conservation** means literally, "off-site *conservation*". It is the process of protecting an *endangered species* of plant or animal outside its natural habitat; for example, by removing part of the *population* from a threatened *habitat* and placing it in a new location, which may be a wild area or within the care of humans. While ex-situ conservation comprises some of the oldest and best known conservation methods, it also involves newer, sometimes controversial laboratory methods.

Ex-situ conservation, while helpful in man's efforts to sustain and protect our environment, is rarely enough to save a species from extinction. It is to be used as a last resort, or as a supplement to *in-situ conservation* because it cannot recreate the habitat as a whole: the entire *genetic variation* of a species, its *symbiotic* counterparts, or those elements which, over time, might help a species adapt to its changing surroundings. Instead, ex-situ conservation removes the species from its natural ecological contexts, preserving it under semi-isolated conditions whereby natural evolution and adaptation processes are either temporarily halted or altered by introducing the specimen to an unnatural habitat. In the case of *cryogenic* storage methods, the preserved specimen's adaptation processes are frozen altogether.

17. The calorific value of a fuel is the **quantity of heat produced by its combustion** - at constant pressure and under "normal" ("standard") conditions (i.e. to *0°C* and under a pressure of *1,013 mbar*).

Hydrogen	141,790
Natural gas	43,000
Petroleum	43,000
Coal (Lignite - Anthrasite)	15,000 - 27,000

18. **Plutonium-239** is an *isotope* of *plutonium*. Plutonium-239 is the primary *fissile* isotope used for the production of *nuclear weapons*, although *uranium-235* has also been used and is currently the secondary isotope. Plutonium-239 is also one of the three main isotopes demonstrated usable as fuel in *nuclear reactors*, along with *uranium-235* and *uranium-233*. Plutonium-239 has a *half-life* of 24,100 years.

19. **Cracking** is the process whereby complex *organic molecules* such as *kerogens* or heavy *hydrocarbons* are broken down into simpler molecules such as light hydrocarbons, by the breaking of *carbon*-carbon *bonds* in the precursors. The *rate* of cracking and the end products are strongly dependent on the *temperature* and presence of *catalysts*. Cracking is the breakdown of a large *alkane* into smaller, more useful *alkanes* and *alkenes*.

22. A **radionuclide** is an *atom* with an unstable *nucleus*, characterized by excess energy available to be imparted either to a newly created radiation particle within the nucleus or via *internal conversion*. During this process, the radionuclide is said to undergo *radioactive decay*, resulting in the emission of *gamma ray*(s) and/or *subatomic particles* such as *alpha* or *beta particles*. These emissions constitute *ionizing radiation*. Radionuclides occur naturally, or can be produced artificially.

The half-life of Carbon-14 is 5730 years. The half-life of Sr-90 is 29.1 years, I-131 has a half-life of 8 days. Cs-137 has a biological half-life of 70 days.

24. **Municipal Solid Waste**

Garbage is generally referred to "Waste" and is also termed as rubbish, trash, junk, unwanted or undesired material. As per the Municipal Solid Waste (Management & Handling) Rule, 2000 garbage is defined as Municipal Solid Waste which includes commercial and residential wastes generated in a municipal or notified areas in either solid or semi-solid form excluding industrial hazardous wastes but including treated bio-medical wastes. Municipal solid waste consists of household waste, construction and demolition debris, sanitation residue, and waste from streets. This garbage is generated mainly from residential and commercial complexes.

Average composition of biodegradable waste in Municipal Solid Waste (MSW) of India is 40 – 45%.

25. **Incineration** is a *waste treatment process* that involves the *combustion* of *organic* substances contained in waste materials. Incineration and other high temperature waste treatment systems are described as *"thermal treatment"*. Incineration of waste materials converts the waste into *ash*, *flue gas*, and heat. The ash is mostly formed by the *inorganic* constituents of the waste, and may take the form of solid lumps or *particulates* carried by the flue gas. The flue gases must be cleaned of gaseous and particulate pollutants before they are dispersed into the *atmosphere*. In some cases, the heat generated by incineration can be used to generate *electric power*.

27. Acceptable risk: That risk for which the probability of a hazard-related incident or exposure occurring and the severity of harm or damage that may result are as low as reasonably practicable (ALARP) and tolerable in the setting being considered.

29. A logarithmic scale used to rate the strength or total energy of earthquakes. The scale has no upper limit but usually ranges from 1 to 9. Because it is logarithmic, an earthquake rated as 5 is ten times as powerful as one rated as 4. An earthquake with a magnitude of 1 is detectable only by seismographs; one with a magnitude of 7 is a major earthquake. The Richter scale is named after the American seismologist Charles Francis Richter.

Less than 2.0: Micro - *not felt.*

2.0-2.9: Minor - *not felt, but recorded.*

3.0-3.9: Minor - *felt, but rarely causes damage.*

4.0-4.9: Light - *noticeable shaking of items, damage unlikely.*

5.0-5.9: Moderate - *damage to poorly constructed buildings, unlikely damage to specially designed buildings.*

6.0-6.9: Strong - *destructive for up to 100 miles across populated areas.*

7.0-7.9: Major - *serious damage over large areas.*

8.0-8.9: Great - *serious damage over areas of several hundred miles.*

9.0-9.9: Great - *devastating damage in areas thousands of miles across.*

31. Human visual perception is limited to three independent coordinates.

39. Ultraviolet (UV) "light" is a type of *electromagnetic radiation*. UV light has a shorter *wavelength* than *visible light*. The solar UV spectrum is continuous, it is a scientific convenience to describe the light within three specific wavebands - UVA, UVB and UVC - classified according to their wavelength. UVA is long wavelength (320-400 nm) UV and accounts for up to 95 per cent of the solar UV radiation reaching the Earth's surface. It can penetrate into the deeper layers of the skin and has for years been thought to play a major part in skin aging and wrinkling. Importantly, recent studies strongly suggest that it may also initiate and exacerbate the development of skin cancers.

UVA rays are present during all daylight hours and throughout the winter months.

43. A method of separating and identifying the components of a complex mixture by differential movement through a two-phase system, in which the movement is effected by a flow of a liquid or a gas (mobile phase) which percolates through an adsorbent (stationary phase) or a second liquid phase chromatograph.

48. Henry's law helps to predict the amount of each gas which will go into solution, but different gases have different solubilities and this also affects the rate. The constant of proportionality in Henry's law must take this into account. For example, in the gas exchange processes in respiration, the solubility of carbon dioxide is about 22 times that of oxygen when they are in contact with the plasma of the human body.

49. Limestone containing about 45% CaO and above is usually preferred for the manufacturing of cement. Limestone Lumps are calcareous sedimentary rock composed of mineral calcite ($CaCO_3$) which upon calcination yields lime (CaO) for commercial use. Besides, Limestone Lumps are used as fluxing material in Ferro-alloys, pelletization plants, foundries and in the production of sponge from iron, as refining materials in the production of sugar; as an additive in glass industry; as a coating material in fertilizers industry; and in the cooking of range and grass in the paper industry.

51. Algae are primary producers in freshwater and marine ecosystems. Exponentially-growing cultures of selected fresh water algae or Cyanobacteria are exposed over multiple generations under defined conditions. Usually five concentrations in a geometric row are tested, but in some cases a limit test is performed.

54. In *ecology*, **commensalism** is a class of relationship between two organisms where one organism benefits but the other is neutral. An example of commensalism: *cattle egrets* foraging in fields among *cattle* or other

livestock. As cattle, *horses*, and other livestock graze on the field, they cause movements that stir up various insects. As the insects are stirred up, the cattle egrets following the livestock catch and feed upon them. The egrets benefit from this relationship because the livestock have helped them find their meals, while the livestock are typically unaffected by it.

56. France with about 80% of their electricity generated by nuclear power. France is the world's largest net exporter of electricity due to its very low cost of generation, and gains over Euro 3 billion per year from this. France has been very active in developing nuclear technology. Reactors and fuel products and services are a major export.

58. Ultrafiltration is a separation process using membranes with pore sizes in the range of 0.1 to 0.001 micron. Typically, ultrafiltration will remove high molecular-weight substances, colloidal materials, and organic and inorganic polymeric molecules. Low molecular-weight organics and ions such as sodium, calcium, magnesium chloride, and sulfate are not removed. Because only high-molecular weight species are removed, the osmotic pressure differential across the membrane surface is negligible. Low applied pressures are therefore sufficient to achieve high flux rates from an ultrafiltration membrane. Flux of a membrane is defined as the amount of permeate produced per unit area of membrane surface per unit time.

60. The criteria for an ideal fuel is as follows :

1. The fuel should have high calorific value. A fuel that gives more calories per unit of weight would be an ideal choice. We have seen earlier that fuels that have oxygen in them have less calorific value.

2. The fuel should have a suitable ignition temperature. We have seen that a fuel will catch fire only if its ignition temperature is reached. If the ignition temperature is too low, then the fuel is not suitable as it will cause fire easily. If the ignition temperature is too high, then again it is not suitable, as reaching the ignition temperature will not be practical. Thus the ignition temperature of an ideal fuel should not be too high nor too low.

3. The fuel should have low content of non combustible materials. Non combustible materials in a fuel are its impurities. When heated these impurities may cause pollution and give out undesirable harmful gases. Thus an ideal fuel should not pollute the air by emanating harmful gases.

61. Algae can either be **autotrophic or heterotrophic** in nature. Most of them are **photoautotrophic** i.e. they need only **light and Carbon Dioxide** as their chief source of energy and carbon. **Chemoheterotrophic** algae require **other external organic compounds** as carbon and energy sources **Reserved food materials** present in algae include Starch, Oils, Floridean starch, Laminarin, Paramylon, soluble carbohydrates and Chrysolaminarin..

67. A niche is the role an organism plays in its environment. The organism uses physical & biological conditions to perform their role. Say for example, the niche of vultures is to feed on dead bodies.

70. Black foot disease has caused significant economic damage in California grape vineyards since the 1990s. Young vines are most susceptible. Plant symptoms are black, sunken root lesions, necrotic root crowns and black vascular streaking. Leaves appear scorched or water stressed and may be chlorotic. Vines are often stunted and may be killed.

71. Most of the world's ice is in Antarctica which is covered to an average depth of more than two kilometers of ice (2133 meters or 7000 feet). Ice at the North Pole is not nearly as thick. There is also a significant amount of ice on Greenland. Total water on earth (estimated): 326,000,000 cubic miles (1360,000,000 cubic km); 3% of that is fresh. 90% of all fresh water is frozen in ice.

UGC-NET ENVIRONMENTAL SCIENCE, JUNE 2012

PAPER-II

Note : *This paper contains fifty (50) objective type questions, each question carrying two (2) marks. Attempt all the questions.*

1. If the standard deviation of a population is 20 and the standard error of mean is 4, then the sample size is
   - A. 25
   - B. 80
   - C. 5
   - D. 100

2. In a multiple regression model, the explained variance per d.f. is 50 and unexplained variance per d.f. is 10. The F-ratio is
   - A. 2.5
   - B. 5
   - C. 25
   - D. 0.2

3. Which one of the following is not a random sampling method?
   - A. Stratified Sampling
   - B. Cluster Sampling
   - C. Systematic Sampling
   - D. Judgement Sampling

4. In the Gaussian Plume Model, the plume size is estimated considering buoyancy of exhaust gases, stack diameter, wind speed and stability of the atmosphere. The plume size Δh depends on inside radius of stack (r) as
   - A. $\Delta h \propto r$
   - B. $\Delta h \propto r^{1/3}$
   - C. $\Delta h \propto r^{2/3}$
   - D. $\Delta h \propto r^2$

5. The acidity of normal rain water is due to
   - A. CO_2
   - B. Cl_2
   - C. NO_2
   - D. SO_2

6. Per cent of water on the world's surface representing fresh water is
   - A. 97
   - B. 50
   - C. 10
   - D. 3

7. Concentration of CO_2 in present day atmosphere is
   - A. ~ 220 ppm
   - B. ~ 280 ppm
   - C. ~ 360 ppm
   - D. ~ 390 ppm

8. Hardness of diamond is due to
   - A. Coordinate bonding
   - B. Covalent bonding
   - C. Electrovalent bonding
   - D. van der Waals forces

9. In biological systems sulphur is largely bound in
   - A. Lipids
   - B. Proteins
   - C. Nucleic acids
   - D. Proteins and nucleic acids

10. pH of 0.01 M HNO_3 is
    - A. 0.1
    - B. 1
    - C. 2
    - D. 10

11. Which is a correct food chain in the Antarctic ecosystem?
    - A. Phytoplankton – Krill – Carnivorous Plankton – Emperor Penguin
    - B. Phytoplankton – Krill – Carnivorous Plankton – Squid – Elephant Seal – Leopard Seal
    - C. Phytoplankton – Herbivorous Zoo Plankton – Carnivorous Plankton – Adelic Penguin – Emperor Penguin
    - D. Herbivorous Zoo Plankton – Phytoplankton – Carnivorous Plankton – Elephant Seal – Leopard Seal

12. Given below are two statements, one labelled as Assertion (A) and the other labelled as Reason (R) :

    Assertion (A) : The phosphorous cycle in an ecosystem is a sedimentary cycle.

    Reason (R) : Phosphorous does not occur naturally as gas.
    - A. Both (A) and (R) are true and (R) is the correct explanation of (A).
    - B. Both (A) and (R) are true, but (R) is not the correct explanation of (A).

C. (A) is true, but (R) is false.

D. (A) is false, but (R) is true.

13. Pyramid of trophic levels is always upright in case of
A. Biomass   B. Energy
C. Number   D. All of the above

14. Which of the following is a correct match?
A. Periyar – Kerala
B. Ranthambore – M.P.
C. Panna – U.P.
D. Bandhvgarh – Bihar

15. Replacement of existing communities by any external condition is termed
A. Primary succession
B. Secondary succession
C. Autogenic succession
D. None of the above

16. The area where two major communities meet and blend together is termed as
A. Ecotype   B. Biotype
C. Ecotone   D. Meeting place

17. Indian wolf has become an important animal because
A. It's name appears in Red Data Book.
B. It is only an important member of food chain of almost all Indian forests.
C. Wild dogs disappeared due to their presence.
D. It has been chosen as a State animal.

18. Walkley and Black rapid titration method is used for the determination of
A. Organic carbon content of soil
B. Nitrate content of soil
C. Phosphate content of soil
D. Fluoride content of soil

19. Which one of the following is an endoenzyme in soil?
A. Cellulase   B. Invertase
C. Protease   D. Dehydrogenase

20. Of the following humic groups which is not soluble in both acid and alkali?
A. Fulvic acid   B. Humic acid
C. Humin   D. All of the above

21. The sources of thermal pollution are
A. Power plants
B. Cooling forests
C. Industrial effluents
D. All of the above

22. Which one of the following radionuclides has the longest half life?
A. C^{14} B. Sr^{90}
C. I^{131} D. Cs^{137}

23. What is the importance of the 42nd Amendment to the Constitution brought in the year 1976?
A. Insertion of Article 48-A
B. Insertion of Article 51-A (g)
C. Insertion of Article 48-A and 51-A (g)
D. None of the above

24. Who issues the Ecomark notification?
A. Ministry of Environment and Forest, Govt. of India
B. Ministry of Human Health and Family Welfare, Govt. of India
C. Department of Science and Technology, Govt. of India
D. Bureau of Indian Standards

25. Which one of the following is a waste recycling method of solid waste management?
A. Pelletisation   B. Composting
C. Incineration   D. Sanitary Landfill

26. A hazardous waste is characterised by
A. Ignitibility   B. Reactivity
C. Toxicity   D. All of the above

27. How many hot spots have been identified in the world and Indian Subcontinent respectively?
A. 17, 2   B. 12, 3
C. 35, 2   D. 17, 3

28. Which one of the following chemical species of mercury is highly toxic to living system?
A. Mercurous ion   B. Mercuric ion
C. Organo mercurials   D. Atomic mercury

29. Natural gas is composed primarily of
A. Methane
B. n-butane
C. n-octane
D. A mixture of n-octane and n-butane

30. Which of the following is true regarding the Leopold interaction matrix used in Environmental Impact Assessment Process?

A. It can be expanded.
B. It can be contracted.
C. It can be contracted and expanded.
D. It cannot be contracted and expanded.

31. Which of the following can be considered in Environmental Risk Assessment?
A. Exposure period
B. Potency of a toxic material
C. Quality of models
D. All of the above

32. In India, Environmental Impact Assessment report of a proposed river valley project after environmental clearance is applicable for a maximal period of how many years?
A. 5   B. 10
C. 30   D. 2

33. An earthquake is rated as 'major' if its magnitude in Richter Scale is in the range of
A. 4.0-4.9   B. 7.0-7.9
C. 6.0-6.9   D. 5.0-5.9

34. What is the proportion of the frequency of occurrence of La Nina compared to El Nino?
A. Half   B. One-third
C. Twice   D. Two-third

35. An element in soil will be considered as a trace element if its concentration is
A. 1-2 wt %   B. < 0.1 wt %
C. > 2 wt %   D. < 1 wt %

36. Which of the following is correct about attribute data in Geographic Information System?
A. Attributes are pieces of data that are connected or related to the points, lines or polygons mapped in the GIS.
B. Attribute data can be analysed to determine patterns of importance.
C. Attribute data is entered directly into a database where it is associated with element data.
D. All of the above

37. At Nadir, the LISS-IV camera in IRS-P6 has a spatial resolution of
A. 5.8 m   B. 5.9 m
C. 5.7 m   D. 5.6 m

38. Which one of the following can be estimated by Flame Photometer?

A. Sodium and Potassium
B. Cadmium and Cobalt
C. Chlorine and Bromine
D. Mercury and Arsenic

39. The contribution of CO_2 towards global warming has been estimated to be about
A. 57-60%   B. 60-75%
C. 80-85%   D. 45-55%

40. The principal components of photochemical smog in urban areas are
A. SO_2 and NO_2
B. SPM and CO
C. SPM and NO_2
D. Hydrocarbons and Ozone

41. Match List-I and List-II and choose the correct answer from the codes given below:

List-I (Aerosol Constituents)	List-II (Sources)
(i) Si	1. Gases in the ambient atmosphere
(ii) V	2. Natural sources
(iii) Benzo(a)pyrene	3. Combustion of certain kinds of fuel oil
(iv) Sulphuric acid droplets	4. Incomplete combustion

Codes:

	(i)	(ii)	(iii)	(iv)
A.	2	4	3	1
B.	3	1	2	4
C.	4	1	2	3
D.	1	4	3	2

42. A river flowing at 20.0 m³/sec has a tributary feeding into it with a flow rate of 5.0 m³/sec. Upstream from the point of junction. The fluoride concentration is 5 mg/L in the river and 10 mg/L in the tributary. Assuming fluoride to be conservative substance and rapid mixing in the river, the downstream concentration in the river is
A. 6 mg/L   B. 8 mg/L
C. 8.5 mg/L   D. 7.5 mg/L

43. The power obtained from a horizontal wind turbine operating at maximum efficiency is proportional to its diameter (D) as
A. D
B. D^2
C. $D^{3/2}$
D. $\sqrt{D}$

44. Noise of 90 dB for 8 hours represents 100% dose. If the noise of 93 dB is for 1 hour duration, it represents a dose of
A. 25%
B. 50%
C. 75%
D. 100%

45. Scale lengths associated with mesoscale phenomenon in atmosphere are typically in the range
A. 10-500 m
B. 1-200 km
C. 100-1000 km
D. 1000-10,000 km

46. When an atmosphere has an isothermal profile, it is
A. very stable
B. slightly stable
C. unstable
D. very unstable (turbulent)

47. The wavelength range of UV-C radiation is
A. 320-400 nm
B. 280-320 nm
C. 100-1500 nm
D. 240-280 nm

48. Lightening in the atmosphere produces
A. NO
B. CO
C. CO_2
D. NH_3

49. The maximum tidal energy potential in India is
A. in Gulf of Khambhat
B. in Gangetic delta in Sundarbans
C. along the coast of Odisha
D. along the coast of Chennai

50. The maximum theoretical efficiency of a silicon solar cell can be
A. 45%
B. 30%
C. 12%
D. 50%

ANSWERS

1	2	3	4	5	6	7	8	9	10
A	B	D	C	A	D	D	B	B	C
11	12	13	14	15	16	17	18	19	20
B	B	B	A	B	C	A	A	D	C
21	22	23	24	25	26	27	28	29	30
D	D	C	A	B	D	C	C	A	C
31	32	33	34	35	36	37	38	39	40
D	B	B	A	B	D	A	A	A	D
41	42	43	44	45	46	47	48	49	50
A	A	B	A	B	B	D	A	A	A

PAPER-III

*Note : This paper contains **seventy five (75)** objective type questions, each question carrying **two (2)** marks. **All** questions are compulsory.*

1. If the standard deviation of a population is 20, the population and sample means are 35 and 33, respectively and the t-statistic at 95% confidence level is 2.5, the sample size is
A. 100
B. 125
C. 250
D. 625

2. For 5 degrees of freedom, the variance of χ^2 distribution is
A. 10
B. 5
C. 16
D. 4

3. Identify the random sampling method among the following :
A. Judgement sampling

B. Quota sampling
C. Convenience sampling
D. Stratified sampling

4. Consider a Box model for an urban area. Assuming that the pollutants are conservative and that the mixing is rapid inside the Box, the concentration (C) of pollutants varies with the mixing height as

A. $C \propto \dfrac{1}{H}$ B. $C \propto \dfrac{1}{H^2}$

C. $C \propto \dfrac{1}{\sqrt{H}}$ D. $C \propto H^{-3/2}$

5. At higher pH, majority of iron is present as
A. Fe^{2+}
B. Fe^{3+}
C. Fe^{2+} and Fe^{3+}
D. $Fe(OH)_2$ and $Fe(OH)_3$

6. In living organisms phosphorous is largely associated with
A. Carbohydrate   B. Lipids
C. Nucleic acids   D. Proteins

7. Molar extinction coefficient of malondialdehyde at 532 nm is 0.155 $M^{-1}cm^{-1}$. The concentration of malondialdehyde in a solution which has absorbance of 0.31 in a 1 cm curette will be
A. 0.5 M   B. 1.0 M
C. 1.5 M   D. 2.0 M

8. pOH of 0.001 M solution of HCl is
A. 0.1   B. 1
C. 10   D. 11

9. The molecular weight of DDT is 354.5. The quantity of DDT required to prepare one litre of 10 ppm DDT solution is
A. 10 mg   B. 35.45 mg
C. 354.5 mg   D. 354.5 μg

10. Which one of the following is referred to as superoxide radical?
A. O   B. O_2
C. $O_2^{\circ-}$ D. O_3

11. The net primary productivity of an ecosystem is
A. the gross primary productivity minus plant respiration
B. the primary productivity at herbivore level
C. the primary productivity at consumer level
D. the productivity at top consumer level minus respiration at all levels

12. Which of the following habitats has not been included as Indian biodiversity hot spots?
A. The Eastern Ghats
B. The Western Ghats
C. North-Eastern Hills
D. South-Eastern Hills

13. The area of the biosphere which is protected entirely, without any experimentation and research and no biotic interference, is known as
A. Undisturbed zone   B. Buffer zone
C. Core zone   D. Principal zone

14. When a mixture of Azospirillum, Azotobacter and Vibrio was applied to rhizosphere, fixation of atmospheric nitrogen was increased. It was due to activity of
A. All the three
B. Azospirillum and Vibrio
C. Azotobacter and Vibrio
D. Azotobacter and Azospirillum

15. Which type of forests are found at an altitude of 5300 ft chiefly on mountains of Himalayas and Nilgiri?
A. Dry deciduous forest
B. Moist tropical forest
C. Temperate forest
D. Tropical moist deciduous forest

16. The sequence of events that occur during primary succession is as follows :
A. Nudation – Colonisation – Ecesis – Aggregation
B. Aggregation – Colonization – Ecesis – Nudation
C. Ecesis – Nudation – Aggregation – Colonization
D. Nudation – Ecesis – Colonization – Aggregation

17. As per Raunkaiers law of frequency, five different frequency classes (A, B, C, D and E) in a natural undisturbed community exhibit one of the following relationship :

A. $A < B > C \gtreqless D < E$

B. $A > B > C \gtreqless D < E$

C. $A < B > C \gtreqless D > E$

D. $A < B < C \gtreqless D > E$

18. Which one of the following category of earth-worms is most suitable for Vermicomposting?
A. Epigeic   B. Anecic
C. Endogeic   D. All of the above

19. Which one of the following is an in situ method of biodiversity conservation?
A. Reserve forest   B. National parks
C. Sanctuaries   D. All of the above

20. Match the contaminant in Column-I with the disease in Column-II :

Column-I	Column-II
(i) Mercury	1. Methamoglobinemia
(ii) Nitrate Nitrogen	2. Itai Itai
(iii) Cadmium	3. Silicosis
(iv) Coal	4. Minamata

Choose the correct code :
Codes :

	(i)	(ii)	(iii)	(iv)
A.	2	3	4	1
B.	3	4	2	1
C.	1	2	3	4
D.	4	1	2	3

21. Which of the following types of coal contains higher percentage of volatile matter?
A. Peat   B. Lignite
C. Bituminous   D. Anthracite

22. Carbon dioxide evolved from soil mainly comes from
A. Microbial respiration
B. Root respiration
C. Soil animals respiration
D. All of the above

23. Which one of the following pesticides persists for a long period in soil?
A. Lindane   B. Monocrotophos
C. Carbaryl   D. Parathion

24. Organic matter (OM) content of soil can be calculated from organic carbon (OC) by using the formula
A. OM (%) = OC (%) × 1.724
B. OM (%) = OC (%) × 1.247
C. OM (%) = OC (%) × 1.472
D. OM (%) = OC (%) × 1.427

25. The problem of thermal pollution can be alleviated by using
A. Cooling ponds
B. Cooling towers
C. More efficient electricity generating plants
D. All of the above

26. According to Recycled Plastics (Manufacture and Usage) Rules 1999, the minimum thickness of carry bags shall not be less than
A. 10 microns   B. 20 microns
C. 30 microns   D. 50 microns

27. Match the Act mentioned in Column-I with the year of enactment mentioned in Column-II :

Column-I	Column-II
(i) The Water (Prevention and Control of Pollution) Act	1. 2002
(ii) The Air (Prevention and Control of Pollution) Act	2. 1986
(iii) The Environmental (Protection) Act	3. 1974
(iv) The Biological Diversity Act	4. 1981

Choose the correct code :
Codes :

	(i)	(ii)	(iii)	(iv)
A.	1	4	3	2
B.	3	4	2	1
C.	3	2	1	4
D.	2	4	3	1

28. Which one of the following is not an energy recovery method of solid waste management?
A. Pelletisation   B. Biomethanation
C. Pyrolysis   D. Composting

29. The colour code of the container for collection of waste scrap generated from Hospitals is

A. Red   B. Blue
C. White   D. Green

30. Given below are two statements, one labelled as Assertion (A) and the other labelled as Reason (R) :

    Assertion (A) : When quantitative probabilistic risk assessment is performed on hazardous waste sites they usually turn out to be of relatively low threats.

    Reason (R) : In hazardous waste sites the chance of exposure is low because of isolation of drinking water supplies and prevention of access.

    Choose the correct answer :
    A. Both (A) and (R) are true and (R) is the correct explanation of (A).
    B. Both (A) and (R) are true, but (R) is not the correct explanation of (A).
    C. (A) is true, but (R) is false.
    D. (A) is false, but (R) is true.

31. In India, an Environment Impact Assessment report of a proposed mining project after environmental clearance is applicable for a maximal period of how many years?
    A. 5 years   B. 10 years
    C. 30 years   D. 2 years

32. An increase of one unit of Richter Scale represents an increase in amplitude by a factor of
    A. 10   B. 100
    C. 1000   D. 2

33. Which rare earth element is not present in the earth's crust but for commercial purpose comes from the Nuclear reactors?
    A. Promethium   B. Lanthanum
    C. Cerium   D. Samarium

34. To display green colour in the monitor the amount of RGB should be
    A. 255 : 0 : 0   B. 255 : 255 : 255
    C. 0 : 0 : 0   D. 0 : 255 : 0

35. When the temperature range in geothermal resource is generally low, electrical power generation from such resources require the use of secondary low boiling point fluid. This is generally known as

A. Rankine cycle
B. Production well cycle
C. Flash stem cycle
D. Hard Dry Rock cycle

36. The Global Warming Potential (GWP) is the least for which of the following greenhouse gases?
    A. CH_4 B. CO_2
    C. N_2O D. SF_6

37. The maximum specific power output (p) from a MHD power generator varies with the velocity (u) of hot ionized gas as
    A. $p \propto u$ B. $p \propto u^2$
    C. $p \propto u^{3/2}$ D. $p \propto u^3$

38. Given below are two statements. One labelled as Assertion (A) and the other labelled as Reason (R).

    Assertion (A) : Electrostatic precipitators (ESPs) can be harmful if not operated properly.

    Reason (R) : Corona discharge in ESPs produces ozone.

    Choose the correct answer :
    A. Both (A) and (R) are correct and (R) is the correct explanation of (A).
    B. Both (A) and (R) are correct and (R) is not the correct explanation of (A).
    C. (A) is true, but (R) is false.
    D. Both (A) and (R) are false.

39. Given below are two statements. One labelled as Assertion (A) and the other labelled as Reason (R) :

    Assertion (A) : Vegetation hedges are the best way to control noise.

    Reason (R) : Vegetation hedges scatter noise.

    Choose the correct answer.
    A. Both (A) and (R) are correct and (R) is the correct explanation of (A).
    B. Both (A) and (R) are correct, but (R) is not the correct explanation of (A).
    C. (A) is true, but (R) is false.
    D. (A) is false, but (R) is true.

40. If w and ws are mixing ratio and saturation mixing ratio respectively; T and Td are the ambient temperature and dew point temperature

respectively, then identify the correct expression of relative humidity (RH).

A. $RH = \dfrac{w \text{ at } Td}{w \text{ at } T}$ B. $RH = \dfrac{w \text{ at } T}{w \text{ at } Td}$

C. $RH = \dfrac{ws \text{ at } Td}{ws \text{ at } T}$ D. $RH = \dfrac{ws \text{ at } T}{ws \text{ at } Td}$

41. Identify mesoscale phenomenon.
   A. Tornado   B. Sea breeze
   C. Cyclone   D. Eddies

42. For elevations less than few hundred metres, if the wind speeds are u_1 and u_2 at elevations z_1 and z_2 respectively, the following equation holds $\left(\dfrac{u_1}{u_2}\right) = \left(\dfrac{z_1}{z_2}\right)^p$. The value of the exponent p is
   A. ≤ 0.6 B. $= 1$
   C. ≥ 0.6 D. negative

43. Given below are two statements. One labelled as Assertion (A) and the other labelled as Reason (R).

   Assertion (A) : Noise gets attenuated more in dry atmosphere.

   Reason (R) : Moist air is less denser than dry air.

   Choose the correct answer :
   A. Both (A) and (R) are true and (R) is the correct explanation of (A).
   B. Both (A) and (R) are true and (R) is not the correct explanation of (A).
   C. (A) is true, but (R) is false.
   D. (A) is false, but (R) is true.

44. OH˙ radicals in atmosphere play a role of
   A. scavenger   B. acidifier
   C. reducing agent   D. greenhouse gas

45. The slow neutrons initiating nuclear fission with U^{235} have energies of the order of
   A. 0.25 MeV   B. 0.15 MeV
   C. 0.25 eV   D. 0.025 eV

46. The most suitable range of wind speeds for wind power generation is
   A. 1-5 m/s   B. 4-12 m/s
   C. 10-20 m/s   D. 20-50 m/s

47. For energy to be produced from nuclear fusion of Deuterium (D) and Tritium (T), the mixture of D + T has to be heated up to energies of at least
   A. 1 KeV   B. 10 KeV
   C. 500 eV   D. 1 MeV

48. Element contaminating the water body is determined and quantified by using one of the following methods :
   A. Colorimeter
   B. Spectrophotometer
   C. Atomic absorption spectrometer
   D. All of the above

49. In which type of chromatography four modes viz, Absorption, partition, Ion exchange and exclusion, are present?
   A. HPLC
   B. Liquid-liquid chromatography
   C. Ion-exchange chromatography
   D. Adsorption chromatography

50. The metal which is generally absorbed by plants along with Zn and causes "Ouch Ouch" disease in human beings is
   A. Pb   B. Cd
   C. Hg   D. Cr

51. Radioactive isotopes of which of the elements in human body decay every second?
   A. K^{40} and C^{14}
   B. C^{14} and N^{6}
   C. N^{16} and K^{40}
   D. None of the above

52. Which of the following techniques is most appropriate for determining crystalline structure of environmental samples?
   A. Infrared spectroscopy
   B. X-ray diffraction
   C. Microspectrophotometry
   D. Raman spectroscopy

53. Which one of the following is the most predominant element in a majority of igneous rocks?
   A. Al   B. Fe
   C. O   D. Si

54. Match the entries in Group-I with the process parameters in Group-II :

Group-I	Group-II
(i) Clark electrode	1. Dissolved Oxygen
(ii) Redox Probe	2. pH
(iii) Load cell	3. Liquid level
(iv) Diaphragm gauge	4. Vessel pressure

Choose the correct code :

Codes :

	(i)	(ii)	(iii)	(iv)
A.	1	2	3	4
B.	2	1	4	3
C.	1	4	3	2
D.	4	3	2	1

55. Which one of the following is used to determine total organic matter by Walkley and Black method?
A. KOH and H_2SO_4
B. $Na_2S_2O_3$ and H_2SO_4
C. $K_2Cr_2O_7$ and H_2SO_4
D. HNO_3 and H_2SO_4

56. As per WHO standards the maximum permissible level of coliform organisms per 100 ml of drinking water is
A. 10   B. 100
C. 150   D. 1000

57. Progressive increase in concentration of a xenobiotic compound when it passes through the food chain is called
A. Biomagnification
B. Hyper accumulation
C. Bioaccumulation
D. None of the above

58. Highest level of biotic interaction is
A. Mutualism   B. Predation
C. Parasitism   D. Amensalism

59. Which one of the following is considered as indicator of aquatic pollution?
A. Rotifers   B. Copepods
C. Mysids   D. Calanoids

60. Poorly nourished lakes are known as
A. Oligotrophic   B. Eutrophic
C. Mesotrophic   D. Xerotrophic

61. Identify a sampling method which is not non-destructive.

A. Sub-surface coring
B. Using of neutron probes to measure soil water
C. Fourier transform infrared spectroscopy
D. Time domain refractometry to measure soil water

62. Ministry of Environment and Forests amended the EIA notification making public hearing mandatory for environmental clearance on
A. 27th January 1996
B. 10th April 1997
C. 27th January 1997
D. None of the above

63. The allochthonous microorganisms of an ecosystem are
A. Indigenous microorganisms
B. Migrant
C. Parasitic
D. Pathogenic

64. The rate of evaporation of oil spilled into the sea depends on
A. The elemental concentration of sea water
B. The composition of sea water microflora
C. Composition of the crude oil
D. The temperature of the sea

65. The most dangerous and heat resistant spoilage organism in canning industry is
A. Clostridium cellulolyticum
B. Bacillus subtilis
C. E.coli
D. Clostridium botulinum

66. Oxygen concentrations in compost developed in static piles usually
A. Ten times lower than in ambient air
B. Five times lower than in ambient air
C. Two times more than in ambient air
D. Five times more than in ambient air

67. If a bacterium with a 20 minute generation time is grown under optimal conditions (37°C), one cell would multiply to 10^3 (1000) cells in 3.3 hours, then how much time it will take to multiply to 10^6 cells?
A. 5.3 hrs.   B. 6.6 hrs.
C. 9.9 hrs.   D. 6.3 hrs.

68. The biodegradation of plant material is slow because of presence of
A. Cellulose B. Xylene
C. Extensin/protein D. Lignin

69. The widely used aerobic suspension type of liquid waste treatment system is
A. Rotating Biological Contactor (RBC)
B. Percolating filter
C. Activated sludge process
D. Septic tank

70. The treatment designed to remove non-biodegradable organic pollutants and mineral nutrients from waste water is
A. Lagoons
B. Imhoff tank
C. Secondary treatment
D. Tertiary treatment

71. An ecotype is
A. Genetically different forms of the same organisms
B. Genetically similar forms of the same organisms
C. Morphologically different forms of the same organisms
D. Both A and B

72. Ultraviolet radiations are lethal due to inactivation of
A. Proteins, nucleic acids and pigments
B. Minerals, water and air
C. Carbohydrates, fats and vitamins
D. O_2, CO_2 and water

73. The following are the characters of species diversity :
(i) More richness
(ii) More evenness
(iii) More dominance
(iv) Less dominance
(v) Less richness
(vi) Less evenness

Point out the combination of conditions in which species diversity of an ecosystem will be more.
A. (i), (ii) and (iii)
B. (v), (ii) and (iii)
C. (i), (ii) and (iv)
D. (i), (vi) and (iv)

74. Given below are two statements, one labelled as Assertion (A) and the other labelled as Reason (R).

Assertion (A) : If natality is greater than mortality, it leads to population explosion.

Reason (R) : The scientific study of various species of human population is called demography.

Choose the correct answer :
A. Both (A) and (R) are true and (R) is the correct explanation of (A).
B. Both (A) and (R) are true, but (R) is not the correct explanation of (A).
C. (A) is true, but (R) is false.
D. Both (A) and (R) are false.

75. Match Column-I with Column-II :

Column-I	Column-II
(i) Chipko Movement	1. Medha Patkar
(ii) Narmada Bacchao Andolan	2. Al Gore
(iii) Climate Change	3. Rachel Carson
(iv) Silent Spring	4. Sundarlal Bahuguna

Choose the correct code :
Codes :

	(i)	(ii)	(iii)	(iv)
A.	1	2	3	4
B.	2	3	4	1
C.	4	1	2	3
D.	3	4	1	2

ANSWERS

1	2	3	4	5	6	7	8	9	10
D	A	D	A	D	C	D	D	A	C

11	12	13	14	15	16	17	18	19	20
A	D	C	D	C	A	B	A	D	D

21	22	23	24	25	26	27	28	29	30
A	A	A	A	D	B	B	D	B	A

31	32	33	34	35	36	37	38	39	40
C	A	A	D	A	B	B	A	D	C

41	42	43	44	45	46	47	48	49	50
B	A	B	A	D	B	B	D	A	B

51	52	53	54	55	56	57	58	59	60
A	B	C	A	C	A	A	B	A	A

61	62	63	64	65	66	67	68	69	70
A	B	B	C	D	B	B	D	C	D

71	72	73	74	75
A	A	C	B	C

UGC-NET ENVIRONMENTAL SCIENCE, DECEMBER 2011

PAPER-II

Note : *This paper contains fifty (50) objective type questions, each question carrying two (2) marks. Attempt all the questions.*

1. What are the steps necessary for sustainable management of renewable resources?
   A. Avoiding over-exploitation and pollution of biotic systems.
   B. Strengthening the resource base and augmenting regenerability of biotic systems.
   C. Use of alternative resources.
   D. All of these

2. Fluxes of heat, water vapour and momentum are constant in
   A. upper atmosphere
   B. middle atmosphere
   C. Ekman layer
   D. surface boundary layer

3. Inversions occur when atmosphere is
   A. unstable   B. neutral
   C. slightly stable D. most stable

4. When one species limits access of another species to a resource regardless of whether the resource is abundant or scarce, it is called
   A. interspecific competition
   B. intraspecific competition
   C. interference competition
   D. exploitative competition

5. Nanda Devi and Sunderbans are examples of Indian
   A. National Parks
   B. Sanctuaries
   C. International heritage areas
   D. Biosphere reserves

6. Match the List-I and List-II and select the correct answer from the codes given below the lists :

List-I (Analytical techniques)	List-II (Measured items)
(a) XRF	1. Functional groups
(b) Nephelometry	2. Elements
(c) IR spectroscopy	3. Turbidity
(d) UV-visible spectroscopy	4. Aromatics

Codes :

	(a)	(b)	(c)	(d)
A.	4	2	3	1
B.	1	3	4	2
C.	3	2	4	1
D.	2	3	1	4

7. The pH of a 0.001 M solution of HCl is
   A. 2   B. 4
   C. 3   D. 1

8. The primitive atmosphere of earth consisted of
   A. CO_2, NO_2, NH_3, SO_2
   B. H_2, NH_3, CH_4, H_2O
   C. CO, N_2O_3, SO_3, H_3N
   D. He, Ne, Ar, Kr

9. Which of the following is the major source of mercury pollution in India?
   A. Coal based thermal power plants
   B. Pesticides
   C. Dental amalgam fillings
   D. Electrical and electronic gadgets

10. Nitrite causes methaemoglobinemia by
    A. oxidizing membrane proteins
    B. reacting with calcium of bones
    C. oxidizing haemoglobin
    D. oxidizing membrane lipids

11. Solubility (S) of a sparingly soluble salt of the type AB is related to the solubility product (K_{SP}) by the relation

A. $S = K_{SP}^2$ B. $S = 2 K_{SP}$

C. $S = \sqrt{K_{SP}}$ D. $S = K_{SP}$

12. The amount of biomass which can be sustained under steady state condition of an ecosystem is termed as
    A. Primary productivity
    B. System homeostasis
    C. Sustainable yield
    D. Carrying capacity

13. Which of the following regions generally possess large diversity in their species composition?
    A. Arctic regions
    B. Antarctic regions
    C. Snow-clad mountains
    D. Subtropical regions

14. Match the items under List-I and List-II and select the correct answer using codes given below :

List-I	List-II
(a) Tissue culture technique	(i) Green revolution
(b) Vermiculture technique	(ii) Storage of propagules
(c) Breeding technique	(iii) Micro-propagation
(d) Cryo preservation technique	(iv) Organic farming

    Codes :

	(a)	(b)	(c)	(d)
A.	(ii)	(iv)	(iii)	(i)
B.	(iii)	(iv)	(i)	(ii)
C.	(i)	(ii)	(iv)	(iii)
D.	(iv)	(i)	(ii)	(iii)

15. Successive increase in concentration of some chemicals through different food level organisms is called
    A. Biogeochemical cycle
    B. Biological magnification
    C. Chemical production
    D. Biodegradation

16. Which of the following is a correct sequence found in a grassland ecosystem?
    A. Grasses → Diatoms → deer → dog
    B. Grasses → rabbit → wolves → tiger
    C. Trees → birds → hawks → wolves
    D. Grasses → snakes → deer → dog

17. Reservoir triggered seismicity in case of hydropower projects with large pondage is most likely to occur when
    A. Thrust fault passes through the reservoir
    B. Strike-slip fault passes through the reservoir
    C. Large flood strikes the project
    D. Final reservoir level drops

18. At the present time volcanoes are confined to certain limited areas of the Earth's surface. This special zone is called
    A. Trans-Atlantic volcanic zone
    B. Circum-Pacific Ring of fire
    C. Central-Asian inter-continental zone
    D. Indian-Ocean volcanic belt

19. Given below are scales of four topographic maps. Maps of which scale will have more clarity?
    A. 1 : 50,000   B. 1 : 25,000
    C. 1 : 250,000   D. 1 : 1,000,000

20. Soil surveys involve which of the following?
    A. Soil series mapping
    B. Soil depth mapping
    C. Soil horizons mapping
    D. All of these

21. In which of the following frequency ranges the human ear is most sensitive to noise?
    A. 1-2 KHz   B. 100-500 Hz
    C. 10-12 KHz   D. 13-16 KHz

22. The maximum value of power coefficient for a wind turbine can be
    A. 0.59   B. 0.49
    C. 0.92   D. 0.72

23. Average value of solar insolation $\left(\dfrac{w}{m^2}\right)$ at the earth's surface is
    A. 250   B. 350
    C. 450   D. 550

24. Fuel cells are devises that generate electricity by converting the energy released by
    A. electrochemical reactions without going through combustion process.

B. biochemical reactions without going through combustion process.

C. electrochemical reactions involving combustion process

D. biochemical reactions involving combustion process

25. Chemically coal is composed of
   (i) Carbon
   (ii) Hydrogen
   (iii) Oxygen
   (iv) Sulphur and/or Nitrogen
   A. All of the above
   B. Only (i) and (ii)
   C. Only (i), (ii) and (iii)
   D. Only (i), (ii) and (iv)

26. Which of the following gases has the maximum global warming potential (GWP)?
   A. Carbon di-oxide   B. Methane
   C. Nitrous oxide   D. Water vapour

27. Acid rain has pH
   A. < 7.6   B. > 7
   C. ≤ 5.6   D. < 1.6

28. Which of the following gases facilitates formation of tropospheric ozone?
   A. NO_2 B. SO_2
   C. CO   D. NH_3

29. The sound power from a voice shouting is 0.001 Watt. The sound level in dB is
   A. 90 dB   B. 60 dB
   C. 30 dB   D. 120 dB

30. According to WHO maximum permissible level of iron in drinking water is
   A. 1 mg/L   B. 5 mg/L
   C. 10 mg/L   D. 50 mg/L

31. The particle sizes associated with ambient aerosols in the atmosphere have the range
   A. < 100 μm   B. 5-10 μm
   C. 1-5 μm   D. < 1 μm

32. Which of the following indices represents the background noise level in the ambient environment?
   A. L_{dn} B. L_{10}
   C. L_{90} D. L_{50}

33. Which species of chromium is toxic in water?
   A. Cr^{+2} B. Cr^{+3}
   C. Cr^{+6} D. Cr^0

34. Identify the correct sequence of stages of obtaining Environmental clearance for new projects
   A. Appraisal, Screening, Scoping, Public Consultation
   B. Screening, Public Consultation, Scoping, Appraisal
   C. Screening, Appraisal, Scoping, Public Consultation
   D. Screening, Scoping, Public Consultation, Appraisal

35. **Assertion (A) :** Cost benefit analysis converts the benefits from the development, damages and control measures into monetary values.

   Reason (R) : Cost benefit analysis compares the cost of damage caused by developmental activity with the cost of control measures adopted and provides the optimum solution for a given environmental quality.

   Which one of the following codes is correct?
   Codes :
   A. Both (A) and (R) are true and (R) is the correct explanation of (A).
   B. Both (A) and (R) are true, but (R) is not the correct explanation of (A).
   C. (A) is true but (R) is false.
   D. (A) is false but (R) is true.

36. Match the items in List-I with List-II and select the correct answers using codes given below :

List-I (Developmental project)	List-II (Validity time period for Environmental Impact Assessment Report)
(a) Mining Projects	(i) 10 years
(b) River Valley Projects	(ii) 30 years
(c) Area Development Projects	(iii) 5 years
(d) Other Projects	(iv) Limited period

Codes :

	(a)	(b)	(c)	(d)
A.	(iv)	(iii)	(ii)	(i)
B.	(i)	(ii)	(iii)	(iv)
C.	(ii)	(i)	(iv)	(iii)
D.	(ii)	(iii)	(i)	(iv)

37. Match the List-I and List-II. Identify the correct answer from the codes given below the lists:

List-I (Domain)	List-II (Effects)
(a) Socioeconomics	(i) Barrier to travel corridors
(b) Wildlife	(ii) Employment opportunities
(c) Water quality	(iii) Erosivity & Erodability
(d) Soil environment	(iv) BOD and COD

Codes :

	(a)	(b)	(c)	(d)
A.	(ii)	(i)	(iv)	(iii)
B.	(i)	(iii)	(ii)	(iv)
C.	(iv)	(ii)	(iii)	(i)
D.	(iii)	(iv)	(i)	(iii)

38. Hazardous substances have the following attributes
    A. Ignitability
    B. Ignitability, Reactivity and Corrosivity
    C. Reactivity and Toxicity
    D. Corrosivity and Toxicity

39. Among bio-medical wastes, human anatomical wastes fall under category
    A. 4   B. 2
    C. 3   D. 1

40. To test whether there is a significant difference between the means of two sets of observations, one employs the following statistical technique
    A. Regression
    B. χ^2 test (chi square test)
    C. t-test
    D. F-test

41. For any finite set of positive numbers, which is the correct relationship involving Harmonic Mean (HM), Geometric Mean (GM) and Arithmetic Mean (AM)?

A. $HM \leq GM \leq AM$
B. $AM \leq GM \leq HM$
C. $AM \leq HM \leq GM$
D. $GM \leq HM \leq AM$

42. The population (N) of an ecosystem follows logistic growth. If K is its carrying capacity, then the environmental resistance is

A. $\dfrac{N}{K}$ B. $1 - \dfrac{N}{K}$

C. $\dfrac{N^2}{K}$ D. NK

43. Chemical compounds having same crystal structure are called
    A. Polymorphic   B. Pseudomorphic
    C. Isomorphic   D. None of the above

44. In the Gaussian Plume Model, the plume rise, under neutral or unstable atmospheric conditions, varies with the average wind speed (u m/sec) at stack height as

A. u   B. $\dfrac{1}{u}$

C. $\dfrac{1}{u^2}$ D. $\dfrac{1}{u^{1/3}}$

45. Micas having an atomic structure defined as continuous sheets of tetrahedrons, sharing 3-oxygen atoms, are called
    A. Inosilicate   B. Phyllosilicate
    C. Tectosilicate   D. Sorosilicate

46. Kyoto Protocol on climate change was envisaged in which year?
    A. 1992   B. 1994
    C. 1997   D. 2002

47. Alkalinity in river waters in caused due to
    A. Presence of SO_4^{2-}
    B. Na^+ and K^+
    C. Cl^-
    D. CO_3^- and HCO_3^-

48. 'Ring of Fire' surrounds which ocean?
    A. Indian Ocean   B. Atlantic Ocean
    C. Arctic Ocean   D. Pacific Ocean

49. Assertion (A) : Available data suggest that the first cells on earth were anaerobic heterotrophs.

Reason (R) : In the beginning, the earth's atmosphere probably lacked free oxygen.
Identify the correct answer :
Codes :
A. Both (A) and (R) are true and (R) is the correct explanation of (A).

B. Both (A) and (R) are true and (R) is not the correct explanation of (A).
C. (A) is true and (R) is false.
D. (A) is false and (R) is true.

50. Chemical formula for CFC-113 is
A. CCl_2F_2
B. CCl_3F_3
C. $C_2Cl_3F_3$
D. CCl_2F_3

ANSWERS

1	2	3	4	5	6	7	8	9	10
D	D	D	C	D	D	C	B	A	C
11	**12**	**13**	**14**	**15**	**16**	**17**	**18**	**19**	**20**
C	D	D	B	B	B	A	B	B	D
21	**22**	**23**	**24**	**25**	**26**	**27**	**28**	**29**	**30**
B	A	A	A	A	A	C	D	A	A
31	**32**	**33**	**34**	**35**	**36**	**37**	**38**	**39**	**40**
A	D	B	D	A	C	A	B	D	C
41	**42**	**43**	**44**	**45**	**46**	**47**	**48**	**49**	**50**
A	A	C	B	D	C	B	D	A	C

UGC-NET ENVIRONMENTAL SCIENCE, JUNE 2011

PAPER-II

Note : *This paper contains fifty (50) objective type questions, each question carrying two (2) marks. Attempt all the questions.*

1. Identify the correct sequence of energy flow through various levels of an ecosystem
   A. Sun's energy → Primary producers → Carnivores
   B. Sun's energy → Primary producers → Carnivores → Herbivores
   C. Sun's energy → Herbivores → Primary producers
   D. Sun's energy → Primary producers → Herbivores → Carnivores

2. When environmental lapse rate is more than dry adiabatic lapse rate, the atmosphere is said to be in
   A. Stable state
   B. Unstable state
   C. Neutral state
   D. Conditionally stable state

3. Which of the following accounts for nearly 75% of the available fresh water in the world?
   A. Groundwater   B. Glaciers
   C. River water   D. Lakes

4. The summers in Taiga climatic zone are
   A. hot, humid and long
   B. warm and short
   C. cool, rainy and short
   D. hot and dry

5. Utilitarian conservation theory was established by
   A. Roosevelt and Pinchot
   B. John Muir
   C. Rachel Carson
   D. Brundtland

6. Ozone undergoes photolysis due to ultraviolet radiations of wavelength
   A. < 315 nm   B. < 400 nm
   C. < 500 nm   D. < 600 nm

7. Which of the following types of pesticides are least biodegradable?
   A. Organo chloro compounds
   B. Organo phosphorous compounds
   C. Organo carbamates
   D. All of the above

8. $MgSO_4$ can be expressed as
   A. 120 equivalent of $CaCO_3$
   B. 117 equivalent of $CaCO_3$
   C. 195 equivalent of $CaCO_3$
   D. 84 equivalent of $CaCO_3$

9. SDS-PAGE of tissue proteins under denaturation determines the
   A. Hydrogen bond breakage
   B. Sulphide bridge breakage
   C. Subunits of protein
   D. None of the above

10. In urban areas, the main constituents of photochemical smog in winter season are
    A. SO_2 + NO_x + PAN
    B. Hydrocarbons + CO + PAN
    C. Hydrocarbons + SO_2 + PAN
    D. Hydrocarbons + NO_x + O_3 + PAN

11. Redox potential in soil is governed by
    A. strong oxidizing agent
    B. weak oxidizing agent
    C. organic matter
    D. soil particle size

12. The process of invasion is completed through the following stages :
    A. Migration and establishment of species in bare area
    B. Migration, ecesis and aggregation
    C. Ecesis and aggregation
    D. Migration, aggregation and settlement of species

13. Which one is not matched correctly?
    A. Kaziranga   – Assam (Asom)
    B. Periyar   – Kerala

C. Ranthambore   –   Rajasthan

D. Hemis High   –   Himachal Pradesh
     Altitude

14. Hyporhric biodiversity is linked with
    A. Ecotone of surface water and groundwater
    B. Ecotone of terrestrial and aquatic ecosystem
    C. Groundwater
    D. Asian region

15. E. coli displays diauxic growth pattern when grown in a medium containing
    A. glucose and fructose
    B. glucose and citrate
    C. glucose and lactose
    D. glucose alone

16. El Nino effect refers to the periodic extension of warm equatorial current along which coast?
    A. Peru Coast
    B. African Coast
    C. East Coast of India
    D. Somalia Coast

17. Which of the following options is correct for concentration of elements in sea water?
    A. $Na > Mg > Ca$
    B. $Ca > Na > Mg$
    C. $Mg > Na > Ca$
    D. $CO_3 > SO_4 > Cl$

18. Land use planning requires which of the following base maps?
    A. Soil type map
    B. Slope map
    C. Soil depth map
    D. All of the above

19. Gutenberg discontinuity is found at the depth of
    A. 333 km
    B. 700 km
    C. 1500 km
    D. 2900 km

20. Landslides are generally associated with heavy rainfall because
    A. Water is universal solvent.
    B. Water enhances chemical weathering.
    C. Water increases the weight of overburden.
    D. Water reduces the shear strength of rock.

21. The optimal pH for Methane production ranges between
    A. 7 to 7.2
    B. 5 to 5.6
    C. 8 to 9.5
    D. 2.3 to 4.5

22. Average life time (τ) and half life ($T_{1/2}$) of a radioactive substances are related as
    A. $\tau = 1.44 \, T_{1/2}$
    B. $\tau = 0.5 \, T_{1/2}$
    C. $\tau = 0.63 \, T_{1/2}$
    D. $\tau = 2 \, T_{1/2}$

23. The maximum contribution to world electricity generation from non-hydro renewable energy sources is from
    A. Wind
    B. Biomass
    C. Solar PV
    D. Geothermal

24. The maximum efficiency of a commercial solar photovoltaic cell attainable today is in the range
    A. 3% to 10%
    B. 12% to 20%
    C. 30% to 40%
    D. 40% to 50%

25. Which of the following does not lead to global warming?
    A. Stratospheric ozone
    B. Tropospheric ozone
    C. Black carbon aerosols
    D. N_2O

26. The instrument used for determination of transparency of water is
    A. Spectrophotometer
    B. Ekman dredge
    C. Conductivity bridge
    D. Sechhi disc

27. Which of the following is an aerobic waste water treatment method?
    A. Sludge digester
    B. Septic tank
    C. Percolating filter
    D. Imhoff tank

28. Nitrogen Oxides (NO_x) consist of
    A. $NO + NO_2$
    B. $NO + NO_2 + N_2O$
    C. $NO + NO_2 + N_2O_5$
    D. $NO + NO_2 + N_2O + N_2O_5$

29. An increase of 10 ppm in the concentration of CO_2 in atmosphere represents approximately an addition of carbon of amount:
    A. 1.2 Kilotons
    B. 2.12 Megatons
    C. 21.2 Geiga tons
    D. 2120 tons

30. Winds blowing down an incline often due to cold air drainage is called
    A. Anabatic winds
    B. Mountain winds
    C. Cyclonic winds
    D. Katabatic winds

31. ISO 14040 is related to
    A. Environmental audit
    B. Energy audit
    C. Cost benefit analysis
    D. Life cycle analysis

32. Definition of Impact Assessment was given by
    A. Kozlowski (1989)
    B. Graham Smith (1993)
    C. Heer and Hagerty (1977)
    D. Bartlett (1989)

33. **Assertion (A)** : Environmental and social impact assessment never overlap with each other.

    Reason (R) : Environmental and social impact assessment are effectively opposite ends of the same spectrum.
    A. Both (A) and (R) are true and (R) is the correct explanation of (A).
    B. Both (A) and (R) are true but (R) is not the correct explanation of (A).
    C. (A) is true but (R) is false.
    D. (A) is false but (R) is true.

34. One of the best known matrix methods for environmental impact assessment is
    A. Leopold Matrix
    B. Sphere Matrix
    C. Saratoga Matrix
    D. Component Interaction Method

35. The method for systematically evaluating alternative development schemes and weighing relevant social cost with social benefits is known as
    A. Cost – benefit analysis
    B. Social cost – benefit analysis
    C. Social benefit – cost analysis
    D. Cost – effectiveness analysis

36. Gases emitted from municipal landfill sites include
    A. SO_2 and CH_4
    B. NH_4, CO, SO_2, CH_4
    C. NH_4, H_2S, CO
    D. CH_4, H_2S, CO_2, NH_4

37. The Air (Prevention and Control of Pollution) Act, 1981 was first amended in the year
    A. 1986   B. 1987
    C. 1988   D. 1990

38. Identify the correct sequence of materials in order of their heating values
    A. Methane > fuel oil > coal > wood
    B. Fuel oil > coal > methane > wood
    C. Coal > wood > fuel oil > garbage
    D. Methane > coal > garbage > wood

39. Urban air quality is basically decided by
    A. CO, SPM, SO_2, NO_2, Surface ozone
    B. SPM, NO_2, SO_2
    C. SPM, NO_2, CO
    D. SPM, SO_2, Surface ozone

40. If N is the population size at any given instant t, r its growth rate in an environment having carrying capacity K, the environmental resistance to population growth is given by

    A. $\dfrac{N}{K}$ B. $1 - \dfrac{N}{K}$

    C. $\dfrac{N}{K}e^{-tr}$ D. $\dfrac{N}{K}e^{tr}$

41. Which of the following statistical attributes is used to test the null hypothesis in Regression Analysis?
    A. Mean
    B. Standard deviation
    C. t-statistic
    D. Chi-square Test

42. Given 'd' as particle size and 'V' settling velocity in cm/sec., the correct relationship between 'd' and 'V' is given by

    A. $V \propto \dfrac{1}{d^n}$ B. $V \propto d^n$

    C. $V \propto d$ D. $V = \dfrac{1}{d^n}$

43. The geometric mean of 5, 5 and 40 is
    A. 16.66   B. 25
    C. 31.6   D. 10

44. The Eigen values of the matrix $\begin{bmatrix} 1 & 1 \\ 1 & 1 \end{bmatrix}$ are
    A. 1, 1   B. 0, 1
    C. 0, 2   D. 1, –1

45. In a simple regression model $y = \alpha + \beta x + E$ (where the symbols have their usual meanings), the expectation value of $<E>$ is assumed as
    A. 0
    B. $\bar{y}$

C. $\dfrac{\sigma}{\sqrt{2}}$; where σ is standard deviation

D. σ^2

46. In the Earth Summit at Rio de Janeiro, 1992, which of the following was not an agenda?
   A. Ozone depletion
   B. Global warming
   C. CO_2 reduction targets
   D. Biodiversity conservation

47. **Assertion (A)** : Most of the corporate sector in India has become conscious of the ethical dimensions pertaining to its impact on environment.

   Reason (R) : Indian people are increasingly becoming aware of the environmental issues.
   Codes :
   A. Both (A) and (R) are true and (R) is the correct explanation of (A).
   B. Both (A) and (R) are true but (R) is not the correct explanation of (A).
   C. (A) is true but (R) is false.
   D. (A) is false but (R) is true.

48. 'Slash and Burn' or milpa farming is often blamed for
   A. habitat destruction
   B. forest destruction
   C. hydrological imbalance
   D. mine destruction

49. **Assertion (A)** : Climate change is going to increase social tensions in India.

   Reason (R) : The frequency and intensity of the extreme weather events will have serious consequences for food security.
   Codes :
   A. Both (A) and (R) are true and (R) is the correct explanation of (A).
   B. Both (A) and (R) are true but (R) is not the correct explanation of (A).
   C. (A) is true but (R) is false.
   D. (A) is false but (R) is true.

50. Snow blindness is caused due to
   A. Ultraviolet radiations
   B. Excessive flux of visible radiations
   C. Infra-red radiations
   D. Microwave radiations

ANSWERS

1	2	3	4	5	6	7	8	9	10
D	B	B	C	A	A	A	A	A	D
11	12	13	14	15	16	17	18	19	20
C	B	D	A	C	A	A	D	D	D
21	22	23	24	25	26	27	28	29	30
A	A	A	B	A	D	C	A	B	B
31	32	33	34	35	36	37	38	39	40
D	C	A	A	B	D	B	A	A	A
41	42	43	44	45	46	47	48	49	50
D	A	C	C	A	C	A	B	A	A

UGC-NET ENVIRONMENTAL SCIENCES DECEMBER, 2010

PAPER-II

Note : *This paper contains* **fifty (50)** *objective type questions, each question carrying* **two (2)** *marks. Attempt* **all** *the questions.*

1. Across the boundaries of a closed thermodynamical system
   A. matter flows but the energy doesn't.
   B. energy flows but the matter doesn't.
   C. both energy and matter flow.
   D. both energy and matter do not flow.

2. The largest soil group in India is of
   A. Red soil
   B. Black soil
   C. Sandy soil
   D. Mountain soil

3. Sustainable development is about
   A. Social justice and equity
   B. Avoiding depletion of non-renewable resources
   C. Environmental protection
   D. All of the above

4. The mixing height is maximum in the
   A. morning   B. noon time
   C. evening   D. mid-night

5. Synoptic scale in meteorology is of the order of
   A. 100 m   B. 1 km
   C. 10 km   D. 1000 km

6. Polychlorinated biphenyls (PCBs) are known to cause
   A. deformities in foetus
   B. nervous disorders
   C. liver and stomach cancer
   D. All of the above

7. Match the List-I and List-II and select the correct answer from the codes given below the lists :

List-I (Analytical techniques)	List-II (Measureed items)
(a) XRF	1. Functional groups
(b) Nephelometry	2. Elements
(c) IR spectroscopy	3. Turbidity
(d) Gas chromatography	4. PAH

   Codes :

	(a)	(b)	(c)	(d)
A.	4	2	3	1
B.	1	3	4	2
C.	3	2	4	1
D.	2	3	1	4

8. An antibacterial chemical present in wood smoke is
   A. Formaldehyde   B. Cellulose
   C. Acetone   D. Methane

9. Microfilteration generally employs
   A. thin polymer film with uniform pore size and a high pore density
   B. thin microfilm with smaller pore size and low pore density
   C. thin micro-bioplastic with regular pore size and a high pore density
   D. thin membrane filter with uniform pore size and a high pore density

10. In natural waters with pH near 7.0, the redox potential lies between
    A. .81 Volt and 0.85 Volt
    B. – 0.41 Volt and 0.06 Volt
    C. – 0.41 Volt and 0.82 Volt
    D. 0.06 Volt and 1.23 Volt

11. BIOCLAIM® – a metal biosorbent includes microorganisms, mainly bacteria of the genus
    A. *Bacillus*   B. *Escherichia*
    C. *Pseudomonas*   D. *Rhizobium*

12. *Saccharomyces cerevisae* is a
    A. Alga   B. Bacterium
    C. Protozoan   D. Yeast

13. Method used to select growth of a specific type of bacteria in microbial ecology is
    A. FISH test   B. Enrichment culture
    C. Biofilms   D. DNA sequencing

14. About half of earth's photosynthesis is carried out by
    A. Cyanobacteria
    B. Rainforest flora
    C. Protists
    D. Marine phytoplankton

15. Ramsar Convention is associated with
    A. Forest conservation
    B. Soil conservation
    C. Wetland conservation
    D. Wildlife conservation

16. In tropical cyclones, mean wind speeds are
    A. between 10 to 20 knots
    B. between 20 to 40 knots
    C. between 40 to 60 knots
    D. greater than 63 knots

17. **Assertion (A):** Process involving living organisms are associated with sedimentation which is more closely linked with hydrosphere and the atmosphere.

    Reason (R) : In the biosphere geochemical differentiation takes place through the metabolic action of organisms.

    A. Both (A) and (R) are correct and (R) is the correct explanation of (A).
    B. Both (A) and (R) are correct and (R) is not the correct explanation of (A).
    C. (A) is true, but (R) is false.
    D. (A) is false, but (R) is true.

18. A mountain slope of slope angle 45° corresponds to which of the following in per cent slope notation?
    A. 10%   B. 50%
    C. 45%   D. 100%

19. Elastic-Rebound Theory suggests that an earthquake results due to change in the state of rock from
    A. Elastic to brittle
    B. Elastic to plastic
    C. Plastic to elastic
    D. Elastic to underformed

20. How many Universal Transverse Mercator (UTM) zones are there on earth?
    A. 45   B. 50
    C. 60   D. 90

21. Match the List-I and List-II. Identify the correct answer from the codes given below the lists :

List-I	List-II
(a) Noamundi Mines	1. Gold ore
(b) Khetri Mines	2. Pb – Zn ore
(c) Zawar Mines	3. Iron ore
(d) Kolar Mines	4. Copper ore

    Codes :

	(a)	(b)	(c)	(d)
A.	2	4	1	3
B.	1	3	2	4
C.	4	3	2	1
D.	4	3	1	2

22. The second generation resource for biofuel production.
    A. Coal   B. Petrol
    C. Corn and molasses D. Crop residues

23. The maximum temperature that can be obtained in a flat plate box type solar collection is between
    A. 50°C – 90°C   B. 100°C – 150°C
    C. 200°C – 250°C   D. 45°C – 50°C

24. At present, the total installed capacity of power generation from all sources in India is between
    A. 60 GW to 90 GW
    B. 30 GW to 60 GW
    C. 100 GW to 200 GW
    D. 200 GW to 250 GW

25. Which of the following materials is not used as moderator to slow down the fast neutrons produced in a nuclear reactor?
    A. Water   B. Heavy water
    C. Graphite   D. Lead

26. If equivalent sound pressure level of 90 dB(A) for 8 hours represents 100% dose of noise, noise dose of 25% implies
    A. 87 dB(A) for 4 hours
    B. 84 dB(A) for 4 hours
    C. 22.5 dB(A) for 8 hours
    D. 84 dB(A) for 2 hours

27. Maximum photodissociation of NO_2 molecules in atmosphere occurs due to solar radiations in the wavelength range
   A. 300 nm – 400 nm
   B. 400 nm – 500 nm
   C. 500 nm – 550 nm
   D. 550 nm – 600 nm

28. The time scale for vertical transport of pollutants in the troposphere is typically
   A. minutes   B. minutes to hours
   C. days to weeks   D. years

29. For domestic drinking water supply the total dissolved solids should not exceed
   A. 250 ppm   B. 500 ppm
   C. 600 ppm   D. 100 ppm

30. Which of the following sewage treatment relies on removing the suspended solids from water?
   A. Primary treatment
   B. Secondary treatment
   C. Tertiary treatment
   D. Breaking down of organic matter

31. The concept of Environmental Impact Assessment originated from
   A. Findings of a Royal Commission investigating the 'Weald Iron Mills and Furnaces' in Southern England in 1548.
   B. Report of the 'Volta Preparatory Commission' (HMSO, 1956).
   C. Discretionary guidelines of the National Environmental Policy Act in 1971.
   D. Report of copper mining in Puerto Rico commissioned in February 1967.

32. **Assertion (A):** Impact Assessment enables the planners and decision makers to think carefully about the project proposals.

   Reason (R) : Impact Assessment can help in ensuring that planners and decision makers are more accountable for their actions
   A. Both (A) and (R) are true and (R) is the correct explanation of (A).
   B. Both (A) and (R) are true but (R) is not the correct explanation of (A).

   C. (A) is true, but (R) is false.
   D. (A) is false, but (R) is true.

33. Eco-auditing focuses on
   A. Assessment of actual effects of existing activities
   B. Assessment of project decisions
   C. Policy assessment
   D. Post project assessment

34. Match the List-I and List-II. Select the correct answer from the codes given below the lists :

List-I	List-II
(a) Ad-hoc Method	(i) Gives some measurements and describes the impacts
(b) Checklist Method	(ii) Limited value for scoping
(c) Overlay Method	(iii) Used for screening and for impact assessment, especially for impact identification
(d) Matrix Method	(iv) Acts as an aid in screening sites or routes for impacts

   Codes :

	(a)	(b)	(c)	(d)
A.	(i)	(ii)	(iii)	(iv)
B.	(ii)	(iii)	(i)	(iv)
C.	(iii)	(iv)	(ii)	(i)
D.	(ii)	(i)	(iv)	(iii)

35. Eco-labelling is governed by
   A. ISO 14001   B. ISO 14020
   C. ISO 14010   D. ISO 14040

36. The predominant gas emitted during the early life of a MSW landfill is
   A. CO   B. CO_2
   C. CH_4 D. VOCs

37. Black foot disease is caused by
   A. excess of fluoride in water
   B. deficiency of iodine in water
   C. excess of arsenic in water
   D. excess of iodine in water

38. The Water Cess Act 1977 was amended in the year
A. 1991   B. 1978
C. 1988   D. 1987

39. Public Liability Insurance Act was enacted in which year?
A. 1991   B. 1986
C. 1990   D. 1984

40. In a multiple regression model $Y_i = \alpha + \beta_{1i}X_i + \beta_2X_{2i} + \beta_{3i}X_3 + \epsilon_i$, if i = N, the number of degrees of freedom required for determining the t-value at 5% level of significance
A. N – 3   B. N – 2
C. N – 4   D. N – 1

41. For large population sizes, the t-distribution approaches
A. Normal distribution
B. Poisson distribution
C. Binomial distribution
D. Chi-square distribution

42. Lotka-Volterra Model deals with
A. Prey-Predator interactions
B. Predicting CO_2 concentrations
C. Study of pollutant concentration in river streams
D. Study of pollutant concentration in atmospheric environment

43. Eigen values of the matrix $\begin{bmatrix} 1 & 1 & 1 \\ 1 & 1 & 1 \\ 1 & 1 & 1 \end{bmatrix}$ are
A. 0, 0, 1
B. 0, 1, 1
C. 0, 2, 1
D. 0, 0, 3

44. The second moment of the data set 2, 3, 7, 8, 10 is
A. 6   B. 378
C. 45.2   D. 22.51

45. In Gaussian dispersion model, the effective stack height is taken as sum of physical stack height and the plume rise ΔH. The plume rise varies with stack velocity V_S in the following manner :
A. $\Delta H \propto V_S$ B. $\Delta H \propto V_S^2$
C. $\Delta H \propto V_S^{-1}$ D. $\Delta H \propto V_S^{3/2}$

46. **Assertion (A):** A large number of districts in States of India have become water stressed.
Reason (R) : The population in India has increased appreciably since independence.
Codes :
A. Both (A) and (R) are ture and (R) is the correct explanation of (A).
B. Both (A) and (R) are true but (R) is not the correct explanation of (A).
C. (A) is true, but (R) is false.
D. (A) is false, but (R) is true.

47. Copenhagen Conference on climate change was held as a sequel to
A. Montreal Protocol
B. Ramsar Convention
C. Basel Convention
D. Kyoto Protocol

48. Under the Climate Change Action Plan of Government of India which of the renewable-source of energy has been identified as a priority for exploitation?
A. Solar energy
B. Wind energy
C. Tidal energy
D. Geothermal energy

49. International Ozone Day is celebrated on
A. 21st April
B. 5th June
C. 22nd April
D. 16th September

50. Sardar Sarovar Dam is built on
A. Sabarmati river   B. Narmada river
C. Tapti river   D. Chambal river

ANSWERS

1	2	3	4	5	6	7	8	9	10
B	A	C	B	D	D	B	A	D	B
11	**12**	**13**	**14**	**15**	**16**	**17**	**18**	**19**	**20**
A	D	C	D	C	B	A	D	D	C
21	**22**	**23**	**24**	**25**	**26**	**27**	**28**	**29**	**30**
C	C	B	C	A	C	A	D	B	A
31	**32**	**33**	**34**	**35**	**36**	**37**	**38**	**39**	**40**
A	A	A	D	A	C	C	C	A	D
41	**42**	**43**	**44**	**45**	**46**	**47**	**48**	**49**	**50**
A	A	D	A	C	A	D	A	D	B

PAPER-III

Note: This paper is of ***two hundred (200)*** *marks containing* ***four (4)*** *sections. Candidates are required to attempt the questions contained in these sections according to the detailed instructions given therein.*

SECTION-I

Note: This section consists of ***two*** *essay type questions of* ***twenty (20)*** *marks each, to be answered in about* ***five hundred (500)*** *words each.*   **(2 × 20 = 40 marks)**

1. **Municipal solid waste management.**

OR

Environmental problems associated with megathermal power plants.

OR

Ground water provinces of India.

OR

Agro-climatic regions of India.

OR

Biodiversity and climate change.

OR

Biodegradation of plant biomass.

Ans. Based on the homogeneity in agrocharacteristics such as rainfall, temperature, soil, topography, cropping and farming systems the country has been divided into 15 agroclimatic regions.

   (i) **Western Himalayan Region :** This consists of three distinct zones of Jammu and Kashmir, Himachal pradesh, and uttar hills. The regions has podsolic soils, mountain meadow soil and hilly brown soils. Cropping intensity is lowest in J&K and highest in Himachal Pradesh. Productivity level is also lower. The strategies for the development of this region may be:

(a) Intensification of soil and water conservation programme through watershed management.

(b) Land use planning based on the concept that land up to 30% slope is suitable for agriculture on terraces, 30–50% slope for horticulture and 50% for forestry.

(c) High value and low volume crops such as pomology, floriculture medicinal and aromatic plants etc. should be preferred.

(d) More facilities of storage and cold storage facilities for fruits and vegetables.

(e) Irrigation management through water harvesting techniques.

(f) Livestock management through integrated approach to breeding feeding and adequate health cover.

(ii) **Eastern Himalayan Region :** It includes Sikkim and Darjeeling Hills, Arunachal Pradesh, Meghalaya, Nagaland, Manipur, Tripura, Mizoram, Assam, Jalpaiguri & Coochbehar districts of west Bengal. The region has high rainfall and high rain cover. Shifting cultivation is practised in almost one–third of the area.

(iii) **Lower Gangetic Plains :** The west Bengal lower gangetic plains consist of four sub-regions. Barind plains, Central alluvial plains, Alluvial coastal plains, and Rarh plains. It is a rice producing region. Mustard, Maize and Potato are the new emerging crops of the region. Here, the potential for enhancing production through higher productivity in crops, livestock and fisheries is enormous. Dairying has also a good scope.

(iv) **Middle Gangetic Plain :** This zone consist of 12 districts of Uttar Pradesh and 27 districts of Bihar plains, The rainfall is high and 39% of GCA is irrigated and cropping intensity of the region is 142%. Rice productivity is low in the region so it should be increased. Poultry, dairying, and inland fishery should also be given priority.

(v) **Upper Gangetic Plain :** This zone consist of 32 districts of Uttar Pradesh divided in to three sub-zones of central, North West and South-West U.P. The zone has 131% irrigation intensity and 144% cropping intensity. A good potential for exploitation of ground water exists. Productivity of rice and wheat is high.

(vi) **Trans-Gangetic Plains :** This zone consist of Punjab and Haryana, union territories of Delhi and Chandigarh and Sriganganagar district of Rajasthan. It has been divided into three sub-zones namely, foothills of Shiwalik and the Himalayas; plains and arid zone bordering the Thar desert. The region has highest net sown area, highest irrigated area, lowest poverty level, high cropping intensity and high ground water utilisation.

(vii) **Eastern Plateau and Hills :** The region consists of

(a) Sub-region of wainganga, Madhya Pradesh, Eastern hills and Orissa inland.

(b) Northern Orissa and MP, Eastern hills and plateau.

(c) North Chhotanagpur, eastern hills & plateau.

(d) South Chhotanagpur, West Bengal hills & plateau.

(e) Chhattisgarh and South-Western hills of Orissa.

Rice is the most dominant Kharif crop, pulses and oilseeds also occupy some area.

(viii) **Central Plateau and Hills :** The zone comprises of 46 districts of Madhya Pradesh, Uttar Pradesh and Rajasthan. The topography is ravines in certain parts and hilly in others. Irrigation and intensity of cropping are very low. 75% of the area is rainfed. Watershed management should be implemented properly. Low value coarse cereal crops should be replaced by high value crops.

(ix) **Western Plateau and Hills :** The zone comprises of major part of Maharashtra, parts of M.P. and one district of Rajasthan. The region forms a major part of peninsula having average rainfall of 904 mm. Net sown area is around 64% and forestry occupy 11% area. Irrigated area is only 12.4% with canals being the main source. Jowar and cotton are the main crops of the region. However, best quality oranges, grapes and bananas are found here. The area under fruit crop is 1 lakh hectares. Scope of growing high value crop are quite good.

(x) **Southern Plateau and Hills :** This zone comprises of 35 districts of Andhra Pradesh, Karnataka and Tamil Nadu which are typically semi arid zones. Rainfed farming is adopted in 81% of the area and cropping intensity is 111. Low value cereal crops and millets dominates the cropping pattern.

(xi) **East Coast Plains and Hills :** This zone consist of six sub-zones.

    (a) Orissa coastal part

    (b) Andhra North Coast and Gaujam

    (c) South Coast of Andhra

    (d) North Coastal part of Tamil Nadu

    (e) Thanjavur, and

    (f) South Coastal Tamil Nadu.

The area account for 20.33% of the total rice production of India and 17.05% of the total ground nut production of India. Alkaline and Saline Soils are found in the Coastal areas and Cover 4.9 lakh hectares. There is need for the reclamation of this soil and there are also common problems of water logging.

Nearly 70% of the cultivated area does not have irrigation facilities and therefore a watershed management programme can be taken up in 64.49 lakh hectares.

(xii) **West Coast Plains and Ghats :** This zone covers the West Coast of Tamil Nadu, Kerala, Karnataka, Maharashtra and Soil types. This zone is also important for plantation of crops and spices.

(xiii) **Gujarat Plains and Hills :** This zone consists of 19 districts of Gujarat. The zone is arid with low rainfall in most parts and only 22.5% of the area is irrigated. Only 50% of the cultivated area is occupied by food crop. It is an important oilseed zone. The cropping intensity is only 114% and nearly 60% of the zone is drought prone.

Nearly 78% of farming is rainfed, so major thrust should be on rain water harvesting and management, dryland farming and canal and ground water management. Agroforestry, grassland development should also be given priority.

(xiv) **Western Dry region :** The region comprises of nine districts of Rajasthan and characterised by hot sandy desert, erratic rainfall, high evaporation, no perennial river and scanty vegetation. The ground is often very deeply located and famine and drought are the common features. The average annual rainfall is only 395 mm with wide fluctuation from year to year. Forest area is only 1.2%. The land under pasture is also low only 4.3% cultivable waste and follow land account for nearly 42% of the geographic area. The net irrigation area is only 6.3% of the net sown area (44.4%) cropping intensity is 105% cropping pattern of the region reveals the importance of Bajra, gwar, month, wheat and gram. Livestock contribute greatly to desert ecology.

The acute shortage of fuel, fodder and forage warrants concentrating at efforts on silvipastoral and energy plantations to meet the scarcity and to establish partially the sand dunes. Indira Gandhi canal project and Desert Development programme are two main programmes of great potential in this region. Increasing tree cover is also necessary to

    (a) Check desertification

    (b) Provide fodder to livestock

    (c) Meet the fuel needs of the population and

    (d) Provide timber for implements.

(xv) **Island region :** The zone covers the Island territories of Andaman and Nicobar Island and Lakshadweep, here the typical equatorial climate with a rainfall of 3000 mm spread over eight to nine months are observed. It is largely a forest zone having large undulating areas leading to heavy loss of soil due to runoff. Nearly half of the cropped area in under coconut.

The main thrust in development of this zone should be on crop improvement water managment and fisheries.

2. Wetland Conservation.

OR

Clean Development Mechanism (CDM) and Environmental protection.

OR

The types, sources and consequences of water pollution.

OR

Soil bioremediation – An emerging technology.

OR

An ecosystem, its structure and functions.

OR

Environmental Impacts of thermochemical and photochemical reactions in atmosphere.

Ans. Water pollution simply means contamination of water due to any external material, or in other words, introduction of something to natural water which makes unsuitable for human comsumption. WHO has defined water pollution as any foreign material either from natural or other sources that may contaminate the water supply and makes it harmful to life, cause of their toxicity leads to reduction of normal oxygen level of water, causes aesthetically unpollutable effects and spread of epidemic diseases, "Owen has defined it as many unreasonable contamination of water which lessens its value to man". In general water, "water pollution may be defined as the adverse change in composition or reduction of the water such that it becomes less suitable for the purposes for which it would be suitable in its natural state". The changes include, physical changes, chemical changes and biological changes. 2. According to Gilpil, "the deterioration in chemical, physical and biological properties of water brought about mainly by human activities". 3 is the water pollution. Whatever additions are done to the water either by natural processes or by human activities invariably, they change the natural qualities. The problem of water pollution was recognized by hippocrates (450 BC), who suggested filtration and boiling as remedial measures. With the fast increase in our industrial civilization, the demand for water is also increasing day by day. At the same time, population increase urbanization, improper sewage disposal, unsafe, industrial wastes, readioactives wastes oil etc., have polluted our water resources so much so that 70%, rivers and streams not only of India but of all the countries contain the polluted water.

Sources of Water Pollution

Water pollution is caused by several sources which are not independent in nature but interact with one another. Generally water pollution can be classified into the following categories

 (i) Domestic effluents and sewage,

 (ii) Industrial effluents

 (iii) Agricultral effluents

 (iv) Radio-active water

 (v) Thermal pollution, and

 (vi) Oil pollution.

 (i) **Domestic effluents sewage :** Man for his various domestic purposes such as drinking, preparation of food, bathing, for cleaning the house, cooling etc. Uses on averages 135 litres of water per day. About 70 to 80 per cent of this is discharged and drained out which although municipal drains poured into, in many cases, a river tank or lake.

This water is known as domestic waste water in which when other waste material such as paper, plastic, detergents, cloth, other waste materials are mixed, is known as municipal waste or sewage. The domestic waste water and sewage is the main source of the water pollution. This is the inevitable and unfortunate fall out of urbanization. As it decays, this organic waste depletes the oxygen from water and upsets the natural balance of the aquatic ecosystem.

Municipal sewage is considered to be the main polluted water. Most of the sewage receives no treatment before discharge, especially in developing countries like India in Delhi alone, 120 crore litres of water is consumed per day out of which 96 crore litres waste water is drained in to the Yamuna river through 17 big drains. All the 47 towns located on the bank of river Ganga drain their sewage into it. With the growth of populaiton the quantity of waste water is also increasing sewage contains decomposable organic mattter and exert on oxygen demand on receiving waters. The common organic materials found in a sewage are soaps, synthetic detergents, fatty acids, proteinaceous matters such as amines, amino acids, amides and amino sugars. In addition to the above components it also contains numerous micro-organisms. Sewage also contains pathegenic bacteria and viruses derived from human faces. Untreated waste water is often the carrier of viruses and bacteria and along with household sanitation practices.

Sewage supports the growth of other forms of life that consume oxygen.

It is measured in terms of Biochemical Oxygen Demand (BOD). It is the lack of oxygen that kills fish and aquatic life.

In recent years, there has been considerable growth in the use of detergents, which causes the severe water pollution, many component of agricultural fertilizers. When phosphate detergents are discharged into water ways, they supply nutrients and promote rapid growth of algae. This enrichment process is known as Eutrophication in many areas of world, aquatic weeds have multiplied explosively. They have interfered with fishing, navigation, irrigation and even production of hydroelectrocity. In developing countries, human population and settlements are growing fast, often faster than waste water treatment facilities can be provided. Thus much of the untreated waste water and sewage is discharged into rivers and other water bodies, making the water unsuitable for drinking and is a main cause of water pollution.

(ii) **Industrial Effluents :** Industrial activities generate a wide variety of waste products which are generally discharged into water caurses. Major contributors are the pulp and paper, chemicals, petro-chemicals and refining, metal working, food processing, textile, distillery, etc.

The wastes, broadly categorized as heavy metals or synthetic organic compounds reach bodies of water either through direct discharge or by leaching from waste dumps. Indeveloped countries of the world, many industrial discharges are strictly controlled. Yet, water pollution continues from accumulations of wastes discharged over the past 100 years. But, in developing countries, industrial discharges are largely uncontrolled, thus a main cause of water pollution.

All the Indian rivers have been polluted by industrial effluents. The holy river Ganga has become a highly polluted river due to various types of industrial discharges. Along the Ganga, several chemical, textile tanning, pulp and paper petrochemicals, rubber, fertilizers and other heavy industries are located and all of them discharge their waste waster and other effluent, directly or indirectly, into the river, resulting in the pollution to such an extent that even the Ganga action plan, to control water pollution, has failed. From Delhi industrial alone more than 8 lakh tonnes of industrial waste is discharged into the river Yamuna.

Damodar river of Jharkhand is a highly polluted river due to industrial wastes discharged from Bokaro, Rourkela, Tata Iron and Steel Company, Bengal paper mills, Sindhri fertilizer factory, etc. A study reveals that from Durgapur plant 1800 cu/m washed coal has been discharged into the river. Similarly, from ISCO 15,000 cu/m and from Bengal paper mills 12,000 cu/m per day industrial waste is discharged into river water.

The story of the Hooghly river of West Bengal is also similar. Its water has been polluted to such an extent that even fish fertilization becomes difficult.

Chambal, Narmada, Kaveri, Godavari, Mahanadi and other small rivers have been polluted and more pollutants have been discharged, resulting in greater water pollution.

Pulp and paper industries effluents from paper and pulp destroy include wood chips, bits of park, cellulose fibres dissolved liginin, in addition to a mixture of chemicals.

All these produce sludge which blankets fish spawning grounds and destroies certain types of aquatic life.

Textile industries, effluents are alkaline in nature and have a higher demand for oxygen food processing industries include dairies.

Textile industries, effluents are alkaline in nature and a higher demand from oxygen.

Food processing industries include dairies, breweries, distilleries meat packing etc., where the waste products include fats, proteins and organics coastes. These industries, discharge wastes containing nitrogen, sugar, proteins etc. All these coastes have a higher BOD and responsible for water pollution.

Chemical industries include acid manufacturing, alkali manufacturing, fertilizers, pesticides and several other industries. The effluents from these industries contain acids which have corrosive effects. The effluents from fertilizer industries contain phosphorus, fluorine, silica and large amounts of suspended solids.

Metal industries usually discharge effluents containing, copper, lead, chromium, cadmium, zinc, etc., which are toxic to man as well as to acquatic life.

These wastes also contain acids, oils, greases and cleansing agents.

Petroleum industries include oil refinery and petro-chemical plants. The effluents include hydro carbons, phonolic compounds and other organic and inorganic sulphur compounds.

Other industries which pollute water are tanneries, soaps and detergents industries, glass, electroplating, bleaching, atomic plants, explosive factories, etc.

Mining operations can result in metals leaching into the acid effluents, the adding to the metal load in rivers, lakes and ground water. Discharge of the mercury from gold mining of activities has polluted some streams in Brazil and Ecuador and created serious health problems, with the reference to the water pollution through mercury, mention of Minimata gulf incident must be made. In 1950 near the Japanese coast, in Minimata gulf fishermen suffered from blindness, weakness, mental illness, paralysis etc. It was found that effluents discharged from a plastic factory contained mercury which entered the fish and eating those fish, all the fishermen suffered from effects of mercury poisoning. The problem of water pollution through industrial effluents has become a major environmental problem and sufficient measures should be taken to control it.

(iii) **Agricultural Effluents :** Agricultural water pollution is caused by fertilizers, insecticides and pesticides, from animal wastes and sediments. In recent years, use of chemical fertilizers has increased manifold. The green revolution of India is a reflection of the increased use of fertilizers. The chemicals used in fertilizers enter the ground water by leaching and the surfaces by run off. The nitrates, when mixed with waters may cause naethemoglobinemia in infants.

Incidences of nitrates poisoning are also there in livestock. The plants nutrients, nitrogen and phosphorus are reported to stimulate the growth of algae and other aquatic plants.

The use of various types of pesticides and insecticides in agriculture is also one of the causes of the water pollution. There presence in water is highly toxic to man and animals, because all these have a high persistance capacity, *i.e.,* their reduces remain for long periods.

The farm animal wastes often pose serious problems of odour and water pollution.

These wastes also contain pathogenic organisms which get transmitted to humans. Sediments of soil and mineral particles washed out, from fields also cause water pollution. They fill stream channels and reservoirs and reduce the sunlight available to acquatic plants.

(iv) **Radio active wastes:** Radio active elements such as uranium and radium possess highly unstable atomic nuclei. This disintegration results in radiation emission which may be highly injurious. During nuclear tests, radio active dusts may encircle the globe at altitudes of 3,000 metres or more, the same of ten comes down to the earth as rain. Eventually, some of radio active material, such as strontium 90 (which can cause bone cancer), percolated down through the soil into groundwater reservoirs or its carried out into streams and rivers. In both cases, public water supplies may be contaminated. The construction of more nuclear reactors and the increasing of radioactive materials in medical research represent other potential contamination sources.

(v) **Thermal pollution:** Most of the thermal and electric power plants also discharge considerable quantities (about 66%) of hot effluent/water into nearby streams or rivers. This has resulted in thermal pollution of our water courses. Thermal pollution is undesirable for several reasons. Warm water does not have the same oxygen hloding capacity as cold water. Therefore, fishes like black bass, trout and walleyes, etc, which require a minimal oxygen concentrate of about 4 ppm would either have to emigrate from the polluted area or die in large numbers. When the temperature of the receiving water is raised, the dissolved O_2 level decreases and demand for O_2 increases hence anaerobic conditions will set in resulting in the release of soul gases.

Thermal pollution is considered hazardous for the whole aquatic ecosystem.

Several industries have installed cooling towers where the heated water is cooled. But even so, thermal pollution has become a serious problem for water bodies located near thermal plants.

SECTION-II

Note: This section contains **three (3)** *questions of* **fifteen** *marks each to be answered in about* **three hundred (300)** *words.*

(3 × 15 = 45 marks)

3. Describe the effects of Cd, Hg and As contamination on soil health.

Ans. Heavy metals have a density of 6.0 g/cm^3 or more (much higher than the average particle density of soils which is 2.65 g/cm^3) and occur naturally in rocks but concentrations are frequently elevated as a result of contamination. The most important heavy metals with regard to potential hazards and occurrence in contaminated soils are: arsenic (As), cadmium (Cd), chromium (Cr), mercury (Hg), lead (Pb) and zinc (Zn).

The sources of heavy metal pollurtants are metal mining, metal smelting metallurgical industries industries, and other metal-using industries, waste disposal, corrosions of metals in use, agriculture and forestry, forestry, fossil fuel combustion, and sports and leisure activities. Heavy metal contamination affects large areas worldwide. Hot spots of heavy metal pollution are located close to industrial sites, around large cities and in the vicinity of mining and smelting plants. Agriculture in these areas faces major problems due to heavy metal transfer into crops and subsequently into the food chain.

Health effects of selected heavy metals

Cadmium (Cd): Its toxicity is linked with reproduction problem because it affects sperm and reduces birth weight. It is a potential carcinogen and seems to be a causal factor in cardiovascular diseases and hypertension. Large concentrations of Cd in the soil are associated with parent material (black slates) and most are manmade (burning of fossil fuels, application of fertilizers, sewage sludge, plastic waste).

Mercury (Hg): This heavy metal is toxic even at low concentrations to a wide range of organisms including humans. The organic form of mercury can be particularly toxic, and the methyl-and ethyl-forms have been the cause of several major epidemics of poisoning in humans resulting from the ingestion of contaminated food, e.g. fish. Two major epidemics in Japan were caused by the release of methyl and other mercury compounds from an industrial site followed by accumulation of the chemicals in edible fish. The poisoning became well-known as Minamata disease.

Arsenic (As): Arsenic is well-known as a poison and a carcinogen. It has an average concentration in the soil of 5 to 6 mg/kg. Its amount in the soil is related to rock type and industrial activity.

4. How does an electrostatic precipitator (ESP) remove particles from flue gases? On what factors the efficiency of ESP depends?

Ans. Electrostatic precipitators, use electrical fields to remove particulate from boiler flue gas. Because precipitators act only on the particulate to be removed, and only minimally hinder flue gas flow, they have very low pressure drops, and thus low energy requirements and operating costs.

In an electrostatic precipitator, an intense electric field is maintained between high-voltage discharge electrodes, typically wires or rigid frames, and grounded collecting electrodes, typically plates. A corona discharge from the discharge electrodes ionizes the gas passing through the precipitator, and gas ions subsequently ionize fly ash (or other) particles. The electric field drives the negatively charge particles to the collecting electrodes. Periodically, the collecting electrodes are rapped mechanically to dislodge collected particulate, which falls into hoppers for removal.

In a typical electrostatic precipitator, collecting plates are arranged parallel to the gas flow, normally 9-18 inches apart, with discharge electrodes between them. Most precipitators have 3-5 independent electrical sections, *i.e.*, sets of discharge and collecting electrodes with independent power supplies, in series. Each independent section removes a fraction of the particulate in the gas stream. This arrangement allows the use of higher voltages in the first sections of the precipitator, where there is more particulate to be removed. Lower voltages must be used in the final, cleaner precipitator sections to avoid excessive sparking between the discharge and collecting electrodes. In a precipitator with only one electrical section, the power input would be limited to the input which would cause sparking at the precipitator exit, thus limiting the performance of the entire precipitator.

Precipitator sectionalization has the added advantage that particles reentrained in the flue gas stream by rapping may be collected in downstream sections of the precipitator, thus minimizing net rapping reentrainment losses.

While several factors determine electrostatic precipitator removal efficiency, precipitator size is of paramount importance. Size determines treatment time: the longer a particle spends in the precipitator, the greater its chance of being collected, other things being equal.

Precipitator size also is related to the specific collection area (SCA), the ratio of the surface area of the collection electrodes to the gas flow. Higher collection areas lead to better removal efficiencies. Collection areas normally are in the range of 200-800 ft^2/1000 acfm. In order to achieve collection efficiencies of 99.5%, specific collection areas of 350-400 ft^2/1000 acfm are typically used. Some older precipitators on utility boilers are small, with specific collection areas below 200 ft^2/1000 acfm and correspondingly short treatment times. Expansion of these precipitators, or their replacement with larger precipitators, can lead to greatly enhanced performance.

Maximizing electric field strength will maximize precipitator collection efficiency. Automatic voltage controllers are used to maintain and electric field strength as high as possible to ensure maximum particle charging and collection, consistent with preventing electrical breakdown of the gas and sparking between the discharge and collecting electrodes, which would extinguish the electric field. These controllers detect spark onset, and maintain voltages just below the level at which sparking would occur.

5. Write about the constitutional provisions pertaining to environment.

Ans. To protect and improve the environment is a constitutional mandate. It is a commitment for a country wedded to the ideas of welfare state. The Indian constitution contains specific provisions for environmental protection under the chapters of directive principles of state policy and fundamental rights.

Directive Principles of State Policy: Our constitution makers were very much aware of the pitiable condition of the people. They realized that the condition of the poor, the illiterate and the backward masses had to be improved, if India was to progress. There was a need for certain steps and definite directives to improve the conditions of our people.

The Directive Principles of State Policy were, therefore, added to the constitution of improve the condition of the people and to bring in progress. These are called Directive Priniciples because they are meant to be directives to the Govts. at all levels in India. It is the duty of every Govt. of India to apply these Directive Principles in the making of laws. These principles help the governments to make social and economic reform in the country. These principles, if put into practice by our Government, can improve our life in every sphere.

Fundamental Rights: The Hon'ble SC in several cases interpreted the right to life and personal liberty to include the right to a wholesome environment.

The Law of Torts on Public and Private Nuisance: A polluter may also be liable in Tort for causing private and public nuisance. Sending deleterious substance like gas, smoke or filth on the property of another person is private nuisance. A civil action can also lie for public nuisance in those circumstance in which a criminal action U/S 268 of IPC can be taken.

Indian Easements Act, 1882: Section 28(D) deals with the prescriptive right to pollute air or water and provides, "the extent of the perspective right to pollute air or water is the extent to the pollution at the commencement of the period of user on completion of which the right arose."

The Indian Forests Act, 1927: The Act contains provisions for prevention of land pollution by deforestation. The states Government have been empowered to make rules or for protection and conservation of forests.

Special legaislation to Prevent and Control Pollution: The deepest doctrine roots of environmental law are found in the common law principles of nuisance. It may be caused through escape of waste water, filthy liquids or substances, smoke, fumes, gases, noise, heat, vibrations, electricity, disease, bacteria etc. India enacted the special legislation on Environmental problems reflecting fuller effect to the resolutions of the Stockholm Conference of 1972.

The Water (Prevention and Control of Pollution) Act, 1974: This comprehensive piece of legislation was passed under Article 252 of the constitution mainly with the object of prevention and control of water pollution. The Act contemplates establishment of one Central Board for prevention and control of water pollution and similar Boards at the state level. The penalties against the pollutant vary from rigorous imprisonment for 6 months to 6 yrs.

The Air (Prevention and Control of Pollution) Act, 1981: The Central Enactment came into force from 16.05.1981. This Act was intended-to achieve effective control over air pollution caused by various reasons. The Act contemplates establishment of the central and state Boards rested with wide powers to enable them to devise means to improve the quality of air and to prevent, control or abate pollution in the country.

The Act is visualised as a measure to implement some of the decisions taken at the UN Conference on Human Environment held at Stockholm in June 1972 to take appropriate steps for the prevention of the natural resources of the earth and control of pollution.

Section 39 of the Act provides for penalty for violation of the provisions of the Act, which may extend to a fine of Rs. 5000/- with an additional fine which may extend to Rs. 100/- per day the contravention continues

The Environmental (Protection) Act, 1986: One of the most noted legislation passed in the wake of Bhopal tragedy, in order to cover the areas not covered by other laws regarding environmental (Protection) act, 1986. It aims at checking the environmental hazards especially connected with the manufacturing and handling of dangerous substances. This is said to be a more effective and bold measure to fight the problem of pollution as compared to all the previous laws in this regard.

SECTION-III

Note: This section contains nine (9) questions of ten (10) marks, each to be answered in about fifty (50) words.

(9 × 10 = 90 marks)

6. What is redox potential? Discuss its significance.

Ans. Redox potential is an electrical measurement that shows the tendency of a soil solution to transfer electrons to or from a reference electrode. From this measurement we can estimate whether the soil is aerobic, anaerobic, and whether chemical compounds such as Fe oxides or nitrate have been chemically reduced or are present in the oxidized forms. Marking these measurements requires three basic pieces of equipment:

1. Platinum electrode
2. Voltmeter
3. Reference electrode

7. Write about chemical reactions leading to ozone depletion.

Ans. Ozone (O_3) is an important natural component of the stratosphere. Ozone occurs in scant amounts between about 6 and 31 miles (10 and 50 km) above sea level and is most strongly concentrated at an altitude of 12 to 16 miles (20–25 km)—the ozone layer. Ozone is formed in the stratosphere when high-energy ultraviolet (UV) radiation splits normal oxygen molecules (O_2) into atomic oxygen (O). The atomic oxygen may then combine with a standard diatomic oxygen molecule (O_2) to form triatomic ozone (O_3). Under natural conditions, ozone is not only formed in the atmosphere, but it is also removed by various reactions.

Depletion of stratospheric ozone has been found to occur mainly due to the three following constituents of the stratosphere:

1. Nitric Oxide Molecules: Nitric oxide usually present in stratosphere, reacts with ozone to form nitrogen dioxide which in turn reacts with atomic oxygen to produce nitric oxide again.

$$NO + O_3 \rightarrow NO_2 + O_2$$
$$NO_2 + O \rightarrow NO + O_2$$

2. Chlorine Atoms: Chlorine atoms react with ozone to yield chlorine monoxide which reacts with atomic oxygen to regenerate chlorine atoms again.

$$Cl + O_3 \rightarrow ClO + O_2$$
$$ClO + O \rightarrow Cl + O_2$$

3. Hydroxyl Ions: Hydroxyl ions produced by photodissociation of water molecules in the stratosphere, react with ozone molecules to produce HO_2 which reacts with another ozone molecule to yield hydroxyl ions again.

$$OH + O_3 \rightarrow HO_2 + O_2$$
$$HO_2 + O_3 \rightarrow OH + 2O_2$$

8. Write about the solid state fermentation

Ans. See Q.No. 7, Paper-III, Dec-2007.

9. What are the essential components of a rain water harvesting system?

Ans. See Q.No. 25, Paper-III, June-2008.

10. Define mixing height. Explain its significance in dispersal of air pollutions.

Ans. Mixing heigh may be defined M the average height traveled by an eddy which is transporting heat, momentum of water wapour is the atmosphere.

11. What are five-R policies for waste minimization?

Ans. Five-R policies (Reduction, Replacement, Recovery, Recycling and Reutilisation of industrial products, residues or waste) are related to waste management.

These policies aim at recognizing the value of sources of energy, and at the minimization of cost, liability and environmetal and health problems associated with waste disposal, as waste is regarded as a potential secondary resource, namely ma-terial and/or energy for which the generator has no further use for its own purposes of production, transformation or consumption and which has no current or perceived market value at the time and place of discard.

12. What is meant by a 'genetically engineered' bacterium? How is this accomplished?

Ans. A genetically engineered organism is an organism whose genetic material has been altered using genetic engineering techniques. These techniques are generally known as recombinatnt DNA technology. With this technology, DNA molecules from different sources are combined into one molecule to create a new set of genes. This DNA is then transferred into an organism, giving it modified or novel genes. These organisms are also called transgenic organisms.

Transgenic Microbes: Genetically engineered (transgenic) microbes are microbes whose genetic material is modified for using it for various purposes such as Research, production of vaccines etc.

Bacteria were the first organisms to be modified in the laboratory, due to their simple genetic make up. These organisms are now used in a variety of tasks, and are particularly important in producing large amounts of pure human proteins for use in medicine.

Uses: Genetically modified bacteria are used to produce the protein insulin to treat diabetes. Similar bacteria have bee used to produce clotting factors to treat haemophilia, and human growth hormone to treat various forms of dwarfism. These recombinant proteins are much safer than the products they replaced, since the older products were purified from cadavers and could transmit diseases.

In addition to bacteria being used for producing proteins, genetically modified viruses allow gene therapy. Gene therapy. Gene therapy is a relatively new idea in medicine. A virus reproduces by injecting its own genetic material into an existing cell. That cell then follows the instructions in this genetic material and produces more viruses. In medicine, this process is engineered to deliver a gene that could cure disease into human cells. It has been used to treat genetic disorders such as severe combined immunodeficiency, and treatments are being developed for a range of other currently incurable diseases, such as cystic fibrosis, sickle cell anemia, and muscular dystrophy.

For instance, the bacteria found that cause tooth decay are called Streptococcus mutans. These bacteria consume left over sugars in the mouth, producing lactic acid that corrodes tooth enamel and ultimately causes cavities. Scientists have recently modified Streptococcus mutans to produce no lactic acid. These transgenic bacteria, if properly colonized in a person's mouth, could reduce the formation of cavities.

Transgenic microbes have also been used in recent research to kill or hinder tumors, and fight Crohn's disease. Genetically modified bacteria are also used in some soils to facilitate crop growth, and can also produce chemicals which are toxic to crop pests.

Microbes are gentically modified for exploiting its use in two important fields, namely

1. Medicine (including research field)

2. Agriculture

The main reason for developing genetically engineered microbes is for doing researches in the field of medicine, These researches could lead to discovery of medicines for many deadly diseases.

13. How does a solar photovolatic (PV) cell work? On what factors its efficiency depends?

Ans. See Q.No. 8, Paper-III, June, 2010.

14. Write down the equation governing the concentration of pollutants in a Gaussian plume dispersion model.

Ans. See Q.No. 8, Paper-III, June, 2006.

SECTION-IV

Note: *This section contains five (5) questions of five (5) marks each based on the following passage. Each question should be answered in about thirty (30) words.*   **(5 × 5 = 25 marks)**

Around 1960, Lake Erie was declared dead, its DO decreased in deeper layer of water, its surface almost covered by overgrowth of algae, and some of its predators became endangered. Investigations were carried out by many scientists, who concluded that the major cause of the destruction of the Lake Erie ecosystem was too much phosphorous from municipal waste. In order to overcome the problems of Lake Erie, it was thought that there should be a strong cooperation between USA and Canada. The International Joint Commission was established and the governments of the two countries worked together for improving waste treatment in communities surrounding Lake Erie. By 1985, the annual release of phosphorous from these sources reduced by 84% and the phosphorous levels in the Detroit River, which feeds Lake Erie, was reduced by 65%. As the water quality improved with phosphorous abatement, algal growth declined and oxygen levels improved. The small planktonic crustaceans that feed on the algae became less abundant and fishes, such as undesirable alewife and shiner, that feed on them, also decreased. By 1991, the total phosphorous level in lake Erie was reduced to a level very close to the permissible level. The decline in algal population resulted in the improvement of water clarity in the Lake. Moreover, the decline in algal population has also been achieved by invading zebra mussels in Lake Erie.

15. How does phosphorous enrichment of water body cause algal growth?

Ans. In deeper layer of water surface almost covered by over growth of alga. When predators of alga became endangered due to waste, phosphorous enrichment of water body cause algal growth.

16. How did the process of eutrophication in Lake Erie lead to oxygen depletion?

Ans. Due to eutrophication, almost surface of Lake Erie was covered by overgrowth of algae. The major cause of the oxygen depletion of the Lake Erie was too much phosphorous from muncipal waste.

17. How the invasion of zebra mussels will affect the ecology of Lake Erie?

Ans. The decline in algal population resulted in the improvement of water clarity in the Lake. Moreover, the decline in algal population has also been achieved by invading zebra mussels in Lake Frie.

18. What was the institutional mechanism set up to address the problems of Lake Erie?

Ans. To address the problem of Lake Erie, USA and Canada were estabished a joint commssion for worked together and improving waste treatment in communities surrounding Lake Erie.

19. What were the positive results due to the institutional intervention?

Ans. Due to the institutional intervention, the annual release of phosphorous reduced by 84% and the phosphorus levels in the detroit River, which feeds Lake Erie, was reduced by 65%. The positive results was, the water quality improved with phosphorous abatement, algal growth declined and oxygen level improved.

UGC-NET ENVIRONMENTAL SCIENCE, JUNE 2010

PAPER-II

Note : *This paper contains **fifty** (50) objective type questions, each question carrying **two** (2) marks. Attempt **all** the questions.*

1. PIXEL is used in evaluation of satellite imageries. It refers to
   A. Photo ionic radiation
   B. Photo induced x-rays emitted light
   C. Printed in x-radiation region
   D. An image of 100 km × 100 km region

2. Geostationary satellites orbit above the earth at about
   A. 10 km above the earth
   B. 500 km above the earth
   C. 1500 km above the earth
   D. 5 km above the earth

3. Environmental assessment of a developmental projects follow the following sequence to achieve sustainable development.
   A. EA → EMP → EIA
   B. EIA → EA → EMP
   C. EMP → EA → EIA
   D. EIA → EMP → EA

4. Dolomite is
   A. an isomorphic substitution between $CaCO_3$ & $MgCO_3$
   B. a fixed composition of $Ca_{0.52} Mg_{0.48} CO_3$
   C. a polygraph of limestone
   D. an isomorph of calcite

5. In order of increasing cation exchange capacity
   A. Illite > Kaolinite > Sericite > Gibbsite
   B. Kaolinite > Gibbsite > Sericite > Illite
   C. Kaolinite > Illite > Montmorillonite
   D. Montmorillonite > Kaolinite > Illite

6. In order of increasing energy content
   A. Lignite, Peat, Anthracite, Bituminous coal
   B. Peat, Lignite, Anthracite, Bituminous coal
   C. Anthracite, Lignite, Bituminous coal, Peat
   D. Bituminous coal, Anthracite, Lignite, Peat

7. Agenda 21 is blue-print for environment & development. Agenda 21 was an outcome of the meeting at
   A. Rio de Janeiro   B. Stockholm
   C. Vienna   D. Washington

8. BOD of the effluents discharged on land for irrigation should not exceed
   A. 30 mg/l   B. 100 mg/l
   C. 300 mg/l   D. 60 mg/l

9. Atmospheric radioactive window permits thermal radiation of which wavelength to leave the earth ?
   A. 4.3 to 9.3 μm   B. 9.5 to 10.6 μm
   C. 7 to 12 μm   D. 7.3 to 10.3 μm

10. Three constituents that contribute towards stratospheric ozone depletion
    A. CFC-11, CFC-12, N_2O
    B. CFC-11, CFC-16, NO_2
    C. CFC-11, CFC-12, O_2
    D. CFC-11, CFC-13, H_2

11. In an ecological succession there is a progressive change in biological community over time & space
    A. Old species are replaced by new one.
    B. Old species evolved into new species.
    C. New species moves in displacing previous one.
    D. Each stage there is a modification in the environment to adopt new species.

12. In nitrogen cycle elemental nitrogen returned to the atmosphere by the following process.
    A. Nitrogen fixing bacteria.

B. Nitrogen fixation by bluegreen algae.

C. Nitrification process.

D. Denitrification process.

13. Fe & Mg silicates from ideal solid solution in
    A. Pyroxene   B. Feldspar
    C. Olivine   D. Mica

14. One of the following represent plygioclases:
    A. $NaAl_2Si_2O_6$ B. $KAlSi_3^-O_8$
    C. $Mg_2Al_2Si_2O_6$ D. $Na_xK_{1-x}Al_2Si_2O_6$

15. Government of India has enacted various Acts for protection & conservation of environment. However, more inclusive Act is
    A. Water (Prevention & Control of Pollution) Act
    B. Air (Prevention & Control of Pollution) Act
    C. Forest Act
    D. Environment (Protection) Act

16. CRZ notification of Government of India specify the stretches of sea, bays, estuaries etc. as coastal areas requires protection from developmental activities.
    A. upto 500 metre from High Tide Level
    B. upto 150 metre from High Tide Level
    C. upto 500 metre from Low Tide Level
    D. upto 100 metre from Low Tide Level

17. An objective of environmental audit is
    A. Raw-material & Waste minimization.
    B. Energy conservation & monitoring.
    C. To improve technical competency.
    D. All of the above.

18. Biome is a natural community of
    A. Plants in a geographical area.
    B. Animals in a geographical area.
    C. Plants and animals in a geographical area.
    D. Plants in Arctic region.

19. Who proposed that succession is not orderly and directional but is heterogenous?
    A. Clements
    B. Egler
    C. Tansley
    D. Reiter

20. In an ecosystem a food chain is represented as:
    Dead organic matter → Earthworm → Sparrow → Falcon.
    This is a type of
    A. Predator food chain
    B. Grazing food chain
    C. Detritus food chain
    D. Auxiliary food chain

21. The rate of biogenetic nutrients between the abiotic and biotic components of an ecosystem is often referred to as
    A. Turn over rate   B. Production rate
    C. Standing state   D. Cycling rate

22. Which of the following pair is not correctly matched regarding National Parks and their locations?
    A. Nilgiri → Tamil Nadu
    B. Sunderbans → West Bengal
    C. Nanda Devi → Uttar Pradesh
    D. Kanha → MP

23. Ecotone is
    A. ecosystem
    B. a zone of an ecosystem
    C. an ecological study
    D. a zone between two ecosystem

24. When solid becomes liquid at its melting point, the entropy
    A. increases   B. decreases
    C. zero   D. remains unaltered

25. The CNS poisoning by methyl mercury is known as
    A. Methamoglobinemia
    B. Minamata disease
    C. Anemic disease
    D. All of the above

26. Topographic factors affect indirectly one of the following :
    A. Edaphic factors
    B. Biotic factors
    C. Climatic factors
    D. All of the above

27. Atmosphere contains various layers each having characteristic composition. The correct sequence starting from earth surface is
   A. Stratosphere → Ionosphere → Toposphere.
   B. Toposphere → Ionosphere → Stratosphere.
   C. Ionosphere → Stratosphere → Toposphere.
   D. Toposphere → Stratosphere → Ionosphere.

28. One of the following in biogeochemical cycle has not involved biological fixation :
   A. Oxygen   B. Carbon
   C. Nitrogen   D. Phosphorus

29. One of the following 'P' values indicates significance of the test :
   A. $P > 0.05$ B. $P < 0.05$
   C. $P = 0.05$ D. All of the above

30. The calorific value of natural gas varies from
   A. 12,000 – 14,000 kCal/m^3
   B. 13,000 – 18,000 kCal/m^3
   C. 16,000 – 18,000 kCal/m^3
   D. 10,000 – 11,000 kCal/m^3

31. Biogas is composed of
   A. Ethane, CO_2, H_2 & N_2
   B. Methane, CO_2, H_2 & N_2
   C. Methane, CO_2 & N_2
   D. Ethane, Methane & CO_2

32. Which of the following is the concentration of CO_2 in the atmosphere (water vapour free)?
   A. 0.32 %
   B. 0.032 %
   C. 0.38 %
   D. 0.038 %

33. Methanization is carried out by the process of
   A. Incineration
   B. Alcoholic fermentation
   C. Thermo-chemical transformation
   D. Anaerobic fermentation

34. Diesel oil is a fraction obtained between
   A. 40-120°C
   B. 180-250°C
   C. 250-320°C
   D. 280-360°C

35. In a trickling filter biological method of domestic waste treatment a layer of biological community growing on the substrate is
   A. Algal film
   B. Bacterial layer
   C. Protozon community
   D. Zoogloea film

36. Primary clarifier basically designed to remove which of the following from waste water ?
   A. Particulate matter
   B. Heavy materials & large size materials
   C. Particulate matter & oily substances
   D. Dissolved substances

37. Solubility of $NaCl$ in water is 10^{-1} m/l. The concentration of Na^+ in water will be

   A. $\left[\dfrac{10^{-1}}{2}\right]$ m/l   B. $\left[\dfrac{10^1}{2}\right]$ m/l

   C. 10^{-1} m/l   D. $\left[\sqrt{10^{-1}}\right]$ m/l

38. In a river with symmetric channel
   A. Maximum velocity is at the bottom
   B. Minimum velocity is at the surface
   C. Maximum velocity is at the borders
   D. Maximum velocity is at 0.7 of the depth

39. Reciprocal of arithmetic mean of the reciprocal of individual observation refers to
   A. weighted mean
   B. geometric mean
   C. median mean
   D. harmonic mean

40. If the size of the sample is very small, then suitable sampling method for better result is obtained by
   A. Random sampling
   B. Stratified sampling
   C. Census sampling
   D. Purposive sampling

41. In an unbalanced or skewed distribution, which measures of central tendency is leased biased?
   A. Mean

B. Median

C. Mode

D. Range

42. Proposed fuel for controlled nuclear fusion is lithium deuteride, LiD.

Which of the following reactions would possibly contribute to energy production?

I. $^6_3Li + ^1_0h \rightarrow ^4_2H + ^3_1H$

II. $^6_3Li + ^2_1H \rightarrow 2^4_2He$

III. $2^2_1H + ^3_2He + ^1_0h$

A. All of them

B. I

C. III

D. I and II

43. What is the free energy, DG, when 1.0 mole of water is converted, at 100 °C and 1.0 atm, to steam at 100 °C and 1.0 atm in a reversible manner ?

[ΔH_{vap} (H_2O) = 9.7 kCalmole^{-1}]

A. 9700 Cal

B. 970 Cal

C. –970 Cal

D. 0.0 Cal

44. Silver oxalate $Ag_2(C_2O_4)$ is dissolved in pure water. The concentration of Ag+ in the saturated solution is 2.2×10^{-4} mole liter.

What is the ksp value of $Ag_2(C_2O_4)$?

A. 5.3×10^{-12}

B. 5.0×10^{-8}

C. 2.2×10^{-4}

D. 11×10^{-12}

45. The bond distance in A-B is 0.917 Å and the di pole moment is 1.91 D. The partial character of the bond is

A. 43 %

B. 50 %

C. 45 %

D. 38.5 %

46. One of the chief ores of uranium (Z = 92) is pitch blende (U_3O_8). When pitch blende is treated with nitric acid, uranyl nitrate [$UO_2(NO_3)_2$] is formed. What is the change in the oxidation number of uranium when this conversion takes place ?

A. + 6

B. no change

C. + 2/3

D. + 2

47. The silicate ion in chrysotile consists of double strands of SiO_4^{-4} tetrahedra as shown below :

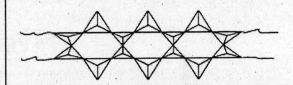

What is the general composition of the silicate ion in chrysolite ?

A. $(S_iO_2)_n$

B. $Si_2O_7^{-6}$

C. $(Si_4O_{11})_n^{-6n}$

D. $(SiO_3)_n^{-2n}$

48. One of the following categories of CRZ, there is no developmental activities are allowed :

A. CRZ-II

B. CRZ-I

C. CRZ-III

D. CRZ-IV

49. Rapid EIA is called

A. a study of three months

B. a study of four months

C. a study of six months

D. a study of one year

50. Development of 'Green Belts' around industries are

A. to control ground leachates

B. to mitigate the gaseous pollutant

C. to increase bioaesthetic

D. all of the above

ANSWERS

1	2	3	4	5	6	7	8	9	10
B	C	B	A	C	B	A	A	B	A
11	12	13	14	15	16	17	18	19	20
C	A	A	B	D	A	D	C	B	A
21	22	23	24	25	26	27	28	29	30
D	C	D	A	D	A	D	B	C	A
31	32	33	34	35	36	37	38	39	40
D	B	D	C	A	B	D	B	D	D
41	42	43	44	45	46	47	48	49	50
B	C	B	A	B	B	B	B	A	D

PAPER-III

Note: This paper is of two hundred (200) marks containing four (4) sections. Candidates are required to attempt the questions contained in these sections according to the detailed instructions given therein.

SECTION-I

*Note: This section consists of **two** essay type questions of **twenty (20)** marks each, to be answered in about **five hundred (500)** words each.*

(2 × 20 = 40 marks)

1. How do you differentiate **in vitro** and **in vivo** conservation of biodiversity? Explain the main steps involved in cryopreservation of a particular genom through micro propagation.

OR

Compare & contrast the availability of ground water in hard rocks & in sedimentary rock region with suitable example from India.

OR

Explain the techniques of nuclear power generation. Add a note on various methods of radioactive waste disposal.

OR

Estimation of iron (5-10 ppm) from a waste water sample can be achieved by any of the following techniques.

- volumetric titration with external indicator.
- volumetric titration involving potentiometry.
- spectrophotometry.
- atomic absorption spectrometry.

Identify the most suitable techniques keeping in mind the selectivity and sensitivity of the technique. Justify your answer.

Ans. Most nuclear power plants produce power at competitive costs and with a positive cash flow. Others are closed in bankruptcy. In the USA, more than half the nuclear sites are considered competitive in changing markets. More than two-thirds of the US units are reported to be producing power for under US $0.02/kWh, about the national average generating cost; some generate for less, yet others have costs of US $0.06-0.13/kWh. In the United Kingdom, each of British Energy's eight privatized nuclear stations produces and sells power at a profit at competitive market set prices (an average of around US $0.03/kWh), while the Magnox plants assigned to BNFL are still producing at around US $0.05/kWh.

What causes these differences? The answer often lies in astute decisions concerning financing, and choices of technology, and successful estimates of demand growth, coupled with good plant management that provides cost control and efficiency gains while maintaining high standards of safety and operational performance. Of these, only good plant management is readily within the control of current NPP managers. The key question is the same though: can the NPP operate profitably? For existing NPPs this translates into whether the plant's incremented revenues can cover marginal operation costs.

2. Describe the impacts of noise pollution on human health. Add a note on noise standards.

OR

Principal component analysis is used for certain types of environmental statistical interpretation. Explain PCA, the eigen values & factors that is part of data calculations. Explain these values with suitable examples.

OR

Define wildlife. Name five wildlife sanctuaries of India. What major steps can be adopted to save mangrove ecosystem of the country?

OR

Describe methods enumerating the reasons in site selection and the parameters adopted in assessing the water quality.

Ans. The generation of unreasonable noise within the environment is regarded as a form of pollution because it lowers the quality of life. There have been several specific ways in which excessive noise can affect people adversely.

Noise has been found to interfere with our activities at three levels; (*a*) audio logical level in referring with the satisfactory performance of the hearing mechanism; (*b*) biological level interfering with the biological functioning of the body; and (*c*) behavioural level affecting the sociological behaviour of the subjects. Because of this the noise affects categorically, performance, physiology and psychology.

Noxious has been known to cause of nervous disorder, headache, high blood pressure and short memory. The various effects of noise may be as follows. Various psychological effect of noise pollution are summarized below:

(*a*) Depression and fatigue, which considerably reduces the efficiency of a person.

(*b*) Insomnia as a result of lack of undisturbed and refreshing sleep.

(*c*) Straining of senses and annoyance as a result of slow but persistent noise from motorcycles, alarm clocks, call bells, telephone rings etc.

(*d*) Affecting of psychomotor performance of a person by a sudden loud noise (sound).

(*e*) It is a cause of frustration and is associated with difficulty in concentration, disturbance of rest, physical and mental fatigue. Low frequency noise of 50 to 60 dB affects the higher centre of brain and causes an alternation in the normal sleep pattern and prevents sound sleep.

(f) Noise, which is an annoyance also causes irritation dis-satisfaction, dis-interest and affects work performance. Noise has been reported both to improve and to decrease work efficiency, depending on its intensity, duration and frequency distribution etc.

Various physiological as well as pathologic effects of noise pollution are as under:

(a) Noise pollution affects human health, comfort and efficiency. It cause contraction of blood vessels, makes, the skin pale, leads to excessive secretion of adrenalin hormone into blood stream with is responsible for high blood pressure.

(b) It causes muscles to contract leading to nervous break down, tension and even insanity.

(c) Noise effects are axiently, stress reaction and fright. These adverse reactions are coupled with a change in hormone content of blood, which in turn produces increased rate of heart beat, constriction of blood vessels, digestive sperms and dilation of pupil of eye.

(d) The most immediate and acute effect of noise is the impairment of hearing, which diminishes by the damage of some part of autitory system. When exposed to very loud and sudden noise acute damage occurs to the eardrum. Prolonged exposure to noise of certain frequency pattern will lead to chronic damage to the hair cells in the inner ear.

(e) Auditory fatigue appears in the 90 dB associated with whistling and buzzing in ears. Temporary deafness occurs at 4000-6000 Hz, and this effect is known as Temporary Threshold Shift (TTS), Permanent loss of hearing occurs at 100 dB due to continuous noise exposure. Under such conditions, the auditory threshold shift is called Permanent Threshold Shift (PTS). Besides chronic hearing loss, there may be instantaneous damage or acoustic trauma, which may be caused by very high intensity impulsive noise resulting from an explosion or sudden excessive noise of more than 150 dB.

(f) Physiological effects of noise pollution include neurosis, hypertension, increase in sweating, hepatic diseases, giddiness, peptic ulcers, undesirable change in gastro intestinal activities behavioural and emotional stress.

(g) Noise mainly interferes with man's communication. It is easily visualized that a conversation can be carried on in whisper in a still place, while one his to shout to make sense in a noisy factory.

(h) Blood gets thickened by excessive noise. Changes in breathing amplitude have also been reported due to impulsive noise.

(i) Noise causes cosinophilia, hyperglycarmia, hypokalaemia and hypoglycarmia by a change in blood and other body fluids.

(j) Noise causes chronic headache and irritability; work, which needs a high degree of skill, is considerably affected. The overall working efficiency goes down when noise level goes up.

(k) Loud and sudden noise such as sonic boom produces a startle effect, which may damage the brain. Sonic booms can also cause physical damage to property i.e. windows may break due to it. Sudden noise can be much more harmful than a continuous noise.

Permissible Noise Limits

Under *Central Motor Vehicle Rules, 1989,* the following limits were imposed on 26th March 1993.

S.No.	Type of Vehicle	Limit in dB
1.	Two wheelers (petrol run)	80
2.	Passenger car, petrol runs three-wheelers, diesel run two wheelers.	82

3.	Passenger or commercial vehicles of upto 4 MT	85
4.	Passenger or commerical vehicles of above 4 MT and upto 12 MT	89
5.	Passenger or commerical vehicles exceeding 12 MT.	91

Noise limits implemented from 1st Jan. 2003:

S. No.	Type of Vehicle	Permissible limit in dB (w.e.f from 1.1.2003)
1.	Two wheelers	
	upto 80 CC	75
	80CC-175 CC	77
	Above 175 CC	80
2.	Three Wheelers	
	Upto 175 CC	77
	Above 175 CC	80
3.	Passenger Car	75
4.	Passenger vehicles	
	Upto 4 tonn	77
	4-12 tonn	80
	Above 12 tonn	82

Permissible noise limits for household goods

S. No.	Appliance	Standard Limit (dB)
1.	Refrigerator	46
2.	Air cooler	60
3.	Air conditioner upto 1 to 1.5 tonn	68
4.	Compactor (Roller), Front loads, Mixer, Crance, Vibrator etc.,	75
5.	Diesel Generator installed in household	85 to 90

Ambient Noise Standards (India)

S. No.	Areas	Leq db (A)	
		Day Time	Night time
1.	Industrial Area	75	70
2.	Commercial Area	65	55
3.	Residential Area	55	45
4.	Silence Zone	50	40

SECTION-II

*Note: This section contains **three (3)** questions of **fifteen** marks each to be answered in about **three hundred (300)** words.*

(3 × 15 = 45 marks)

3. Describe Carbon & Nitrogen Cycles in the Environment.

Ans. Carbon Cycle: Carbon is the basis building block of the carbohydrates, fats, proteins, nucleic acids such as DNA and RNA, and other organic compounds necessary for life. Most land plants get their carbon by absorbing carbon dioxide gas, which makes up about 0.04% of the gaseous atmosphere, through pores in their leaves, Phytoplankton, the microscopic plants that float in aquatic ecosystems, get their carbon from atmospheric carbon dioxide that has dissolved in water.

These producer plants then carry out photosynthesis, which converts the carbon in carbon dioxide to carbon in complex organic compounds such as glucose:

carbon dioxide + water + **solar energy** $\rightarrow$ glucose + oxygen

Then the cells in oxygen-consuming plants, animals, and decomposers carry out aerobic cellular respiration, which breaks down glucose and other complex organic compounds and converts the carbon back to carbon dioxide for reuse by producers:

glucose + oxygen $\rightarrow$ carbon dioxide + water + **energy**

This linkage between photosynthesis and aerobic respiration circulates carbon in the ecosphere and is a major part of the **carbon cycle.** This part of the gaseous cycle is shown in greatly simplified in carbon cycle. And some of the ways plants, animals, and decomposers in the biosphere depend on one another for survival. Oxygen and hydrogen, the other elements in glucose and other carbohydrates, cycle almost in step with carbon.

Carbon cycles rapidly between the atmosphere and hydrosphere and living organisms. It shows that some of the earth's carbon is tied up for long periods in fossil fuels–coal, petroleum, natural gas, peat, oil shale, tar sand, and lignite—formed over millions of years in the lithosphere. The carbon in these mineral deposits remains locked up until it is released to the atmosphere as carbon dioxide when fossil fuels are extracted and burned.

Nitrogen Cycle: Organisms require nitrogen in various chemical forms to make proteins and genetically important nucleic acids such as DNA. Most green plants need nitrogen in the form of nitrate ions (NO_3^-) and ammonium ions (NH_4^+). The nitrogen gas (N_2) that makes up about 78% of the volume of the earth's atmosphere is useless to such plants, people, and most other organisms. Fortunately, nitrogen gas is converted into water-soluble ionic compounds containing nitrate ions and ammonium ions, which are taken up by plant roots as part of the **nitrogen cycle.**

The conversion of atmospheric nitrogen gas into other chemical forms useful to plants is called **nitrogen fixation.** It is carried out mostly by blue-green algae and certain kinds of bacteria in soil and water and by rhizobium bacteria living in small swellings called nodules on the roots of alfalfa, clover, peas, beans, and other legume plants. Also playing a role in nitrogen fixation, lightning converts nitrogen gas and oxygen gas in the atmosphere to nitric oxide and nitrogen dioxide gas. These gases react with water vapor in the atmosphere and are converted to nitrate ions that return to the earth as nitric acid dissolved in precipitation and as particles of nitrate salts.

Plants convert inorganic nitrate ions and ammonium ions obtained from soil water into proteins, DNA, and other large, nitrogen-containing organic compounds they require. Animals get most of their nitrogen-containing nutrients by eating plants or other animals that have eaten plants.

4. Discuss scope & content of EIA of any river valley project.

Ans. Environmental Impact Assessment can be defined as the study of impact on environment of proposed action like policy, plan or project. It is a process of anticipating or establishing the changes in physical, ecological and socio-economic components of the environment before, during and after an impending developmental project so that undesirable effects, if any can be mitigated. Environemtal impact assessment has to try to answer the following set of questions.

1. What are the environmental issues associated with the project?

2. What will be extend of changes?

3. Whether the benefits derived from the project arc worth the environmental damages sustained?

4. What can be done about adverse impacts?

A developmental activity is under taken or the state. The socio-economic quality of life cannot be sustained indefinitely if the activity causes adverse changes in the environment however small these changes may be at some point of time in future the entire system could deteriorate. A through assessment of the likely impact which a proposed plan or project shall cause, is therefore, essential so that even the minor seemingly insignificant changes are brought to the notice of policy makers.

The process of environmental impact assessment has to be conducted in three stages i.e.,

(i) Initial Scrutiny

(ii) Rapid Assessment

(iii) Comprehensive Assessment

Tungabhadra is considered as a major river of Karnataka state. In Shimoga District, rivers Tunga and Bhadra merge to form this river. The gross capacity of reservoir is 3767 mm^3. The main purpose of project are power generation and irrigation. The total area irrigated under this project amounts to 3.63 lac hac. Main environmental impacts observed during the operation of project are waterlogging and Salinity of water and soil.

By spot visual examination, it is found that the approx, 33,000 hac of land in the area underwent water logging in 35 years of irrigation. Salt efflorescence, water stagnation, poor germination etc. are the systems of land affects from water logging.

Salinity is several wells in command area is common. The content of soluble salt in the soil moisture varies from 0.036% to 0.20% in root zones and goes beyond 2.5% at salt concentrations zones. The soil electrical conductivity is more than 1 mho/cm, pH greater than 8.5 and exchangeable Sodium higher than 15% indicating saline character. Because of low rainfall (18 to 20 cm) the leaching of salt is difficult and hence salt deposits can be seen on the surface of soil. Other impacts includes change in cropping pattern, rise in ground water table etc.

5. Discuss linkages between 'Green-House effect', 'Ozone depletion' and 'Global Climate Change'.

Ans. Green House Effect: The best-known greenhouse gas is **carbon dioxide** (CO_2). Carbon dioxide is breathed out or otherwise given off by living organisms (including plants) as they undergo aerobic respiration, and is taken in by green plants during photosynthesis. A small amount of cabon dioxide in the atmosphere is an absolute necessity for life on Earth; without it the planet would be too cold to support living organisms, and plants would lack an essential raw ingredient. But an excess of carbon dioxide will cause the Earth's surface to heat up abnormally.

Clearly, we humans are very quickly adding to the amount of carbon dioxide in the atmosphere. In 1950 the average annual concentration of carbon dioxide was about 250 ppm (parts per million); this increased to 316 ppm by 1950 and by 2007 it had grown to nearly 460 ppm. The CO_2 content of the atmosphere continues to increase.

The primary way we are increasing the CO_2 content of the atmosphere is through the burning of fossil fuels: coal, oil, and gas. For millions of years, the carbon in these fuels has been out of atmospheric circulation, buried deep under the surface of the Earth. But suddenly, over a period of just two centuries (and especially during the last few decades), we have released massive amounts of this fossilized carbon back in the atmosphere. In 2004, for instance, an estimated 6.5 billion tons (5.9 billion metric tons of carbon were released worldwide by the combination of fossil fuels–slightly over 1.1 tons of metric ton) of cabon per person on Earth. E ton of pure carbon released forms approximate of 3.66 tons of CO_2, so approximately 23.8 billion tons (21.6 billion metric tons) of CO_2 were leased into the atmosphere simply by the burning of fossil fuels in 2004 or 21 trillion kg of CO_2. Given that 500g of CO_2 occupies about 8.75 cubic feet at room temperature at sea level, 21 trillion kg of CO_2 is equivalent to more than 400 trillion cubic feet of trillion m^3 of CO_2, of course, the actual volume of CO_2 depends on temperature and pressure conditions in various parts of the atmosphere.

Ozone depletion: It may appear that the ozone story has come to a happy closure; however, despite the 1990 and 1992 agreements, the story is not over yet. Even with the complete phaseout of CFCs and other Clorine-bearing chemicals, stratospheric chlorine concentrations are expected to remain high well into the twenty-first century as already released CFC molecules rise from the troposphere into the stratosphere (a CFC molecule can take 15 years to make it away up from the Earth's surface to the stratospheric ozone layer). Furthermore, despite the Montreal Protocol and its amendments, as of the early 1990s some developing countries had actually increased their use of CFCs (most CFCs still originate from the industrialized world, however). Realizing the urgency of the situation, some countries have moved up the phaseout schedules; for instance, the 12 members of the European Union promised to stop producing CFCs by the end of 1994.

Even with the accelerated phaseout, the problem will persist. Some of the more common CFCs have life expectancies of between 75 and 110 years, and the chlorine catalyst in the stratosphere can also be quite long-lived. The estimated background level of chlorine in the atmosphere, derived from natural sources such as volcanoes, is about 0.6 ppb (parts per billion). Currently, due to human releases of chlorine-bearing chemicals like CFCs, the concentration of chlorine is about 3.5 ppb, and this number is increasing at a rate of about 5% a year. Assuming that CFC production is phased out by the year 1998 (or 2008 in the case of some developing countries), atmospheric chlorine concentrations are still expected to reach 4.1 ppb by the end of the twentieth century.

Scientists estimate that the ozone layer will continue to be depleted until at least 2050, resulting in ozone losses of as high as 10 to 30% over the northern latitudes where most of the world's population resides. During the latter half of the next century, the ozone may start to build up again, but measurable amounts of CFCs will continue to reside in the atmosphere well into the twenty-fourth century. Thus, even if the 1990 and 1992 agreements are upheld by all nations (perhaps an overly optimistic assumption), the Earth will be subjected to an increasingly thin ozone layer for decades to come.

Climate Change: Atmospheric circulation, which ultimately causes what we see as weather (in the short term) and climate (in the longer term), is caused by the differential heating of air masses on the Earth's surface. Although establishing the exact effects global warming will have on these patterns is extremely difficult, some educated predictions can be ventured. As more heat is retained in the system, more air will move across the Earth's surface producing winds, clashing warm and cold fronts, and generally more violent weather conditions. Hurricanes, tornadoes, and other dangerous storms will increase in intensity. Some researchers attribute the record number of extremely damaging storms in the last decade to global warming.

Global warming will also dramatically change overall climatic patterns. With increased warming, evaporation from the oceans and other large water masses may increase, which will lead to higher levels of precipitation. But the increased precipitation will not necessarily occur where it falls now–with the changing air currents, the areas of rainfall will be displaced. The American Midwest, often referred to as the "breadbasket" of America (and the world), may experience such intense droughts that it will become a desert. The rain that would have fallen in this area may well be pushed north into Canada. Rainfall may also shift from one season to another; some agricultural regions may receive more rain on average than at present, but the bulk of it will come during the winter months when it is of little use for crops. Changing rainfall patterns, coupled with the generally more violent weather, will cause increasing incidences of flash floods. Ironically some areas will experience droughts and floods simultaneously; during the height of a drought, a violent cloudburst will cause rivers to swell and flood, but it will not replenish reservoirs, which require gentle, protracted rains in order to recharge.

SECTION-III

*Note: This section contains **nine (9)** questions of **ten (10)** marks, each to be answered in about **fifty (50)** words.*   (9 × 10 = 90 marks)

6. 0.2 molor solution of formic acid is ionized to 3.2%. Calculate its ionization constant.

Ans. $pH = 14 - pK_p - \log \dfrac{[Salt]}{[Base]} = 14 - 5 - \log \dfrac{10.01}{0.1} = 9 - \log 10^{-1} = 9 + 1 = 10$

7. In a pond ecosystem, the pyramid of number and energy are upright whereas that of biomass is inverted. Explain it.

Ans. The pyramid of biomass, showing total dry weight and other suitable measure of the total amount of living matter and pyramid of energy showing the rate of energy flow and/or productivity at successive trophic levels. The pyramid of numbers and biomass may be upright or inverted depending upon the nature of food chain in the particular ecosystem, where as pyramid of energy are always upright.

8. Describe the principle of photovoltaic cell. Add a note on various types of photovoltaic cells.

Ans. A class of photoelectic cell which acts as a sources of emf and so does not need a seperate battery. The effect in which irradiation of a p-n-junction or the junction of a metal and a semiconductor by electromagnetic radiation (ultra violet to infrared) generate an e.m.f., which can be used to deliver power to an external circuit. A solar cell consists of such a p-n junction.

9. Describe the effects of particulate matters of various sizes in our atmosphere on plants and human health.

Ans. Particulate matter remain in the atmosphere for different lengths of time depending mostly on the relative size of particles and on the climate. Large particles with diameters greator than 10 micrometers normally remain in the troposphere only a day or two day before being brought to earth by gravity or precipitation. Medium sized particles with diameters between 1 and 10 micrometers, are lighter and tend.

10. Differentiate clay and clay minerals. What are their major properties that are important to environment?

Ans. Clay: A fine textured, sedimentary or residual deposit. It consists of hydrated silicates of aluminium mixed with various impurities. A fine graded sediment of variable composition having a grain size less than 1/256 mm (4 μm).

Clay mineral: Any mineral of clay grade but specifically, one of a complex group of finely crystalline, metacolloidal or amaphous hydrous alumino silicates. They have sheet like lattices and most are formed by the weathering of primary silicate minerals. Clay are used in manufacture or pottery.

11. Radioactive decay equation is similar to some aspects of Lodka-Volterra equation.

Ans. Radioactive decay: Radioactive decay by the emission of nuclei heavier than the alpha particle. The probability of this occurring is very small but carbon-14 rather than alpha decay has been observed from radium-223.

Lotka-Volterra equation: The Lotka-Volterra equations, also known as the predator-prey equations, are a pair of first order, non-linear, differential equations frequently used to describe the dynamics of biological systems in which two species interact, one a predator and one its prey. They evolve in time according to the pair of equations:

$$\frac{dx}{dt} = x(\alpha - \beta y)$$

$$\frac{dy}{dt} = -\dot{y}(\gamma - \delta x)$$

where, y is the number of some predator (for example, wolves);

x is the number of its prey (for example, rabbits);

$\frac{dy}{dt}$ and $\frac{dx}{dt}$ represent the growth of the two populations against time; t represents the time; and

α, β, γ and δ are parameters representing the interaction of the two species.

Thus radioactive decay is similar to some aspects of Lodka Voltera equation.

12. Describe the principle of electrophoresis. Why does SDS-PAGE used to identify the effects of any hazardous chemical?

Ans. Migration of ions in an electric field at a definite pH is called elecrophoresis. This method was developed by Arne W.K. Tiselius in 1937 and is based on the principle that the proteins migrate in an electric field except at the pH of their isoelectric point. And in a mixture of proteins/chemicals, each sample with its characteristic electrical charge will respond differently to an applied electric potential. The rate of this electrophoretic migration (or mobility) depends on the pH of medium, strength of the electric field, magnitude of the net charge on the molecule and the size of the molecule.

13. Explain the concept of 'Gondwana Pond' and discuss the economic importance.

Ans. Gondwana Ponds is most important from water lake. Natural lake systems were generally formed during the ice ages because of tectonic or volcanic activities. It play a vital role in the survival of many species of flora and fauna.

14. Describe in brief methods used in reducing desertification.

Ans. The techniques for combating desertification consists of practices that are effective in controlling several desertification processes, that in aggregate represent desertification. Soil, climate and land slopes are variables, and that must be known to develope appropriate control measures likes conserving soil and rain water, soil fertility management, management of non-arable lands as alternative land-use systems and watershed approach.

SECTION-IV

Note: *This section contains five (5) questions of five (5) marks each based on the following passage. Each question should be answered in about thirty (30) words.*   **(5 × 5 = 25 marks)**

Rapid development activities over the last few decades and the consequent increase in urbanization in our country has led to an ever growing problem of disposal of waste of all types. The waste generated are commonly classified based on characteristics in terms of its impacts on the environment. The hazardous waste (HW) such as chemical and the specific biological one is of great concern due to its toxicity even at low levels and some are greatly infectious. The disposal of these HW requires very specialized methods. These HW may be gaseous, liquid and solids, which may be reactive, toxic, flammable, corrosive, radio-active and particularly of biological origin may be infectious. All such wastes are directly or indirectly involved in health and environmental hazards.

In order to tackle the problem of hazardous waste, authorities have identified types of industries generating HW. These industries store and transport as per the guidelines and unload at the specific designated disposal sites. There are also well defined criteria for selection and preparation of the disposal sites. The Government of India has issued management and handling rules for such chemical and bio-chemical waste. There are various categories of HW and the steps involved in its management. The steps involved in this process also include the EIA in the selection and preparation of disposal sites.

15. Define hazardous waste. Describe various types of hazardous waste.

Ans. Hazardous waste is a waste that, due to its chemical activity or flammable explosive, toxic or corrosive properties, is likely to the result in danger to human health or the environment.

Hazardous waste posses following characteristics (i) Igntability (ii) corrosivity (iii) reactivity (iv) toxicity.

The above four characteristics given as above provide guidelines for considering a substance to be hazardous.

16. Explain colour for segregation of biomedical waste.

Ans. Categories and colour coding recommended for segregation in health-care establishment, including the categories mentioned in the Bio-Medical Waste Regulations of the Ministry of Environment and Forests, Government of India.

Category	Type of Waste	Container	Colour
Cat. 1	Human Anatomical Waste, blood and body fluids, bandages, animal and slaughter house waste, microbiology and biotechnology waste, extremely sailed linen	Tubs, buckets with lids	Yellow
Cat. 2	Sharps—Two types *Reusable sharps* such as some needles, scalpels, surgical instruments separated by needle/sharp separator	Veterinary institutions, dispensaries and animal houses	White or Translucent

	Waste sharps such as broken glass, disposable needles, blades, etc.	Cardboard cartor	
Cat. 3	Disposable plastics, rubber/latex gloves	Bags or buckets, stainless steel drums	Blue
Cat. 4	Chemical wastes, all hazardous wastes	Bucket with lid cardboard container	Red
Cat. 5	Compostable waste	Buckets/drums/trolley	Black
Cat. 6	Office paper	Cardboard boxes	Green

17. What are the steps involved in management of chemical hazardous waste?

Ans. There are various alternative waste treatment technologies e.g. physical treatment, chemical treatment, biological treatment, incineration etc. These process are used to recycle and reuse waste materials reduce the volume and toxicity of a waste stream or produce a final residual material that is suitable for disposal.

Physical Treatment

This includes processes that separate components of a waste stream or change the physical form of the waste without alterning the chemical structure of the material. Commonly used physical processes are as follows:

1. *Screening and Sedimentation.*
2. *Flotation*–Removes solids from liquids by floating the particles to the surface by using tiny air bubbles.
3. *Filtration*–Process for separating liquids and solids by using various types of porous materials.
4. *Centrifugation*–Process for separating solid and liquid components by rapidly rotating a mixture of solids and liquids indise a vessel.
5. *Dialysis*–Process for separating components in a liquid steam by using membrane components of a liquid stream will diffuse through the membrane if a stream with greater concentration of the component is on the other side of membrane.
6. *Electrodialysis*–It is an extension of dialysis. This process is used to separate the components of an ionic solution by applying electric current.
7. *Reverse Osmosis*–It separates components by applying external pressures to one side of membrane.
8. *Ultra filtration*–It is similar to reverse osmosis but the separation beings at higher molecular weights.
9. *Distillation*–Process of separating liquids with deferent boilings poings. The mixed liquid stream is exposed to increasing amounts of heat and the various components of the mixture are vaporized and recovered.

Chemical Treatment

These alter the chemical structure of the constituents of the waste to produce less hazardous material. Chemical processes are attractive because they produce minimal air emissions, they can be carried out on the site. Commonly used chemical treatments are given below :

1. *Neutralization*–Process for reducing the acidity or alkalinity by mixing acids and bases.

2. *Precipitation*–Process for removing soluble compounds.

3. *Dechlorination*–A process for stripping chlorine atoms from chlorinated compounds.

4. *Oxidation-reduction-Process* for detoxifying toxic wastes in which the chemical bonds are broken.

Biological Treatment

It includes processes that use microorganisms to decompose organic wastes either into water, CO_2 and simple inorganic substances.

The purpose of biological treatment system is to control the environment for microorganisms so their growth and activity are enhanced.

Various biological treatments are:

1. Activated sludge Process

2. Aerated Lagoon

3. Trickling filters

4. Stabilization Pond

5. Anaerobic digestion

18. Describe rules & regulations in safe disposal of hazardous waste.

Ans. 41-A Constitution of Site Appraisal Committees: (1) The State Government may, for purposes of advising it to consider applications for grant of permission for the initial location of a factory involving a hazardous process or for the expansion of any such factory, appoint a Site Appraisal Committee consisting of ..

(a) the Chief Inspector of the State who shall be its Chairman;

(b) a representative of the Central Board for the Prevention and Control of Water Pollution appointed by the Central Government under Section 3 of the Water (Prevention and Control of Pollution) Act, 1974;

(c) a representative of the Central Board for the Prevention and Control of Air Pollution referred to in Section 3 of the Air (Prevention and Control of Pollution) Act, 1981;

(d) a representative of the State Board appointed under Section 4 of the Water (Prevention and Control of Pollution) Act, 1974.

(e) a representative of the State Board for the Prevention and Control of Air Pollution referred to in Section 5 of the Air (Prevention and Control of Pollution) Act, 1981;

(f) a representative of the Department of Environment in the State;

(g) a representative of the Meteorological Department of the Government of India;

(h) an expert in the field of occupational health; and

(i) a representative of the Town Planning Department of the State Government,

Hazardous Waste (Management & Handling) Rules 1989

To regulate the special wastes generation, disposal and input and treatment.

Main Features :

A list of 44 processes has been listed out which generate hazardous waste.

89 type of waste have been listed based on concentrated limits.

Every occupier generating hazardous waste and having a facility for collection reception, treatment, transport, storage and disposal of such waste has to obtain authorization from state board.

Responsibilities & Duties of Occupier and Operation of a Facility.

Proper collection, reception, treatment, storage and disposal of hazardous waste. To give information to operator of a waste disposal facility operation as specified by Pollution Control Boards Property handle and dispose off waste so that there is no adverse affect to the environment.

Duties: To contain containments and prevent accidents and limit their consequence on human health and environment.

Provide persons working on site with information, training and equipment necessarily to ensure their safely.

Ensuring that hazardous waste are packed as per Rules specified in Motor Vehicle Act 1988.

Import & Export of Hazardous Wastes:

No import/export without permission of Ministry of Environment Forest.

19. List the categories of industries based on generation of hazardous waste.

Ans. Although the words **trash, garbage, rubbish** and **refuse**—are often used as synonyms in casual discussions, each has a different and specific technical meaning. *Trash* refers to things like old paper, newspaper, boxes, cans, containers, and so on— generally, objects that are "dry" and nonedible. *Garbage* refers to "wet" discarded matter, such as old food remains, yard waste like grass clippings, dead animals, leftovers from meat packing operations and butcher shops (such as the viscera of slaughtered animals), and so on. Generally, garbage is edible and was often kept separate from trash in the past so that it could be fed to pigs. Today some types of garbage are useful for composting. *Refuse* technically refers to both trash and garbage, while *rubbish* includes not only refuse but also construction and demolition debris, such as old boards, bricks, cinderblocks, beams, tar paper, shingles, and so on. Ultimately, all of these sorts of rubbish are finding their way into our modern landfills.

Here we should point out that no matter what we want to call it or how we wish to define it, waste is a characteristically human concept. Generally, waste is not found in nature (although "pollution" may occur naturally in some instances, as when a volcano releases gases that promote acid rain). In a typical ecosystem, there is no waste—the "waste" of one organism is the necessary raw material that another organism depends upon. Only humans typically discard waste that cannot be readily recycled and reused by other parts of the biosphere.

Solid waste, "Materials (non liquid or gaseous) which are mainly generated through anthropogenic activities and are discarded as useless or unwanted are called solid wastes." Certainly, household garbage, trash, refuse, and rubbish are all solid waste, but so too are solids, various semisolids, liquids, and even gases that result from mining, agricultural, commercial, and industrial activities. Often substance such as liquids and gases are confined in solid containers and disposed of with more conventional solid wastes. Sewage effluent, and wastewater from commercial enterprises, organizations, and private homes are not solid waste, but once wastewater is treated and various residues are removed from the water to form sludge, the sludge is usually treated as a form of solid waste. Solid waste may be divided into two broad categories depending on its origination : municipal solid waste (produced by various institutions, businesses, and private homes) and industrial solid waste. Another useful distinction is between **hazardous waste** and nonhazardous waste.

Note : *This paper contains **fifty** (50) objective type questions, each question carrying **two** (2) marks. Attempt **all** the questions.*

1. The use of anthropoid hazard chemicals like DDT causes reduction in fish population because the chemical mimics the effect of
   A. Luteinizing hormone
   B. Testosterone
   C. Estrogen
   D. All of the above

2. The ionizing radiation, which affects the activities of most of the enzymes is due to
   A. Photoemission of electron
   B. Interaction of α-particles, β-and γ-rays with enzymes
   C. Interaction of electron with body.
   D. Interaction of radiation with tissues.

3. SDS-PAGE of tissue proteins under denaturation determines the
   A. Hydrogen bond breakage
   B. Sulfide bridge breakage
   C. Subunits of protein
   D. None of the above

4. Intake of lead may primarily cause the damage of
   A. Brain   B. Lung
   C. Liver   D. Kidney

5. Parallelism among the standard curves can be determined by one of the following.
   A. ANOVA   B. Student's-t test
   C. Chi square   D. ANCOVA

6. Liquid ammonia can be used in refrigeration because of its
   A. High basicity
   B. High dipole moment
   C. High heat of vaporization
   D. Non-toxic nature

7. The pair of molecules forming strongest intermolecular hydrogen bonds are
   A. H_2O and H_2
   B. HCOOH and CH_3COOH
   C. CH_3COCH_3 and $CHCl_3$
   D. SiH_4 and SiF_6

8. Which of these requires quantum nature of light for their explanation?
   A. Diffraction
   B. Polarisation
   C. Black body spectrum
   D. Interference

9. The mass of 1 mole of electron is equal to
   A. $9.1094 \times 6.16 \times 10^{-28}$ g
   B. $9.1094 \times 10^{-31} \times 6.023 \times 10^{23}$ kg
   C. $(9.1094 \times 10^{-31}) / 6.023 \times 10^{23}$ kg
   D. $(6.023 \times 10^{23}) / 6.1094 \times 10^{-28}$ gm

10. Which set of stoichiometric coefficient correctly balance the equation
    a. H_2O_2 + b. $KMnO_4$ + c. $H_2SO_4 \rightarrow$ d. K_2SO_4 + e. $Mn\,SO_4$ + f. H_2O + g. O_2

	a	b	c	d	e	f	g
A.	1	1	1	1	1	1	1
B.	1	2	3	1	2	4	3
C.	2	5	3	2	1	8	5
D.	5	2	3	1	2	8	5

11. Which of the transmutation does not take place by α-decay?
    A. $^{238}U_{92} \longrightarrow\ ^{234}Th_{90}$
    B. $^{213}Bi_{83} \longrightarrow\ ^{213}Po_{84}$
    C. $^{226}Ra_{88} \longrightarrow\ ^{222}Rn_{86}$
    D. $^{227}Ac_{89} \longrightarrow\ ^{223}Fr_{87}$

12. Which radioactive element is considered under Indoor pollutants category?
    A. O –16   B. N –13
    C. Carbon 14   D. Radon

13. Industries generating hazardous waste are classified as
    A. Brown
    B. Green
    C. Yellow
    D. Red

14. One of the following methods for disposal of municipal solid waste known to be scientific is
    A. Open land disposal
    B. Incerination
    C. Landfill method
    D. Sanitary landfill method

15. One of the following is not an In situ conservation for biological resources.
    A. Biosphere reserve
    B. National Parks
    C. Protected areas
    D. Breeding under confined areas

16. Solar ponds are used for
    A. Salt production
    B. Aquaculture
    C. Power generation
    D. All of the above

17. Biodiesel is produced in India presently from
    A. Calotropis sp
    B. Catharanthus sp
    C. Jatropha sp
    D. Delonix sp

18. Ozone depletion is caused by the increase in the level of
    A. Water vapour
    B. Chlorofluro carbon
    C. Oxygen
    D. Carbon monoxide

19. Thermal power generation in India is carried out by burning
    A. Natural gas
    B. Coal
    C. Oil
    D. All of the above

20. Biogas production is the outcome of
    A. Methanogenesis
    B. Pyrolysis
    C. Methanogenesis and Gasification
    D. Gasification

21. Mauna Loa, in Hawaii is famous for
    A. Botanical Garden
    B. Monitoring sea level rise since 1950
    C. Biggest collection of mammals fossils
    D. Continuous monitoring of atmospheric CO_2 since 1957.

22. To generate environmental awareness Paryavaran Vahini Scheme was launched in
    A. 1998
    B. 1968
    C. 1992
    D. 1994

23. General Circulation Model (GGM's) are used to
    A. predict climate
    B. predict cyclones
    C. study ocean currents
    D. study temperature on wind

24. Among the following which country has lowest per capita green house gas emission?
    A. France
    B. India
    C. China
    D. Mexico

25. Water (Prevention & Control of Pollution) Act 1974, industries are allowed to release waste in inland water having BOD level
    A. 100 mg/l
    B. 30 mg/l
    C. 150 mg/l
    D. 80 mg/l

26. Richael Carsson in her book Silent Spring has raised concern on
    A. Economical & social impacts
    B. Deforestation
    C. Climate change
    D. Impacts of agro-chemicals on ecological functions

27. The term oligotrophic refers to
    A. Higher nutrients in water
    B. High aquatic productivity
    C. Low nutrients and low productivity
    D. Algal blooms

28. Following initiative under International efforts made to have household eco-friendly refrigerators :
    A. Kyoto Protocol
    B. Basal Convention
    C. Montreal Protocol
    D. CITES

29. The 'mean' that stands for relative importance of different items in a data set is
    A. Weighted mean
    B. Harmonic mean
    C. Arithmetic mean
    D. Geometric mean

30. In symmetrical distribution pattern
    A. Median, Mean and Mode coincide
    B. Mean & Median coincide
    C. Mean & Mode coincide
    D. Mode & Median coincide

31. Which statistical device helps in analysing the co-variation of two or more variables?
    A. Regression

B. Correlation

C. Standard deviation

D. Mean of the variables

32. Stoke's Law of Settling Velocity is represented by

A. $V \propto d$

B. $V \propto \dfrac{1}{a}n$

C. $V = \dfrac{1}{d}$

D. $V = cd$

33. Correct arrangement in order of decreasing soil particle size

A. Sand, clay, silt

B. Silt, sand, clay

C. Sand, silt, clay

D. Clay, silt, sand

34. Comparing continental and oceanic crust

A. the chemical composition of crust does not vary.

B. the Fe content in continental crust is more than that of oceanic crust.

C. the Si and A*l* content in continental crust is more than that of oceanic crust.

D. the Na, Ca, A*l* content in oceanic crust is more than that of continental crust.

35. The size distribution of particles in soil and sediments generally follow

A. binomial distribution

B. normal distribution

C. linear distribution

D. log-normal distribution

36. Maximum density of water is at

A. 0 °C

B. 100 °C

C. –4 °C

D. 4 °C

37. The geochemical weathering process can be viewed as

A. Clay minerals + $CO_2 \rightleftharpoons$ Quartz + Al_2O_3

B. Primary silicate + CO_2 + $H_2O \rightleftharpoons$ clay minerals + cations + HCO_3^- + H_4SiO_4 + H^+

C. Primary silicate + $H_2O \rightleftharpoons Al_2O_3$ + SiO_2 + CaO + H^+

D. Clay minerals + $H_2O \rightleftharpoons Fe_2O_3$ + Al_2O_3 + SiO_2 + CaO

38. Which group of minerals represent

A. Polymorphic transformation

B. Non-substitutional representation

C. Isomorphic substitution

D. Unmixed presence of different non silicates

39. Garnet is a metamorphic product of

A. Feldspar

B. Quartzite

C. Mica

D. Serpentine

40. Formation of marble can be represented by

A. $CaSiO_3 \rightleftharpoons Ca^{+2} + SiO_3^{-2}$

B. $CaO + CO_2 \rightleftharpoons CaCO_3$

C. $CaCO_3 \rightleftharpoons CaO + CO_2$

D. $CaCO_3 + SiO_2 \rightleftharpoons CaSiO_3 + CO_2$

41. For the precipitation of $CaCO_3$ from water

$Ca^{+2} + CO_3^{-2} - CaCO_3$

the equilibrium constant K is $10^{-8.3}$. This indicates that

A. Ca^{+2} & CO_3^{-2} concentration are equal in water

B. $m_{CO_3^{-2}} >> m_{Ca^{+2}}$

C. $m_{Ca^{+2}} < m_{Co_3^{-2}}$

D. $m_{Ca^{+2}} = \dfrac{1}{m_{Co_3^{-2}}}$

42. How many sites as potential areas for biosphere reserves have been identified by the National MAB Committee for the Department of Environment?

A. 13

B. 23

C. 33

D. 43

43. Which one of the following is not a permitting cryoprotectant?

A. Glycerol

B. DMSO

C. Sucrose

D. 1, 2 –propanediol

44. The aggregation of all eco systems on the earth is referred to as

A. Atmosphere

B. Ecosphere

C. Stratosphere

D. Ionosphere

45. Which one of the following is not a biofertilizer?

A. Aquatic ferns

B. Blue-green algae

C. Phosphate-Solubilising micro-organisms

D. Vermicompost

46. Who first used and defined "Ecology" in 1866?

A. H. Reiter

B. Haeckel

C. Charles Elton

D. Odum

47. CITES has following schedules in order of priority to protect animals and plants from trade:
    A. Schedule I, II, III   B. Schedule I, I, III
    C. Schedule III, III, I   D. Schedule II, I, III

48. Methamoglobinemia is actually caused by water pollution containing
    A. NO_2
    B. NO_3^-
    C. NH_4^+
    D. NO_2^-

49. Environmental Impact Assessment is mandatory for certain developmental project under one of the following legislation:

    A. The Factories' Act
    B. Forest Act
    C. Environment (Protection) Act
    D. Air (Pollution and Control) Act

50. Which one of the following air pollution control device has highest efficiency in controlling dust?
    A. Wet Scruber
    B. Electrostatic precipitator
    C. Venturi Scruber
    D. Cyclonic spray scruber

ANSWERS

1	2	3	4	5	6	7	8	9	10
A	B	A	D	A	B	A	A	B	C
11	**12**	**13**	**14**	**15**	**16**	**17**	**18**	**19**	**20**
B	D	D	B	D	C	C	B	B	C
21	**22**	**23**	**24**	**25**	**26**	**27**	**28**	**29**	**30**
D	D	D	B	B	D	C	C	C	D
31	**32**	**33**	**34**	**35**	**36**	**37**	**38**	**39**	**40**
B	B	D	B	A	D	B	B	C	B
41	**42**	**43**	**44**	**45**	**46**	**47**	**48**	**49**	**50**
C	A	B	B	A	B	D	B	C	B

PAPER-III

Note: *This paper is of two hundred (200) marks containing four (4) sections. Candidates are required to attempt the questions contained in these sections according to the detailed instructions given therein.*

SECTION-I

Note: *This section contains five (5) questions based on the following paragraph. Each question should be answered in about thirty (30) words and each carries five (5) marks.*

(5 × 5 = 25 marks)

Read the passage below and answer the questions that follow based on your understanding of the passage.

Biomes are defined as plants, which are evolved in response to climatic conditions and animals adapted to plants as per source food and shelter. This means types of plants and animals communities present in a defined climatic conditions are different from other climatic zones. There are basically three broad climatic conditions influencing biotic communities (temperature, sunshine and precipitation). In addition, local edaphic factors play important role in variation of biological communities with same climatic conditions.

Biome classification is based on average rainfall, potential evapo-transpiration and mean annual temperatures. These factors may also vary depending on longitude, latitude and altitude. Whittakar also proposed biome classification based on gradient analysis. There are extreme climatic conditions in certain types of biomes while other have uniform climatic throughout the years. These biomes also differ in species diversity, stratification and canopy cover. Biomes occurring on both sides of equator are known to be rich in biodiversity, evergreen and stratified, while polar and hot desert biomes are very characteristic due to limitation in various climatic factors. Within tropical bromes, there are a number of different units which are known as desert, moist deciduous, deciduous, thorny and grasslands, each having set of climatic ranges and biotic communities.

These naturally occurring biological communities are under threat due to various developmental activities, trade, rapid utilization for health, food and economical purposes etc.

As these biomes play an important role in regulating various ecological functions, their protection and conservation have been undertaken under various initiatives, rules and regulations and legislation.

1. Explain basis of biome classification with example.

Ans. Biome classification is based on overage rainfall, potential evapo-transpiration and mean annual temperatures.

1. Tundra Biome: e.g. Fragile ecosystem.
2. Alpine Biome: e.g. insects.
3. Forest Biome: e.g. grizzly bear.
4. Tropical savanna Biomes: e.g. tropical grasslands.
5. Grassland Biomes: e.g. wild horse.
6. Desert Biomes: e.g. fruit pat.

2. Describe the role of altitudinal changes in biotic communities.

Ans. The average rainfall, potential eve transpiration and man annual temperatures factors may also vary depending on longitude, latitude and altitude. Within tropical biomes these are numbers of different units when are know as desert, moist deciduous, deciduous thorny and grasslands, each having set of climatic ranges and biotic communities.

3. Explain characteristics of desert biome.

Ans. Deserts are the biome formed in the driest of environments. Temperature may range from very hot deserts to very cold as in cold deserts. Major hot deserts of the world are situated near the tropics of cancer and Capricorn, with a rainfall of less than 10 mm. The hot and cold deserts may also be distinguished by differences in plant population which are mostly succulent type (e.g. cactus, palo verde trees, creosote bush etc.) Most clod desert have sage bush.

4. Is CITES relevant in protection and conservation of biomes ?

Ans. CITES (Conventional on International Trade in Endangered Species of Wild Fauna and Flora, also known as the Washington Convention) is an international agreement between governments, drafted as a result of a resolution adopted in 1963 at a meeting of members of the International Union for Conservation of Nature (IUCN). The text of the convention was agreed upon in 1973, and CITES entered into force on 1 July, 1975. Its aim is to ensure that international trade in specimens of wild animals and plants does not threaten their survival and it accords varying degrees of protection to more than 40,000 species of animals and plants.

CITES is an international agreement to which States (countries) adhere voluntarily. States that have agreed to be bound by the Convention ('joined' CITES) are known as Parties. Although CITES is legally binding on the Parties—in other words they have to implement the Convention—it does not take the place of national laws. Rather it provides a framework to be respected by each Party, which has to adopt its own domestic legislation to ensure that CITES is implemented at the national level.

5. Mention types of protected areas in India. Explain their significance.

Ans. They are ecological/biogeographical areas where biological diversity alongwith natural and cultural resources is protected, maintained and managed through legal or other effective measures. They are delimited on the basis of biological diversity, e.g., cold desert (Ladakh and Spiti), hot desert (Thar), wetland (Assam), saline swampy area (Sunderbans) etc. Protected areas include national parks, sanctuaries and biosphere reserves.

- **National Parks:** They are areas maintained by government and reserved for betterment of wildlife. Cultivation, grazing forestry and habital manipulation are not allowed. There are 89 national parks in India (2005) occupying nearly 1.1% of geographical area.
- **Sanctuaries:** They are tracts of land with or without lake where wild animals/fauna can take refuge without being hunted. Other activities like collection of forest products, harvesting of timber, private ownership of land, tilling of land, etc. are allowed.
- **Biosphere reserves:** They are multipurpose protected areas which are meant for preserving genetic diversity in representative ecosystems of various natural biomes and unique biological communities by protecting wild populations, traditional life style of tribals and domesticated plant/animal genetic resources.

SECTION-II

*Note: This section contains **fifteen (15)** questions each to be answered in about **thirty (30)** words. Each question carries **five (5)** marks.*

(5 × 15 = 75 marks)

6. Discuss the importance of sensitivity and detection limit in analytical method.

Ans. Ethod validation is the process used to confirm that the analytical procedure employed for a specific test is suitable for its intended use. Results from method validation can be used to judge the quality, reliability and consistency of analytical results; it is an integral part of any good analytical practice.

Analytical methods need to be validated or revalidated

- before their introduction into routine use;
- whenever the conditions change for which the method has been validated (e.g., an instrument with different characteristics or samples with a different matrix); and
- whenever the method is changed and the change is outside the original scope of the method.

7. Heavy metals (As, Cd, Hg, Pb etc.) are known to be toxic for human beings and animals. Suggest remedial measures for any one of the above mentioned metal.

Ans. Remedial measures for Hg: Environmental pollution by Hg can be prevented by adopting the following measures, as recommended by the Environmental Protection Agencies of USA and Sweden:

(*i*) All chlor alkali plants must stop using Hg electrodes and swith to new technology.

(*ii*) All alkale mercury pesticides must be banned.

(*iii*) All other mercurial pesticides must be restricted to some selected areas.

8. Different models have been suggested to describe energy flow in an ecosystem. What do the two arms of a Y-shaped energy flow model represent?

Ans. There are two types of energy flow models in ecosystem.

1. Single channel energy models/energy flow diagrams.

2. Y-shaped or 2 channel energy flow models/diagrams.

Y-shaped energy flow models as pioneered by H.T. odum in 1956. This model shows a common boundary, light and heat flows as well as the import, export and storage of organic matter. Decomposers as placed in a separate box as a means of partially separating the grazing and detritus food chains. In terms of energy levels, decomposers are, in fact, a mixed group.

It separates the two chains i.e. grazing food chain and detritus food chain in both time and space.

9. What is cryo-preservation? Is this technique useful in germ plasm conservation through somatic embryogenesis?

Ans. Preservation of germplasm at ultra low temperatures of around – 196 °C is called Cryopreservation. At such low temperatures, the biological activities essentially cease, the cell division stops and the genetic changes to not occur.

It is important to note that besides the crop plants, freeze preservation is also utilized for cultured animal cells, spermatozoa, ovarian and embryonic tissue and also the whole animal embryos. It is also used for live stock breeding programmer.

10. Comment on the energy content of different types of coal.

Ans. The classification of coal is generally based on the content of volatiles. However, the exact classification varies between countries. According to the German classification, coal is classified as follows:

Name	Volatiles %	C Carbon %	H Hydrogen %	O Oxygen %	S Sulfur %	Heat content kJ/kg
Braunkohle (Lignite)	45-65	60-75	6.0-5.8	34-17	0.5-3	<28470
Flammkohle (Flame coal)	40-45	75-82	6.0-5.8	>9.8	~1	<32870
Gasflammkohle (Gas flame coal)	35-40	82-85	5.8-5.6	9.8-7.3	~1	<33910
Gaskohle (Gas coal)	28-35	85-87.5	5.6-5.0	7.3-4.5	~1	<34960
Fettkohle (Fat coal)	19-28	87.5-89.5	5.0-4.5	4.5-3.2	~1	<35380
Esskohle (Forge coal)	14-19	89.5-90.5	4.5-4.0	3.2-2.8	~1	<35380
Magerkohle (Non baking coal)	10-14	90.5-91.5	4.0-3.75	2.8-3.5	~1	35380
Anthrazit (Anthracite)	7-12	>91.5	<3.75	<2.5	~1	<35300

Percent by weight

11. Discuss the water quality index.

Ans. A member of indices have been developed for assessment of qualities of water and bita and there have been reviewed by Hellawell (1978), Laglar (1956) and Hanes (1980). The indices are as under.

(i) Boitic Indices (ii) Dominance Index (iii) Trophic state Index (iv) Species Diversity Index
(v) Similarity Index (vi) Percentage Similarity Index.

12. Explain health hazards associated with fly ash.

Ans. The bulk of the mineral particulate matter in a polluted atmosphere exists as oxides and other compounds resulting from combustion of high as fossil fuel. Smaller as particles called fly ash.

The fine particle ($< 3\mu$) from fly ash causes lung damage due to their ability to penetrate into the deep air passages. Larger particles ($> 3\mu$) are trapped in the nose and throat from which they are easily eliminated but finer particles can stay infact for years in the innermost region.

13. What are the criteria used in identification of 'Hot Spots' ?

Ans. To identify as hot-spot, the main determining criterion is species endesim. A second criterion is degree of threat, to qualify an area must reatain on 30% or less of its original primary vegetation.

14. Explain the principles and working of aerobic pond used in sewage treatment.

Ans. Basically the stabilization pond is a complex system comprises of actions and interactions between different groups of microbes. Aerobic ponds are shallow structures of about 0.3 m depth or less, so designed as to maximise light penetration and growth of algae. Photosynthetic action, aerobic conditions are maintained thoughout the depth of the pond at all times.

15. Describe the process involved in formation of secondary air pollutants.

Ans. In the process of secondary air pollutants the substances are not emitted directly into the atmosphere, but are formed by various physical processes in the atmosphere.

For example ozone, which is formed through some chemical process i.e. not obtained directly but through secondary reactions.

$$N_2O + h\nu \ (\lambda \leq 337 \text{ nm}) \rightarrow N_2 + O$$
$$N_2O + h\nu \ (\lambda \leq 250 \text{ nm}) \rightarrow NO + N$$
$$NO + N_2 \rightarrow O_3 + N_2$$
$$NO + O_3 \rightarrow NO_2 + O_2$$

16. How important is environmental audit as a part of EIA?

Ans. Environment audit report provides the necessary information on how well the management system are performing to keep pace with sustainable level of development. It provides performance evaluation of industrial working facilities and its possible effect in the surroundings. Environmental audit for safe guarding our environment and ensures optimal usage of all resources. It provides assurance of compliance with environmental regulation, standards etc. It help in placing environmental information to the public.

17. Enlist various processes involved in environmental planning.

Ans. The central theme of environmental planning is the reduction or minimisation of the impact of human activities on the environment, thus an endeavour to avoid the over use, misuse and abuse of environmental resources. The cornerstones in any environmental strategy are:

(*i*) environmental planning (*ii*) environmental status evaluation (*iii*) environmental impact assessment and (*iv*) environmental legislation and administration.

18. Explain the principles of coastal regulation zones.

Ans. The Ministry of Environment and Forests (MoEF) has issued the draft CRZ Notification, 2010 under the Environment (Protection) Act, 1986 on 15th September, 2010 inviting suggestions and objections from public within 60 days from date of its issue. The following are the new additions to the original 1991 notification:

(i) Inclusion of 'Aquatic' Part

(ii) Hazard Mapping Mechanism to be revised

(iii) Preparation of Action Plans

(iv) Classification of Erosion-Prone Areas

19. Define Skewness, Kurtosis and Median.

Ans. Skewness: Skewness is defined as the degree of asymmetry about the central value of distribution. Skewness can be positive as well as negative. If the mean is greater than mode or the median, the skewness will be positive. If it is less Skewness will be negative.

Kurtosis: Kurtosis is defined as the degree to which a distribution is sharply peaked at its centre. Kurotosis is denoted by B_2.

Median: The median (M) is a statistics of location occasionally useful in biological research. St is defined as the value of the variable that has an equal number of items on either side of it. Thus, the median divides a frequency distribution of two halves.

20. Explain methanogenesis in biogas production.

Ans. Biogas is composed of methane, CO_2, H_2 and N_2. At 40% methane content, calorific value is 3,214 k cal/m^3, at 50% is 4,429 k cal/m^3 and at 55% is 4,713 k cal/m^3. In order to make best use of biogas technology, two things are relevant restricted use of water and better strains of methane generating bacteria. There is to be developed a dry process, that requires less of water. Also there is need for methanogens, able to operate at temperatures lower than 20ºC. The ideal temperatures for methane generation is 35ºC or more.

SECTION-III

Note: *This section contains five (5) questions. Each question carries twelve (12) marks and is to be answered in about two hundred (200) words.*

(5 × 12 = 60 marks)

21. Discuss an appropriate chromatographic method for separation of organic pollutants in water on the basis of their relative size.

Ans. High performance liquid chromatography (HPLC) has become a standard and routine method for separation and concentration of analytes. An HPLC system consists of a solvent reservoir, high pressure pumps, sample injection port, separation column, detector, and recorder units. HPLC is the result of attempts to increase the efficiency of liquid chromatography to the same level as that of gas chromatography. This is achieved by using particles of 2–20 μm size to overcome diffusion-related problems in the liquid and solid phase. The resulting high inlet pressure in the column is overcome by resorting to high pressure pumping of solutions. A pump forces one or more mobile phases through the tightly packed high efficiency column. The sample is introduced through an injection system into the entrance to the column. Sample introduction can be improved by flow-injection method, by injecting the sample into a flowing stream, which carries the analyte through a chemical modulator into a detector. There is no universal detector for HPLC. Detectors based on refractive index (RI), optical absorbance, fluorescence, thermal conductivity, and flame ionization are in use.

Reverse-phase HPLC (RP-HPLC) is very well suited for the analysis of non-volatile polar compounds, such as polycyclic aromatic hydrocarbons (PAHs). Adsorbed PAHs on filters are recovered using Soxhlet extraction. The sample is then separated into fractions by column chromatography on silica gel using hexane-chloroform as the mobile phase, and individual components are detected by fluorescence. Advent of HPLC has resulted in tremendous progress in the separation of a wide variety of inorganic and organic compounds, with high sensitivity of detection.

22. How do the moist tropical deciduous forest differ from dry tropical deciduous forest? Explain with example.

Ans. The tropical and subtropical dry broadleaf forest biome, also known as tropical dry forest, is located at tropical and subtropical latitudes. Though these forests occur in climates that are warm year-round, and may receive several hundred centimeters of rain per year, they have long dry seasons which last several months and vary with geographic location. These seasonal droughts have great impact on all living things in the forest.

Deciduous trees predominate in most of these forests, and during the drought a leafless period occurs, which varies with species type. Because trees lose moisture through their leaves, the shedding of leaves allows trees such as teak and mountain ebony to conserve water during dry periods. The newly bare trees open up the canopy layer, enabling sunlight to reach ground level and facilitate the growth of thick underbrush. Trees on moister sites and those with access to ground water tend to be evergreen. Infertile sites also tend to support evergreen trees. Three tropical dry broadleaf forest ecoregions, the East Deccan dry evergreen forests, the Sri Lanka dry-zone dry evergreen forests, and the Southeastern Indochina dry evergreen forests, are characterized by evergreen trees.

Though less biologically diverse than rainforests, tropical dry forests are home to a wide variety of wildlife including monkeys, deer, large cats, parrots, various rodents, and ground dwelling birds. Mammalian biomass tends to be higher in dry forests than in rain forests, especially in Asian and African dry forests. Many of these species display extraordinary adaptations to the difficult climate.

This biome is alternately known as the tropical and subtropical dry forest biome or the tropical and subtropical deciduous forest biome. Locally some of these forests are also called monsoon forests, and they tend to merge into savannas.

Dry forests tend to exist north and south of the equator rain forest belt, south or north of the subtropical deserts, generally in two bands, one between 10° and 20°N latitude and the other between 20° and 30°S latitude. The most diverse dry forests in the world occur in southern Mexico and in the Bolivian lowlands. The dry forests of the Pacific Coast of northwestern South America support a wealth of unique species due to their dry climate. The subtropical forests of Maputo land-Ponderousin the subtropical regions of the united states of America and in southeastern Africa are diverse and support many endemic species. The dry forests of central India and Indochina are notable for their diverse large vertebrate faunas. Madagascar dry deciduous forests and New Caledonia dry forests are also highly distinctive (pronounced extremism and a large number of reliquary taxa) for a wide range of taxa and at higher taxonomic levels. Trees use underground water during the dry seasons.

Species tend to have wider ranges than moist forest species, although in some regions many species do display highly restricted ranges; most dry forest species are restricted to tropical dry forests, particularly in plants; beta diversity and alpha diversity high but typically lower than adjacent moist forests.

Effective conservation of dry broadleaf forests requires the preservation of large and continuous areas of forest. Large natural areas are required to maintain larger predators and other vertebrates, and to buffer sensitive species from hunting pressure. The persistence of riparian forests and water sources is critical for many dry forest species. Large swathes of intact forest are required to allow species to recover from occasional large events, like forest fires.

Dry forests are highly sensitive to excessive burning and deforestation; overgrazing and exotic species can also quickly alter natural communities; restoration is possible but challenging, particularly if degradation has been intense and persistent. Degrading dry broadleaf often leaves thorny shrublands, thickets, or dry grasslands in their place.

23. Discuss green energy options.

Ans. Green energy, there is any source of power that is sustainable and not excessively harmful to human health or the environment. A strict definition would include water, wind and solar power. A more expensive definition would include nuclear power, biofuel and biogas.

Hydro power: Some scientists have suggested that we use hydrogen gas (H_2) to fuel cars, heat homes, and provide hot water when oil and natural gas run out. Hydrogen gas does not occur in significant quantities in nature. However, it can be produced by chemical processes from nonrenewable coal or natural gas or by using heat, electricity, or perhaps sunlight to decompose fresh water or seawater. Hydrogen gas can be burned in a reaction with oxygen gas in a power plant, a specially designed automobile engine, or a fuel cell that converts the chemical energy produced by the reaction into direct- current electricity. Fuel cells running on a mixture of hydrogen and air have efficiencies of 60% to 80%.

Wind Power: Humans have been utilizing wind power for thousands of years for such applications as wind- mills and sailing ships. In the first quarter of the twentieth century, wind-powered irrigation pumps were very common in many countries (India, USA, Japan, Austria), but their use gradually declined as inexpensive oil and gas become more readily available.

Despite its drawbacks, wind power capacity continues to expand. In 1990 the global wind energy–generating capacity was a mere 10 megawatts; by 2004 it has grown to 3710 megawatts, and the growth shows no signs of abating. In the United States, wind power received a boost from the passage of the National Energy Policy Act of 1992, which includes a tax credit of 1.5 cents per kilowatt-hour of wind-generated electricity. The United States and Ukraine are discussing a cooperative venture to build a 500-megawatt wind farm to replace power currently supplied by one of the chernobyl nuclear reactors. All told, the immediate future of wind power looks very bright.

Solar energy: The largest, mostly untapped sources of energy for all countries are perpetual and renewable energy from the sun, wind, flowing water, biomass, and the earth's internal heat (geothermal energy). Currently India gets about 21% of its energy from perpetual and renewable energy resources but could easily get much more using available technology. California currently gets roughly 30% of its electricity from perpetual and renewable sources of energy; by the year 2009 this figure could rise to 50%.

According to the Department of Energy, reserves and potential supplies of perpetual and renewable energy sources in India make up 93% of the country's total energy resources. Developing these untapped resources could meet up to 80% of the country's projected energy needs by 2010 and virtually all energy needs if coupled with improvements in energy efficiency. Doing this would save money, eliminate the need for oil imports, produce less pollution and environmental degradation per unit of energy used, and increase economic environmental, and military security. The rest of this chapter evaluates the various perpetual and renewable energy resources available to us.

24. Explain the principles and working of an aerobic pond used in sewage treatment.

Ans. Although waste water treatment in oxidation pond is considered to be aerobic process, both aerobic and anaerobic processes operate together. The aerobic decomposition mainly takes place near the surface and anaerobic process, at the bottom. The oxygen required for the metabolism of bacteria is obtained from the surface through aeration as well as from the algae present in the pond, and in turn the bacteria supplies CO_2 by decomposing the waste. For good supply of oxygen by algae, the ponds are made shallow so that sunlight can penetrate well, helping photosynthesis. The waste thus, present at the upper part of the pond, undergoes aerobic decomposition into CO_2 and H_2O. The solids present in the waste get settled to the bottom, and undergo anaerobic decomposition to form CH_4, CO_2 and NH_3. The oxidation pond, with both the aerobic and anaerobic conditions prevailing is called facultative pond. The bad odors due to anaerobic decomposition however, creates problem and thus waste water before being released into the pond should be treated to remove the solid materials which may settle down, and aeration should be provided throughout the pond by mechanical stirring. Secondly, in winters when photosynthesis gets retarded, oxygen supply is reduced creating an anaerobic condition and causes same problem with odors.

25. Describe in brief methods used in reclamation of wastelands.

Ans. Land is a precious resource. since it is put to diverse use by man. India with a land area of $32,88000$ km^2 which is about 2.4% of the world supports 15% of the worlds population. The percapita land resource available now in India is less than 0.4 hectares, in comparision to more than 0.9 hectare in China. About 44% of our land is used for agriculture, 23% is covered with forests, 4% is used for pastures and grazing fields, 8% for housing, agroforestry, industrial areas, roads and so on. The 14% land is barren and about 8% is used for miscellaneous purposes. The rapid increase of urbanisation and migration of population to towns and cities has created many problems. All this has led to the utilization of agricultural land for housing construction, industries etc.

The rational use of land resource is possible by adopting and integrated land-use policy which involves prevention of land misuse and reclamation of degraded and under-utilised land, wastelands, fallows, etc. Reclamation of abandoned mines and brick kilns may yield some much required land. Fertile agricultural land should not be sacrificed for non-agricultural purposes, such as road building, development of industries or construction of water reservoirs. Urban areas should not be developed on agricultural lands. Waste lands arc lands which are unproductive, unfit for cultivation grazing and other economic uses due to rough terrain and eroded soils. The lands which are water-logged and saline are also termed as waste lands.

The geomorphic processes become active in the absence of land management practices. As a result, these processes erode and transport soil layers making those lands infertile, stony and useless.

The deforestation leads to soil erosion and the eroded soils exhibit droughtly tendency. Further, the falling trees aggravate the lowering of water table and dry conditions. The loss of fertility followed by crosion also leads to the transformation of marginal forest lands into wastelands.

Waste lands are broadly categorized under two groups: barren and uncultivable waste land and cultivable wasteland. The first category includes lands which cannot be brought under cultivation or economic use except at a very high cost whether they exist as isolated pockets or within cultivated holdings. They are mostly lands such as hilly slopes, rocky exposures, stony or leached or gully land and sandy deserts.

The second category lands are cultivable but not cultivated for more than five years. It comprises all lands available for cultivation, but not taken up for cultivation. Next to 'fallow' lands, cultivable waste lands are important for agricultural purposes because they can be reclaimed through conservational practices for cultivation or grazing or agro-forestry.

Reclamation: Some of the measures used to reclaim these waste lands are the following:

(i) these lands can be brought under cultivation by using abundant water and fertilizers.

(ii) afforestation and agronomical practices are adopted to conserve the soil. So that they can be used for agriculture.

(iii) contour bunds are constructed affording safe disposal of water of the catchment areas.

These lands are also used for settlement of landless agricultural workers.

SECTION-III

Note: This section consists of one essay type question of forty (40) marks to be answered in about one thousand (1000) words on any one of the following topics.

(40 × 1 = 40 marks)

26. Discuss the linkages between El Nino, La Nino, thermahyaline balance and the global climate change.

OR

Integrate EIA, EMP & Environmental Audit as requirement of life cycle-use coal based thermal power plant for elaborating your answer.

OR

What is bio-remediation ? Is bioremediation eco-friendly method in restoration of soil quality ? Justify your answer.

OR

Discuss various guidelines and notification required in developing new township with reference to environmental issues. Add a note on methods used to make eco-friendly township.

OR

What are wetlands ? Discuss the role of wetlands in ecosystem. Explain criteria used in identification of ecologically important wetlands under Ramsar convention.

OR

Explain method for removal of interference caused by the emission intensities in the measurement of absorption intensities using atomic absorption spectrometer (AAS).

OR

Describe the various methods of energy production from ocean ? Add a note on the feasibility of power production through ocean thermal energy conversion.

OR

What is ecological succession? How many types of ecological successions are there? Discuss in detail the structural and functional changes taking place from a baren to climax stage in a water habitat giving suitable examples.

Ans. Climate: Climate change is a long-term shift in the climate of a specific location, region or planet. The shift is measured by changes in features associated with average weather, such as temperature, wind patterns and precipitation. What most people don't know is that a change in the variability of climate is also considered climate change, even if average weather conditions remain the same.

Climate change occurs when the climate of a specific area or planet is altered between two different periods of time. This usually occurs when something changes the total amount of the sun's energy absorbed by the earth's atmosphere and surface. It also happens when something changes the amount of heat energy from the earth's surface and atmosphere that escapes to space over an extended period of time.

Such changes can involve both changes in average weather conditions and changes in how much the weather varies around these averages. The changes can be caused by natural processes like volcanic eruptions, variations in the sun's intensity, or very slow changes in ocean circulation or land surfaces which occur on time scales of decades, centuries or longer.

But humans also cause climates to change by releasing greenhouse gases and aerosols into the atmosphere, by changing land surfaces, and by depleting the stratospheric ozone layer. Both natural and human factors that can cause climate change are called 'climate forcings', since they push, or 'force' the climate to shift to new values.

Climate change refers to a statistically significant variation in either the mean state of the climate or in its variability, persisting for an extended period (typically decades or longer). Climate change may be due to natural internal processes or external forcing, or to persistent anthropogenic changes in the composition of the atmosphere or in land use.

Climate change is commonly used to describe any systematic alteration or statistically significant variation in either the average state of the climate elements such as precipitation, temperature, winds, or pressure; or in its variability, sustained over a finite time period (decades or longer). It can be referred to as the long-term change in global weather patterns, associated especially with increases in temperature, precipitation, and storm activity.

The work of climatologists has found evidence to suggest that only a limited number of factors are primarily responsible for most of the past episodes of climate change on the Earth. These factors can be categorized into two broad categories:

A. Natural Causes of Climate Change:

1. Variations in the Earth's orbital characteristics (Milankovitch theory).
2. Volcanic eruptions
3. Variations in solar output
4. Change in composition of atmosphere

B. Anthropogenic Causes of Climate Change

1. Green house gas emission
    I. carbon dioxide
    II. methane
    III. CFCs
    IV. Nitrogen Oxide
    V. Water Vapour
2. Industrialization
3. Deforestation

El Nino and La Nino

El-Nino is a warm ocean current that flows along the equator from the date line and south off the coast of Ecuador at Christmas time. The water along the barren coast of Peru are cold and flow northward during most of the year, but around Christmas time, they are warm and flow southward. The latter current was originally given the name El-Nino, Spanish term for "the boy." Because of its timing, and because it is associated with refreshing rains, the name also refers to Child Jesus.

Every few years the current is exceptionally intense and persistent, bringing very heavy rains that transform parts of the coastal desert into a garden. At such times the fish that usually are abundant in the cold water, disappear temporarily.

Today, the term El Nino is reserved for these interannual events which now are perceived as disasters even though they originally were welcomed as blessings. El Nino was originally regarded as a regional phenomenon, confined to the shores of Peru, but is now recognized as part of the changes in oceanic conditions across the entire tropical Pacific Ocean. Furthermore, El Nino is not a sporadic departure from "normal" conditions, but is one phase of a continual oscillation with a period of 3 to 5 years; the complementary phase is known as La Nina. (This oscillation is evident in a record of sea surface temperature variations in the eastern equatorial Pacific over the past century.

Early in the 20th century, Gilbert Walker's attempts to predict failures of the monsoons in India led to his discovery of the Southern Oscillation, which includes oscillations in the intensity of the trade winds over the tropical Pacific. Those oscillations, it turns out, are the ones that induce El Nino and La Nina. From a meteorological perspective, the changes in the wind patterns are a consequence of the changes in the sea surface temperature patterns associated with El Nino and La Nina.

This circular argument—sea surface temperature changes are both the cause and the consequence of changes in the winds—implies that interactions between the ocean and atmosphere are at the heart of the matter. Those interactions are unstable, capable of amplifying small, random disturbances, such as a burst of strong winds, into a major climate fluctuation.

———————

UGC-NET ENVIRONMENTAL SCIENCE, JUNE 2008

PAPER-II

Note : *This paper contains fifty (50) multiple-choice questions, each question carrying two (2) marks. Attempt all of them.*

1. **Assertion A.:** Sustainable development is necessary for the survival of human race.

   Reason (R): Rapid economic growth without environmental concerns cannot be sustained.
   A. (A) is true and (R) is false
   B. (A) is false and (R) is true
   C. Both (A) and (R) true but (R) is not the correct explanation
   D. Both (A) and (R) true and (R) is the correct explanation

2. The spatial scale of meso scale meteorological phenomena is approximately :
   A. 2 - 3 km to 5 - 6 km
   B. few km to 100 km
   C. few 100 m to few km
   D. 10 mm to 1 km

3. The mass of the earth's mantle is approximately:
   A. 2×10^{25} gm
   B. 8.1×10^{17} gm
   C. 4.05×10^{27} gm
   D. 3.1×10^{22} gm

4. When the environmental lapse rate is less than the adiabatic lapse rate, the atmosphere is:
   A. Stable
   B. Moderately unstable
   C. Highly unstable
   D. Neutral

5. The standard hydrogen electrode, the pressure of hydrogen and hydrogen ion concentration respectively are:
   A. 1 atm ; 10 m
   B. 10 atm ; 1m
   C. 1 atm ; 1 m
   D. 1 atm ; m/10

6. Consider the following statements:
   (i) Entropy in a spontaneous reaction increases
   (ii) Free energy in a spontaneous reaction increases
   (iii) Free energy remains constant when reaction is in equilibrium

   (iv) Free energy increases in a reverse reaction
   Which of these are *correct:*
   A. (i) and (ii)
   B. (ii) and (iii)
   C. (i), (iii) and (iv)
   D. none of the above

7. **Assertion (A):** Increased level of Arsenic in water is a health hazard.

   Reason (R) : Arsenic has antagonistic behaviour with other metals, its dietary requirement is in trace amount and shows speciation.
   A. Both (A) and (R) true
   B. Both (A) and (R) true but (R) is not the correct explanation of (A)
   C. (A) is true but (R) is false
   D. (A) is false but (R) is true

8. One liter of water contains:
   A. $55.5 \times 6.02 \times 10^{23}$ H_2O molecules
   B. $25.5 \times 6.02 \times 10^{23}$ H_2O molecules
   C. $1.0 \times 6.02 \times 10^{23}$ H_2O molecules
   D. $1000 \times 6.02 \times 10^{23}$ H_2O molecules

9. When terrestrial plant communities progress with time from successional to climax stage:
   (i) Standing crop biomass increases
   (ii) Net ecosystem productivity increases
   (iii) Gross productivity per unit of standing crop biomass decreases
   (iv) Biomass supported per unit of energy flow decreases.

   Which of the following combination is *correct:*
   A. (i) and (ii)
   B. (i) and (iii)
   C. (i)) and (iv)
   D. (ii) and (iii)

10. **Assertion (A):** 'Hot spots' are the region showing richness of endemic species.

    Reason (R): The distribution of endemic species are confined to a specific region.
    A. Both (A) and (R) are true and (R) is correct explanation of (A)
    B. Both (A) and (R) are true but (R) is not the correct explanation

C. **(A)** is true but **(R)** is false

D. **(A)** is false but **(R)** is true

11. Trophic structure may be shown graphically by ecological pyramids; which of the following ecological pyramid will always have a true upright pyramid shape:
   A. Pyramid of numbers B. Pyramid of biomass
   C. Pyramid of energy D. All of the above

12. Species diversity is generally higher in ecosystem experiencing:
   A. No disturbance
   B. Moderate disturbance
   C. High disturbance
   D. Drastic disturbance

13. Those Planktons which have dimensions in the range of 2 - 20μm are known as:
   A. Micro plankton   B. Nano plankton
   C. Peri plankton   D. Pico plankton

14. **Assertion (A):** Plants are not auxotrophs.

   Reason (R): Plants can synthesize all the growth factors they need.
   A. Both **(A)** and **(R)** are true and **(R)** is the correct explanation of **(A)**
   B. Both **(A)** and **(R)** are true but **(R)** is not the correct explanation of **(A)**
   C. **(A)** is false and **(R)** is true
   D. **(A)** is true and **(R)** is false

15. **Assertion (A):** Decomposition of hydrocarbons is favoured in neutral soil.

   Reason (R): Neutral pH favours the greatest populations of micro-organisms.
   A. Both **(A)** and **(R)** are true and **(R)** is not the correct explanation of **(A)**
   B. Both **(A)** and **(R)** are true and **(R)** is the correct explanation of **(A)**
   C. **(A)** is false **(R)** is true
   D. **(A)** is true **(R)** is false

16. A majority of the antibiotics are derived from actinomycetes come from members of the genus:
   A. *Nocardia*   B. *Streptomyces*
   C. *Micromonospora*   D. *Actinomyces*

17. Germany's poison gas in World War I was developed by:

A. Knowels   B. Haber

C. Hitlor   D. Stevenson

18. Which of the following nitrogen fixers is found in philosophers:
   A. *Azotobacter*   B. *Clostridium*
   C. *Klebsiella*   D. *Rhodospirillum*

19. Thiobacillus and Beggiatoa play an important role in the:
   A. water cycle on Earth
   B. Phosphorus cycle
   C. Sulfur cycle in the soil
   D. Breakdown of sewage

20. One of the purpose of secondary treatment of industrial waste water and sewage is to:
   A. increase the chlorine content
   B. reduce the BOD
   C. encourage the formation of PCBs
   D. discourage ammonification

21. AGENDA 21 specifically advocates to devise strategies to:
   A. Promote economic growth to support increasing human population with adequate environment care
   B. Control human population explosion, resource over use and deteriorating environmental quality
   C. Halt and reverse the effects of environmental degradation to promote sustainable and environmentally sound development
   D. Promote economic development and environmental with a view to reduce poverty and faster human welfare

22. Eutrophication of water bodies is triggered by:
   A. Excessive growth of phytoplanktons
   B. Excessive growth of fishes
   C. Excessive inflow of nutrients
   D. Bright sunlight

23. Under montreal protocol, developing countries are required to phase out the HCFCs by the year:
   A. 2030   B. 2010
   C. 2020   D. 2040

24. Identify the correct sequence of gases in the increasing order of their global warming potential:

A. $CH_4 < N_2O < CFC < SF_6$
B. $CO_2 < N_2O < CH_4 < CFC$
C. $CO_2 < CH_4 < SF_6 < CFC$
D. $N_2O < CH_4 < CO_2 < CFC$

25. In a simple regression consisting of dependent variable Y, independent variable X and random error term $\in$, $Y = \alpha + \beta X + \in$, the expectation value $< \in >$ is:
A. 0
B. α/β
C. β/α
D. $(\beta - \alpha)$

26. If p and q are the probabilities of success and failure, respectively in a trial and N is the total number of trials, the variance is:
A. $\sqrt{npq}$
B. npq
C. $n\dfrac{p}{q}$
D. $n\dfrac{q}{p}$

27. If $S = 4$ is the standard deviation of sample size 20 drawn from a normal distribution with standard deviation $\sigma = 2$, the value of Ψ^2 (chi-square) statistic is:
A. 40
B. 10
C. 20
D. 80

28. Under unstable atmospheric conditions, the plum rise (Δh) above the stack varies with wind speed (u) at stack height as:
A. $\Delta h \propto u$
B. $\Delta h \propto 1/u$
C. $\Delta h \propto u^{1/3}$
D. $\Delta h \propto u^{-1/3}$

29. The geometric mean of the data 2, 4, 27 is:
A. 6
B. $6\sqrt{6}$
C. 16.5
D. $\sqrt{33}$

30. Bulking of sewage sludge is frequently associated with:
A. High C : N ratio
B. High C : P ratio
C. High dissolved oxygen
D. All of the above

31. Which of the following is removed from waste water by:
A. Phosphates
B. Organic Compounds
C. Ammonia
D. Sulphates

32. The bacteria responsible for deposition of iron oxide in water pipes:
A. *Gallionella*
B. *Klebsiella*
C. *Thermococcus*
D. *Helicobacter*

33. **Assertion (A):** In electrostatic precipitator corona discharge is used for removing participate particles from the gas stream.

Reason (R) : The corona discharge creates an electric field, which makes the particles settle down.
A. Both (A) and (R) are true and (R) is the correct explanation of (A)
B. Both (A) and (R) are true but (R) is not the correct explanation of (A)
C. (A) is true but (R) is false
D. (A) is false but (R) is true

34. Which of the following affects the ozone concentration in troposphere:
A. CO
B. N_2
C. SO_2
D. CO_2

35. **Assertion (A):** While characterizing the size of an aerosol particle aerodynamic diameter is used.

Reason (R): The aerosol particle may be of irregular shape.
A. Both (A) and (R) are true and (R) is correct explanation of (A)
B. Both (A) and (R) are true but (R) is not the correct explanation of (A)
C. (A) is true but (R) is false
D. (A) is false but (R) is true

36. The noise index Lgo refers to:
A. Background noise level
B. Peak noise level
C. Average noise level
D. 90%

37. Fission of 1 gm of ^{235}U liberates energy equivalent to about:
A. 5.7 barrels of crude oil
B. 13.7 barrels of crude oil
C. 18.7 barrels of crude oil
D. 22.7 barrels of crude oil

38. To increase the power output from a MHD power plant, which of the following compounds is used:

A. ZnO   B. Fe_2O_3

C. Cs_2O_3 D. SiO_2

39. **Assertion (A):** Geothermal reservoirs with temperatures above 180°C are useful for generating electric power.

    Reason (R): High temperature steam can be used to drive turbines to generate electricity.

    A. Both **(A)** and **(R)** are true and **(R)** is the correct explanation of **(A)**

    B. Both **(A)** and **(R)** are true but **(R)** is not the correct explanation of **(A)**

    C. **(A)** is true but **(R)** is false

    D. **(A)** is false but **(R)** is true

40. The optimum range of wind speeds for wind power generation is:

    A. 2 - 4 m/sec   B. 1 - 2 m/sec

    C. 4 -12 m/sec   D. 15 - 20 m/sec

41. Deep sea ferromanganese nodules are found on:

    A. Oceanic plateau   B. Oceanic ridges

    C. Oceanic islands   D. Oceanic plains

42. In ocean regime carbonate compensation depth (CCD) implies:

    A. Precipitation of carbonate

    B. Dissolution of carbonate

    C. Evaporation of carbonate

    D. Sublimation of carbonate

43. Which of the following statement is *NOT* correct:

    Carcinogenic agents like pesticides are mutagens which may cause.

    A. Change in chromosome

    B. Change in nucleotide sequence in DNA of sperms or eggs, which is inherited

    C. Change in nucleotide sequence in DNA of somatic cells is inherited

    D. Change in DNA sequence may be due to generation of free radicals in the cells

44. According to the Public Liability Insurance Act 1991, what is the upper monetary limit for drawing insurance policies by the owners for handling any hazardous substance:

A. Rs. 5 Crores   B. Rs. 50 Crores

C. Rs. 500 Crores   D. Rs. 1000 Crores

45. Hospital waste has to be disposed off by:

    A. handing over to hazardous waste management site

    B. burring 3 meters below the ground

    C. burring 10 meters below the ground

    D. incineration

46. Which of the following industries do not produce hazardous waste:

    A. Electroplating   B. Chemical

    C. Sugar   D. Pharmaceutical

47. Four stages viz Initiation, Inventory analysis, Impact assessment and improvement assessment are associated with:

    A. LCA

    B. EIA

    C. Environmental Audit

    D. Environmental Impact - Statement

48. When industry with 'Red' category is to be established, it is necessary to have public hearing or inquiry under the procedure called as:

    A. Environmental Health Hazard (EHH)

    B. Environmental Litigation (EL)

    C. Environmental Management System (EMS)

    D. Environmental Impact Assessment (EIA)

49. The National Ambient Air Quality Standard for 1 hour average concentration (mg/m^3) of CO in restricted area is:

    A. 2   B. 4

    C. 16   D. 20

50. For aerosol particles of size comparable to wavelengths of either shortwave radiation or infra-red radiation, the following type of scattering takes place :

    A. Rayleigh scattering

    B. Mie scattering

    C. Raman scattering

    D. Brillouin scattering

ANSWERS

1	2	3	4	5	6	7	8	9	10
C	C	D	B	C	B	C	C	C	B

11	12	13	14	15	16	17	18	19	20
C	D	B	D	B	D	A	A	D	B

21	22	23	24	25	26	27	28	29	30
A	A	C	B	A	B	B	A	A	B

31	32	33	34	35	36	37	38	39	40
B	B	A	B	C	C	B	B	B	C

41	42	43	44	45	46	47	48	49	50
B	A	D	B	D	A	D	A	A	A

PAPER-III

Note: This paper is of two hundred (200) marks containing four (4) sections. Candidates are required to attempt the questions contained in these sections according to the detailed instructions given therein.

SECTION-I

Note: This section contains five (5) questions based on the following paragraph. Each question should be answered in about thirty (30) words and each carries five (5) marks.

(5 × 5 = 25 marks)

Read the passage below and answer the questions that follow based on your understanding of the passage.

Biodiversity refers to the number variety and population sizes of living species in their various physical habitats. It is mainly of three types viz., genetic biodiversity, species biodiversity and ecosystem biodiversity.

Biodiversity is partly a function of the process of evolution by natural selections. These ensure that the ecological niches are colonised by population of organisms that are best adapted to survive in the face of climatic extremes, predators and competition from other species. The constant process of mutation and selection guarantee the production of new species. However, the evolution of species is tempered by fluctuations in numbers of organisms including population explosion, where conditions are exceptionally favourable to reproduction, survival and population 'overshoot', and die-back when numbers start exceeding the carrying capacity of a species habitat. Environmental stress and many forms of exploitation and predation can also regulate the numbers or cause them to fluctuate over time.

In natural world and in pre-history large scale reduction in biodiversity have resulted from climatic and geological extremes that have ended in loss, fragmentation as sterilization of habitats and the collapse of food chain and webs. In the modern era, the principle cause of biodiversity loss is human activity. Land is being transformed at an ever increasing rate and usually towards the simplification and uniformitization of ecosystems. As population size and living standards rise, pollution, industrialisation of agriculture and forestry tend to affect the species negatively, while overharvesting has had devastating effects on fisheries, marine products, wild animals and plants. The accidental and deliberate introduction of exotic species has often led to a reduction in the diversity of indegenous organisms which are outcompeted by the newcomers. The tendency of humans to treat exotic species as commodities has caused the demise of the more prominent reptiles, amphibians, pachyderms, birds and flowering plants. Poaching, smuggling and trade of ivory and furs has depleted stocks of rare animals at an accelerated rate.

Many ways have been suggested to conserve the biodiversity. It can be maintained by identifying species in danger of loss and protecting their population and habitats. One alternative is the biosphere reserve concept in which protected core area is separated from unprotected area with buffer zone where limited activity is allowed. To address the problem of loss of biodiversity, scientific, political and administrative actions are necessary alongwith local participation of communities.

1. The author is primarily concerned with:
A. How biodiversity came into existence on earth?
B. Loss and conservation of biodiversity
C. Distribution of species
D. Number of threatened species

Ans. The author is primarily concerned with loss and conservation of biodiversity. In modern era, the principle cause of biodiversity loss is human activity. To address the problem of loss of biodiversity, scientific, political and administrative actions are necessary alongwith local participation of communities.

2. According to the passage, which of the most important points are being discussed:
(*i*) Origin of biodiversity
(*ii*) Effect of loss of biodiversity on humans
(*iii*) Rapid rate of extinction of species due to anthropogenic activities
(*iv*) Biodiversity and its inter-relation with economic aspects
A. (*i*), (*iii*) and (*iv*) only
B. (*i*), (*ii*) and (*iii*) only
C. (*iv*) only
D. (*ii*) and (*iii*) only

Ans. According to the passage the most important points are being discussed origin of biodiversity effect of loss of biodiversity on humans and rapid rate of extinction of species due to economic aspects.

3. The material in the passage could best be used in an argument for:
A. Boosting the economic growth of the country
B. Sustainable existence of humans on the earth
C. Proving the supremacy of humans
D. Fullfilling the needs of humans on the earth

Ans. The material in the passage could best be used in an argument for sustainable existence of humans on the earth. To conserve the loss of biodiversity for sustainable existence of humans on the earth; the scientific, political and administrative actions are necessary alongwith local participation of communities.

4. The author strongly advocates which of the following ways to conserve the biodiversity?
A. Biotechnology
B. Ex-situ protection methods
C. Formulation of laws to protect certain species
D. Identification of endangered species and protecting their habitats and creation of biosphere reserve

Ans. The author strongly advocates the ways to conserve the biodiversity identification of endangered species and protecting their habitats and creation of biosphere reserve to address the problem of loss of biodiversity, scientific, political and administrative actions are necessary alongwith local participation of communities.

5. Which is the basic reason that is responsible for loss of biodiversity:
A. Ecotourism
B. Construction of dams
C. Agricultural activity
D. Rise in living standards of humans and population growth

Ans. The rise in living standards of humans and population growth is the basic reason that is responsible for loss of biodiversity. As population size and living standards rise, pollution, industrialisation of agriculture and forestry tend to affect the species negatively.

SECTION-II

Note: This section contains fifteen (15) questions each to be answered in about thirty (30) words. Each question carries five (5) marks.

(5 × 15 = 75 marks)

6. Deltic Environment.

Ans. A delta, in the geographic sense, is a deltoid-shaped area determined by the major bifurcations of a river and resulting from relatively rapid deposition of river-borne sediment into a more or less still standing body of water. A delta, in the geologic sense, is defined as a deposit of sediment partly subaerial and made by a stream at the place of entrance into a permanent body of water. The major portion of the deltaic sediments is deposited subaqueously in the permanent body of water where waves and currents aid in the transportation and deposition.

7. Aerosols.

Ans. A dispersion in which a finely divided solid is suspended in air and the particles are of colloidal dimensions, e.g. smoke. Aerosols can often be formed by the rapid condensation of a vapour such as that of a metal oxide.

Aerosol sprays consist of a material dissolved or suspended in a liquid under pressure which when released volatilizes to produce a fine sprays.

8. Biopesticides.

Ans. Biopesticides are those biological agents that are used for control of weeds, insects and pathogens. The microorganisms used as biopesticides are viruses, bacteria, protozoa, fungi and mites. Some of the biopesticides are being used at a commercial sacle. Most important example is the soil bacterium, *Bacillus thuringiensis (Bt)*.

9. Air quality index.

Ans. The Air Quality Index (AQI) (also known as the Air Pollution Index (API) or Pollutant Standard Index (PSI) is a number used by government agencies to characterize the quality of the air at a given location. As the AQI increases, an increasingly large percentage of the population is likely to experience increasingly severe adverse health effects. To compute the AQI requires an air pollutant concentration from a monitor or model. The function used to convert from air pollutant concentration to AQI varies by pollutant, and is different in different countries. Air quality index values are divided into ranges, and each range is assigned a descriptor and a color code. Standardized public health advisories are associated with each AQI range. An agency might also encourage members of the public to take public transportation or work from home when AQI levels are high.

10. Endangered species.

Ans. It is facing a high risk of extinction in the wild in the near future due to decrease in its habitat, excessive predation or poaching. The percentage number of endangered species in the list of threatened ones is 19% mammals, 17% birds, 21% reptiles, 22% of amphibians and 19% angiosperms. e.g., Red panda, Blue whale, Asiatic wild ass, Lion tailed macaque.

11. Primary productivity.

Ans. Primary Productivity: It is defined as the rate at which radiant energy is stored by photosynthesic and chemosynthetic activity of producers. Primary productivity is of two types i.e. Gross primary productivity and Net primary productivity.

12. Trophic level.

Ans. Trophic level is a step or division of food chain which is characterised by the method of obtaining its food. The number of trophic levels is equal to the number of steps in the food chain. The two fundamental trophic levels are producers and consumers. A fundamental similarity of all trophic levels is that it uses a part of food in body building while a major part of it is consumed in liberation of energy during respiration.

13. BOD.

Ans. The amount of oxygen in (mg/l) taken up by micro-organisms that decompose organic waste matter in water. It is therefore used as the measure of the amount of certain types of organic pollutants in water. BOD is calculated by keeping a sample of water, containing a known amount of oxygen for five days at 20°C in BOD inclubator. The oxygen content is measured again after 5 days period. A high BOD indicates the presence of a large number of micro-organisms, which suggest a high level of pollution.

These are the conditions associated with eutrophication. BOD is thus an indicator of degraded conditions in a body of water, but it cannot tell us specifically what may be causing the degradation. The BOD value is an index of contamination of water. It is an important consideration in sewage treatment, in which proper aeration of the organic material is essential.

14. Ecological succession.

Ans. A gradual process incurred by the change in number of individuals of each species of a community and by the establishment of new species populations that may gradually replace the original inhabitants. The introduction of pollution can hasten the onset of ecological recession, which is the reverse of ecological succession in that during recession the complex community begins to loose its diversity of species and becomes simple again.

15. Wet and dry deposition.

Ans. Wet deposition: In this nutrients are present in the dissolved state e.g. rainfall, siltation etc. It is deposited by siltation or running water or rainfall.

Dry deposition: It is the bringing of nutrients in the particulate state e.g. dust fall. In this nutrients are brought by air.

16. Biofuels.

Ans. Biofuels are a wide range of fuels which are in some way derived from biomass. The term covers solid biomass, liquid fuels and various biogases. Biofuels are gaining increased public and scientific attention, driven by factors such as oil price spikes, the need for increased energy security, and concern over greenhouse gas emissions from fossil fuels.

17. Saturation mixing ratio.

Ans. Saturation mixing ratio (Ws) is the theoretical maximum amount of water vapor that air at a specific temperature and pressure can hold. When air is saturated, it cannot hold any additional water vapor. To find this value at any pressure level, use the dashed green saturation mixing ratio lines on either side of your plotted temperature. Interpolate the value of your temperature plot using the scale on the mixing ratio lines printed just above the 1,000-millibar level.

18. Radionuclides.

Ans. Some important radionuclides, their largest tissue and half life are given in the Table.

S.No.	Radio Nuclide	Half Life	Target Tissue
1.	Calcium-45	165 days	Bone
2.	Carbon-14	5760 days	Whole Body
3.	Caesium-137	25 years	Soft Tissue
4.	Iodine-129	17 Million Years	Thyroid
5.	Iodine-131	8 days	Thyroid
6.	Radium-226	1620 Years	Bone
7.	Strontium-90	28 Years	Bone

19. Coefficient of determination (R^2).

Ans. In statistics, the coefficient of determination, R^2, is used in the context of statistical models whose main purpose is the prediction of future outcomes on the basis of other related information. It is the proportion of variability in a data set that is accounted for by the statistical model. It provides a measure of how well future outcomes are likely to be predicted by the model.

20. Carbon credits.

Ans. A carbon credit is a generic term for any tradable certificate or permit representing the right to emit one tonne of carbon dioxide or carbon dioxide equivalent (CO_2-e).

Carbon credits and carbon markets are a component of national and international attempts to mitigate the growth in concentrations of greenhouse gases (GHGs). One carbon credit is equal to one ton of carbon dioxide, or in some markets, carbon dioxide equivalent gases. Carbon trading is an application of an emissions trading approach. Greenhouse gas emissions are capped and then markets are used to allocate the emissions among the group of regulated sources.

SECTION-III

Note: This section contains five (5) questions. Each question carries twelve (12) marks and is to be answered in about two hundred (200) words.

(12 × 5 = 60 marks)

21. Noise indices.

Ans. In our technological age the sources of noise seem almost infinite. Industrialization and Modernization have contributed towards the noise pollution to a great extent. Radios, TVs, vacuum cleaners, power loom movers and outside air conditioners, the list are endless.

Because of the paper thin walls in most new apartment buildings, today's apartment dweller is frequently assaulted by the noise from his neighbour's appliances as well as his own. In some communities, instruction of noise from early industrial areas is a serious problem. But in most of the world's major metropolitan areas construction and transportation sources, particularly trucks, motorcycle, sports cars, and aircraft (both civil and military) are the most serious offenders.

In matters related to noise pollution, as in air and water pollution problems, economic considerations have generally taken precedence over environment considerations. Furthermore, the machines that make noise frequently benefit certain groups of people while imposing the noise nuisance on another group that does not share in the benefits.

Sources of Noise

Sources of noise are numerous but may be broadly classified into two classes such as :
1. Industrial
2. Non-Industrial

Industrial

The industrial may include noises from various industries operating in cities like transportation, vehicular movements such as car, motor, truck, train, tempo, motor cycle, aircrafts, rockets, defence equipments, explosions etc.

The disturbing qualities of noise emitted by industrial premises are generally its loudness, its distinguishing features such as tonal or impulsive components, and its intermittency and duration.

Non-Industrial

Among the non-industrial sources, important ones are as follows:
1. Loudspeaker
2. Construction work
3. Road Traffic
4. Trains
5. Aircrafts
6. Radios and Microphones
7. Agricultural Machines
8. Defence Equipment

Permissible Noise Limits

Under *Central Motor Vehicle Rules, 1989*, the following limits were imposed on 26th March 1993.

S.No.	Type of Vehicle	Limit in dB
1.	Two wheelers (petrol run)	80
2.	Passenger car, petrol runs three-wheelers, diesel run two wheelers.	82
3.	Passenger or commercial vehicles of upto 4 MT	85
4.	Passenger or commerical vehicles of above 4 MT and upto 12 MT	89
5.	Passenger or commerical vehicles exceeding 12 MT.	91

Noise limits implemented from 1st Jan. 2003:

S. No.	Type of Vehicle	Permissible limit in dB (w.e.f from 1.1.2003)
1.	Two wheelers	
	upto 80 CC	75
	80CC-175 CC	77
	Above 175 CC	80
2.	Three Wheelers	
	Upto 175 CC	77
	Above 175 CC	80
3.	Passenger Car	75
4.	Passenger vehicles	
	Upto 4 tonn	77
	4-12 tonn	80
	Above 12 tonn	82

22. Energy flow in ecosystems.

Ans. At each transfer from one trophic level to another in a food chain or web, work is done, low-quality heat is given off to the environment, and the availability of high-quality energy to organisms at the next trophic level is reduced. This reduction in high-quality energy available at each trophic level is the result of the inevitable energy quality tax imposed by the second law of energy.

The percentage of available high-quality energy transferred from one trophic level to another varies from 2% to 30%, depending on the types of species involved and the ecosystem in which the transfer takes place. In the wild, ecologists estimate that an average of about 10% of the high-quality chemical energy available at one trophic level is transferred and stored in usable form as chemical energy in the bodies of the organisms at the next level. The rest of the energy is used to keep the organisms alive, and most is eventually degraded and lost to the environment as low-quality heat in compliance with the second law of energy. Some of it is transferred to decomposers, which use a small amount to stay alive and degrade the rest to low-quality heat.

There is a (in figure) loss of usable-quality energy at each step in a simple food chain. The **pyramids of energy flow and energy loss** in this diagram show that the greater the number of trophic levels or steps in a food chain or web, the greater the cumulative loss of usable high-quality energy.

The energy flow pyramid explains why a larger population of people can be supported if people shorten the food chain by eating grains directly (for example, rice → human) rather than eating animals that feed on grains (grain → steer → human). To prevent protein malnutrition, a vegetarian diet must include a variety of plants that provide enough of the 10 nitrogen-containing amino acid molecules used to make proteins that our bodies cannot synthesize. Poor people surviving on a plant diet often don't have enough money to grow or purchase the variety of plants needed to avoid protein malnutrition.

23. Biofertilizers.

Ans. Biofertilizer are the biologically active products or microbial inoculants of bacteria, algae and fungi, which may help biological nitrogen fixation for the benefit of plants. Biofertilizers also include organic fertilizers (manures, etc.), which are rendered in an available form due to the interaction of micro-organisms or due to the interaction of micro-organisms or due to their association with plants. Biiofertilizers thus include (i) symbiotic nitrogen fixers e.g. *Rhizobium* spp.; (ii) asymbiotic free nitrogen fixer e.g.

Azotobacter, Azospirillum, etc. (*iii*) algae biofertillizers e.g. blue green algae or BGA in association with *Azolla;* (*iv*) phosphate solubilising bacteria; (*v*) mycorrhizae; (*vi*) organic fertilizers.

The need for the use of biofertilzers has arisen, primarily of two reasons. First, because increase in the use of fertilizers leads to increased usage of chemical fertiliizer leads to damage in soil texture and raises other environmental problems. Therefore, the use of biofertilzers is both economical and environmetns friendly. The pragmatic approach will be to develop the integrated nutrient supply system involving a combination of the use of chemical fertilizers and biofertilizers.

Rhizobia are able to enter into symbiotic relationship with legumes (pulses, etc.). They fix atmospheric nitrogen and thus not only increase the production of the inoculated crops, but also leave a fair amount of nitrogen in the soil, which benefits the subsequent crop. Following seven groups of *Rhizobia* have been recognised for inoculating legumes in India: *R. leguminosarum, R. japonicum* and *Rhizobium spp.* The new technology for industrial preparation for rhizobial cultures included the following : (*i*) seed pelleting with gum arabic or crboxy methyl cellulose as percoated seed (*ii*) polyacrylamide entrapped rhizobia; (*iii*) frezedried or lyophilzed culture of rhizobia; (*iv*) *Rhizobium* paste; (*v*) inoculants in liquid/frozen concentrate form; (*vi*) granular soil inoculants to be applied by aerial application; (*vii*) natural peat granule as soil implant inoculum.

24. Hazardous waste management.

Ans. There are various alternative waste treatment technologies e.g. physical treatment, chemical treatment, biological treatment, incineration etc. These process are used to recycle and reuse waste materials reduce the volume and toxicity of a waste stream or produce a final residual material that is suitable for disposal.

Physical Treatment

This includes processes that separate components of a waste stream or change the physical form of the waste without alterning the chemical structure of the material. Commonly used physical processes are as follows:

1. *Screening and Sedimentation.*
2. *Flotation*–Removes solids from liquids by floating the particles to the surface by using tiny air bubbles.
3. *Filtration*–Process for separating liquids and solids by using various types of porous materials.
4. *Centrifugation*–Process for separating solid and liquid components by rapidly rotating a mixture of solids and liquids indise a vessel.
5. *Dialysis*–Process for separating components in a liquid steam by using membrane components of a liquid stream will diffuse through the membrane if a stream with greater concentration of the component is on the other side of membrane.
6. *Electrodialysis*–It is an extension of dialysis. This process is used to separate the components of an ionic solution by applying electric current.
7. *Reverse Osmosis*–It separates components by applying external pressures to one side of membrane.
8. *Ultra filtration*–It is similar to reverse osmosis but the separation beings at higher molecular weights.
9. *Distillation*–Process of separating liquids with deferent boilings poings. The mixed liquid stream is exposed to increasing amounts of heat and the various components of the mixture are vaporized and recovered.

Chemical Treatment

These alter the chemical structure of the constituents of the waste to produce less hazardous material. Chemical processes are attractive because they produce minimal air emissions, they can be carried out on the site. Commonly used chemical treatments are given below :

1. *Neutralization*–Process for reducing the acidity or alkalinity by mixing acids and bases.
2. *Precipitation*–Process for removing soluble compounds.
3. *Dechlorination*–A process for stripping chlorine atoms from chlorinated compounds.
4. *Oxidation-reduction-Process* for detoxifying toxic wastes in which the chemical bonds are broken.

Biological Treatment

It includes processes that use microorganisms to decompose organic wastes either into water, CO_2 and simple inorganic substances.

The purpose of biological treatment system is to control the environment for microorganisms so their growth and activity are enhanced.

Various biological treatments are:

1. Activated sludge Process
2. Aerated Lagoon
3. Trickling filters
4. Stabilization Pond
5. Anaerobic digestion

25. Rainwater harvesting.

Ans. Collection of rain water from paved or G.I. corrugated roofs and paved courts yards of houses, known as rainwater harvesting, is common in areas having high rainfall intensity well distributed in the years. Such areas include: Himalayan areas, north eastern states, Andaman and Nicobar islands, Lakshadweep, Rajasthan and southern parts of Kerela and Tamil Nadu.

Rainwater harvesting is now being increasingly used for meeting the drinking water needs of rural areas, particularly during the periods of drought.

Many methods are available for harvesting of rainwater. The choice of a method depends upon the suitability of a particular site. Following steps are followed in rainwater harvesting from roofs:

1. Collection of rainwater
2. Separation of first rain flush
3. Filtration of rainwater
4. Storage of rainwater
5. Distribution of water

Before supplying for human consumption, the raw water from the pond should, however, be filtered through a sand filter and kept in a PVC tank connected to a hand pump for withdrawal. Despite certain limitations, rain water harvesting will be beneficial for providing drinking water to human beings as well as cattle in areas lacking alternative sources.

SECTION-IV

Note: This section consists of one essay type question of forty (40) marks to be answered in about one thousand (1000) words on any of the following topics.

(40 × 1 = 40 marks)

26. Write on *any one* of the following:

(a) Discuss various methods of solid waste management.

OR

(b) Use of plant biomass for biofuel production.

OR

(c) "Hotspots" of biodiversity with special reference to India.

OR

(d) Environmental priorities in India and sustainable development.

OR

(e) Salient features of Kyoto protocol and various mechanisms for its implementation.

OR

(f) Toxic chemicals in air and water. Methodologies of Environmental Impact Assessment.

OR

(g) Remote sensing and its application to Environmental Sciences.

Ans. The activities involved with the management of solid wastes from the point generation to final disposal have been grouped into six functional element:

1. Waste generation
2. On-site handling, storage and processing
3. Collection
4. Transfer and transport
5. Processing and recovery
6. Disposal

The functional elements are described in the table below:

Description of the functional elements of a solid managements system

TABLE

Functional element	Description
Waste generation	Those activities in which materials are identified as no longer being of value and are either thrown away or gathered together for disposal.
On-site handling, storageing and processing	Those activities associated with the handling, storage and process of solid waste at or near the point of generation.
Collection	Those activities associated with the gathering of solid wastes and the hauling of wastes after collection to the location where the collection vehicle is emptied.
Transfer and transport	Those activities associated with (1) the transfer to wastes from the smaller collection vehicle to the larger transport equipment and (2) the subsequent transport of the wastes to the disposal site.

| Processing and recovery | Those techniques, cover equipment and facilities used both to improve the efficiency of the other functional elements and to recover materials or energy from solid wastes. |
| Disposal | Those activities associated with ultimate disposal of solid waste, including those waste collected and transported directly to landfill site. |

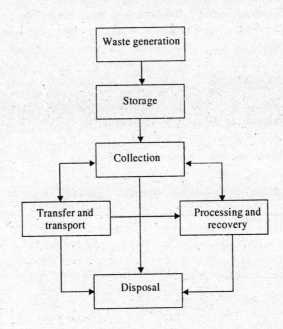

Interrelationship of functional elements of a solid waste management system

On-Site Handling

On-site handling refers to the activities associated with the handling of solid wastes until they are placed in the containers used for their storage before collection. Depending on the type of collection service, handling may also be required to move loaded containers to the collection point and to return the empty containers to the point where they are stored between collections.

On-Site Storage

The factors that must be considered in the on-site storage of solid wastes include:
1. The type of container to be used
2. The container location
3. Public health and aesthetics
4. Collection methods to be used

Containers

To a large extent, the types and capacities of containers used depend on the characteristics of the solid waste to be collected, the collection frequency and the space available for the placement of containers.

Container Locations

In newer residential areas, containers for solid waste usually are placed by the side or near of the house. In older residential areas containers are located in allyes. In low-rise multi family appart-ments large containers are often placed in specially designed and designated enclosures.

On-Site Processing of Solid Wastes

On-site processing methods are used to recover usable materials from solid wastes, to reduce volume, or to alter the physical form. The most common on-site processing operations include manual sorting, compaction and incineration.

COLLECTION ON SOLID WASTES

Information on collection, one of the most costly functional elements, is presented in four parts dealing with

1. The types of collection services
2. The types of collection systems
3. An analysis of collection systems
4. The general methodology involved in setting up collection routes

Hauled-Container Systems (HCS)

Collection systems in which the containers used for the storage of wastes are hauled to the processing, transfer, or disposal site, emptied and returned to either their original location or some other location are defined as hauled-container systems. There are two main types of hauled-container systems:

1. Tilt-frame container
2. Trash-trailer

TRANSFER MEANS AND METHODS OF SOLID WASTE

Motor vehicles, railroads, and ocean going vessels are the principal means now used to transport solid wastes. Pneumatic and hydraulic systems have also been used.

Motor Vehicle Transport

Motor vehicles used to transport solid wastes on highways should satisfy the following requirements

1. the vehicles must transport wastes at minimum costs
2. waste must be covered during the haul operation
3. vehicles must be designed for highway traffic
4. vehicles capacity must be such that allowable weight limits are not exceeded
5. methods used for unloading must be simple and dependable

Railroad Transport

Although railroad were commonly used for the transport of solid wastes in the past, they are now used by only a few communities. However, renewed interests is again developing in the use of railroads for hauling solid wastes, especially to remote areas were highway travel is difficult and railroad lines now exist.

Water Transport

Barges, scows, and special boats have been used in the past to transport solid wastes to processing locations and to sea side and ocean disposal sites, but ocean disposal is no longer practiced now.

TRADITIONAL MEANS OF WASTE MANAGEMENT

In the twentieth century, humans have dealt with solid wastes in three basic ways: (1) by burning the waste, thus essentially injecting much of it, converted to gases and smoke, into the atmosphere (2) by storing wastes, including the leftover as from burning, in dumps, impoundments, and most recently sanitary landfills; and (3) by injecting or burying wastes in rock cavities deep underground (a method proposed for the disposal of industrial and conventional toxic or hazardous waste, as described below, and also for radioactive waste. Each of these waste disposal methodologies has its proponents and its critics. In the next few sections, we will consider each briefly.

Incineration

In the industrial technique of incineration, trash and garbage and burned in large furnace at high temperatures to get rid off much of the refuse as possible. Of course, burning trash is a time-honored procedure, but use of large incinerators dates back only to the late nineteenth century. .

During their first 50 years of existence, incinerators were in and out of fashion. Many early incinerators were relatively inefficient caused massive pollution, and left large quantities of ash and other nonburables. But by World War II, some seven hundred new and improved incinerators were operating throughout the world.

Some appartment buildings even had small incinerators to burn the residents' trash. Nevertheless, incinerators continued to cause problems. Aesthetically, incinerators were an offensive intrusion on the skyline, and people who lived near them complained of the odours and said the smoke and gases caused respiratory problems. The increasing environmental awareness of the late 1960s and early 1970s continued to erode people's confidence in, and tolerance of, incinerators. The Air Quality Act of 1967 and Clean Air Act Amendments of 1970 established new emission standards that many existing incinerators did not meet; most operators simply closed their incinerators rather than adding costly emission control devices.

But shutting down the incinerators meant that the trash and garbage had to be disposed of some other way. The preferred alternative was sanitary landfills. But by the late 1970s and early 1980s, many cities and municipalities were finding that their landfills were running out of space, and there were fewer and fewer sites available, at least politically. An apparent solution to this predicament was presented by a new breed of incinerators known as resource recovery plants.

Mass-burn incinerators take a more direct approach to the waste. The unsorted trash and garbage are simply fed into a furnace that burns the refuse at very high temperatures 980 to 1100°C). The heat from the burning refuse is used to produce steam that drives a turbine to generate electricity. Whatever is not burned in the incinerator is removed and simple disposed of (for instance, in a landfill).

UGC-NET ENVIRONMENTAL SCIENCE, DECEMBER 2008

PAPER-II

Note : *This paper contains **fifty** (50) multiple-choice questions, each question carrying **two** (2) marks. Attempt **all** of them.*

1. Plants suitable for biomonitoring of SO_2 pollution are:
   A. White pine, moss and lichens
   B. Tobacco, grapes and garden bean
   C. Apricot, peach and gladiolas
   D. Tomato and lettuce

2. Which of the following survive by forming spores?
   A. *Escherichia coli*   B. *Rhizobium*
   C. *Clostridium*   D. *Salmonella*

3. *Deinococcus* and *Deinobacter* are radiation resistant bacteria because:
   A. They have effective repair mechanism for damaged DNA and have high concentration of carotenoids
   B. They do not absorb radiations
   C. They have RNA instead of DNA
   D. They grow in ice

4. The orchid seeds do not germinate under ordinary conditions because :
   A. Orchid seeds are too large for dispersal
   B. Orchid seeds do not have endosperm
   C. Orchid seeds undergo a dormancy period
   D. They germinate under very dry conditions

5. Which of the following is for rhizosphere?
   A. Region where soil and roots make contact
   B. Apical part of root
   C. Epidermal part of the root
   D. Root hairs

6. Suppose the number of individual prey population is N_1 and their intrinsic rate of population increase N_1, where:
   $r_1 = b - m$
   b = birth rate per individual

   m = mortality rate per individual, then the rate of change of the prey population (dN_1/dt) (without immigration and emigration) is as below :
   A. $\frac{1}{2}r_1N_1$ B. r_1N_1
   C. $(r_1N_1)^2$ D. $(r_1N_1)^{1/2}$

7. The photosynthetic zone is limited to the upper layers of water in the soil with a high intensity of productivity per unit volume, yielding an average of about:
   A. 300 mg c m^{-2} hr^{-1} B. 250 mg c m^{-2} hr^{-1}
   C. 100 mg c m^{-2} hr^{-1} D. 75 mg c m^{-2} hr^{-1}

8. **Assertion (A):** Copper - T is used as a contraceptive.

   Reason (R): Copper of Copper - T disrupts production of some reproductive hormone.
   A. Both **(A)** and **(R)** are true and **(R)** is correct explanation of **(A)**
   B. Both **(A)** and **(R)** are true but **(R)** is not correct explanation of **(A)**
   C. **(A)** is true but **(R)** is false
   D. **(A)** is false but **(R)** is true

9. Asbestos use is banned in many countries. It is known to cause
   A. Cardiac diseases   B. Urinary diseases
   C. Lung cancer   D. Cataract

10. Which of the following is used as a carrier for the *Rhizobium* biofertilization?
    A. Peat bog   B. Salt
    C. Sand   D. Cow dung

11. The flow in natural streams is almost always turbulent and may be assumed to be incompressible, consequently the applicable equations of motion for the fluid are the:
    A. Bed-load equation   B. Reynolds equation
    C. Lane's model   D. Lacey's equation

12. Suspended sediment load is that part of the sediment load which is transported within the main body flow. The primary mechanism of maintaining the sediment particles in suspension is:
  A. Channel flow
  B. Particle size
  C. Turbulent diffusion
  D. Dissolved gasses

13. A highly vesicular material derived from acidic lavas and produced in very large quantities is known as:
  A. Scoriae
  B. Volcanic bomb
  C. Pumice
  D. Tuff

14. Half life (T) of a radioactive sample is given by:
  A. $0.693/\lambda$
  B. $1.693/\lambda$
  C. $0.693/2\lambda$
  D. $1.693/2\lambda$
  Where λ is the disintegration constant

15. At the present time volcanoes are confined to certain limited areas of the Earth's surface. This special zone is called:
  A. Trans-Atlantic volcanic zone
  B. Circum-Pacific Ring of fire
  C. Central-Asian inter-continental zone
  D. Indian-Ocean volcanic belt

16. When the cavities between the mineral grains in a rock contains fluid, it is called
  A. Permeable rock
  C. Cavernous rock
  B. Porous rock
  D. Fractured rock

17. Temperature in the troposphere:
  A. Decreases with height
  B. Rapidly increases with height
  C. Slowly increases with height
  D. Remains constant

18. Failure to explain the black body radiation emission spectrum in the ultraviolet region (ultraviolet catastrophe) has occurred in:
  A. Plancks radiation law
  B. Rayleigh Jeans law
  C. Wiens Displacement law
  D. Stephans Boltzmann law

19. A noise signal can be characterized through its amplitude/energy content in the signal. The signal can be expressed in various forms like root mean square value, given as:

A. $\left[\dfrac{1}{T} \int_0^T a^2(t)dt \right]^{1/2}$

B. $\left[\dfrac{1}{2T} \int_0^T a^2(t)dt \right]^{1/2}$

C. $\left[\dfrac{1}{T} \int_0^T |a| \cdot dt \right]$

D. $\left[\dfrac{1}{2T} \int_0^T |a| \cdot dt \right]$

Where T is the relevant time period over which the averaging takes place and a(t) the instantaneous amplitude.

20. Sound pressure level (dB) can be expressed as:

A. $20 \log_{10} \left(\dfrac{\text{Measured pressure}}{\text{Reference pressure}} \right)$

B. $20 \log_{10} \left(\dfrac{\text{Reference pressure}}{\text{Measured pressure}} \right)$

C. $20 \log_{10} \left(\dfrac{\text{Reference pressure}}{\text{Measured pressure}} \right)^{1/2}$

D. $20 \log_{10} \left(\dfrac{\text{Measured pressure}}{\text{Reference pressure}} \right)^{1/2}$

21. Relationship regarding wave particle duality ($P = h/\lambda$, P = momentum, h = Plancks constant and λ, The wave length), was given by:
  A. Heisenberg
  B. de Broglie
  C. Neils Bohr
  D. Schroedinger

22. The effect of low level non-ionizing electromagnetic radiation effects on bilogical systems can be classified in the following category:
  A. Instantaneous
  B. Delayed
  C. Not at all
  D. Prolonged

23. Which of the following is a recalcitrant?
  A. Sugarcane waste
  B. DDT
  C. Lignin
  D. Cellulose

24. A small reduction in ozone concentration can lead to a large increase in the amount of harmful ultraviolet radiations reaching the earth in the wavelength region:
  A. 200 – 205 nm
  B. 220 – 225 nm
  C. 260 – 265 nm
  D. 295 – 300 nm

25. The planet nearest to the Sun is:
  A. Earth
  B. Mercury
  C. Moon
  D. Jupitor

26. Steel units generate which of the following air pollutants:
    A. Particulates, smoke, carbon monoxide, fluoride
    B. SO_2, acid mist
    C. NO_X, SO_2, particulates
    D. SO_2, NO_X, particulates, smoke

27. In a soil profile, O_2 concentration:
    A. Increases vertically from top to bottom
    B. Increases horizontally but not vertically
    C. Decreases vertically from top to bottom
    D. Both vertically and horizontally increases randomly

28. Mobile phone frequencies are in the range of:
    A. 1kHz – 100kHz
    B. 100kHz – 100MHz
    C. 100MHz – 700MHz
    D. 800MHz – 2200MHz

29. Elements in sea water present in order of increasing residence time:
    A. Na > Cl > Mg > Ca > K > Fe > P
    B. Cl > Na > Mg > Ca > K > P > Fe
    C. Cl > Mg > Ca > Na > K > Fe > P
    D. Mg > Ca > Cl > Na > K > P > Fe

30. **Assertion (A):** Aerosols heave potential for modifying the climate.
    Reason (R): Aerosols interact with both short wave and infra-red radiation.
    A. Both (A) and (R) are true and (R) is the correct explanation of (A)
    B. Both (A) and (R) are true but (R) is not the correct explanation of (A)
    C. (A) is true but (R) is false
    D. (A) is false but (R) is true

31. Out of the following which is not a greenhouse gas:
    A. CH_4
    B. CO_2
    C. N_2O
    D. SO_2

32. Ozone "hole" in the stratosphere was discovered over the continent of:
    A. North America
    B. Australia
    C. Antarctica
    D. Greenland

33. Which of the following layers of Earth have the composition of peridotite?

A. Upper Mantle
B. Inner Core
C. Outer Core
D. Continental Crust

34. Sedimentary component which is produced in-situ within the pore spaces is called :
    A. Primary
    B. Authigenic
    C. Allogenic
    D. Orogenic

35. Stoke's law of settling velocity simplified as $V \propto \frac{1}{d^n}$ suggest that:
    A. A large particle 100μm in diameter will settle slowly compared to a smaller 10μm particle
    B. A large particle 100μm in diameter, will settle faster than a smaller particle 10 μm
    C. Both a large 100 μm particle and a small 10 μm particle will settle in a column of 10 cm. at the same time.
    D. Small particle 10 μm in diameter will settle faster, while coarser particle of 100 μm diameter will remain in suspension.

36. Which of these remote sensing tool is commonly used for groundwater exploration and soil moisture determinations:
    A. Colour composite imageries
    B. Band 5 spectra
    C. Infra Red spectra
    D. Black and white Aerial photos

37. The atmosphere is divided in four layers. The layer in contact with the surface of the Earth is called:
    A. Stratosphere
    B. Troposphere
    C. Mesosphere
    D. Ionosphere

38. A ship (X) moving due North with a velocity (v) observes that another ship (Y) is moving due west, the actual velocity of (Y) is:
    A. (v) is due East
    B. ($\sqrt{2}v$) is towards North West
    C. (v) is towards South East
    D. ($\sqrt{2}v$) is towards North East

39. The solubility of Fe in water:
    A. Increases with increasing pH
    B. Decreases with increasing pH
    C. Independent of pH
    D. Dependent only on redox potential and not pH

40. A cube of ice with radius of 100 mm is formed at 3° C. When ice melts, the final volume will be:
   A. 1000 cm³   B. 1250 cm³
   C. 1000 mm³   D. 1750 mm³

41. Which of the following phenomena can be explained by the wave model of light, but not by the particle model?
   A. Pressure is exerted by a light beam
   B. All of the energy emitted by an atom, as light can later be completely transferred to another atom
   C. A light beam changes direction when passing from one medium to another
   D. Light can reach the geometrical shadow of an obstacle in its path

42. 2 ppm of CO at 25°C and 760 mm of Hg pressure is equivalent to
   A. 1250 µg/m³   B. 1145 µg/m³
   C. 2500 µg/m³   D. 2290 µg/m³

43. Which waves carry most energy?
   A. UV light   B. Infra-red light
   C. Microwaves   D. Millimeter waves

44. If one wishes to measure total As, As^{+3} and As^{+5} in a sample the most suitable analytical tool is:
   A. Atomic Absorption spectrophotometer
   B. Ion chromatograph
   C. Scanning Electron Microscope
   D. Gas chromatograph

45. The acid rains result from chemical transformation and transport of:
   A. Sulfur dioxide and nitrogen oxide
   B. Phosphorus pentaoxide and sulfur compound
   C. Chlorine gas and nitrous oxide
   D. Iron oxide and copper nitrate

46. Any particulate matter, gas, or combination thereof other than water vapour is called:
   A. Air curtain   B. Air emission
   C. Air monitoring   D. Air contaminant

47. The chemical system for removal of the ions of salt, is called:
   A. Ion transfer   B. Ionization
   C. Ion exchange   D. Ion vaporization

48. At ordinary temperatures, the molecules of a diatomic gas have only translational and rotational kinetic energies. At high temperatures, they may have vibrational energy. As a result of this, compared to lower temperatures, a diatomic gas at higher temperatures will have :
   A. Lower molar heat capacity
   B. Higher molar heat capacity
   C. Lower isothermal compressibility
   D. Higher isothermal compressibility

49. In the periodic table of elements :
   A. Non-metallic property increases vertically
   B. Metallic property increases from right to left
   C. Non-metallic property increases from right to left
   D. Metallic property increases left to right and from top to bottom

50. Polychlorinated biphenyls (PCBs) which cause environmental exposure risk have these important properties:
   A. Very high volatility in air
   B. Chemically unstable and highly reactive
   C. Heat stable and have no flash or fire point
   D. Highly soluble in water and poorly soluble in oils and organic solvents

ANSWERS

1	2	3	4	5	6	7	8	9	10
A	C	B	D	D	B	A	C	C	A
11	12	13	14	15	16	17	18	19	20
D	A	C	A	B	A	A	B	C	A

21	22	23	24	25	26	27	28	29	30
D.	A	C	A	B	D	C	B	A	B

31	32	33	34	35	36	37	38	39	40
D	C	B	C	D	D	B	C	B	D

41	42	43	44	45	46	47	48	49	50
C	D	B	A	A	B	C	C	D	D

PAPER-III

Note: This paper is of two hundred (200) marks containing four (4) sections. Candidates are required to attempt the questions contained in these sections according to the detailed instructions given therein.

SECTION-I

Note: This section contains five (5) questions based on the following paragraph. Each question should be answered in about thirty (30) words and each carries five (5) marks. (5 × 5 = 25 marks)

The eutrophication is the nutrient enrichment in a water body. A freshly formed body of water has a very low concentration of plant nutrients. Little plant life develops in such waters. Low primary production limits animal communities as well. Surface runoffs, wind borne dust and organic debris, excreta and exudates of animals which use water, slowly raise the nutrient content. Bacteria and cyanobacteria fix atmospheric nitrogen. Phosphates in rocks and detritus at the bottom are solubilized by the microbial activity. In gradual stages the nutrient status of the water improves. A moderate population of plants, animals, aquatic fungi and other microorganisms develop. With the passage of time further nutrient enrichment occurs. Dense population of plants, phytoplanktons and animals now appears. At this stage, the aquatic system becomes highly productive in terms of fish yield and other produce. Based on nutrient status and productivity an aquatic system can be classified into the following three types: The oligotrophic or water with poor nutrient status and productivity; the mesotrophic or water with intermediate or moderate nutrient status and productivity; and eutrophic or water with rich nutrient status with high productivity. In some eutrophic waters dense population of planktonic algae develops, water turns green followed by unpleasant odour referred to as water bloom.

Answer the following questions :

1. Define the term eutrophication.

Ans. The process of again of a body of water by the growth of vegetation particularly algae, these plants flourish and then die, their decay using up the dissolved Oxygen of water with serious impairment of water quality, in lakes, rivers, harbors, and estuaries, the accumulation of nutrients.

2. What results eutrophication?

Ans. In eutrophication, algal bloom release chemicals which kill fish and other aquatic animals when oxygen fall to zero i.e., anaerobic zone same bacteria drive oxygen through reduction of nitrates on complete exhaustion of nitrate, oxygen may be last resort be obtained by reduction of sulphate yielding hydrogen sulphide (H_2S) causing foul smell and bad taste of water.

3. Which are the organisms that fix up nitrogen?

Ans. Certain bacteria e.g. *Azotobacter* and blue-green algae e.g. *Anabaena,* Phizobium are able to fix nitrogen in association with cells in the roots of leguminous plants such as pear and beans, in which they form characteristic root nodules, cultivation of legumes is therefore one way of increasing soil nitrogen.

4. Name the types of eutrophication.

Ans. Eutrophication is of two types.

(*i*) *Cultural Eutrophication:* St is due to human activities which are responsible for 80% nitrogen and 75% of phosphorous to streams and lakes.

(*ii*) *Natural Eutrophication:* It is due to natural activities/reasons.

5. What is water bloom?

Ans. An algal bloom is a rapid increase or accumulation in the population of algae in an aquatic system. Algal blooms may occur in freshwater as well as marine environments. Typically, only one or a small number of phytoplankton species are involved, and some blooms may be recognized by discoloration of the water resulting from the high density of pigmented cells.

SECTION-II

Note: This section contains fifteen (15) questions each to be answered in about thirty (30) words. Each question carries five (5) marks.

(5 × 15 = 75 marks)

6. Repetitive DNA.

Ans. Repetitive DNA: Part of DNA containing the same sequence of N_2 bases repeated several times in tandem occur near telomere, centromere, pericontric and other heterochromatic area.

7. Transgenic plants.

Ans. Transgenic plants are those plants, which carry additional, stably integrated and expressed, foreign gene(s) from transpecies. The whole process involving introduction, integration and expression of foreign gene(s) in the host, is called genetic transformation. The combined use of recombinant DNA technology, gene transfer methods and tissue culture techniques has led to the efficient transformation and production of transgenics, in a wide variety of crop plants. Unlike conventional breeding, only the cloned gene(s) of agronomic importance is being introduced without the cotransfer of other undesirable gene from the donor. The recipient genotype is least disturbed and there is no need for repeated back crosses. This will serve as an effective means of removing certain specific defect of otherwise well adopted cultivars.

8. 'Hot spots' of biodiversity.

Ans. The concept of 'hot spots' of biodiversity was developed in the year 1988 by Norman Myes. According to him " 'hot spots' are the richest and the most threatened reservoirs of plants and animal life on earth." This concept was developed on the basis of two important consideration (*i*) The species which are not founds elsewhere and (*ii*) difference of loss of habitat.

9. Acid rain

Ans. Acid rain is an environmental problem that knows no boundaries. Increasing acidity in natural waters and soil has become a global concern. Acidification and climate change are interrelated, as the sources responsible for acidification of environment and green house gases are same. Normally unpolluted rain water is always slightly acidic, because CO_2 in atmosphere dissolve in it forming carbonic acid H_2CO_3. The pH of unpolluted rain water is about 5.5–5.7. But due to presence of SO_2 and NO_2 gases as pollutants in the atmosphere, the pH of rain is further lowered. Often as low as 2.4 and this type of precipitation is generally referred to as acid rain.

10. Air quality monitoring (AAQ)

Ans. Monitoring Air Quality: The Air Quality Index (AQI) is a rating scale for outdoor air in Ontario. The lower the AQI, the better the air quality.

Based on data from its network of air monitoring stations, the Ministry of the Environment reports an AQI for many communities across Ontario to all major media outlets and the Ministry web site hourly.

These pollutants were chosen because they have an adverse effect on humans and the environment at high levels.

The air monitoring data are sent to a computer centre at the ministry. Data are compared to ambient air quality standards for each of the six air pollutants. These scientifically-based standards, which are updated from time to time, indicate the maximum safe level for a pollutant. Above this level, the pollutant begins to have an undesirable impact on people and the environment.

The monitoring data are converted into the AQI scale. The scale ranges from 0-15 (very good) to 100+ (very poor).

11. Marine spillage.

Ans. Oil spills can have serious effects on marine life, as highlighted by the photos of dead birds which regularly appear in the news after such an event. Such images fuel the perception of widespread and permanent environmental damage after every spill, and an inevitable loss of marine resources with serious economic repercussions. A science-based appraisal of the effects reveals that whilst damage occurs and may be profound at the level of individual organisms, populations are more resilient and natural recovery processes are capable of repairing the damage and returning the system to normal functions.

12. Role of algae in biodiesel production.

Ans. Several companies and government agencies are funding efforts to reduce capital and operating costs and make algae fuel production commercially viable. The production of biofuels from algae does not reduce atmospheric carbon dioxide (CO_2), because any CO_2 taken out of the atmosphere by the algae is returned when the biofuels are burned. They do however potentially reduce the introduction of new CO_2 by displacing fossil hydrocarbon fuels.

13. Scanning Electron Microscopy (SEM).

Ans. The scanning electron microscope (SEM) is a type of electron microscope that images the sample surface by scanning it with a high-energy beam of electrons in a raster scan pattern. The electrons interact with the atoms that make up the sample producing signals that contain information about the sample's surface topography, composition and other properties such as electrical conductivity.

14. Applications of Diatoms

Ans. Diatoms are algae and they are capable of photosynthesis. They can be found in almost everywhere in the world especially in aquatic environments. Even though they are considered as non motile, they are capable of limited movements. Since they depend on photosynthesis for their energy, they are restricted in environment where sunlight is available. They have a skeleton composed of silicon. Two forms of diatoms are existing; benthic and planktic. The dimensions of diatoms are measured in microns. The length of diatoms range from 20 to 200 microns but they can grow up to few millimeters. They have an economical value as they are used to produce filters, paints and toothpaste.

15. Internal structure of Earth.

Ans. The Earth is composed of a thin crust, a thick mantle, and a core. The three layers are distinguished by different chemical compositions. In turn, both the mantle and core contain finer layers based on changing physical properties. Scientists have learned a remarkable amount about the Earth's structure even though the deepest well is only a 12 kilometer hole in northern Russia.

16. Carrying capacity of a river.

Ans. Geomatics tools have been used as aide to study the carrying capacity of a river. In order to facilitate future planning for the river basis, it carrying capacity studied with reference to its resources and degradation in land and water.

17. Biomagnification and bioaccumulation.

Ans. *Biomagnification:* There are many pesticides e.g. DDT, aldrin, and dieldrin, which have a long life in the environment. They are fat soluble and non-biodegradable. They get magnified in the higher trophie level which is called bio magnification or biological amplification. Bioaccumulation. Accumulation of elements and compounds in living organisms which is a frequent phenomenon in alga and aquatie used species in waters. Some of the known harmful accumulates are DDT, aldrin, dieldrin, cadmium, lead and Mercury.

18. Environmental audit.

Ans. Environmental audit is defined as basic management tool which comprises, a systematic, documented, periodic and objective evaluation of how well organization, management systems and equipment's are performing."

It can also be defined as "A systematic, documented verification process of objectively obtaining and evaluating evidence to determine whether specified environmental activities, events, conditions, management, systems or information about there matters conform with audit criteria and communicating the results of this process to the client.

19. Carbonate compensation depth.

Ans. Carbonate compensation depth (CCD) is the depth in the oceans below which the rate of supply of calcite (calcium carbonate) lags behind the rate of solvation, such that no calcite is preserved. Aragonite compensation depth (hence ACD) describes the same behaviour in reference to aragonitic carbonates. By the time the CCD is reached all calcium carbonate has dissolved according to this equation:

$$CaCO_3 + CO_2 + H_2O \rightleftharpoons Ca^{2+} (aq) + 2HCO_3^- (aq)$$

20. Water quality index

Ans.   **Water Quality Standards**

Constituents	Indian Standard (1993)		WHO	
	Desirable Limits	Maximum Permissible Limits (ppm)	Desirable Limits (ppm)	Maximum Permissible Limits (ppm)
1. pH	6.5-8.5	6.5-9.5	7.0-8.5	6.5-8.2
2. Total Hardness	300	600	100	500
3. Calcium	75	200	75	200
4. Magnesium	30	100	–	150
5. Sodium	–	100	–	80
6. Chloride	250	1000	200	600
7. Copper	0.05	1.5	0.05	1.5
8. Iron	0.3	1.0	0.1	1.0

9.	Manganese	0.1	0.5	0.05	0.5
10.	Cadmium	0.01	NR	–	0.1
11.	Lead	0.1	NR	–	0.1
12.	Zinc	0.05	0.15	0.05	0.15
13.	Chromium	0.05	NR	–	0.05

SECTION-III

Note: *This section contains five (5) questions. Each question carries twelve (12) marks and is to be answered in about two hundred (200) words.*

(12 × 5 = 60 marks)

21. Ecological succession.

Ans. Every community undergoes a series of changes until a group in the area. This is called biotic succession. Succession is a sequence of changes in time of the species which inhabit an area from an initial pioneer community to a final climax community. In other word, the development of community by the action of vegetation on the environment leading to the development of new species is called succession.

Why Succession

Succession involves a series of complex processes. It is because of this reason that the occurrence of succession is associated with many causes. These exist three primary causes of succession.

(i) The first cause is concerned with climatic and biotic in nature. The climatic causes are erosion, deposits, wind and fire etc. All of these are responsible for destroying the existing population in the concerned area.

(ii) The second cause is concerned with migration, aggregation, completition reaction etc. These are responsible for changing the soil features of this area.

(iii) The third cause is concerned with factors such as climate of the area responsible for stabilisation of the community.

Types of Succession

The succession is of different types, which are as under :

(1) The succession which starts from a primitive substrate without any previous living matter is called **primary succession.** It starts on an area which is not occupied previously by a community.

(2) The succession starting from an area where living matter already exists, is known as **secondary succession.** Secondary succession is faster than primary succession.

(3) In case the existing community causes its own community as a result of its reaction with the environment, it is known as **autogenic succession.**

(4) In case the replacement of one community takes place by another due to forces other than the effects of communities on the environment, the succession is called **allogenic succession.** Such a kind of succession may occur in highly disturbed area or in ponds where the nutrients and pollutants enter from outside which in turn modify the environment and thus communities.

(5) The early and continued dominance of autotrophic organisms such as green plants is called **autotrophic succession.** This type of succession take place in an inorganic environment.

(6) The early dominance of heterotrophic organisms such as bacteria, fungi, animals and actinomycetes is called **heterotrophic succession.**

22. Kyoto Protocol.

Ans. The Kyoto Protocol is a protocol to the United Nations Framework Convention on Climate Change (UNFCCC or FCCC), aimed at fighting global warming. The UNFCCC is an international environmental treaty with the goal of achieving "stabilization of greenhouse gas concentrations in the atmosphere at a level that would prevent dangerous anthropogenic interference with the climate system.

The protocol was initially adopted on 11 December 1997 in Kyoto, Japan and entered into force on 16 February 2005. As of July 2010, 191 states have signed and ratified the protocol.

Under the Protocol, 37 countries ("Annex I countries") commit themselves to a reduction of four greenhouse gases (GHG) (carbon dioxide, methane, nitrous oxide, sulphur hexafluoride) and two groups of gases (hydroflurocarbons and perfluorocarbons) produced by them, and all member countries give general commitments. Annex I countries agreed to reduce their collective greenhouse gas emissions by 5.2% from the 1990 level. Emission limits do not include emissions by international aviation and shipping, but are in addition to the industrial gases, chlorofluorocarbons, or CFCs, which are death with under the 1987 Montreal Protocol on Substances that Deplete the Ozone Layer.

The benchmark 1990 emission levels were accepted by the Conference of the Parties of UNFCCC (decision 2/CP.3) were the values of "global warming potential" calculated for the IPCC Second Assessment Report. These figures are used for converting the various greenhouse gas emissions into comparable CO_2 equivalents (CO_2-eq) when computing overall sources and sinks.

The Protocol allows for several "flexible mechanisms", such as emissions trading, the clean development mechanism (CDM) and joint implementation to allow Annex I countries to meet their GHG emission limitations by purchasing GHG emission reductions credits from elsewhere, through financial exchanges, projects that reduce emissions in non-Annex I countries, from other Annex I countries, or from annex I countries with excess allowances.

Each Annex I country is required to submit an annual report of inventories of all anthropogenic greenhouse gas emissions from sources and removals from sinks under UNFCCC and the Kyoto Protocol. These countries nominate a person (called a "designated national authority") to create the manage its greenhouse gas inventory. Virtually all of the non-Annex I countries have also established a designated national authority to manage its Kyoto obligations, specifically the "CDM process" that determines which GHG projects they wish to propose for accreditation by the CDM Executive Board.

23. Plastic waste management.

Ans. Plastic waste management is a collective term for various approaches and strategies used to recycle plastic materials that would otherwise be dumped into landfills, or bodies of water, or otherwise contaminate the environment. The idea behind this type of waste management is to utilize those discarded material to manufacture new plastic products without the need to actually generate additional plastic materials. Doing so can help lower production costs as well as protect the environment.

Many different types of industries participate in some type of plastic waste management process. Some are specifically geared toward collecting plastic items for recycling. For example, many supermarkets encourage customers to contribute unwanted plastic bags into a recycling container located near the front of the store. The collected bags are then forwarded to recycling centers where the material is processed for use in the production of new products made from the recycled plastic.

Businesses that produce plastic products also engage in the task of plastic waste management. This often focuses on finding ways to recycle or reuse excess plastic that is discarded as units of different goods are produced. These plastic remnants can often be collected and ran through an internal recycling process to create additional products for sale. Not only does this approach prevent the disposal of the used materials into a landfill, it also allows the company to lower the actual a cost associated with manufacturing each unit of its product line.

In some cases, businesses outsource the process of plastic waste management. Contracting with a waste management company makes it possible for unwanted plastic items to be collected and removed from the premises without expending additional company resources. Municipalities sometimes work with a waste management disposal company in creating plastic recycling programs that allow households to conveniently dispose of plastic milk jugs, broken plastic toys, and other plastic items without placing them into the trash. Depending on the nature of the arrangement with the plastic waste management company, the municipality may actually earn a small amount from the arrangement, creating another stream of revenue for the city or town that can be used to fund services offered to residents.

Any type of plastic waste management must be conducted in compliance with regulations set by local, state, and federal governments. This includes using recycling methods that are considered to be environmentally friendly, and that are not likely to create health risks for individuals living and working in the community. Since regulations regarding recycling vary somewhat from one jurisdiction to another, it is important to determine what is and is not allowed before establishing any type of ongoing program to deal with plastic waste.

24. Utility of biofertilizers in agriculture.

Ans. Biofertilizer are the biologically active products or microbial inoculants of bacteria, algae and fungi, which may help biological nitrogen fixation for the benefit of plants. Biofertilizers also include organic fertilizers (manures, etc.), which are rendered in an available form due to the interaction of micro-organisms or due to the interaction of micro-organisms or due to their association with plants. Biiofertilizers thus include (*i*) symbiotic nitrogen fixers e.g. *Rhizobium* spp.; (*ii*) asymbiotic free nitrogen fixer e.g. *Azotobacter, Azospirillum,* etc. (*iii*) algae biofertillizers e.g. blue green algae or BGA in association with *Azolla;* (*iv*) phosphate solubilising bacteria; (*v*) mycorrhizae; (*vi*) organic fertilizers.

The need for the use of biofertilzers has arisen, primarily of two reasons. First, because increase in the use of fertilizers leads to increased usage of chemical fertiliizer leads to damage in soil texture and raises other environmental problems. Therefore, the use of biofertilzers is both economical and environmetns friendly. The pragmatic approach will be to develop the integrated nutrient supply system involving a combination of the use of chemical fertilizers and biofertilizers.

Rhizobia spp.

Rhizobia are able to enter into symbiotic relationship with legumes (pulses, etc.). They fix atmospheric nitrogen and thus not only increase the production of the inoculated crops, but also leave a fair amount of nitrogen in the soil, which benefits the subsequent crop. Following seven groups of *Rhizobia* have been recognised for inoculating legumes in India: *R. leguminosarum, R. japonicum* and *Rhizobium spp.* The new technology for industrial preparation for rhizobial cultures included the following : (*i*) seed pelleting with gum arabic or crboxy methyl cellulose as percoated seed (*ii*) polyacrylamide entrapped rhizobia; (*iii*) frezedried or lyophilzed culture of rhizobia; (*iv*) *Rhizobium* paste; (*v*) inoculants in liquid/frozen concentrate form; (*vi*) granular soil inoculants to be applied by aerial application; (*vii*) natural peat granule as soil implant inoculum.

Asymbiotic Nitrogen-Fixers

Azotobacter and *Azopirillum,* when applied to rhizosphere, fix atmospheric Nitrogen and make it available to crop plants. They also synthesize growth promoting antibioic substance, helpful to the plant. Most efficient strains of *Azotobacter* fix 30 kg of Nitrogen from 1000 kg of organic matter. When applied to fields, positive responses by field crops were observed leading to saving of 10-25 kg/ha of Nitrogen. Similarly, *Azospirllum* with farmyard manure, led to saving of 15-25 kg equivalent to Nitrogen per hectare in crops like sorghum and other millets.

Algal Fertilizers

Blue green algae (BGA) and *Azolla* constitute a system, which is the main source of algal biofertiliizer in south and southeast Asia, particularly for lowland paddy. BGA inoculatoin with composite cultures of algal genera *Anabaena, Nostoc, Plectonema, Aulosiro, Oscillatoria, Tolypothrix,* etc. have been found to be more effective than single cultures. Besides being a source of Nitrogen, BGA use has the following advantages : (*i*) algal biomass accumulates as organic mattr; (*ii*) growth promoting substances are produced, which stimulate growth of rice seedling; (*iii*) it provides partial tolerance to pesticides and fungicides; (*iv*) it also helps in reclamation of saline and alkaline soils.

Mycorrhiza

Mycorrhiza is a symbiotic associatin of fungi with roots of plants, so that the nutrients absorbed from soil by the fungus are released to the host cels and in turn, the fungus takes its food requirements from the host. Mycorrhizae are of two types *viz.,* ectomycorrhiza and endomycorrhiza. Ectomycorrhiza are found on the roots of forest trees such as pine, oak, beech, eucalyptus, etc. They absorb niitrogen, phosphorus, potassium and calcium. They also convert complex organic molecules into simpler available forms, protect the roots from the pathogen, and produce growth promoting substances. Endomycorrhiza are found in the roots of most fruits and other horticultural crops such as coffee, pepper, cardamon betelvine, *etc*. They particularly help in phosphorus nutrition. They also produce growth promoting substances and offer resistane against pathogens.

25. Use of EIA in environment management.

Ans. Environmental impact assessment is usually conducted in three stages which optimize the resources and increases the effectively of the assessment. The process of environmental impact assessment has to be integrated with the development. The effects of a development activity should be examined at an early stage in the planning of the project and not after the decisions regarding its design and location at an early sates in the planning of the project and not after the decisions regarding its design and location have been decided by other factors. Three stages or environmental impact assessment precede every decision making step of the project—extending and intensifying itself as the project planning is elaborated. These steps are:

1. Initial scrutiny
2. Rapid Assessment
3. Comprehensive Assessment

1. Initial Screening

The first step in the process of Environmental Impact Assessment is to decide whether the impact assessment is actually needed for the development project being undertaken or it is simply unnecessary. Screening helps to clear the type of project which are not likely to cause serious environmental problems quickly.

2. Rapid Assessment

If it is felt that the project is likely to cause some detrimental effects on the environment, it is subjected to Rapid Environmental Assessment which involves:

1. Identification of the important impacts of the project on the environment.
2. Evaluation of the impact of the project on the locality or entire region; cost benefit analysis.
3. Listing of the issues which are unresolved and which need examination in detail.

Rapid Environmental Impact Assessment, thus, attempts to identify the key issues in a particular case to that attention or resources could be directed to relevant aspects. Issues which are not important enough to deserve further studies are omitted. This helps in optimizing our resources. Rapid Environmental Assessment usually involves interactions and discussion between public, various private organizations and experts as well as the scientific examination of impact caused by critical elements of project on the environment.

3. Comprehensive Assessment

Comprehensive Environmental Assessment is usually undertaken after the initial screeing and Rapid Impact Assessment has been performed. The earlier work has already generated some information about the project and its likely impact on the environment and it is now a comprehensive study of the critical aspects of project which is taken-up in the Comprehensive Environmental Impact Assessment. It usually involves collection and evaluation of the following set of information.

1. Base-line data about the project.
2. Impact Identification.
3. Impact Prediction.
4. Evaluation of the impacts.
5. Mitigative measures and monitoring plans
6. Informing the society and the decision makers.

SECTION-IV

Note: *This section consists of one essay type question of forty (40) marks to be answered in about one thousand (1000) words on any of the following topics.*

(40 × 1 = 40 marks)

26. Write an eassy on *any one* of the following:
(a) Groundwater provinces and resources of India.

OR

(b) Environmental aspects related to large dams such as Tehri Dam or Narmada Dam.

OR

(c) Mineral resources of India.

OR

(d) Recycling of agricultural waste and bioremidiation.

OR

(e) Causes of air pollution and the role played by greenhouse gases and aerosols.

OR

(f) What are natural hazards? Discuss causes effects, mitigation of floods and droughts in India.

OR

(g) "Nuclear energy is important for energy needs of India"- Critically evaluate the statement.

OR

(h) Give a description account of evolution of organisms for their adaptability in present day environment.

Ans. Air is available in abundance in the surface of the earth. It is never found clean in nature. A number of gases are continually released into the atmosphere through natural activity. The tiny particles of solids or liquid are distributed throughout the air by winds, volcanic explosions and similar other natural sources. Man-made pollutants resulting from chemical and biological processes are also released into the atmosphere. These impurities lead to pollution of air. The contents of clean air and polluted air are given in table-8.

Air pollution may be defined as any atmospheric condition in which certain substances are present in such concentration that they can produce undesirable effects on man and environment. These substances are gases such as sulphur oxides, nitrogen oxides, carbon monoxides, hydrocarbons and particulate matter such as smoke, dust, fumes, aerosols as well as radioactive materials etc.

Table: Contents of air

S. No.	Components	Clean air (ppm)	Polluted air (ppm)
1.	Sulphur dioxide	0.001-0.01	0.02-2.0
2.	Carbon dioxide	310-330	350-370
3.	Carbon monoxide	1.0	5-200
4.	Nitrogen oxides	0.001-0.01	0.01-0.05
5.	Hydrocarbons	1.0	1-20
6.	Particulate	10-20	70-700

A hypothetical representation of some important pollutants causing air pollution is shown as follows:

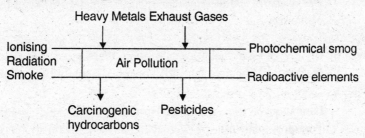

Fig. A hypothetical representation of important pollutants causing air pollution.

Classification of Air Pollutants

Air pollutants are classified on the basis of origin of pollutants, chemical composition and states of matter. These are:

(I) Primary Pollutants: The primary pollutants are emitted directly from the sources *e.g.,* Ash smoke, dust, fumes, dust and spray, sulphur dioxides, hydrogen sulphide, nitric oxide, ammonia, carbon monoxide, hydrogen fluoride, olefinic, aromatic hydrocarbons and radioactive compounds.

(II) Secondary Pollutants: The primary pollutants discharged into the atmosphere undergo chemical changes in the presence of water, oxygen and ultraviolet rays of sunlight to form secondary pollutants. Some secondary pollutants are given in the table.

Table: Formation of Secondary Pollutants

S. No.	Primary Pollutants	Reaction	Secondary Pollutants
1.	Carbon dioxide	Water	Bicarbonate
2.	Hydrogen sulphide	Oxygen	Sulphuric Acid
3.	Sulphur dioxide	Water	Sulphuric Acid
4.	Nitrogen dioxide	Hydrogen	Nitrous
			Nitric Acid
5.	Silicon Tetrafluoride	Water	Fluorosilicic Acid

SOURCES OF AIR POLLUTANTS

The major air pollutants and their sources are given in the table.

Table: Sources of Air pollutants

S. No.	Pollutants	Sources
1.	Oxides of Carbon CO, CO_2.	Coal and oil used for energy production, biomass burning.
2.	Oxides of Sulphur, SO_2 and SO_3.	Burning of coal, containing sulphur, ore smelting for extraction of metals e.g., Copper and iron from their sulphide ore, industrial processes, municipal incine-ration process.
3.	Oxides of Nitrogen NO and NO_2.	Use of petrol and diesel for transport of vehicles, Nitrogen fertilisers, Burning of biomass.
4.	Methane and other hydrocarbons	Burning of fossil fuel, Rice cultivation, Breeding of domestic animals, Burning of forests. Municipal land fill, microbial activity of sewage.
5.	Suspended Particulate Matter	Formation of soot, smoke on burning of coal, building constructions, Transport vehicles.
6.	Chlorofluoro-carbons and chloro compounds	Refrigerants, aerosol sprays, foam, plastic for making disposable fast food containers.
7.	Photochemical oxidants, ozone and PAN	Photochemical reactions in the lower troposphere. Reactions of oxides of nitrogen and hydrocarbons with oxygen.

Major Air Pollution

The emissions of air pollutants depends upon the method of combustion and the type of fuel used. The combustion of all fuels results in exothermic oxidation of carbon, hydrogen, sulphur and nitrogen. In case of complete combustion, carbon dioxide, water vapour, nitrogen oxides, volatile and non-volatile trace metals such as Arsenic, Cadmium, Lead and Mercury would be the principal emission. However, in practice complete combustion does not occur and as a result of additional particulate and gaseous pollutants result in the production of secondary pollutants. Certain pollutants undergo atmospheric oxidation to form acidic precipitation.

In addition, indoor air pollution is also considered to be of great importance in terms of personal exposure. The principal air pollutants are divided from combustion of stoves, heaters, cigarettes, building materials and furnishing air products. House hold dust is also believed to be of importance in the indoor air pollution. The impact of indoor emissions depends upon the strength of the source and the ventilation rate.

Status of Vehicular Air Pollution in India

Air Quality, with respect to sulphur dioxide (SO_2), oxides of nitrogen (NO_x) and suspended particulate matter (SPM) are presented as under:

Sulphur Dioxide (SO_2)

The locations having highest top ten values of annual mean concentration of sulphur dioxide are listed in Table. The annual mean concentration of Sulphur dioxide exceeded the standards in the city of Jharia and Dhanbad in Jharkhand.

Table: Highest Concentration of Sulphur Dioxide During 2007 in Selected Location

Industrial Location	State	Annual mean conc. ($\mu g/m^3$)	Residential Location	State	Annual mean ($\mu g/m^3$)
MADA, Jharia	Jharkhand	91	Regional Office, Dhanbad	Jharkhand	91
Near Police Station (FCI Main Hospital Sindri)	Jharkhand	73	Sakchi water tower, Jamshedpur	Jharkhand	65
Cossilpore, Kolkata	West Bengal	74	Lal Bazar (Dalhousie), Kolkata	West Bengal	61
Anpara Colony, Anpara	U.P.	93	Anand Rao Circle, Bangalore	Karnataka	54
Burmamines Water tower, Jamshedpur	Jharkhand	61	Nasik Municipal Corporation, Building, Nasik	Maharashtra	43

Oxides of Nitrogen

The location where annual standards of industrial areas, exceeded in the city of Udaipur, Pune and Kota (one sensitive), Alwar is a satellite town and Delhi with a high concentration of industries. Due to inadequatic power supply, the industrial, commercial and residential activities often resort to captive power generation resulting in high emissions of Oxides of Nitrogen. Table enlists locations having top eight highest values of annual mean concentration of Nitrogen dioxide.

Table: Highest Concentration of Nitrogen Dioxide in Selected Locations

S. No.	Industrial Location	State	Annual mean conc. ($\mu g/m^3$)	S. No.	Residential Location	State	Annual mean ($\mu g/m^3$)
1.	RIICO Pump House, Alwar	Rajasthan	79	5.	Regional Office Udaipur	Rajasthn	98
2.	Gaurav Solvex, Alwar	Rajasthan	75	6.	Regional Office, Alwar	Rajasthan	74
3.	Renusagar Colony, Anpara	U.P.	62	7.	University Gate, Pune	Maharashtra	61
4.	Poud Phata (Kothrud),	Maharashtra	56	8.	Town Hall, Delhi	Delhi	55

Suspended Particulate Matter (SPM)

Locations, where the concentration of suspended particulate matter in ambient air was found highest are presented in Table.

Table: Highest Concentration of SPM in Selected Locations

S. No.	Industrial Location	State	Annual Mean Conc. ($\mu g/m^3$)	S. No.	Residential Location	State	Annual Cone ($\mu g/m^3$)
1.	Rita Sewing Machine, Ludhiana	Punjab	515	4.	Clock Tower, MC Office, Ludhiana	Punjab	528
2.	M/s A. Chem. P. Ltd. Fazalganj, Kanpur	U.P.	467	5.	Gandhi Maidan, Test Centre, Patna	Bihar	515
3.	MADA, Jharia	Jharkhand	458	6.	Sojati Gate, Jodhpur	Rajasthan	458

UGC-NET (JRF) EXAM JUNE, 2008

PAPER–I

Note : This paper contains **fifty (50)** multiple-choice questions, each question carrying **two (2)** marks. Attempt **all** of them.

1. The teacher has been glorified by the phrase "Friend, philosopher and guide" because :
   A. He has to play all vital roles in the context of society
   B. He transmits the high value of humanity to students
   C. He is the great reformer of the society
   D. He is a great patriot

2. The most important cause of failure for teacher lies in the area of :
   A. inter personal relationship
   B. lack of command over the knowledge of the subject
   C. verbal ability
   D. strict handling of the students

3. A teacher can establish rapport with his students by :
   A. becoming a figure of authority
   B. impressing students with knowledge and skill
   C. playing the role of a guide
   D. becoming a friend to the students

4. Education is a powerful instrument of :
   A. Social transformation
   B. Personal transformation
   C. Cultural transformation
   D. All the above

5. A teacher's major contribution towards the maximum self-realization of the student is affected through :
   A. Constant fulfilment of the students' needs
   B. Strict control of class-room activities
   C. Sensitivity to students' needs, goals and purposes
   D. Strict reinforcement of academic standards

6. Research problem is selected from the stand point of :
   A. Researcher's interest
   B. Financial support
   C. Social relevance
   D. Availability of relevant literature

7. Which one is called non-probability sampling?
   A. Cluster sampling
   B. Quota sampling
   C. Systematic sampling
   D. Stratified random sampling

8. Formulation of hypothesis may NOT be required in :
   A. Survey method
   B. Historical studies
   C. Experimental studies
   D. Normative studies

9. Field-work based research is classified as :
   A. Empirical   B. Historical
   C. Experimental   D. Biographical

10. Which of the following sampling method is appropriate to study the prevalence of AIDS amongst male and female in India in 1976, 1986, 1996 and 2006 ?

A. Cluster sampling
B. Systematic sampling
C. Quota sampling
D. Stratified random sampling

Read the following passage and answer the questions 11 to 15 :

The fundamental principle is that Article 14 forbids class legislation but permits reasonable classification for the purpose of legislation which classification must satisfy the twin tests of classification being founded on an intelligible differentia which distinguishes persons or things that are grouped together from those that are left out of the group and that differentia must have a rational nexus to the object sought to be achieved by the Statute in question. The thrust of Article 14 is that the citizen is entitled to equality before law and equal protection of laws. In the very nature of things the society being composed of unequals a welfare State will have to strive by both executive and legislative action to help the less fortunate in society to ameliorate their condition so that the social and economic inequality in the society may be bridged. This would necessitate a legislative application to a group of citizens otherwise unequal and amelioration of whose lot is the object of state affirmative action. In the absence of the doctrine of classification such legislation is likely to flounder on the bed rock of equality enshrined in Article 14. The Court realistically appraising the social and economic inequality and keeping in view the guidelines on which the State action must move as constitutionally laid down in Part IV of the Constitution evolved the doctrine of classification. The doctrine was evolved to sustain a legislation or State action designed to help weaker sections of the society or some such segments of the society in need of succour. Legislative and executive action may accordingly be sustained if it satisfies the twin tests of reasonable classification and the rational principle correlated to the object sought to be achieved.

The concept of equality before the law does not involve the idea of absolute equality among human beings which is a physical impossibility. All that Article 14 guarantees is a similarity of treatment contra-distinguished from identical treatment. Equality before law means that among equals the law should be equal and should be equally administered and that the likes should be treated alike. Equality before the law does not mean that things which are different shall be as though they are the same. It ofcourse means denial of any special privilege by reason of birth, creed or the like. The legislation as well as the executive government, while dealing with diverse problems arising out of an infinite variety of human relations must of necessity have the power of making special laws, to attain any particular object and to achieve that object it must have the power of selection or classification of persons and things upon which such laws are to operate.

11. Right to equality, one of the fundamental rights, is enunciated in the constitution under Part III, Article :
   A. 12   B. 13
   C. 14   D. 15

12. The main thrust of Right to equality is that it permits :
   A. class legislation
   B. equality before law and equal protection under the law
   C. absolute equality
   D. special privilege by reason of birth

13. The social and economic inequality in the society can be bridged by :
   A. executive and legislative action
   B. universal suffrage
   C. identical treatment
   D. none of the above

14. The doctrine of classification is evolved to :
   A. Help weaker sections of the society
   B. Provide absolute equality
   C. Provide identical treatment
   D. None of the above

15. While dealing with diverse problems arising out of an infinite variety of human relations, the government :
   A. must have the power of making special laws

B. must not have any power to make special laws

C. must have power to withdraw equal rights

D. none of the above

16. Communication with oneself is known as :
A. Group communication
B. Grapevine communication
C. Interpersonal communication
D. Intrapersonal communication

17. Which broadcasting system for TV is followed in India ?
A. NTSE   B. PAL
C. SECAM   D. NTCS

18. All India Radio before 1936 was known as :
A. Indian Radio Broadcasting
B. Broadcasting Service of India
C. Indian State Broadcasting Service
D. All India Broadcasting Service

19. The biggest news agency of India is :
A. PTI   B. UNI
C. NANAP   D. Samachar Bharati

20. Prasar Bharati was launched in the year :
A. 1995   B. 1997
C. 1999   D. 2001

21. A statistical measure based upon the entire population is called parameter while measure based upon a sample is known as :
A. Sample parameter
B. Inference
C. Statistics
D. None of these

22. The importance of the correlation co-efficient lies in the fact that :
A. There is a linear relationship between the correlated variables.
B. It is one of the most valid measure of statistics.
C. It allows one to determine the degree or strength of the association between two variables.
D. It is a non-parametric method of statistical analysis.

23. The F-test:
A. is essentially a two tailed test.
B. is essentially a one tailed test.

C. can be one tailed as well as two tailed depending on the hypothesis.
D. can never be a one tailed test.

24. What will be the next letter in the following series : DCXW, FEVU, HGTS, _____
A. AKPO   B. JBYZ
C. JIRQ   D. LMRS

25. The following question is based on the diagram given below. If the two small circles represent formal class-room education and distance education and the big circle stands for university system of education, which figure represents the university systems.

A. ⭕⭕⭕ B. ⭕⭕
C. ⭕⭕ D. ⭕⭕

26. The statement, *'To be non-violent is good'* is a :
A. Moral judgement
B. Factual judgement
C. Religious judgement
D. Value judgement

27. **Assertion (A):** Man is a rational being.
Reason (R): Man is a social being.
A. Both A. and (R) are true and (R) is the correct explanation of A.
B. Both A. and (R) are true but (R) is not the correct explanation of A.
C. A. is true but (R) is false
D. A. is false but (R) is true

28. Value Judgements are :
A. Factual Judgements
B. Ordinary Judgements
C. Normative Judgements
D. Expression of public opinion

29. Deductive reasoning proceeds from :
A. general to particular
B. particular to general
C. one general conclusion to another general conclusion
D. one particular conclusion to another particular conclusion

30. AGARTALA is written in code as 14168171, the code for AGRA is :
A. 1641   B. 1416
C. 1441   D. 1461

31. Which one of the following is the most comprehensive source of population data ?
A. National Family Health Surveys
B. National Sample Surveys
C. Census
D. Demographic Health Surveys

32. Which one of the following principles is *not* applicable to sampling ?
A. Sample units must be clearly defined
B. Sample units must be dependent on each other
C. Same units of sample should be used throughout the study
D. Sample units must be chosen in a systematic and objective manner

33. If January 1st, 2007 is Monday, what was the day on 1st January 1995 ?
A. Sunday   B. Monday
C. Friday   D. Saturday

34. Insert the missing number in the following series :
4   16   8   64   ?   256
A. 16   B. 24
C. 32   D. 20

35. If an article is sold for Rs. 178 at a loss of 11%; what would be its selling price in order to earn a profit of 11% ?
A. Rs. 222.50   B. Rs. 267
C. Rs. 222   D. Rs. 220

36. WYSIWYG - describes the display of a document on screen as it will actually print
A. What you state is what you get
B. What you see is what you get
C. What you save is what you get
D. What you suggest is what you get

37. Which of the following is *not a* Computer language ?
A. PASCAL   B. UNIX
C. FORTRAN   D. COBOL

38. A key-board has at least :
A. 91 keys   B. 101 keys
C. 111 keys   D. 121 keys

39. An E-mail address is composed of
A. two parts   B. three parts
C. four parts   D. five parts

40. Corel Draw is a popular :
A. Illustration programme
B. Programming language
C. Text programme
D. None of the above

41. Human ear is most sensitive to noise in which of the following ranges :
A. 1-2 KHz   B. 100 - 500 Hz
C. 10 - 12 KHz   D. 13 - 16 KHz

42. Which one of the following units is used to measure intensity of noise ?
A. decible   B. Hz
C. Phon   D. Watts/m^2

43. If the population growth follows a logistic curve, the maximum sustainable yield :
A. is equal to half the carrying capacity.
B. is equal to the carrying capacity.
C. depends on growth rates.
D. depends on the initial population.

44. Chemical weathering of rocks is largely dependent upon :
A. high temperature
B. strong wind action
C. heavy rainfall
D. glaciation

45. Structure of earth's system consists of the following :

Match *List-I* with *List-II* and give the correct answer.

List-I (Zone)	List-II (Chemical Character)
(a) Atmosphere	(i) Inert gases
(b) Biosphere	(ii) Salt, fresh water, snow and ice
(c) Hydrosphere	(iii) Organic substances, skeleton matter
(d) Lithosphere	(iv) Light silicates

Codes :

	(a)	(b)	(c)	(d)
A.	(ii)	(iii)	(i)	(iv)
B.	(i)	(iii)	(ii)	(iv)
C.	(ii)	(i)	(iii)	(iv)
D.	(i)	(i)	(ii)	(iv)

46. NAAC is an autonomous institution under the aegis of :
A. ICSSR
B. CSIR
C. AICTE
D. UGC

47. National Council for Women's Education was established in :
A. 1958
B. 1976
C. 1989
D. 2000

48. Which one of the following is *not* situated in New Delhi ?
A. Indian Council of Cultural Relations
B. Indian Council of Scientific Research
C. National Council of Educational Research and Training
D. Indian Institute of Advanced Studies

49. Autonomy in higher education implies freedom in :
A. Administration
B. Policy-making
C. Finance
D. Curriculum development

50. Match *List-I* with *List-II* and select the correct answer from the code given below
List-I (Institutions)
(a) Dr. Hari Singh Gour University
(b) S.N.D.T. University
(c) M.S. University
(d) J.N. Vyas University *Codes :*
List-II (Locations)
(i) Mumbai   (ii) Baroda
(iii) Jodhpur   (iv) Sagar

	(a)	(b)	(c)	(d)
A.	(iv)	(i)	(ii)	(iii)
B.	(i)	(ii)	(iii)	(iv)
C.	(iii)	(i)	(ii)	(iv)
D.	(ii)	(iv)	(i)	(iii)

ANSWERS

1	2	3	4	5	6	7	8	9	10
B	B	B	D	C	C	B	B	A	D
11	12	13	14	15	16	17	18	19	20
C	B	A	A	A	D	B	C	A	B
21	22	23	24	25	26	27	28	29	30
A	C	C	C	B	A	B	C	A	D
31	32	33	34	35	36	37	38	39	40
C	B	D	A	C	B	B	B	A	A
41	42	43	44	45	46	47	48	49	50
B	A	A	C	B	D	A	D	C	A

SOME SELECTED EXPLANATORY ANSWERS

24.
D C X W
F E V U

H G T S
∴ J I R Q

6

30. Since,

A G A R T A L A
↓ ↓ ↓ ↓ ↓ ↓ ↓ ↓
1 4 1 6 8 1 7 1

Therefore

A G R A
↓ ↓ ↓ ↓
| 1 4 6 1 |

34.

35. S.P. = 89% of C.P.

$$\Rightarrow \quad 178 = \text{C.P.} \times \frac{89}{100}$$

$$\Rightarrow \quad \text{C.P.} = \frac{100 \times 178}{89} = 200$$

∴ For 11% Profit, the selling price will be

$$\text{S.P.} = 200 \times \frac{111}{100} = \text{Rs. } 222$$

||||||||||

UGC-NET (JRF) EXAM DECEMBER, 2008

PAPER–I

Note : This paper contains **fifty** (50) multiple-choice questions, each question carrying **two** (2) marks. Attempt **all** of them.

1. According to Swami Vivekananda, teacher's success depends on:
   A. His renunciation of personal gain and service to others
   B. His professional training and creativity
   C. His concentration on his work and duties with a spirit of obedience to God
   D. His mastery on the subject and capacity in controlling the students

2. Which of the following teacher, will be liked most:
   A. A teacher of high idealistic attitude
   B. A loving teacher
   C. A teacher who is disciplined
   D. A teacher who often amuses his students

3. A teacher's most important challenge is:
   A. To make students do their home work
   B. To make teaching-learning process enjoyable
   C. To maintain discipline in the class room
   D. To prepare the question paper

4. Value-education stands for:
   A. making a student healthy
   B. making a student to get a job
   C. inculcation of virtues
   D. all-round development of personality

5. When a normal student behaves in an erratic manner in the class, you would:
   A. pull up the student then and there
   B. talk to the student after the class
   C. ask the student to leave the class
   D. ignore the student

6. The research is always—
   A. verifying the old knowledge
   B. exploring new knowledge
   C. filling the gap between knowledge
   D. all of these

7. The research that applies the laws at the time of field study to draw more and more clear ideas about the problem is:
   A. Applied research
   B. Action research
   C. Experimental research
   D. None of these

8. When a research problem is related to heterogeneous population, the most suitable sampling method is:
   A. Cluster Sampling
   B. Stratified Sampling
   C. Convenient Sampling
   D. Lottery Method

9. The process not needed in experimental research is:
   A. Observation
   B. Manipulation and replication
   C. Controlling
   D. Reference collection

10. A research problem is not feasible only when:
    A. it is researchable

B. it is new and adds something to knowledge
C. it consists of independent and dependent variables
D. it has utility and relevance

Read the following passage carefully and answer the questions 11 to 15 :

Radically changing monsoon patterns, reduction in the winter rice harvest and a quantum increase in respiratory diseases all part of the environmental doomsday scenario which is reportedly playing out in South Asia. According to a United Nations Environment Programme report, a deadly three-kilometer deep blanket of pollution comprising a fearsome, cocktail of ash, acids, aerosols and other particles has enveloped in this region. For India, already struggling to cope with a drought, the implication of this are devastating and further crop failure will amount to a life and death question for many Indians. The increase in premature deaths will have adverse social and economic consequences and a rise in morbidities will place an unbearable burden on our crumbling health system. And there is no one to blame but ourselves. Both official and corporate India has always been allergic to any mention of clean technology. Most mechanical two wheelers roll of the assembly line without proper pollution control system. Little effort is made for R&D on simple technologies, which could make a vital difference to people's lives and the environment.

However, while there is no denying that South Asia must clean up its act, skeptics might question the timing of the haze report. The Kyoto meet on climate change is just two weeks away and the stage is set for the usual battle between the developing world and the West, particularly the Unites States of America. President Mr. Bush has adamantly refused to sign any protocol, which would mean a change in American consumption level. U.N. environment report will likely find a place in the U.S. arsenal as it plants an accusing finger towards controls like India and China. Yet the U.S.A. can hardly deny its own dubious role in the matter of erasing trading quotas.

Richer countries can simply buy up excess credits from poorer countries and continue to pollute. Rather than try to get the better of developing countries, who undoubtedly have taken up environmental shortcuts in their bid to catch up with the West, the USA should take a look at the environmental profigacy, which is going on within. From opening up virgin territories for oil exploration to relaxing the standards for drinking water, Mr. Bush's policies are not exactly beneficial, not even to America's interests. We realize that we are all in this together and that pollution anywhere should be a global concern otherwise there will only be more tunnels at the end of the tunnel.

11. Both official and corporate India is allergic to:
A. Failure of Monsoon
B. Poverty and Inequality
C. Slowdown in Industrial Production
D. Mention of Clean Technology

12. If the rate of premature death increases it will:
A. Exert added burden on the crumbling economy
B. Have adverse social and economic consequences
C. Make positive effect on our effort to control population
D. Have less job aspirants in the society

13. According to the passage, the two wheeler industry is not adequately concerned about:
A. Passenger safety on the roads
B. Life cover insurance of the vehicle owner
C. Pollution control system in the vehicle
D. Rising cost of the two wheelers

14. What could be the reason behind timing of the haze report just before the Kyoto meet ?
A. United Nations is working hand-in-glove with U.S.A.
B. Organizers of the forthcoming meet to teach a lesson to the U.S.A.
C. Drawing attention of the world towards devastating effects of environment degradation.
D. U.S.A. wants to use it as a handle against the developing countries in the forthcoming meet

15. Which of the following is the indication of environmental degradation in South Asia ?
   A. Social and economic inequality
   B. Crumbling health care system
   C. Inadequate pollution control system
   D. Radically changing monsoon pattern

16. Community Radio is a type of radio service that caters to the interest of :
   A. Local audience   B. Education
   C. Entertainment   D. News

17. Orcut is a part of :
   A. Intra personal Communication
   B. Mass Communication
   C. Group Communication
   D. Interpersonal Communication

18. Match List-I with List-II and select the correct answer using the codes given below:

List - I (Artists)	List - II (Art)
(a) Amrita Shergill	(i) Flute
(b) T. Swaminathan Pillai	(ii) Classical Song
(c) Bhimsen Joshi	(iii) Painting
(d) Padma Subramaniyam	(iv) Bharat Natyam

   Codes :

	(a)	(b)	(c)	(d)
A.	(iii)	(i)	(ii)	(iv)
B.	(ii)	(iii)	(i)	(iv)
C.	(iv)	(ii)	(iii)	(i)
D.	(i)	(iv)	(ii)	(iii)

19. Which is not correct in latest communication award ?
   A. Salman Rushdie – Booker's Prize - July 20, 2008
   B. Dilip Sanghavi – Business Standard CEO Award July 22, 2008
   C. Tapan Sinha – Dada Saheb Falke Award, July 21, 2008
   D. Gautam Ghosh – Osians Lifetime Achievement Award July 11, 2008

20. Firewalls are used to protect a communication network system against:
   A. Unauthorized attacks
   B. Virus attacks
   C. Data-driven attacks
   D. Fire-attacks

21. Insert the missing number in the following :
   $$\frac{2}{3}, \frac{4}{7}, ?, \frac{11}{21}, \frac{16}{31}$$
   A. $\frac{10}{8}$ B. $\frac{6}{10}$
   C. $\frac{5}{10}$ D. $\frac{7}{13}$

22. In a certain code, GAMESMAN is written as AGMEMSAN. How would DISCLOSE be written in that code ?
   A. IDSCOLSE
   B. IDCSOLES
   C. IDSCOLES
   D. IDSCLOSE

23. The letters in the first set have a certain relationship. On the basis of this relationship mark the right choice for the second set :
   AST : BRU : : NQV : ?
   A. ORW   B. MPU
   C. MRW   D. OPW

24. On what dates of April 1994 did SUNDAY fall?
   A. 2, 9, 16, 23, 30
   B. 3, 10, 17, 24
   C. 4, 11, 18, 25
   D. 1, 8, 15, 22, 29

25. Find out the wrong number in the sequence:
   125, 127, 130, 135, 142, 153, 165
   A. 130   B. 142
   C. 153   D. 165

26. There are five books A, B, C, D and E. The book C lies above D, the book E is below A and B is below E. Which is at the bottom ?
   A. E   B. B
   C. A   D. D

27. Logical reasoning is based on:
   A. Truth of involved propositions
   B. Valid relation among the involved propositions

C. Employment of symbolic language
D. Employment of ordinary language

28. Two propositions with the same subject and predicate terms but different in quality are :
   A. Contradictory   B. Contrary
   C. Subaltern   D. Identical

29. The premises of a valid deductive argument:
   A. Provide some evidence for its conclusion
   B. Provide no evidence for its conclusion
   C. Are irrelevant for its conclusion
   D. Provide conclusive evidence for its conclusion

30. Syllogistic reasoning is :
   A. Deductive
   B. Inductive
   C. Experimental
   D. Hypothetical

Study the following Venn diagram and answer questions nos. 31 to 33.
Three circles representing GRADUATES, CLERKS and GOVERNMENT EMPLOYEES are intersecting. The intersections are marked A, B, C, e, f, g and h. Which part best represents the statements in questions 31 to 33 ?

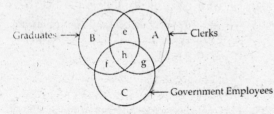

31. Some Graduates are Government employees but not as Clerks.
   A. h   B. g
   C. f   D. e

32. Clerks who are graduates as well as government employees :
   A. e   B. f
   C. g   D. h

33. Some graduates are Clerks but not Government employees.
   A. f   B. g
   C. h   D. e

Study the following graph and answer questions numbered from 34 to 35

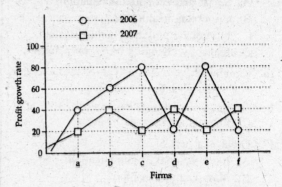

34. Which of the firms got maximum profit growth rate in the year 2006.
   A. ab   B. ce
   C. cd   D. ef

35. Which of the firms got maximum profit growth rate in the year 2007.
   A. bdf   B. acf
   C. bed   D. ace

36. The accounting software 'Tally' was developed by :
   A. HCL   B. TCS
   C. Infosys   D. Wipro

37. Errors in computer programmes are called :
   A. Follies   B. Mistakes
   C. Bugs   D. Spam

38. HTML is basically used to design :
   A. Web-page
   B. Web-site
   C. Graphics
   D. Tables and Frames

39. 'Micro Processing' is made for :
   A. Computer
   B. Digital System
   C. Calculator
   D. Electronic Goods

40. Information, a combination of graphics, text, sound, video and animation is called :
   A. Multiprogramme
   B. Multifacet

C. Multimedia

D. Multiprocess

41. Which of the following pairs regarding typical composition of hospital wastes is incorrect ?
A. Plastic- 9-12%
B. Metals- 1-2%
C. Ceramic - 8 - 10%
D. Biodegradable - 35 - 40%

42. Fresh water achieves its greatest density at :
A. –4°C
B. 0° C
C. 4°C
D. –2.5° C

43. Which one of the following is not associated with earthquakes ?
A. Focus
B. Epicenter
C. Seismograph
D. Swells

44. The tallest trees in the world are found in the region :
A. Equatorial region
B. Temperate region
C. Monsoon region
D. Mediterranean region

45. Match List-I with List-II and select the correct answer from the codes given below :

List - I (National Parks)	List - II (States)
(a) Periyar	(i) Orissa
(b) Nandan Kanan	(ii) Kerala
(c) Corbett National Park	(iii) Rajasthan
(d) Sariska Tiger Reserve	(iv) Uttarakhand

Codes :

	(a)	(b)	(c)	(d)
A.	(ii)	(i)	(iv)	(iii)
B.	(i)	(ii)	(iv)	(iii)
C.	(iii)	(ii)	(i)	(iv)
D.	(i)	(ii)	(iii)	(iv)

46. According to Radhakrishnan Commission, the aim of Higher Education is :
A. To develop the democratic values, peace and harmony
B. To develop great personalities who can give their contributions in politics, administration, industry and commerce

C. Both A. and B.

D. None of these

47. The National Museum at New Delhi is attached to:
A. Delhi University
B. a Deemed University
C. a Subordinate Office of the JNU
D. Part of Ministry of Tourism and Culture

48. Match List-I with List-II and select the correct answer from the code given below :

List - I (Institutions)	List - II (Locations)
(a) National Law Institute	(i) Shimla
(b) Indian Institute of Advanced Studies	(ii) Bhopal
(c) National Judicial Academy	(iii) Hyderabad
(d) National Savings Institute	(iv) Nagpur

Codes :

	(a)	(b)	(c)	(d)
A.	(iii)	(ii)	(iv)	(i)
B.	(i)	(ii)	(iii)	(iv)
C.	(iv)	(iii)	(i)	(ii)
D.	(iii)	(i)	(ii)	(iv)

49. Election of Rural and Urban local bodies are conducted and ultimately supervised by :
A. Election Commission of India
B. State Election Commission
C. District Collector and District Magistrate
D. Concerned Returning Officer

50. Which opinion is not correct ?
A. Education is a subject of concurrent list of VII schedule of Constitution of India
B. University Grants Commission is a statutory body
C. Patent, inventions, design, copyright and trade marks are the subject of concurrent list
D. Indian Council of Social Science Research is a statutory body related to research in social sciences

ANSWERS

1	2	3	4	5	6	7	8	9	10
D	C	B	C	B	D	A	B	D	B
11	**12**	**13**	**14**	**15**	**16**	**17**	**18**	**19**	**20**
D	B	C	C	D	A	D	A	B	A
21	**22**	**23**	**24**	**25**	**26**	**27**	**28**	**29**	**30**
D	A	D	B	D	B	B	A	D	A
31	**32**	**33**	**34**	**35**	**36**	**37**	**38**	**39**	**40**
C	D	D	B.	A	B	C	A	A	C
41	**42**	**43**	**44**	**45**	**46**	**47**	**48**	**49**	**50**
D	C	D	B	A	C	D	D	B	C

SOME SELECTED EXPLANATORY ANSWERS

21. Since,

$$\frac{2}{3} = \frac{2}{2 \times 2 - 1}$$

$$\frac{4}{7} = \frac{4}{4 \times 2 - 1}$$

$$\frac{11}{21} = \frac{11}{11 \times 2 - 1}$$

and $\frac{16}{31} = \frac{16}{16 \times 2 - 1}$

Therefore $\frac{7}{13} = \frac{7}{7 \times 2 - 1}$

22. Since,

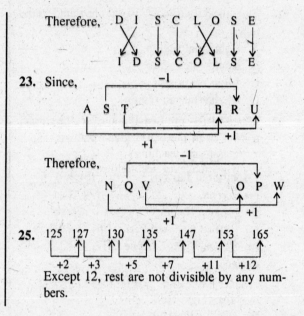

23. Since,

25.

Except 12, rest are not divisible by any numbers.

UGC-NET (JRF) Exam DECEMBER, 2009

PAPER–I

Note : This paper contains **sixty** (60) multiple-choice questions, each question carrying **two** (2) marks. Candidate is expected to answer any **fifty** (50) questions. In case more than 50 questions are attempted, only the first 50 questions will be evaluated.

1. The University which telecasts interaction educational programmes through its own channel is
   A. Osmania University
   B. University of Pune
   C. Annamalai University
   D. Indira Gandhi National University (IGNOU)

2. Which of the following skills are needed for present day teacher to adjust effectively with the classroom teaching?
   1. Knowledge of technology
   2. Use of technology in teaching learning
   3. Knowledge of students' needs
   4. Content mastery
   A. 1 & 3   B. 2 & 3
   C. 2, 3 & 4   D. 2 & 4

3. Who has signed as MOU for Accreditation of Teacher Education Institutions in India?
   A. NAAC and UGC
   B. NCTE and NAAC
   C. UGC and NCTE
   D. NCTE and IGNOU

4. The primary duty of the teacher is to
   A. raise the intellectual standard of the students
   B. improve the physical standard of the students
   C. help all round development of the students
   D. imbibe value system in the students

5. Micro teaching is more effective
   A. during the preparation for teaching-practice
   B. during the teaching-practice
   C. after the teaching-practice
   D. always

6. What quality the students like the most in a teacher ?
   A. Idealist philosophy
   B. Compassion
   C. Discipline
   D. Entertaining

7. A null hypothesis is
   A. when there is no difference between the variables
   B. the same as research hypothesis
   C. subjective in nature
   D. when there is difference between the variables

8. The research which is exploring new facts through the study of the past is called
   A. Philosophical research
   B. Historical research
   C. Mythological research
   D. Content analysis

9. Action research is
   A. An applied research
   B. A research carried out to solve immediate problems
   C. A longitudinal research
   D. Simulative research

10. The process not needed in Experimental Researches is
  A. Observation B. Manipulation
  C. Controlling D. Content Analysis

11. Manipulation is always a part of
  A. Historical research
  B. Fundamental research
  C. Descriptive research
  D. Experimental research

12. Which correlation co-efficient best explains the relationship between creativity and intelligence ?
  A. 1.00 B. 0.6
  C. 0.5 D. 0.3

Read the following passage and answer the Question Nos. 13 to 18 :

The decisive shift in British Policy really came about under mass pressure in the autumn and winter of 1945 to 46 - the months which Perderel Moon while editing Wavell's Journal has perceptively described as 'The Edge of a Volcano'. Very foolishly, the British initially decided to hold public trials of several hundreds of the 20,000 I.N.A. prisoners (as well as dismissing from service and detaining without trial no less than 7,000). They compounded the folly by holding the first trial in the Red Fort, Delhi in November 1945, and putting on the dock together a Hindu, a Muslim and a Sikh (P.K. Sehgal, Shah Nawaz, Gurbaksh Singh Dhillon). Bhulabhai Desai, Tejbahadur Sapru and Nehru appeared for the defence (the latter putting on his barrister's gown after 25 years), and the Muslim League also joined the countrywide protest. On 20 November, an Intelligence Bureau note admitted that "there has seldom been a matter which has attracted so much Indian public interest and, it is safe to say, sympathy ... this particular brand of sympathy cuts across communal barriers.' A journalist (B. Shiva Rao) visiting the Red Fort prisoners on the same day reported that 'There is not the slightest feeling among them of Hindu and Muslim ... A majority of the men now awaiting trial in the Red Fort is Muslim. Some of these men are bitter that Mr. Jinnah is keeping alive a controversy about Pakistan.' The British became extremely nervous about the I.N.A. spirit spreading to the Indian Army, and in January the Punjab Governor reported that a Lahore reception for released I.N.A. prisoners had been attended by Indian soldiers in uniform.

13. Which heading is more appropriate to assign to the above passage ?
  A. Wavell's Journal
  B. Role of Muslim League
  C. I.N.A. Trials
  D. Red Fort Prisoners

14. The trial of P.K. Sehgal, Shah Nawaz and Gurbaksh Singh Dhillon symbolises
  A. communal harmony
  B. threat to all religious persons
  C. threat to persons fighting for the freedom
  D. British reaction against the natives

15. I.N.A. stands for
  A. Indian National Assembly
  B. Indian National Association
  C. Inter-national Association
  D. Indian National Army

16. 'There has seldom been a matter which has attracted so much Indian Public Interest and, it is safe to say, sympathy ... this particular brand of sympathy cuts across communal barriers.' Who sympathises to whom and against whom ?
  A. Muslims sympathised with Shah Nawaz against the British
  B. Hindus sympathised with P.K. Sehgal against the British
  C. Sikhs sympathised with Gurbaksh Singh Dhillon against the British
  D. Indians sympathised with the persons who were to be trialled

17. The majority of people waiting for trial outside the Red Fort and criticising Jinnah were the
  A. Hindus
  B. Muslims
  C. Sikhs
  D. Hindus and Muslims both

18. The sympathy of Indian soldiers in uniform with the released I.N.A. prisoners at Lahore indicates

A. Feeling of Nationalism and Fraternity
B. Rebellious nature of Indian soldiers
C. Simply to participate in the reception party
D. None of the above

19. The country which has the distinction of having the two largest circulated newspapers in the world is
A. Great Britain
B. The United States
C. Japan
D. China

20. The chronological order of non-verbal communication is
A. Signs, symbols, codes, colours
B. Symbols, codes, signs, colours
C. Colours, signs, codes, symbols
D. Codes, colours, symbols, signs

21. Which of the following statements is not connected with communication ?
A. Medium is the message.
B. The world is an electronic cocoon.
C. Information is power.
D. Telepathy is technological.

22. Communication becomes circular when
A. the decoder becomes an encoder
B. the feedback is absent
C. the source is credible
D. the channel is clear

23. The site that played a major role during the terrorist attack on Mumbai (26/11) in 2008 was
A. Orkut
B. Facebook
C. Amazon.com
D. Twitter

24. **Assertion (A):** For an effective classroom communication at times it is desirable to use the projection technology.
Reason (R): Using the projection technology facilitates extensive coverage of course contents.
A. Both A. and (R) are true, and (R) is the correct explanation.
B. Both A. and (R) are true, but (R) is not the correct explanation.
C. A. is true, but (R) is false.
D. A. is false, but (R) is true.

25. January 1, 1995 was a Sunday. What day of the week lies on January 1, 1996 ?
A. Sunday
B. Monday
C. Wednesday
D. Saturday

26. When an error of 1% is made in the length and breadth of a rectangle, the percentage error (%) in the area of a rectangle will be
A. 0
B. 1
C. 2
D. 4

27. The next number in the series 2, 5, 9, 19, 37, ? will be
A. 74
B. 75
C. 76
D. None of the above

28. There are 10 true-false questions in an examination. Then these questions can be answered in
A. 20 ways
B. 100 ways
C. 240 ways
D. 1024 ways

29. What will be the next term in the following? DCXW, FEVU, HGTS, ?
A. AKPO
B. ABYZ
C. JIRQ
D. LMRS

30. Three individuals X, Y, Z hired a car on a sharing basis and paid Rs. 1,040. They used it for 7, 8, 11 hours, respectively. What are the charges paid by Y ?
A. Rs. 290
B. Rs. 320
C. Rs. 360
D. Rs. 440

31. Deductive argument involves
A. sufficient evidence
B. critical thinking
C. seeing logical relations
D. repeated observation

32. Inductive reasoning is based on or presupposes
A. uniformity of nature
B. God created the world
C. unity of nature
D. laws of nature

33. To be critical, thinking must be
A. practical
B. socially relevant
C. individually satisfying
D. analytical

34. Which of the following is an analogous statement ?
- A. Man is like God
- B. God is great
- C. Gandhiji is the Father of the Nation
- D. Man is a rational being.

Questions from 35 - 36 are based on the following diagram in which there are three intersecting circles. H representing The Hindu, 1 representing Indian Express and T representing The Times of India. A total of 50 persons were surveyed and the number in the Venn diagram indicates the number of persons reading the newspapers.

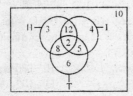

35. How many persons would be reading at least two newspapers ?
- A. 23
- B. 25
- C. 27
- D. 29

36. How many persons would be reading almost two newspapers ?
- A. 23
- B. 25
- C. 27
- D. 48

37. Which of the following graphs does not represent regular (periodic) behaviour of the variable f(t) ?

1.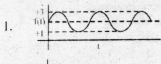

2.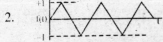

3.

4.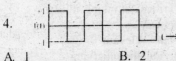

- A. 1
- B. 2
- C. 3
- D. 4

Study the following graph and answer the questions 38 to 40.

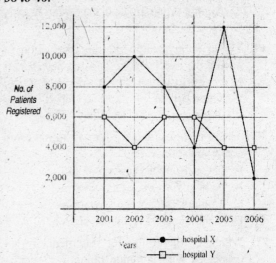

38. In which year total number of patients registered in hospital X and hospital Y was the maximum ?
- A. 2003
- C. 2005
- B. 2004
- D. 2006

39. What is the maximum dispersion in the registration of patients in the two hospitals in a year?
- A. 8000
- C. 4000
- B. 6000
- D. 2000

40. In which year there was maximum decrease in registration of patients in hospital X ?
- A. 2003
- B. 2004
- C. 2005
- D. 2006

41. Which of the following sources of data is not based on primary data collection ?
- A. Census of India
- B. National Sample Survey
- C. Statistical Abstracts of India
- D. National Family Health Survey

42. Which of the four data sets have more dispersion ?

A.	88	91	90	92	89	91
B.	0	1	1	0	−1	−2
C.	3	5	2	4	1	5
D.	0	5	8	10	−2	−8

43. Which of the following is *not* related to information security on the Internet ?
   A. Data Encryption
   B. Water marking
   C. Data Hiding
   D. Information Retrieval

44. Which is the largest unit of storage among the following ?
   A. Terabyte   B. Megabyte
   C. Kilobyte   D. Gigabyte

45. bit stands for
   A. binary information term
   C. binary tree
   B. binary digit
   D. Bivariate Theory

46. Which one of the following is *not* a linear data structure ?
   A. Array   B. Binary Tree
   C. Queue   D. Stack

47. Which one of the following is *not* a network device ?
   A. Router   B. Switch
   C. Hub   D. CPU

48. A compiler is used to convert the following to object code which can be executed
   A. High-level language
   B. Low-level language
   C. Assembly language
   D. Natural language

49. The great Indian Bustard bird is found in
   A. Thar Desert of Rajasthan
   B. Malabar Coast
   C. Coastal regions of India
   D. Delta regions

50. The Sagarmanthan National Park has been established to preserve the eco-system of which mountain peak ?
   A. Kanchenjunga   B. Mount Everest
   C. Annapurna   D. Dhaulavira

51. Maximum soot is released from
   A. Petrol vehicles
   B. CNG vehicles
   C. Diesel vehicles
   D. Thermal Power Plants

52. Surface Ozone is produced from
   A. Transport sector
   B. Cement plants
   C. Textile industry
   D. Chemical industry

53. Which one of the following non-conventional energy sources can be exploited most economically ?
   A. Solar
   B. Wind
   C. Geo-thermal
   D. Ocean Thermal Energy Conversion (OTEC)

54. The most recurring natural hazard in India is
   A. Earthquakes   B. Floods
   C. Landslides   D. Volcanoes

55. The recommendation of National Knowledge Commission for the establishment of 1500 Universities is to
   A. create more teaching jobs
   B. ensure increase in student enrolment in higher education
   C. replace or substitute the privately managed higher education institutions by public institutions
   D. enable increased movement of students from rural areas to urban areas

56. According to Article 120 of the Constitution of India, the business in Parliament shall be transacted in
   A. English only
   B. Hindi only
   C. English and Hindi both
   D. All the languages included in Eighth Schedule of the Constitution

57. Which of the following is more interactive and student centric ?
   A. Seminar   B. Workshop
   C. Lecture   D. Group Discussion

58. The Parliament in India is composed of
   A. Lok Sabha & Rajya Sabha
   B. Lok Sabha, Rajya Sabha & Vice President
   C. Lok Sabha, Rajya Sabha & President
   D. Lok Sabha, Rajya Sabha with their Secretariats

59. The enrolment in higher education in India is contributed both by Formal System of Education and by System of Distance Education Distance education contributes
A. 50% of formal system
B. 25% of formal system
C. 10% of the formal system
D. Distance education system's contribution is not taken into account while considering the figures of enrolment in higher education

60. **Assertion A :** The U.G.C. Academic Staff Colleges came into existence to improve the quality of teachers.
Reason (R) : University and college teachers have to undergo both orientation and refresher courses.
A. Both A. and (R) are true and (R) is the correct explanation.
B. Both A. and (R) are correct but (R) is not the correct explanation of A..
C. A. is correct and (R) is false.
D. A. is false and (R) is correct.

ANSWERS

1	2	3	4	5	6	7	8	9	10
D	C	B	C	B	C	A	B	B	B
11	**12**	**13**	**14**	**15**	**16**	**17**	**18**	**19**	**20**
C	B	C	A	D	D	B	A	C	A
21	**22**	**23**	**24**	**25**	**26**	**27**	**28**	**29**	**30**
D	A	A	A	B	C	B	D	C	B
31	**32**	**33**	**34**	**35**	**36**	**37**	**38**	**39**	**40**
C	A	B	A	C	D	C	C	A	D
41	**42**	**43**	**44**	**45**	**46**	**47**	**48**	**49**	**50**
C	D	D	A	B	B	D	A	A	B
51	**52**	**53**	**54**	**55**	**56**	**57**	**58**	**59**	**60**
D	A	A	B	B	C	D	C	B	A

SOME SELECTED EXPLANATORY ANSWERS

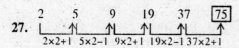

27. 2 5 9 19 37 75
2×2+1 5×2-1 9×2+1 19×2-1 37×2+1

44. Kilobyte < Megabyte < Gigabyte < Terabyte

49. The great Indian Bustard bird is found in Thar Desert.

58. The Parliament in India is composed of Lok Sabha, Rajya Sabha & President.

UGC-NET (JRF) Exam June, 2010

PAPER–I

Note : This paper contains **sixty** (60) multiple-choice questions, each question carrying **two** (2) marks. C ndidate is expected to answer any **fifty** (50) questions. In case more than 50 questions are attempted, only the first 50 questions will be evaluated.

1. Which one of the following is the most important quality of a good teacher ?
   A. Punctuality and sincerity
   B. Content mastery
   C. Content mastery and reactive
   D. Content mastery and sociable

2. The primary responsibility for the teacher's adjustment lies with
   A. The children
   B. The principal
   C. The teacher himself
   D. The community

3. As per the NCTE norms, what should be the staff strength for a unit of 100 students at B.Ed, level ?
   A. 1 + 7   B. 1 + 9
   C. 1 + 10   D. 1 + 5

4. Research has shown that the most frequent symptom of nervous instability among teachers is
   A. Digestive upsets
   B. Explosive behaviour
   C. Fatigue
   D. Worry

5. Which one of the following statements is correct ?
   A. Syllabus is an annexure to the curriculum.
   B. Curriculum is the same in all educational institutions.
   C. Curriculum includes both formal, and informal education.
   D. Curriculum does not include methods of evaluation.

6. A successful teacher is one who is
   A. Compassionate and disciplinarian
   B. Quite and reactive
   C. Tolerant and dominating
   D. Passive and active

Read the following passage carefully and answer the questions 7 to 12.

The phrase "What is it like ?" stands for a fundamental thought process. How does one go about observing and reporting on things and events that occupy segments of earth space ? Of all the infinite variety of phenomena on the face of the earth, how does one decide what phenomena to observe ? There is no such thing as a complete description of the earth or any part of it, for every microscopic point on the earth's surface differs from every other such point. Experience shows that the things observed are already familiar, because they are like phenomena that occur at home or because they resemble the abstract images and models developed in the human mind.

How are abstract images formed ? Humans alone among the animals possess language; their words symbolize not only specific things but also mental images of classes of things. People can remember what they have seen or experienced because they attach a word symbol to them.

During the long record of our efforts to gain more and more knowledge about the face of the earth as the human habitat, there has been a continuing interplay between things and events. The direct observation through the senses is described as a percept; the mental image is described as a concept. Percepts are what some people describe as reality, in contrast to mental images, which are theoretical, implying that they are not real.

The relation of Percept to Concept is not as simple as the definition implies. It is now quite clear that people of different cultures or even individuals in the same culture develop different mental images of reality and what they perceive is a reflection of these preconceptions. The direct observation of things and events on the face of the earth is so clearly a function of the mental images of the mind of the observer that the whole idea of reality must be reconsidered.

Concepts determine what the observer perceives, yet concepts are derived from the generalizations of previous percepts. What happens is that the educated observer is taught to accept a set of concepts and then sharpens or changes these concepts during a professional career. In any one field of scholarship, professional opinion at one time determines what concepts and procedures are acceptable, and these form a kind of model of scholarly behaviour.

7. The problem raised in the passage reflects on
   A. thought process
   B. human behaviour
   C. cultural perceptions
   D. professional opinion

8. According to the passage, human beings have mostly in mind
   A. Observation of things
   B. Preparation of mental images
   C. Expression through language
   D. To gain knowledge

9. Concept means
   A. A mental image
   B. A reality
   C. An idea expressed in language form
   D. All the above

10. The relation of Percept to Concept is
    A. Positive   B. Negative
    C. Reflective   D. Absolute

11. In the passage, the earth is taken as
    A. The Globe
    B. The Human Habitat
    C. A Celestial Body
    D. A Planet

12. Percept means
    A. Direct observation through the senses
    B. A conceived idea
    C. Ends of a spectrum
    D. An abstract image

13. Action research means
    A. A longitudinal research
    B. An applied research
    C. A research initiated to solve an immediate problem
    D. A research with socio-economic objective

14. Research is
    A. Searching again and again
    B. Finding solution to any problem
    C. Working in a scientific way to search for truth of any problem
    D. None of the above

15. A common test in research demands much priority on
    A. Reliability   B. Useability
    C. Objectivity   D. All of the above

16. Which of the following is the first step in starting the research process ?
    A. Searching sources of information to locate problem.
    B. Survey of related literature
    C. Identification of problem
    D. Searching for solutions to the problem

17. If a researcher conducts a research on finding out which administrative style contributes more to institutional effectiveness ? This will be an example of
    A. Basic Research
    B. Action Research
    C. Applied Research
    D. None of the above

18. Normal Probability Curve should be
    A. Positively skewed
    B. Negatively skewed
    C. Leptokurtic skewed
    D. Zero skewed

19. In communication, a major barrier to reception of messages is
    A. audience attitude
    B. audience knowledge
    C. audience education
    D. audience income

20. Post-modernism is associated with
    A. newspapers   B. magazines
    C. radio   D. television

21. Didactic communication is
    A. intra-personal B. inter-personal
    C. organisational D. relational

22. In communication, the language is
    A. the non-verbal code
    B. the verbal code
    C. the symbolic code
    D. the iconic code

23. Identify the correct sequence of the following:
    A. Source, channel, message, receiver
    B. Source, receiver, channel, message
    C. Source, message, receiver, channel
    D. Source, message, channel, receiver

24. **Assertion** A.: Mass media promote a culture of violence in the society.

    Reason (R) : Because violence sells in the market as people themselves are violent in character.
    A. Both A. and (R) are true and (R) is the correct explanation of A..
    B. Both A. and (R) are true, but (R) is not the correct explanation of A..
    C. A. is true, but (R) is false.
    D. Both A. and (R) are false.

25. When an error of 1% is made in the length of a square, the percentage error in the area of a square will be
    A. 0   B. 1/2
    C. 1   D. 2

26. On January 12, 1980, it was a Saturday. The day of the week on January 12, 1979 was

    A. Thursday   B. Friday
    C. Saturday   D. Sunday

27. If water is called food, food is called tree, tree is called earth, earth is called world, which of the following grows a fruit ?
    A. Water   B. Tree
    C. World   D. Earth

28. E is the son of A, D is the son of B, E is married to C, C is the daughter of B. How is D related to E ?
    A. Brother   B. Uncle
    C. Father-in-law D. Brother-in-law

29. If INSURANCE is coded as ECNARUSNI, how HINDRANCE will be coded ?
    A. CADNfflWCE   B. HANODEINR
    C. AENIRHDCN   D. ECNARDNIH

30. Find the next number in the following series: 2, 5, 10, 17, 26, 37, 50, ?
    A. 63   B. 65
    C. 67   D. 69

31. Which of the following is an example of circular argument ?
    A. God created man in his image and man created God in his own image.
    B. God is the source of a scripture and the scripture is the source of our knowledge of God.
    C. Some of the Indians are great because India is great.
    D. Rama is great because he is Rama.

32. Lakshmana is a morally good person because
    A. he is religious B. he is educated
    C. he is rich   D. he is rational

33. Two statements I and II given below are followed by two conclusions (a) and (b). Supposing the statements are true, which of the following conclusions can logically follow ?
    I. Some religious people are morally good.
    II. Some religious people are rational.

    Conclusions :
    (a) Rationally religious people are good morally.

(b) Non-rational religious persons are not morally good.
A. Only (a) follows.
B. Only (b) follows.
C. Both (a) and (b) follow.
D. Neither (a) nor (b) follows.

34. Certainty is
A. an objective fact
B. emotionally satisfying
C. logical
D. ontological

Questions from 35 to 36 are based on the following diagram in which there are three intersecting circles I, S and P where circle I stands for Indians, circle S stands for scientists and circle P for politicians. Different regions of the figure are lettered from a to g.

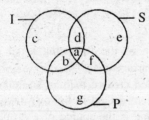

35. The region which represents non-Indian scientists who are politicians.
A. f   B. d
C. a   D. c

36. The region which represents politicians who are Indians as well as scientists.
A. b   B. c
C. a   D. d
A. an objective fact

37. The population of a city is plotted as a function of time (years) in graphic form below:

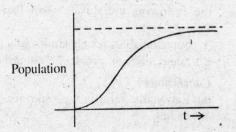

Which of the following inference can be drawn from above plot ?
A. The population increases exponentially. The population increases in parabolic fashion.
The population initially increases in a linear fashion and then stabilizes.
The population initially increases exponentially and then stabilizes.

In the following chart, the price of logs is shown in per cubic metre and that of Plywood and Saw Timber in per tonnes. Study the chart and answer the following questions 38, 39 and 40.

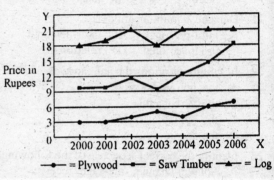

38. Which product shows the maximum percentage increase in price over the period?
A. Saw timber
B. Plywood
C. Log
D. None of the above

39. What is the maximum percentage increase in price per cubic metre of log ?
A. 6   B. 12
C. 18   D. None of these

40. In which year the prices of two products increased and that of the third increased ?
A. 2000   B. 2002
C. 2003   D. 2006

41. Which one of the following is the oldest Archival source of data in India ?
A. National Sample Surveys
B. Agricultural Statistics
C. Census
D. Vital Statistics

42. In a large random data set following normal distribution, the ratio (%) of number of data points which are in the range of (mean ± standard deviation) to the total number of data points, is
    A. ~ 50%   B. ~ 67%
    C. ~ 97%   D. ~ 47%

43. Which number system is usually followed in a typical 32-bit computer?
    A. 2   B. 8
    C. 10   D. 16

44. Which one of the following is an example of Operating System ?
    A. Microsoft Word
    B. Microsoft Excel
    C. Microsoft Access
    D. Microsoft Windows

45. Which one of the following represent the binary equivalent of the decimal number 23?
    A. 01011   B. 10111
    C. 10011   D. None of the above

46. Which one of the following is different from other members?
    A. Google   B. Windows
    C. Linux   D. Mac

47. Where does a computer add and compare its data?
    A. CPU   B. Memory
    C. Hard disk   D. Floppy disk

48. Computers on an internet are identified by
    A. e-mail address
    B. street address
    C. IP address
    D. None of the above

49. The Right to Information Act, 2005 makes the provision of
    A. Dissemination of all types of information by all Public authorities to any person.
    B. Establishment of Central, State and District Level Information Commissions as an appellate body.

C. Transparency and accountability in Public authorities.
D. All of the above

50. Which type of natural hazards cause maximum damage to property and lives?
    A. Hydrological
    B. Hydro-meteorological
    C. Geological
    D. Geo-chemical

51. Dioxins are produced from
    A. Wastelands
    B. Power plants
    C. Sugar factories
    D. Combustion of plastics

52. The slogan "A tree for each child" was coined for
    A. Social forestry programme
    B. Clean Air programme
    C. Soil conservation programme
    D. Environmental protection programme

53. The main constituents of biogas are
    A. Methane and Carbon di-oxide
    B. Methane and Nitric oxide
    C. Methane, Hydrogen and Nitric oxide
    D. Methane and Sulphur di-oxide

54. Assertion (A): In the world as a whole, the environment has degraded during past several decades.
    Reason (R) : The population of the world has been growing significantly.
    A. A. is correct, (R) is correct and (R) is the correct explanation of A..
    B. A. is correct, (R) is correct and (R) is not the correct explanation of A..
    C. A. is correct, but (R) is false.
    D. A. is false, but (R) is correct.

55. Climate change has implications for
    1. soil moisture   2. forest fires
    3. biodiversity   4. ground water
    Identify the correct combination according to the code :
    Codes :
    A. 1 and 3   B. 1, 2 and 3
    C. 1, 3 and 4   D. 1, 2, 3 and 4

56. The accreditation process by National Assessment and Accreditation Council (NAAC) differs from that of National Board of Accreditation (NBA) in terms of
   A. Disciplines covered by both being the same, there is duplication of efforts.
   B. One has institutional grading approach and the other has programme grading approach.
   C. Once get accredited by NBA or NAAC, the institution is free from renewal of grading, which is not a progressive decision.
   D. This accreditation amounts to approval of minimum standards in the quality of education in the institution concerned.

57. Which option is not correct ?
   A. Most of the educational institutions of National repute in scientific and technical sphere fall under 64th entry of Union list.
   B. Education, in general, is the subject of concurrent list since 42nd Constitutional Amendment Act 1976.
   C. Central Advisory Board on Education (CABE) was first established in 1920.
   D. India had implemented the right to Free and Compulsory Primary Education in 2002 through 86th Constitutional Amendment.

58. Which statement is not correct about the "National Education Day" of India ?
   A. It is celebrated on 5th September every year.
   B. It is celebrated on 11th November every year.
   C. It is celebrated in the memory of India's first Union Minister of Education, Dr. Abul Kalam Azad.
   D. It is being celebrated since 2008.

59. Match List-I with List-II and select the correct answer from the codes given below:

List -1 (Articles of the Constitution)	List - II (Institutions)
(a) Article 280	(i) Administrative Tribunals
(b) Article 324	(ii) Election Commission of India
(c) Article 323	(iii) Finance Commission at Union level
(d) Article 315	(iv) Union Public Service Commission

Codes :

	(a)	(b)	(c)	(d)
A.	(i)	(ii)	(iii)	(iv)
B.	(iii)	(ii)	(i)	(iv)
C.	(ii)	(iii)	(iv)	(i)
D.	(ii)	(iv)	(iii)	(i)

60. Deemed Universities declared by UGC under Section 3 of the UGC Act 1956, are not permitted to
   A. offer programmes in higher education and issue degrees.
   B. give affiliation to any institute of higher education.
   C. open off-campus and off-shore campus anywhere in the country and overseas respectively without the permission of the UGC.
   D. offer distance education programmes without the approval of the Distance Education Council.

ANSWERS

1	2	3	4	5	6	7	8	9	10
B	C	C	B	C	A	C	A	A	C
11	12	13	14	15	16	17	18	19	20
B	A	C	C	D	C	C	D	C	D
21	22	23	24	25	26	27	28	29	30
B	B	D	D	D	B	C	D	D	B

31 B	32 A	33 D	34 C	35 A	36 C	37 D	38 C	39 D	40 B
41 C	42 B	43 A	44 D	45 B	46 B	47 A	48 C	49 D	50 C
51 D	52 D	53 A	54 B	55 D	56 C	57 A	58 A	59 B	60 B

SOME SELECTED EXPLANATORY ANSWERS

29. Since,

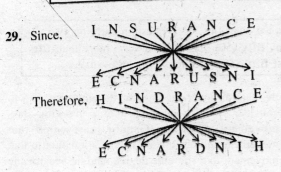

Therefore,

30.

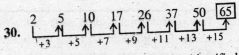

48. Computers on an internet are identified by IP address.

53. Main constituents of biogas are: Methane and Carbon di-oxide.

||||||||

UGC-NET (JRF) EXAM DECEMBER, 2010

PAPER–I

Note : This paper contains **sixty** (60) multiple-choice questions, each question carrying **two** (2) marks. Candidate is expected to answer any **fifty** (50) questions. In case more than **fifty** (50) questions are attempted, only the first **fifty** (50) questions will be evaluated.

1. Which of the following variables cannot be expressed in quantitative terms?
   A. Socio-economic Status
   B. Marital Status
   C. Numerical Aptitude
   D. Professional Attitude

2. A doctor studies the relative effectiveness of two drugs of dengue fever. His research would be classified as
   A. Descriptive Survey
   B. Experimental Research
   C. Case Study
   D. Ethnography

3. The term 'phenomenology' is associated with the process of
   A. Qualitative Research
   B. Analysis of Variance
   C. Correlational Study
   D. Probability Sampling

4. The 'Sociogram' technique is used to study
   A. Vocational Interest
   B. Professional Competence
   C. Human Relations
   D. Achievement Motivation

Read the following passage carefully and answer questions from 5 to 10.

It should be remembered that the nationalist movement in India, like all nationalist movements, was essentially a bourgeois movement. It represented the natural historical stage of development, and to consider it or to criticise it as a working-class movement is wrong. Gandhi represented that movement and the Indian masses in relation to that movement to a supreme degree, and he became the voice of Indian people to that extent. The main contribution of Gandhi to India and the Indian masses has been through the powerful movements which he launched through the National Congress. Through nation-wide action he sought to mould the millions, and largely succeeded in doing so, and changing them from a demoralised, timid and hopeless mass, bullied and crushed by every dominant interest, and incapable of resistance, into a people with self-respect and self-reliance, resisting tyranny, and capable of united action and sacrifice for a larger cause.

Gandhi made people think of political and economic issues and every village and every bazaar hummed with argument and debate on the new ideas and hopes that filled the people. That was an amazing psychological change. The time was ripe for it, of course, and circumstances and world conditions worked for this change. But a great leader is necessary to take advantage of circumstances and conditions. Gandhi was that leader, and he released many of the bonds that imprisoned and disabled our minds, and none of us who experienced it can ever forget that great feeling of release and exhilaration that came over the Indian people.

Gandhi has played a revolutionary role in India of the greatest importance because he knew how to make the most of the objective conditions and could reach the heart of the masses, while groups with a more advanced ideology functioned largely in the air because they did not fit in with those conditions and could therefore not evoke any substantial response from the masses.

It is perfectly true that Gandhi, functioning in the nationalist plane, does not think in terms of the conflict of classes, and tries to compose their differences. But the action he has indulged and taught the people has inevitably raised mass consciousness tremendously and made social issues vital. Gandhi and the Congress must be judged by the policies they pursue and the action they indulge in. But behind this, personality counts and colours those policies and activities. In the case of very exceptional person like Gandhi the question of personality becomes especially important in order to understand and appraise him. To us he has represented the spirit and honour of India, the yearning of her sorrowing millions to be rid of their innumerable burdens, and an insult to him by the British Government or others has been an insult to India and her people.

5. Which one of the following is true of the given passage?
   A. The passage is a critique of Gandhi's role in Indian movement for independence.
   B. The passage hails the role of Gandhi in India's freedom movement.
   C. The author is neutral on Gandhi's role in India's freedom movement.
   D. It is an account of Indian National Congress's support to the working-class movement.

6. The change that the Gandhian movement brought among the Indian masses was
   A. Physical   B. Cultural
   C. Technological   D. Psychological

7. To consider the nationalist movement or to criticise it as a working-class movement was wrong because it was a
   A. historical movement
   B. voice of the Indian people

C. bourgeois movement
D. movement represented by Gandhi

8. Gandhi played a revolutionary role in India because he could
   A. preach morality
   B. reach the heart of Indians
   C. see the conflict of classes
   D. lead the Indian National Congress

9. Groups with advanced ideology functioned in the air as they did not fit in with
   A. objective conditions of masses
   B. the Gandhian ideology
   C. the class consciousness of the people
   D. the differences among masses

10. The author concludes the passage by
    A. criticising the Indian masses
    B. the Gandhian movement
    C. pointing out the importance of the personality of Gandhi
    D. identifying the sorrows of millions of Indians

11. Media that exist in an interconnected series of communication – points are referred to as
    A. Networked media
    B. Connective media
    C. Nodal media
    D. Multimedia

12. The information function of mass communication is described as
    A. diffusion   B. publicity
    C. surveillance   D. diversion

13. An example of asynchronous medium is
    A. Radio   B. Television
    C. Film   D. Newspaper

14. In communication, connotative words are
    A. explicit   C. abstract
    B. simple   D. cultural

15. A message beneath a message is labelled as
    A. embedded text   B. internal text
    C. inter-text   D. sub-text

16. In analog mass communication, stories are
    A. static   B. dynamic
    C. interactive   D. exploratory

17. Determine the relationship between the pair of words ALWAYS : NEVER and then select from the following pair of words which have a similar relationship
   A. often : rarely
   B. frequently : occasionally
   C. constantly : frequently
   D. intermittently : casually

18. Find the wrong number in the sequence
   52, 51, 48, 43, 34, 27, 16
   A. 27   B. 34
   C. 43   D. 48

19. In a certain code, PAN is written as 31 and PAR as 35, then PAT is written in the same code as
   A. 30   B. 37
   C. 39   D. 41

20. The letters in the first set have certain relationship. On the basis of this relationship, make the right choice for the second set :
   AF : IK : : LQ : ?
   A. MO   B. NP
   C. OR   D. TV

21. If 5472 = 9, 6342 = 6, 7584 = 6, what is 9236?
   A. 2   B. 3
   C. 4   D. 5

22. In an examination, 35% of the total students failed in Hindi, 45% failed in English and 20% in both. The percentage of those who passed in both subjects is
   A. 10   B. 20
   C. 30   D. 40

23. Two statements I and II given below are followed by two conclusions (a) and (b). Supposing the statements are true, which of the following conclusions can logically follow?

   Statements :
   I.   Some flowers are red.
   II. Some flowers are blue.

   Conclusions :
   (a) Some flowers are neither red nor blue.
   (b) Some flowers are both red and blue.

   A. Only (a) follows.
   B. Only (b) follows.
   C. Both (a) and (b) follows.
   D. Neither (a) nor (b) follows.

24. If the statement 'all students are intelligent' is true, which of the following statements are false?
   (i) No students are intelligent.
   (ii) Some students are intelligent.
   (iii) Some students are not intelligent.
   A. (i) and (ii)
   B. (i) and (iii)
   C. (ii) and (iii)
   D. (i) only

25. A reasoning where we start with certain particular statements and conclude with a universal statement is called
   A. Deductive Reasoning
   B. Inductive Reasoning
   C. Abnormal Reasoning
   D. Transcendental Reasoning

26. What is the smallest number of ducks that could swim in this formation — two ducks in front of a duck, two ducks behind a duck and a duck between two ducks?
   A. 5   B. 7
   C. 4   D. 3

27. Mr. A, Miss B, Mr. C and Miss D are sitting around a table and discussing their trades.
   (i) Mr. A sits opposite to the cook.
   (ii) Miss B sits right to the barber.
   (iii) The washerman sits right to the barber.
   (iv) Miss D sits opposite to Mr. C.

   What are the trades of A and B?
   A. Tailor and barber
   B. Barber and cook
   C. Tailor and cook
   D. Tailor and washerman

28. Which one of the following methods serve to measure correlation between two variables?
   A. Scatter Diagram
   B. Frequency Distrubution
   C. Two-way table
   D. Coefficient of Rank Correlation

29. Which one of the following is not an Internet Service Provider (ISP)?
A. MTNL   B. BSNL
C. ERNET India   D. Infotech India Ltd.

30. The hexadecimal number system consists of the symbols
A. 0 – 7   2. 0 – 9, A – F
C. 0 – 7, A – F   D. None of these

31. The binary equivalent of $(-15)_{10}$ is (2's complement system is used)
A. 11110001   B. 11110000
C. 10001111   D. None of these

32. 1 GB is equal to
A. 2^{30} bits   B. 2^{30} bytes
C. 2^{20} bits   D. 2^{20} bytes

33. The set of computer programs that manage the hardware/software of a computer is called
A. Compiler system
B. Operation system
C. Operating system
D. None of these

34. S/MIME in Internet technology stands for
A. Secure Multipurpose Internet Mail Extension
B. Secure Multimedia Internet Mail Extension
C. Simple Multipurpose Internet Mail Extension
D. Simple Multimedia Internet Mail Extension

35. Which of the following is **not** covered in 8 missions under the Climate Action Plan of Government of India?
A. Solar power
C. Waste to energy conversion
B. Afforestation
D. Nuclear energy

36. The concentration of Total Dissolved Solids (TDS) in drinking water should not exceed
A. 500 mg/L   B. 400 mg/L
C. 300 mg/L   D. 200 mg/L

37. 'Chipko movement was first started by
A. Arundhati Roy
B. Medha Patkar
C. Ila Bhatt
D. Sunderlal Bahuguna

38. The constitutents of photochemical smog responsible for eye irritation are
A. SO_2 and O_3
B. SO_2 and NO_2
C. HCHO and PAN
D. SO_2 and SPM

39. **Assertion (A) :** Some carbonaceous aerosols may be carcinogenic.

Reason (R) : They may contain polycyclic aromatic hydrocarbons (PAHs).
A. Both (A) and (R) are correct and (R) is the correct explanation of (A).
B. Both (A) and (R) are correct but (R) is not the correct explanation of (A).
C. (A) is correct, but (R) is false.
D. (A) is false, but (R) is correct.

40. Volcanic eruptions affect
A. atmosphere and hydrosphere
B. hydrosphere and biosphere
C. lithosphere, biosphere and atmosphere
D. lithosphere, hydrosphere and atmosphere

41. India's first Defence University is in the State of
A. Haryana   B. Andhra Pradesh
C. Uttar Pradesh   D. Punjab

42. Most of the Universities in India
A. conduct teaching and research only
B. affiliate colleges and conduct examinations
C. conduct teaching/research and examinations
D. promote research only

43. Which one of the following is not a Constitutional Body?
A. Election Commission
B. Finance Commission
C. Union Public Service Commission
D. Planning Commission

44. Which one of the following statements is not correct?
A. Indian Parliament is supreme.
B. The Supreme Court of India has the power of judicial review.

C. There is a division of powers between the Centre and the States.

D. There is a Council of Ministers to aid and advise the President.

45. Which one of the following statements reflects the republic character of Indian democracy?
A. Written constitution
B. No State religion
C. Devolution of power to local Government institutions
D. Elected President and directly or indirectly elected Parliament

46. Who among the following appointed by the Governor can be removed by only the President of India?
A. Chief Minister of a State
B. A member of the State Public Service Commission
C. Advocate-General
D. Vice-Chancellor of a State University

47. If two small circles represent the class of the 'men' and the class of the 'plants and the big circle represents 'mortality', which one of the following figures represent the proposition 'All men are mortal.'?

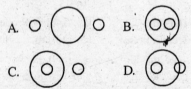

The following table presents the production of electronic items (TVs and LCDs) in a factory during the period from 2006 to 2010. Study the table carefully and answer the questions from **48** to **52** :

Year	2006	2007	2008	2009	2010
TVs	6000	9000	13000	11000	8000
LCDs	7000	9400	9000	10000	12000

48. In which year, the total production of electronic items is maximum?
A. 2006　　　　B. 2007
C. 2008　　　　D. 2010

49. What is the difference between averages of production of LCDs and TVs from 2006 to 2008?
A. 3000　　　　B. 2867
C. 3015　　　　D. None of these

50. What is the year in which production of TVs is half the production of LCDs in the year 2010?
A. 2007　　　　B. 2006
C. 2009　　　　D. 2008

51. What is the ratio of production of LCDs in the years 2008 and 2010?
A. 4 : 3　　　　B. 3 : 4
C. 1 : 3　　　　D. 2 : 3

52. What is the ratio of production of TVs in the years 2006 and 2007?
A. 6 : 7　　　　B. 7 : 6
C. 2 : 3　　　　D. 3 : 2

53. Some students in a class exhibit great curiosity for learning. It may be because such children
A. Are gifted
B. Come from rich families
C. Show artificial behaviour
D. Create indiscipline in the class

54. The most important quality of a good teacher is
A. Sound knowledge of subject matter
B. Good communication skills
C. Concern for students' welfare
D. Effective leadership qualities

55. Which one of the following is appropriate in respect of teacher-student relationship.
A. Very informal and intimate
B. Limited to classroom only
C. Cordial and respectful
D. Indifferent

56. The academic performance of students can be improved if parents are encouraged to
A. supervise the work of their wards
B. arrange for extra tuition
C. remain unconcerned about it
D. interact with teachers frequently

57. In a lively classroom situation, there is likely to be
A. occasional roars of laughter
B. complete silence
C. frequent teacher-student dialogue
D. loud discussion among students

58. If a parent approaches the teacher to do some favour to his/her ward in the examination, the teacher should
A. try to help him
B. ask him not to talk in those terms
C. refulse politely and firmly
D. ask him rudely to go away

59. Which of the following phrases is not relevant to describe the meaning of research as a process?
A. Systematic Activity
B. Objective Observation
C. Trial and Error
D. Problem Solving

60. Which of the following is not an example of a continuous variable?
A. Family size
B. Intelligence
C. Height
D. Attitude

ANSWERS

1	2	3	4	5	6	7	8	9	10
D	B	A	C	B	D	C	B	A	C
11	**12**	**13**	**14**	**15**	**16**	**17**	**18**	**19**	**20**
A	C	D	D	D	A	A	B	B	D
21	**22**	**23**	**24**	**25**	**26**	**27**	**28**	**29**	**30**
A	B	C	D	B	A	C	D	D	B
31	**32**	**33**	**34**	**35**	**36**	**37**	**38**	**39**	**40**
D	B	C	A	D	A	D	B	A	D
41	**42**	**43**	**44**	**45**	**46**	**47**	**48**	**49**	**50**
A	C	D	B	D	B	C	C	D	B
51	**52**	**53**	**54**	**55**	**56**	**57**	**58**	**59**	**60**
B	C	A	B	C	D	C	C	C	C

SOME SELECTED EXPLANATORY ANSWERS

18.
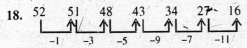

Only 9 is divisible by 3 and rest are not divisible by any number.

19.

A	B	C	D	E	F	G	H	I
1	2	3	4	5	6	7	8	9
J	K	L	M	N	O	P	Q	R
10	11	12	13	14	15	16	17	18

S	T	U	V	W	X	Y	Z
19	20	21	22	23	24	25	26

$\therefore$ PAN $\Rightarrow$ 16 + 1 + 14 = 31
PAR $\Rightarrow$ 16 + 1 + 18 = 35
$\therefore$ PAT $\Rightarrow$ 16 + 1 + 20 = $\boxed{37}$.

21. $\therefore$ 5472 $\Rightarrow$ 5 + 4 + 7 + 2 = 18 $\Rightarrow$ 1 + 8 = 9
6342 $\Rightarrow$ 6 + 3 + 4 + 2 = 15 $\Rightarrow$ 1 + 5 = 6
7584 $\Rightarrow$ 7 + 5 + 8 + 4 = 24 $\Rightarrow$ 2 + 4 = 6
$\therefore$ 9236 $\Rightarrow$ 9 + 2 + 3 + 6 = 20 $\Rightarrow$ 2 + 0 = 2

UGC-NET (JRF) Exam June, 2011

PAPER-I

Note : This paper contains **sixty (60)** multiple-choice questions, each question carrying **two (2)** marks. Candidate is expected to answer any **fifty (50)** questions. In case more than **fifty (50)** questions are attempted, only the first **fifty (50)** questions will be evaluated.

1. A research paper is a brief report of research work based on
   A. Primary Data only
   B. Secondary Data only
   C. Both Primary and Secondary Data
   D. None of the above

2. Newton gave three basic laws of motion. This research is categorized as
   A. Descriptive Research
   B. Sample Survey
   C. Fundamental Research
   D. Applied Research

3. A group of experts in a specific area of knowledge assembled at a place and prepared a syllabus for a new course. The process may be termed as
   A. Seminar B. Workshop
   C. Conference D. Symposium

4. In the process of conducting research "Formulation of Hypothesis" is followed by
   A. Statement of Objectives
   B. Analysis of Data
   C. Selection of Research Tools
   D. Collection of Data

Read the following passage carefully and answer questions from 5 to 10:

All historians are interpreters of text if they be private letters, Government records or parish birthlists or whatever. For most kinds of historians, these are only the necessary means to understanding something other than the texts themselves, such as a political action or a historical trend, whereas for the intellectual historian, a full understanding of his chosen texts is itself the aim of his enquiries. Of course, the intellectual history is particularly prone to draw on the focus of other disciplines that are habitually interpreting texts for purposes of their own, probing the reasoning that ostensibly connects premises and conclusions. Furthermore, the boundaries with adjacent subdisciplines are shifting and indistinct : the history of art and the history of science both claim a certain autonomy, partly just because they require specialised technical skills, but both can also be seen as part of a wider intellectual history, as is evident when one considers, for example, the common stock of knowledge about cosmological beliefs or moral ideals of a period.

Like all historians, the intellectual historian is a consumer rather than a producer of 'methods'. His distinctiveness lies in which aspect of the past he is trying to illuminate, not in having exclusive possession of either a corpus of evidence or a body of techniques. That being said, it does seem that the label 'intellectual history' attracts a disproportionate share of misunderstanding.

It is alleged that intellectual history is the history of something that never really mattered. The long dominance of the historical profession by political historians bred a kind of philistinism, an unspoken belief that power and its exercise was 'what mattered'. The prejudice was reinforced by the assertion that political action was never really the outcome of principles or ideas that were 'more flapdoodle'. The legacy of this precept is still discernible in the tendency to require ideas to have 'licensed' the political class before they can be deemed worthy of intellectual attention, as if there were some reasons why the history of art or science, of philosophy or literature, were somehow of interest and significance than the history of Parties or Parliaments. Perhaps in recent years the mirror-image of this philistinism has been more common in the claim that ideas of any one is of systematic expression or sophistication do not matter, as if they were only held by a minority.

Answer the following questions :

5. An intellectual historian aims to fully understand
   A. the chosen texts of his own
   B. political actions
   C. historical trends
   D. his enquiries

6. Intellectual historians do not claim exclusive possession of
   A. conclusions
   B. any corpus of evidence
   C. distinctiveness
   D. habitual interpretation

7. The misconceptions about intellectual history stem from
   A. a body of techniques
   B. the common stock of knowledge
   C. the dominance of political historians
   D. cosmological beliefs

8. What is philistinism?
   A. Reinforcement of prejudice
   B. Fabrication of reasons
   C. The hold of land-owning classes
   D. Belief that power and its exercise matter

9. Knowledge of cosmological beliefs or moral ideas of a period can be drawn as part of
   A. literary criticism
   B. history of science
   C. history of philosophy
   D. intellectual history

10. The claim that ideas of any one is of systematic expression do not matter, as if they were held by a minority, is
    A. to have a licensed political class
    B. political action
    C. a philosophy of literature
    D. the mirror-image of philistinism

11. Public communication tends to occur within a more
    A. complex structure
    B. political structure
    C. convenient structure
    D. formal structure

12. Transforming thoughts, ideas and messages into verbal and non-verbal signs is referred to as
    A. channelisation   B. mediation
    C. encoding   D. decoding

13. Effective communication needs a supportive
    A. economic environment
    B. political environment
    C. social environment
    D. multi-cultural environment

14. A major barrier in the transmission of cognitive data in the process of communication is an individual's
    A. personality   C. expectation
    B. social status   D. coding ability

15. When communicated, institutionalised stereotypes become
    A. myths   B. reasons
    C. experiences   D. convictions

16. In mass communication, selective perception is dependent on the receiver's
    A. competence   B. pre-disposition
    C. receptivity   D. ethnicity

17. Determine the relationship between the pair of words NUMERATOR : DENOMINATOR and then select the pair of words from the following which have a similar relationship :
    A. fraction : decimal
    B. divisor : quotient
    C. top : bottom
    D. dividend : divisor

18. Find the wrong number in the sequence
125, 127, 130, 135, 142, 153, 165
A. 130   B. 142
C. 153   D. 165

19. If HOBBY is coded as IOBY and LOBBY is coded as MOBY; then BOBBY is coded as
A. BOBY   B. COBY
C. DOBY   D. OOBY

20. The letters in the first set have certain relationship. On the basis of this relationship, make the right choice for the second set :
K/T : 11/20 : : J/R : ?
A. 10/8   B. 10/18
C. 11/19   D. 10/19

21. If A = 5, B = 6, C = 7, D = 8 and so on, what do the following numbers stand for?
17, 19, 20, 9, 8
A. Plane   B. Moped
C. Motor   D. Tonga

22. The price of oil is increased by 25%. If the expenditure is not allowed to increase, the ratio between the reduction in consumption and the original consumption is
A. 1 : 3   B. 1 : 4
C. 1 : 5   D. 1 : 6

23. How many 8's are there in the following sequence which are preceded by 5 but not immediately followed by 3?
5 8 3 7 5 8 6 3 8 5 4 5 8 4 7 6
5 5 8 3 5 8 7 5 8 2 8 5
A. 4   B. 5
C. 7   D. 3

24. If a rectangle were called a circle, a circle a point, a point a triangle and a triangle a square, the shape of a wheel is
A. Rectangle   B. Circle
C. Point   D. Triangle

25. Which one of the following methods is best suited for mapping the distribution of different crops as provided in the standard classification of crops in India?
A. Pie diagram
B. Chorochromatic technique
C. Isopleth technique
D. Dot method

26. Which one of the following does not come under the methods of data classification?
A. Qualitative   B. Normative
C. Spatial   D. Quantitative

27. Which one of the following is not a source of data?
A. Administrative records
B. Population census
C. GIS
D. Sample survey

28. If the statement 'some men are cruel' is false, which of the following statements/statement are/is true?
(i) All men are cruel.
(ii) No men are cruel.
(iii) Some men are not cruel.
A. (i) and (iii)   B. (i) and (ii)
C. (ii) and (iii)   D. (iii) only

29. The octal number system consists of the following symbols:
A. 0 – 7   B. 0 – 9
C. 0 – 9, A – F   D. None of the above

30. The binary equivalent of $(-19)_{10}$ in signed magnitude system is
A. 11101100   B. 11101101
C. 10010011   D. None of these

31. DNS in internet technology stands for
A. Dynamic Name System
B. Domain Name System
C. Distributed Name System
D. None of these

32. HTML stands for
A. Hyper Text Markup Language
B. Hyper Text Manipulation Language
C. Hyper Text Managing Links
D. Hyper Text Manipulating Links

33. Which of the following is type of LAN?
A. Ethernet   B. Token Ring
C. FDDI   D. All of the above

34. Which of the following statements is true?
A. Smart cards do not require an operating system.
B. Smart cards and PCs use some operating system.

C. COS is smart card operating system.

D. The communication between reader and card is in full duplex mode.

35. The Ganga Action Plan was initiated during the year
A. 1986   C. 1988
B. 1990   D. 1992

36. Identify the correct sequence of energy sources in order of their share in the power sector in India:
A. Thermal > nuclear > hydro > wind
B. Thermal > hydro > nuclear > wind
C. Hydro > nuclear > thermal > wind
D. Nuclear > hydro > wind > thermal

37. Chromium as a contaminant in drinking water in excess of permissible levels, causes
A. Skeletal damage
B. Gastrointestinal problem
C. Dermal and nervous problems
D. Liver/Kidney problems

38. The main precursors of winter smog are
A. N_2O and hydrocarbons
B. NO_x and hydrocarbons
C. SO_2 and hydrocarbons
D. SO_2 and ozone

39. Flash floods are caused when
A. the atmosphere is convectively unstable and there is considerable vertical wind-shear
B. the atmosphere is stable
C. the atmosphere is convectively unstable with no vertical windshear
D. winds are catabatic

40. In mega cities of India, the dominant source of air pollution is
A. transport sector
B. thermal power
C. municipal waste
D. commercial sector

41. The first Open University in India was set up in the State of
A. Andhra Pradesh
B. Delhi
C. Himachal Pradesh
D. Tamil Nadu

42. Most of the Universities in India are funded by
A. the Central Government
B. the State Governments
C. the University Grants Commission
D. Private bodies and Individuals

43. Which of the following organizations looks after the quality of Technical and Management education in India?
A. NCTE
B. MCI
C. AICTE
D. CSIR

44. Consider the following statements :
Identify the statement which implies natural justice.
A. The principle of natural justice is followed by the Courts.
B. Justice delayed is justice denied.
C. Natural justice is an inalienable right of a citizen
D. A reasonable opportunity of being heard must be given.

45. The President of India is
A. the Head of State
B. the Head of Government
C. both A and B
D. None of the above

46. Who among the following holds office during the pleasure of the President of India?
A. Chief Election Commissioner
B. Comptroller and Auditor General of India
C. Chairman of the Union Public Service Commission
D. Governor of a State

Questions 47 to 49 are based upon the following diagram in which there are three interlocking circles A, P and S where A stands for Artists, circle P for Professors and circle S for Sportspersons.

Different regions in the figure are lettered from a to f :

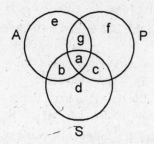

47. The region which represents artists who are neither sportsmen nor professors.
    A. d   B. e
    C. b   D. g

48. The region which represents professors, who are both artists and sportspersons.
    A. a   B. c
    C. d   D. g

49. The region which represents professors, who are also sportspersons, but not artists.
    A. e   B. f
    C. c   D. g

Questions 50 to 52 are based on the following data :

Measurements of some variable X were made at an interval of 1 minute from 10 A.M. to 10:20 A.M. The data, thus, obtained is as follows :

   X : 60, 62, 65, 64, 63, 61, 66, 65, 70, 68
        63, 62, 64, 69, 65, 64, 66, 67, 66, 64

50. The value of X, which is exceeded 10% of the time in the duration of measurement, is
    A. 69   B. 68
    C. 67   D. 66

51. The value of X, which is exceeded 90% of the time in the duration of measurement, is
    A. 63   B. 62
    C. 61   D. 60

52. The value of X, which is exceeded 50% of the time in the duration of measurement, is
    A. 66   B. 65
    C. 64   D. 63

53. For maintaining an effective discipline in the class, the teacher should
    A. Allow students to do what they like.
    B. Deal with the students strictly.
    C. Give the students some problem to solve.
    D. Deal with them politely and firmly.

54. An effective teaching aid is one which
    A. is colourful and good looking
    B. activates all faculties
    C. is visible to all students
    D. easy to prepare and use

55. Those teachers are popular among students who
    A. develop intimacy with them
    B. help them solve their problems
    C. award good grades
    D. take classes on extra tuition fee

56. The essence of an effective classroom environment is
    A. a variety of teaching aids
    B. lively student-teacher interaction
    C. pin-drop silence
    D. strict discipline

57. On the first day of his class, if a teacher is asked by the students to introduce himself, he should
    A. ask them to meet after the class
    B. tell them about himself in brief
    C. ignore the demand and start teaching
    D. scold the student for this unwanted demand

58. Moral values can be effectively inculcated among the students when the teacher
    A. frequently talks about values
    B. himself practices them
    C. tells stories of great persons
    D. talks of Gods and Goddesses

59. The essential qualities of a researcher are
    A. spirit of free enquiry
    B. reliance on observation and evidence

C. systematization or theorizing of knowledge
D. All of the above

60. Research is conducted to
I. Generate new knowledge
II. Not to develop a theory

III. Obtain research degree
IV. Reinterpret existing knowledge
Which of the above are correct?
A. I, III & II   B. III, II & IV
C. II, I & III   D. I, III & IV

ANSWERS

1	2	3	4	5	6	7	8	9	10
C	C	B	C	A	B	C	D	D	D
11	**12**	**13**	**14**	**15**	**16**	**17**	**18**	**19**	**20**
D	C	D	C	D	B	D	D	B	B
21	**22**	**23**	**24**	**25**	**26**	**27**	**28**	**29**	**30**
B	C	A	C	A	B	A	B	A	D
31	**32**	**33**	**34**	**35**	**36**	**37**	**38**	**39**	**40**
B	A	D	C	A	B	D	C	A	A
41	**42**	**43**	**44**	**45**	**46**	**47**	**48**	**49**	**50**
A	C	C	D	B	D	B	A	C	C
51	**52**	**53**	**54**	**55**	**56**	**57**	**58**	**59**	**60**
B	D	D	B	B	B	B	B	D	D

SOME SELECTED EXPLANATORY ANSWERS

18.

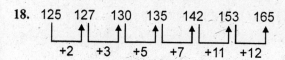

Except 12, all others are odd numbers.

19.

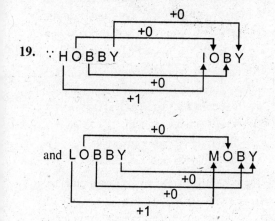

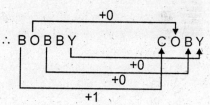

20.

A	B	C	D	E	F	G	H	I	J
1	2	3	4	5	6	7	8	9	10
K	L	M	N	O	P	Q	R	S	T
11	12	13	14	15	16	17	18	19	20
U	V	W	X	Y	Z				
21	22	23	24	25	26				

∵   K → 11
and   T → 20
∴   J → 10
        R → 18

21. ∵ A = 5, B = 6, C = 7, D = 8,
∴ E = 9, F = 10, G = 11, H = 12, I = 13.

J = 14, K = 15, L = 16, M = 17, N = 18, O = 19, P = 20, Q = 21, R = 22, S = 23 ....

Therefore,

$$17 = \boxed{M}$$
$$19 = \boxed{O}$$
$$20 = \boxed{P}$$
$$9 = \boxed{E}$$
$$8 = \boxed{D}$$

23. There are four 8's in the sequence which are preceded by 5 but not immediately followed by 3.

24. Since

□ → ○ → · → △ → □

Rectangle circle   point   triangle   square

∴ The shape of a wheel is Point.

29. An octal number is a number that consists of

any of the following eight symbols – 0, 1, 2, 3, 4, 5, 6 and 7.

Hints : 47 to 49

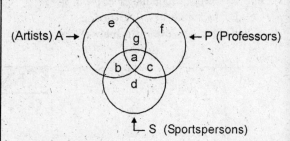

(Artists) A →   ← P (Professors)

└ S (Sportspersons)

47. 'e' represents artists who are neither sportsmen nor professors.

48. 'a' represents professors, who are both artists and sportspersons.

49. 'c' represents professors, who are also sports persons but not artists.

UGC-NET (JRF) Exam
December, 2011

PAPER–I

Note : This paper contains **Sixty (60)** multiple-choice questions, each question carrying **two (2)** marks. Candidate is expected to answer any **Fifty (50)** questions. In case more than **Fifty (50)** questions are attempted, only the first **Fifty (50)** questions will be evaluated.

1. Photo bleeding means
   A. Photo cropping
   B. Photo placement
   C. Photo cutting
   D. Photo colour adjustment

2. While designing communication strategy feed-forward studies are conducted by
   A. Audience
   B. Communicator
   C. Satellite
   D. Media

3. In which language the newspapers have highest circulation ?
   A. English
   B. Hindi
   C. Bengali
   D. Tamil

4. Aspect ratio of TV Screen is
   A. 4 : 3
   B. 3 : 4
   C. 2 : 3
   D. 2 : 4

5. Communication with oneself is known as
   A. Organisational Communication
   B. Grapewine Communication
   C. Interpersonal Communication
   D. Intrapersonal Communication

6. The term 'SITE' stands for
   A. Satellite Indian Television Experiment
   B. Satellite International Television Experiment
   C. Satellite Instructional Television Experiment
   D. Satellite Instructional Teachers Education

7. What is the number that comes next in the sequence ?
   2, 5, 9, 19, 37, ___
   A. 76
   B. 74
   C. 75
   D. 50

8. Find the next letter for the series MPSV.....
   A. X
   B. Y
   C. Z
   D. A

9. If '367' means 'I am happy'; '748' means 'you are sad' and '469' means 'happy and sad' in a given code, then which of the following represents 'and' in that code ?
   A. 3
   B. 6
   C. 9
   D. 4

10. The basis of the following classification is 'animal', 'man', 'house', 'book', and 'student':
    A. Definite descriptions
    B. Proper names
    C. Descriptive phrases
    D. Common names

11. **Assertion (A) :** The coin when flipped next time will come up tails.

    Reason (R) : Because the coin was flipped five times in a row, and each time it came up heads.

    Choose the correct answer from below :
    A. Both (A) and (R) are true, and (R) is the correct explanation of (A).

B. Both (A) and (R) are false, and (R) is the correct explanation of (A).

C. (A) is doubtful, (R) is true, and (R) is not the correct explanation of (A).

D. (A) is doubtful, (R) is false, and (R) is the correct explanation of (A).

12. The relation 'is a sister of ' is
A. non-symmetrical
B. symmetrical
C. asymmetrical
D. transitive

13. If the proposition "Vegetarians are not meat eaters" is false, then which of the following inferences is correct ? Choose from the codes given below :
1. "Some vegetarians are meat eaters" is true.
2. "All vegetarians are meat eaters" is doubtful.
3. "Some vegetarians are not meat eaters" is true.
4. "Some vegetarians are not meat eaters" is doubtful.
Codes:
A. 1, 2 and 3   B. 2, 3 and 4
C. 1, 3 and 4   D. 1, 2 and 4

14. Determine the nature of the following definition :

'Poor' means having an annual income of ₹ 10,000.
A. persuasive   B. precising
C. lexical   D. stipulative

15. Which one of the following is not an argument ?
A. If today is Tuesday, tomorrow will be Wednesday.
B. Since today is Tuesday, tomorrow will be Wednesday.
C. Ram insulted me so I punched him in the nose.
D. Ram is not at home, so he must have gone to town.

16. Venn diagram is a kind of diagram to
A. represent and assess the truth of elementary inferences with the help of Boolean Algebra of classes.

B. represent and assess the validity of elementary inferences with the help of Boolean Algebra of classes.

C. represent but not assess the validity of elementary inferences with the help of Boolean Algebra of classes.

D. assess but not represent the validity of elementary inferences with the help of Boolean Algebra of classes.

17. Inductive logic studies the way in which a premise may
A. support and entail a conclusion
B. not support but entail a conclusion
C. neither support nor entail a conclusion
D. support a conclusion without entailing it

18. Which of the following statements are true ? Choose from the codes given below.
1. Some arguments, while not completely valid, are almost valid.
2. A sound argument may be invalid.
3. A cogent argument may have a probably false conclusion.
4. A statement may be true or false.
Codes:
A. 1 and 2   B. 1, 3 and 4
C. 4 alone   D. 3 and 4

19. If the side of the square increases by 40%, then the area of the square increases by
A. 60 %   B. 40 %
C. 196 %   D. 96 %

20. There are 10 lamps in a hall. Each one of them can be switched on independently. The number of ways in which hall can be illuminated is
A. 10^2 B. 1023
C. 2^{10} D. 10 !

21. How many numbers between 100 and 300 begin or end with 2 ?
A. 100   B. 110
C. 120   D. 180

22. In a college having 300 students, every student reads 5 newspapers and every newspaper is read by 60 students. The number of newspapers required is

A. at least 30   B. at most 20
C. exactly 25   D. exactly 5

The total CO_2 emissions from various sectors are 5 mmt. In the Pie Chart given below, the percentage contribution to CO_2 emissions from various sectors is indicated.

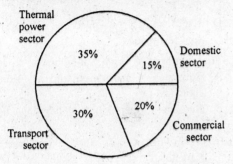

23. What is the absolute CO_2 emission from domestic sector ?
A. 1.5 mmt   B. 2.5 mmt
C. 1.75 mmt   D. 0.75 mmt

24. What is the absolute CO_2 emission for combined thermal power and transport sectors?
A. 3.25 mmt   B. 1.5 mmt
C. 2.5 mmt   D. 4 mmt

25. Which of the following operating system is used on mobile phones?
A. Windows Vista   B. Android
C. Windows XP   D. All of the above

26. If $(y)_x$ represents a number y in base x, then which of the following numbers is smallest of all?
A. $(1111)_2$ B. $(1111)_8$
C. $(1111)_{10}$ D. $(1111)_{16}$

27. High level programming language can be converted to machine language using which of the following?
A. Oracle   B. Compiler
C. Mat lab   D. Assembler

28. HTML is used to create
A. machine language program
B. high level program
C. web page
D. web server

29. The term DNS stands for
A. Domain Name System
B. Defense Nuclear System
C. Downloadable New Software
D. Dependent Name Server

30. IPv4 and IPv6 are addresses used to identify computers on the internet. Find the correct statement out of the following :
A. Number of bits required for IPv4 address is more than number of bits required for IPv6 address.
B. Number of bits required for IPv4 address is same as number of bits required for IPv6 address.
C. Number of bits required for IPv4 address is less than number of bits required for IPv6 address.
D. Number of bits required for IPv4 address is 64.

31. Which of the following pollutants affects the respiratory tract in humans?
A. Carbon monoxide
B. Nitric oxide
C. Sulphur di-oxide
D. Aerosols

32. Which of the following pollutants is not emitted from the transport sector?
A. Oxides of nitrogen
B. Chlorofluorocarbons
C. Carbon monoxide
D. Poly aromatic hydrocarbons

33. Which of the following sources of energy has the maximum potential in India?
A. Solar energy
B. Wind energy
C. Ocean thermal energy
D. Tidal energy

34. Which of the following is not a source of pollution in soil ?
A. Transport sector
B. Agriculture sector
C. Thermal power plants
D. Hydropower plants

35. Which of the following is *not* a natural hazard?
    A. Earthquake   B. Tsunami
    C. Flash floods   D. Nuclear accident

36. Ecological footprint represents
    A. area of productive land and water to meet the resources requirement
    B. energy consumption
    C. CO_2 emissions per person
    D. forest cover

37. The aim of value education to inculcate in students is
    A. the moral values
    B. the social values
    C. the political values
    D. the economic values

38. Indicate the number of Regional Offices of University Grants Commission of India.
    A. 10   B. 07
    C. 08   D. 09

39. One-rupee currency note in India bears the signature of
    A. The President of India
    B. Finance Minister of India
    C. Governor, Reserve Bank of India
    D. Finance Secretary of Government of India

40. Match the List – I with the List – II and select the correct answer from the codes given below:

List – I (Commissions and Committees)	List – II (Year)
(a) First Administrative Reforms Commission	(i) 2005
(b) Paul H. Appleby Committee I	(ii) 1962
(c) K. Santhanam Committee	(iii) 1966
(d) Second Administrative Reforms Commission	(iv) 1953

Codes :

	(a)	(b)	(c)	(d)
A.	(i)	(iii)	(ii)	(iv)
B.	(iii)	(iv)	(ii)	(i)
C.	(iv)	(ii)	(iii)	(i)
D.	(ii)	(i)	(iv)	(iii)

41. Constitutionally the registration and recognition of political parties is the function performed by
    A. The State Election Commission of respective States
    B. The Law Ministry of Government of India
    C. The Election Commission of India
    D. Election Department of the State Governments

42. The members of Gram Sabha are
    A. Sarpanch, Upsarpanch and all elected Panchas
    B. Sarpanch, Upsarpanch and Village level worker
    C. Sarpanch, Gram Sevak and elected Panchas
    D. Registered voters of Village Panchayat

43. By which of the following methods the true evaluation of the students is possible?
    A. Evaluation at the end of the course.
    B. Evaluation twice in a year.
    C. Continuous evaluation.
    D. Formative evaluation.

44. Suppose a student wants to share his problems with his teacher and he visits the teacher's house for the purpose, the teacher should
    A. contact the student's parents and solve his problem.
    B. suggest him that he should never visit his house.
    C. suggest him to meet the principal and solve the problem.
    D. extend reasonable help and boost his morale.

45. When some students are deliberately attempting to disturb the discipline of the class by making mischief, what will be your role as a teacher?
    A. Expelling those students.
    B. Isolate those students.
    C. Reform the group with your authority.
    D. Giving them an opportunity for introspection and improve their behaviour.

46. Which of the following belongs to a projected aid?
    A. Blackboard   B. Diorama
    C. Epidiascope   D. Globe

47. A teacher is said to be fluent in asking questions, if he can ask
    A. meaningful questions
    B. as many questions as possible
    C. maximum number of questions in a fixed time
    D. many meaningful questions in a fixed time

48. Which of the following qualities is most essential for a teacher ?
    A. He should be a learned person.
    B. He should be a well dressed person.
    C. He should have patience.
    D. He should be an expert in his subject.

49. A hypothesis is a
    A. law   B. canon
    C. postulate   D. supposition

50. Suppose you want to investigate the working efficiency of nationalised bank in India, which one of the following would you follow?
    A. Area Sampling
    B. Multi-stage Sampling
    C. Sequential Sampling
    D. Quota Sampling

51. Controlled group condition is applied in
    A. Survey Research
    B. Historical Research
    C. Experimental Research
    D. Descriptive Research

52. Workshops are meant for
    A. giving lectures
    B. multiple target groups
    C. showcase new theories
    D. hands on training/experience

53. Which one of the following is a research tool?
    A. Graph   B. Illustration
    C. Questionnaire D. Diagram

54. Research is not considered ethical if it
    A. tries to prove a particular point.
    B. does not ensure privacy and anonymity of the respondent.
    C. does not investigate the data scientifically.
    D. is not of a very high standard.

Directions (Qs. 55 to 60): *Read the following passage carefully and answer the questions.*

The catalytic fact of the twentieth century is uncontrollable development, consumerist society, political materialism, and spiritual devaluation. This inordinate development has led to the transcendental 'second reality' of sacred perception that biologically transcendence is a part of human life. As the century closes, it dawns with imperative vigour that the 'first reality' of enlightened rationalism and the 'second reality' of the Beyond have to be harmonised in a worthy state of man. The *de facto* values describe what we are, they portray the 'is' of our ethic, they are *est* values (Latin *est* means is). The ideal values tell us what we ought to be, they are *esto* values (Latin *esto* 'ought to be'). Both have to be in the ebb and flow of consciousness. The ever new science and technology and the ever-perennial faith are two modes of one certainty, that is the wholeness of man, his courage to be, his share in Being.

The materialistic foundations of science have crumbled down. Science itself has proved that matter is energy, processes are as valid as facts, and affirmed the non-materiality of the universe. The encounter of the 'two cultures', the scientific and the humane, will restore the normal vision, and will be the bedrock of a 'science of understanding' in the new century. It will give new meaning to the ancient perception that quantity (measure) and quality (value) coexist at the root of nature. Human endeavours cannot afford to be humanistically irresponsible.

55. The problem raised in the passage reflects overall on
    A. Consumerism
    B. Materialism
    C. Spiritual devaluation
    D. Inordinate development

56. The '*de facto*' values in the passage means
    A. What is   B. What ought to be
    C. What can be   D. Where it is

57. According to the passage, the 'first reality' constitutes
A. Economic prosperity
B. Political development
C. Sacred perception of life
D. Enlightened rationalism

58. Encounter of the 'two cultures', the scientific and the human implies
A. Restoration of normal vision
B. Universe is both material and non-material

C. Man is superior to nature
D. Co-existence of quantity and quality in nature

59. The contents of the passage are
A. Descriptive   B. Prescriptive
C. Axiomatic   D. Optional

60. The passage indicates that science has proved that
A. universe is material
B. matter is energy
C. nature has abundance
D. humans are irresponsible

ANSWERS

1	2	3	4	5	6	7	8	9	10
A	B	B	A	D	C	C	B	C	D
11	12	13	14	15	16	17	18	19	20
C	B	A	B	A	B	D	D	D	B
21	22	23	24	25	26	27	28	29	30
B	C	D	A	B	A	B	C	A	C
31	32	33	34	35	36	37	38	39	40
A	B	B	D	D	A	A	B	D	B
41	42	43	44	45	46	47	48	49	50
C	D	D	D	D	C	D	C	D	B
51	52	53	54	55	56	57	58	59	60
C	D	C	B	C	A	D	A	A	B

SOME SELECTED EXPLANATORY ANSWERS

7.
$2 \times 2 + 1 = 5$
$5 \times 2 - 1 = 9$
$9 \times 2 + 1 = 19$
$19 \times 2 - 1 = 37$
$\therefore 37 \times 2 + 1 = \boxed{75}$

8. M   P   S   V   Y
+2   +2   +2   +2

9.
I am happy = 367 ...(1)
You are sad = 748 ...(2)

Happy and sad = 469 ...(3)
From (1) and (3)
Happy = 6
and from (2) and (3)
Sad = 4
$\therefore$ and = 9

19. Let the side of the square be 100 m.
$\therefore$ Area = side^2 = 10000 m^2
After increase, side of the square = 100 + 40
= 140 cm

$\therefore$ Area = $140 \times 140 = 19600$ cm^2

$\therefore$ Percentage increase = $\dfrac{19600-10000}{10000} \times 100$

$= \dfrac{9600 \times 100}{10000} = 96\%$

21. The required numbers are—

Numbers from 200 to 299

And 102, 112, 122, 132, 142, 152, 162, 172, 182, 192

Hence total required number = 100 + 10
$= 110$

22. Here we suppose group of 5 students as 1 unit.

so, number of units = $\dfrac{300}{60} = 5$ units

Now, each unit requires sets of papers

Total requirement = $5 \times 5 = \boxed{25}$

23. Domestic sector emission = $5 \times \dfrac{15}{100}$

$= 0.75$ mmt.

24. Combined % of emission of CO_2 from thermal and transport sector = 30 + 35 = 65%

Required emission = $5 \times \dfrac{65}{100} = 3.25$ mmt

26. $(1111)_2 = 2^3 + 2^2 + 2^1 + 2^0 = \boxed{15}$

UGC-NET (JRF) Exam June, 2012

PAPER–I

Note : This paper contains **sixty (60)** multiple-choice questions, each question carrying **two (2)** marks. Candidate is expected to answer any **fifty (50)** questions. In case more than **fifty (50)** questions are attempted, only the first **fifty (50)** questions will be evaluated.

1. Video-Conferencing can be classified as one of the following types of communication:
   (A) Visual one way
   (B) Audio-Visual one way
   (C) Audio-Visual two way
   (D) Visual two way

2. MC National University of Journalism and Communication is located at:
   (A) Lucknow   (B) Bhopal
   (C) Chennai   (D) Mumbai

3. All India Radio (A.I.R.) for broadcasting was named in the year:
   (A) 1926   (B) 1936
   (C) 1946   (D) 1956

4. In India for broadcasting TV programmes which system is followed?
   (A) NTCS   (B) PAL
   (C) NTSE   (D) SECAM

5. The term 'DAVP' stands for:
   (A) Directorate of Advertising & Vocal Publicity
   (B) Division of Audio-Visual Publicity
   (C) Department of Audio-Visual Publicity
   (D) Directorate of Advertising & Visual Publicity

6. The term "TRP" is associated with TV shows stands for:
   (A) Total Rating Points
   (B) Time Rating Points
   (C) Thematic Rating Points
   (D) Television Rating Points

7. Which is the number that comes next in the following sequence?
   2, 6, 12, 20, 30, 42, 56, _____
   (A) 60   (B) 64
   (C) 72   (D) 70

8. Find the next letter for the series YVSP ....
   (A) N   (B) M
   (C) O   (D) L

9. Given that in a code language, '645' means 'day is warm'; '42' means 'warm spring' and '634' means 'spring is sunny'; which digit represents 'sunny'?
   (A) 3   (B) 2
   (C) 4   (D) 5

10. The basis of the following classification is: 'first President of India', 'author of *Godan*', 'books in my library', 'blue things' and 'students who work hard'
    (A) Common names
    (B) Proper names
    (C) Descriptive phrases
    (D) Indefinite description

11. In the expression 'Nothing is larger than itself' the relation 'is larger than' is:
    (A) antisymmetric

(B) asymmetrical
(C) intransitive
(D) irreflexive

12. **Assertion (A)** : There are more laws on the books today than ever before, and more crimes being committed than ever before.
Reason (R) : Because to reduce crime we must eliminate the laws.
Choose the correct answer from below:
(A) (A) is true, (R) is doubtful and (R) is not the correct explanation of (A).
(B) (A) is false, (R) is true and (R) is the correct explanation of (A).
(C) (A) is doubtful, (R) is doubtful and (R) is not the correct explanation of (A).
(D) (A) is doubtful, (R) is true and (R) is not the correct explanation of (A).

13. If the proposition "All men are not mortal" is true then which of the following inferences is correct? Choose from the code given below:
1. "All men are mortal" is true.
2. "Some men are mortal" is false.
3. "No men are mortal" is doubtful.
4. "All men are mortal" is false.
Code :
(A) 1, 2 and 3
(B) 2, 3 and 4
(C) 1, 3 and 4
(D) 1 and 3

14. Determine the nature of the following definition:
"Abortion" means the ruthless murdering of innocent beings.
(A) Lexical
(B) Persuasive
(C) Stipulative
(D) Theoretical

15. Which one of the following is **not** an argument?
(A) Devadutt does not eat in the day so he must be eating at night.
(B) If Devadutt is growing fat and if he does not eat during the day, he will be eating at night.
(C) Devadutt eats in the night so he does not eat during the day.
(D) Since Devadutt does not eat in the day, he must be eating in the night.

16. Venn diagram is a kind of diagram to:
(A) represent and assess the validity of elementary inferences of syllogistic form.
(B) represent but not assess the validity of elementary inferences of syllogistic form.
(C) represent and assess the truth of elementary inferences of syllogistic form.
(D) assess but not represent the truth of elementary inferences of syllogistic form.

17. Reasoning by analogy leads to:
(A) certainty
(B) definite conclusion
(C) predictive conjecture
(D) surety

18. Which of the following statements are false? Choose from the code given below:
1. Inductive arguments always proceed from the particular to the general.
2. A cogent argument must be inductively strong.
3. A valid argument may have a false premise and a false conclusion.
4. An argument may legitimately be spoken of as 'true' or 'false'.
Code :
(A) 2, 3 and 4
(B) 1 and 3
(C) 2 and 4
(D) 1 and 2

19. Six persons A, B, C, D, E and F are standing in a circle. B is between F and C, A is between E and D, F is to the left of D. Who is between A and F?
(A) B
(B) C
(C) D
(D) E

20. The price of petrol increases by 25%. By what percentage must a customer reduce the consumption so that the earlier bill on the petrol does not alter?
(A) 20%
(B) 25%
(C) 30%
(D) 33.33%

21. If Ram knows that y is an integer greater than 2 and less than 7 and Hari knows that y is an integer greater than 5 and less than 10, then they may correctly conclude that
(A) y can be exactly determined
(B) y may be either of two values

(C) y may be any of three values

(D) there is no value of y satisfying these conditions

22. Four pipes can fill a reservoir in 15, 20, 30 and 60 hours respectively. The first one was opened at 6 AM, second at 7 AM, third at 8 AM and the fourth at 9 AM. When will the reservoir be filled?

(A) 11 AM   (B) 12 Noon

(C) 1 PM   (D) 1:30 PM

The total electricity generation in a country is 97 GW. The contribution of various energy sources is indicated in percentage terms in the Pie Chart given below:

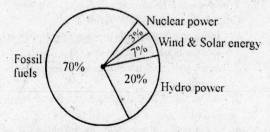

23. What is the contribution of wind and solar power in absolute terms in the electricity generation?

(A) 6.79 GW   (B) 19.4 GW

(C) 9.7 GW   (D) 29.1 GW

24. What is the contribution of renewable energy sources in absolute terms in the electricity generation?

(A) 29.1 GW   (B) 26.19 GW

(C) 67.9 GW   (D) 97 GW

25. TCP/IP is necessary if one is to connect to the:

(A) Phone lines

(B) LAN

(C) Internet

(D) Server

26. Each character on the keyboard of computer has an ASCII value which stands for:

(A) American Stock Code for Information Interchange

(B) American Standard Code for Information Interchange

(C) African Standard Code for Information Interchange

(D) Adaptable Standard Code for Information Change

27. Which of the following is not a programming language?

(A) Pascal

(B) Microsoft Office

(C) Java

(D) C++

28. Minimum number of bits required to store any 3 digit decimal number is equal to:

(A) 3   (B) 5

(C) 8   (D) 10

29. Internet explorer is a type of

(A) Operating System

(B) Compiler

(C) Browser

(D) IP address

30. POP3 and IMAP are e-mail accounts in which:

(A) One automatically gets one's mail everyday

(B) One has to be connected to the server to read or write one's mail

(C) One only has to be connected to the server to send and receive e-mail

(D) One does not need any telephone lines

31. Irritation in eyes is caused by the pollutant:

(A) Sulphur di-oxide

(B) Ozone

(C) PAN

(D) Nitrous oxide

32. Which is the source of chlorofluorocarbons?

(A) Thermal power plants

(B) Automobiles

(C) Refrigeration and Airconditioning

(D) Fertilizers

33. Which of the following is not a renewable natural resource?

(A) Clean air   (B) Fertile soil

(C) Fresh water   (D) Salt

34. Which of the following parameters is not used as a pollution indicator in water?

(A) Total dissolved solids
(B) Coliform count
(C) Dissolved oxygen
(D) Density

35. S and P waves are associated with:
(A) floods
(B) wind energy
(C) earthquakes
(D) tidal energy

36. Match Lists I and II and select the correct answer from the codes given below:

List-I	List-II
(i) Ozone hole	(a) Tsunami
(ii) Greenhouse effect	(b) UV radiations
(iii) Natural hazards	(c) Methane
(iv) Sustainable development	(d) Eco-centrism

Codes :

	(i)	(ii)	(iii)	(iv)
(A)	(b)	(c)	(a)	(d)
(B)	(c)	(b)	(a)	(d)
(C)	(d)	(c)	(a)	(b)
(D)	(d)	(b)	(c)	(a)

37. Indian Institute of Advanced Study is located at:
(A) Dharmshala
(B) Shimla
(C) Solan
(D) Chandigarh

38. Indicate the number of Regional Offices of National Council of Teacher Education.
(A) 04   (B) 05
(C) 06   (D) 08

39. Which of the following rights was considered the "Heart and Soul" of the Indian Constitution by Dr. B.R. Ambedkar?
(A) Freedom of Speech
(B) Right to Equality
(C) Right to Freedom of Religion
(D) Right to Constitutional Remedies

40. Who among the following created the office of the District Collector in India?
(A) Lord Cornwallis
(B) Warren Hastings

(C) The Royal Commission on Decentralisation
(D) Sir Charles Metcalf

41. The Fundamental Duties of a citizen include:
1. Respect for the Constitution, the National Flag and the National Anthem
2. To develop the scientific temper.
3. Respect for the Government.
4. To protect Wildlife.

Choose the correct answer from the codes given below:
Codes :
(A) 1, 2 and 3   (B) 1, 2 and 4
(C) 2, 3 and 4   (D) 1, 3, 4 and 2

42. The President of India takes oath:
(A) to uphold the sovereignty and integrity of India.
(B) to bear true faith and allegiance to the Constitution of India.
(C) to uphold the Constitution and Laws of the country.
(D) to preserve, protect and defend the Constitution and the law of the country.

43. If you get an opportunity to teach a visually challenged student along with normal students, what type of treatment would you like to give him in the class?
(A) Not giving extra attention because majority may suffer.
(B) Take care of him sympathetically in the class-room.
(C) You will think that blindness is his destiny and hence you cannot do anything.
(D) Arrange a seat in the front row and try to teach at a pace convenient to him.

44. Which of the following is not a characteristic of a good achievement test?
(A) Reliability   (B) Objectivity
(C) Ambiguity   (D) Validity

45. Which of the following does not belong to a projected aid?
(A) Overhead projector
(B) Blackboard

(C) Epidiascope

(D) Slide projector

46. For a teacher, which of the following methods would be correct for writing on the blackboard?
(A) Writing fast and as clearly as possible.
(B) Writing the matter first and then asking students to read it.
(C) Asking a question to students and then writing the answer as stated by them.
(D) Writing the important points as clearly as possible.

47. A teacher can be successful if he/she:
(A) helps students in becoming better citizens
(B) imparts subject knowledge to students
(C) prepares students to pass the examination
(D) presents the subject matter in a well organized manner

48. Dynamic approach to teaching means:
(A) Teaching should be forceful and effective
(B) Teachers should be energetic and dynamic
(C) The topics of teaching should not be static, but dynamic
(D) The students should be required to learn through activities

49. The research that aims at immediate application is:
(A) Action Research
(B) Empirical Research
(C) Conceptual Research
(D) Fundamental Research

50. When two or more successive footnotes refer to the same work which one of the following expressions is used?
(A) ibid
(B) et.al
(C) op.cit :
(D) loc.cit.

51. Nine year olds are taller than seven year olds. This is an example of a reference drawn from:
(A) Vertical study
(B) Cross-sectional study
(C) Time series study
(D) Experimental study

52. Conferences are meant for:
(A) Multiple target groups

(B) Group discussions
(C) Show-casing new Research
(D) All the above

53. Ex Post Facto research means:
(A) The research is carried out after the incident
(B) The research is carried out prior to the incident
(C) The research is carried out along with the happening of an incident.
(D) The research is carried out keeping in mind the possibilities of an incident.

54. Research ethics do not include:
(A) Honesty   (B) Subjectivity
(C) Integrity   (D) Objectivity

Directions (Qs. 55 to 60): *Read the following passage carefully and answer the questions:*

James Madison said, "A people who mean to be their own governors must arm themselves with power that knowledge gives." In India, the Official Secrets Act, 1923 was a convenient smokescreen to deny members of the public access to information. Public functioning has traditionally been shrouded in secrecy. But in a democracy in which people govern themselves, it is necessary to have more openness. In the maturing of our democracy, right to information is a major step forward; it enables citizens to participate fully in the decision-making process that affects their lives so profoundly. It is in this context that the address of the Prime Minister in the Lok Sabha is significant. He said, "I would only like to see that everyone, particularly our civil servants, should see the Bill in a positive spirit; not as a draconian law for paralyzing Government, but as an instrument for improving Government-Citizen interface resulting in a friendly, caring and effective Government functioning for the good of our People." He further said, "This is an innovative Bill, where there will be scope to review its functioning as we gain experience. Therefore, this is a piece of legislation, whose working will be kept under constant reviews."

The Commission, in its Report, has dealt with the application of the Right to Information in Executive, Legislature and Judiciary. The judiciary could be a pioneer in implementing the Act in letter and spirit because much of the work that the Judiciary does is open to public scrutiny, Government of India has sanctioned an e-governance project in the Judiciary for about ₹ 700 crores which would bring about systematic classification, standardization and categorization of records. This would help the judiciary to fulfil its mandate under the Act. Similar capacity building would be required in all other public authorities. The transformation from non-transparency to transparency and public accountability is the responsibility of all three organs of State.

55. A person gets power:
(A) by acquiring knowledge
(B) from the Official Secrets Act, 1923
(C) through openings
(D) by denying public information

56. Right to Information is a major step forward to:
(A) enable citizens to participate fully in the decision-making process
(B) to make the people aware of the Act
(C) to gain knowledge of administration
(D) to make the people Government friendly

57. The Prime Minister considered the Bill:
(A) to provide power to the civil servants
(B) as an instrument for improving Government-citizen interface resulting in a friendly, caring and effective Government

(C) a draconian law against the officials
(D) to check the harassment of the people

58. The Commission made the Bill effective by:
(A) extending power to the executive authorities
(B) combining the executive and legislative power
(C) recognizing Judiciary a pioneer in implementing the act in letter and spirit
(D) educating the people before its implementation

59. The Prime Minister considered the Bill innovative and hoped that
(A) It could be reviewed based on the experience gained on its functioning.
(B) The civil servants would see the Bill in a positive spirit.
(C) It would not be considered as a draconian law for paralyzing Government
(D) All the above

60. The transparency and public accountability is the responsibility of three organs of the State. These three organs are:
(A) Lok Sabha, Rajya Sabha and Judiciary
(B) Lok Sabha, Rajya Sabha and Executive
(C) Judiciary, Legislature and the Commission
(D) Legislature, Executive and Judiciary

ANSWERS

1	2	3	4	5	6	7	8	9	10
(C)	(B)	(B)	(B)	(D)	(D)	(C)	(B)	(A)	(C)
11	12	13	14	15	16	17	18	19	20
(D)	(A)	(B)	(B)	(B)	(A)	(C)	(C)	(C)	(A)
21	22	23	24	25	26	27	28	29	30
(A)	(C)	(A)	(B)	(C)	(B)	(B)	(D)	(C)	(C)
31	32	33	34	35	36	37	38	39	40
(C)	(C)	(D)	(D)	(C)	(A)	(B)	(A)	(D)	(B)
41	42	43	44	45	46	47	48	49	50
(B)	(D)	(D)	(C)	(B)	(D)	(D)	(D)	(A)	(A)
51	52	53	54	55	56	57	58	59	60
(B)	(D)	(A)	(B)	(A)	(A)	(B)	(C)	(D)	(D)

SOME SELECTED EXPLANATORY ANSWERS

1. Video-conferencing is the conduct of a video-conference by a set of tele-communication technologies which allow two or more locations to communicate by simultaneous two-way video and audio transmissions. It has also been called visual collaboration and is a type of groupware.

2. Makhanlal Chaturvedi National University of Journalism and Communication, officially known as MC Rashtriya Patrakarita Vishwavidyalaya is a government University located in Bhopal, Madhya Pradesh. It was set up by the Act 15 of 1990 of the Madhya Pradesh Legislative Assembly. This University was formally inaugurated by Dr. Shankar Dayal Sharma, the then Vice President of India, on 16th January, 1990.

3. In June 1923, the Radio Club of Bombay made the first ever broadcast in the country. This was followed by the setting up of the Calcutta Radio Club five month later. The first radio station of the Indian Broadcasting Company (IBC) at Bombay (now Mumbai), formally inaugurated by the then Viceroy of India, Lord Irwin, on January 23, 1927, heralded the beginning of organised broadcasting in India. Interestingly, this was the year in which the British Broadcasting Corporation (BBC) was formed. The IBC was liquidated in 1930.

4. PAL (Phase Alternating Line) is a analogue television colour encoding system used in broadcast television systems in many countries. Other common analogue television systems are NTSC (National Television System Committee) and SECAM (Sequential Couleur Avec Memoire).

   North America, most of South America, Japan, South Korea and Taiwan adopted NTSC. Most of Western Europe, India, Iceland, Australia, parts of Africa and the Middle East, and a few countries in South America adopted PAL. SECAM was mainly adopted in France, Eastern Europe and parts of Africa.

5. The Directorate of Advertising & Visual Publicity (DAVP) is the nodal agency to undertake multi-media advertising and publicity for various Ministries and Departments of Governments of India. Some of the Autonomous Bodies also route their advertisements through DAVP. As a service agency, it endeavours to Communicate at grass roots level on behalf of various Central Government Ministries.

7.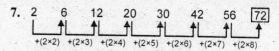

8.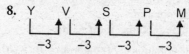

14. **Persuasive Definitions:** The purpose of a persuasive definition is to convince us to believe that something is the case and to get us to act accordingly. Frequently definitions of words like "freedom," "democracy," and "communism," are of this type. (E.g., taxation is the means by which bureaucrats rip off the people who have elected them.) While these sorts of definitions might be emotionally useful, we should avoid them when we are attempting to be logical.

   Theoretical Definitions: Theoretical definitions are designed to explain a theory. Whether they are correct or not will depend, largely, on whether the theory they are an integral part of is correct. Newton's famous formula "F = ma" (*i.e.*, Force = mass x acceleration), provides a good example of such a definition.

   Stipulative Definitions: Stipulative definitions are frequently provided when we need to refer to a complex idea, but there simply is no word for that idea. A word is selected and assigned a meaning without any pretense that this is what that word really means. (E.g., by "a blue number" we mean any number greater than 17 but less than 36.)

Lexical Definitions: Unlike stipulative definitions, lexical definitions do attempt to capture the real meaning of a word and so can be either correct or incorrect. When we tell someone that "intractable" means not easily governed, or obstinate, this is the kind of definition we are providing. Roughly, lexical definitions are the kinds of definitions found in dictionaries.

16. Kind of diagram invented by Venn in 1881, for representing and assessing the validity of elementary inferences either of a syllogistic form, or from the Boolean algebra of classes (Venn was attempting to illustrate Boole's own methods). In a Venn diagram for the syllogism there are three circles, corresponding to S, M and P. Shaded areas indicate which combinations are empty, and a cross indicates which ones have members, while a cross on a border between two classes represents that at least one class has a member. For example, to illustrate the syllogism 'Some S is M, all M is P, so some S is P', the first premise is represented by (i). Here, the cross hovers between the area of P and the area outside P. However, the second premise adds the shading of (ii), since any M region outside P is empty. Hence, the cross cannot be there, and is driven into the P area. This shows that some S is indeed P; hence the syllogism is valid. Venn generalized the method. For statements in the algebra of classes involving four terms, ellipses can be drawn, but the method becomes cumbersome. Strips and charts of various kinds were invented in the late 19th and early 20th centuries to give graphical representations of such problems.

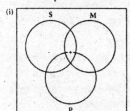
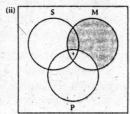

18. A valid argument is one where true premises necessitate a true conclusion.

1. All unicorns are beautiful.
2. Dave is a unicorn.
It follows that Dave is beautiful. (Valid)
An inductive argument is one based on a likely or probable relationship between the premises and the conclusion.

Strong Inductive: If we have true premises, then our conclusion is probably true.
Example:
1. Almost everyone likes chocolate.
2. I give you some chocolate.
Thus, you will probably like the chocolate.

Weak Inductive: An argument is weak when the conclusion probably does not follow from the premises.
Example:
1. When I put a match in water, it goes out.
2. Gasoline is like water.

When I put a match in gasoline, it will probably go out.
An inductive argument is cogent if it is strong and all the premises in the argument are true. Otherwise it is uncogent.
Example:
1. Most people think that torturing people for fun is morally wrong.
2. Mr. Gacy tortured people for fun.
Thus, most people probably think that Mr. Gacy acted wrongly.

20. Let the price of petrol be ₹ 100 per litre. Let the user use 1 litre of petrol. Therefore, his expense on petrol = $100 \times 1 = ₹ 100$
Now, the price of petrol increases by 25%. Therefore, the new price of petrol = ₹ 125.
As he has to maintain his expenditure on petrol constant, he will be spending only ₹ 100 on petrol.
Let 'x' be the number of litres of petrol he will use at the new price.
Therefore,
$$125 \times x = 100$$
$$\Rightarrow x = \frac{100}{125} = \frac{4}{5} = 0.8 \text{ litres}$$
He has cut down his petrol consumption by
0.2 litres $= \frac{0.2}{1} \times 100 = 20\%$.

22. Upto 9 A.M. 1st pipe has worked for 3 hrs; 2nd pipe for 2 hrs. and 3rd pipe for 1 hr.

∴ Part filled up to 9 A.M.

$$= 3 \times \frac{1}{15} + 2 \times \frac{1}{20} + \frac{1}{30}$$

$$= \frac{1}{5} + \frac{1}{10} + \frac{1}{30}$$

$$= \frac{1}{3}$$

Unfilled part at 9 A.M. $= 1 - \frac{1}{3} = \frac{2}{3}$

From 9 A.M. onwards all four pipes are functioning.

Part filled (by all four pipes) in 1 hr.

$$= \frac{1}{15} + \frac{1}{20} + \frac{1}{30} + \frac{1}{60} = \frac{1}{6}$$

∴ $\frac{2}{3}$ of reservoir will be filled up in

$6 \times \frac{2}{3} = 4$ hr.

Counting 4 hrs. from 9 A.M. reservoir will be full at 1.00 P.M.

23. Contribution of wind and solar power in absolute terms $= 97 \times \frac{7}{100} = 6.79$ GW.

24. Contribution of renewable energy sources in absolute terms $= \frac{97 \times 27}{100} = 26.19$ GW.

25. TCP/IP is the communication protocol for communication between computers on the Internet.
TCP/IP stands for **T**ransmission **C**ontrol **P**rotocol/**I**nternet **P**rotocol.
TCP/IP defines how electronic devices (like computers) should be connected to the Internet, and how data should be transmitted between them.

26. ASCII stands for the "American Standard Code for Information Interchange". It was designed in the early 60's, as a standard character-set for computers and hardware devices like teleprinters and tapedrives.
ASCII is a 7-bit character set containing 128 characters.
It contains the numbers from 0-9, the uppercase and lowercase English letters from A to Z, and some special characters.
The character-sets used in modern computers, HTML, and Internet are all based on ASCII.

29. Internet Explorer is a free web browser from Microsoft.
Internet Explorer was released in 1995 and is one of the most popular browsers today.

30. POP3 stands for a Post Office Protocol version 3. The POP3 protocol is designed to allow the users to retrieve e-mail messages when they are connected to the e-mail server (via Internet, Ethernet or VPN network connection). Once the e-mail messages are downloaded from the server they can be modified, read and manipulated offline.
The IMAP (Internet Message Access Protocol) is a newer and modern alternative to the POP3 protocol. Unlike it, the IMAP allows the users to work with their messages in both online and offline modes. The IMAP-capable e-mail client programs retrieve the messages' headers from the server and can store local copies of the messages in a local (temporary) cache. All the messages are left on the server until they are deleted by the user. This mechanism allows multiple e-mail clients to access a single mailbox and is often used for corporate/ business e-mails (*e.g.* sales@company-domain.com).

31. Peroxyacyl nitrates (PANs) are powerful respiratory and eye irritants present in photochemical smog.

35. There are two types of seismic waves, *body waves* and *surface waves*. Body waves travel through the interior of the Earth, while surface waves travel only within the top surface layers. Most earthquakes take place at depths of less than 80 km below the Earth's surface. There are two types of body waves, *P waves* and *S waves*. P waves bunch together and then spread apart when they move. It is a bit like the movement of an inch worm or a slinky. S waves are like rolling ocean waves or like when you snap a rope. The oscillations are in a waveform.

37. The Indian Institute of Advanced Study (IIAS) is a prestigious research institute based in Shimla. It was set up by the Ministry of Education, Government of India in 1964 and it started functioning from October 20, 1965. The building that houses the Institute was originally built as a home for Lord Dufferin, Viceroy of India from 1884-1888 and was called the Viceregal Lodge. It housed all the subsequent viceroys and governors general of India. It occupied the Observatory Hill, one of the seven hills that Shimla is built upon.

38. NCTE has 4 Regional offices which are as follows:
    1. Eastern Regional Committee (ERC) located at Bhubaneshwar.
    2. Southern Regional Committee (SRC) located at Bangalore.
    3. Western Regional Committee (WRC) located at Bhopal.
    4. Northern Regional Committee (NRC) located at Jaipur.

39. Right to Constitutional Remedies (Article 32) was regarded as the heart and soul of the Indian Constitution by Dr. B.R. Ambedkar.

45. **Non-projected Aids:** Visual instructional devices which are simply presented without any projection equipment are non-projected aids. **Examples:** blackboard, chart, etc.
    Projected Aids: Visual instructional devices which are shown with a projector are called projected aids. **Examples:** slides, filmstrip, silent films, cartoons, etc. projected through an opaque projector (epidiascope), or an over head projector.

50. Ibid is a contraction of *ibidem*, a Latin word meaning "the same place." This term is most commonly used for footnoting in scholarly texts, allowing the author to say "ibid" instead of citing a lengthy title. In legal texts, people may use "id," a shortening of "idem," a word which means "as mentioned previously."

53. *Ex-post facto* research is systematic empirical inquiry in which the scientist does not have direct control of independent variables because their manifestations have already occurred or because they are inherently not manipulated.

UGC-NET (JRF) Exam December, 2012

PAPER–I

Note : This paper contains **sixty (60)** multiple-choice questions, each question carrying **two (2)** marks. Candidate is expected to answer any **fifty (50)** questions. In case more than **fifty (50)** questions are attempted, only the first **fifty (50)** questions will be evaluated.

1. The English word 'Communication' is derived from the words:
   A. Communis and Communicare
   B. Communist and Commune
   C. Communism and Communalism
   D. Communion and Common sense

2. Chinese Cultural Revolution leader Mao Zedong used a type of communication to talk to the masses is known as:
   A. Mass line communication
   B. Group communication
   C. Participatory communication
   D. Dialogue communication

3. Conversing with the spirits and ancestors is termed as:
   A. Transpersonal communication
   B. Intrapersonal communication
   C. Interpersonal communication
   D. Face-to-face communication

4. The largest circulated daily newspaper among the following is:
   A. The Times of India
   B. The Indian Express
   C. The Hindu
   D. The Deccan Herald

5. The Pioneer of the silent feature film in India was:
   A. K.A. Abbas
   B. Satyajit Ray
   C. B.R. Chopra
   D. Dada Sahib Phalke

6. Classroom communication of a teacher rests on the principle of:
   A. Infotainment
   B. Edutainment
   C. Entertainment
   D. Power equation

7. The missing number in the series :
   0, 6, 24, 60, 120, ?, 336, is:
   A. 240
   B. 220
   C. 280
   D. 210

8. A group of 7 members having a majority of boys is to be formed out of 6 boys and 4 girls. The number of ways the group can be formed is:
   A. 80
   B. 100
   C. 90
   D. 110

9. The number of observations in a group is 40. The average of the first 10 members is 4.5 and the average of the remaining 30 members is 3.5. The average of the whole group is:
   A. 4
   B. 15/2
   C. 15/4
   D. 6

10. If MOHAN is represented by the code KMFYL, then COUNT will be represented by:
    A. AMSLR
    B. MSLAR
    C. MASRL
    D. SAMLR

11. The sum of the ages of two persons A and B is 50. 5 years ago, the ratio of their ages was 5/3. The present age of A and B are:
    A. 30, 20
    B. 35, 15
    C. 38, 12
    D. 40, 10

12. Let a means minus (–), b means multiplied by (×), C means divided by (÷) and D means plus (+). The value of 90 D 9 a 29 C 10 b 2 is:
    A. -8
    B. 10
    C. 12
    D. 14

13. Consider the Assertion-I and Assertion-II and select the right code given below :
    Assertion-I : Even Bank-lockers are not safe. Thieves can break them and take away your

wealth. But thieves can not go to heaven. So you should keep your wealth in heaven.

Assertion-II : The difference of skin-colour of beings is because of the distance from the sun and not because of some permanent traits. Skin-colour is the result of body's reaction to the sun and its rays.

Codes :

A. Both the assertions-I and II are forms of argument.

B. The assertion-I is an argument but the assertion-II is not.

C. The assertion-II is an argument but the assertion-I is not.

D. Both the assertions are explanations of facts.

14. By which of the following proposition, the proposition 'some men are not honest' is contradicted?

A. All men are honest
C. Some men are honest
B. No men are honest
D. All of the above

15. A stipulative definition is:

A. always true
B. always false
C. sometimes true sometimes false
D. neither true nor false

16. Choose the appropriate alternative given in the codes to replace the question mark.

Examiner – Examinee, Pleader – Client, Preceptor – ?

A. Customer   B. Path-finder
C. Perceiver   D. Disciple

17. If the statement 'most of the students are obedient' is taken to be true, which one of the following pair of statements can be claimed to be true?

I. All obedient persons are students.
II. All students are obedient.
III. Some students are obedient.
IV. Some students are not disobedient.

Codes:

A. I & II   B. II & III
C. III & IV   D. II & IV

18. Choose the right code :

A deductive argument claims that :

I. The conclusion does not claim something more than that which is contained in the premises.

II. The conclusion is supported by the premise/premises conclusively.

III. If the conclusion is false, then premise/premises may be either true or false.

IV. If premise/combination of premises is true, then conclusion must be true.

Codes:

A. I and II   B. I and III
C. II and III   D. All of the above

Direction (Qs. 19 to 24): *On the basis of the data given in the following table, give answers to questions.*

Government Expenditures on Social Services
(As per cent of total expenditure)

S.I. No.	Items	2007-08	2008-09	2009-10	2010-11
	Social Services	11.06	12.94	13.06	14.02
(a)	Education, sports & youth affairs	4.02	4.04	3.96	4.46
(b)	Health & family welfare	2.05	1.91	1.90	2.03
(c)	Water supply, housing, etc,	2.02	2.31	2.20	2.27
(d)	Information & broadcasting	0.22	0.22	0.20	0.22
(e)	Welfare to SC/ST & OBC	0.36	0.35	0.41	0.63
(f)	Labour and employment	0.27	0.27	0.22	0.25
(g)	Social welfare & nutrition	0.82	0.72	0.79	1.06
(h)	North-eastern areas	0.00	1.56	1.50	1.75
(i)	Other social services	1.29	1.55	1.87	1.34
	Total Government expenditure	100.00	100.00	100.00	100.00

19. How many activities in the social services are there where the expenditure has been less than 5 per cent of the total expenditures incurred on the social services in 2008-09?
A. One   B. Three
C. Five   D. All of the above

20. In which year, the expenditures on the social services have increased at the highest rate?
A. 2007-08   B. 2008-09
C. 2009-10   D. 2010-11

21. Which of the following activities remains almost stagnant in terms of share of expenditures?
A. North-eastern areas
B. Welfare to SC/ST & OBC
C. Information & broadcasting
D. Social welfare and nutrition

22. Which of the following item's expenditure share is almost equal to the remaining three items in the given years?
A. Information & broadcasting
B. Welfare to SC/ST and OBC
C. Labour and employment
D. Social welfare & nutrition

23. Which of the following items of social services has registered the highest rate of increase in expenditures during 2007-08 to 2010-11?
A. Education, sports & youth affairs
B. Welfare to SC/ST & OBC
C. Social welfare & nutrition
D. Overall social services

24. Which of the following items has registered the highest rate of decline in terms of expenditure during 2007-08 to 2009-10?
A. Labour and employment
B. Health & family welfare
C. Social welfare & nutrition
D. Education, sports & youth affairs

25. ALU stands for:
A. American Logic Unit
B. Alternate Local Unit
C. Alternating Logic Unit
D. Arithmetic Logic Unit

26. A Personal Computer uses a number of chips mounted on a circuit board called:
A. Microprocessor   B. System Board
C. Daughter Board   D. Mother Board

27. Computer Virus is a:
A. Hardware   B. Bacteria
C. Software   D. None of these

28. Which one of the following is correct?
A. $(17)_{10} = (17)_{16}$
B. $(17)_{10} = (17)_{8}$
C. $(17)_{10} = (10111)_{2}$
D. $(17)_{10} = (10001)_{2}$

29. The file extension of MS-Word document in Office 2007 is ....
A. .pdf   B. .doc
C. .docx   D. .txt

30. .... is a protocol used by e-mail clients to download e-mails to your computer.
A. TCP   B. FTP
C. SMTP   D. POP

31. Which of the following is a source of methane?
A. Wetlands
B. Foam Industry
C. Thermal Power Plants
D. Cement Industry

32. 'Minamata disaster' in Japan was caused by pollution due to:
A. Lead   B. Mercury
C. Cadmium   D. Zinc

33. Biomagnification means increase in the:
A. concentration of pollutants in living organisms
B. number of species
C. size of living organisms
D. biomass

34. Nagoya Protocol is related to:
A. Climate change   B. Ozone depletion
C. Hazardous waste   D. Biodiversity

35. The second most important source after fossil fuels contributing to India's energy needs is:
A. Solar energy   C. Nuclear energy
B. Hydropower   D. Wind energy

36. In case of earthquakes, an increase of magnitude 1 on Richter Scale implies:
    A. a ten-fold increase in the amplitude of seismic waves.
    B. a ten-fold increase in the energy of the seismic waves.
    C. two-fold increase in the amplitude of seismic waves.
    D. two-fold increase in the energy of seismic waves.

37. Which of the following is not a measure of Human Development Index?
    A. Literacy Rate   B. Gross Enrolment
    C. Sex Ratio   D. Life Expectancy

38. India has the highest number of students in colleges after:
    A. the U.K.
    B. the U.S.A.
    C. Australia
    D. Canada

39. Which of the following statement(s) is/are not correct about the Attorney General of India?
    1. The President appoints a person, who is qualified to be a Judge of a High Court, to be the Attorney General of India.
    2. He has the right of audience in all the Courts of the country.
    3. He has the right to take part in the proceedings of the Lok Sabha and the Rajya Sabha.
    4. He has a fixed tenure.
    Select the correct answer from the codes given below :
    Codes:
    A. 1 and 4   B. 2, 3 and 4
    C. 3 and 4   D. 3 only

40. Which of the following prefix President Pranab Mukherjee desires to be discontinued while interacting with Indian dignitaries as well as in official notings?
    1. His Excellency   2. Mahamahim
    3. Hon'ble   4. Shri/Smt.
    Select the correct answer from the codes given below:

Codes:
A. 1 and 3   B. 2 and 3
C. 1 and 2   D. 1, 2 and 3

41. Which of the following can be done under conditions of financial emergency?
    1. State Legislative Assemblies can be abolished.
    2. Central Government can acquire control over the budget and expenditure of States.
    3. Salaries of the Judges of the High Courts and the Supreme Court can be reduced.
    4. Right to Constitutional Remedies can be suspended.
    Select the correct answer from the codes given below :
    Codes :
    A. 1, 2 and 3   B. 2, 3 and 4
    C. 1 and 2   D. 2 and 3

42. Match List-I with List-II and select the correct answer from the codes given below :

List-I	List-II
(a) Poverty Reduction Programme	(i) Mid-day Meals
(b) Human Development Scheme	(ii) Indira Awas Yojna (IAY)
(c) Social Assistance Scheme	(iii) National Old Age Pension (NOAP)
(d) Minimum Need Scheme	(iv) MNREGA

Codes :

	(a)	(b)	(c)	(d)
A.	(iv)	(i)	(iii)	(ii)
B.	(ii)	(iii)	(iv)	(ii)
C.	(iii)	(iv)	(i)	(ii)
D.	(iv)	(iii)	(ii)	(i)

43. For an efficient and durable learning, learner should have:
    A. ability to learn only
    B. requisite level of motivation only
    C. opportunities to learn only
    D. desired level of ability and motivation

44. Classroom communication must be:
    A. Teacher centric   B. Student centric
    C. General centric   D. Textbook centric

45. The best method of teaching is to:
A. impart information
B. ask students to read books
C. suggest good reference material
D. initiate a discussion and participate in it

46. Interaction inside the classroom should generate:
A. Argument   B. Information
C. Ideas   D. Controversy

47. "Spare the rod and spoil the child", gives the message that:
A. punishment in the class should be banned.
B. corporal punishment is not acceptable.
C. undesirable behaviour must be punished.
D. children should be beaten with rods.

48. The type of communication that the teacher has in the classroom, is termed as:
A. Interpersonal
B. Mass communication
C. Group communication
D. Face-to-face communication

49. Which one of the following is an indication of the quality of a research journal?
A. Impact factor   B. h-index
C. g-index   D. i10-index

50. Good 'research ethics' means:
A. Not disclosing the holdings of shares/stocks in a company that sponsors your research.
B. Assigning a particular research problem to one Ph.D./research student only.
C. Discussing with your colleagues confidential data from a research paper that you are reviewing for an academic journal.
D. Submitting the same research manuscript for publishing in more than one journal.

51. Which of the following sampling methods is based on probability?
A. Convenience sampling
B. Quota sampling
C. Judgement sampling
D. Stratified sampling

52. Which one of the following references is written according to American Psychological Association (APA) format?
A. Sharma, V. (2010). Fundamentals of Computer Science.
New Delhi : Tata McGraw Hill
B. Sharma, V. 2010. Fundamentals of Computer Science.
New Delhi : Tata McGraw Hill
C. Sharma. V. 2010. Fundamentals of Computer Science,
New Delhi : Tata McGraw Hill
D. Sharma, V. (2010), Fundamentals of Computer Science,
New Delhi : Tata McGraw Hill

53. Arrange the following steps of research in correct sequence:
1. Identification of research problem
2. Listing of research objectives
3. Collection of data
4. Methodology
5. Data analysis
6. Results and discussion
A. 1 – 2 – 3 – 4 – 5 – 6
B. 1 – 2 – 4 – 3 – 5 – 6
C. 2 – 1 – 3 – 4 – 5 – 6
D. 2 – 1 – 4 – 3 – 5 – 6

54. Identify the **incorrect** statement :
A. A hypothesis is made on the basis of limited evidence as a starting point for further investigations.
B. A hypothesis is a basis for reasoning without any assumption of its truth.
C. Hypothesis is a proposed explanation for a phenomenon.
D. Scientific hypothesis is a scientific theory.

Directions (Qs. 50 to 60) : *Read the following passage carefully and answer the questions:*

The popular view of towns and cities in developing countries and of urbanization process is that despite the benefits and comforts it brings, the emergence of such cities connotes environmental degradation, generation of slums and squatters, urban poverty, unemployment, crimes, lawlessness, traffic chaos etc. But what is the reality? Given the unprecedental increase in urban population over the last 50 years from 300 million in 1950 to 2 billion in 2000 in developing countries, the wonder really is how well the world has coped, and not how badly.

In general, the urban quality of life has improved in terms of availability of water and sanitation, power, health and education, communication and transport. By way of illustration, a large number of urban residents have been provided with improved water in urban areas in Asia's largest countries such as China, India, Indonesia and Philippines. Despite that, the access to improved water in terms of percentage of total urban population seems to have declined during the last decade of 20th century, though in absolute numbers, millions of additional urbanites, have been provided improved services. These countries have made significant progress in the provision of sanitation services too, together, providing for an additional population of more than 293 million citizens within a decade (1990-2000). These improvements must be viewed against the backdrop of rapidly increasing urban population, fiscal crunch and strained human resources and efficient and quality-oriented public management.

55. The popular view about the process of urbanization in developing countries is:
A. Positive
B. Negative
C. Neutral
D. Unspecified

56. The average annual increase in the number of urbanites in developing countries, from 1950 to 2000 A.D. was close to:
A. 30 million
B. 40 million
C. 50 million
D. 60 million

57. The reality of urbanization is reflected in:
A. How well the situation has been managed.
B. How badly the situation has gone out of control.
C. How fast has been tempo of urbanization.
D. How fast the environment has degraded.

58. Which one of the following is not considered as an indicator of urban quality of life?
A. Tempo of urbanization
B. Provision of basic services
C. Access to social amenities
D. All of the above

59. The author in this passage has tried to focus on
A. Extension of Knowledge
B. Generation of Environmental Consciousness
C. Analytical Reasoning
D. Descriptive Statement

60. In the above passage, the author intends to state:
A. The hazards of the urban life
B. The sufferings of the urban life
C. The awareness of human progress
D. The limits to growth

ANSWERS

1	2	3	4	5	6	7	8	9	10
A	A	A	A	D	B	D	B	C	A
11	12	13	14	15	16	17	18	19	20
A	*	B	A	D	D	C	A	D	B
21	22	23	24	25	26	27	28	29	30
C	D	B	A	D	D	C	D	C	D
31	32	33	34	35	36	37	38	39	40
A	B	A	D	C	A	C	B	A	C
41	42	43	44	45	46	47	48	49	50
D	A	D	B	D	C	C	C	A	B
51	52	53	54	55	56	57	58	59	60
D	A	B	D	B	A	A	A	C	D

SOME SELECTED EXPLANATORY ANSWERS

7. 0, 6, 24, 60, 120, x, 336.

Let missing term is x

Now,

$$\frac{0}{6}, \frac{6}{24}, \frac{24}{60}, \frac{60}{120}, \frac{120}{x}, \frac{x}{336}$$

$$= 0, \frac{1}{4}, \frac{2}{5}, \frac{3}{6}, \frac{120}{x}, \frac{x}{336}$$

From the pattern

$$\frac{120}{x} \text{ should be } \frac{4}{7}$$

so, $\dfrac{120}{x} = \dfrac{4}{7}$ or, $x = 210$.

8. The group must formed by 4, 5 or 6 boys and 3, 2 or 1 girls

the required number of ways

when group formed by 4 boys and 3 girls

Number of ways for this selection

$$^6C_4 \times {}^4C_3$$

when group formed by 5 boys and 2 girls

Number of ways for this selection

$$^6C_5 \times {}^4C_2$$

when group formed by 6 boys and 1 girl

the number of ways for this selection

$$^6C_6 \times {}^4C_1$$

total number of ways

$$= {}^6C_4 \times {}^4C_3 + {}^6C_5 \times {}^4C_2 + {}^6C_6 \times {}^4C_1$$

$= 15 \times 4 + 6 \times 6 + 1 \times 4$

$= 60 + 36 + 4 = 100$.

9. Observation of first 10 members

$= 4.5 \times 10 = 45$

observation of last 30 members

$= 3.5 \times 30 = 105$

total observation done by 40 members

$= 45 + 105 = 150$

Average observation $= \dfrac{150}{40} = \dfrac{15}{4}$.

11. Let present age of A is x and B is y.

According to the question

$$x + y = 50 \qquad \text{...(i)}$$

5 years ago, ratio of their age

$$\frac{x-5}{y-5} = \frac{5}{3}$$

$$3(x - 5) = 5(y - 5)$$

or, $\qquad 3x - 5y = -10 \qquad \text{...(ii)}$

from (i) and (ii)

$$8x = 250 - 10$$

$$x = \frac{240}{8} = 30$$

$$y = 20$$

Present Age of A = 30 years

Present Age of B = 20 years.

28. $(10001)_2 = 1 \times 2^4 + 0 \times 2^3 + 0 \times 2^2 + 0 \times 2$

$$+ 1 \times 2^0$$

$= 16 + 0 + 0 + 0 + 1 = 17$

so, $(17)^{10} = (10001)_2$.

UGC-NET (JRF) Exam June, 2013

PAPER–I

Note: *This paper contains Sixty (60) objective type questions, each question carrying two (2) marks. Attempt all the questions.*

1. Which one of the following references is written as per Modern Language Association (MLA) format?
   A. Hall, Donald. Fundamentals of Electronics, New Delhi : Prentice Hall of India, 2005
   B. Hall, Donald, Fundamentals of Electronics, New Delhi : Prentice Hall of India, 2005
   C. Hall, Donald, Fundamentals of Electronics, New Delhi – Prentice Hall of India, 2005
   D. Hall, Donald. Fundamentals of Electronics. New Delhi : Prentice Hall of India, 2005

2. A workshop is
   A. a conference for discussion on a topic.
   B. a meeting for discussion on a topic.
   C. a class at a college or a university in which a teacher and the students discuss a topic.
   D. a brief intensive course for a small group emphasizing the development of a skill or technique for solving a specific problem.

3. A working hypothesis is
   A. a proven hypothesis for an argument.
   B. not required to be tested.
   C. a provisionally accepted hypothesis for further research.
   D. a scientific theory.

Read the following passage carefully and answer the questions (4 to 9) :

The Taj Mahal has become one of the world's best known monuments. This domed white marble structure is situated on a high plinth at the southern end of a four-quartered garden, evoking the gardens of paradise, enclosed within walls measuring 305 by 549 metres. Outside the walls, in an area known as Mumtazabad, were living quarters for attendants, markets, serais and other structures built by local merchants and nobles. The tomb complex and the other imperial structures of Mumtazabad were maintained by the income of thirty villages given specifically for the tomb's support. The name Taj Mahal is unknown in Mughal chronicles, but it is used by contemporary Europeans in India, suggesting that this was the tomb's popular name. In contemporary texts, it is generally called simply the Illuminated Tomb (Rauza-i-Munavvara).

Mumtaz Mahal died shortly after delivering her fourteenth child in 1631. The Mughal court was then residing in Burhanpur. Her remains were temporarily buried by the griefstricken emperor in a spacious garden known as Zainabad on the bank of the river Tapti. Six months later her body was transported to Agra, where it was interred in land chosen for the mausoleum. This land, situated south of the Mughal city on the bank of the Jamuna, had belonged to the Kachhwaha rajas since the time of Raja Man Singh and was purchased from the current raja, Jai Singh. Although contemporary chronicles indicate Jai Singh's willing cooperation in this exchange, extant *farmans* (imperial commands) indicate that the final price was not settled until almost two years after the mausoleum's commencement. Jai Singh's further cooperation was insured by imperial orders issued between 1632 and 1637 demanding that he provide stone masons and carts to transport marble from the mines at Makrana, within his "ancestral domain", to Agra where both the Taj Mahal and Shah Jahan's additions to the Agra fort were constructed concurrently.

Work on the mausoleum was commenced early in 1632. Inscriptional evidence indicates much of the tomb was completed by 1636. By 1643, when Shah Jahan most lavishly celebrated the 'Urs ceremony for Mumtaz Mahal', the entire complex was virtually complete.

4. Marble stone used for the construction of the Taj Mahal was brought from the ancestral domain of Raja Jai Singh. The name of the place where mines of marble is
   A. Burhanpur   B. Makrana
   C. Amber   D. Jaipur

5. The popular name Taj Mahal was given by
   A. Shah Jahan
   B. Tourists
   C. Public
   D. European travellers

6. Point out the true statement from the following:
   A. Marble was not used for the construction of the Taj Mahal.
   B. Red sand stone is non-visible in the Taj Mahal complex.
   C. The Taj Mahal is surrounded by a four-quartered garden known as Chahr Bagh.
   D. The Taj Mahal was constructed to celebrate the 'Urs ceremony for Mumtaz Mahal'.

7. In the contemporary texts the Taj Mahal is known
   A. Mumtazabad
   B. Mumtaz Mahal
   C. Zainabad
   D. Rauza-i-Munavvara

8. The construction of the Taj Mahal was completed between the period
   A. 1632 – 1636 A.D. B. 1630 – 1643 A.D.
   C. 1632 – 1643 A.D. D. 1636 – 1643 A.D.

9. The documents indicating the ownership of land, where the Taj Mahal was built, known as
   A. Farman
   B. Sale Deed
   C. Sale-Purchase Deed
   D. None of the above

10. In the process of communication, which one of the following is in the chronological order?
    A. Communicator, Medium, Receiver, Effect, Message
    B. Medium, Communicator, Message, Receiver, Effect
    C. Communicator, Message, Medium, Receiver, Effect
    D. Message, Communicator, Medium, Receiver, Effect

11. Bengal Gazette, the first Newspaper in India was started in 1780 by
    A. Dr. Annie Besant
    B. James Augustus Hicky
    C. Lord Cripson
    D. A.O. Hume

12. Press censorship in India was imposed during the tenure of the Prime Minister
    A. Rajeev Gandhi   B. Narasimha Rao
    C. Indira Gandhi   D. Deve Gowda

13. Communication via New media such as computers, teleshopping, internet and mobile telephony is termed as
    A. Entertainment
    B. Interactive communication
    C. Developmental communication
    D. Communitarian

14. Classroom communication of a teacher rests on the principle of
    A. Infotainment   B. Edutainment
    C. Entertainment   D. Enlightenment

15. _____ is important when a teacher communicates with his/her student.
    A. Sympathy   B. Empathy
    C. Apathy   D. Antipathy

16. In a certain code GALIB is represented by HBMJC. TIGER will be represented by
    A. UJHFS   B. UHJSF
    C. JHUSF   D. HUJSF

17. In a certain cricket tournament 45 matches were played. Each team played once against each of the other teams. The number of teams participated in the tournament is
    A. 8   B. 10
    C. 12   D. 14

18. The missing number in the series 40, 120, 60, 180, 90,?, 135 is
   A. 110   B. 270
   C. 105   D. 210

19. The odd numbers from 1 to 45 which are exactly divisible by 3 are arranged in an ascending order. The number at 6th position is
   A. 18   B. 24
   C. 33   D. 36

20. The mean of four numbers a, b, c, d is 100. If c = 70, then the mean of the remaining numbers is

   A. 30   B. $\dfrac{85}{2}$

   C. $\dfrac{170}{3}$ D. 110

21. If the radius of a circle is increased by 50%, the perimeter of the circle will increase by
   A. 20%   B. 30%
   C. 40%   D. 50%

22. If the statement 'some men are honest' is false, which among the following statements will be true.
   Choose the correct code given below :
   (i) All men are honest.
   (ii) No men are honest.
   (iii) Some men are not honest.
   (iv) All men are dishonest.
   Codes :
   A. (i), (ii) and (iii)
   B. (ii), (iii) and (iv)
   C. (i), (iii) and (iv)
   D. (ii), (i) and (iv)

23. Choose the proper alternative given in the codes to replace the question mark.
   Bee – Honey, Cow – Milk, Teacher – ?
   A. Intelligence   B. Marks
   C. Lessons   D. Wisdom

24. P is the father of R and S is the son of Q and T is the brother of P. If R is the sister of S, how is Q related to T?
   A. Wife   B. Sister-in-law
   C. Brother-in-law   D. Daughter-in-law

25. A definition put forward to resolve a dispute by influencing attitudes or stirring emotions is called
   A. Lexical   B. Persuasive
   C. Stipulative   D. Precisions

26. Which of the codes given below contains only the correct statements?
   Statements :
   (i) Venn diagram is a clear method of notation.
   (ii) Venn diagram is the most direct method of testing the validity of categorical syllogisms.
   (iii) In Venn diagram method the premises and the conclusion of a categorical syllogism is diagrammed.
   (iv) In Venn diagram method the three overlapping circles are drawn for testing a categorical syllogism.
   Codes :
   A. (i), (ii) & (iii)   B. (i), (ii) & (iv)
   C. (ii), (iii) & (iv)   D. (i), (iii) & (iv)

27. Inductive reasoning presupposes
   A. unity in human nature
   B. integrity in human nature
   C. uniformity in human nature
   D. harmony in human nature

Read the table below and based on this table answer questions from 28 to 33 :

Area under Major Horticulture Crops

(in lakh hectares)

Year	Fruits	Vegetables	Flowers	Total Horticulture Area
2005–06	53	72	1	187
2006–07	56	75	1	194
2007–08	58	78	2	202
2008–09	61	79	2	207
2009–10	63	79	2	209

28. Which of the following two years have recorded the highest rate of increase in area under the total horticulture?
   A. 2005–06 & 2006–07
   B. 2006–07 & 2008–09
   C. 2007–08 & 2008–09
   D. 2006–07 & 2007–08

29. Shares of the area under flowers, vegetables and fruits in the area under total horticulture are respectively :
    A. 1, 38 and 30 percent
    B. 30, 38 and 1 percent
    C. 38, 30 and 1 percent
    D. 35, 36 and 2 percent

30. Which of the following has recorded the highest rate of increase in area during 2005–06 to 2009–10?
    A. Fruits
    B. Vegetables
    C. Flowers
    D. Total horticulture

31. Find out the horticultural crop that has recorded an increase of area by around 10 percent from 2005–06 to 2009–10
    A. Fruits
    B. Vegetables
    C. Flowers
    D. Total horticulture

32. What has been the share of area under fruits, vegetables and flowers in the area under total horticulture in 2007–08?
    A. 53 percent
    B. 68 percent
    C. 79 percent
    D. 100 percent

33. In which year, area under fruits has recorded the highest rate of increase?
    A. 2006–07
    B. 2007–08
    C. 2008–09
    D. 2009–10

34. 'www' stands for
    A. work with web
    B. word wide web
    C. world wide web
    D. worth while web

35. A hard disk is divided into tracks which is further subdivided into
    A. Clusters
    B. Sectors
    C. Vectors
    D. Heads

36. A computer program that translates a program statement by statement into machine language is called a/an
    A. Compiler
    B. Simulator
    C. Translator
    D. Interpreter

37. A Gigabyte is equal to
    A. 1024 Megabytes
    B. 1024 Kilobytes
    C. 1024 Terabytes
    D. 1024 Bytes

38. A Compiler is a software which converts
    A. characters to bits
    B. high level language to machine language

C. machine language to high level language
D. words to bits

39. Virtual memory is
    A. an extremely large main memory.
    B. an extremely large secondary memory.
    C. an illusion of extremely large main memory.
    D. a type of memory used in super computers.

40. The phrase 'tragedy of commons' is in the context of
    A. tragic event related to damage caused by release of poisonous gases.
    B. tragic conditions of poor people.
    C. degradation of renewable free access resources.
    D. climate change.

41. Kyoto Protocol is related to
    A. Ozone depletion
    B. Hazardous waste
    C. Climate change
    D. Nuclear energy

42. Which of the following is a source of emissions leading to the eventual formation of surface ozone as a pollutant?
    A. Transport sector
    B. Refrigeration and Airconditioning
    C. Wetlands
    D. Fertilizers

43. The smog in cities in India mainly consists of
    A. Oxides of sulphur
    B. Oxides of nitrogen and unburnt hydrocarbons
    C. Carbon monoxide and SPM
    D. Oxides of sulphur and ozone

44. Which of the following types of natural hazards have the highest potential to cause damage to humans?
    A. Earthquakes
    B. Forest fires
    C. Volcanic eruptions
    D. Droughts and Floods

45. The percentage share of renewable energy sources in the power production in India is around
    A. 2–3%
    B. 22–25%
    C. 10–12%
    D. < 1%

46. In which of the following categories the enrolment of students in higher education in 2010–11 was beyond the percentage of seats reserved?
A. OBC students
B. SC students
C. ST students
D. Woman students

47. Which one of the following statements is not correct about the University Grants Commission (UGC)?
A. It was established in 1956 by an Act of Parliament.
B. It is tasked with promoting and coordinating higher education.
C. It receives Plan and Non-plan funds from the Central Government.
D. It receives funds from State Governments in respect of State Universities.

48. Consider the statement which is followed by two arguments (I) and (II) :
Statement : Should India switch over to a two party system?
Arguments : (I) Yes, it will lead to stability of Government.
(II) No, it will limit the choice of voters.
A. Only argument (I) is strong.
B. Only argument (II) is strong.
C. Both the arguments are strong.
D. Neither of the arguments is strong.

49. Consider the statement which is followed by two arguments (I) and (II) :
Statement : Should persons with criminal background be banned from contesting elections?
Arguments : (I) Yes, it will decriminalise politics.
(II) No, it will encourage the ruling party to file frivolous cases against their political opponents.
A. Only argument (I) is strong.
B. Only argument (II) is strong.
C. Both the arguments are strong.
D. Neither of the arguments is strong.

50. Which of the following statement(s) is/are correct about a Judge of the Supreme Court of India?
1. A Judge of the Supreme Court is appointed by the President of India.
2. He holds office during the pleasure of the President.
3. He can be suspended, pending an inquiry.
4. He can be removed for proven misbehaviour or incapacity.
Select the correct answer from the codes given below :
Codes :
A. 1, 2 and 3   B. 1, 3 and 4
C. 1 and 3   D. 1 and 4

51. In the warrant of precedence, the Speaker of the Lok Sabha comes next only to
A. The President
B. The Vice-President
C. The Prime Minister
D. The Cabinet Ministers

52. The black-board can be utilised best by a teacher for
A. putting the matter of teaching in black and white
B. making the students attentive
C. writing the important and notable points
D. highlighting the teacher himself

53. Nowadays the most effective mode of learning is
A. self study
B. face-to-face learning
C. e-learning
D. blended learning

54. At the primary school stage, most of the teachers should be women because they
A. can teach children better than men.
B. know basic content better than men.
C. are available on lower salaries.
D. can deal with children with love and affection.

55. Which one is the highest order of learning?
A. Chain learning
B. Problem-solving learning
C. Stimulus-response learning
D. Conditioned-reflex learning

56. A person can enjoy teaching as a profession when he
A. has control over students.
B. commands respect from students.
C. is more qualified than his colleagues.
D. is very close to higher authorities.

57. "A diagram speaks more than 1000 words." The statement means that the teacher should
A. use diagrams in teaching.
B. speak more and more in the class.
C. use teaching aids in the class.
D. not speak too much in the class.

58. A research paper
A. is a compilation of information on a topic.
B. contains original research as deemed by the author.
C. contains peer-reviewed original research or evaluation of research conducted by others.
D. can be published in more than one journal.

59. Which one of the following belongs to the category of good "research ethics"?
A. Publishing the same paper in two research journals without telling the editors.
B. Conducting a review of the literature that acknowledges the contributions of other people in the relevant field or relevant prior work.
C. Trimming outliers from a data set without discussing your reasons in a research paper.
D. Including a colleague as an author on a research paper in return for a favour even though the colleague did not make a serious contribution to the paper.

60. Which of the following sampling methods is not based on probability?
A. Simple Random Sampling
B. Stratified Sampling
C. Quota Sampling
D. Cluster Sampling

ANSWERS

1	2	3	4	5	6	7	8	9	10
D	D	C	B	D	C	D	C	A	C
11	12	13	14	15	16	17	18	19	20
B	C	B	B	B	A	B	B	C	D
21	22	23	24	25	26	27	28	29	30
D	B	D	B	B	B	C	D	A	C
31	32	33	34	35	36	37	38	39	40
B	B	A	C	B	D	A	B	C	C
41	42	43	44	45	46	47	48	49	50
C	A	B	D	C	A	D	C	A	D
51	52	53	54	55	56	57	58	59	60
C	C	D	D	D	B	C	C	B	C

SOME SELECTED EXPLANATORY ANSWERS

16.

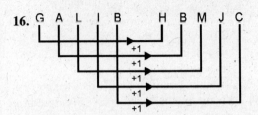

Similarly,

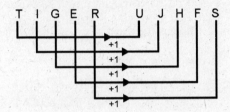

17. Let number of teams participated in the tournament are n

then, number of game played by,

first team $= (n - 1)$

Second team $= (n - 2)$

....

....

....

$(n - 1)^{th}$ team $= 1$

According to the question,

$(n - 1) + (n - 2) + (n - 3) + ... + 1 = 45$

This is equivalent to, Selection of two teams out of n teams $^nc_2$

$\therefore \qquad ^nc_2 = 45$

$\dfrac{n(n-1)}{2} = 45$

or, $\qquad n(n-1) = 90$

$n^2 - n - 90 = 0$

$(n - 10)(n + 9) = 0$

$\Rightarrow \qquad\qquad n = 10.$

18.

| 40 | 120 | 60 | 100 | 90 | 270 | 135 |

$\times 3 \quad \times (0.5) \quad \times 3 \quad \times (0.5) \quad \times 3 \quad \times (0.5)$

19. Odd numbers from 1 to 45 which are exactly divisible by 3 are following.

3, 9, 15, 21, ..., 45

This is an arithmetic series with first term $a = 3$, and common difference $d = 6$

Sixth term of this series

$t_6 = a + (6 - 1).d$

$= 3 + 5 \times 6 = 33.$

20. Mean of four numbers $\dfrac{a+b+c+d}{4} = 100$

or, $\quad a + b + c + d = 400$

or, $\quad a + b + 70 + d = 400$

$a + b + d = 400 - 70 = 330$

Mean $\qquad = \dfrac{a+b+d}{3}$

$= \dfrac{330}{3}$

$= 110.$

21. Perimeter of circle $(p) = 2\pi r$

when radius (r) increased by 50%

$r' = r + \dfrac{r \times 50}{100}$

$= \dfrac{3r}{2}$

New Perimeter $(p') = 2\pi\, r'$

$= 3\pi r$

Increase in perimeter

$p' - p = 3\pi r - 2\pi r = \pi r$

Percentage increment $= \dfrac{\pi r}{2\pi r} \times 100 = 50\%.$

23. Bee give us honey and Cow gives milk, similarly from teacher we get wisdom.

24.

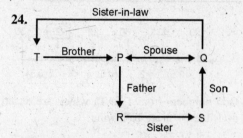

28. Increase in total horticulture area

from 2005-06 & 2006-07

194 – 187 = 7 Lakh hect.

from 2006-07 & 2007-08

202 – 194 = 8 Lakh hect.

from 2007-08 & 2008-09

207 – 202 = 5 Lakh hect.

from 2006-07 & 2008-09

207 – 194 = 13 Lakh hect.

Hence, highest rate of increase is registered in 2006-07 & 2007-08.

29. Total horticultural area

= 187 + 194 + 202 + 207 + 209

= 999 lakh hect.

Total flowers area

= 1 + 1 + 2 + 2 + 2

= 8 lakh hect.

Percentage area under flowers

$= \dfrac{8}{999} \times 100 \cong 0.8\%$

Total area under Vegetation

= 72 + 75 +78 + 79 + 79

= 383 Lakh hect.

Percentage area under vegetation

$= \dfrac{383}{999} \times 100 \cong 38.3\%$

Total area under Fruits

= 53 + 56 + 58 + 61 + 63

= 291 Lakh hect.

Percentage area under fruits

$= \dfrac{291}{999} \times 100 \cong 29.1\%$

Hence, Correct option is (A).

30. Increase in area under

Fruits = 63 – 53

= 10 lakh hect.

Rate of increase $= \dfrac{10}{5} = 2$ lakh hect

Increase in area under

Vegetables = 79 – 72

= 7 lakh hect.

Rate of increase $= \dfrac{7}{5}$

= 1.4 lakh hect.

Increase in area under flowers

= 2 – 1

= 1 Lakh hect.

Rate of increase $= \dfrac{1}{5}$

= 0.2 lakh hect.

Increase in area under total horticulture

= 209 – 187

= 22 lakh hect.

Rate of increase $= \dfrac{22}{5}$

= 4.4 lakh hect.

Hence correct option is (D).

31. Percentage increase in area under

fruits $= \dfrac{63-53}{53} \times 100 = 18.89\% \cong 20\%$

Vegetables $= \dfrac{79-72}{72} \times 100 = 9.77\% \cong 10\%$

Flowers $= \dfrac{2-1}{1} \times 100 = 100\%$

Total horticulture

$= \dfrac{209-187}{187} \times 100$

$= 11.7\% \cong 12\%$

Hence, correct option is (B).

32. Area under fruits, vegetables and flowers in year 2007 – 08

$= 58 + 78 + 2$

$= 138$ lakh hect.

Area under horticulture in year 2007 – 08

$= 202$ lakh hect.

Percentage of area $= \dfrac{138}{202} \times 100$

$= 68.33\%.$

33. Rate of increase of area under flowers

in year 2006-07 $= \dfrac{56-53}{1} = 3$

in year 2007-08 $= \dfrac{58-56}{1} = 2$

in year 2008-09 $= \dfrac{61-58}{1} = 3$

in year 2009-10 $= \dfrac{63-61}{1} = 2.$

UGC-NET (JRF) EXAM, DECEMBER– 2013

PAPER–I

Note: *This paper contains* **Sixty (60)** *multiple choice questions, each question carrying* **two (2)** *marks. Attempt any* **Fifty (50)** *questions.*

1. Which is the main objective of research ?
   A. To review the literature
   B. To summarize what is already known
   C. To get an academic degree
   D. To discover new facts or to make fresh interpretation of known facts

2. Sampling error decreases with the
   A. decrease in sample size
   B. increase in sample size
   C. process of randomization
   D. process of analysis

3. The principles of fundamental research are used in
   A. action research
   B. applied research
   C. philosophical research
   D. historical research

4. Users who use media for their own ends are identified as
   A. Passive audience
   B. Active audience
   C. Positive audience
   D. Negative audience

5. Classroom communication can be described as
   A. Exploration
   B. Institutionalisation
   C. Unsignified narration
   D. Discourse

6. Ideological codes shape our collective
   A. Productions   B. Perceptions
   C. Consumptions   D. Creations

7. In communication, myths have power, but are
   A. uncultural.   B. insignificant.
   C. imprecise.   D. unpreferred.

8. The first multi-lingual news agency of India was
   A. Samachar
   B. API
   C. Hindustan Samachar
   D. Samachar Bharati

9. Organisational communication can also be equated with
   A. intra-personal communication.
   B. inter-personal communication.
   C. group communication.
   D. mass communication.

10. If two propositions having the same subject and predicate terms are such that one is the denial of the other, the relationship between them is called
    A. Contradictory   B. Contrary
    C. Sub-contrary   D. Sub-alternation

11. Ananya and Krishna can speak and follow English. Bulbul can write and speak Hindi as Archana does. Archana talks with Ananya also in Bengali. Krishna can not follow Bengali. Bulbul talks with Ananya in Hindi. Who can speak and follow English, Hindi and Bengali?
    A. Archana   B. Bulbul
    C. Ananya   D. Krishna

12. A stipulative definition may be said to be
    A. Always true
    B. Always false
    C. Sometimes true, sometimes false
    D. Neither true nor false

13. When the conclusion of an argument follows from its premise/premises conclusively, the argument is called
  A. Circular argument
  B. Inductive argument
  C. Deductive argument
  D. Analogical argument

14. Saturn and Mars are planets like the earth. They borrow light from the Sun and moves around the Sun as the Earth does. So those planets are inhabited by various orders of creatures as the earth is. What type of argument is contained in the above passage ?
  A. Deductive   B. Astrological
  C. Analogical   D. Mathematical

15. Given below are two premises. Four conclusions are drawn from those two premises in four codes. Select the code that states the conclusion validly drawn.
  Premises:
    (i) All saints are religious. (major)
    (ii) Some honest persons are saints. (minor)
  Codes:
  A. All saints are honest.
  B. Some saints are honest.
  C. Some honest persons are religious.
  D. All religious persons are honest.

Following table provides details about the Foreign Tourist Arrivals (FTAs) in India from different regions of the world in different years. Study the table carefully and answer questions from 16 to 19 based on this table.

Region	Number of Foreign Tourist Arrivals		
	2007	2008	2009
Western Europe	1686083	1799525	1610086
North America	1007276	1027297	1024469
South Asia	982428	1051846	982633
South East Asia	303475	332925	348495
East Asia	352037	355230	318292
West Asia	171661	215542	201110
Total FTAs in India	5081504	5282603	5108579

16. Find out the region that contributed around 20 per cent of the total foreign tourist arrivals in India in 2009.
  A. Western Europe   B. North America
  C. South Asia   D. South East Asia

17. Which of the following regions has recorded the highest negative growth rate of foreign tourist arrivals in India in 2009?
  A. Western Europe   B. North America
  C. South Asia   D. West Asia

18. Find out the region that has been showing declining trend in terms of share of foreign tourist arrivals in India in 2008 and 2009.
  A. Western Europe   B. South East Asia
  C. East Asia   D. West Asia

19. Identify the region that has shown hyper growth rate of foreign tourist arrivals than the growth rate of the total FTAs in India in 2008.
  A. Western Europe   B. North America
  C. South Asia   D. East Asia

20. The post-industrial society is designated as
  A. Information society
  B. Technology society
  C. Mediated society
  D. Non-agricultural society

21. The initial efforts for internet based communication was for
  A. Commercial communication
  B. Military purposes
  C. Personal interaction
  D. Political campaigns

22. Internal communication within institutions is done through
  A. LAN   B. WAN
  C. EBB   D. MMS

23. Virtual reality provides
  A. Sharp pictures
  B. Individual audio
  C. Participatory experience
  D. Preview of new films

24. The first virtual university of India came up in
  A. Andhra Pradesh   B. Maharashtra
  C. Uttar Pradesh   D. Tamil Nadu

25. Arrange the following books in chronological order in which they appeared. Use the code given below :
    (*i*) Limits to Growth
    (*ii*) Silent Spring
    (*iii*) Our Common Future
    (*iv*) Resourceful Earth
    Codes:
    A. (*i*), (*iii*), (*iv*), (*ii*)
    B. (*ii*), (*iii*), (*i*), (*iv*)
    C. (*ii*), (*i*), (*iii*), (*iv*)
    D. (*i*), (*ii*), (*iii*), (*iv*)

26. Which one of the following continents is at a greater risk of desertification?
    A. Africa
    B. Asia
    C. South America
    D. North America

27. "Women are closer to nature than men." What kind of perspective is this?
    A. Realist
    B. Essentialist
    C. Feminist
    D. Deep ecology

28. Which one of the following is not a matter a global concern in the removal of tropical forests?
    A. Their ability to absorb the chemicals that contribute to depletion of ozone layer.
    B. Their role in maintaining the oxygen and carbon balance of the earth.
    C. Their ability to regulate surface and air temperatures, moisture content and reflectivity.
    D. Their contribution to the biological diversity of the planet.

29. The most comprehensive approach to address the problems of man-environment interaction is one of the following:
    A. Natural Resource Conservation Approach
    B. Urban-industrial Growth Oriented Approach
    C. Rural-agricultural Growth Oriented Approach
    D. Watershed Development Approach

30. The major source of the pollutant gas, carbon mono-oxide (CO), in urban areas is
    A. Thermal power sector
    B. Transport sector
    C. Industrial sector
    D. Domestic sector

31. In a fuel cell driven vehicle, the energy is obtained from the combustion of
    A. Methane
    B. Hydrogen
    C. LPG
    D. CNG

32. Which one of the following Councils has been disbanded in 2013?
    A. Distance Education Council (DEC)
    B. National Council for Teacher Education (NCTE)
    C. National Council of Educational Research and Training (NCERT)
    D. National Assessment and Accreditation Council (NAAC)

33. Which of the following statements are correct about the National Assessment and Accreditation Council?
    1. It is an autonomous institution.
    2. It is tasked with the responsibility of assessing and accrediting institutions of higher education.
    3. It is located in Delhi.
    4. It has regional offices.

    Select the correct answer from the codes given below:
    Codes:
    A. 1 and 3
    B. 1 and 2
    C. 1, 2 and 4
    D. 2, 3 and 4

34. The power of the Supreme Court of India to decide disputes between two or more States falls under its
    A. Advisory Jurisdiction
    B. Appellate Jurisdiction
    C. Original Jurisdiction
    D. Writ Jurisdiction

35. Which of the following statements are correct?
    1. There are seven Union Territories in India.
    2. Two Union Territories have Legislative Assemblies
    3. One Union Territory has a High Court.
    4. One Union Territory is the capital of two States.

Select the correct answer from the codes given below :
A. 1 and 3 only   B. 2 and 4 only
C. 2, 3 and 4 only   D. 1, 2, 3 and 4

36. Which of the following statements are correct about the Central Information Commission?
1. The Central Information Commission is a statutory body.
2. The Chief Information Commissioner and other Information Commissioners are appointed by the President of India.
3. The Commission can impose a penalty upto a maximum of ₹ 25,000/-
4. It can punish an errant officer.

Select the correct answer from the codes given below:
Codes:
A. 1 and 2 only   B. 1, 2 and 4
C. 1, 2 and 3   D. 2, 3 and 4

37. Who among the following conducted the CNN-IBN – The Hindu 2013 Election Tracker Survey across 267 constituencies in 18 States?
A. The Centre for the Study of Developing Societies (CSDS)
B. The Association for Democratic Reforms (ADR)
C. CNN and IBN
D. CNN, IBN and The Hindu

38. In certain code TEACHER is written as VGCEJGT. The code of CHILDREN will be
A. EKNJFTGP   B. EJKNFTGP
C. KNJFGTP   D. None of these

39. A person has to buy both apples and mangoes. The cost of one apple is ₹ 7/- whereas that of a mango is ₹ 5/-. If the person has ₹ 38, the number of apples he can buy is
A. 1   B. 2
C. 3   D. 4

40. A man pointing to a lady said, "The son of her only brother is the brother of my wife". The lady is related to the man as
A. Mother's sister
B. Grand mother
C. Mother-in-law
D. Sister of Father-in-law

41. In this series
6, 4, 1, 2, 2, 8, 7, 4, 2, 1, 5, 3, 8, 6, 2, 2, 7, 1, 4, 1, 3, 5, 8, 6,
how many pairs of successive numbers have a difference of 2 each ?
A. 4   B. 5
C. 6   D. 8

42. The mean marks obtained by a class of 40 students is 65. The mean marks of half of the students is found to be 45. The mean marks of the remaining students is
A. 85   B. 60
C. 70   D. 65

43. Anil is twice as old as Sunita. Three years ago, he was three times as old as Sunita. The present age of Anil is
A. 6 years   B. 8 years
C. 12 years   D. 16 years

44. Which of the following is a social network?
A. amazon.com   B. eBay
C. gmail.com   D. Twitter

45. The population information is called parameter while the corresponding sample information is known as
A. Universe   B. Inference
C. Sampling design   D. Statistics

Read the following passage carefully and answer questions 46 to 51 :

Heritage conservation practices improved worldwide after the International Centre for the Study of the Preservation and Restoration of Cultural Property (ICCROM) was established with UNESCO's assistance in 1959. The inter-governmental organisation with 126 member states has done a commendable job by training more than 4,000 professionals, providing practice standards, and sharing technical expertise. In this golden jubilee year, as we acknowledge its key role in global conservation, an assessment of international practices would be meaningful to the Indian conservation movement. Consistent investment, rigorous attention, and dedicated research and dissemination are some of the positive lessons to imbibe. Countries such as Italy have demonstrated that prioritising heritage with significant budget provision pays. On the other hand, India, which is no less endowed in terms of cultural capital, has a long way to go. Surveys indicate that in addition to the 6,600 protected monuments, there are over 60,000 equally valuable heritage structures that await attention. Besides the small group in the service of Archaeological Survey of India, there are only about 150 trained conservation professionals. In order to overcome this severe shortage the emphasis has been on setting up dedicated labs and training institutions. It would make much better sense for conservation to be made part of mainstream research and engineering institutes, as has been done in Europe. Increasing funding and building institutions are the relatively easy part. The real challenge is to redefine international approaches to address local contexts. Conservation cannot limit itself to enhancing the art-historical value of the heritage structures, which international charters perhaps overemphasise. The effort has to be broad-based : It must also serve as a means to improving the quality of life in the area where the heritage structures are located. The first task therefore is to integrate conservation efforts with sound development plans that take care of people living in the heritage vicinity. Unlike in western countries, many traditional building crafts survive in India, and conservation practices offer an avenue to support them. This has been acknowledged by the Indian National Trust for Art and Cultural Heritage charter for conservation but is yet to receive substantial state support. More strength for heritage conservation can be mobilised by aligning it with the green building movement. Heritage structures are essentially eco-friendly and conservation could become a vital part of the sustainable building practices campaign in future.

46. The outlook for conservation heritage changed
    A. after the establishment of the International Centre for the Study of the Preservation and Restoration of Cultural Property.
    B. after training the specialists in the field.
    C. after extending UNESCO's assistance to the educational institutions.

D. after ASI's measures to protect the monuments.

47. The inter-government organization was appreciated because of
    A. increasing number of members to 126.
    B. imparting training to professionals and sharing technical expertise.
    C. consistent investment in conservation.
    D. its proactive role in renovation and restoration.

48. Indian conservation movement will be successful if there would be
    A. Financial support from the Government of India.
    B. Non-governmental organisations role and participation in the conservation movement.
    C. consistent investment, rigorous attention, and dedicated research and dissemination of awareness for conservation.
    D. Archaeological Survey of India's meaningful assistance.

49. As per the surveys of historical monuments in India, there is very small number of protected monuments. As per given the total number of monuments and enlisted number of protected monuments, percentage comes to
    A. 10 per cent   B. 11 per cent
    C. 12 per cent   D. 13 per cent

50. What should India learn from Europe to conserve our cultural heritage ?
    (i) There should be significant budget provision to conserve our cultural heritage.
    (ii) Establish dedicated labs and training institutions.
    (iii) Force the government to provide sufficient funds.
    (iv) Conservation should be made part of mainstream research and engineering institutes.

Choose correct answer from the codes given below :
    A. (i), (ii), (iii), (iv)   B. (i), (ii), (iv)
    (C. (i), (ii)   D. (i), (iii), (iv)

51. INTACH is known for its contribution for conservation of our cultural heritage. The full form of INTACH is
    A. International Trust for Art and Cultural Heritage
    B. Intra-national Trust for Art and Cultural Heritage
    C. Integrated Trust for Art and Cultural Heritage
    D. Indian National Trust for Art and Cultural Heritage

52. While delivering lecture if there is some disturbance in the class, a teacher should
    A. keep quiet for a while and then continue.
    B. punish those causing disturbance.
    C. motivate to teach those causing disturbance.
    D. not bother of what is happening in the class.

53. Effective teaching is a function of
    A. Teacher's satisfaction.
    B. Teacher's honesty and commitment.
    C. Teacher's making students learn and understand.
    D. Teacher's liking for professional excellence.

54. The most appropriate meaning of learning is
    A. Acquisition of skills
    B. Modification of behaviour
    C. Personal adjustment
    D. Inculcation of knowledge

55. Arrange the following teaching process in order :
    (i) Relate the present knowledge with previous one
    (ii) Evaluation
    (iii) Reteaching
    (iv) Formulating instructional objectives
    (v) Presentation of instructional materials
    A. (i), (ii), (iii), (iv), (v)
    B. (ii), (i), (iii), (iv), (v)

C. (v), (iv), (iii), (i), (ii)
D. (iv), (i), (v), (ii), (iii)

56. CIET stands for
    A. Centre for Integrated Education and Technology
    B. Central Institute for Engineering and Technology
    C. Central Institute for Education Technology
    D. Centre for Integrated Evaluation Techniques.

57. Teacher's role at higher education level is to
    A. provide information to students.
    B. promote self learning in students.
    C. encourage healthy competition among students.
    D. help students to solve their problems.

58. The Verstehen School of Understanding was popularised by
    A. German Social Scientists
    B. American Philosophers
    C. British Academicians
    D. Italian Political Analysts

59. The sequential operations in scientific research are
    A. Co-variation, Elimination of Spurious Relations, Generalisation, Theorisation
    B. Generalisation, Co-variation, Theorisation, Elimination of Spurious Relations
    C. Theorisation, Generalisation, Elimination of Spurious Relations, Co-variation
    D. Elimination of Spurious Relations, Theorisation, Generalisation, Co-variation.

60. In sampling, the lottery method is used for
    A. Interpretation
    B. Theorisation
    C. Conceptualisation
    D. Randomisation

ANSWERS

1	2	3	4	5	6	7	8	9	10
D	B	B	B	D	B	C	C	C	A
11	12	13	14	15	16	17	18	19	20
C	D	C	C	C	B	D	A	C	A
21	22	23	24	25	26	27	28	29	30
B	A	C	D	C	A	B	A	D	B
31	32	33	34	35	36	37	38	39	40
B	A	B	C	D	C	A	B	D	D
41	42	43	44	45	46	47	48	49	50
C	A	C	D	D	A	B	C	B	B
51	52	53	54	55	56	57	58	59	60
D	C	C	B	D	C	B	A	A	D

SOME SELECTED EXPLANATORY ANSWERS

11. **Language:** Hindi   English   Bengali

    Name: Bulbul   Ananya   Archana

                  Archana Krishna   Ananya

                  Ananya

Hence, Ananya can speak & follow English, Hindi and Bengali.

15.

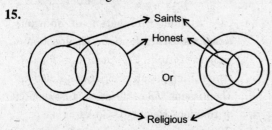

Here, there is no premises given to whether some or all saints are honests.

Hence, clear validly drawn is some honest persons are religious.

16. FTA contribution (in per cent) by different region in year 2009.

$$\text{Western Europe} = \frac{1610086}{5108579} \times 100 = 31.5\%$$

$$\text{North America} = \frac{1024469}{5108579} \times 100 = 20\%$$

$$\text{South Asia} = \frac{982633}{5108579} \times 100 = 19.23\%$$

$$\text{South East Asia} = \frac{348495}{5108579} \times 100 = 6.82\%$$

Hence, North America's contribution is around 20% of the total FTAs.

22. LAN — Local Area Network

This is an interconnection technique use to connect different PC installed within a small area like institutions.

24. The government of Tamil Nadu established the Tamil Virtual University (TVU) on 17 February 2001 as a Society. The university provides internet-based educational resources and opportunities for the Tamil diaspora as well as for others interested in learning the Tamil language and acquiring knowledge of the history, art, literature and culture of the Tamils.

30. Transport contributes to ambient air pollution, one of the most serious public health problems.

The main source of ambient air pollution is the combustion of fossil fuels by both stationary and mobile sources. The transportation sector is in general responsible for a significant share of the ambient air pollution in urban areas by emission of carbon monoxide. Ambient air quality problems tend to be most severe in urban areas where both population and pollution sources, particularly automobiles and industry, are most concentrated.

31. A hydrogen vehicle is a vehicle that uses hydrogen as its onboard fuel for motive power. Hydrogen vehicles include hydrogen fueled space rockets, as well as automobiles and other transportation vehicles. The power plants of such vehicles convert the chemical energy of hydrogen to mechanical energy either by burning hydrogen in an internal combustion engine, or by reacting hydrogen with oxygen in a fuel cell to run electric motors. Widespread use of hydrogen for fueling transportation is a key element of a proposed hydrogen economy.

38. T E A C H E R — V G C E J G T

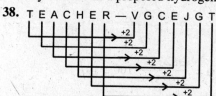

Similarly,

C H I L D R E N — E J K N F T G P

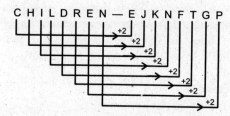

39. Let number of apples and mangoes bought by man is x and y respectively.

then,

$$7x + 5y = 38$$

for x, y an integer number, this is satisfied for $x = 4$, $y = 2$

Hence, number of apples = 4

41. Such pairs are (6, 4), (4, 2), (5, 3), (8, 6), (3, 5), (8, 6).

42. Total marks obtained by 40 students

$$= 65 \times 40 = 2600$$

Total marks obtained by 20 students

$$= 45 \times 20 = 900$$

Marks obtained by remaining 20 students

$$= 2600 - 900 = 1700$$

So, Average of marks obtained by remaining

20 students $= \dfrac{1700}{20} = 85$.

43. Let Sunita's age is x yrs.

Then Anil's age is $2x$ yrs.

According to the question,

$$2x - 3 = 3(x - 3)$$
$$2x - 3 = 3x - 9$$
$$x = 6 \text{ yrs}$$

Hence, Anil's present age $= 2x = 12$ yrs.

44. amazon.com and gmail.com are websites used for mailing services. eBay is marketing site used for online sale/purchase while Twitter is a social networking site.

UGC-NET (JRF) EXAM JUNE, 2014*

> **Note :** This paper contains **Sixty (60)** multiple-choice questions, each question carrying **two (2)** marks. Candidate is expected to answer any **fifty (50)** questions. In case more than **fifty (50)** questions are attempted, only the first **fifty (50)** questions will be evaluated.

1. "If a large diamond is cut up into little bits, it will lose its value just as an army is divided up into small units of soldiers, it loses its strength."
   The argument put above may be called as
   A. Analogical   B. Deductive
   C. Statistical   D. Causal

2. Given below are some characteristics of logical argument. Select the code which expresses a characteristic which is not of inductive in character.
   A. The conclusion is claimed to follow from its premises.
   B. The conclusion is based on causal relation.
   C. The conclusion conclusively follows from its premises.
   D. The conclusion is based on observation and experiment.

3. If two propositions having the same subject and predicate terms can both be true but can not both be false, the relation between those two propositions is called
   A. contradictory   B. contrary
   C. subcontrary   D. subaltern

4. One writes all numbers from 50 to 99 without the digits 2 and 7. How many numbers have been written?
   A. 32   B. 36
   C. 40   D. 38

5. Given below is a diagram of three circles A, B and C enter-related with each other. The circle A represents the class of Indians, the circle B represents the class of scientists and circle C represents the class of politicians. *p, q, r, s* ... represent different regions. Select the code containing the region that indicates the class of Indian scientists who are not politicians.

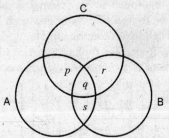

   Codes :
   A. *q* and *s* only   B. *s* only
   C. *s* and *r* only   D. *p, q* and *s* only

6. Given below are two premises and four conclusions drawn from those premises. Select the code that expresses conclusion drawn validly from the premises (separately or jointly).
   Premises :
   (*a*) All dogs are mammals
   (*b*) No cats are dogs
   Conclusions :
   (*i*) No cats are mammals
   (*ii*) Some cats are mammals
   (*iii*) No dogs are cats
   (*iv*) No dogs are non-mammals
   Codes :
   A. (*i*) only   B. (*i*) and (*ii*)
   C. (*iii*) and (*iv*) D. (*ii*) and (*iii*)

Read the following table carefully. Based upon this table answer questions from 7 to 11 :

Net area under irrigation by sources in a country

(in Thousand Hectares)

Year	Government canals	Private canals	Tanks	Tube-wells & other wells	Other Sources	Total
1997-98	17117	211	2593	32090	3102	55173
1998-99	17093	212	2792	33988	3326	57411
1999-00	16842	194	2535	34623	2915	57109
2000-01	15748	203	2449	33796	2880	55076
2001-02	15031	209	2179	34906	4347	56672
2002-03	13863	206	1802	34250	3657	53778
2003-04	14444	206	1908	35779	4281	56618
2004-05	14696	206	1727	34785	7453	58867
2005-06	15268	207	2034	35372	7314	60196

7. Find out the source of Irrigation that has registered the maximum improvement in terms of percentage of Net irrigated area during 2002-03 and 2003-04.
   A. Government canals
   B. Tanks
   C. Tube-wells and other wells
   D. Other sources

8. In which of the following years, Net irrigation by tanks increased at the highest rate?
   A. 1998-99   B. 2000-01
   C. 2003-04   D. 2005-06

9. Identify the source of Irrigation that has recorded the maximum incidence of negative growth in terms of Net irrigated area during the years given in the table.
   A. Government canals
   B. Private canals
   C. Tube-wells and other wells
   D. Other sources

10. In which of the following years, share of the tube-wells and other wells in the total net irrigated area was the highest?
    A. 1998-99   B. 2000-01
    C. 2002-03   D. 2004-05

11. Which of the following sources of Irrigation has registered the largest percentage of decline in Net area under irrigation during 1997-98 and 2005-06?
    A. Government canals
    B. Private canals
    C. Tanks
    D. Other sources

12. Which one of the following is not a/an image/graphic file format?
    A. PNG   B. GIF
    C. BMP   D. GUI

13. The first web browser is
    A. Internet Explorer   B. Netscape
    C. World Wide Web   D. Firefox

14. When a computer is booting, BIOS is loaded to the memory by
    A. RAM   B. ROM
    C. CD-ROM   D. TCP

15. Which one of the following is not the same as the other three?
    A. MAC address   B. Hardware address
    C. Physical address   D. IP address

16. Identify the IP address from the following:
    A. 300 · 215 · 317 · 3
    B. 302 · 215 @ 417 · 5
    C. 202 · 50 · 20 · 148
    D. 202 - 50 - 20 - 148

17. The acronym FIP stands for
    A. File Transfer Protocol
    B. Fast Transfer Protocol
    C. File Tracking Protocol
    D. File Transfer Procedure

18. Which of the following cities has been worst affected by urban smog in recent times?
    A. Paris   B. London
    C. Los Angeles   D. Beijing

19. The primary source of organic pollution in fresh water bodies is
    A. run-off urban areas
    B. run-off from agricultural forms
    C. sewage effluents
    D. industrial effluents

20. 'Lahar' is a natural disaster involving
    A. eruption of large amount of material
    B. strong winds
    C. strong water waves
    D. strong winds and water waves

21. The population of India is about 1.2 billion. Take the average consumption of energy per person per year in India as 30 Mega Joules. If this consumption is met by carbon based fuels and the rate of carbon emissions per kilojoule is 15 × 106 kgs, the total carbon emissions per year from India will be
   A. 54 million metric tons
   B. 540 million metric tons
   C. 5400 million metric tons
   D. 2400 million metric tons

22. The National Disaster Management Authority functions under the Union Ministry of
   A. Environment
   B. Water Resources
   C. Home Affairs
   D. Defence

23. Match List-I and List-II and select the correct answer from the codes given below:

List-I	List-II
(a) Flood	1. Lack of rainfall of sufficient duration
(b) Drought	2. Tremors produced by the passage of vibratory waves through the rocks of the earth
(c) Earthquake	3. A vent through which molted substances come out
(d) Volcano	4. Excess rain and uneven distribution of water

   Codes :

	(a)	(b)	(c)	(d)
A.	4	1	2	3
B.	2	3	4	1
C.	3	4	2	1
D.	4	3	1	2

24. Which one of the following greenhouse gases has the shortest residence time in the atmosphere?
   A. Chlorofluorocarbon
   B. Carbon dioxide
   C. Methane
   D. Nitrous oxide

25. In order to avoid catastrophic consequences of climate change, there is general agreement among the countries of the world to limit the rise in average surface temperature of earth compared to that of pre-industrial times by
   A. 1.5 °C to 2 °C
   B. 2.0 °C to 3.5 °C
   C. 0.5 °C to 1.0 °C
   D. 0.25 °C to 0.5 °C

26. Who among the following is the de facto executive head of the Planning Commission?
   A. Chairman
   B. Deputy Chairman
   C. Minister of State for Planning
   D. Member Secretary

27. Education as a subject of legislation figures in the
   A. Union List   B. State List
   C. Concurrent List   D. Residuary Powers

28. Which of the following are Central Universities?
   1. Pondicherry University
   2. Vishwa Bharati
   3. H.N.B. Garhwal University
   4. Kurukshetra University
   Select the correct answer from the code given below:
   Codes:
   A. 1, 2 and 3   B. 1, 3 and 4
   C. 2, 3 and 4   D. 1, 2 and 4

29. Consider the following statements and select the correct answer from the code given below:
   (i) Rajasthan receives the highest solar radiation in the country.
   (ii) India has the fifth largest installed wind power in the world.
   (iii) The maximum amount of wind power is contributed by Tamil Nadu.
   (iv) The primary source of uranium in India is Jaduguda.
   Codes :
   A. (i) and (ii)   B. (i), (ii) and (iii)
   C. (ii) and (iii)   D. (i) and (iv)

30. Which of the following universities has adopted the meta university concept?
A. Assam University
B. Delhi University
C. Hyderabad University
D. Pondicherry University

31. Which of the following statements are correct about a Central University?
1. Central University is established under an Act of Parliament
2. The President of India acts as the visitor of the University.
3. The President has the power to nominate some members to the Executive Committee or the Board of Management of the University.
4. The President occasionally presides over the meetings of the Executive Committee or Court.

Select the correct answer from the code given below:
A. 1, 2 and 4   B. 1, 3 and 4
C. 1, 2 and 3   B. 1, 2, 3 and 4

32. Consider the statement which is followed by two arguments (*i*) and (*ii*).

Statement : India should have a very strong and powerful Lokpal.

Arguments : (*i*) Yes, it will go a long in eliminating corruption in bureaucracy.

(*ii*) No, it will discourage honest officers from making quick decisions.

Codes:
A. Only argument (*i*) is strong.
B. Only argument (*ii*) is strong.
C. Both the arguments are strong.
D. Neither of the arguments is strong.

33. Which one of the following is the best method of teaching?
A. Lecture   B. Discussion
C. Demonstration   D. Narration

34. Dyslexia is associated with
A. mental disorder
B. behavioural disorder
C. reading disorder
D. writing disorder

35. The e-content generation for under-graduate courses has been assigned by the Ministry of Human Resource Development to
A. INFLIBNET
B. Consortium for Educational Communication.
C. National Knowledge Commission
D. Indira Gandhi National Open University

36. Classroom communication is normally considered as
A. effective   B. cognitive
C. affective   D. selective

37. Which one of the following is considered a sign of motivated teaching?
A. Students asking questions
B. Maximum attendance of the students
C. Pin drop silence in the classroom
D. Students taking notes

38. In a thesis, figures and tables are included in
A. the appendix
B. a separate chapter
C. the concluding chapter
D. the text itself

39. A thesis statement is
A. an observation   B. a fact
C. an assertion   D. a discussion

40. The research approach of Max Weber to understand how people create meanings in natural settings is identified as
A. positive paradigm
B. critical paradigm
C. natural paradigm
D. interpretative paradigm

41. Which one of the following is a non-probability sampling?
A. Simple random   B. Purposive
C. Systematic   D. Stratified

42. Identify the category of evaluation that assesses the learning progress to provide continuous feedback to the students during instruction.
A. Placement   B. Diagnostic
C. Formative   D. Summative

43. The research stream of immediate application is
   A. Conceptual research
   B. Action research
   C. Fundamental research
   D. Empirical research

44. Who among the following, propounded the concept of paradigm?
   A. Peter Haggett   B. Von Thunen
   C. Thomas Kuhn   D. John K. Wright

Read the following passage carefully and answer questions 45 to 49:

Traditional Indian Values must be viewed both from the angle of the individual and from that of the geographically delimited agglomeration of peoples or groups enjoying a common system of leadership which we call the 'State'. The Indian 'State's' special feature is the peaceful, or perhaps mostly peaceful, co-existence of social groups of various historical provenances which mutually adhere in a geographical, economic, and political sense, without ever assimilating to each other in social terms, in ways of thinking, or even in language. Modern Indian law will determine certain rules, especially in relation to the regime of the family, upon the basis of how the loin-cloth is tied, or how the turban is worn, for this may identify the litigants as members of a regional group, and therefore as participants in its traditional law, though their ancestors left the region three or four centuries earlier. The use of the word 'State' above must not mislead us. There was no such thing as a conflict between the individual and the State, atleast before foreign governments became established, just as there was no concept of state 'sovereignty' or of any church-and-state dichotomy.

Modern Indian 'secularism' has an admittedly peculiar feature : It requires the state to make a fair distribution of attention and support amongst all religions. These blessed aspects of India's famed tolerance (Indian kings so rarely persecuted religious groups that the exceptions prove the rule) at once struck Portuguese and other European visitors to the West Coast of India in the sixteenth century, and the impression made upon them in this and other ways gave rise, at one remove, to the basic constitution of Thomas More's Utopia. There is little about modern India that strikes one at once as Utopian : but the insistence upon the inculcation of norms, and the absence of bigotry and institutionalized exploitation of human or natural resources, are two very different features which link the realities of India and her tradition with the essence of all Utopians.

45. The author uses the world 'State' to highlight.
   A. Antagonistic relationship between the state and the individual throughout the period of history.
   B. Absence of conflict between the state and the individuals upto a point in time.
   C. The concept of state sovereignty.
   D. Dependence on religion.

46. Which one is the peculiar feature of modern Indian 'Secularism'?
   A. No discrimination on religious considerations
   B. Total indifference to religion.
   C. No space for social identity
   D. Disregard for social law

47. The basic construction of Thomas More's Utopia was inspired by
   A. Indian tradition of religious tolerance.
   B. Persecution of religious groups by Indian rulers.
   C. Social inequality in India.
   D. European perception of Indian State.

48. What is the striking feature of modern India?
   A. A replica of Utopian State
   B. Uniform laws
   C. Adherence to traditional values
   D. Absence of Bigotry

49. Which of the following is a special feature of the Indian State?
   A. Peaceful co-existence of people under a common system of leadership.
   B. Peaceful co-existence of social groups of different historical provenances attached to each other in a geographical, economic and political sense.
   C. Social integration of all groups.
   D. Cultural assimilation of all social groups.

50. The Telephone Model of Communication was first developed in the area of
A. Technological theory
B. Dispersion theory
C. Minimal effects theory
D. Information theory

51. The Dada Saheb Phalke Award for 2013 has been conferred on
A. Karan Johar   B. Amir Khan
C. Asha Bhonsle   D. Gulzar

52. Photographs are not easy to
A. publish   B. secure
C. decode   D. change

53. The grains that appear on a television set when operated are also referred to as
A. sparks   B. green dots
C. snow   D. rain drops

54. In circular communication, the encoder becomes a decoder when there is
A. noise   B. audience
C. criticality   D. feedback

55. Break-down in verbal communication is described as
A. Short circuit   B. Contradiction
C. Unevenness   D. Entropy

56. In certain coding method, the word QUESTION is encoded as DOMESTIC. In this coding, what is the code word for the word RESPONSE?
A. OMESUCEM   B. OMESICSM
C. OMESICEM   D. OMESISCM

57. If the series, 4, 5, 8, 13, 14, 17, 22, ... is continued in the same pattern, which one of the following is not a term of this series?
A. 31   B. 32
C. 33   D. 35

58. Complete the series BB, FE, II, ML, PP, ... by choosing one of the following option given:
A. TS   B. ST
C. RS   D. SR

59. A man started walking from his house towards south. After walking 6 km, he turned to his left and walked 5 km. Then he walked further 3 km after turning left. He then turned to his left and continued his walk for 9 km. How far is he away from his house?
A. 3 km   B. 4 km
C. 5 km   D. 6 km

60. In a post-office, stamps of three different denominations of ₹ 7, ₹ 8, ₹ 10 are available. The exact amount for which one cannot buy stamps is
A. 19   B. 20
C. 23   D. 29

ANSWERS

1	2	3	4	5	6	7	8	9	10
A	B	D	A	B	C	D	D	A	C

11	12	13	14	15	16	17	18	19	20
A	D	C	B	D	C	A	D	C	A

21	22	23	24	25	26	27	28	29	30
C	C	A	C	A	B	C	A	B	B

31	32	33	34	35	36	37	38	39	40
C	A	C	C	B	B	A	D	D	D

41	42	43	44	45	46	47	48	49	50
B	C	B	C	B	A	A	A	B	B

51	52	53	54	55	56	57	58	59	60
D	C	C	D	C	C	C	A	C	A

SOME SELECTED EXPLANATORY ANSWERS

4. 50 51 (52) 53 54 55 56 (57) 58 59

60 61 (62) 63 64 65 66 (67) 68 69

(70) (71) (72) (73) (74) (75) (76) (77) (78) (79)

80 81 (82) 83 84 85 86 (87) 88 89

90 91 (92) 93 94 95 96 (97) 98 99

∴ 50 – 18 = 32

He has written 32 numbers.

5.

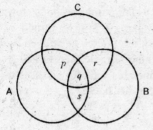

⊙ A represents – Indians
⊙ B represents – Scientists
⊙ C represents – Politicians
p, q, r, s.... represents different regions
Required code is (B) s only.

6.

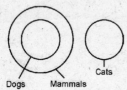

or

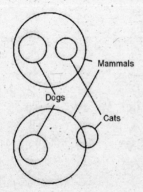

As from premise-II,

No cats are dogs,

So, No dogs are cats.

Again from premise-I

All dogs are mammals

So, No dogs are non-mammals.

7. A. Government canals

= 14444 – 13863 = 581

$\% = \dfrac{581}{13863} \times 100 = \dfrac{58100}{13863} = 4\%$

B. Tanks = 1908 – 1802 = 106

$\% = \dfrac{106}{1802} \times 100 = \dfrac{10600}{1802} = 5.9\%$

C. Tube-wells and other wells

= 35779 – 34250 = 1529

$\% = \dfrac{1529}{34250} \times 100 = \dfrac{152900}{34250} = 4\%$

D. Other sources

= 4281 – 3657 = 624

$\% = \dfrac{624}{3657} \times 100 = \dfrac{62400}{3657} = 17\%$

Clearly (D) gives maximum.

Hence, correct answer is (D).

8. A. 1998-99 ⇒ 2792 – 2593 = 199

$\% = \dfrac{199}{2593} \times 100 = \dfrac{19900}{2593} = 7\%$

B. 2000-01 ⇒ 2449 – 2535 = –86
negative sign shows not increase.

C. 2003-04 ⇒ 1908 – 1802 = 106

$\% = \dfrac{106}{1802} \times 100 = \dfrac{10600}{1802} = 5.8\%$

D. 2005-06 ⇒ 2034 – 1727 = 307

$\% = \dfrac{307}{1727} \times 100 = \dfrac{30700}{1727} = 17\%$

Hence, 2005-06 net irrigation by tanks increases at the highest rate.

9. Required answer is (A) Government canals.

10. Required year is 2002-03.

11. Required Sources of irrigation is Government canals.

16. The correct format to write IP address is to use dots between each set of digits.

17. FTP stands for file transfer protocol and is a method by which you can transfer files from one computer to another.

18. Beijing along with Tianjin and Hebei province & central and western Shandong province is affected by the worst urban smog in recent times. Bejing has a four-tier alert system, using blue, yellow, orrange and red to indicate the air pollution level. A red alert indicates the most serious air pollution (AQI above 300) for 3 consecutive days. An orange alert indicates heavy to serious air pollution (AQI between 200 and 300) alternately for 3 consecutive days. A yellow alert means severe pollution for 1 day or heavy pollution for 3 consecutive days.

19. The main source of freshwater pollution can be attributed to discharge of untreated waste mainly sewage effluents.

20. Lahar is a natural disaster that involves eruption of large amount of material from volcano. The material flows down from a volcano, typically along a river valley is known as lahar.

56.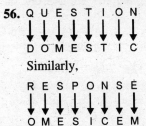

57.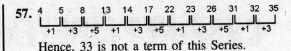

Hence, 33 is not a term of this Series.

58.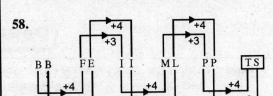

59.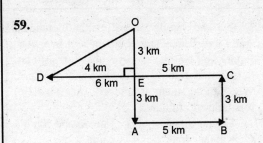

In △OED,

$$(OD)^2 = (4)^2 + (3)^2$$
$$= 16 + 9 = 25$$
$$\therefore \quad OD = \sqrt{25} = 5 \text{ km.}$$

Hence, he is 5 km away from his house.

60. B.　$20 = 10 \times 2 = 20$

C.　$23 = 8 \times 2 + 7 \times 1$
$$= 16 + 7 = 23$$

D.　$29 = 7 \times 3 + 8 \times 1$
$$= 21 + 8 = 29$$

A.　$19 = 7 \times 2 + 5 = 8 \times 2 + 3$
$$= 10 \times 1 + 8 \times 1 + 1$$
$$= 10 \times 1 + 7 \times 1 + 2$$

Hence, the exact amount for which one can not buy stamps is 19.

CBSE-NET (JRF) Exam December, 2014*

PAPER–I

> **Note :** This paper contains **Sixty (60)** multiple choice questions, each question carrying **two (2)** marks. Candidate is expected to answer any **Fifty (50)** questions. In case more than **Fifty (50)** questions are attempted, only the first **Fifty (50)** questions will be evaluated.

1. Namita and Samita are brilliant and studious. Anita and Karabi are obedient and irregular. Babita and Namita are irregular but brilliant. Samita and Kabita are regular and obedient. Who among them is/are brilliant, obedient, regular and studious?
   A. Samita alone
   B. Namita and Samita
   C. Kabita alone
   D. Anita alone

2. Warrior is related to sword, carpenter is related to saw, farmer is related to plough. In the same way, the author is related to
   A. Book
   B. Fame
   C. Reader
   D. Pen

3. Given below is a diagram of three circles A, B and C over-lapping each other. The circle A represents the class of honest people, the circle B represents the class of sincere people and circle C represents the class of politicians. p, q, r, s, U, X, Y represent different regions. Select the code that represents the region indicating the class of honest politicians who are not sincere.

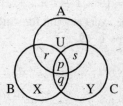

   Codes:
   A. X
   B. q
   C. p
   D. s

4. "A man ought no more to value himself for being wiser than a woman if he owes his advantage to a better education, than he ought to boast of his courage for beating a man when his hands were tied."
   The above passage is an instance of
   A. Deductive argument
   B. Hypothetical argument
   C. Analogical argument
   D. Factual argument

5. By which of the following proposition, the proposition 'wise men are hardly afraid of death' is contradicted?
   A. Some wise men are afraid of death
   B. All wise men are afraid of death
   C. No wise men is afraid of death
   D. Some wise men are not afraid of death

6. When in a group of propositions, one proposition is claimed to follow from the others, that group of propositions is called
   A. An argument
   B. A valid argument
   C. An explanation
   D. An invalid argument

Directions (Qs. 7 to 12): *For a country CO_2 emissions (million metric tons) from various sectors are given in the following table. Answer the questions based on the data given:*

	\multicolumn{5}{c}{CO_2 emissions (million metric tons)}
Sector / Year	Power	Industry	Commercial	Agriculture	Domestic
2005	500	200	150	80	100
2006	600	300	200	90	110
2007	650	320	250	100	120
2008	700	400	300	150	150
2009	800	450	320	200	180

7. Which sector has recorded maximum growth in CO_2 emissions during 2005 to 2009?
   A. Power
   B. Industry
   C. Commercial
   D. Agriculture

8. By what percentage (%), the total emissions of CO_2 have increased from 2005 to 2009?
   A. ~89.32%
   B. ~57.62%
   C. ~40.32%
   D. ~113.12%

9. What is the average annual growth rate of CO_2 emissions in power sector?
   A. ~12.57%   B. ~16.87%
   C. ~30.81%   D. ~50.25%

10. What is the percentage contribution of power sector to total CO_2 emissions in the year 2008?
    A. ~30.82%   B. ~41.18%
    C. ~51.38%   D. ~60.25%

11. In which year, the contribution (%) of industry to total sectoral CO_2 emissions was minimum?
    A. 2005   B. 2006
    C. 2007   D. 2009

12. What is the percentage (%) growth of CO_2 emissions from power sector during 2005 to 2009?
    A. 60   B. 50
    C. 40   D. 80

13. Which one of the following is not a search engine?
    A. Google   B. Chrome
    C. Yahoo   D. Bing

14. CSS stands for
    A. Cascading Style Sheets
    B. Collecting Style Sheets
    C. Comparative Style Sheets
    D. Comprehensive Style Sheets

15. MOOC stands for
    A. Media Online Open Course
    B. Massachusetts Open Online Course
    C. Massive Open Online Course
    D. Myrind Open Online Course

16. Binary equivalent of decimal number 35 is
    A. 100011   B. 110001
    C. 110101   D. 101011

17. gif, jpg, bmp, png are used as extensions for files which store
    A. audio data
    B. image data
    C. video data
    D. text data

18. Symbols A-F are used in which one of the following?
    A. Binary number system
    B. Decimal number system
    C. Hexadecimal number system
    D. Octal number system

19. One of the anthropogenic sources of gaseous pollutants chlorofluorocarbons (CFCs) in air is
    A. Cement industry
    B. Fertiliser industry
    C. Foam industry
    D. Pesticide industry

20. In terms of total CO_2 emissions from a country, identity the correct sequence:
    A. U.S.A. > China > India > Russia
    B. China > U.S.A. > India > Russia
    C. China > U.S.A. > Russia > India
    D. U.S.A. > China > Russia > India

21. Match List-I and List-II and identify the correct code:

List-I	List-II
(a) World Health Day	(i) 16th September
(b) World Population Day	(ii) 1st December
(c) World Ozone Day	(iii) 11th July
(d) World AIDS Day	(iv) 7th April

    Codes:

	(a)	(b)	(c)	(d)
A.	(i)	(ii)	(iii)	(iv)
B.	(iv)	(iii)	(i)	(ii)
C.	(ii)	(iii)	(iv)	(i)
D.	(iii)	(iv)	(ii)	(i)

22. Which of the anthropogenic activity accounts for more than $\frac{2}{3}$rd of global water consumption?
   A. Agriculture
   B. Hydropower generation
   C. Industry
   D. Domestic and Municipal usage

23. Which of the following is *not* a renewable natural resource?
   A. Clean air   B. Fresh water
   C. Fertile soil   D. Salt

24. The maximum number of fake institutions/universities as identified by the UGC in the year 2014 are in the State/Union territory of
   A. Bihar   B. Uttar Pradesh
   C. Tamil Nadu   D. Delhi

25. Which of the following institutions are empowered to confer or grant degrees under the UGC Act, 1956?
   1. A university established by an Act of Parliament.
   2. A university established by an Act of Legislature.
   3. A university/institution established by a linguistic minority.
   4. An institution which is a deemed to be university.
   Select the correct answer from the codes given below:
   A. 1 and 2   B. 1, 2 and 3
   C. 1, 2 and 4   D. 1, 2, 3 and 4

26. Which of the following are the tools of good governance?
   1. Social Audit
   2. Separation of Powers
   3. Citizen's Charter
   4. Right to Information
   Select the correct answer from the codes given below:
   A. 1, 3 and 4
   B. 2, 3 and 4
   C. 1 and 4
   D. 1, 2, 3 and 4

27. The cyclone 'Hudhud' hit the coast of which State?
   A. Andhra Pradesh
   B. Karnataka
   C. Kerala
   D. Gujarat

28. The interval between two sessions of parliament must not exceed
   A. 3 months   B. 6 months
   C. 4 months   D. 100 days

29. Right to Privacy as a Fundamental Right is implied in
   A. Right to Freedom
   B. Right to Life and Personal Liberty
   C. Right to Equality
   D. Right against Exploitation

30. Which of the following organizations deals with 'capacity building program' on Educational Planning?
   A. NCERT   B. UGC
   C. NAAC   D. NUEPA

31. Which of the following powers, the President has in relation to Lok Sabha?
   1. Summoning
   2. Adjournment – sine die
   3. Prorogation
   4. Dissolution
   Select the correct answer from the codes given below:
   A. 1 and 4   B. 1, 2 and 3
   C. 1, 3 and 4   D. 1, 2, 3 and 4

32. Which of the following is not a prescribed level of teaching?
   A. Memory
   B. Understanding
   C. Reflective
   D. Differentiation

33. Maximum participation of students during teaching is possible through
   A. Lecture method
   B. Demonstration method
   C. Inductive method
   D. Textbook method

34. Diagnostic evaluation ascertains
    A. Students performance at the beginning of instructions
    B. Learning progress and failures during instructions
    C. Degree of achievement of instructions at the end
    D. Causes and remedies of persistent learning problems during instructions

35. Instructional aids are used by the teacher to
    A. glorify the class
    B. attract the students
    C. clarify the concepts
    D. ensure discipline

36. Attitude of the teacher that affects teaching pertains to
    A. Affective domain
    B. Cognitive domain
    C. Connative domain
    D. Psychomotor domain

37. "Education is the manifestation of perfection already in man" was stated by
    A. M.K. Gandhi
    B. R.N. Tagore
    C. Swami Vivekanand
    D. Sri Aurobindo

38. When academicians are called to deliver lecture or presentation to an audience on certain topics or a set of topics of educational nature, it is called
    A. Training Program B. Seminar
    C. Workshop   D. Symposium

39. The core elements of a dissertation are
    A. Introduction; Data Collection; Data Analysis; Conclusions and Recommendations
    B. Executive Summary; Literature review; Data gathered; Conclusions; Bibliography
    C. Research Plan; Research Data; Analysis; References
    D. Introduction; Literature Review; Research Methodology; Results; Discussion and Conclusion

40. What is a Research Design?
    A. A way of conducting research that is not grounded in theory
    B. The choice between using qualitative or quantitative methods
    C. The style in which you present your research findings e.g. a graph
    D. A framework for every stage of the collection and analysis of data

41. 'Sampling Cases' means
    A. Sampling using a sampling frame
    B. Identifying people who are suitable for research
    C. Literally the researcher's brief case
    D. Sampling of people, newspapers, television programmes etc.

42. The frequency distribution of a research data which is symmetrical in shape similar to a normal distribution but center peak is much higher, is
    A. Skewed   B. Mesokurtic
    C. Leptokurtic   D. Platykurtic

43. When planning to do as social research, it is better to
    A. approach the topic with an open mind
    B. do a pilot study before getting stuck into it
    C. be familiar with literature on the topic
    D. forget about theory because this is a very practical

44. In the classroom, the teacher sends the message either as words or images. The students are really
    A. Encoders   B. Decoders
    C. Agitators   D. Propagators

45. Media is known as
    A. First Estate   B. Second Estate
    C. Third Estate   D. Fourth Estate

46. The mode of communication that involves a single source transmitting information to a large number of receivers simultaneously, is called
    A. Group Communication

B. Mass Communication

C. Intrapersonal Communication

D. Interpersonal Communication

47. A smart classroom is a teaching space which has

  (*i*) Smart portion with a touch panel control system

  (*ii*) PC/Laptop connection and DVD/VCR player

  (*iii*) Document camera and specialized software

  (*iv*) Projector and screen

Select the correct answer from the codes given below:

A. (*i*) and (*ii*) only

B. (*ii*) and (*iv*) only

C. (*i*), (*ii*) and (*iii*) only

D. (*i*), (*ii*), (*iii*) and (*iv*)

48. The term 'Yellow Journalism' refers to

A. sensational news about terrorism and violence

B. sensationalism and exaggeration to attract readers/viewers

C. sensational news about arts and culture

D. sensational news prints in yellow paper

49. The next term in the series:

2, 7, 28, 63, 126, ...

is

A. 215   B. 245

C. 276   D. 296

50. The next term in the series:

AB, ED, IH, NM, ...

is

A. TS   B. ST

C. TU   D. SU

51. If STREAMERS is coded as UVTGALDQR, then KNOWLEDGE will be coded as

A. MQPYLCDFD   B. MPQYLDCFD

C. PMYQLDFCD   D. YMQPLDDFC

52. A is brother of B. B is the brother of C. C is the husband of D. E is the father of A. D is related to E as

A. Daughter   B. Daughter-in-law

C. Sister-in-law   D. Sister

53. Two numbers are in the ratio 3 : 5. If 9 is subtracted from the numbers, the ratio becomes 12 : 23. The numbers are

A. 30, 50   B. 36, 60

C. 33, 55   D. 42, 70

54. The mean of the ages of father and his son is 27 years. After 18 years, father will be twice as old as his son. Their present ages are

A. 42, 12   B. 40, 14

C. 30, 24   D. 36, 18

55. Digital Empowerment means

  (*i*) Universal digit literacy.

  (*ii*) Universal access to all digital resources.

  (*iii*) Collaborative digital platform for participative governance.

  (*iv*) Probability of all entitlements for individuals through cloud.

Choose the correct answer from the codes given below:

A. (*i*) and (*ii*) only

B. (*ii*) and (*iii*) only

C. (*i*), (*ii*) and (*iii*) only

D. (*i*), (*ii*), (*iii*) and (*iv*)

Directions (Qs. 56 to 60): *Read the following passage carefully and answer questions.*

The literary distaste for politics, however, seems to be focused not so much on the largely murky practice of politics in itself as a subject of literary representation but rather more on how it is often depicted in literature, *i.e.,* on the very politics of such representation. A political novel often turns out to be not merely a novel about politics but a novel with a politics of its own, for it seeks not merely to show us how things are but has fairly definite ideas about how things should be, and precisely what one should think and do in order to make things move in that desired direction. In short, it seeks to convert and enlist the reader to a particular cause or ideology: it often is (in an only too familiar phrase) not literature but propaganda. This is said to violate the very spirit of literature which is to broaden our understanding of the world and the range of our sympathies rather than to narrow them down through partisan commitment. As John Keats said, 'We hate poetry that has a palpable design upon us'.

Another reason why politics does not seem amenable to the highest kind of literary representation seems to arise from the fact that politics by its very nature is constituted of ideas and ideologies. If political situations do not lend themselves to happy literary treatment, political ideas present perhaps an even greater problem in this regard. Literature, it is argued, is about human experiences rather than about intellectual abstractions; it deals in what is called the 'felt reality' of human flesh and blood, and in sap and savour (*rasa*) rather than in arid and lifeless ideas. In an extensive discussion of the matter in her book *Ideas and the Novel,* the American novelist Mary McCarthy observed that 'ideas are still today felt to be unsightly in the novel' though that was not so in 'former days', *i.e.,* in the 18th and 19th centuries. Her formulation of the precise nature of the incompatibility between ideas on the one hand and the novel no the other betrays perhaps a divided conscience in the matter and a sense of dilemma shared by many writers and readers: 'An idea cannot have loose ends, but a novel. I almost think, needs them. Nevertheless, there is enough in common for the novelists to feel .... the attraction of ideas while taking up arms against them – most often with weapons of mockery.'

56. A political novel reveals
   A. Reality of the things
   B. Writer's perception
   C. Particular ideology of the readers
   D. The spirit of literature

57. The constructs of politics by its nature is
   A. Prevalent political situation
   B. Ideas and Ideologies
   C. Political propaganda
   D. Understanding of human nature

58. Literature deals with
   A. Human experiences in politics
   B. Intellectual abstractions
   C. Dry and empty ideas
   D. Felt reality of human life

59. The observation of the novelist, Mary McCarthy reveals
   A. unseen felt ideas of today in the novel
   B. dichotomy of conscience on political ideas and novels
   C. compatibility between idea and novel
   D. endless ideas and novels

60. According to the passage, a political novel often turns out to be a
   A. Literary distaste for politics
   B. Literary representation of politics
   C. Novel with its own politics
   D. Depiction of murky practice of politics

ANSWERS

1	2	3	4	5	6	7	8	9	10
A	D	D	C	B	A	D	A	A	B
11	**12**	**13**	**14**	**15**	**16**	**17**	**18**	**19**	**20**
A	A	B	A	C	A	B	C	C	B
21	**22**	**23**	**24**	**25**	**26**	**27**	**28**	**29**	**30**
B	A	D	B	C	A	A	B	B	D
31	**32**	**33**	**34**	**35**	**36**	**37**	**38**	**39**	**40**
C	D	B	D	C	A	C	B	D	D
41	**42**	**43**	**44**	**45**	**46**	**47**	**48**	**49**	**50**
D	C	C	B	D	B	D	B	A	A
51	**52**	**53**	**54**	**55**	**56**	**57**	**58**	**59**	**60**
B	B	C	A	D	B	B	D	A	C

SOME SELECTED EXPLANATORY ANSWERS

3. Elements of A = u, r, p, s (honest)

Elements of B = x, r, p, q (sincere)

Elements of C = p, q, s, y (politician)

Hence (honest and politician but not sincere)

p, q, s are sincere.

∴ Required code is S which is in A and C.

7. Power $800 - 500 = 300$

$$\% = \frac{300}{500} \times 100 = 60\%$$

Industry $450 - 200 = 250$

$$\% = \frac{250}{200} \times 100 = 125\%$$

Commercial $320 - 150 = 170$

$$\% = \frac{170}{150} \times 100$$

$$= \frac{340}{3} = 113\%$$

Agriculture $200 - 80 = 120$

$$\% = \frac{120}{80} \times 100 = 150\%$$

Domestic $180 - 100 = 80$

$$\% = \frac{80}{100} \times 100 = 80\%$$

Hence, maximum growth in CO_2 is Agriculture.

8. Total emissions of CO_2 in 2005

$$= 500 + 200 + 150 + 80 + 100$$
$$= 1030$$

Total emissions of CO_2 in 2009

$$= 800 + 450 + 320 + 200 + 180$$
$$= 1950$$

increased $= 1950 - 1030 = 920$

$$\% \text{ increased} = \frac{920}{1030} \times 100 = 89.32\%.$$

9. In power sector 2005 to 2006

$$= \frac{100}{500} \times 100 = 20\%$$

In 2006 to 2007 $= \frac{50}{600} \times 100 = 8.33\%$

In 2007 to 2008 $= \frac{50}{650} \times 100 = 7.69\%$

In 2008 to 2009 $= \frac{100}{700} \times 100 = 14.28\%$

Average Annual growth rate

$$= \frac{50.30}{4} = 12.57\%.$$

10. Required % in 2008 $= \frac{700}{1700} \times 100$

$$= \frac{700}{17} = 41.18\%.$$

11. Required year = 2005.

12. Growth of CO_2 from power sector during 2005 to 2009

$$= 800 - 500 = 300$$

$$\% \text{ growth} = \frac{300}{500} \times 100 = 60\%.$$

49. 2   7   28   63   126   215

↓   ↓   ↓   ↓   ↓

$2^3 - 1$ $3^3 - 1$ $4^3 - 1$ $5^3 - 1$ $6^3 - 1$

Hence, the next term in the series will be 215.

53. Let the numbers are $3x$ and $5x$

According to the question,

$$\frac{3x - 9}{5x - 9} = \frac{12}{23}$$

$\Rightarrow$ $69x - 207 = 60x - 108$

$\Rightarrow$ $9x = 99$

$\Rightarrow$ $x = 11$

∴ Numbers are 33 and 55.

54. Let present age of father = x years
and present age of son = y years
$$x + y = 2 \times 27 = 54$$
$\Rightarrow$ $\qquad x = 54 - y$
After 18 years, father's age = $(x + 18)$ years
After 18 years, son's age = $(y + 18)$ years
According to the question,
$$x + 18 = 2\,(y + 18)$$
$\Rightarrow \qquad x + 18 = 2y + 36$
$\Rightarrow \qquad x - 2y = 18$
$\Rightarrow \quad 54 - y - 2y = 18$
$\Rightarrow \qquad\quad -3y = -36$
$\Rightarrow \qquad\qquad y = 12$
$$x = 54 - 12 = 42$$

Hence, present age of father
$$= 42 \text{ years}$$
and present age of son
$$= 12 \text{ years.}$$

16. Remainder
$$35 \div 2 = 17 + 1$$
$$17 \div 2 = 8 + 1$$
$$8 \div 2 = 4 + 0$$
$$4 \div 2 = 2 + 0$$
$$2 \div 2 = 1 + 0$$
$$1 \div 2 = 0 + 1$$
$\therefore \qquad\qquad 35 = 100011$
Hence, binary equivalent of decimal number
$$35 = 100011.$$

UGC-NET (JRF) Exam June, 2015*

PAPER–I

> **Note :** This paper contains **Sixty (60)** multiple choice questions, each question carrying **two (2)** marks. Candidate is expected to answer any **Fifty (50)** questions. In case more than **Fifty (50)** questions are attempted, only the first **Fifty (50)** questions will be evaluated.

1. Which of the following is the highest level of cognitive ability?
   A. Knowing   B. Understanding
   C. Analysing   D. Evaluating

2. Which of the following factors does **not** impact teaching?
   A. Teacher's knowledge
   B. Class-room activities that encourage learning
   C. Socio-economic background of teachers and students
   D. Learning through experience

3. Which of the following statements about teaching aids are correct?
   (a) They help in retaining concepts for longer duration.
   (b) They help students learn better.
   (c) They make teaching learning process interesting.
   (d) They enhance rote learning.
   Select the correct answer from the codes given below:
   A. (a), (b), (c) and (d)   B. (a), (b) and (c)
   C. (b), (c) and (d)   D. (a), (b) and (d)

4. Techniques used by a teacher to teach include:
   (a) Lecture
   (b) Interactive lecture
   (c) Group work
   (d) Self study
   Select the correct answer from the codes given below :

A. (a), (b) and (c)   B. (a), (b), (c) and (d)
C. (b), (c) and (d)   D. (a), (b) and (d)

5. Achievement tests are commonly used for the purpose of :
   A. Making selections for a specific job
   B. Selecting candidates for a course
   C. Identifying strengths and weaknesses of learners
   D. Assessing the amount of learning after teaching

6. A good teacher is one who:
   A. gives useful information
   B. explains concepts and principles
   C. gives printed notes to students
   D. inspires students to learn

7. Which of the following statements regarding the meaning of research are correct?
   (a) Research refers to a series of systematic activity or activities undertaken to find out the solution of a problem.
   (b) It is a systematic, logical and an unbiased process wherein verification of hypothesis, data analysis, interpretation and formation of principles can be done.
   (c) It is an intellectual enquiry or quest towards truth.
   (d) It leads to enhancement of knowledge.
   Select the correct answer from the codes given below :
   A. (a), (b) and (c)   B. (b), (c) and (d)
   C. (a), (c) and (d)   D. (a), (b), (c) and (d)

8. A good thesis writing should involve:
   (a) reduction of punctuation and grammatical errors to a minimum.
   (b) careful checking of references.
   (c) consistency in the way the thesis is written.
   (d) a clear and well written abstract.

   Select the correct answer from the codes given below:
   A. (a), (b), (c) and (d)   B. (a), (b) and (c)
   C. (a), (b) and (d)   D. (b), (c) and (d)

9. Jean Piaget gave a theory of cognitive development of humans on the basis of his:
   A. Fundamental Research
   B. Applied Research
   C. Action Research
   D. Evaluation Research

10. "Male and female students perform equally well in a numerical aptitude test." This statement indicates a :
    A. research hypothesis
    B. null hypothesis
    C. directional hypothesis
    D. statistical hypothesis

11. The conclusions/findings of which type of research cannot be generalized to other situations?
    A. Historical Research
    B. Descriptive Research
    C. Experimental Research
    D. Causal Comparative Research

12. Which of the following steps are required to design a questionnaire?
    (a) Writing primary and secondary aims of the study.
    (b) Review of the current literature.
    (c) Prepare a draft of questionnaire.
    (d) Revision of the draft.

    Select the correct answer from the codes given below:
    A. (a), (b) and (c)   B. (a), (c) and (d)
    C. (b), (c) and (d)   D. (a), (b), (c) and (d)

Directions (Qs. 13-18): *Read the following passage carefully and answer the questions given below:*

Story telling is not in our genes. Neither it is an evolutionary history. It is the essence of what makes us Human.

Human beings progress by telling stories. One event can result in a great variety of stories being told about it. Sometimes those stories differ greatly. Which stories are picked up and repeated and which ones are dropped and forgotten often determines how we progress. Our history, knowledge and understanding are all the collections of the few stories that survive. This includes the stories that we tell each other about the future. And how the future will turn out depends partly, possibly largely, on which stories we collectively choose to believe.

Some stories are designed to spread fear and concern. This is because some story-tellers feel that there is a need to raise some tensions. Some stories are frightening, they are like totemic warnings: "Fail to act now and we are all doomed." Then there are stories that indicate that all will be fine so long as we leave everything upto a few especially able adults. Currently, this trend is being led by those who call themselves "rational optimists". They tend to claim that it is human nature to compete and to succeed and also to profit at the expense of others. The rational optimists however, do not realize how humanity has progressed overtime through amiable social networks and how large groups work in less selfishness and in the process accommodate rich and poor, high and low alike. This aspect in story-telling is considered by the 'Practical Possibles', who sit between those who say all is fine and cheerful and be individualistic in your approach to a successful future, and those who ordain pessimism and fear that we are doomed.

What the future holds for us is which stories we hold on to and how we act on them.

13. Our knowledge is a collection of:
    A. all stories that we have heard during our life-time

B. some stories that we remember
C. a few stories that survive
D. some important stories

14. Story telling is:
   A. an art
   B. a science
   C. in our genes
   D. the essence of what makes us human

15. How the future will turn out to be, depends upon the stories?
   A. We collectively choose to believe in
   B. Which are repeatedly narrated
   C. Designed to spread fear and tension
   D. Designed to make prophecy

16. Rational optimists:
   (a) Look for opportunities
   (b) Are sensible and cheerful
   (c) Are selfishly driven

Identify the correct answer from the codes given below:
   A. (a), (b) and (c)   B. (a) only
   C. (a) and (b) only   D. (b) and (c) only

17. Humans become less selfish when:
   A. they work in large groups
   B. they listen to frightening stories
   C. they listen to cheerful stories
   D. they work in solitude

18. 'Practical Possibles' are the ones who:
   A. follow Midway Path
   B. are doom-mongers
   C. are self-centred
   D. are cheerful and carefree

19. Effectiveness of communication can be traced from which of the following?
   (a) Attitude surveys
   (b) Performance records
   (c) Students attendance
   (d) Selection of communication channel

Select the correct answer from the codes given below:
   A. (a), (b), (c) and (d)   B. (a), (b) and (c)
   C. (b), (c) and (d)   D. (a), (b) and (d)

20. **Assertion (A):** Formal communication tends to be fast and flexible.

   Reason (R): Formal communication is a systematic and orderly flow of information.
   A. Both (A) and (R) are correct and (R) is correct explanation of (A)
   B. Both (A) and (R) are correct, but (R) is not correct explanation of (A)
   C. (A) is correct, but (R) is false
   D. (A) is false, but (R) is correct

21. Which of the following are the characteristic features of communication?
   (a) Communication involves exchange of ideas, facts and opinions.
   (b) Communication involves both information and understanding.
   (c) Communication is a continuous process.
   (d) Communication is a circular process.

Select the correct answer from the codes given below:
   A. (a), (b) and (c)   B. (a), (b) and (d)
   C. (b), (c) and (d)   D. (a), (b), (c) and (d)

22. The term 'grapevine' is also known as :
   A. Downward communication
   B. Informal communication
   C. Upward communication
   D. Horizontal communication

23. Which of the following is **not** a principle of effective communication?
   A. Persuasive and convincing dialogue
   B. Participation of the audience
   C. One-way transfer of information
   D. Strategic use of grapevine

24. In communication, the language is:
   A. The verbal code
   B. Intrapersonal
   C. The symbolic code
   D. The non-verbal code

25. The next term in the series is:
   2, 5, 9, 19, 37, ?
   A. 73   B. 75
   C. 78   D. 80

26. In certain code MATHURA is coded as JXQEROX. The code of HOTELS will be :
   A. LEQIBP   B. ELQBIP
   C. LEBIQP   D. ELIPQB

27. One day Prakash left home and walked 10 km towards south, turned right and walked 5 km, turned right and walked 10 km and turned left and walked 10 km. How many km will he have to walk to reach his home straight?
   A. 10   B. 20
   C. 15   D. 30

28. A girl introduced a boy as the son of the daughter of the father of her uncle. The boy is related to the girl as :
   A. Brother   B. Uncle
   C. Nephew   D. Son

29. In an examination 10,000 students appeared. The result revealed the number of students who have:

   passed in all five subjects   = 5583
   passed in three subjects only = 1400
   passed in two subjects only   = 1200
   passed in one subject only   = 735
   failed in English only   =   75
   failed in Physics only   = 145
   failed in Chemistry only   = 140
   failed in Mathematics only   = 200
   failed in Bio-science only   = 157

   The number of students passed in at least four subjects is:
   A. 6300   B. 6900
   C. 7300   D. 7900

30. At present a person is 4 times older than his son and is 3 years older than his wife. After 3 years the age of the son will be 15 years. The age of the person's wife after 5 years will be:
   A. 42   B. 48
   C. 45   D. 50

31. If we want to seek new knowledge of facts about the world, we must rely on reason of the type:
   A. Inductive   B. Deductive
   C. Demonstrative   D. Physiological

32. A deductive argument is invalid if :
   A. Its premises and conclusions are all false
   B. Its premises are true but its conclusion is false
   C. Its premises are false but its conclusion is true
   D. Its premises and conclusions are all true

33. Inductive reasoning is grounded on:
   A. Integrity of nature
   B. Unity of nature
   C. Uniformity of nature
   D. Harmony of nature

34. Among the following statements **two** are contradictory to each other. Select the correct code that represents them:
   Statements:
   (a) All poets are philosophers.
   (b) Some poets are philosophers.
   (c) Some poets are not philosophers.
   (d) No philosopher is a poet.
   Codes:
   A. (a) and (b)   B. (a) and (d)
   C. (a) and (c)   D. (b) and (c)

35. Which of the codes given below contains only the **correct** statements? Select the code:
   Statements:
   (a) Venn diagram represents the arguments graphically.
   (b) Venn diagram can enhance our understanding.
   (c) Venn diagram may be called valid or invalid.
   (d) Venn diagram is clear method of notation.
   Codes:
   A. (a), (b) and (c)
   B. (a), (b) and (d)
   C. (b), (c) and (d)
   D. (a), (c) and (d)

36. When the purpose of a definition is to explain the use or to eliminate ambiguity the definition is called:
   A. Stipulative   B. Theoretical
   C. Lexical   D. Persuasive

Direction (Qs. 37-42): *Answer the question based on the tabulated data given below:*

A company has 20 employees with their age (in years) and salary (in thousand rupees per month) mentioned against each of them:

S.No.	Age (in years)	Salary (in thousand rupees per month)
1.	44	35
2.	32	20
3.	54	45
4.	42	35
5.	31	20
6.	53	60
7.	42	50
8.	51	55
9.	34	25
10.	41	30
11.	33	30
12.	31	35
13.	30	35
14.	37	40
15.	44	45
16.	36	35
17.	34	35
18.	49	50
19.	43	45
20.	45	50

37. Classify the data of age of each employee in class interval of 5 years. Which class interval of 5 years has the maximum average salary?
A. 35-40 years
B. 40-45 years
C. 45-50 years
D. 50-55 years

38. What is the frequency (%) in the class interval of 30-35 years?
A. 20%
B. 25%
C. 30%
D. 35%

39. What is the average age of the employees?
A. 40.3 years
B. 38.6 years
C. 47.2 years
D. 45.3 years

40. What is the fraction (%) of employees getting salary ≥ 40,000 per month?
A. 45%
B. 50%
C. 35%
D. 32%

41. What is the average salary (in thousand per month) in the age group 40-50 years?
A. 35
B. 42.5
C. 40.5
D. 36.5

42. What is the fraction of employees getting salary less than the average salary of all the employees?
A. 45%
B. 50%
C. 55%
D. 47%

43. Encoding or scrambling data for transmission across a network is known as :
A. Protection
B. Detection
C. Encryption
D. Decryption

44. Which of the following is **not** an output device?
A. Printer
B. Speaker
C. Monitor
D. Keyboard

45. Which of the following represents one billion characters ?
A. Kilobyte
B. Megabyte
C. Gigabyte
D. Terabyte

46. Which of the following is **not** open source software?
A. Internet explorer
B. Fedora Linux
C. Open office
D. Apache HTTP server

47. Which one of the following represents the binary equivalent of the decimal number 25?
A. 10101
B. 01101
C. 11001
D. 11011

48. Which is an instant messenger that is used for chatting?
A. Altavista
B. MAC
C. Microsoft Office
D. Google Talk

49. In which of the countries per capita use of water is maximum?
A. USA
B. European Union
C. China
D. India

50. India's contribution to total global carbon dioxide emissions is about:
A. ~ 3%
B. ~ 6%
C. ~ 10%
D. ~ 15%

51. Two earthquakes A and B happen to be of magnitude 5 and 6 respectively on Richter Scale. The ratio of the energies released E_B/E_A will be approximately:
A. ~8
B. ~16
C. ~32
D. ~64

52. Which of the following combinations represent renewable natural resources?
A. Fertile soil, fresh water and natural gas
B. Clean air, phosphates and biological diversity
C. Fishes, fertile soil and fresh water
D. Oil, forests and tides

53. In the recently launched Air Quality Index in India, which of the following pollutants is **not** included?
A. Carbon monoxide
B. Fine particulate matter
C. Ozone
D. Chlorofluorocarbons

54. The factors which are most important in determining the impact of anthropogenic activities on environment are :
A. Population, affluence per person, land available per person
B. Population, affluence per person and the technology used for exploiting resources
C. Atmospheric conditions, population and forest cover
D. Population, forest cover and land available per person

55. The session of the Parliament is summoned by:
A. The President
B. The Prime Minister
C. The Speaker of the Lok Sabha
D. The Speaker of the Lok Sabha and the Chairman of the Rajya Sabha

56. Civil Service Day is celebrated in India on:
A. 21st April
B. 24th April
C. 21st June
D. 7th July

57. The South Asia University is situated in the city of :
A. Colombo
B. Dhaka
C. New Delhi
D. Kathmandu

58. The University Grants Commission was established with which of the following aims?
(a) Promotion of research and development in higher education
(b) Identifying and sustaining institutions of potential learning
(c) Capacity building of teachers
(d) Providing autonomy to each and every higher educational institution in India.
Select the correct answer from the codes given below :
A. (a), (b), (c) and (d)
B. (a), (b) and (c)
C. (b), (c) and (d)
D. (a), (b) and (d)

59. The Gross Enrolment Ratio (GER) in institutions of higher education in India at present (2015) is about:
A. 8 per cent
B. 12 per cent
C. 19 per cent
D. 23 per cent

60. The total number of central universities in India in April 2015 was:
A. 08
B. 14
C. 27
D. 43

ANSWERS

1	2	3	4	5	6	7	8	9	10
D	C	B	A	D	D	D	A	A	B
11	**12**	**13**	**14**	**15**	**16**	**17**	**18**	**19**	**20**
A	D	C	D	A	A	A	A	B	D
21	**22**	**23**	**24**	**25**	**26**	**27**	**28**	**29**	**30**
D	B	C	A	B	B	C	A	A	D

31	32	33	34	35	36	37	38	39	40
A	B	C	C	B	C	D	D	A	A

41	42	43	44	45	46	47	48	49	50
B	C	C	D	C	A	C	D	B	B

51	52	53	54	55	56	57	58	59	60
C	C	D	B	A	A	C	B	C	D

SOME SELECTED EXPLANATORY ANSWERS

1. Bloom identified six levels within the cognitive domain, from the simple recall or recognition of facts, as the lowest level, through increasingly more complex and abstract mental levels, to the highest order which is classified as evaluation.

Evaluation is concerned with the ability to judge the value of material (statement, novel, poem, research report) for a given purpose. The judgements are to be based on definite criteria. These may be internal criteria (organization) or external criteria (relevance to the purpose) and the student may determine the criteria or be given them. Learning outcomes in this area are highest in the cognitive hierarchy because they contain elements of all the other categories, plus conscious value judgements based on clearly defined criteria.

5. An **achievement test** is a test of developed skill or knowledge. It is the assessment of the amount of the learning after teaching. The most common type of achievement test is a standardized test developed to measure skills and knowledge learned in a given grade level, usually through planned instruction, such as training or classroom instruction. Achievement tests are often contrasted with tests that measure aptitude, a more general and stable cognitive trait.

6. It is not an exaggeration to say that a great teacher can change a student's life. As some of the most influential role models for developing students, teachers are responsible for more than just academic enrichment. If you want to be a great educator, you must connect with your pupils and reach them on multiple levels, because the best teachers are committed to their students' well-being both inside and outside the classroom.

Inspiring students is integral to ensuring their success and encouraging them to fulfil their potential. Students who are inspired by their teachers can accomplish amazing things, and that motivation almost always stays with them. Inspiration can also take many forms, from helping a pupil through the academic year and their short-term goals, to guiding them towards their future career. Years after graduation, many working professionals will still cite a particular teacher as the one who fostered their love of what they currently do and attribute their accomplishments to that educator.

9. Piaget's theory of cognitive development is a comprehensive theory about the nature and development of human intelligence. Piaget believed that one's childhood plays a vital and active role in a person's development. Piaget's idea is primarily known as a developmental stage theory. It is based on his fundamental research.

To Piaget, cognitive development was a progressive reorganization of mental processes resulting from biological maturation and environmental experience.

10. In inferential statistics the **null hypothesis** usually refers to a general statement or default position that there is no relationship between two measured phenomena, or no difference among groups.

For example "Male and female students perform equally well in a numerical aptitude test".

19. Communication is an exchange of feelings, ideas, and information, whether by speaking, writing, signals, or behaviours. Effective communication is an essential component of organizational success at all levels.

It can be traced out by following points:

(a) Attitude surveys

(b) Performance records

(c) Students attendance

20. Formal communication refers to the communication transmitted through the officially established chain of command in the organisation structure. The organisation structure reflecting superior subordinate relationships determines the flow of formal communication. Formal communication, according to the direction or flow may be of three types-(a) upward, (b) downward, and (c) horizontal. Formal communication is generally in writing and includes transmission of orders, instructions and decisions. Speed of communication is abit slow and time consuming. By Nature, it is systematic and orderly flow of information.

22. Informal communication is also known as grapevine communication because there is no definite route of communication for sharing information.

In this form of communication, information converges a long way by passing from one person to another person leaving no indication from which point it started. This is quite similar to the vine of grapes. It is also difficult to find out the beginning and the end of the grapevine.

23. One-way communication is a misnomer. The one-way process is not communication; it is simply the dispensing of information to another person, incormation that may or may not be received in the form intended. It is not a way of effective communication because the one-way posture inhibits interchange, and limits feedback.

24. Verbal means "consisting of words". Therefore, a verbal code is a set of rules about the use of words in the creation of messages. It is language we use for communication. Words can obviously be either spoken or written. Verbal codes, then, include both oral (spoken) language and non-oral (written) language.

25.

2	5	9	19	37	75
×2+1	×2−1	×2+1	×2−1	×2+1	

Hence, the next term in the series is 75.

26. M A T H U R A
−3↓ −3↓ −3↓ −3↓ −3↓ −3↓ −3↓
J X Q E R O X

Similarly,

H O T E L S
−3↓ −3↓ −3↓ −3↓ −3↓ −3↓
E L Q B I P

27.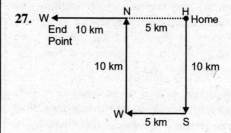

He has to walk 15 km to reach his home straight.

28.

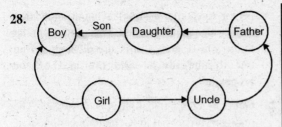

Hence the relation between boy and girl is brother and sister.

∴ The boy is related to the girl as brother.

29. Required no. of Students passed in at least four subjects is 5583 + 717 = 6300.

30. Let present age of son = x years

Present age of father = $4x$ years

Wife's present age = $4x - 3$ years

According to the question,

$$x + 3 = 15 \implies x = 12$$

Wife's present age = $4 \times 12 - 3 = 45$ years

After 5 years wife's age = $45 + 5 = 50$ years.

31. Inductive reasoning is one in which the premises seek to supply strong evidence for the truth of the conclusion. While the conclusion of a deductive argument is certain, the truth of the conclusion of an inductive argument is *probable*, based upon the evidence given.

Inductive reasoning is also known as hypothesis construction because any conclusions made are based on current knowledge and predictions. As with deductive arguments, biases can distort the proper application of inductive argument, thereby preventing the reasoner from forming the most logical conclusion based on the clues. Examples of these biases include the availability heuristic, confirmation bias, and the predictable-world bias.

32. An argument is said to be deductive if its conclusion is claimed to *necessarily* follow from its premises. That is, if it is claimed that since the premises are true or acceptable, the conclusion must also be true or acceptable,

then the argument is deductive. We can also define deduction by saying that in a deductive argument, the logical relation between the premises and the conclusion is claimed to be 100% supporting.

36. A lexical definition simply reports the way in which a term is already used within a language community. The goal here is to inform someone else of the accepted meaning of the term, so the definition is more or less correct depending upon the accuracy with which it captures that usage. In these pages, my definitions of technical terms of logic are lexical because they are intended to inform you about the way in which these terms are actually employed within the discipline of logic.

37. 35-40 years:

Average Salary

$$= \frac{40 + 35}{2} = \frac{75}{2} = 37.5 \text{ thousand/month}$$

40-45 years:

$$\text{Average} = \frac{35 + 35 + 50 + 30 + 45 + 45}{6}$$

$$= \frac{240}{6} = 40 \text{ thousand/month}$$

45-50 years:

$$\text{Average} = \frac{50 + 50}{2} = \frac{100}{2}$$

$$= 50 \text{ thousand/month}$$

50-55 years:

$$\text{Average} = \frac{45 + 60 + 55}{3} = \frac{160}{3}$$

$$= 53.3 \text{ thousand/month}$$

Hence, the 50-55 class interval has the maximum average salary.

38. Required % = $\frac{7}{20} \times 100 = 35\%$.

39. Total age of 20 employees

$$= 424 + 382 = 806 \text{ years}$$

$$\text{Average} = \frac{806}{20} = 40.3 \text{ years.}$$

105

UGC-COMP. P-I (E)–14

40. Required % $= \dfrac{9}{20} \times 100 = 45\%$.

41. 40-50 years:

Total salary $= 35 + 35 + 50 + 30 + 45 +$
$$50 + 45 + 50$$

$$= 340 \text{ thousand}$$

Required average salary $= \dfrac{340}{8} = 42.5$.

42. Total salary of 20 workers

$= (375 + 400)$ thousand $= 775$ thousand

Average salary $= \dfrac{775}{20} = 38.75$ thousand

Required% $= \dfrac{11}{20} \times 100 = 55\%$.

43. *Encryption* involves scrambling and perhaps compressing the data prior to transmission; the receiving device is provided with the necessary logic to decrypt and decompress the trasmitted information. Encryption generally resides in firmware included in stand-alone devices, although it can be built into virtually any device. Encryption logic, for example, often is incorporated into routers, which can encrypt data on a packet-by-packet basis. Encryption comes in two basic flavors: private key and public key. *Private key* is a symmetric encryption method that uses the same key to encrypt and decrypt data and requires that the key be kept secret. *Public key* is an asymmetric encryption method with two keys—an encryption (encoding) key that can be used by all authorized network users and a decryption (decoding) key that is kept secret.

44. A computer **keyboard** is one of the primary input devices used with a computer that looks similar to those found on electric typewriters, but with some additional keys. Keyboards allow you to input letters, numbers, and other symbols into a computer that often function as commands.

45. A Gigabyte is approximately 1,000 Megabytes or 1 billion characters. A Gigabyte is still a very common term used these days when referring to disk space or drive storage. 1 Gigabyte of data is almost twice the amount of data that a CD-ROM can hold. But it's about one thousand times the capacity of a 3-1/2 floppy disk. 1 Gigabyte could hold the contents of about 10 yards of books on a shelf. 100 Gigabytes could hold the entire library floor of academic journals.

46. Open source software (OSS) as "software for which the human-readable source code is available for use, study, re-use, modification, enhancement, and re-distribution by the users of that software".

The Internet Explorer Developer Relations Team at Microsoft have hinted at the possibility that the browser may one day become "Open Source".

"Open Source" is a term referring to software that whose source code is available for modification or enhancement by anyone. All other major web browsers (Mozilla Firefox, Google Chrome, Opera and Safari are based on open-source components). Presently, Internet Explorer is the only one of the big 5 browsers to remain entirely "closed source".

47.

2	25	1
2	12	0
2	6	0
2	3	1
	1	

$\therefore (25)_{10} = (11001)_2$.

48. Google Talk is an instant messaging service that provides both text and voice communication. The instant messaging service is colloquially known as "gtalk", "gchat", or "gmessage" to its users, although Google does not endorse those names.

50. Carbon dioxide (CO_2) emissions from fossil fuel burning and cement production increased by 2.3% in 2013, with a total of 9.9 ± 0.5 GtC (billion tonnes of carbon) (36 $GtCO_2$) emitted to the atmosphere, 61% above 1990 emissions (the Kyoto Protocol reference year).

India and China are among the world's biggest contributors to fossil fuel emissions with India's carbon dioxide discharge increasing by a whopping ~ 6 per cent.

52. **Renewable Resources:** These are the resources that are replenished through rapid natural cycles. Common examples of such resources are:

(i) Oxygen in the air, which is replenished through photosynthesis.

(ii) Fresh water, which is replenished through the water cycle.

(iii) All biological products (food, fishes, timber, etc.,) which are replenished through natural cycles of growth and reproduction.

(iv) Solar energy is also considered as renewable as on a human time scale and it is inexhaustible. It is expected that sun will last at least 6.5 billion years.

(v) Some other renewable resources that can be renewed (hours to several decades) through natural processes include forests, grassland grasses, wild animals, fishes, fresh air & water and fertile soil. However, potentially renewable resources can be depleted when resources utilization rate exceeds the natural replacement rate.

53. The Centre for Science and Environment (CSE), which has been demanding adoption of an **Air Quality Index** (AQI) for "an important step forward for building awareness and protecting public health".

There are six AQI categories, namely: Good, Satisfactory, Moderately polluted, Poor, Very poor and Severe.

The index considers eight pollutants — PM10, PM2.5, NO_2, SO_2, CO, O_3, NH_3 and Pb (CFC is not included). The likely health implications of the six categories would also be provided with a colour code. CSE said that with this step, India has joined the global league of countries like the US, China, Mexico and France that have implemented smog alert systems.

55. A **joint session** or **joint convention** is, most broadly, when two normally separate decision-making groups meet together, often in a special session or other extraordinary meeting, for a specific purpose.

Most often it refers to when both houses of a bicameral legislature sit together. A joint session typically occurs to receive foreign or domestic diplomats or leaders, or to allow both houses to consider bills together.

In India, if a bill has been rejected by any house of the parliament and if more than six months have elapsed, the President may summon a joint session for purpose of passing the bill. The bill is passed by a simple majority of a joint sitting. Since the lower house (Lok Sabha) has more than twice the members of the upper house (Rajya Sabha), a group commanding a majority in the lower house of the Government of India can pass such a bill even if it was previously rejected by the upper house.

So far, only three bills - the Dowry Prohibition Act, 1960, the Banking Service Commission Repeal Bill, 1977, and the Prevention of Terrorism Act, 2002 - have been passed at joint sessions.

56. The **Civil Services of India** refer to the civil service and the permanent bureaucracy of the Government of India. The civil service system is the backbone of the administrative machinery of the country.

Every year, on the 21st of April, the "Civil Service Day" is observed by all Civil Services to re-dedicate and re-commit themselves to the cause of the people. It provides a unique opportunity for introspection as also chalking out future strategies to deal with the challenges being posed by the changing times.

57. **South Asian University** (SAU) is an International University sponsored by the eight

Member States of the South Asian Association for Regional Cooperation (SAARC). The eight countries are : Afghanistan, Bangladesh, Bhutan, India, Maldives, Nepal, Pakistan and Sri Lanka. South Asian University started admitting students in 2010, at a temporary campus at Akbar Bhawan, India. Its permanent campus will be at Maidan Garhi in South Delhi, India, next to Indira Gandhi National Open University (IGNOU). First academic session of the university started in August 2010 with two post-graduate academic programmes, in economics and computer sciences. As of 2014 SAU offered Master's and MPhil/PhD programs in applied mathematics, biotechnology, computer science, development economics, international relations, law and sociology. The degrees of the university are recognized by all the member nations of the SAARC according to an inter-governmental agreement signed by the foreign ministers of the 8 countries.

59. The UGC had chalked out several plans to increase gross enrolment ratio (GER) of students (in the age group of 18 to 22) in higher education. He was optimistic of increasing the GER from the present 19 per cent to 30 per cent by the end of the 12th Five Year Plan (2012-17). The enrolment of candidates for degree courses would be increased from the present 20 million to 29 million by the end of 12th Plan period. The number of students enrolled in distance education would go up from 4.6 million to 6.3 million by 2017.

60. A **Central University** or a **Union University** in India is established by Act of Parliament and are under the purview of the Department of Higher Education in the Union Human Resource Development Ministry. In general, universities in India are recognised by the University Grants Commission (UGC), which draws its power from the *University Grants Commission Act, 1956*. In addition, 15 Professional Councils are established, controlling different aspects of accreditation and coordination. Central universities, in addition, are covered by the *Central Universities Act, 2009*, which regulates their purpose, powers governance etc., and established 12 new universities.

The number of central universities published by the UGC includes 43 central universities as on April 2015.

UGC-NET (JRF) Exam December, 2015

PAPER–I

> **Note :** This paper consists **Sixty (60)** multiple-choice type of questions, out of which the candidate would be required to answer **any Fifty (50)** questions. In the event of candidate attempting more than **Fifty (50)** questions, the **first Fifty (50)** questions attempted by the Candidate would be evaluated.

1. Greater the handicap of the students coming to the educational institutions, greater the demand on the:
   A. Family
   B. Society
   C. Teacher
   D. State

2. What are the characteristics of Continuous and Comprehensive Evaluation?
   (a) It increases the workload on students by taking multiple tests.
   (b) It replaces marks with grades.
   (c) It evaluates every aspect of the student.
   (d) It helps in reducing examination phobia.

   Select the **correct** answer from the codes given below:
   A. (a), (b), (c) and (d)   B. (b) and (d)
   C. (a), (b) and (c)   D. (b), (c) and (d)

3. Which of the following attributes denote great strengths of a teacher?
   (a) Full-time active involvement in the institutional management
   (b) Setting examples
   (c) Willingness to put assumptions to the test
   (d) Acknowledging mistakes

   Select the **correct** answer from the codes given below:
   A. (a), (b) and (d)   B. (b), (c) and (d)
   C. (a), (c) and (d)   D. (a), (b), (c) and (d)

4. Which one of the following statements is **correct** in the context of multiple - choice type questions?

   A. They are more objective than true-false type questions.
   B. They are less objective than essay type questions.
   C. They are more subjective than short-answer type questions.
   D. They are more subjective than true-false type questions.

5. As Chairman of an independent commission on education, Jacques Delors report to UNESCO was titled:
   A. International Commission on Education Report
   B. Millennium Development Report
   C. Learning : The Treasure Within
   D. World Declaration on Education for All

6. What are required for good teaching?
   (a) Diagnosis   (b) Remedy
   (c) Direction   (d) Feedback

   Select the **correct** answer from the codes given below:
   A. (a), (b), (c) and (d)
   B. (a) and (b)
   C. (b), (c) and (d)
   D. (c) and (d)

7. Which of the following statements is **not** true in the context of participatory research?
   A. It recognizes knowledge as power.
   B. It emphasises on people as experts.
   C. It is a collective process of enquiry.
   D. Its sole purpose is production of knowledge.

8. Which of the following statements is **true** in the context of the testing of a hypothesis?

A. It is only the alternative hypothesis, that can be tested

B. It is only the null hypothesis, that can be tested

C. Both, the alternative and the null hypotheses can be tested

D. Both, the alternative and the null hypotheses cannot be tested

9. Which of the following are the basic rules of APA style of referencing format?

(a) Italicize titles of shorter works such as journal articles or essays

(b) Invert authors' names (last name first)

(c) Italicize titles of longer works such as books and journals

(d) Alphabetically index reference list

Select the **correct** answer from the codes given below:

A. (a) and (b)   B. (b), (c) and (d)
C. (c) and (d)   D. (a), (b), (c) and (d)

10. Which of the following are the characteristics of a seminar?

(a) It is a form of academic instruction

(b) It involves questioning, discussion and debates

(c) It involves large groups of individuals

(d) It needs involvement of skilled persons

Select the **correct** answer from the codes given below:

A. (b) and (c)   B. (b) and (d)
C. (b), (c) and (d)   D. (a), (b) and (d)

11. A researcher is interested in studying the prospects of a particular political party in an urban area. What tool should he prefer for the study?

A. Rating scale   B. Interview
C. Questionnaire   D. Schedule

12. Ethical norms in research do **not** involve guidelines for:

A. Thesis format
B. Copyright
C. Patenting policy
D. Data sharing policies

Direction (Qs. 13 to 17): *Read the following passage carefully and answer the question.*

I did that thing recently where you have to sign a big card - which is a horror unto itself, especially as the keeper of the Big Card was leaning over me at the time. Suddenly I was on the spot, a rabbit in the headlights, torn between doing a fun message or some sort of in-joke or a drawing. Instead overwhelmed by the myriad options available to me, I decided to just write : "Good luck, best, Joel".

It was then that I realised, to my horror, that I had forgotten how to write. My entire existence is "tap letters into computer". My shopping lists are hidden in the notes function of my phone. If I need to remember something I send an e-mail to myself. A pen is something I chew when I'm struggling to think. Paper is something I pile beneath my laptop to make it a more comfortable height for me to type on.

A poll of 1,000 teens by the stationers, Bic found that one in 10 don't own a pen, a third have never written a letter, and half of 13 to 19 years - old have never been forced to sit down and write a thank you letter. More than 80% have never written a love letter, 56% don't have letter paper at home. And a quarter have never known the unique torture of writing a birthday card. The most a teen ever has to use a pen is on an exam paper.

Bic, have you heard of mobile phones? Have you heard of e-mail, facebook and snap chatting? This is the future. Pens are dead. Paper is dead. Handwriting is a relic.

"Handwriting is one of the most creative outlets we have and should be given the same importance as other art forms such as sketching, painting or photography."

Answer the following questions:

13. When confronted with signing a big card, the author felt like "a rabbit in the headlight". What does this phrase mean?

A. A state of confusion
B. A state of pleasure
C. A state of anxiety
D. A state of pain

14. According to the author, which one is **not** the most creative outlet of pursuit?
A. Handwriting   B. Photography
C. Sketching   D. Reading

15. The entire existence of the author revolves round:
(a) Computer
(b) Mobile phone
(c) Typewriter
Identify the **correct** answer from the codes given below:
A. (b) only   B. (a) and (b) only
C. (a), (b) and (c)   D. (b) and (c) only

16. How many teens, as per the Bic survey, do **not** own a pen?
A. 800   B. 560
C. 500   D. 100

17. What is the main concern of the author?
A. That the teens use social networks for communication
B. That the teens use mobile phones
C. That the teens use computer
D. That the teens have forgotten the art of handwriting

18. The main objectives of student evaluation of teachers are:
(a) To gather information about student weaknesses.
(b) To make teachers take teaching seriously.
(c) To help teachers adopt innovative methods of teaching.
(d) To identify the areas of further improvement in teacher traits.
Identify the **correct** answer from the codes given below:
A. (a) and (b) only   B. (b), (c) and (d) only
C. (a), (b) and (c) only   D. (a) only

19. Using the central point of the classroom communication as the beginning of a dynamic pattern of ideas is referred to as:
A. Systemisation
B. Problem - orientation
C. Idea protocol
D. Mind mapping

20. Aspects of the voice, other than the speech are known as:
A. Physical language   B. Personal language
C. Para language   D. Delivery language

21. Every type of communication is affected by its:
A. Reception   B. Transmission
C. Non-regulation   D. Context

22. Attitudes, actions and appearances in the context of classroom communication are considered as:
A. Verbal   B. Non-verbal
C. Impersonal   D. Irrational

23. Most often, the teacher - student communication is:
A. Spurious   B. Critical
C. Utilitarian   D. Confrontational

24. In a classroom, a communicator's trust level is determined by:
A. the use of hyperbole
B. the change of voice level
C. the use of abstract concepts
D. eye contact

25. The next term in the series
2, 5, 10, 17, 26, 37, __?__ is :
A. 50   B. 57
C. 62   D. 72

26. A group of 210 students appeared in some test. The mean of $\frac{1}{3}$rd of students is found to be 60. The mean of the remaining students is found to be 78. The mean of the whole group will be :
A. 80   B. 76
C. 74   D. 72

27. Anil after travelling 6 km towards East from his house realized that he has travelled in a wrong direction. He turned and travelled 12 km towards West, turned right and travelled 8 km to reach his office. The straight distance of the office from his house is:
A. 20 km   B. 14 km
C. 12 km   D. 10 km

28. The next term in the series:
B2E, D5H, F12K, H27N, __?__ is:
A. J56I B. I62Q
C. Q62J D. J58Q

29. A party was held in which a grandmother, father, mother, four sons, their wives and one son and two daughters to each of the sons were present. The number of females present in the party is:
A. 12 B. 14
C. 18 D. 24

30. P and Q are brothers. R and S are sisters. The son of P is brother of S. Q is related to R as:
A. Son B. Brother
C. Uncle D. Father

31. Consider the argument given below:

'Pre - employment testing of teachers is quite fair because doctors, architects and engineers who are now employed had to face such a testing.'

What type of argument it is ?
A. Deductive B. Analogical
C. Psychological D. Biological

32. Among the following propositions two are related in such a way that they can both be true although they cannot both be false. Which are those propositions? Select the **correct** code.
Propositions:
(a) Some priests are cunning.
(b) No priest is cunning.
(c) All priests are cunning.
(d) Some priests are not cunning.
Codes:
A. (a) and (b) B. (c) and (d)
C. (a) and (c) D. (a) and (d)

33. A Cluster of propositions with a structure that exhibits some inference is called:
A. An inference B. An argument
C. An explanation D. A valid argument

34. Consider the following **assertion (A)** and **reason (R)** and select the **correct** code given below :
Assertion (A): No man is perfect.

Reason (R): Some men are not perfect.
A. Both (A) and (R) are true but (R) does not provide sufficient reason for (A)
B. Both (A) and (R) are true and (R) provides sufficient reason for (A)
C. (A) is true but (R) is false
D. (A) is false but (R) is true

35. A definition that has a meaning that is deliberately assigned to some symbol is called:
A. Lexical B. Precising
C. Stipulative D. Persuasive

36. If the proposition 'No men are honest' is taken to be false which of the following proposition/ propositions can be claimed certainly to be true?
Propositions:
A. All men are honest
B. Some men are honest
C. Some men are not honest
D. No honest person is man

Given below in the table is the decadal data of Population and Electrical Power Production of a country.

Year	Population (million)	Electrical Power Production (GW)*
1951	20	10
1961	21	20
1971	24	25
1981	27	40
1991	30	50
2001	32	80
2011	35	100
	* 1 GW = 1000 million watt	

Directions (Qs. 37 to 42): *Based on the above table answer the questions.*

37. Which decade registered the maximum growth rate (%) of population?
A. 1961-71 B. 1971-81
C. 1991-2001 D. 2001-2011

38. Average decadal growth rate (%) of population is:
A. ~ 12.21% B. ~ 9.82%
C. ~ 6.73% D. ~ 5%

39. Based on the average decadal growth rate, what will be the population in the year 2021?
A. 40.34 million
B. 38.49 million
C. 37.28 million
D. 36.62 million

40. In the year 1951, what was the power availability per person?
A. 100 W
B. 200 W
C. 400 W
D. 500 W

41. In which decade, the average power availability per person was maximum?
A. 1981-1991
B. 1991-2001
C. 2001-2011
D. 1971-1981

42. By what percentage (%) the power production increased from 1951 to 2011?
A. 100%
B. 300%
C. 600%
D. 900%

43. NMEICT stands for:
A. National Mission on Education through ICT
B. National Mission on E-governance through ICT
C. National Mission on E-commerce through ICT
D. National Mission on E-learning through ICT

44. Which of the following is an instant messaging application?
(a) WhatsApp
(b) Google Talk
(c) Viber

Select the **correct** answer from the codes given below:
A. (a) and (b) only
B. (b) and (c) only
C. (a) only
D. (a), (b) and (c)

45. In a Computer a byte generally consists of:
A. 4 bits
B. 8 bits
C. 16 bits
D. 10 bits

46. Which of the following is **not** an input device?
A. Microphone
B. Keyboard
C. Joystick
D. Monitor

47. Which of the following is an open source software?
A. MS Word
B. Windows
C. Mozilla Firefox
D. Acrobat Reader

48. Which of the following enables us to send the same letter to different persons in MS Word?
A. Mail join
B. Mail copy
C. Mail insert
D. Mail merge

49. Inside rural homes, the source/sources of Nitrogen Oxide Pollution may be:
(a) Unvented gas stoves
(b) Wood stoves
(c) Kerosene heaters

Choose the **correct** code:
A. (a) and (b) only
B. (b) and (c) only
C. (b) only
D. (a), (b) and (c)

50. Which of the following pollutants can cause cancer in humans?
A. Pesticides
B. Mercury
C. Lead
D. Ozone

51. **Assertion (A):** People population control measures do not necessarily help in checking environmental degradation.

Reason (R): The relationship between population growth and environmental degradation is rather complex.

Choose the **correct** answer from the following:
A. Both (A) and (R) are true and (R) is the correct explanation of (A)
B. Both (A) and (R) are true but (R) is not the correct explanation of (A)
C. (A) is true but (R) is false
D. (A) is false but (R) is true

52. Which of the following phenomena is **not** a natural hazard?
A. Wildfire
B. Lightning
C. Landslide
D. Chemical contamination

53. As part of National Climate Change Policy, Indian government is planning to raise the installed capacity of renewable energy by the year 2030 to:
A. 175 GW
B. 200 GW
C. 250 GW
D. 350 GW

54. At present, in terms of per capita energy consumption (kWh/year), identify the **correct** sequence.
A. Brazil > Russia > China > India
B. Russia > China > India > Brazil
C. Russia > China > Brazil > India
D. China > Russia > Brazil > India

55. Which of the following are the objectives of Rashtriya Uchchatar Shiksha Abhiyan (RUSA)?
(a) To improve the overall quality of state institutions.
(b) To ensure adequate availability of quality faculty.
(c) To create new institutions through upgradation of existing autonomous colleges.
(d) To downgrade universities with poor infrastructure into autonomous colleges.
Select the **correct** answer from the codes given below :
A. (a), (b), (c) and (d)   B. (a), (b) and (c)
C. (a), (c) and (d)   D. (a), (b) and (d)

56. The grounds on which discrimination in admission to educational institutions is constitutionally prohibited are:
(a) Religion
(b) Sex
(c) Place of birth
(d) Nationality
Select the **correct** answer from the codes given below:
A. (b), (c) and (d)   B. (a), (b) and (c)
C. (a), (b) and (d)   D. (a), (b), (c) and (d)

57. Which of the following statements are **correct** about Lok Sabha?
(a) The Constitution puts a limit on the size of the Lok Sabha.
(b) The size and shape of the Parliamentary Constituencies is determined by the Election Commission.
(c) First - past - the Post electoral system is followed.
(d) The Speaker of Lok Sabha does not have a casting vote in case of an equality of votes.
Select the **correct** answer from the codes given below:
A. (a) and (c)
B. (a), (b) and (c)
C. (a), (c) and (d)
D. (a), (b), (c) and (d)

58. Public Order as an item in the Constitution figures in:
A. the Union List
B. the State List
C. the Concurrent List
D. the Residuary Powers

59. The term of office of the Advocate General of a State is:
A. 4 years
B. 5 years
C. 6 years or 65 years of age whichever is earlier
D. not fixed

60. Which among the following States has the highest number of seats in the Lok Sabha?
A. Maharashtra   B. Rajasthan
C. Tamil Nadu   D. West Bengal

ANSWERS

1	2	3	4	5	6	7	8	9	10
C	D	B	A	C	A	D	B	B	D
11	12	13	14	15	16	17	18	19	20
C	A	A	D	B	D	D	B	D	C
21	22	23	24	25	26	27	28	29	30
D	B	C	D	A	D	D	D	B	C

31	32	33	34	35	36	37	38	39	40
B	D	B	A	C	B	A	B	B	D

41	42	43	44	45	46	47	48	49	50
C	D	A	D	B	D	C	D	D	A

51	52	53	54	55	56	57	58	59	60
A	D	D	C	B	B	A	B	D	A

SOME SELECTED EXPLANATORY ANSWERS

5. Jacques Delors is the chairman of the International Commission on Education for the Twenty-first Century. The result of three years of research and debate by an international panel of 14 specialists on how education should confront the complex challenges of the next century, the 266-page report is being published simultaneously in English and French.

Entitled "Learning: the Treasure Within," the report revolves around six main lines of enquiry which will guide UNESCO's future education policies and those of its 184 Member States. The lines focus on the relationship between education and the six subject areas of development, science, citizenship, culture, social cohesion, and work.

20. Paralanguage is a component of meta-communication that may modify or nuance meaning, or convey emotion, such as prosody, pitch, volume, intonation etc. It is sometimes defined as relating to nonphonemic properties only.

The paralinguistic properties of speech play an important role in human communication. There are no utterances or speech signals that lack paralinguistic properties, since speech requires the presence of a voice that can be modulated. This voice must have some properties, and all the properties of a voice as such are paralinguistic.

21. Each context has an influence on the communication process. Contexts can overlap, creating an even more dynamic process. You have been communicating in many of these contexts across your lifetime, and you'll be able to apply what you've learned through experience in each context to business communication.

25.

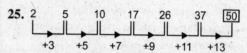

28.

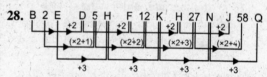

33. Argument: An argument is any group of propositions of which one is claimed to follow from the others, which are regarded as providing support or grounds for the truth of that one.

35. A definition that has a meaning which is deliberately assigned to some symbol is called stipulative. One who introduces a new symbol is free to assign, or stipulate, whatever meaning he cares to. Even an old term in a new context may also have its present meaning stipulated. What are here called *stipulative* definitions are sometimes referred to as *nominal* or *verbal* definitions.

37. Growth rate (%) of population in decade

1961-71 :

$$\left(\frac{24-21}{21}\right) \times 100 = \frac{100}{7} = 14.285\%$$

1971-81 :

$$\left(\frac{27-24}{24}\right) \times 100 = \frac{3}{24} \times 100 = 12.5\%$$

1991-2001 :

$$\left(\frac{32-30}{30}\right) \times 100 = \frac{2}{30} \times 100 = 6.67\%$$

2001-2011 :

$$\left(\frac{35-32}{32}\right) \times 100 = \frac{2}{32} \times 100 = 9.375\%$$

$\therefore$ Maximum growth rate (%) of population registered on 1961-71.

38. Average decadal growth rate (%) of population

$$= \frac{5+14.28+12.5+11.11+6.67+9.38}{6}$$

$= 9.82\%.$

39. Projected Population in 2021

$$= 35 + \frac{35 \times 9.82}{100}$$

$$= 35 + 3.4$$

$$= 38.4 \text{ million.}$$

40. Power availabilty per person in year 1951

$$= \frac{10 \times 1000}{20} = 500 \text{ W.}$$

41. Average Power availability per person in decade

1981-91 : $\dfrac{(40+50) \times 1000}{(27+30)} \cong 1579$ W

1991-2001 : $\dfrac{(50+80) \times 1000}{(30+32)} \cong 2097$ W

2001-2011 : $\dfrac{(80+100) \times 1000}{(32+35)} \cong 2686.5$ W

1971-1981 : $\dfrac{(25+40) \times 1000}{(24+27)} \cong 1274.5$ W

So, Average Power availability per person was maximum in 2001-2011.

42. Percentage (%) increase in power production from 1951 to 2011

$$= \left(\frac{100-10}{10}\right) \times 100$$

$= 900\%.$

43. National Mission on Education through Information and Communication Technology is abbreviated as NMEICT .

45. The byte is a unit of digital information that most commonly consists of eight bits. Historically, the byte was the number of bits used to encode a single character of text in a computer and for this reason it is the smallest addressable unit of memory in many computer architectures.

50. Pesticides are the only toxic substances released intentionally into our environment to kill living things. Pesticides are used in our schools, parks, and public lands. Pesticides are sprayed on agricultural fields and wood lots. Pesticides can be found in our air, our food, our soil, our water and even in our breast milk.

Pesticides can cause many types of cancer in humans. Some of the most prevalent forms include leukemia, non-Hodgkins lymphoma, brain, bone, breast, ovarian, prostate, testicular and liver cancers.

YOUR SPACE

UGC-NET (JRF) EXAM JULY, 2016*

PAPER–I

> **Note :**
> - This paper contains **Sixty (60)** multiple choice questions, each question carrying **two (2)** marks.
> - Candidate is expected to answer any **Fifty (50)** questions.
> - In case more than **Fifty (50)** questions are attempted, only the first **Fifty (50)** questions will be evaluated.

1. Select the alternative which consists of positive factors contributing to effectiveness of teaching :

   List of factors :
   (a) Teacher's knowledge of the subject.
   (b) Teacher's socio-economic background.
   (c) Communication skill of the teacher.
   (d) Teacher's ability to please the students.
   (e) Teacher's personal contact with students.
   (f) Teacher's competence in managing and monitoring the classroom transactions.

   Codes :
   A. (b), (c) and (d)   B. (c), (d) and (f)
   C. (b), (d) and (e)   D. (a), (c) and (f)

2. The use of teaching aids is justified on the grounds of :
   A. attracting students' attention in the classroom.
   B. minimising indiscipline problems in the classroom.
   C. optimising learning outcomes of students.
   D. effective engagement of students in learning tasks.

3. **Assertion (A) :** The purpose of higher education is to promote critical and creative thinking abilities among students.
   Reason (R) : These abilities ensure job placements.

Choose the correct answer from the following code :
A. Both (A) and (R) are true and (R) is the correct explanation of (A).
B. Both (A) and (R) are true, but (R) is not the correct explanation of (A).
C. (A) is true, but (R) is false.
D. (A) is false, but (R) is true.

4. Match the items of the first set with that of the second set in respect of evaluation system. Choose the correct code :

Set–I	Set–II
(a) Formative evaluation	1. Evaluating cognitive and co-cognitive aspects with regularity
(b) Summative evaluation	2. Tests and their interpretations based on a group and certain yardsticks
(c) Continuous and comprehensive evaluation	3. Grading the final learning outcomes
(d) Norm and criterion referenced tests	4. Quizzes and discussions

   Codes :

	(a)	(b)	(c)	(d)
A.	4	3	1	2
B.	1	2	3	4
C.	3	4	2	1
D.	1	3	4	2

5. A researcher intends to explore the effect of possible factors for the organization of effective mid-day meal interventions. Which research method will be most appropriate for this study?
A. Historical method
B. Descriptive survey method
C. Experimental method
D. Ex-post-facto method

6. Which of the following is an initial mandatory requirement for pursuing research?
A. Developing a research design
B. Formulating a research question
C. Deciding about the data analysis procedure
D. Formulating a research hypothesis

7. The format of thesis writing is the same as in :
A. preparation of a research paper/article
B. writing of seminar presentation
C. a research dissertation
D. presenting a workshop / conference paper

8. In qualitative research paradigm, which of the following features may be considered critical?
A. Data collection with standardised research tools.
B. Sampling design with probability sample techniques.
C. Data collection with bottom-up empirical evidences.
D. Data gathering to take place with top-down systematic evidences.

9. From the following list of statements identify the set which has negative implications for 'research ethics' :
(i) A researcher critically looks at the findings of another research.
(ii) Related studies are cited without proper references.
(iii) Research findings are made the basis for policy making.
(iv) Conduct of practitioner is screened in terms of reported research evidences.
(v) A research study is replicated with a view to verify the evidences from other researches.

(vi) Both policy making and policy implementing processes are regulated in terms of preliminary studies.
Codes :
A. (i), (ii) and (iii)
B. (ii), (iii) and (iv)
C. (ii), (iv) and (vi)
D. (i), (iii) and (v)

10. In a research on the effect of child-rearing practices on stress-proneness of children in completing school projects, the hypothesis formulated is that 'child rearing practices do influence stress-proneness'. At the data-analysis stage a null hypothesis is advanced to find out the tenability of research hypothesis. On the basis of the evidence available, the null hypothesis is rejected at 0.01 level of significance. What decision may be warranted in respect of the research hypothesis?
A. The research hypothesis will also be rejected.
B. The research hypothesis will be accepted.
C. Both the research hypothesis and the null hypothesis will be rejected.
D. No decision can be taken in respect of the research hypothesis.

Directions (Qs. Nos. 11-16) : *Read the following passage carefully and answer the questions.*

In terms of labour, for decades the relatively low cost and high quality of Japanese workers conferred considerable competitive advantage across numerous durable goods and consumer-electronics industries (*e.g.,* Machinery, automobiles, televisions, radios). Then labour-based advantages shifted to South Korea, then to Malaysia, Mexico and other nations. Today, China appears to be capitalizing best on the basis of labour. Japanese firms still remain competitive in markets for such durable goods, electronics and other products, but the labour force is no longer sufficient for competitive advantage over manufacturers in other industrializing nations. Such shifting of labour-based advantage is clearly not limited to manufacturing industries. Today, a huge number of IT and service jobs are moving from Europe and North America to India, Singapore, and like countries with relatively well-educated, low-cost workforces possessing technical skills. However, as educational levels and technical skills continue to rise in other countries, India, Singapore, and like nations enjoying labour-based competitive advantage today are likely to find such advantage cannot be sustained through emergence of new competitors.

In terms of capital, for centuries the days of gold coins and later even paper money restricted financial flows. Subsequently regional concentrations were formed where large banks, industries and markets coalesced. But today capital flows internationally at rapid speed. Global commerce no longer requires regional interactions among business players. Regional capital concentrations in places such as New York, London and Tokyo still persist, of course, but the capital concentrated there is no longer sufficient for competitive advantage over other capitalists distributed worldwide. Only if an organization is able to combine, integrate and apply its resources (*e.g.* Land, labour, capital, IT) in an effective manner that is not readily imitable by competitors can such an organization enjoy competitive advantage sustainable overtime.

In a knowledge-based theory of the firm, this idea is extended to view organizational knowledge as a resource with atleast the same level of power and importance as the traditional economic inputs. An organization with superior knowledge can achieve competitive advantage in markets that appreciate the application of such knowledge. Semiconductors, genetic engineering, pharmaceuticals, software, military warfare, and like knowledge-intensive competitive arenas provide both time-proven and current examples. Consider semiconductors (*e.g.* computer chips), which are made principally of sand and common metals. These ubiquitous and powerful electronic devices are designed within common office buildings, using commercially available tools, and fabricated within factories in many industrialized nations. Hence, land is not the key competitive resource in the semiconductor industry.

Based on the passage answer the following questions :

11. Which country enjoyed competitive advantages in automobile industry for decades?
    A. South Korea   B. Japan
    C. Mexico   D. Malaysia

12. Why labour-based competitive advantages of India and Singapore cannot be sustained in IT and service sectors?
    A. Due to diminishing levels of skill.
    B. Due to capital-intensive technology making inroads.
    C. Because of new competitors.
    D. Because of shifting of labour-based advantage in manufacturing industries.

13. How can an organisation enjoy competitive advantage sustainable overtime?
    A. Through regional capital flows.
    B. Through regional interactions among business players.
    C. By making large banks, industries and markets coalesced.
    D. By effective use of various instrumentalities.

14. What is required to ensure competitive advantages in specific markets?
    A. Access to capital
    B. Common office buildings
    C. Superior knowledge
    D. Common metals

15. The passage also mentions about the trend of :
    A. Global financial flow
    B. Absence of competition in manufacturing industry
    C. Regionalisation of capitalists
    D. Organizational incompatibility

16. What does the author lay stress on in the passage?
    A. International commerce
    B. Labour-intensive industries
    C. Capital resource management
    D. Knowledge-driven competitive advantage

17. Imagine you are working in an educational institution where people are of equal status. Which method of communication is best suited and normally employed in such a context?
A. Horizontal communication
B. Vertical communication
C. Corporate communication
D. Cross communication

18. Identify the important element a teacher has to take cognizance of while addressing students in a classroom.
A. Avoidance of proximity
B. Voice modulation
C. Repetitive pause
D. Fixed posture

19. What are the barriers to effective communication?
A. Moralising, being judgemental and comments of consolation.
B. Dialogue, summary and self-review.
C. Use of simple words, cool reaction and defensive attitude.
D. Personal statements, eye contact and simple narration.

20. The choice of communication partners is influenced by factors of :
A. Proximity, utility, loneliness
B. Utility, secrecy, dissonance
C. Secrecy, dissonance, deception
D. Dissimilarity, dissonance, deviance

21. As a teacher, select the best option to ensure your effective presence in the classroom.
A. Use of peer command
B. Making aggressive statements
C. Adoption of well-established posture
D. Being authoritarian

22. Every communicator has to experience :
A. Manipulated emotions
B. Anticipatory excitement
C. The issue of homophiles
D. Status dislocation

23. In certain code, SELECTION is coded as QCJCARGML. The code of AMERICANS will be :

A. YKCPGAYLQ   B. BNFSJDBMR
C. QLYAGPCKY   D. YQKLCYPAG

24. In the series
3, 11, 23, 39, 59, ...
The next term will be :
A. 63   B. 73
C. 83   D. 93

25. Two railway tickets from city A to B and three tickets from city A to C cost ₹ 177. Three tickets from city A to B and two tickets from city A to C cost ₹ 173. The fare for city B from city A will be ₹ :
A. 25   B. 27
C. 30   D. 33

26. A person walks 10 m infront and 10 m to the right. Then every time turning to his left, he walks 5, 15 and 15 m respectively. How far is he now from his starting point?
A. 20 m   B. 15 m
C. 10 m   D. 5 m

27. A is sister of B. F is daughter of G. C is mother of B. D is father of C. E is mother of D. A is related to D as :
A. Grand daughter   B. Daughter
C. Daughter-in-law   D. Sister

28. In the series
AB, EDC, FGHI, ...?...., OPQRST, the missing term is :
A. JKLMN   B. JMKNL
C. NMLKJ   D. NMKLJ

29. Among the following propositions two are related in such a way that one is the denial of the other. Which are those propositions? Select the correct code :
Propositions :
(a) All women are equal to men
(b) Some women are equal to men
(c) Some women are not equal to men
(d) No women are equal to men
Codes :
A. (a) and (b)
B. (a) and (d)
C. (c) and (d)
D. (a) and (c)

30. If the proposition 'All thieves are poor' is false, which of the following propositions can be claimed certainly to be true?
Propositions :
A. Some thieves are poor.
B. Some thieves are not poor.
C. No thief is poor.
D. No poor person is a thief.

31. Consider the following statement and select the correct code stating the nature of the argument involved in it :
To suppose that the earth is the only populated world in the infinite space is as absurd as to assert that in an entire field of millet only one grain will grow.
A. Astronomical   B. Anthropological
C. Deductive   D. Analogical

32. Select the code which is not correct about Venn diagram :
A. Venn diagram represents propositions as well as classes.
B. It can provide clear method of notation.
C. It can be either valid or invalid.
D. It can provide the direct method of testing the validity.

33. Select the code which is not correct in the context of deductive argument with two premises :
A. An argument with one true premise, one false premise and a false conclusion may be valid.
B. An argument with two true premises and a false conclusion may be valid.
C. An argument with one true premise, one false premise and a true conclusion may be valid.
D. An argument with two false premises and a false conclusion may be valid.

34. Given below are two premises and four conclusions are drawn from them (taking singly or together). Select the code that states the conclusions validly drawn.
Premises :
(*i*) All religious persons are emotional.

(*ii*) Ram is a religious person.
Conclusions :
(*a*) Ram is emotional.
(*b*) All emotional persons are religious.
(*c*) Ram is not a non-religious person.
(*d*) Some religious persons are not emotional.
Codes :
A. (*a*), (*b*), (*c*) and (*d*)
B. (*a*) only
C. (*a*) and (*c*) only
D. (*b*) and (*c*) only

Directions (Qs. Nos. 35-37) : *The following table shows the percentage profit (%) earned by two companies A and B during the years 2011-15. Answer these questions based on the data contained in the table :*

Profit earned by two companies

Year	Percentage Profit (%)	
	A	**B**
2011	20	30
2012	35	40
2013	45	35
2014	40	50
2015	25	35

Where, per cent (%) Profit
$$= \frac{\text{Income} - \text{Expenditure}}{\text{Expenditure}} \times 100$$

35. If the total expenditure of the two companies was ₹ 9 lakh in the year 2012 and the expenditure of A and B were in the ratio 2 : 1, then what was the income of the company A in that year?
A. ₹ 9.2 lakh   B. ₹ 8.1 lakh
C. ₹ 7.2 lakh   D. ₹ 6.0 lakh

36. What is the average percentage profit earned by the company B?
A. 35%   B. 42%
C. 38%   D. 40%

37. In which year, the percentage profit earned by the company B is less than that of company A?
A. 2012   B. 2013
C. 2014   D. 2015

Directions (Qs. Nos. 38-40) : *The following table shows the number of people in different age groups who responded to a survey about their favourite style of music. Use this information to answer the questions that follow, to the nearest whole percentage :*

	Number of people		
Style of Music ↓ Age →	(Years) 15-20	(Years) 21-30	(Years) 31+
Classical	6	4	17
Pop	7	5	5
Rock	6	12	14
Jazz	1	4	11
Blues	2	3	15
Hip-Hop	9	3	4
Ambient	2	2	2

38. Approximately what percentage of the total sample were aged 21-30?
- A. 31%
- B. 23%
- C. 25%
- D. 14%

39. Approximately what percentage of the total sample indicates that Hip-Hop is their favourite style of music?
- A. 6%
- B. 8%
- C. 14%
- D. 12%

40. What percentage of respondents aged 31+ indicated a favourite style other than classical music?
- A. 64%
- B. 60%
- C. 75%
- D. 50%

41. The statement "the study, design, development, implementation, support or management of computer-based information systems, particularly software applications and computer Hardware" refers to :
- A. Information Technology (IT)
- B. Information and Collaborative Technology (ICT)
- C. Information and Data Technology (IDT)
- D. Artificial Intelligence (AI)

42. If the binary equivalent of the decimal number 48 is 110000, then the binary equivalent of the decimal number 51 is given by :
- A. 110011
- B. 110010
- C. 110001
- D. 110100

43. The process of copying files to a CD-ROM is known as :
- A. Burning
- B. Zipping
- C. Digitizing
- D. Ripping

44. An unsolicited e-mail message sent to many recipients at once is a :
- A. Worm
- B. Virus
- C. Threat
- D. Spam

45. _____ is a type of memory circuitry that holds the computer's start-up routine.
- A. RIM (Read Initial Memory)
- B. RAM (Random Access Memory)
- C. ROM (Read Only Memory)
- D. Cache Memory

46. An ASCII is a character-encoding scheme that is employed by personal computers in order to represent various characters, numbers and control keys that the computer user selects on the keyboard. ASCII is an acronym for :
- A. American Standard Code for Information Interchange
- B. American Standard Code for Intelligent Information
- C. American Standard Code for Information Integrity
- D. American Standard Code for Isolated Information

47. Identify the air pollutant in urban areas which irritates eyes and also respiratory tract of human beings.
- A. Particulate matter
- B. Oxides of nitrogen
- C. Surface ozone
- D. Carbon monoxide

48. Which of the following is the largest source of water pollution in major rivers of India?
- A. Untreated sewage
- B. Agriculture run-off
- C. Unregulated small scale industries
- D. Religious practices

49. Sustainable development goals have specific targets to be achieved by :
A. 2022 B. 2030
C. 2040 D. 2050

50. Indian government's target of producing power from biomass by the year 2022, is :
A. 50 MW B. 25 MW
C. 15 MW D. 10 MW

51. Assertion (A) : Conserving our soil resources is critical to human survival.
Reason (R) : Soil is home to many micro-organisms and contains minerals.
Choose the correct code :
A. Both (A) and (R) are correct and (R) is the correct explanation of (A).
B. Both (A) and (R) are correct, but (R) is not the correct explanation of (A).
C. (A) is true and (R) is false.
D. (A) is false and (R) is true.

52. World Meteorological Organisation's (WMO) objective has been to reduce the number of deaths due to hydrometeorological disasters over the decade 2010-2019 by (with reference to the decade 1994-2003) :
A. 25% B. 50%
C. 75% D. 80%

53. Which of the following core values among the institutions of higher education are promoted by the NAAC (National Assessment and Accreditation Council)?
(a) Contributing to national development.
(b) Fostering global competencies among the students.
(c) Inculcating a value system among students and teachers.
(d) Promoting the optimum utilization of the infrastructure.
Select the correct answer from the codes given below :
Codes :
A. (b), (c) and (d)
B. (a), (b) and (c)
C. (a), (c) and (d)
D. (a), (b), (c) and (d)

54. The best way for providing value education is through :
A. discussions on scriptural texts
B. lectures / discourses on values
C. seminars / symposia on values
D. mentoring / reflective sessions on values

55. The National Judicial Appointments Commission (NJAC) has been declared unconstitutional by :
A. The Supreme Court of India
B. The High Court
C. The High Court and the Supreme Court both
D. The President of India

56. Which of the following statements about the Indian political system is/are correct?
(a) The President is both Head of the State and Head of the Government.
(b) Parliament is Supreme.
(c) The Supreme Court is the guardian of the Constitution.
(d) The Directive Principles of State Policy are justiciable.
Select the correct answer from the codes given below :
A. (a), (b), (c) and (d) B. (b), (c) and (d)
C. (b) and (c) D. (c) only

57. Which of the following are the fundamental duties?
(a) To respect the National Flag.
(b) To protect and improve the natural environment.
(c) For a parent to provide opportunities for education to his/her child.
(d) To protect monuments and places of national importance.
Select the correct answer from the codes given:
Codes :
A. (a), (b) and (c) B. (a), (b) and (d)
C. (a), (c) and (d) D. (a), (b), (c) and (d)

58. Which of the following statements are correct in respect of NITI Aayog?
(a) It is a constitutional body.
(b) It is a statutory body.

(c) It is neither a constitutional body nor a statutory body.

(d) It is a think-tank.

Select the correct answer from the codes given below :

A. (a) and (d) B. (b) and (d)
C. (c) and (d) D. (b), (c) and (d)

59. A college level assistant professor has planned his/her lectures with an intent to develop cognitive dimensions of students centered on skills of analysis and synthesis. Below, given are two sets of items Set–I consisting of levels of cognitive interchange and Set–II comprising basic requirements for promoting them. Match the two sets and indicate your answer by choosing the correct alternative from the code:

Set–I
(Levels of Cognitive Interchange)

Set–II
(Basic requirements for promoting cognitive interchange)

(a) Memory level

1. Giving opportunity for discriminating examples and non-examples of a point.

(b) Understanding level

2. Recording the important points made during the presentations.

(c) Reflective level

3. Asking the students to discuss various items of information.

4. Critically analyzing the points to be made and discussed.

Codes :

	(a)	(b)	(c)
A.	2	4	1
B.	3	4	2
C.	2	1	4
D.	1	2	3

60. Which set of learner characteristics may be considered helpful in designing effective teaching-learning systems? Select the correct alternative from the codes given below :

(i) Prior experience of learners in respect of the subject.

(ii) Interpersonal relationships of learner's family friends.

(iii) Ability of the learners in respect of the subject.

(iv) Student's language background.

(v) Interest of students in following the prescribed dress code.

(vi) Motivational-orientation of the students.

Codes :

A. (i), (ii), (iii) and (iv)
B. (i), (iii), (iv) and (vi)
C. (ii), (iii), (iv) and (v)
D. (iii), (iv), (v) and (vi)

ANSWERS

1	2	3	4	5	6	7	8	9	10
D	C	B	A	D	B	C	C	C	B
11	12	13	14	15	16	17	18	19	20
B	C	D	C	A	D	A	B	A	A
21	22	23	24	25	26	27	28	29	30
C	B	A	C	D	D	A	C	D	B
31	32	33	34	35	36	37	38	39	40
D	C	B	C	B	C	B	C	D	C
41	42	43	44	45	46	47	48	49	50
A	A	A	D	C	A	C	A	B	D
51	52	53	54	55	56	57	58	59	60
B	B	B	D	A	D	A	C	C	B

EXPLANATORY ANSWERS

7. Documentation is important in writing a research paper, thesis and dissertation to determine if a researcher has read and used several research works and other materials as reference. A research paper, thesis and dissertation is worthless without documentation to serve as proof of the research.

Generally speaking, a research paper, thesis or dissertation is *scientific* if it has several documented materials. But it is *unscientific* if the writer does not explain the relationships of the documented materials to his study and most of the writings of his research paper, thesis or dissertation are documented materials where he has no ideas of his own.

17. Horizontal communication is the transmission of information between people, divisions, departments or units within the same level of organizational hierarchy. You can distinguish it from vertical communication, which is the transmission of information between different levels of the organizational hierarchy. Horizontal communication is often referred to as 'lateral communication'.

Horizontal communication presents some distinct advantages. It decreases misunderstanding between departments working on the same project, thereby increasing efficiency and productivity. It may result in better implementation of top-level decisions because employees on lower levels are permitted to coordinate directly with each other in the implementation of the decision made at the top.

23. SELECTION is coded as

S	E	L	E	C	T	I	O	N
−2	−2	−2	−2	−2	−2	−2	−2	−2
Q	C	J	C	A	R	G	M	L

∴ AMERICANS will be coded as

A	M	E	R	I	C	A	N	S
−2	−2	−2	−2	−2	−2	−2	−2	−2
Y	K	C	P	G	A	Y	L	Q

24. In the series

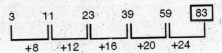

Hence, the next term will be 83.

25. Let fare of A to B = ₹ x
and fare of A to C = ₹ y

According to the question,

$$2x + 3y = ₹\ 177 \quad ...(i)\ ] \times 3$$
$$3x + 2y = ₹\ 173 \quad ...(ii)\ ] \times 2$$
$$6x + 9y = 531$$
$$6x + 4y = 346$$

$$\underline{\qquad\qquad\qquad}$$

$$5y = 185 \Rightarrow y = 37$$

Putting the value of y in (i)

$$2x + 3 \times 37 = 177$$
$$\Rightarrow \qquad 2x = 177 - 111$$
$$\Rightarrow \qquad 2x = 66$$
$$\Rightarrow \qquad x = 33$$

∴ Fare of A to B = ₹ 33

Hence, the fare for city B from A will be ₹ 33.

27.

$$(-)\ E$$
$$|$$
$$D\ (+)$$
$$|$$
$$(-)\ C \qquad और \qquad G\ (?)$$
$$| \qquad\qquad\qquad |$$
$$(-)\ A - B\ (?) \qquad P\ (-)$$

Relation between A to D is Grand daughter.

28. AB, EDC, FGHI, NMLKJ, OPQRST

Hence, the missing term is NMLKJ.

32. The Venn diagrams constitute an *iconic* representation of the standard form categorical propositions, in which spatial inclusions and exclusions correspond to the nonspatial inclusions and exclusions of classes. They provide an exceptionally clear method of notation. They also provide the basis for the simplest and most direct method of testing the validity of categorical syllogisms.

34.

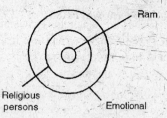

Hence, Ram is emotional and also Ram is not a non-religious person.

35. In 2012, Total expenditure = ₹ 9 lakh

$$\therefore \text{ Expenditure of A} = \frac{2}{3} \times 9 = 6 \text{ lakh}$$

$$\text{Expenditure of B} = \frac{1}{3} \times 9 = 3 \text{ lakh}$$

Let income of Company A = ₹ x

$$35\% = \left(\frac{x - 6 \text{ lakh}}{6} \right) \times 100$$

$$\frac{35}{100} = \frac{(x - 6)}{6}$$

$$\Rightarrow \quad \frac{35 \times 6}{100} = (x - 6)$$

$$\Rightarrow \quad \frac{21}{10} = (x - 6)$$

$$\Rightarrow \quad 10x - 60 = 21$$

$$\Rightarrow \quad 10x = 81$$

$$\Rightarrow \quad x = \frac{81}{10} \text{ lakh} = 8.1 \text{ lakh}$$

∴ Income of company A = 8.1 lakh.

36. Total % profit of Company B

= (30 + 40 + 35 + 50 + 35) = 190

$$\text{Required average} = \frac{190}{5} = 38\%.$$

37. Required year is 2013, the percentage profit earned by the company B is less than that of company A.

38. Total no. of people = 134

No. of people (21 – 30) years = 33

$$\text{Required \%} = \frac{33}{134} \times 100$$

$$= 25\% \text{ (Approx.).}$$

39. $\text{Required \%} = \frac{16}{134} \times 100$

$$= \frac{800}{67} = 12\% \text{ (Approx.).}$$

40. $\text{Required \%} = \frac{68}{134} \times 100$

$$= 50\% \text{ (Approx.).}$$

41. Information Technology (IT), as defined by the Information Technology Association of America (ITAA), is "the study, design, development, implementation, support or management of computer-based information systems, particularly software applications and computer hardware". IT deals with the use of electronic computers and computer software to convert, store, protect, process, transmit, and securely retrieve information. Information Technology (IT) is a general term that describes any technology that helps to produce, manipulate, store, communicate, and/or disseminate information.

42. Decimal to Binary Conversion

2	51	1
2	25	1
2	12	0
2	6	0
2	3	1
	1	

$$\therefore \qquad (51)_{10} = (110011)_2.$$

43. Copying files to a CD or DVD is often called "burning". To burn to one of these optical disc drives you need a disc of the appropriate type. Disc types you're likely to encounter include:

- CD-R (a recordable disc that you can only write data to once)
- CD-RW (a rewritable disc that you can erase and burn again)
- DVD-R and DVD+R
- DVD-RW and DVD+RW.

44. Spam, an unsolicited e-mail message sent to many recipients at once, is commonly known as Internet junk mail. The content of spam ranges from selling a product or service, to promoting a business opportunity, to advertising offensive material. It is strongly advised not to reply to spam messages for any reason if you want to keep your personal data private.

45. ROM (read-only memory) is a type of memory circuitry that holds the computer's startup routine. ROM is housed in a single integrated circuitusually a fairly large, caterpillar-like DIP package—which is plugged into the system board.

46. ASCII is an acronym of "American Standard Code for Information Interchange". The ASCII coding system is an agreement made by organizations working in the computing business. As its name implies, the coding system was developed in the United States where the commercial use of computers began.

47. Ozone, nitrogen oxide and organic compounds (PAN, $CH_2 = O$, $CH_2 = CHCHO$) are main constituents of photochemical smog each of which produce hazardous effects.

- Aldehydes and PAN components of smog cause irritation to eyes and affect the respiratory tract of human beings.
- Ozone causes cracks in rubber materials and is also harmful to fabric, crops and ornamental plants.

- The toxic nature of photochemical smog cause coughing, wheezing, bronchial constrictions and irritation to respiratory mucous system.
- The highly toxic PAN attacks newly grown leaves and causes bronzing and glazing of their surfaces.
- The brownish colour of photochemical smog due to NO_2 reduces visibility. NO_2 also produces throat and eye irritation and leads to several chronic disease of throat, eyes, lungs and heart.

48. Water pollution is a major environmental issue in India. The largest source of water pollution in India is untreated sewage. Other sources of pollution include agricultural runoff and unregulated small scale industry. Most rivers, lakes and surface water in India are polluted.

A 2007 study found that discharge of untreated sewage is the single most important source of pollution of surface and groundwater in India. There is a large gap between generation and treatment of domestic waste water in India. The problem is not only that India lacks sufficient treatment capacity but also that the sewage treatment plants that exist do not operate and are not maintained.

49. In September, 2015 the UN General Assembly adopted the 17 Sustainable Development Goals (the SDGs), with 169 specific targets, to guide the world's development agenda through 2030. One of the goals is to "Ensure availability and sustainable management of water and sanitation for all", and one of the six targets to be achieved under this is "By 2030, implement integrated water resources management at all levels, including through transboundary cooperation as appropriate".

55. The National Judicial Appointments Commission (NJAC) is unconstitutional, ruled the Supreme Court of India. The verdict effectively rejects a major law passed by Parliament last year, which was subsequently ratified by 20 state Assemblies, and restores the collegium system of appointing judges.

56. The Supreme Court of India is the guardian of the Constitution. There are two points of significance of the Supreme Court's rule as the protector and guardian of the Constitution.

- First, as the highest Federal Court, it is within the power and authority of the Supreme Court to settle any dispute regarding division of powers between the Union and the States.

- Secondly, it is in the Supreme Court's authority to safeguard the fundamental rights of the citizens.

In order to discharge these two functions it is sometimes necessary for the Supreme Court to examine or review the legality of the laws enacted by both the Union and the State Governments. This is known as the power of Judicial Review. Indian Supreme Court enjoys limited power of Judicial Review.

57. Fundamental Duties

The Forty-second Constitution Amendment Act has inserted Part IVA with Art. 51A having a set of Fundamental Duties. It says that it shall be the duty of every citizen of India:

(*a*) to abide by the Constitution and respect its ideals and institutions, the National Flag and the National Anthem;

(*b*) to cherish and follow the noble ideals which inspired our national struggle for freedom;

(*c*) to uphold and protect the sovereignty, unity and integrity of India;

(*d*) to defend the country and render national service when called upon to do so;

(*e*) to promote harmony and the spirit of common brotherhood amongst all the people of India transcending religious, linguistic and regional or sectional diversities; to renounce practices derogatory to the dignity of women;

(*f*) to value and preserve the rich heritage of our composite culture;

(*g*) to protect and improve the natural environment including forests, lakes, rivers and wildlife and to have compassion for living creatures;

(*h*) to develop the scientific temper, humanism and the spirit of inquiry and reform;

(*i*) to safeguard public property and to abjure violence;

(*j*) to strive for excellence in all spheres of individual and collective activity so that the nation constantly rises to higher levels of endeavour and achievement.

(*k*) to provide as a parent or a guardian opportunities for education to his/her child or ward between the age of 6 to 14 years.

58. NITI Aayog is a Think tank for Government policy formulation. NITI Aayog too is a non-Constitutional, non-statutory body formed by a cabinet resolution. It is not accountable to parliament, and if line-ministries fail to achieve targets, NITI Aayog cannot punish them.

UGC-NET (JRF) Exam January, 2017*

PAPER–I

> **Note :**
> - This paper contains **Sixty (60)** multiple choice questions, each question carrying **two (2)** marks.
> - Candidate is expected to answer any **Fifty (50)** questions.
> - In case more than **Fifty (50)** questions are attempted, only the first **Fifty (50)** questions will be evaluated.

1. The principal of a school conducts an interview session of teachers and students with a view to explore the possibility of their enhanced participation in school programmes. This endeavour may be related to which type of research?
   A. Evaluation Research
   B. Fundamental Research
   C. Action Research
   D. Applied Research

2. In doing action research what is the usual sequence of steps?
   A. Reflect, observe, plan, act
   B. Plan, act, observe, reflect
   C. Plan, reflect, observe, act
   D. Act, observe, plan, reflect

3. Which sequence of research steps is logical in the list given below?
   A. Problem formulation, Analysis, Development of Research design, Hypothesis making, Collection of data, Arriving at generalizations and conclusions.
   B. Development of Research design, Hypothesis making, Problem formulation, Data analysis, Arriving at conclusions and data collection.
   C. Problem formulation, Hypothesis making, Development of a Research design, Collection of data, Data analysis and formulation of generalizations and conclusions.
   D. Problem formulation, Deciding about the sample and data collection tools, Formulation of hypothesis, Collection and interpretation of research evidence.

4. Below are given two sets – research methods (Set-I) and data collection tools (Set-II). Match the two sets and indicate your answer by selecting the correct code :

Set-I (Research Methods)	Set-II (Data Collection Tools)
(a) Experimental method	(i) Using primary and secondary sources
(b) Ex post-facto method	(ii) Questionnaire
(c) Descriptive survey method	(iii) Standardized tests
(d) Historical method	(iv) Typical characteristic tests

Codes:

	(a)	(b)	(c)	(d)
A.	(ii)	(i)	(iii)	(iv)
B.	(iii)	(iv)	(ii)	(i)
C.	(ii)	(iii)	(i)	(iv)
D.	(ii)	(iv)	(iii)	(i)

5. The issue of 'research ethics' may be considered pertinent at which stage of research?
   A. At the stage of problem formulation and its definition
   B. At the stage of defining the population of research
   C. At the stage of data collection and interpretation
   D. At the stage of reporting the findings.

6. In which of the following, reporting format is formally prescribed?
   A. Doctoral level thesis
   B. Conference of researchers
   C. Workshops and seminars
   D. Symposia

Read the following passage carefully and answer questions from 7 to 12:

The last great war, which nearly shook the foundations of the modern world, had little impact on Indian literature beyond aggravating the popular revulsion against violence and adding to the growing disillusionment with the 'humane pretensions' of the Western World. This was eloquently voiced in Tagore's later poems and his last testament, Crisis in Civilisation. The Indian intelligentsia was in a state of moral dilemma. On the one hand, it could not help sympathising with England's dogged courage in the hour of peril, with the Russians fighting with their backs to the wall against the ruthless Nazi hordes, and with China groaning under the heel of Japanese militarism; on the other hand, their own country was practically under military occupation of their own soil, and an Indian army under Subhas Bose was trying from the opposite camp to liberate their country. No creative impulse could issue from such confusion of loyalties. One would imagine that the achievement of Indian Independence in 1947, which came in the wake of the Allies' victory and was followed by the collapse of colonialism in the neighbouring countries of South-East Asia, would have released an upsurge of creative energy. No doubt it did, but unfortunately it was soon submerged in the great agony of partition, with its inhuman slaughter of the innocents and the uprooting of millions of people from their homeland, followed by the martyrdom of Mahatma Gandhi. These tragedies, along with Pakistan's invasion of Kashmir and its later atrocities in Bangladesh, did indeed provoke a poignant writing, particularly in the languages of the regions most affected, Bengali, Hindi, Kashmiri, Punjabi, Sindhi and Urdu. But poignant or passionate writing does not by itself make great literature. What reserves of enthusiasm and confidence survived these disasters have been mainly absorbed in the task of national reconstruction and economic development. Great literature has always emerged out of chains of convulsions. Indian literature is richer today in volume, range and variety than it ever was in the past.

Based on the passage answer the following questions from 7 to 12:

7. What was the impact of the last great war on Indian literature?
   A. It had no impact.
   B. It aggravated popular revulsion against violence.
   C. It shook the foundations of literature.
   D. It offered eloquent support to the Western World.

8. What did Tagore articulate in his last testament?
   A. Offered support to Subhas Bose.
   B. Exposed the humane pretensions of the Western World.
   C. Expressed loyalty to England.
   D. Encouraged the liberation of countries.

9. What was the stance of Indian intelligentsia during the period of great war?
   A. Indifference to Russia's plight.
   B. They favoured Japanese militarism.
   C. They prompted creativity out of confused loyalties.
   D. They expressed sympathy for England's dogged courage.

10. Identify the factor responsible for the submergence of creative energy in Indian literature.

A. Military occupation of one's own soil.
B. Resistance to colonial occupation.
C. Great agony of partition.
D. Victory of Allies.

11. What was the aftermath that survived tragedies in Kashmir and Bangladesh?
A. Suspicion of other countries
B. Continuance of rivalry
C. Menace of war
D. National reconstruction

12. The passage has the message that
A. Disasters are inevitable.
B. Great literature emerges out of chains of convulsions.
C. Indian literature does not have a marked landscape.
D. Literature has no relation with war and independence.

13. Effective communication pre-supposes
A. Non-alignment   B. Domination
C. Passivity   D. Understanding

14. When verbal and non-verbal messages are contradictory, it is said that most people believe in
A. indeterminate messages
B. verbal messages
C. non-verbal messages
D. aggressive messages

15. The typical feature of an information-rich classroom lecture is in the nature of being
A. Sedentary   B. Staggered
C. Factual   D. Sectoral

16. Expressive communication is driven by
A. Passive aggression
B. Encoder's personality characteristics
C. External clues
D. Encoder-decoder contract

17. Positive classroom communication leads to
A. Coercion   B. Submission
C. Confrontation   D. Persuasion

18. Classroom communication is the basis of
A. Social identity
B. External inanities

C. Biased passivity
D. Group aggression

19. The missing term in the series 1, 4, 27, 16, ?, 36, 343, ... is
A. 30   B. 49
C. 125   D. 81

20. The next term in the following series YEB, WFD, UHG, SKI, ? will be
A. TLO   B. QOL
C. QLO   D. GQP

21. If A is coded as C, M as I, N as P, S as O, I as A, P as N, E as M, O as E and C as S, then the code of COMPANIES will be
A. SPEINMOAC   B. NCPSEIOMA
C. SMOPIEACN   D. SEINCPAMO

22. Among the following, identify the continuous type of data:
A. Number of languages a person speaks
B. Number of children in a household
C. Population of cities
D. Weight of students in a class

23. Ali buys a glass, a pencil box and a cup and pays ₹ 21 to the shopkeeper. Rakesh buys a cup, two pencil boxes and a glass and pays ₹ 28 to the shopkeeper. Preeti buys two glasses, a cup and two pencil boxes and pays ₹ 35 to the shopkeeper. The cost of 10 cups will be
A. ₹ 40   B. ₹ 60
C. ₹ 80   D. ₹ 70

24. Out of four cities given below three are alike in some manner while the fourth one is different. Identify the odd one
A. Lucknow   B. Rishikesh
C. Allahabad   D. Patna

25. Given below are some characteristics of reasoning. Select the code that states a characteristic which is not of deductive reasoning:
A. The conclusion must be based on observation and experiment.
B. The conclusion should be supported by the premise/premises.
C. The conclusion must follow from the premise/premises necessarily.
D. The argument may be valid or invalid.

26. If two standard form categorical propositions with the same subject and predicate are related in such a manner that if one is undetermined the other must be undetermined, what is their relation?
    A. Contrary
    B. Subcontrary
    C. Contradictory
    D. Sub-altern

27. Men and woman may have different reproductive strategies but neither can be considered inferior or superior to the other, any more than a bird's wings can be considered superior or inferior to a fish's fins. What type of argument it is?
    A. Biological
    B. Physiological
    C. Analogical
    D. Hypothetical

28. Among the following propositions two are related in such a way that they cannot both be true but can both be false. Select the code that states those two propositions.
    Propositions:
    (a) Every student is attentive.
    (b) Some students are attentive.
    (c) Students are never attentive.
    (d) Some students are not attentive.
    Codes:
    A. (a) and (b)
    B. (a) and (c)
    C. (b) and (c)
    D. (c) and (d)

29. Given below are two premises (a) and (b). From those two premises four conclusions (i), (ii), (iii) & (iv) are drawn. Select the code that states the conclusions validly drawn from the premises (taking singly or jointly).

    Premises: (a) Untouchability is a curse.
    (b) All hot pans are untouchable.
    Conclusions:
    (i) All hot pans are curse.
    (ii) Some untouchable things are hot pans.
    (iii) All curses are untouchability.
    (iv) Some curses are untouchability.
    Codes:
    A. (i) and (ii)
    B. (ii) and (iii)
    C. (iii) and (iv)
    D. (ii) and (iv)

30. If the statement 'None but the brave wins the race' is false which of the following statements can be claimed to be true?

Select the correct code:
    A. All brave persons win the race.
    B. Some persons who win the race are not brave.
    C. Some persons who win the race are brave.
    D. No person who wins the race is brave.

The table below embodies data on the sales revenue (₹ in lakh) generated by a publishing house during the years 2012-15 while selling books, magazines and journals as three categories of items. Answer questions 31 – 33 based on the data contained in the table.

Items ↓ \ Year→	Sales Revenue (₹ in lakh)			
	2012	2013	2014	2015
Journals	46	47	45	44
Magazines	31	39	46	51
Books	73	77	78	78
Total				

31. In 2015, approximately what percent of total revenue came from books?
    A. 45%
    B. 55%
    C. 35%
    D. 25%

32. The number of years in which there was an increase in revenue from at least two categories of items, is
    A. 0
    B. 1
    C. 2
    D. 3

33. If the year 2016 were to show the same growth in terms of total sales revenue as the year 2015 over the year 2014, then the revenue in the year 2016 must be approximately:
    A. ₹ 194 lakh
    B. ₹ 187 lakh
    C. ₹ 172 lakh
    D. ₹ 177 lakh

A University professor maintains data on MCA students tabulated by performance and gender of the students. The data is kept on a computer hard disk, but accidently some of it is lost because of a computer virus. Only the following could be recovered:

Performance → / Gender ↓	Number of MCA Students			
	Average	Good	Excellent	Total
Male			10	
Female				32
Total		30		

Panic buttons were pressed but to no avail. An expert committee was formed, which decided that the following facts were self evident:

(a) Half the students were either excellent or good.

(b) 40% of the students were females.

(c) One-third of the male students were average.

Answer questions 34 – 36 based on the data given above:

34. How many female students are excellent?
- A. 0
- B. 8
- C. 16
- D. 32

35. What proportion of female students are good?
- A. 0
- B. 0.25
- C. 0.50
- D. 0.75

36. Approximately, what proportion of good students are male?
- A. 0
- B. 0.73
- C. 0.43
- D. 0.27

37. Which of the following statement(s) is/are TRUE?

S1: The decimal number 11 is larger than the hexadecimal number 11.

S2: In the binary number 1110.101, the fractional part has the decimal value as 0.625.
- A. S1 only
- B. S2 only
- C. Both S1 and S2
- D. Neither S1 nor S2

38. Read the following two statements:

I: Information and Communication Technology (ICT) is considered a subset of Information Technology (IT).

II: The 'right to use' a piece of software is termed as copyright.

Which of the above statement(s) is/are CORRECT?
- A. Both I and II
- B. Neither I nor II
- C. II only
- D. I only

39. Which of the following correctly lists computer memory types from highest to lowest speed?
- A. Secondary Storage; Main Memory (RAM); Cache Memory; CPU Registers
- B. CPU Registers; Cache Memory; Secondary Storage; Main Memory (RAM)
- C. CPU Registers; Cache Memory; Main Memory (RAM); Secondary Storage
- D. Cache Memory; CPU Registers; Main Memory (RAM); Secondary Storage

40. Which of the following is a characteristic of Web2.0 applications?
- A. Multiple users schedule their time to use Web2.0 applications one by one.
- B. Web2.0 applications are focused on the ability for people to collaborate and share information online.
- C. Web2.0 applications provide users with content rather than facilitating users to create it.
- D. Web2.0 applications use only static pages.

41. With regard to a word processing software, the process of combining static information in a publication together with variable information in a data source to create one merged publication is called
- A. Electronic mail
- B. Data sourcing
- C. Mail merge
- D. Spam mail

42. DVD technology uses an optical media to store the digital data. DVD is an acronym for
- A. Digital Vector Disc
- B. Digital Volume Disc
- C. Digital Versatile Disc
- D. Digital Visualization Disc

43. **Assertion (A):** Sustainable development is critical to well being of human society.

Reason (R): Environmentally sound policies do not harm the environment or deplete the natural resources.

Choose the correct code:
A. Both (A) and (R) are correct and (R) is the correct explanation of (A).
B. Both (A) and (R) are correct, but (R) is not the correct explanation of (A).
C. (A) is true, but (R) is false.
D. (A) is false, but (R) is true.

44. The dominant source of pollution due to oxides of nitrogen (NO_x) in urban areas is
A. road transport
B. commercial sector
C. energy use in industry
D. power plants

45. Which of the following is **not** a water-brone disease?
A. Typhoid   B. Hepatitis
C. Cholera   D. Dengue

46. Indian government's target for power production from small hydro projects by the year 2022 is
A. 1 Giga-Watt   B. 5 Giga-Watt
C. 10 Giga-Watt   D. 15 Giga-Watt

47. In which country, the recent international agreement on phasing out Hydro Fluoro Carbons (HFCs) was signed?
A. Rwanda   B. Morocco
C. South Africa   D. Algeria

48. Which of the following natural hazards is **not** hydro-meteorological?
A. Snow avalanche   B. Sea erosion
C. Tropical cyclone   D. Tsunami

49. Which of the following are the demerits of globalisation of higher education?
(a) Exposure to global curriculum
(b) Promotion of elitism in education
(c) Commodification of higher education
(d) Increase in the cost of education

Select the correct answer from the codes given below:
Codes:
A. (a) and (d)   B. (a), (c) and (d)
C. (b), (c) and (d)   D. (a), (b), (c) and (d)

50. Which of the following statements are correct about Deemed Universities?

(a) The Governor of the State is the chancellor of Deemed Universities.
(b) They can design their own syllabus and course work.
(c) They can frame their own guidelines regarding admission and fees.
(d) They can grant degrees.

Select the correct answer from the codes given below:
Codes:
A. (a), (b) and (c)   B. (b), (c) and (d)
C. (a), (c) and (d)   D. (a), (b), (c) and (d)

51. The purpose of value education is best served by focussing on
A. Cultural practices prevailing in the society.
B. Norms of conduct laid down by a social group.
C. Concern for human values.
D. Religious and moral practices and instructions.

52. Which of the following statements are correct?
(a) Rajya Sabha is a Permanent House which can be dissolved only during national emergency.
(b) Rajya Sabha does not represent the local interests of the States.
(c) Members of the Rajya Sabha are not bound to vote at the dictates of the states they represent.
(d) No Union territory has a representative in the Rajya Sabha.

Select the correct answer from the codes given below:
Codes:
A. (a) and (d)   B. (b) and (c)
C. (b), (c) and (d)   D. (a), (b), (c) and (d)

53. Which of the following are not necessarily the immediate consequences of the proclamation of the President's Rule in a State?
(a) Dissolution of the State Assembly.
(b) Removal of the Council of Ministers in the State.
(c) Takeover of the State administration by the Union Government.
(d) Appointment of a new Chief Secretary.

Select the correct answer from the codes given below:

Codes:

A. (*a*) and (*d*)   B. (*a*), (*b*) and (*c*)
C. (*a*), (*b*), (*c*) and (*d*) D. (*b*) and (*c*)

54. Instead of holding the office during the pleasure of the President who among the following hold(s) office during good behaviour?
(*a*) Governor of a State
(*b*) Attorney General of India
(*c*) Judges of the High Court
(*d*) Administrator of a Union Territory

Select the correct answer from the codes given below:

Codes:

A. (*a*) only   B. (*c*) only
C. (*a*) and (*c*)   D. (*a*), (*b*), (*c*) and (*d*)

55. Which of the following set of statements represents acceptable propositions in respect of teaching-learning relationships ? Choose the correct code to indicate your answer.
(*i*) When students fail in a test, it is the teacher who fails.
(*ii*) Every teaching must aim at ensuring learning.
(*iii*) There can be teaching without learning taking place.
(*iv*) There can be no learning without teaching.
(*v*) A teacher teaches but learns also.
(*vi*) Real learning implies rote learning.

Codes:

A. (*ii*), (*iii*), (*iv*) and (*v*)
B. (*i*), (*ii*), (*iii*) and (*v*)
C. (*iii*), (*iv*), (*v*) and (*vi*)
D. (*i*), (*ii*), (*v*) and (*vi*)

56. **Assertion (A):** Learning is a life long process.

Reason (R) : Learning to be useful must be linked with life processes.

Choose the correct answer from the following code:
A. Both (A) and (R) are true and (R) is the correct explanation of (A).
B. Both (A) and (R) are true, but (R) is not the correct explanation of (A).
C. (A) is true, but (R) is false.
D. (A) is false, but (R) is true.

57. Effectiveness of teaching has to be judged in terms of
A. Course coverage
B. Students' interest
C. Learning outcomes of students
D. Use of teaching aids in the classroom

58. In which teaching method learner's participation is made optimal and proactive ?
A. Discussion method
B. Buzz session method
C. Brainstorming session method
D. Project method

59. One of the most powerful factors affecting teaching effectiveness is related to the
A. Social system of the country
B. Economic status of the society
C. Prevailing political system
D. Educational system

60. **Assertion (A):** Formative evaluation tends to accelerate the pace of learning.

Reason (R): As against summative evaluation, formative evaluation is highly reliable.

Choose the correct answer from the following code :
A. Both (A) and (R) are true and (R) is the correct explanation of (A).
B. Both (A) and (R) are true, but (R) is not the correct explanation of (A).
C. (A) is true, but (R) is false.
D. (A) is false, but (R) is true.

ANSWERS

1	2	3	4	5	6	7	8	9	10
C	B	C	B	C	A	B	B	D	C
11	12	13	14	15	16	17	18	19	20
D	B	D	C	C	B	D	A	C	B

21	22	23	24	25	26	27	28	29	30
D	D	D	A	A	C	C	B	D	B
31	32	33	34	35	36	37	38	39	40
A	C	D	A	B	B	B	B	C	B
41	42	43	44	45	46	47	48	49	50
C	C	B	A	D	B	A	D	C	B
51	52	53	54	55	56	57	58	59	60
C	B	A	B	B	A	C	D	D	C

EXPLANATORY ANSWERS

1. **Action Research:** Action research is focused on immediate application, not on the development of theory or on general application. It emphasises on a problem here and now in a local setting. Its findings are to be evaluated in terms of local applicability, not universal validity. "Its purpose is to improve school practices and to improve those who try to improve the practices, to combine the research processes, habits of thinking, ability to work harmoniously with others, and professional spirit".

   In the field of action research a teacher conducts action research to improve his own teaching. A school administrator conducts action research to improve his administrative behaviour. In action research, the teacher is deliberately more scientific and careful in diagnosing the problem, in collecting facts, in designing hypotheses in experiments with tentative practices and actions, and in evaluating results of the actions taken. He tries to keep experimental approach towards problem solving in close touch with reality. The action-research may be individual or co-operative. But it is found that ultimately utilitarian considerations infiltrate into the high level investigations and pollute the spirit of pure research.

2. Action research is a process by which change and understanding can be pursued at the same time. The action learning process involves a sequence of steps: plan, act, observe and reflect. This sequence should be repeated as many times as necessary to deal with a particular problem.

   Action research, therefore, is practical and it involves the actual workings of people in their workplace, learning from their results so that future problem solving is made more effective.

3. The various steps of research are:
   - formulation of the problem
   - literature study
   - aims, objectives and formulation of the hypothesis
   - research design (methods)
   - research techniques
   - sampling
   - collection of data
   - data analysis
   - the writing and critical evaluation of reports.

5. **Ethical Issues in Data Analysis and Interpretation**

   Data analysis is making sense of the data and interpreting them appropriately so as to not mislead readers. The ethical issue is not about a researcher's honest error or honest differences of data interpretation; rather, it is in regard to the intent to deceive others or misrepresent one's work. Examples of such misconduct include using inappropriate statistical techniques or other methods of measurement to enhance the significance of your research or interpreting your results in a way that supports your opinions and biases. These are ethical issues of fabrication and falsification of data.

Fabrication is making up data or results, and *falsification* is changing data or results to deliberately distort them and then including them in your research report.

13. **Understanding the process:** Important element for effective communication is the need to understand how the process of communication works, *i.e.*, the principles and tools of communication. To appreciate the various steps involved in communication in terms of encoding, decoding, transmission, comprehension, feedback, etc., it is necessary to have a good understanding of the mode, channels, types, instruments, methods and barriers relating to communication and the factors affecting it. Good communicators like good artists, use their tools effectively.

14. Most people believe that nonverbal communication is more reliable than verbal communication in expressing true feelings. This is especially the case when verbal and nonverbal messages are inconsistent. If you say you feel fine, but you are slumping and the corners of your mouth are turned down, others probably will not believe your verbal message.

The fact that people tend to believe nonverbal behaviours doesn't mean that nonverbal behaviours actually are honest or that we can interpret them reliably. It's possible for people to manipulate nonverbal communication, just as we manipulate our verbal communication. Politicians are coached not only in how to speak but also in how to use nonverbal communication to bolster images.

16. Communication is receptive or expressive. Receptive communication is the ability to understand or comprehend communication. Expressive communication means being able to put thoughts into words and sentences. Generally, receptive communication is in advance of expressive communication. Both receptive and expressive communication are supported by a Total Communication Environment.

18. **Classroom communication;** the process by which someone who has a purpose to accomplish, say a teacher, tries to convey something to get someone else, say a student, to act for the achievement of the purpose. Communication involves both exchanging information and transmitting meaning.

19.

1	4	27	16	?	36	343
↓	↓	↓	↓	↓	↓	↓
1^3	2^2	3^3	4^2	5^3	6^2	7^3

Hence, 125 will come at the place of question mark.

20. Y E B   W F D   U HG   S KI   Q OL

Hence, QOL will come at the place of question mark.

21.

A	M	N	S	I	P	E	O	C
↓	↓	↓	↓	↓	↓	↓	↓	↓
C	I	P	O	A	N	M	E	S

C	O	M	P	A	N	I	E	S
↓	↓	↓	↓	↓	↓	↓	↓	↓
S	E	I	N	C	P	A	M	O

Hence, code of COMPANIES will be SEINCPAMO.

22. **Continuous data:** The data which can take any value between two whole numbers are called continuous data. For example,

Weight of students of a class: 42 kg, 45.030 kg, 47.250 kg, 55 kg

Height of students : 145 cm, 151.50 cm, 147.25 cm, 155.49 cm

Measurement of rainfall on differenct days: 30 mm, 32 mm, 35.23 mm, 34.50 mm

Temperature on different days : 25°C, 23.5°C, 32.4°C, 28.7°C.

23. 1 glass + 1 pencil box + 1 cup = 21   ...(*i*)
1 glass + 2 pencil box + 1 cup = 28   ...(*ii*)
2 glass + 2 pencil box + 1 cup = 35   ...(*iii*)

Eqns. (*ii*) – (*i*) gives

Cost of 1 pencil box = 28 – 21 = ₹ 7

Eqns. (*iii*) – (*ii*) gives

Cost of 1 glass = 35 – 28 = ₹ 7

Cost of 1 glass + 1 pencil box + 1 cup = ₹ 21

$$7 + 7 + 1 \text{ cup} = 21$$

Cost of 1 cup = 21 – 14 = ₹ 7

∴ Cost of 10 cups = ₹ 7 × 10

$$= ₹ 70.$$

24. Except Lucknow, other three are situated on the bank of river Ganga.

25. Aristotle identified two fundamental forms of reasoning: inductive and deductive. With either form, there are premises that lead to a conclusion. If the conclusion follows necessarily from the premises and contains no new information, the reasoning is deductive. For example, start with the premise that all lawsuits for personal injury are barred unless filed within three years of the injury. If, as a second premise, it is established that John Jones's lawsuit was filed four years after his injury, it follows necessarily that John Jones's lawsuit is time barred. This argument is based on deductive reasoning. If the premises are true, the conclusion is always true. Thus, in a deductive argument the focus is always on the premises. Once the premises are established as true, the argument is won.

In inductive arguments, focus on the inference. When a conclusion relies upon an inference and contains new information not found in the premises, the reasoning is inductive. For example, if premises were established that the defendant slurred his words, stumbled as he walked, and smelled of alcohol, you might reasonably infer the conclusion that the defendant was drunk. This is inductive reasoning. In an inductive argument the conclusion is, at best, probable. The conclusion is not always true when the premises are true. The probability of the conclusion depends on the strength of the inference from the premises, Thus, when dealing with inductive reasoning,

pay special attention to the inductive leap or inference by which the conclusion follows from the premises.

27. Analogical reasoning is simply reasoning from an analogy. In other words, it is making an argument by comparing two cases. When using analogical reasoning, it is important that the cases are comparable. Remember, although two cases or situations may be very similar, they are never identical. To remedy this situation, once again we suggest using inoculation. You should point out the differences and minimize them. Recently, a small business owner argued in front of the city council that the town should not support a smoking ban in restaurants. He believed that decisions about smoking should be left to the individual business owner. He based his argument on an analogy comparing the limitation of civil liberties when the Nazis first came to power in Germany with the restriction of civil liberties that this ban represented. He stressed that a ban on smoking was among the Nazis' new laws. He also pointed out that he wasn't trying to compare those that supported the ban to Nazis but that the restrictions were similar, His argument was partially persuasive as he was a nonsmoker who had made the choice as a business owner not to allow smoking in his establishment.

31. Required % = $\dfrac{78}{173} \times 100$

$$= \dfrac{7800}{173} = 45\% \text{ (Approx.)}$$

32. 2014   45 - 46 - 78

2015   44 - 51 - 78

33. Revenue in 2015 = 44 + 51 + 78

$$= 173 \text{ lakh}$$

Revenue in 2014 = 45 + 46 + 78

$$= 169 \text{ lakh}$$

Difference = 173 – 169 = 4 lakh

∴ Revenue in 2016 = 173 + 4 = 177 lakh.

37. Hexadecimal number 11 to decimal

$$(11)_{16} = 1 \times 16^1 + 1 \times 16^0.$$

Obviously this will be much bigger than decimal number 11. So first statement (S1) is wrong. In second statement, we've to find the decimal value of $(0.101)_2$

So,

$$1 \times 2^{-1} + 0 \times 2^{-2} + 1 \times 2^{-3}$$
$$= 0.5 + 0 + 0.125$$
$$= 0.625$$

Hence, second statement (S2) is right.

39.	Cache memory	It's extremely fast compared to main memory (RAM).
	CPU registers	They're part of the Control unit and ALU rather than the memory. Hence their contents can be handled much faster than any content of memory.
	Secondary storage	Operating speed is slower than of main memory (RAM).

So, accordingly speed wise: CPU registers > Cache > RAM > secondary memory.

41. **Mail Merge:** The process of merging information into a main document from a data source, such as an address book or database, to create customized documents, such as form letters or mailing labels.

42. **Digital Versatile Disc (DVD):** Also referred to as digital video *disc*. For some people, the *acronym* itself has become its name. Although it has the same dimensions of a *compact disc,* it has higher capacities. A DVD is double-sided; a CD is single-sided.

45. **Vector-borne diseases:** Flies are common culprits that breed diseases. Flies may sit on dirt and garbage when pathogens stick to their bodies. If food is left uncovered, the flies carrying germs sit on it and contaminate it. Drinking water may get contaminated by sewage. Consuming such contaminated food and water causes diseases. Insects like flies and mosquitoes are vectors or carriers of various diseases like malaria and dengue. Malaria is actually caused by a pathogen called *Plasmodium* which is transmitted by the female *Anopheles* mosquito. Dengue is caused by the dengue virus and spread by female *Aedes* mosquito.

48. **Hydro-meteorological hazards:** These hazards are of atmospheric, hydrological or oceanographic nature. Hydro-meteorological hazards include: floods, debris and mud floods; tropical cyclones, storm surges, thunder/hailstorms, rain and wind storms, blizzards and other severe storms, drought, desertification, wild land fires, temperature extremes, sand or dust storms; permafrost and snow or ice avalanches. Hydro-meteorological hazards can be single, sequential or combined in their origin and effects.

50. Deemed University is a status granted to high performing institutes and departments of various universities by the Ministry of Human Resource Development on the advice of the University Grants Commission (UGC).

The Deemed University status allows not just full autonomy in setting course work and syllabus, but also allows it to set its own guidelines for the admissions and fees.

Parent universities may award degrees but cannot control the administration of these Deemed Universities, many of whom also award degrees under their own name.

Most Deemed Universities are affiliated to the UGC or the All India Council of Technical Education and are known and recognized for their quality education.

51. Mere academic knowledge without deep rooting in human values will only give rise to personalities who may become rich in material possessions, but will remain poor in self-understanding, peace and social concern. Emphasizing value education Swami Vivekananda said,

"Excess of knowledge and power, without Values, make human beings devils."

Value education is important to help everyone in improving the value system that he/she holds and put hem to use. Once, everyone has understood their values in life they can examine and control the various choice they make in their life. Thus, value education is always essential to shape one's life and to give him an opportunity of performing himself on the global stage. Value education teaches us that how we do things is more important to our well-being than what we do.

54. The executive holds office during the pleasure of the President. This is true of the civil servants and the Armed Forces. Even for Governors. But the judges are not subject to the doctrine of pleasure. They hold office during good behaviour. The doctrine of pleasure is destructive of independence.

56. With the changing world and globalization, the learning needs of the society around us are also changing. The society is no longer the traditional learning society but has emerged as a "lifelong learning society". The world today realizes the fact that learning occurs at all stages of life, in different forms and in variety of arenas. Learning never ceases and continues till death, hence the concept of 'cradle-to-grave' for lifelong learning gains prominence in the present day world and work environment. Thus we can say that the present society around us is a knowledge society; it is

a human society in which thrust is on knowledge for justice, solidarity, democracy and peace. This is a society in which knowledge is a force for changing society.

Lifelong education covers "formal, non-formal and informal patterns of learning throughout the life cycle of an individual for the conscious and continuous enhancement of the quality of life, his own and that of society". Lifelong learning is the provision or use of both formal and informal learning opportunities throughout people's lives in order to foster the continuous development and improvement of the knowledge and skills needed for employment and personal fulfillment.

57. Teaching effectiveness is a complex and multifactorial concept that involves the teaching – learning dynamics between faculty and students and assessment of students' learning outcomes. To achieve excellence in teaching, faculty analyze feedback from a variety of resources to improve effectiveness, adjust teaching methods according to diverse needs of learners, evaluate teaching effectiveness using valid and reliable instruments, and mentor novice educators to the academic role.

58. In project work-student has an important role to play starting from planning stage to reporting stage. It provides him experiential learning.

UGC-NET (JRF) Exam November, 2017*

PAPER–I

> **Note :** • This paper consists of **Fifty (50)** objective type questions of **two (2)** marks each. All questions are compulsory. **(50 × 2 = 100 marks.)**

1. Which of the following set of statements best represents the nature and objective of teaching and learning?
   (a) Teaching is like selling and learning is like buying.
   (b) Teaching is a social act while learning is a personal act.
   (c) Teaching implies learning whereas learning does not imply teaching.
   (d) Teaching is a kind of delivery of knowledge while learning is like receiving it.
   (e) Teaching is an interaction and is triadic in nature whereas learning is an active engagement in a subject domain.
   Code:
   A. (a), (d) and (e)
   B. (b), (c) and (e)
   C. (a), (b) and (c)
   D. (a), (b) and (d)

2. From the list given below identify the learner characteristics which would facilitate teaching learning system to become effective. Choose the correct code to indicate your answer.
   (a) Prior experience of learner
   (b) Learner's family lineage
   (c) Aptitude of the learner
   (d) Learner's stage of development
   (e) Learner's food habits and hobbies
   (f) Learner's religious affiliation

   Code:
   A. (a), (c) and (d)
   B. (d), (e) and (f)
   C. (a), (d) and (e)
   D. (b), (c) and (f)

3. **Assertion (A):** All teaching implies learning.
   Reason (R) : Learning to be useful must be derived from teaching.

   Choose the correct answer from the following:
   A. Both (A) and (R) are true and (R) is the correct explanation of (A).
   B. Both (A) and (R) are true, but (R) is not the correct explanation of (A).
   C. (A) is true, but (R) is false.
   D. (A) is false, but (R) is true.

4. On the basis of summative tests, a teacher is interpreting his/her students, performance in terms of their wellness life style evident in behaviour. This will be called:
   A. Formative testing
   B. Continuous and comprehensive evaluation
   C. Norm-referenced testing
   D. Criterion-referenced testing

5. Which one of the following is a key behaviour in effective teaching?
   A. Using student ideas and contribution
   B. Structuring
   C. Instructional variety
   D. Questioning

6. Which of the following research types focuses on ameliorating the prevailing situations?
A. Fundamental Research
B. Applied Research
C. Action Research
D. Experimental Research

7. A researcher attempts to evaluate the effect of method of feeding on anxiety - proneness of children. Which method of research would be appropriate for this?
A. Case study method
B. Experimental method
C. Ex-post-facto method
D. Survey method

8. In which of the following arrangements a wider spectrum of ideas and issues may be made possible?
A. Research Article
B. Workshop mode
C. Conference
D. Symposium

9. In finalizing a thesis writing format which of the following would form part of supplementary pages?
A. List of tables and figures
B. Table of contents
C. Conclusions of the study
D. Bibliography and Appendices

10. Which of the following is susceptible to the issue of research ethics?
A. Inaccurate application of statistical techniques
B. Faulty research design
C. Choice of sampling techniques
D. Reporting of research findings

Directions (Qs. No. 11-15): *Read the passage carefully and answer the questions.*

Climate change is considered to be one of the most serious threats to sustainable development, with adverse impacts on the environment, human health, food security, economic activity, natural resources and physical infrastructure. Global climate varies naturally.

According to the Intergovernmental Panel on Climate Change (IPCC), the effects of climate change have already been observed, and scientific findings indicate that precautionary and prompt action is necessary. Vulnerability to climate change is not just a function of geography or dependence on natural resources; it also has social, economic and political dimensions which influence how climate change affects different groups.

Poor people rarely have insurance to cover loss of property due to natural calamities *i.e.,* drought, floods, super cyclones etc. The poor communities are already struggling to cope with the existing challenges of poverty and climate variability and climate change could push many beyond their ability to cope or even survive. It is vital that these communities are helped to adapt to the changing dynamics of nature. Adaptation is a process through which societies make themselves better able to cope with an uncertain future.

Adapting to climate change entails taking the right measures to reduce the negative effects of climate change (or exploit the positive ones) by making the appropriate adjustments and changes. These range from technological options such as increased sea defences or flood - proof houses on stilts to behavioural change at the individual level, such as reducing water use in times of drought. Other strategies include early warning systems for extreme events, better water management, improved risk management, various insurance options and biodiversity conservation. Because of the speed at which climate change is happening due to global temperature rise, it is urgent that the vulnerability of developing countries to climate change is reduced and their capacity to adapt is increased and national adaptation plans are implemented. Adapting to climate change will entail adjustments and changes at every level from community to national and international.

Communities must build their resilience, including adopting appropriate technologies while making the most of traditional knowledge, and diversifying their livelihoods to cope with current and future climate stress. Local coping strategies and knowledge need to be used in synergy with government and local interventions. The need of adaptation interventions depends on national circumstances. There is a large body of knowledge and experience within local communities on coping with climatic variability and extreme weather events. Local communities have always aimed to adapt to variations in their climate. To do so, they have made preparations based on their resources and their knowledge accumulated through experience of past weather patterns.

This includes times when they have also been forced to react to and recover from extreme events, such as floods, drought and hurricanes. Local coping strategies are an important element of planning for adaptation. Climate change is leading communities to experience climatic extremes more frequently, as well as new climate conditions and extremes. Traditional knowledge can help to provide efficient, appropriate and time-tested ways of advising and enabling adaptation to climate change in communities who are feeling the effects of climate changes due to global warming.

11. Given below are the factors of vulnerability of poor people to climate change. Select the code that contains the correct answer.
   (a) Their dependence on natural resources
   (b) Geographical attributes
   (c) Lack of financial resources
   (d) Lack of traditional knowledge
   Code:
   A. (a), (b) and (c)   B. (b), (c) and (d)
   C. (a), (b), (c) and (d) D. (c) only

12. Adaptation as a process enables societies to cope with:
   (a) An uncertain future
   (b) Adjustments and changes
   (c) Negative impact of climate change
   (d) Positive impact of climate change

   Select the most appropriate answer from the following code:
   A. (a), (b), (c) and (d) B. (a) and (c)
   C. (b), (c) and (d)   D. (c) only

13. To address the challenge of climate change, developing countries urgently require:
   A. Imposition of climate change tax
   B. Implementation of national adaptation policy at their level
   C. Adoption of short-term plans
   D. Adoption of technological solutions

14. The traditional knowledge should be used through:
   A. Its dissemination
   B. Improvement in national circumstances
   C. Synergy between government and local interventions
   D. Modern technology

15. The main focus of the passage is on:
   A. Combining traditional knowledge with appropriate technology
   B. Co-ordination between regional and national efforts
   C. Adaptation to climate change
   D. Social dimensions of climate change

16. The interaction between a teacher and students creates a zone of proximal:
   A. Difference   B. Confusion
   C. Development   D. Distortion

17. The spatial audio reproduction in a classroom can reduce the students:
   A. Cognitive load in understanding
   B. Respect for the teacher
   C. Motivation for excellence
   D. Interest in technology-orientation

18. The classroom communication should essentially be:
   A. Contrived
   B. Empathetic
   C. Abstract
   D. Non-descriptive

19. A good communicator begins his/her presentation with a:
   A. Complex question
   B. Non-sequitur
   C. Repetitive phrase
   D. Ice-breaker

20. In a classroom, the probability of message reception can be enhanced by:
A. Establishing a viewpoint
B. Exposing the ignorance of students
C. Increasing the information load
D. Using high decibel audio tools

21. In the series 1, 6, 15, 28, 45, ... the next term will be:
A. 66
B. 76
C. 56
D. 84

22. The next term in the series ABD, DGK, HMS, MTB, ... is:
A. NSA
B. SBL
C. PSK
D. RUH

23. In certain code, "COVALENT" is coded as BWPDUOFM. The code of "ELEPHANT" will be:
A. MFUIQRTW
B. QMUBIADH
C. QFMFUOBI
D. EPHNTEAS

24. Ajay is a friend of Rakesh. Pointing to an old man Ajay asked Rakesh who is he? Rakesh said "His son is my son's uncle". The old man is related to Rakesh as:
A. Grandfather
B. Father-in-law
C. Father
D. Uncle

25. A postman walked 20 m straight from his office, turned right and walked 10 m. After turning left he walked 10 m and after turning right walked 20 m. He again turned right and walked 70 m. How far he is from his office?
A. 50 m
B. 40 m
C. 60 m
D. 20 m

26. It is Truism to say that no one was there when life first appeared on earth. Any assertion about life's origin, thus, should be treated as a theory. The above two statements constitute:
A. A historical explanation
B. A narrative
C. An argument
D. A conjecture

27. Given below are four statements. Among them two are related in such a way that they can both be true but they cannot both be false. Select the code that indicates those two statements:
Statements:
(a) Honest people never suffer.
(b) Almost all honest people do suffer.
(c) Honest people hardly suffer.
(d) Each and every honest person suffers.
Code:
A. (a) and (b)
B. (a) and (c)
C. (a) and (d)
D. (b) and (c)

28. A deductive argument is invalid if:
A. Its premises and conclusion are all true.
B. Its premises and conclusion are all false.
C. Its premises are all false but its conclusion is true.
D. Its premises are all true but its conclusion is false.

29. Given below are two premises (a and b). From those two premises four conclusions (i), (ii), (iii) and (iv) are drawn. Select the code that states the conclusion/conclusions drawn validly (taking the premises singularly or jointly).
Premises   : (a) All bats are mammals.
            (b) No birds are bats.
Conclusions: (i) No birds are mammals.
            (ii) Some birds are not mammals.
            (iii) No bats are birds.
            (iv) All mammals are bats.
Code:
A. (i) only
B. (i) and (ii) only
C. (iii) only
D. (iii) and (iv) only

30. Just as melting ice-cubes do not cause a glass of water to overflow, melting sea-ice does not increase oceanic volume.
What type of argument is it?
A. Analogical
B. Hypothetical
C. Psychological
D. Statistical

Directions (Qs. No. 31-35): *Answer the questions based on the data given in the table below.*

Table: Number of registered vehicles in India and India's population.

Year	Total vehicles (Lakhs)	Two wheelers (Lakhs)	Cars, Jeeps, Taxis (Lakhs)	Buses (Lakhs)	Goods vehicles (Lakhs)	Others (Lakhs)	Population (India) (Millions)
1961	6.65	0.88	3.1	0.57	1.68	0.42	439.23
1971	18.65	5.76	6.82	0.94	3.43	1.70	548.15
1981	53.91	26.18	11.60	1.62	5.54	8.97	683.32
1991	213.74	142.00	29.54	3.31	13.56	25.33	846.42
2001	549.91	385.56	70.58	6.34	29.48	57.95	1028.73
2011	1417.58	1018.65	191.23	16.04	70.64	121.02	1210.19

31. The maximum decadal growth in population of India is registered in the period:
    A. 1961 - 1971
    B. 1991 - 2001
    C. 2001 - 2011
    D. 1981 - 1991

32. In which year the decadal growth (%) in number of cars surpassed that of the two wheelers?
    A. 1991   B. 2001
    C. 1981   D. 2011

33. What was the average decadal growth in the number of cars during 1961 - 2011?
    A. ~ 131%   B. ~ 68%
    C. ~ 217%   D. ~ 157%

34. In the year 2001, out of total number of vehicles, the number of passenger vehicles (4 wheelers) accounted for:
    A. ~ 14%   B. ~ 24%
    C. ~ 31%   D. ~ 43%

35. What was the per capita ownership of two wheelers in India in the year 2011?
    A. ~ 0.084%   B. ~ 0.0084%
    C. ~ 0.84%   D. ~ 0.068%

36. What is the name for a webpage address?
    A. Domain   B. Directory
    C. Protocol   D. URL

37. The data storage hierarchy consists of:
    A. Bytes, bits, fields, records, files and databases
    B. Bits, bytes, fields, records, files and databases
    C. Bits, bytes, records, fields, files and databases
    D. Bits, bytes, fields, files, records and databases

38. Which of the following domains is used for - profit businesses?
    A. .org   B. .net
    C. .edu   D. .com

39. What is the full form of USB as used in computer related activities?
    A. Ultra Security Block
    B. Universal Security Block
    C. Universal Serial Bus
    D. United Serial Bus

40. Which of the following represents billion characters?
    A. Terabytes   B. Megabytes
    C. Kilobytes   D. Gigabytes

41. Which of the following pollutants is the major cause of respiratory diseases?
    A. Suspended fine particles
    B. Nitrogen oxides
    C. Carbon monoxide
    D. Volatile organic compounds

42. Assertion (A): In urban areas, smog episodes occur frequently in winters.

Reason (R) : In winters, a lot of biomass is burnt by people for heating purposes or to keep themselves warm.

Choose the correct answer from the code given below:

A. Both (A) and (R) are true and (R) is the correct explanation of (A)

B. Both (A) and (R) are true, but (R) is not the correct explanation of (A)

C. (A) is true and (R) is false

D. Both (A) and (R) are false

43. Occurrence of natural hazards is affected by:
(a) Land use changes
(b) Drainage and construction
(c) Ozone depletion
(d) Climate change

Choose the correct answer from the code given below:
A. (a), (c) and (d)
B. (a), (b) and (c)
C. (a), (b) and (d)
D. (b), (c) and (d)

44. Which of the following pollutant gases is **not** produced both naturally and as a result of industrial activity?
A. Chlorofluoro carbon
B. Nitrous oxide
C. Methane
D. Carbon dioxide

45. Among the following fuels of energy, which is the most environment friendly?
A. Ethanol   B. Biogas
C. CNG   D. Hydrogen

46. Which of the following are the goals of higher education in India?
(a) Access
(b) Equity
(c) Quality and Excellence
(d) Relevance

(e) Value based education
(f) Compulsory and free education

Select the correct answer from the code given below:
A. (a), (b) and (e) only
B. (a), (b), (e) and (f)
C. (a), (b), (c), (d) and (e)
D. (a), (b), (c), (d), (e) and (f)

47. Which of the following has been ranked the best college in the country (2017) as per the National Institutional Ranking Framework (NIRF)?
A. Miranda House, Delhi
B. St. Stephen's College, Delhi
C. Fergusson College, Pune
D. Maharaja's College, Mysore

48. Which of the following universities has received the Visitor's Award for the best Central University in India in Feb. 2017?
A. Jawaharlal Nehru University
B. Banaras Hindu University
C. Tezpur University
D. University of Hyderabad

49. Who among the following can be removed by the President without Parliament's resolution?
A. Judge of a High Court
B. Governor of a State
C. Chief Election Commissioner
D. Comptroller and Auditor-General

50. Which of the following come(s) within the ambit of the term 'corruption'?
(a) Misuse of official position
(b) Deviation from rules, laws and norms
(c) Non-action when action is required
(d) Harm to public good

Select the correct answer from the code given below:
A. (a) only
B. (a) and (b) only
C. (a), (b) and (d)
D. (a), (b), (c) and (d)

ANSWERS

1	2	3	4	5	6	7	8	9	10
B	A	C	D	C	C	C	C	D	D

11	12	13	14	15	16	17	18	19	20
A	A	B	C	C	C	A	B	D	A

21	22	23	24	25	26	27	28	29	30
A	B	C	C	A	C	D	D	C	A

31	32	33	34	35	36	37	38	39	40
A	D	A	A	*	D	B	D	C	D

41	42	43	44	45	46	47	48	49	50
A	B	C	A	D	C	A	A	B	D

Error in Questions

EXPLANATORY ANSWERS

4. A **criterion-referenced test** is a style of test which uses test scores to generate a statement about the behaviour that can be expected of a person with that score.

Most tests and quizzes that are written by school teachers can be considered criterion-referenced tests.

Criterion-referenced tests (or CRTs) differ in that each examinee's performance is compared to a pre-defined set of criteria or a standard. The goal with these tests is to determine whether or not the candidate has the demonstrated mastery of a certain skill or set of skills.

5. Key behaviours for effective teaching and some indicators pertaining to them are the following:

- **Lesson clarity:** Logical, step-by-step order; clear and audible delivery free of distracting mannerisms.

- **Instructional variety:** Variability in instructional materials, questioning, types of feedback, and teaching strategies.

- **Task orientation:** Achievement (content) orientation as opposed to process orientation, maximum content coverage, and time devoted to instruction.

- **Student engagement:** Limiting opportunities for distraction and getting students to work on, think through, and inquire about the content.

- **Success rate:** 60% to 70% of time spent on tasks that afford moderate-to-high levels of success, especially during expository or didactic instruction.

Instructional variety is a description of the flexibility of an instructor when presenting a lesson.

For a teacher, this means being able to shift from one form of instruction to another in order to maintain the focus of students. This is not easy and is considered a valuable skill in education. If a teacher teaches the same way regardless of what the lesson demands or the students need, this indicates a lack of a variety. This inability to provide instruction in a variety of ways suggest that there may be a lower level of teacher effectiveness.

6. Action research is either research initiated to solve an immediate problem or a reflective process of progressive problem solving led by individuals working with others in teams or as part of a "community of practice" to improve the way they address issues and solve problems.

Action research helps educators be more effective at what they care most about—their teaching and the development of their students. Seeing students grow is probably the greatest joy educators can experience.

When teachers have convincing evidence that their work has made a real difference in their students' lives, the countless hours and endless efforts of teaching seem worthwhile.

The Action Research Process

Educational action research can be engaged in by a single teacher, by a group of colleagues who share an interest in a common problem, or by the entire faculty of a school. Whatever the scenario, action research always involves the same seven-step process.

These seven steps, which become an endless cycle for the inquiring teacher, are the following:

1. Selecting a focus
2. Clarifying theories
3. Identifying research questions
4. Collecting data
5. Analyzing data
6. Reporting results
7. Taking informed action

7. Researcher attempts to evaluate the effect of method of feeding on anxiety-proneness of children. Ex-post-facto method of research would be appropriate for this.

An ex-post-facto research design is a method in which groups with qualities that already exist are compared on some dependent variable.

Also known as "after the fact" research, an ex-post-facto design is considered quasi-experimental because the subjects are not randomly assigned - they are grouped based on a particular characteristic or trait.

Although differing groups are analyzed and compared in regards to independent and dependent variables it is not a true experiment because it lacks random assignment. The assignment of subjects to different groups is based on whichever variable is of interest to the researchers.

8. **A conference** is a gathering of people with a common interest or background, with the purposes of allowing them to meet one another and to learn about and discuss issues, ideas and work that focus on a topic of mutual concern.

The Latin roots of the word "conference" mean, literally, "Bring together." A conference brings together people and ideas.

In the cases of health and community work, conferences often have the goal of generating or working toward solutions to problems or broader social change.

Conferences may be held in places other than the workplaces and neighbourhoods of their participants, so that the people attending can focus on the topic at hand without distractions. Some conferences are even held in another area of the country or the world.

9. A thesis (or dissertation) may be arranged as a thesis by publication or a monograph, with or without appended papers, respectively, though many graduate programs allow candidates to submit a curated collection of published papers.

An ordinary monograph has a title page, an abstract, a table of contents, comprising the various chapters (*e.g.,* introduction, literature review, methodology, results, discussion), and a bibliography or (more usually) a references section.

They differ in their structure in accordance with the many different areas of study (arts, humanities, social sciences, technology, sciences, etc.) and the differences between them. In a thesis by publication, the chapters constitute an introductory and comprehensive review of the appended published and unpublished article documents.

10. **Research** that involves human subjects or participants raises unique and complex ethical, legal, social and political issues.

Research ethics is specifically interested in the analysis of **ethical** issues that are raised when people are involved as participants in research. There are three objectives in research ethics.

16. The **zone of proximal development** is the difference between what a learner can do without help and what he or she cannot do.

The zone of proximal development (ZPD) of a child is not a naturally existing phenomenon that arises by itself every time an adult helps a child achieve greater independence. It is a special form of interaction in which the action of the adult is aimed at generating and supporting the child's initiative.

18. Empathy—the power to understand perspectives other than your own—is an essential skill for all children to master, and it's one of an important set of **teaching strategies** teachers should focus on.

Empathy is foundational for building bridges between individuals, understanding each others' complex emotions, gaining a diverse perspective, and leveraging relationships for collaboration and progress.

19. An ice-breaker is an activity, game, or event that is used to welcome and warm up the conversation among participants in a meeting, training class, team building session, or another event.

Any event that requires people to comfortably interact with each other and a facilitator is an opportunity to use an ice-breaker.

21.

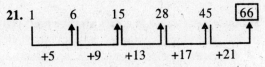

Hence, the next term will be 66.

22. ABD, DGK, HMS, MTB ......
Hence, next term in the series is SBL.

23. C O V A L E N T   is coded as
↓ ↓ ↓ ↓ ↓ ↓ ↓ ↓
B W P D U O F M

Similarly,

E L E P H A N T   is coded as
↓ ↓ ↓ ↓ ↓ ↓ ↓ ↓
Q F M F U O B I

24. The oldman is related to Rakesh as Father.

25.

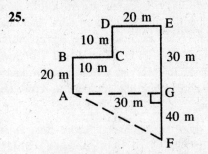

In right Δ AGF,

$$AF^2 = (40)^2 + (30)^2$$
$$= 1600 + 900$$
$$\Rightarrow \quad AF^2 = 2500$$
$$\Rightarrow \quad AF = 50 \text{ m}$$

Hence, Postman is 50 m away from his office.

28. **A deductive argument** is said to be valid if and only if it takes a form that makes it impossible for the premises to be true and the conclusion nevertheless to be false. Otherwise, **a deductive argument** is said to be **invalid**.

A deductive argument is *sound* if and only if it is both valid, and all of its premises are *actually true*. Otherwise, a deductive argument is *unsound*.

37. Data is organized in a **data storage hierarchy** of increasingly complex levels: bits, bytes (characters), fields, records, files, and databases. A **character** is a letter, number, or special character. A **field** consists of one or more characters (bytes). A **record** is a collection of related fields.

A **file** is a collection of related records. A database is, as mentioned, an organized collection of integrated files. Important to data organization is the key field, a field used to uniquely identify a record so that it can be easily retrieved and processed.

38. .com be used primarily for commercial businesses, .net for network related organizations and .org for nonprofit groups. This quickly became unworkable and consequently, in the case of.com, .net and .org, a decision was made to rely on registrants to choose the TLD *(Top Level Domain)* they wish. In fact, many registrants *(domain owners)* order their domain name as .com, .net and .org.

39. USB, short for Universal Serial Bus, is an industry standard that defines cables, connectors and communications protocols for connection, communication, and power supply between computers and devices.

USB was designed to standardize the connection of computer peripherals (including keyboards, pointing devices, digital cameras, printers, portable media players, disk drives and network adapters) to personal computers, both to communicate and to supply electric power.

It has largely replaced a variety of earlier interfaces, such as serial ports and parallel ports, as well as separate power chargers for portable devices—and has become commonplace on a wide range of devices.

Created in the mid-1990s, it is currently developed by the USB Implementers Forum (USB IF).

40. A gigabyte (GB) is a measure of computer data storage capacity that is roughly equivalent to 1 billion bytes. A gigabyte is two to the 30th power or 1,073,741,824 in decimal notation.

41. There is clear evidence that atmospheric pollution is associated with troublesome respiratory symptoms in children but what is less clear is whether specific pollutants have a causal role in the pathogenesis of respiratory diseases.

The principal pollutants of the external (outdoor) environment include nitrogen oxides (NO, NO_2), ozone, sulphur dioxide (SO_2) and particulates.

Respirable suspended particulates or PM10, can get deep into the lungs and cause a broad range of health effects, in particular, respiratory and cardiovascular illnesses, including –

- Increasing respiratory symptoms, such as irritation of the air-ways, coughing, or difficulty in breathing;
- Decreasing lung function;
- Aggravation of asthma;
- Development of chronic bronchitis;
- Adverse effects on the cardiovascular system;
- Premature death in people with heart or lung disease.

People with heart or lung disease, children and the elderly are most likely to be affected by particulate pollution.

43. Natural hazards are naturally occurring phenomena that have disastrous impact on humanity.

These phenomena had been in existence even before the advent of humanity. The hazardous dimension of these natural phenomena are in the context of the impact that such a phenomenon would have on human population in the area affected by that phenomenon.

Geophysical hazards encompass geological and meteorological phenomena such as earthquakes, volcanic eruptions, wildfires, cyclonic storms, floods, droughts, and landslides.

44. Chlorofluoro carbon (CFC) is an organic compound that contains carbon, chlorine, and fluorine, produced as a volatile derivative of methane, ethane and propane.

    The properties of CFCs make them useful for a variety of commercial and industrial purposes: as a propellant in aerosol sprays (now banned in the US and Europe), in refrigeration and air conditioning systems, in foams, in cleaning solvents and in electrical components.

    Most CFCs have been released to the atmosphere through the use of aerosols containing them and as leakages from refrigeration equipment. Other releases may occur from industry producing and using them and other products containing them. There are not thought to be any natural sources of CFCs to the environment.

45. An Eco-Friendly Fuel is an ecologically friendly fuel. Its production and use has a minimum impact on the environment.

    Hydrogen fuel is a zero-emission fuel when burned with oxygen, if one considers water not to be an emission. Hydrogen has been touted as an environmentally friendly wonder fuel that can be used in vehicles and burns to produce only water as a by product. The problem with hydrogen is that producing it is far from environmentally friendly and storing it in a fuel tank is extremely hazardous.

46. India's higher education system is the third largest in the world. The main governing body at the tertiary level is the University Grants Commission, which enforces its standards, advises the government, and helps coordinate between the centre and the state.

The objectives of higher education are:

- **Wisdom and knowledge:** Since education is both a training of minds and training of souls, it should give both knowledge and wisdom. No amount of factual information would take ordinarily into educated men unless something is awakened in them.

- **Aims of the social order:** Our education system must find its guiding principle in the aims of the social order for which it prepares. Unless we preserve the value of democracy, justice, liberty, equality and fraternity, we cannot preserves our freedom.

- **Love for higher values of life:** The greatness of a country does not depend on the extent of its territory, the length of its communication or the amount of its wealth, but on the love for higher values of life. We must develop thought for the poor and sufferings, regards and respect for women, faith in brotherhood regardless of race, colour, religion etc.

- **Training for leadership:** One of the important aims of higher education is the training for leadership in the profession and public life. It is the function of universities to train men and women for wise leadership.

47. The Ministry of Human Resource Development released the NIRF rankings, 2017 as per which the Indian Institute of Science at Bengaluru in Karnataka is No. 1 higher educational institute while the Indian Institute of Management at Ahmedabad in Gujarat is the top management institute.

    The Indian Institute of Technology (IIT) Madras has been ranked as the best engineering college in India. Deemed university Jamia Hamdard in Delhi is numero uno in pharmacy category, while Miranda House in the national capital has been ranked the best college in the country.

    Bengaluru's IISc has also been ranked as the top university in India, as per the second edition of India Rankings under the National Institutional Ranking Framework (NIRF) released by Union Human Resource Development Minister Prakash Javadekar. The Jawaharlal Nehru University (JNU) secured second spot in the top university rankings in India.

In the list of best colleges in India, Miranda House in Delhi was followed by Loyola college in Chennai. This is the first time general colleges have been ranked in the NIRF.

49. The **governors and lieutenant-governors** of the states and union territories of India have similar powers and functions at the state level as that of the President of India at Union level. Governors exist in the states while lieutenant-governors exist in union territories and in the National Capital Territory of Delhi.

The governors and **lieutenant-governors** are appointed by the **President** for a term of **five years**.

The term of governor's office is normally 5 years but it can be terminated earlier by:

- Dismissal by the president (usually on the advice of the prime minister of the country) at whose pleasure the governor holds office. Dismissal of Governors without valid reason is not permitted. However, it is the duty of the President to dismiss a Governor whose acts are upheld by courts as unconstitutional and in bad faith.

- Resignation by the governor: There is no provision for impeachment, as it happens for the president.

50. Corruption is the misuse of *public* power (by elected politician or appointed civil servant) for private gain.

Corruption is a deviation from normal human behaviour in a geopolitical setting whereby causing the derailment of individual and institutional accountability, transparency and natural justice.

Corruption is a barometer of a nations' development and decline which determines its stanching stature and estimation among the country of nation-states. But of late, corruption has become a way of national life and has already been institutionalized beyond the comprehension of ordinary human imagination.